A group of men, their heads and bodies shakin   at
made them forget age & weakness & becoming   of
the chant melody, like the breathing that gives

Thus wrote T.G.H. Strehlow in 1935, during an early j   m
to write *Songs of Central Australia*. That book, now rare and out of print, is generally
acclaimed as one of the great books of world literature, and a seminal text for
Australia. Barry Hill in *Overland* called it 'a huge, marvellous, astonishing gift of a
book – a gem, the great source book of the poetic lore of the region, the text that
most extensively tables, with the authority of the *Torah*, the ancient poetry . . .'

T.G.H. Strehlow was the son of the German Lutheran Pastor Carl Strehlow of the
Hermannsburg mission in Central Australia. He grew up speaking Aranda; he had
Greek and Latin from his father by the time he was 14. After a first-class honours
degree in English at the University of Adelaide, he began collecting songs in 1932;
he inducted himself as bushman, and with his 'camel boy', Tom Ljonga, as his sole
companion, travelled thousands of miles to camp with knowledgeable Aboriginal
men. For the next three decades he continued to collect, regarding himself as *ingkata*,
or ceremonial chief, and writing in the elegiac mode, in the 'sunset', he thought, of
Aboriginal culture.

Strehlow was the first Patrol Officer of Central Australia when economic and
sexual exploitation was rife. He was a friend of the Aborigine: for his trouble he was
branded in the Federal Parliament as a Nazi in 1941. After the war Strehlow was also
translating the New Testament into Aranda. As the translator of songs, he was akin
to Shakespeare's Caliban; but as a man of the Gospel he was Luther's Caliban, who
secretly thought of himself as a 'Black Missionary'. Out of both cultures, he sought
to affirm what was 'eternal', and to articulate the essence of belonging in Australia.

As a public intellectual Strehlow had sharp things to say about religious rights,
assimilation, Max Stuart's conviction, the N.T. Land Rights Act, the 'Aboriginal
industry', customary law and Aboriginal futures: he was never far from controversy.
His huge collection of secret-sacred objects was hotly contested when Aboriginal
identity become politicised. Finally – ironically, and tragically – he was accused
of betraying sacred images he had obtained in trust, a scandal that greatly damaged
his reputation.

Prize-winning poet and historian Barry Hill, with exclusive access to Strehlow's
diaries, offers a deeply layered intellectual recovery of Strehlow's life in translation, and,
by implication, a placement of it in the context of contemporary anxieties about
cultural degeneration and continuity. This is both a critical study of the work
and an intimate narrative of Strehlow's yearnings. *Broken Song* straddles a century of
Australian history, from the race wars on the frontier to the modern era, and flowing
through everything is Strehlow's passionate ambivalence towards Aranda culture's
mode of sustaining desire.

Barry Hill's long narrative poem, *Ghosting William Buckley*, won the 1994 N.S.W. Premier's Award for Poetry, and his labour history, *Sitting In*, won the same award for Non-Fiction in 1992. He is the winner of other national awards for poetry, non-fiction and works for radio. His short fiction has been widely anthologised and translated. His most recent books include *The Rock: Travelling to Uluru*, and *The Inland Sea* (poems). *Broken Song* is his third and final book arising from a decade of work out of Central Australia.

Barry is an Honorary Fellow at the Australian Centre at the University of Melbourne, where he teaches occasionally, and is Poetry Editor for the national newspaper, *The Australian*. He lives in Queenscliff, Victoria.

Also by Barry Hill

Fiction
A Rim of Blue
Near the Refinery
Headlocks and Other Stories
The Best Picture

Non-Fiction
The Schools
Sitting In
The Rock: Travelling to Uluru

Poetry
Raft
Ghosting William Buckley
The Inland Sea

Broken Song

T.G.H. STREHLOW AND ABORIGINAL POSSESSION

Barry Hill

VINTAGE BOOKS
Australia

A Vintage book
Published by Random House Australia Pty Ltd
20 Alfred Street, Milsons Point, NSW 2061
http://www.randomhouse.com.au

Sydney New York Toronto
London Auckland Johannesburg

First published in Australia by Knopf in 2002
This Vintage edition first published 2003

National Library of Australia
Cataloguing-in-Publication Entry

Hill, Barry, 1943– .
Broken song: T.G.H. Strehlow and Aboriginal possession.

Bibliography.
Includes index.
ISBN 978 1 174051 229 9.
ISBN 1 74051 229 4 (pbk).

1. Strehlow, T. G. H. (Theodor George Henry), 1908–1978. 2. Anthropologists – Australia –
Biography. 3. Aborigines, Australian – Australia. I. Title.

301.092

Cover images and map courtesy of the Strehlow Research Centre
Front cover: T.G.H. Strehlow with Hale River elder Ljeraritjinaka
Back cover: Theo and baby Victoria, c. 1913
Map (page xviii) of 'Sub-groups of Aranda Tribe' from *Aranda Traditions*, 1947

Design by Gayna Murphy, Greendot Design
Typeset in 12/14 pt Bembo by Midland Typesetters, Maryborough, Victoria
Printed and bound by The SOS Print and Media Group

10 9 8 7 6 5 4 3 2

To
Hugh Stretton and Peter Latz

A group of men, their heads and bodies shaking rhythmically, chanting with the enthusiasm that made them
forget age & weakness & becoming young again in spirit,
glowing fires . . . a windbreak of boughs, a moon dripping
through fleeing clouds, the rising and falling of the chant
melody, like the breathing that gives us life,—what an
unforgettable scene!

T.G.H. Strehlow, 1935

'. . . poetically, man dwells . . .'

Hölderlin/Martin Heidegger, 1951

Jesus can you mend this broken song?

Neil Murray, 1993

Publisher's Note

Indigenous readers are advised that *Broken Song* includes material which might be regarded as sensitive or distressing. Material from the Strehlow Collection used in the book has been vetted by the Strehlow Research Centre and all attempts have been made to exclude information or images which might offend the cultural values of Aboriginal people.

Contents

Acknowledgments

THERE ARE MANY people to thank for different stages of this book. I should start with Community Aid Abroad and their scheme with an outfit called Desert Tracks, with whom I first travelled in Central Australia, and first met Aboriginal people in their own country. I thank Gus Williams at Hermannsburg, for permission to walk down the Finke and camp on Aboriginal land; and Garry Stoll, for letting me travel with him in his pastoral work at Docker River. Glen Auricht introduced me to Aranda country around the mission, and advised me in important ways. In Alice Springs Rod Moss, Alison French, Kieran Finnane and Erwin Chlanda (and their splendid children, Rainer and Jacquie) gave me hospitality. In Adelaide Ian Davey was always welcoming, as were Hugh and Pat Stretton. When I got closer to the grain of the work, and the various drafts of chapters, the following friends and colleagues were invaluable: Tim Rowse, John Morton, Peter Sutton, Ken Inglis, Dick Kimber, Peter Latz; all generous, patient, knowledgeable. Numerous chapters owe much to one or other of these men, and the errors that remain are mine not theirs. Peter Latz, who grew up on the Hermannsburg Mission, and put me up in his house in the MacDonnell Range countless times, has a special place in this list. Nicolas Peterson, John Mulvaney, Les Murray, Bill Gammage, Ramona Koval, David Turnbull, Kerryn Goldsworthy, Pat Stretton and John Embling helped in precise but different ways when they could.

Walter Veit read what I asked of him, and shared his German files on Carl Strehlow.

The staff at the Commonwealth Archives in Darwin and Canberra deserve medals for their helpfulness, as does Jenny Tonkin at the State Library of South Australia. I also thank the staff of the archive at the Australian National University, and at the University of Adelaide, where Hugh Stretton gave them firm encouragement to trust a freelance writer, as did Harry Medlin, who shared his files with me. Philip Jones at the South Australian Museum gave me crucial initial guidance with Strehlow's early diaries and has been generous beyond that. At the Institute of Aboriginal and Torres Strait Islander Studies I have Kingsley Palmer and Jacquie Lambert to thank; and, leading to that access, Marcia Langton. Thanks also to Lyall Kupke at the Lutheran Archive in Adelaide, and to others with close connections with the former mission at Hermannsburg: the late Philip Scherer and the ever-warm Helene Burns, as well as her brother, Paul Albrecht, who helped with translations. Thanks are due to John Sabel, T.G. Obst, Trudy Johannsen, Kevin Schmidt, John Pfitzner, and the librarian of Immanuel College. Profound thanks go to the official historians of Immanuel College, Dorothy and Ian Hansen, who became close friends and colleagues in the course of my writing this book. John Strehlow has been a steady supporter of this project, and a source of valuable impressions. I have also had the cooperation of his brother Theo and sister Shirley: thanks to them for their trust. In Germany Mr and Mrs Bill Fuggman were delightful hosts and informants. The curator and archivist respectively were helpful at the Museums für Volkerkunde and the Lutheran Seminary in Neuendettelsau. At the Strehlow Research Centre in Alice Springs I have had the help of Chris Torlach, Shane Hersey, Garry Stoll, and most of all the goodwill and industry of Research Director Brett Galt-Smith, whose arrival on the scene a few years ago facilitated the access I eventually gained to a useful selection of Strehlow's diaries and letters. In the years when that access was denied, and when principles of liberal scholarship needed affirming somewhat, I had the invaluable support of John Mulvaney, Hugh Stretton, Ken Inglis, Hilary McPhee, Tom Shapcott, Peter McPhee and Kate Darian-Smith. John Mulvaney's urging that I should press on with the access agreement facilitated by Brett Galt-Smith consolidated my decision to see this book through. Finally, it is to the credit of the Board of the Strehlow Research Centre that they acted on Galt-Smith's advice: I thank the Board.

The Literature Board of the Australia Council funded me with a senior fellowship when this book was one of several Central Australian projects on my drawing board; and then again with a fare to Germany when it counted. At an important stage of this self-funded project the State Library of New South Wales awarded me the 1996 Curry Fellowship. More recently the resources of the Australian Centre at the University of Melbourne have been available to me, along with the colleagueship of another Strehlow scholar, Paul Carter. Beverley Farmer and Jenny Lee helped with early editorial work. The final manuscript benefited from the stamina and exactitude of Carl Harrison-Ford, and the publishing courage of Jane Palfreyman at Random House. And my agent Rose Cresswell had faith in the project's ambitions from the moment I approached her.

For the last laps of the book, when most of the hard writing was done, it was the love and companionship of Rose Bygrave that made the work seem something other than strange punishment.

Barry Hill
May 2002

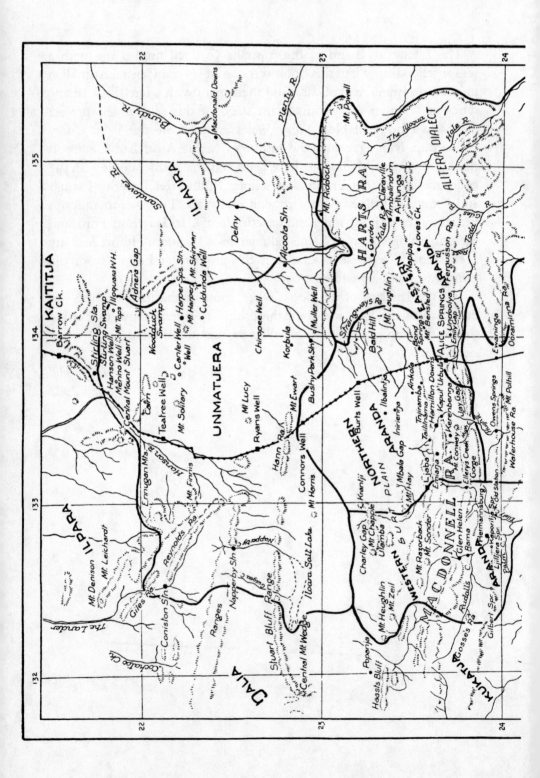

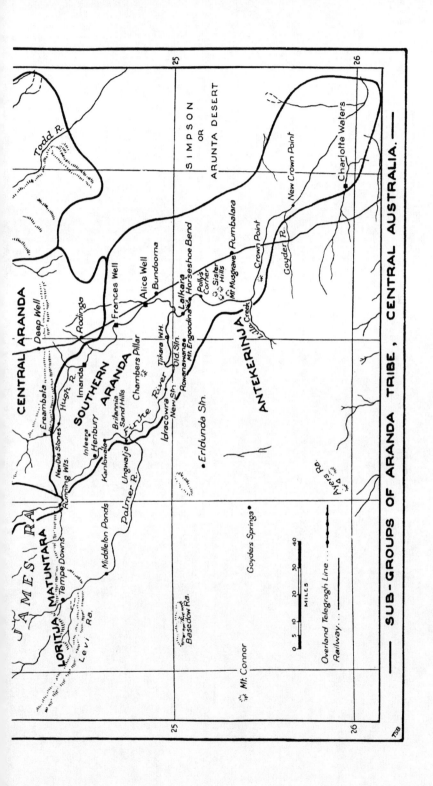

SUB-GROUPS OF ARANDA TRIBE, CENTRAL AUSTRALIA.

Overture

Put colours in the bags
Close it all around
And make the netted bag
All the colours of the rainbow.

THE EARLIEST DESERT song to be written into English belonged to
the people around Lake Eyre. When it was sung it came out of
parched salty ground, and in the pristine air of that country its notes were
as crystal as the Milky Way.

Mull a-a-a—wora-a-a
Yoong-arra-a-a Oondoo-o-o
Ya Pillee-e—e-e Mulka-a-a-a angienie
Kooriekirra-a-a ya-a-a-ya.

The translator was Samuel Gason, a police trooper, who had spent 'a nine
years sojourn' among the 'Dieyerie Tribe.' His Diyari was not flash, but
he had made a fist of the sounds so that one can, with an application of
a certain pitch, at which the Aboriginal singers were soon recognised as
masters, enact them in one's imagination.

Gason was impressed by it as a secret song, or at least one kept from
the women on pain of death, as it was part of the red ochre business.

At certain times of the year men went off for some weeks and came back with loads of the invaluable ochre for their sacred ceremonies. Seeds were collected by women, the camp prepared to receive the honoured men burdened with ochre. And the bags were woven to put the colours in, woven as if to net all the colours of the rainbow. A song of work, and belief, and celebration of beauty rolled as neatly into four lines as can be.

The trooper was, as policemen often were in the Outback, in good Christian company when he published his song. In the same book, *The Native Tribes of South Australia*, published in 1879, only 40 years after the first white people had arrived in Adelaide, the Reverend C.W. Schurmann, a Lutheran, put down a couple of verses and remarked upon their connection with dance in the life of the Port Lincoln people. The verses remained untranslated. In the same book, the Reverend G. Taplin did a little more on behalf of the Narrinyeri people, and took pains to say it was a very imperfect attempt to 'render the corroboree' in English. Gason did, however, have an inkling of 'the idea of the composition,' which was 'first to describe the subject, then in the course of the song to multiply descriptive adjectives giving a vivid idea of the scene, and also to throw in any comparison which may be illustrative, and the whole with abundant interjection of wonder and gesticulations.'[1]

It is evocative enough, especially the abundant interjection of wonder. The singing was strong, it was alive with a verbal and physical energy. But that did not mean the songs would last for ever, for reasons most people are now all too familiar with.

The better translations of the inland people were done by the Lutheran missionaries around Lake Eyre. They wrote down the songs in the course of their Janus work as translators. They wanted to know how the native language worked, and something of native belief and feeling. They sought and often brilliantly gained this knowledge the better to erase heathenism from the shores of the lake so that all the waters of the desert would be available for Christian baptism.

The first inland desert language to be translated into a European language was Diyari: this by the industrious and bookish Pastor Reuther, who laboured in the wilderness of the Lutheran mission built on Lake Killalpaninna, near Cooper Creek. No country to the European eye could be more forsaken, but not, surely, after it was visited by the Word. Reuther translated from his native German: at first hymns, then passages from scripture, then whole Gospels. At the same time he was transcribing legends told to him by men who came in out of the heat and the dust, carrying many flies with them, into the cave of his book-lined study. They told him songs, too, and Reuther wrote them down.

Kana karura tili maltara julkani
ja wodatarana ngamani
Wirda njamenunda ngana ngura
duka wajimana palau wora
Daka pitjeri dakajurari
kana karuru tilli
Wolpa wirra ngalpurungalpuru
wolpa kanala kuturu ngunai
wolpa wirra davadara.

This was the 'Pampo ulu Song,' as Reuther called it. In his notebook he did not render it in anything but Diyari, and I leave it on the page like this as a raw example of an Aboriginal verse written phonetically, and as such, offering to us its physical reality and perhaps something of the sentiment in its sound system. For that is what language is like: it is a somatic act before it is anything else: it goes into the ear before anything else and all our attempts to understand its speaker are bound up with bodies in space together, with a form approaching intimacy. Bodies sing in the company of voices.

These words were for rain making. 'Different men,' Reuther wrote, 'stick a pointed emu bone into their upper arm and pull the bone right through (between the skin and the flesh). The blood lost by the men is caught in a bowl and a man, the Tidnamatuka, goes out to hunt kapiri, and pours the blood into the sandhills as a sacrifice to the maduka earth.'[2]

No songs could have been more serious: they bore upon life that issued from the earth. Reuther translated at least 130 of them, but, in the course of translating his impressive language work into English, they have never turned up.[3] The loss is extreme: they would have been a body of song to rival the preserve that has been the creation of the Strehlows. For Pastor Carl Strehlow arrived to help Reuther in 1892. He was also skilled in language and, as a Lutheran, instructed to enter the native language in order to enter the soul of the people. Strehlow helped Reuther with the New Testament and, no doubt, the extra-curricular Christian work, if it could be called that. The first desert songs the pastor heard would have been these Diyari verses, designed, as the most important ones always were, to work as much magic in the world as fervent Christian prayer.

But no Diyari songs survive,[4] and in 1894 Pastor Strehlow went further inland to become the superintendent of the Hermannsburg Mission on the Finke River. This country, though prone to regular droughts, was a paradise compared to the area he had left: regular water places existed, and game often abounded, along with a profusion of plants that were food to the people who spoke Aranda.* Among the first songs he put into German was the ritual song for the red kangaroo, which is too sensitive to set down here. Some songs are still too alive in Aboriginal belief and practice to be treated as open: they are too integral to the secret-sacred business of men's initiation. Even today they are far from broken, despite a century of mission work designed to bury them; so that the cultural paradox, it could be said, is the fading of Christian 'song' as the 'song' of the Aborigine has revived. T.G.H. Strehlow's feelings about this complex possibility is one theme of this book.

The first song laid out by Pastor Strehlow was what he called 'The two venom gland-men (atua ntjikantja tara)' and it connects from the area not that far from the place he had left: Crown Point, on the Lower Finke, on the edge of the Simpson Desert. It begins:

> *Tjikara in the camp Itirkawara below men venom glands many*
> *They meat fish—eating were—Messenger one below went*
> *Thicket to the camp, there were venom glands two others were, grey wallaby . . .*

And so on for five more pages. The poetic qualities so apparent to the red ochre song are buried in the simple word-for-word translation. Pastor Carl was more interested in the myth that went with it. It tells of the venom gland men who entice the water snake out of a large water hole and feast on it. The men from Crown Point have done so,

---

* *Aranda* was the Finke River Mission's spelling after Strehlow; *Arunta* was Spencer and Gillen's from 1896; *Arrernte* it is by fiat of linguists today. I have kept to *Aranda* to remain closer to the semantic world of Strehlow and the Lutherans, and to avoid the tedium for writer and reader of indicating otherwise throughout a century of texts. With other key terms I have also kept to the period: place names (Yapalpa, Piltardi, Hergott Springs . . .) and slang (half-caste, native, nigger, lubra, gin . . .). With terms now regarded as offensive I trust the reader's intelligence to read the word in the context attempting to speak directly out of the period without cumbersome textual adjustments. There is nothing worse than a page of inverted commas that have to be brushed away like flies. Like apologising for meat that is not off.

it seems, transgressionally. For after eating the fat water snake they climbed up their short spear into the sky. The other men, who had a long spear rising into the sky, took the short spear out of the ground. The Crown Point men called out, 'Stick our spear back into the ground so that we can climb down!' The men did not stick the spear into the ground, but replied, 'Climb down the long spear!' The two said, 'No we cannot climb down the long spear. Stay on earth, you mortals. We will stay here forever and be immortal.' Finally the men laid the long spear on the ground as well. The two remained in the sky and are now two stars in the sky. There they lit a big fire, the smoke of which is known as kulbbura–ilkalama. Thus Aboriginal song is as bound up with teachings as it is with the performances of the body. For the precise meanings of those teachings, those myths, that is a complex issue even today, and not the subject of this book. Pastor Carl translated the songs in various ways and different lengths. His reports of myths are still regarded as invaluable ethnology. As for the songs, he did not give any description of their music or the marriage with performance. As a Christian he could not stomach such intimacy with pagan practice. The work he did was, like Reuther's, from the quiet confines of his study. [5]

This is enough for now. Our story line, a kind of an echo of the 'songlines' falsely attributed to Strehlow,[*] is about the arrival of translated desert songs in Australia which move from the coast of South Australia

---

[*]   Most glibly by Bruce Chatwin in *Songlines* (1987), whereas the first ethnographic authority to be clear about songs that travelled from language group to language group across country was probably W.E. Roth (1984:1:117–25). Educated at Oxford with Baldwin Spencer, an anthropologist and the Protector of Aborigines in Queensland, Roth described the Molonga ceremony and its variations over 90 miles in various directions like articles of exchange along trade routes. Spencer's public discussion of it was noted with interest by Gillen (Spencer 1896: 207). The travelling song was also featured by the prolific author of *Native Tribes of South-East Australia* (1904), A.W. Howitt, a close colleague of Spencer in Australia, who found it 'hard to say how far and how long such songs may travel in the course of time over the Australian continent.' It was Howitt, also, who first noted what T.G.H. Strehlow was to make so much of: that 'the songs . . . including all kinds of Aboriginal poetry, are obtained by the bards from the spirits of the deceased.' Howitt was of the view that 'the bard who composed this song came of a poetic stock' who were 'prototypes of the "sacred singers" of olden times' (1886: 329–30). As to the religious gravity of the songs, the Reverend G.W. Torrance (1886: 339–40) noted that the intonations of the songs resembled Gregorian music, and 'the Temple melodies of some of the most ancient civilised nations, and conducive to the expression of solemnity and grandeur, as well as mystery.' Torrance was exited by the connection with Judaeo-Christian plainsong, 'the Temple worship of the Hebrews, who may themselves have derived it from the ancient Egyptians.' By implication the Aboriginal song was as worthy of reverence.

to the scattered waters of Lake Eyre and onto the German Lutheran mission on the beautiful banks of the Finke River, the oldest of Centralian rivers and perhaps the oldest riverbed in the world. There the last of the pastor's five sons was born: Theodor George Henry Strehlow whose fate it was to become a translator and to create the book that is the world's great treasure trove of Aboriginal song.

So. In the heart of the heart of the country there lies a huge, marvellous, astonishing gift of a book, *Songs of Central Australia,* by T.G.H. Strehlow. This is a book about the nature of that book, its making and the man who composed it. It is about the book's becoming and what became of its author. *Songs* was published in 1971, when Strehlow was 63, though he had written most of it twenty years before. It is a huge and now rare book that tabled—at length and flourishingly—the Aboriginal poetry at the core of the continent. Strehlow designed his book to sing and elucidate the soul of the first inhabitants and it does so with the lyricism of the *Song of Songs* and the gravity of the *Torah.* There have been other renderings of Aboriginal poetry, and they have been splendid reminders of the depth of the culture that has pulsed here for so long, but no other book has been as embracing as Strehlow's, or more honorifically committed to placing the 'first songs' of the 'first people' in the context of world poetry. In *Songs,* Aboriginal life breathes in the company of Greek and Anglo-Saxon, Norse and Hebraic utterance. Strehlow's magnificent achievement was to create for readers the impression that here we have Aboriginal poetry speaking for itself and at the same time inhabiting poetic universals. Culturally speaking, *Songs* is Australia's book of Genesis. It contains words of sacred beginnings. At the same time it is a hymn of praise. Of itself the work sings as it retrieves the ancient lore and poetry that it—as a book—came to possess.

Songs represents Strehlow's life work. Indeed its production, as he grew older, and in the miserable years before his death in 1978, became his *raison d'être.* He began collecting in 1932 and continued for the rest of the decade, when he was the first patrol officer of Central Australia; and then, after the war, when he was an academic at the University of Adelaide. He was in a unique position to do so because he had grown up in the Aranda language: after his infancy he was the only white boy on the Hermannsburg Mission.

Pastor Carl Strehlow was superintendent of the mission from 1896 to 1922. That year the great man died at Horseshoe Bend, after a long tragic buggy ride in the October heat. Theo was fourteen, and his father's death was perhaps the determining event of his life, out of which he mythologised his life, most noticeably when he published *Journey to Horseshoe Bend* in 1969.

After his father's death Strehlow went south to be educated in Adelaide and when he came back to the Centre it was to make a formal study of the Aranda language. In so doing he found himself collecting the songs and myths. Hand in hand with this activity went the business of collecting the sacred objects called *tjurunga*, the carved stones and wooden things which housed the ancestor spirits of which the songs sang. Sometimes an old man might not want to sing the song without handling the *tjurunga*. So Strehlow would go to the secret place where they were stored. And then, after the presentation, a man might want to give him the *tjurunga* for safekeeping. How else to protect the lore? How else to safeguard the remnants of the dying culture? He addressed this matter rather brilliantly as a young man.[6] Then, for the next 30 years collecting songs and sacred things went together. Chance—and then his own enormous industry and hunger—made Strehlow one of Australia's great collectors. To himself he had gathered a museum of things, which were also a spirit world.

Strehlow became—by his own lights—a white custodian of Aboriginal culture. He called himself *ingkata*, Aranda for ceremonial chief. He always said that the senior men had invested their trust in him as a guardian of the last of their culture, and that in this—his intimacy with sacred ceremony—he was unique among anthropologists. He was indeed a friend of the Aborigine for the duration of his life. But he was a friend whose allegiances were complex and whose actions ended in scandal.

This is the profound paradox of his major work's position in our culture. It was written by a man who—after three decades of collecting songs and befriending Aborigines, after a life that ostensibly (some would say ostentatiously) honoured the sacred—acted sacrilegiously. Strehlow's disgrace—the result of a business deal about secret-sacred material—is no simple matter, any more than his character. But the episode mocked the care so often affirmed in the course of his life. When, in good faith, a white chief is anointed as a custodian of the black man's things, and such a fate befalls him, what can we say? What transpired in the crucial years that went into the making of the great book? What becomes of the monumental work? What kind of story are we telling?

At a basic level, it is one that situates T.G.H. Strehlow in the history of Australian ethnology. To do that requires, first of all, a knowledge of his father's work, which remains unpublished in English but which had a galvanising impact on European thinking from 1907, when it began to be published in Germany. The pastor's reports on the beliefs and material life of the Aranda were quickly assimilated by the leading thinkers of nineteenth-century anthropology. Secondly one needs to appreciate that the founders of Central Australian anthropology in English, Baldwin Spencer, Professor of Biology at the University of Melbourne, and Frank Gillen, his wry and intelligent drinking partner at the telegraph station in Alice Springs, were at the turn of the century the authors of a monumental classic, *Native Tribes of Central Australia*. That was published in 1899 and was later reissued in 1927 in two volumes entitled *The Arunta*. The Aranda people had by then become the most studied people in the British Empire, and certainly, in Europe, had found themselves forever in the annals of the romantic and counter-romantic imagination of the primitive. It was only five years after *Native Tribes* was reissued that T.G.H. Strehlow came back to his mission to start his work, taking the first steps to make the book that was and remains the necessary corrective to all that Spencer and Gillen had nobly and ignobly done.

This is the point. Spencer and Gillen's work was essentially the product of evolutionary Darwinism, and a methodology that made objects of its native subjects. Their work is a magnificent documentation of Aboriginal ceremonies, painstaking work of ethnographic observation, the product, very largely, of Spencer and Gillen's ability to persuade their Aranda informants to stage dancing and singing for the purposes of the white man's note taking and photography. Thus Spencer and Gillen's texts honoured the Aranda, even though their premise was that they were a Stone Age people as doomed to extinction as the kangaroo or the platypus.[7] The patron of the 1894 Horn Scientific Expedition, of which Spencer was a member, reported: 'The Central Australian aborigine is the living representative of a stone age . . . His origin and history are lost in the gloomy mists of the past. He has no written records and few oral traditions. In appearance be is a naked, hirsute savage, with a type of features occasionally pronouncedly Jewish . . . He has no private ownership of land, except as regards that which is not over carefully concealed about his person.'[8]

Paradoxically, the relatively uninformed E.C. Stirling, who wrote the chapter on anthropology for the report of the Horn Expedition, was the first to show a sample Central Australian song for English readers. His passage is worth citing in full, as it illustrates the primal place of song in the most sacred ceremony, and the intimacy of song with ritual uses of the body. For the bodies singing here have been decorated with down and ochre, the former fixed with 'freshly coagulated human blood.' Stirling continued:

During the time that the incision in the arm was being made the following is chanted by the bystanders:—

>   Unka chaapani unk na-a-a—
>   Unka cha—chaapani aamen-a-a

While the blood is flowing:—
>   Unka cha chaan ca cha-a-a—
>   Owini amen aa-a—

and
>   Okatain teyn man ca-a-a
>   Tain ma okatain tain ma tain ma-a-a—

With an improvised brush the blood is daubed on to the body and the Portulaca down made to adhere. While this is being done the chant is:—
>   Ai unchun cha la—laaa—a-a-
>   Unchun cha-la-lai.

Stirling went on to say that 'the natives are quite unable to assign any meaning to the words of these and other chants, of which there are a great number.'[9] Stirling credited the sounds of the 'monotonous chants' with 'euphony . . . due to the gentle and even way in which the voices, naturally melodious, fade away to absolute stillness.' But the Aranda was not treated as worthy of attention. Instead, Stirling turned to the sign language said to be well developed. Trooper Gason had told them that the Diyari made copious use of the signs.[10]

These were not ground-breaking remarks about language, or even song. But Stirling had shown two crucial things. Firstly, the sacred in Aboriginal culture, and therefore the most sacred song, is often bound up with erotic transformative ceremonies of men. The details of those ceremonies cannot be printed today without deeply offending Aranda people, but they are the backdrop, the life blood, literally, of all that must be thought and said about the life and the work of Strehlow. Strehlow more than anyone else was to expound on sacred matters of fertility, of the realms of Aranda culture that issued from desire, and his exposition of such matters, his struggle with his material, is a key part of our story too.*

Secondly, Stirling's virgin account makes it clear that the song was always more than the song: it transpired not merely as song, but as a situational performance. It is most interesting that Stirling remarked in the way that he did: 'the voices, naturally melodious, fade away to absolute stillness.'

The image is stark, and goes to the heart of one's experience, even a limited experience, of the singing. When it stops there is the sound of the desert space, the fire, the night, the ground all around. All of a sudden it feels as if the silence is part of the song, which it can be, as an expression of the song's meaning. 'There are sacred performances where no words at all may be sung,' Strehlow wrote, 'even the chorus men being allowed to assist the actor or actors by hitting the ground with a stone or shield or beating together boomerangs.' Only these sounds break the 'reverent silence.' There could be 'songless sacred performances' precisely because all the songs assume a presence.[11] They only exist on the breath of the totemic ancestor.

Stirling, who relied heavily on Gillen, hardly grasped as much, though his sentence hints at it. And that, pretty much, was the end of the Darwinians' interest in songs. Much of Spencer and Gillen's material was accurate and respectful of the Aranda culture; but all of it was an account constructed on the basis of observations derived from limited access to the culture. Spencer spoke no Aranda, and Gillen's was never fluent, despite his years in the Territory and trust of native friends. Still, Gillen was sufficiently skilled in Aranda to penetrate Aranda belief and to be respected as a 'great teacher' and 'initiate.'[12]

---

* The above details are as far as this book seeks to go. I regard them as essential background to its substantive themes, and their absence would constitute a radical neglect of the reader. No offence is intended by citing what is already in the public domain in the classic literature. With regard to material from Strehlow's diaries, hitherto unpublished, painstaking consultation with the Strehlow Research Centre has taken place over my text, the totality of which was submitted to the centre under the access agreement that made this book possible.

One can then read Spencer and Gillen and wonder at the marvel of their texts: it is probably as richly penetrating, as thick a description, as could have been done at the time, especially considering the understanding they had acquired of the sacred objects, the totemic ground, and the Dreaming, the notion they were the first to popularise from their slight mistranslation of the term *Alcheringa*. Their work was unquestionably foundational, but it was nonetheless relatively incomplete until T.G.H. Strehlow did his.

The simple fact is that with Spencer and Gillen we observe the ceremonies as outsiders. Strehlow took us inside. Spencer and Gillen present the ritual performances, and some of the myths that go with them. They made pioneering sound recordings of song and had one notated by Percy Grainger, but their texts did not account for the songs which were at the centre of those rituals. Strehlow, with his intimacy with the language, tabled the songs, and in so doing not only rescued the language from neglect, but placed the religion of the Aranda on a spiritual level with other cultures. With Spencer and Gillen we had a picture drawn for us of gesticulating ethnographic objects. Thanks to Strehlow, the same people have been fully rendered as highly cognisant celebratory subjects, poets and artists of their life, makers of their culture, rather than doomed aspects of nature. To say, then, that Strehlow translated the songs of the Aranda people, is to say much more than that he brought to us the gift of their poetry. It is to say that he credited them with full humanity. That he struggled in his own way with notions of the primitive is also part of our story, but it takes nothing away from his unsurpassable achievement.

There is already a small but important literature out of Strehlow. Paul Carter splendidly writes of Strehlow's work as if it was designed to help us translate ourselves into a post-colonial poetics.[13] John Morton has used Strehlow's *oeuvre* to make the successful case for the claimants in the Alice Springs Native Title case,[14] and written about Strehlow in the company of one of Freud's favourite madmen.[15] Tim Rowse has taken heart from Strehlow as a public intellectual intent on the development of Aboriginal citizenship.[16] Mudrooroo, writing with the polemical identity of an indigenous intellectual, is attuned to Strehlow as one who might be accused of appropriating the Aboriginal culture, but most of all wants us to value Strehlow's text as restitution and conservation: Strehlow recorded the songs before they were lost forever.[17] This book has grown in the same garden as these interpretations but developed differently. Strehlow was a man everyone has found difficult to categorise, including myself and, it must be said, his previous journalistic biographer, Ward McNally. This book is partly written on the assumption that, in the world run by professionals (academics, anthropologists, Aborigines . . .) categories can be studious lies.

Strehlow was a linguist: that was his profession. But he was a linguist who had grown up in the language and whose passion went to poetry, especially poetry that pertained to the myths of the world. Whatever we come to say about his early life on the frontier of Central Australia, and his late, destructive conduct in the trenches of academia, his informing spirit was Orphic. In the last paragraph of *Songs* he wrote: 'It is my belief that when the strong web of future Australian verse comes to be woven, probably some of its strands will be found to be poetic threads spun on the Stone Age hair-spindles of Central Australia.'

Thus the project of the book was thrown forward. It was meant to embody more than the old songs of the old culture. It offered a promise—culturally speaking—of marriage and reproduction; out of the body of song, a reconciling future. It sought reconciliation by means of poetry.

Songs of Central Australia, the book itself, is a monumental object, an exclusive and in some ways excluding text. It commands monological authority. Look, for instance, at the front cover and the frontispiece. There in both is the sand painting which represents Strehlow's totem at *Ntaria*, the Aranda name for Hermannsburg. The ground painting, we are told, became the private property of the author when it was handed over to him by the last surviving custodian of that totemic clan. Who could argue with that? It is Strehlow's claim, as author, that no one can argue with that. His book is Writ.

It might be read as a kind of Scripture. Consider one of its grand pages. There are five categories of writing here: the Aranda line, and the English translation; the prose account of the latter, and the reference to the relevant item in the field journals; and finally, there is the explanatory footnote. The last named usually involves an expansive note by way of comparison to something in European literature, or a biographical entry drawn from Strehlow's journals in the field. As a total text inviting exegesis it is multivalent, and any one of the above solicits all manner of interpretation, including that which is often not evident on the page: that many of the songs have already been translated by Pastor Carl Strehlow. So that the work of a son who has enshrined the work of his father has been put before us as a kind of testament to that work, as well as the older testaments of the senior men of the Aranda tribe. The extent to which Strehlow's writings can be read—as in penetrated—is an endemic problem which any story of his life and work can't escape from.

It is also a book that conjures up the experience of reading as a journey, as a kind of initiation into Aboriginal country. This has been closest to my experience with it, and an aspect of the book I have been writing, since it has been moving in some of Strehlow's tracks. *Songs of Central Australia* is a country rich in sound and sentiment, feeling and meaning, poetry and cultural politics, translation and relationship. Strehlow once remarked that for the Aranda, 'The whole countryside is his living age-old family tree.' When you start in on *Songs* it proliferates like a family tree—roots in blooded earth, branches in night skies of eternity, its trunk in the clear light of day. Its 729 pages have a compass analogous to the imagined experience of singing songs that go on for hours and days and nights. Strehlow does not give you the poems at first, he tables their music. You get the basic tonal pattern of the sounds that have for so long belonged to the earth, and patterns that belong to the kangaroo, the honey ant, bandicoot, dog, fire, rain and so on. Strehlow documents the phonetics of chanting and the shifting stress accents that govern the song and always dramatically interweave with the lyrics, one seldom dominating the other. By the time we reach the second part of the book, 'Language and Verse Structure,' Strehlow has drummed the musicology of the songs into us.

The most spectacular songs are the most sacred. If one had access to Aranda it would perhaps be transgressional to read them because the songs contain the most sacred words connected with the secret names of ancestor beings, and descriptions of events and actions central to initiation rites on the *pmara kutata,* the totemic home place of the Dreaming being. In English—Strehlow's English which has its special stamp—they may be reproduced:

I am red like burning fire
I am covered with a glowing red down

I am red like burning fire
I am gleaming red, glistening with ochre

I am red like burning fire
Red is the hollow in which I am lying

A tjurunga is standing upon my head:
Red is the hollow in which I am lying.

This is from the 'Ankota Song.' The song is, as Strehlow points out, vivid, and its power is obtained by the simple device of repetition that in each stanza pushes forward the description of the figure in eagle down. The technique, which is as old as the Hebrew psalms and the Gilgamesh epic, is open to subtle variations. In the Aranda what also moves songs slowly forward is rhyme, as with the eagle song, where the birds circling over the MacDonnell Ranges can be sensed.

One above the other we are hovering in the air
Both of us are hovering in the air

Off the edge of the mountain bluff we are hovering in the air
Near the jagged mountain edge we are hovering in the air.

With some ti-tree verses we have:

Let the little ti-tree bushes intertwine their branch tips.
Let the little ti-tree bushes sprout blossom clusters on their branch tips!

Let the little ti-tree bushes spread their bushy crested tips;
Let the little ti-tree bushes sprout blossom clusters on their branch tips.

Let the little ti-tree bushes raise high the foreheads of their branches.
Let the little ti-tree bushes sit fast and avert their faces.

Strehlow comments: 'From an examination of these couplets it is clear that we find in the Central Australian songs not merely the balance of rhythms but also balance of thought.' And an interanimation of thought as well. Even after a few couplets you sense that everything in the land-scape is in dialogue with everything else. The eagle-downed ancestor is in communion with rocks that might tell the story as well. In the eagle poem an ancestor voice oversees the country and is in total communion with it. It comes as no surprise that these ti-tree bushes are really mythical alknarintja women, who may not leave their homes, and who must always avert their faces from all men.

Even at this early stage of reading *Songs* the thought occurs that if everything is vitally interconnected then the whole world is a poem, an enchantment simply awaiting notation, or indication. This process is not a matter of art so much as the simple acts of record, of pointing and not pointing, as the case may be. A poem is a manifestation of the seamless web of things, that may be named or not named, depending on the way we have cast ourselves in the greater song. Strehlow is at pains to show—in the context of describing the formal devices of Aranda poetry—what lies between the lines and behind them, what is deliberately masked by the poem, what might be spiritually latent in a song's manifest carnality.

Take the marvellous 'Bandicoot Song of Ilbalintja.' Strehlow lays it out in ten sets of couplets, beginning with the description of the sacred soak from which the ancestors emerge, the place that is the navel of Sire Karora, a supreme ancestor, through events that involve the birth of the sun (since Ilbalintja is also a sun-totem site), right up to the verses of the 'final catastrophe' (as Strehlow calls it). The latter are the couplets that invoke the ancestral powers previously sung. Such verses typically conclude a song cycle, or the last narrative incidents of a myth. They are designed to put to rest or lay to rest ('*gunama*, pushy down, push into the ground') the ancestors. In the case of the bandi-coot song the story concludes with nothing less than a flood of sweet ntjuimabna, the dark nectar of honeysuckle blossom, which descends upon the totemic site from the west. Like a river it roars across the plains sweeping Karora and all his sons back into the depths of the soak:

> *Their sweet dark juice is flowing forth;*
> *From the centre of the chalice it is flowing forth*
>
> *From the slender pistil it is flowing forth;*
> *The sweet dark juice is flowing forth.*

And later:

Let our sweet sap encircle them with rings;
Let the flood of nectar encircle them with rings!

Let our sweet sap ooze from the ground;
Let our dark honey ooze from the ground!

And ending with:

Let the flood of our nectar encircle them with rings
Let our sweet sap encircle them with rings!

I am trying to convey the fecundity of Strehlow's book, its depth and scope as well as its mysteries. As you keep reading *Songs* the marvel is that its fecundity increases. In the section 'Subject Matter and Themes,' the poetry fans out as never before and becomes, as you move through its 400 pages, the great delta, the beauty of which is akin to one of those stunning aerial photographs of Central Australia; all bone and membrane and bloodstream of pale green spirit matter that survived the inland sea.

Enough. This is how I saw the book when I first came upon it.[18] The journey of writing about it has yielded a different set of feelings, other readings, and the realisation that *Songs* is at least as much about 'him' as 'them.' The even more remarkable truth is that this can be said without detracting from Strehlow or the Aranda songs.

Strehlow is primarily a literary figure, as his friend and fellow anthropologist Ronald Berndt remarked to Strehlow's first biographer.[19] Berndt meant that Strehlow was trained in English literature and sought to apply comparative literature to Aboriginal culture. He was also alluding to the fact that Strehlow wrote as a man of letters rather than an ethnologist in the scientific mode: that his work was a literary engagement with and representation of 'the flavour' of Aboriginal life. To some extent this is a book about that: of Strehlow as a writer, about his writing, and his writing in relationship to his 'them'. These remarks play a modern tune without agreeing that Strehlow is a modern subject who calls for that treatment.[20]

In Shakespeare country Strehlow was very much at home. As a student at the University of Adelaide he planned an MA thesis on A.C. Bradley's theory of Shakespearian tragedy. Out of Strehlow's life much could be said about his own flaws, and one writer has reasonably made the comparison with both Macbeth and King Lear.[21] Arising out of *Songs*, I think of Strehlow in the context of *The Tempest*, the play that has increasingly been read in the context of colonial histories. In *Songs* Strehlow manifests himself as a Caliban rising to speak like a Prospero. Or to put this another way: the magic comes from Strehlow as Prospero summoning a Caliban from Aboriginal culture.

When Caliban hisses,

> *You taught me language, and my profit on't*
> *Is I know how to curse*

he is doing more than reply to Miranda's charge of ingratitude. He is rising up, turning the tool of his subjugation against his oppressor, the imperial Prospero. He is asserting his right to speak, and to revel in his lustful claims on the colonist's daughter. To this extent, of course, he is demonstrating Prospero's lack of success in civilising him. But not everything Caliban says is a reaction to Prospero. He has something to affirm for himself when he says:

> *Be not afeard, the isle is full of noises,*
> *Sounds and sweet airs, that give delight, and hurt not.*
> *Sometimes a thousand twanging instruments*
> *Will hum about mine ears; and sometime voices,*
> *That, if I then had wak'd after long sleep,*
> *Will make me sleep again: and then, in dreaming,*
> *The clouds methought would open and show riches*
> *Ready to drop upon me; that, when I wak'd*
> *I cried to dream again.*

> (3.2.133–41)

Arguably, this is Caliban showing himself to be something more than 'a savage and deformed slave' as one critic has called him: more than raw nature. He is gesturing towards a poetics of his own—realms akin to those that Strehlow represents, with all his Prospero-ish command of secret-sacred 'magic' in Aranda. Thanks to *Songs*, we have a strong sense— like hearing Caliban speak fully for himself—of the modalities of the other's speech and song.

But I am not suggesting that Strehlow was cognisant of or even interested in post-colonial constructions of Caliban. There is no sign that he was—even when he found himself defending Rupert Max Stuart in court in 1959, defending on the grounds of language a black man convicted of the savage murder and rape of a young white girl. The point is that Strehlow was in much of his local thinking an advanced critic of colonial racisms, and that in his life in translation he enacted some important dimensions of the Prospero/Caliban dynamic. A case might be put that he was more Prospero than Caliban, especially when we think of mishaps at the end of a life. But for reasons that will emerge, I have settled on Caliban.

But he was Luther's Caliban. The rhetoric of Strehlow's motives was never simple. He was never not the missionary's son. He spent a life in translation and not all of it was translating Aranda into English. True, that was his main work, his *raison d'être*: it was his day work, one might say; labour for which he sought most recognition. But he had other, central, part-time work, his night work, so to speak, his labour of love. This was the business of translating Scripture into Aranda. For all during the years he was working on *Songs*, he was translating the New Testament into Aranda. The work had been begun by his father. The son agreed to continue with it, and proudly saw it come to fruition in 1956 when it was published by the Lutheran Publishing House. In Strehlow's mind the two massive projects went side by side. In a sense— one that he never really spelt out—they were companion pieces: they complemented each other. The Christian work could hardly be presented to the academy. But it was work that came directly from his biographical roots because he too believed in Christ's Word, and also, I think, because he hoped that in the aftermath of the white destruction of Aboriginal culture, the essence of mission work was to heal, and that in the words of Neil Murray's profound song about mission history, 'Jesus might mend their broken song.'[22]

Strehlow's was the elegiac mode, no matter what we might want to say today about continuities and discontinuities in Aboriginal culture. At some moments there seems no reason to challenge Strehlow's sense of midnight. At other times there is. On the issue of continuity, of hope, suffice to say that as recently as 1999, a Land Claim over Strehlow's totemic territory was won on the grounds of a vibrant old man presenting *tjurunga* to the court, the reappearance of which would have astonished Strehlow, since he had come to regard himself as the recipient of all last things. I had the honour to meet that man, who expressed disappointment that Strehlow had failed to honour his father by using the Hermannsburg totemic ground-painting in his *Songs of Central Australia*. But this kind of experience, of meeting such 'informants' where I feel out of my depth, is not what this book is about, either.[23]

The book that celebrated Caliban was, then, written by Luther's man. The complex ramifications of this doubleness in Strehlow is an aspect of his becoming. The life that he spent in translation—misspent, he fell to saying at the end—was always a dual one. He was both 'within and against' the colonial system, 'at once old-fashioned and prescient.'[24] Put in more local terms, Strehlow's fate was to be a twentieth-century Christian saddled on a camel that had to look Hobbes in one eye and Rousseau in the other: his life's journey was with the 'fate of the Aborigines to be caught by the rising tide of disfavour and to be stranded by the ebb of romanticism.'[25]

But let allusions look after themselves as the book unfolds! Strehlow's self-divisions, his doublings in a life of translation, his deep translations from both sides of ardency, are what this book is about.

Still, it is misleading to give the impression that this book has an entirely literary focus. Far from it.[26] It is about Strehlow's travelling, his loving, his uses and abuses of authority, his political conflicts. That he was constructing himself in the writing of his diaries and journals is less important than his role in four decades of Australian history when much was happening on the race frontier of Central Australia. In his search for the poetry of song he was unavoidably political, which signals another truth: that poetry itself is always historical, always a breathing into social situations. Strehlow's early patron A.P. Elkin coined the expression 'literary liaisons' to acknowledge the privileged access Strehlow had to his Aboriginal culture, and it is an expression that highlights the relationships that composed his life as a collector and a white man with authority. His authority was never more stark than between 1936 and 1941 as a patrol officer, when his diaries move the story closer to Conrad than Caliban. At this time the state had oxymoronic policies that tried to combine racism with compassion. Strehlow the son of the missionary was in the thick of it. His story almost tells itself, as it concerns the heart of darkness that lives in that chapter of our colonial history, and the present struggle in the national consciousness to assimilate its truth. His diaries speak vividly—albeit ambivalently—of social fact rather than what is merely 'written.' After years of battling on behalf of Aborigines in 1941 he was called a Nazi on the floor of the Federal parliament: we are dealing with social forces rather than literary tendencies.

As dark stories go, no book on Strehlow can fail to mention his posthumous legacy. By the end of his life he had become the most possessive of collectors, a collector possessed. The Strehlow Collection—the hundreds of objects, photographs, films and sound recordings, manuscripts, diaries and genealogies—has been a matter of controversy for the last 24 years. At one point, Mrs Kathleen Strehlow, his second wife to whom he bequeathed his archive, allegedly removed the collection from Australia, only to meet governmental intervention. At another time state officials raided her premises for objects and documents suspected of being withheld from them. Mrs Strehlow remains an embattled woman. Her husband vowed never to part with his collection unless it was housed in terms that absolutely suited him. The interminable wrangles over the Strehlow Collection have brought little happiness to anybody, least of all (until very recently), Aborigines. Originally, the *tjurunga* came out of a cave. Today, controversy, suspicion and distrust can still make a cave of the Strehlow story.

Some years ago an astonishing profile of Kathleen Strehlow appeared under the title, 'Strehlow Collection Preserved in Vitriol.' It showed Kathleen Strehlow at home in Adelaide, seated at a table ready to defend the Collection, described as 'some 700 objects—15 kilometres of movie film, 7,000 slides, thousands of pages of genealogical records, myths, sound recordings, 42 diaries, paintings, letters, maps, a 1,000-volume library.' The article says that when Strehlow's first wife, Bertha, challenged his will—staking a claim on the diligently collected and identified sacred objects—Kathleen Strehlow said: 'I personally snipped the labels off 400 objects in the collection, so it would be useless to her if she got it, a pyrrhic victory. I'm the only one with the knowledge to re-document those objects.'[27]

There are other lamentable phenomena. Over the years Kathleen Strehlow has provided extracts of genealogies to the Magellan Petroleum Company. The Western Mining Company held copies of Strehlow's field diaries and sound recordings[28], that is to say, the wealth of primary documentation regarding songs, sites and ownership. This during the years of Northern Territory history when Aboriginal land claims were most contested, and when Strehlow's genealogies and totemic maps were of acute political value.

Even so, a positive legacy to Strehlow is flowering as we speak. There was, as I have mentioned, the use of his work in helping make the

Native Title Claim in Alice Springs.[29] There is the play written by Suzanne Spunner, *The Ingkata's Wife*, which sprang out of a compassionate view of the grieving widow. A cantata about *Journey to Horseshoe Bend* is in preparation. The first documentary film has been made. There has been a splendid travelling exhibition of the Strehlows' work in translation . . .* Out of the shadows come the leitmotifs from the treasure trove, and this book is in large part meant to complement the creative legacy in the spirit of Strehlow's highest wishes, which was to facilitate the 'hair-spindles' of Australian poetry. It is a document designed to critically appraise Strehlow as an old-fashioned hero whose life story, whose life-in-translation, creates a large sense of what poetry is finally made of: the inner and outer music of the body politic, of our relationships with our selves and each other, including 'others' who are not, ostensibly, 'us.'

Steven Feld, in his marvellously conceived book about the music and the feeling of the Kululi people and their forest birds in New Guinea, an account of 'weeping that moves men [and women] to song,' and of 'the poetics of loss and abandonment' (a paradigm made for Strehlow's story), begins by reminding us that anthropological writing involves a formidable sense of allegory. The genre is said to tell us significant things about ourselves, our modes of constructing "otherness," our idealisations and self-deceptions, our gender and class biases, our times and historical positions.' Feld is prepared to go along with this only so far. For at a crucial point ethnography is 'a specific yet indefinite encounter, something at once empirically brutal and interpretively subtle. This dynamic creates numerous ironic mysteries for the author, and no less for the people who are trying to figure out what the author is up to. But in the end the ethnographer's accountability for depiction is more than an accountability for representation; it is an accountability to other human beings whose lives, desires and sensitivities are no less complicated than his or her own.'[30]

Self-centred though he was, Strehlow was never in the modern sense burdened by problems of representation, so it would be unfair to his mode to lower the lattice of contemporary self-consciousness upon him. He wrote self-assertively out of himself, but without subjecting himself to much analysis. On balance, therefore, he was looking outward on 'the lives, desires and sensitivities' of his Aranda friends, and

---

*   The cantata was written by Gordon Williams, music by Andrew Schultz; the film was made by Hart Cohen; the installation is by Paul Carter and Ruark Lewis (see *Depth of Translation: The Book of Raft*, 1999).

denied to the end that he had betrayed them. His felt accountability is the subject of this book too, along with the living presence of lives no less complicated than his own. I try to indicate these lives when texts and social realities invite, but that is not my main focus and would require a different kind of book. Calling up Aranda voices in relationship with Strehlow is difficult. I don't speak Aranda. No Aranda speaker I know writes books, or reads books like Strehlow's, or rather, if they do they are a case deserving of special anthropological comment.[31] Strehlow's books are not dialogic in any way: they are not designed to bring other voices in from the veranda. The voices are there, their hushed tones can be heard in Strehlow's diaries and their presence formally recognised in some of his publications, but that is all.

Hero is another old-fashioned notion that is unavoidable, and resonant in anthropology. The biographical subject is inevitably a hero of some kind, even if an anti-hero, which Strehlow also was, considering his bad end. He is a hero if only because we have come through an epoch when the anthropologist has been deemed 'the very model of the twentieth century consciousness.' That is to say, a manly adventurer among the primitives whose world is breaking and crumbling before his eyes, even as he is face to face with his own doubt, his ignorance of them and himself, and so can never 'feel himself "at home" anywhere.' The words are Susan Sontag's, writing about the famous Claude Lévi-Strauss, the Frenchman whose anthropological fame arose from a brief, brilliant stay in Brazil. From Lévi-Strauss Sontag was able to construe the anthropological hero as not only homeless but one who was 'psychologically speaking, an amputee.'[32]

Susan Sontag put her finger on this phenomenon with a gushy fashioning of Lévi-Strauss, but in so doing she embraced the wrong hero. Prior to Lévi-Strauss there was Bronislaw Malinowski, sweating over his Conradian diary in the Trobriand Islands, and rupturing his diary by reference to an iconic code about himself—'Nietzsche breaking with Wagner'[33]—yet surviving the field to write his splendid anthropological treatises that had the descriptive power of Emile Zola's fictions.[34] The British claimed their hero (Pole though he was) before Lévi-Strauss occupied the armchair upholstered by Rousseau. Even before that, though, the Americans had their hero in the form of a German-born physicist called Franz Boas. It was Boas who went furthest first into the field when in 1883–84 he spent a long winter with the Eskimos, recording their songs and their myths with avidity, and at night in his cold dark tent reading 'Mr Kant as a good antidote.' He was writing, as exiles will, to his sweetheart, proving, in his case, that the journey was making him stronger as 'a thinking person.' He thought the 'valuable influence' of what he was doing lay in 'the strengthening of the viewpoint of the relativity of all cultivation (*Bildung*) and that the evil as well as the value of the person lies in the cultivation of the heart.' He had just remarked: 'I often ask myself what advantages our "good society" possesses over that of the "savages" and find, the more I see of their customs, that we have no right to look down on them.'[35] The hero, here, is implicated in a double movement: out and about as he is with the other, he must also face himself.

Into this frame Strehlow fits as hero in the classic mode—a solitary traveller, a dualistic lonely soul, a man who placed his own inner self in the company, physical and imaginary, of the 'savage,' all the while predominantly engaged in a literary endeavour. Malinowski in the field was reading his Kipling and Fenimore Cooper. Admittedly he despised the habit of novel reading, but that was that: he could not stop the literary flow of the imagination. Boas was reading Kant, all the better to reflect on the way consciousness creates its own objects. Strehlow, when he was a young man starting out on the first trips with his camels, was reading Johann Herder, Sigmund Freud, and the Bible. It was Freud's *Totem and Taboo* he had in his saddlebag when he saw his first corroboree, a bloody sacred ceremony. All of which, quite apart from his umbilical link to the natives he studied, whose songs he received from the field (the anthropologist as hero is a kind of grazier in the fields of the Lord), fits him up for the pantheon. And the fact that the subjects he studied were always his subjects and never quite his objects makes him unique in the history of anthropology, even though he was never, strictly speaking, an anthropologist, any more than he was a particularly original thinker. He was, rather, his problematic self. He might be regarded as a case study of what Boas called *Bildung*, 'the relativity of all cultivation.' Partly for this reason colleagues might come to be deeply peeved with him, or admire him patronisingly. So he becomes, to my mind, a fallen hero more interesting than most. When Malinowski was fictionalised, his brilliant friend Stanislaw Witkiewicz called him the 'Duke of Nevermore,' which is a reminder that travelling with heroes who are essentially products of the nineteenth century is bound to invoke Gothic tones here and there. But that does not make them, or the narratives they invoke, entirely anachronistic.

1 S. Gason, 'The Manners and Customs of the Dieyeri Tribe of Australian Aborigines,' in *The Native Tribes of South Australia*, ed. J.D. Wood (Adelaide: Wigg & Son, Adelaide, 1877), 39, 241–43, 282–83.

2 Reuther Papers, Lutheran Archives, Adelaide. My source on the loss of Reuther's songs was Pastor Philip Scherer, formerly of the Hermannsburg Mission, archivist at the above, and translator into English of the Reuther works.

3 Some verses are, however, scattered through Reuther's work. See J.G. Reuther, *The Diari*, trans. P.A. Scherer (Canberra: AIAS, 1981), microfiche no. 2.

4 Apart from some singing by Jimmy Russell up to 1975, which bore out the accuracy of Trooper Gason, and the durability of the song until then. Russell was recorded by Strehlow, and at other times by Luise Hercus (personal conversation, 8 July 2001). See also Luise Hercus and Grace Koch, 'Old Yet Always New: Song Traditions of Southern Central Australia,' Strehlow Research Centre, *Occasional Paper 1* (October 1997): 83–107; Hercus and Koch are also drawing on Philip Jones, 'Red Ochre Expeditions: An Ethnographic and Historical Analysis of Aboriginal Trade in the Lake Eyre Basin,' *Journal of the Anthropological Society of South Australia* 22, no. 7 (1984): 119.

5 Carl Strehlow, 'The Aranda and Loritja Tribes of Central Australia,' ed. M.F. von Leonhardi, trans. Hans D. Oberscheidt, 1907–20 (unpublished), vol. 1, pt I: 42–48.

6 In a series of public talks in Adelaide in 1934–35, eventually published as *Aranda Traditions* (Melbourne: Melbourne University Press, 1947).

7 Baldwin Spencer and Frank Gillen, *The Arunta* (London: Macmillan, 1927), 1:vii.

8 *Report on the Work of the Horn Scientific Expedition . . .* ed. Baldwin Spencer (Melbourne: Melville, Mullen and Slade, 1896), pt 1, ix.

9 Ibid., pt IV, 72–73.

10 Ibid., 111.

11 T.G.H. Strehlow, *Songs of Central Australia* (Sydney: Angus & Robertson, 1971), 128n.

12 For the most favourable account of Spencer and Gillen's work see John Mulvaney, *So Much That Is New* (Melbourne: Melbourne University Press, 1987); George Stocking, *After Tylor: British Social Anthropology, 1888–1951* (Madison: University of Wisconsin Press, 1992); and Richard Kimber, 'Gillen Time: The Creation of an Era,' in *Connection and Disconnection*, ed. Tony Austin and Suzanne Parry (Darwin: Northern Territory University Press, 1998), 59–63, which recounts Gillen's 'breakthrough' understanding about the distant past as 'the dream-times' and Aranda belief that he had powers of communicating with mythic beings and was called Oknirrabata, great teacher. Gillen's letters to Spencer are replete with developing understandings, including the remark that the word for 'Churinga' was 'a blending of the sacred and the miraculous': John Mulvaney, *My Dear Spencer* (Melbourne: Hyland House, 1997), 210.

13 See Paul Carter, *The Lie of the Land* (London: Faber, 1996) and *Depth of Translation: The Book of Raft* (Burnley, Vic.: NMA Publications 1999).

14 Morton was anthropologist for the Central Lands Council that pressed the claim for the Hayes family and others in 1997–99, and which resulted in a finding for the claimants (Hayes v Northern Territory, Federal Court of Australia, 1248, September 1999). He is also among the distinguished company of Spencer and Gillen, Geza Roheim and the Strehlows in having become a specialist in the Aranda; see his 'Sustaining Desire' (PhD thesis, Australian National University, 1985).

15 Freud's madman, psychoanalysis' actually, was Daniel Paul Schreber, a case study in paranoia (Case Histories II, vol. 9 of *Pelican Freud Library*), upon which

Morton essays, 'In Search of Lost Law: T.G.H. Strehlow and his Presentation of the Aranda' (1988, unpublished).

16   Most sustainedly in 1999, 'The Collector as Outsider—T.G.H. Strehlow as "Public Intellectual,"' Strehlow Research Centre, *Occasional Paper 2* (December 1999): 61–121.

17   Mudrooroo, *The Indigenous Literature of Australia* (Melbourne: Hyland House, 1997), 1–32.

18   See my 'Welcoming Dance: On Reading Songs of Central Australia,' *Overland*, Autumn 1992.

19   Ward McNally, *Aborigines, Artefacts and Anguish* (Adelaide: Lutheran Publishing House, 1981), 85. The remark was also in keeping with the emphasis Berndt gave in his oration on the day Strehlow died, where he honoured Strehlow (and his father) for collecting 'Traditional Aboriginal material in its own right—its oral literature and song-poetry, its music and dance, its religious ideology and philosophy . . . knowledge recovered from the jaws of destruction' even after 'the irretrievable loss of vast repertoires of aesthetic expression' ('A Time for Remembering,' October 1978, unpublished, 3, 5, 2).

20   When I draw attention to 'writing' I do not want to lead the reader deeply into the gaming house of relativities so stylishly run by James Clifford, who is splendid on the notion of ethnographic authority but who does not, thank goodness, free writing from truth claims about the world. Thus while he can begin by saying that the subjectivities produced in ethnographic exchange are 'constructed domains of truth, serious fictions' (*The Predicament of Culture* [Cambridge, Mass.; Harvard University Press, 1988], 10), which open the abyss, he goes onto say his discussion remains 'at the experimental boundaries of a *realist* cultural science' (emphasis added, 24n). Similarly, even when speaking so illuminatingly of ethnography as allegory, which opens up vistas for the pure imagination, he carefully adds: 'ethnographic texts are *not only, or predominantly*, allegories.' Indeed, as we have seen, they struggle to limit the play of their 'extra' meanings, subordinating them to mimetic, referential functions. The truth stakes come to ground. And so it goes, really, with the substantive nature of the one who writes: the author of the ethnography, the knowing, biographical self. When Clifford wrote his excellent biography, *Person and Myth: Maurice Leenhardt in the Melanesian World* (Berkeley and Los Angeles: University of California Press, 1982), try as he might 'to avoid the realist mode, the "fable" of identity and so forth, including the notion of an "inner life" or a "real" and "essential" self' (6), he was asserting the alternative model of the biographical subject as 'less than a discrete character than an assembly of relationships' (7), all the better to capture Leenhardt's 'problematic involvement with Melanesia' (129) and the local constructions of self. Well and good, but Clifford's book nevertheless reads like any other biography. And so it must be with Strehlow: even more so in fact, considering the solid state of his diary, testimony to an inner life, and a real self if ever there was one. My general point is that to write about Strehlow as a writer, a literary constructor of himself and of texts, is not to relativise all things at once.

21   R.G. Kimber, *Northern Territory Dictionary of Biography* (Darwin: Northern Territory University Press, 1991), 2:207.

22   Neil Murray's 'Broken Song' goes (in part):
>   *Now the song line is broken*
>   *people are chokin'*
>   *we're losing our direction*
>   *culture is eroding*
>   *I wish I could remember*
>   *what my father tried to show me*

and pick up what's come undone.
Jesus can you mend this broken song …
These Hands (Rondor Music, 1993), track 9.

23 I am referring to the fairly recently deceased Norman Ratara, the father of Conrad Ratara and a relative of Denis Ebarintja. The land claim essentially decided on the basis of Ratara's continuity of knowledge was for key parts of Palm Valley, downriver from *Ntaria*, or Hermannsburg. (The Palm Valley Land Claim No. 48, Report and Recommendation of the former Aboriginal Land Commissioner, Justice Grey, August 1999, 107–18.)

24 The terms are James Clifford's in *Person and Myth*, 1.

25 The resonant phrase is Stanner's, who would not have wanted to apply it to Strehlow, but it stands nonetheless as a diamond embrace of intellectual history. W.H. Stanner, *White Man Got No Dreaming* (Canberra: ANU Press, 1979), 148.

26 That is to say it is also close to Stanner's employment of Caliban in his 1962 'Caliban Discovered,' which situates the Aborigine in the long 'melancholy' history of misunderstanding, or studious ignorance of 'mentality, character and custom.' Stanner, prior to the full post-colonial argument, was able to use Caliban as the European precursor to the Noble Savage, as the Hobbesian preliminary to Rousseau's reaction, whereby the 'The Noble Savage is Caliban humanised and untruly romanticised.' On Stanner's argument, which seems now to have been informed by the melancholia of political impotence, 'Caliban' was in the line of oppressive misunderstanding rather than hope built on rebellious difference. Stanner, *White Man Got no Dreaming*, 144–64, especially 151–52.

27 Janet Hawley, Good Weekend, *The Age*, 28 August 1987.

28 See transcript of Proceedings re Lake Amadeus–Luritja Land Claim at Alice Springs before Justice M.D.A. Maurice, 8 September 1987, Commonwealth Reporting Service, Commonwealth of Australia, at 373, 371. See also David Hugo, former research director of the Strehlow Research Centre: 'Acquisition of the Strehlow Collection by the Northern Territory Government—a Chronology,' in Strehlow Research Centre, *Occasional Paper 1* (October 1997): 130.

29 The Strehlow cards could also have been played another way. His records document much discontinuity of culture: stolen or sold *tjurunga*; songs forgotten or neglected (the lost originals only to be found in his notebooks); disrupted kinship lines. In other words, a general decline in social authority, whatever one wants to argue about the changing basis of that authority. That the Northern Territory government decided not to put Strehlow to these uses was a decision based on politics rather than ethnography.

30 Steven Feld, *Sound and Sentiment: Birds, Weeping, Poetics, and Song in Kaluli Expression* (Philadelphia: University of Pennsylvania Press, 1990), x.

31 Peter Sutton writes (8 July 2001): 'Some Aranda people read books like Strehlow's—or at least some read Spencer and Gillen: I heard of a family who kept their copy with the *tjurunga* in the safe place.' And John Morton reports that 'the late H. Pareroultja, with whom I once worked briefly . . . was schooled in Strehlow's work and was known to authoritatively reiterate Strehlow's texts' (in *Country: Aboriginal Boundaries and Land Ownership in Australia*, ed. Peter Sutton, Aboriginal History Monograph 3 [Canberra: Aboriginal History Inc., 1995], 149).

32 Susan Sontag, 'The Anthropologist as Hero,' in *Claude Lévi-Strauss: The Anthropologist as Hero*, ed. E. Nelson Hayes and Tanya Hayes (Cambridge, Mass.: MIT Press, 1970), 188–90. Sontag is mainly drawing on Lévi-Strauss' chapter, 'The Making of an Anthropologist,' where he writes of anthropology as a mission and a refuge (from the professions): 'One can discover in it oneself,

even though one may have been taught nothing about it . . . it allows me to reconcile my character with my life'. Claude Lévi-Strauss, *Tristes Tropiques* (New York: Atheneum, 1973), 55, 59.

33   Heroic in playfulness as well: 'At night, a little tired, but not exhausted, I sang, to a Wagner melody, the words "Kiss my ass" to chase away *mulukwausi* [flying witches].' Bronislaw Malinowski, *A Diary in the Strict Sense of the Term* (Stanford, Ca.: Stanford University Press, 1967), 157.

34   Malinowski, ibid.; George Stocking, *Observers Observed: Essays on Ethnographic Field Work*. History of Anthropology, vol 1. (Madison: University of Wisconsin Press, 1983) and *After Tylor*, 87–98; Clifford Geertz, *Works and Lives: The Anthropologist as Author* (Cambridge, Mass.: Harvard University Press, 1988), 73–102; E.E. Evans-Pritchard, *A History of Anthropological Thought* (London: Faber, 1981), 197–200.

35   '"The Value of a Person lies in His Herzensbildung": Franz Boas' Baffin Island Letter-Diary, 1883–1884,' in Stocking, *Observers Observed*, 29, 33.

PART I: DESIRE

We are born, so to speak, provisionally, it doesn't matter where;
it is only gradually that we compose, within ourselves, our true
place of origin, so that we may be born there retrospectively.

Rainer Maria Rilke

1   Pentecost Twin

Cradled

IN JUNE 1908, at Hermannsburg in Central Australia, after a 'long period of dryness followed by strong rains sent by the Lord,' Pastor Carl Strehlow wrote to his superiors. He had something to complain about with regard to the blacks, and, rather as an afterthought, a happy event to announce:

> At the moment the countryside looks wonderful; the ground is covered almost everywhere in grass over one foot high and fruits and berries have grown in abundance for the Aborigines. But these good years normally have their disadvantages as well. While the Blacks never think of leaving the station during times of drought, due to material advantages, their Wanderlust is awakened when their local foods are in abundance, and many are unable to resist the urge to visit their relatives and friends; if they do not obtain the permission of the missionary, they go without permission without clearly considering the consequences of their actions . . .
>
> [T]he Committee has finally decided to ask you to send up another missionary to us. I have long complained to the Committee that there is too much work for a married missionary, even if he has an unmarried teacher to assist. The Black boys and girls need a supervisor; but the work involved with the Black women and children is too much

for a single female missionary who must also look after a large household. In my opinion, there should always be two missionaries on a
station as isolated as ours so that in cases of sickness etc. the second
one can help out and the church service does not need to be cancelled. Happily, the work has been spared such interruptions, but they
could occur.

I am able to inform you of happy news. God the Lord blessed us on
the 6th of this month with the birth of a son, who received the name
Theodor Georg Heinrich at Holy Baptism on Whitsunday. The Lord
came to our aid, even though there was no nurse and no doctor here;
thanks be to Him.

With this delivery I send you a notebook that contains myths and
legends of the Aranda; I wrote them down as the Blacks told them to
me, although I have allowed myself some abridgments and have avoided
wordiness as much as possible

With hearty greetings to you and your dear wife, to which my wife
adds hers.

Your thankful

C. Strehlow[1]

The little boy was a month premature. Into his mother's waiting arms
he went, and then, in the same movement really, the arms of the
Aboriginal maid Christina, and the equally warm-hearted and faithful
Marianna. It was Christina who would carry him to the baptismal font.
They were of a pair, these Aboriginal women who had been well
trained on the domestic front: they were his surrogate mothers. They
helped feed him, bathed him and led him to bed. It was their language
they spoke—cooingly, one imagines, softly as they handled him—into
his infant ear. While the household language was German, Theodor was
cradled in Aranda.

There was another thing that would link him to the place forever. As
a child born of *Ntaria*, the Aranda for Hermannsburg, he belonged to the
myth of the *Ratapa** or Spirit Boys: the story of two boys who were
twins. It also has to be said that he had been born on Pentecost, when
Christ's disciples had received the Holy Spirit by speaking in tongues, an
auspicious date, surely, for one who would place translation so ardently at
the centre of his existence. And that date, of course—just to complete this

---

* 'Ratapa' is Strehlow's Germanic spelling. Today we would write 'ratara'.

picture of evolving doubleness and complexity in the world of material and spiritual things—was in pagan terms under the sign of Gemini, the Twins.

The Intellectual Babel

Pastor Strehlow was sending his teacher in Germany 'a few lines from our solitude in the desert.' The almost incidental reference to the birth of a son made sense. He and his wife had been in their desert for twelve years and she had already given birth to four sons and a daughter. The babies had arrived as regularly as drought. The new arrival on 6 June 1908 was bound to add to their labours.

The other casual reference in the letter was to the myths and legends of the Aranda. This casualness also made sense. For it was one thing to have learnt the native language in order to better preach the Gospel, which was Lutheran practice in Africa, India and North America. But it was quite another to dwell on pagan belief. The head of the Mission Board wasted no time in telling Brother Strehlow that while his work on the Aranda was 'a beautiful monument to German diligence . . . the material is conceivably the most worthless that has ever been put into written language':

> It is almost all chaff with barely a grain here and there of moral worth. It obviously took no small amount of self-denial on your part to note down these unimaginative stories that can only be of some interest to an ethnographer. I do not doubt in the least the historiographical worth of your writings as a singular monument to a tribe that is disappearing from the earth. At bottom it is a truly sad tragedy that is occurring before our eyes. The extinction of the Australians is a confirmation of the not always applicable motto: the history of the world is the judgment of the world! Or better the biblical: whosoever does not have from him will be taken what he has.[2]

Strehlow did not reply to this slur. Even if he had been tempted to, how could he, without appearing to deflect from his task? He was going on with the ethnology that would make him as famous as his mission work. Since 1901 it had been his honour to send his observations to Baron Moritz von Leonhardi, who with Bernhard Hagen was to edit the material for the Stadtisches Volkermuseum of Frankfurt. *Die Aranda- und Loritja-Stämme in Zentral-Australien*, seven volumes on philology and myth, including translations of songs, was published by the museum between 1907 and 1920.

Baron Leonhardi had urged Strehlow to take special care to keep to truly original ideas that had not been influenced by the whites— by which he meant also the Christian ideas of missions. The hope was that Strehlow would shed light on the great topic of the day—ideas of the divine amongst the religions of the lowest people, especially since the book that claimed authority on the matter raised some difficult questions. Did, for instance, the natives have an idea of the supreme being? Did they believe in reincarnation? Strehlow was urged to 'preserve [what he could] for science before it is forever too late.' Leonhardi was as seductive in his pleas for Strehlow's time as the head of the Mission Board had been chary about its being wasted. 'Since [the ethnology] goes hand in hand with your profession as missionary you shouldn't hold it against me if I urge you a little towards it.'[3]

And from all of this Leonhardi was urging Strehlow to keep on sending his material in the hope that 'the spell of the book by Spencer and Gillen will hopefully be broken and destroyed by science.'[4] Leonhardi did not mean, necessarily, that the German tradition was compelled to revise all the disparaging terms of the British, empiricist, Darwinian way of thinking. This was the heyday of Empire, both British and German. But nonetheless the terms of ethnographic entry and address with regard to the 'native tribes' of the world were significantly different, and very much turned on attitudes to language.

So, when the little Pentecost boy was born on the desert mission station in 1908 he was in his philological element. How could he fail to grow up with an acute sense of language, of tongues overlapping and contesting, of what was said and then written being of central importance? He had been enfolded into a double life, where looking out presented one set of adjustments, and looking in would always divide him.

The Boy and the Donkey

There is a wonderful photograph of Theo as a toddler, standing beside a pram in which an Aboriginal baby is lying. He has a soft toy under his arm, a teddy bear. The fat little baby is smilingly asleep. Her name was Victoria. Theo is looking rather proudly at the camera, looking out for all the world as if the baby beside him might be a brother or sister. The intimacy of the shot throws the mind forward: it seems hard to imagine these children not growing up together feeling as if they had belonged to the same family all along. At the same time, though, at least half the point of the image seems designed to show something else: the difference between them. The novelty is that the black child is in the white culture's carriage. If the little white boy could speak the signs he might be saying, *Look what we've got.*

It is quite a contrast to another photograph of him which shows him alone on his tricycle on the verandah of the mission house. It is now a comfortable place designed only for his family (the other pastors had their own quarters). Behind him is a cockatoo in a cage. Behind it is an aviary built on to the verandah, with several plump parrots perched against the mesh, as if asking to have their picture taken, or to be set free in their native bush. Everything in the photo speaks of con-finement and European ways of civilising the wild, including young children. *No native in sight.*

There is another splendid shot of Theo about the same age, standing with his arms folded, squinting into the sun, at the centre of a group of 30 Aboriginal children. Some are older than him and they are standing too. The younger ones are sitting or kneeling either side of him. They are wearing the loose shirts or smocks required for school, but he is in knickerbockers and sailor suit. No proud showing off of Aranda com-panions here: he has been positioned as the odd one out, the only white boy in the native school. The Aranda children are shyly leaning against each other. *No one is touching Theo.*

But he is close to other bodies in another photograph, which shows him with his parents, sitting at a table with an embroidered cloth. His father—with collar—is sitting beside his mother in her apron. They are not the glossy couple they once were; it is all too clear that Theo came into their lives when they were close to being worn out by mission work. Both have put on weight, neither looks well, especially Pastor Strehlow, whose weight would soon enough contribute to his death. But Theo is smiling beside them, the black teddy sitting erect in his lap. His is the happiness in this photograph, while the glumness of his parents speaks of their years of toil, and their ambivalence, perhaps, at having only a few years earlier taken their five other children to Germany and left them there. *Theo did not complain about becoming an only child.*

The other happy shot shows Theo on the back of a donkey. Its name was Possum and it was given to him by Bob Buck, the owner at

Henbury station, some miles away to the south. Buck was already a character in the region, well known for his skills as a bushman, his drinking, profanities and intimacy with native women. He lived in a bush hut with a woman he called Looney: he had children by her and probably other native women. Strictly speaking, his flouting of legal marriage should have made him an enemy of the pastor, but Strehlow always made Buck welcome at the mission. At least Buck stuck with his women and treated them well, so the pastor thought. Buck's present delighted everyone, and *Theo was forever grateful to the bushman.*

My Silent Presence

Theo was a silent presence. The phrase was his. 'My silent presence in the house had always been accepted since earliest childhood.' It was his way of emphasising his reliability as a witness. He was the watchful, attentive one who heard everything. He drew a map of the house, and in particular where he slept.

During mealtimes he was present at all the adult talk; and he used to sit on the sofa 'every night.' And then, when he went to bed—here is his point—because he slept so close to his father's study and his parents' bedroom, 'it would have been impossible for me not to overhear most of the conversations carried on by adults speaking at normal voice level in the four rooms set down in this sketch.'[5] [See Plate 12.] He meant, of course, that he was conscious of everything important in the household, from his parents' most intimate joys to their deepest anxieties, most notably those leading up to the death of his father. Then he was acutely suffering with his parents, whose conversations—'sometimes in near despair, sometimes in near panic'—he could hear from his bed. He was listening in to their prayers, even as the prayers came to nothing.

A silent presence then, in an intensely claustrophobic situation. As an only child he had learnt to make a room of his own in his diary, which he kept in German. He seems to have written each day, but for some reason it has been lost to the Strehlow archive. What is on hand is his *Tagebuch*, charmingly illustrated with pen and coloured pencils. In the old Gothic German script he transcribed short verse and hymns. In 1922, he decorated a book he called *Buntes Allerlei* (colourful miscellany). Two years earlier he had worked industriously on two smaller drawing books, in which he recorded numerous plants—sometimes three or four to a page—with botanical precision. Beside them the names are German and English and Aranda. It is as if in these quiet works the silent presence had his head down in the company of other voices, among them those of his Aboriginal friends who were there, just outside the mission house.

Right outside his front door, there it was, the little church in all its stolid glory. It was made of stone and limestone, with a steep pitched roof, a rustic gesture towards the snows of Silesia. Inside, a timber floor and a short row of pews to the altar; and behind the altar a brooding painting of the Crucifix: a poor, dark, peasant image of ultimate suffering. The silence of the little chapel called out for joyous hymns to give it life there, planted in the middle of Australia.

Behind the church was the mortuary. And the school, and the meat house, and the other limestone buildings: all the whitewashed places that made a compound of good order, and which glared brightly, almost bearably, in the hot sun, and at night seemed to squat close to the ground, like little watch-houses, or the stumps of dead trees.

Not far off, on the high flat of the riverbank, was the congregation of Aboriginal homes. They were mainly grass huts, with conical hats, and the impression they made was of a New Guinea village, or even an American Indian encampment of wigwams. A Lutheran missionary in Goroka or Yellowstone Park might well have felt reassured to see that the Good Word in Australia had already convinced natives that it was better to sleep indoors out of sight of the stars than in the open by the fires with their dogs. Thereby they traded warmth for the sky, and instantly acquired the concept of accumulated debris, personal hygiene, domestic filth.

Through the back door of the mission house—as you can also see from Theo's sketch—he could get to the Finke, the 'Father of Centralian rivers' as he was to call it. To the west along the river he would have walked upstream, with the platform of the range to his left. In the gullies of that range the shade tightened among saplings and boulders. There were caves and rock pools, recesses and sacred places; *the* most sacred place was there in one gully. Further west you might pass the wide fat boulder for the rainmaking ceremonies, and then, beyond that, up a little creek you would come to one of the best water places, where springs fanned across black rocks at Kaporilja.

From there the native women carried fresh water down to the mission. In later years a concrete pipe conducted water to mission gardens and water tanks. But when Theo was a boy, that source was some hard walking away, and you had to go past the rain-making rock.

The sky is clouded with water moss
The sky sends down scattered showers

Over the rock plate the flow is echoing,—
Over the rockplates green with moss.

Ceremonial rubbing had created a basin into the rock: it was wide enough to take a boy's hand, a rock worn smooth by song.

Leaving by his back door and going the other way, downriver, Theo had the fan of white sand to follow. You only have to walk for ten minutes and the weight of the gorge is around you. The top of Mount Hermannsburg is ever-present, like some hump to your right. The range is called Pota Uruna, or Range of Doom, and its highest point is Lalkintinerama or 'where the nose bone went through.' Mount Hermannsburg on your right is a shadowy hump as you go, and on the other side, wide of the river's meander, there are sharp cliffs, with wild figs trees growing out of clefts. There are caves high up. The rock shelf at the base of the cliff is a place where a boy could sit and talk or scratch in the rock or dance or chant.

The riverbed is wide for miles down, a swathe of white sand and smooth pebbles. I camped there one night under the stars, still wondering if I might write this book. I cooked lamb chops and watched the dingoes lurking on the edge of the firelight, and wandered around, naked, in the balmy air. I hardly needed a tent, but put it up out of habit. Once inside I took a long time to sleep, electrically conscious of I was not sure what. It is soft sand to sleep on; the river is a welcoming bed. And yet the valley of the Finke is a brooding presence for some miles south of Hermannsburg so that, near the hump of range, you seem to be inside more than sleep. In the middle of the night I was suddenly bolt upright, not knowing what had woken me.

There had been a violent slippage of sound, a metallic racket of some sort. I put my head out. Stars and stillness: the riverbed white under the moon, nothing else. Then the clatter happened again: the stones, I realised, the loose stones on the riverbed. I saw the horse. Seeing me, it shied up, off the stones onto the river sand where, out of sight in the dark, it came to a muffled halt on the soft bank. There was a lovely night silence for a moment. But then, even more violently, the clatter rose up, a crescendo this time. I leapt out of the tent as a pack of shadows bunched and swirled in the dark, galloping off, upriver, away into the dark.

Once the brumbies had gone I fell back into deep sleep, wondering if they could have been descendants of Giles' horses: those he had known so fondly by name, and which had led him into this Aboriginal country.* When the sun came I felt strangely revitalised, sensual; aroused by the bright depth of the river valley, its whole resonance as a place. I do not know what the connections were, but I knew I had to write this book.

The Aboriginal boys, in Theo's time, would have run off down this river: in little bands, or packs; the wild ones. They ran and they jumped. They threw spears and sharpened sticks, boomerangs. They called out—and not to the Lord, or to their mothers and fathers. When there was water in the river they splashed, and tried to swim. One day Theo fell into deeper water, hit his head and sank. He would have drowned if one of the native boys had not pulled him out. His name was Gustav Malbunka.

All these boys would, when the time came, be initiated by their fathers and uncles. All this wild play—a kind of foreplay to the sexual passage they would go through in early adolescence—was grist to their pagan mill. Theo was struck by how tough they had to be. When there was a camp fire they had a game they liked to play: picking up the scorching stones and seeing how long they could hold them or rest them on bare skin.

Strehlow does not tell us the extent to which he felt he belonged to the pack running free along the river. When did his mother, or his father, call him? Was he ever late for dinner? And what was the punishment for being out so long with pagans? Did he, in the company of his black friends, ever strip off that sailor suit? Were they ever naked together? How far downriver, how far off, could the pastor's son go?

At all times the Finke is a powerful presence as it snakes its way around the Range of Doom. In the afternoon light it spreads itself

---

*   Ernest Giles led five expeditions into Central Australia between 1872 and 1876, at first with horses, later with camels, thinking little of the natives, much of Lord Byron, whom he read for breakfast, and a great deal of his horses, the suffering and character of which he described in memorable detail in January 1874, when one of his expeditions was floundering. See Erickson (1978: 153–55).

along as a welcome. At dusk it takes all the day down into itself. At night the stars fall into its sand which, under the flare of the Milky Way, is still white. In the middle of the night the pale belly of the snake has gone: it has rolled over and its course is as dark as the range. At dawn, a pale aqua slips along the horizon. The first pink in the sky also washes the ridgeline. Finally, when the sun shows itself, the whole bed of the river is sitting up again: it wakes with a shout.

The little limestone church on the river's bank might ring its bell, but the note gets lost along the river.

---

1   Carl Strehlow [CS] to the Inspector, 23 June 1908, Walter Veit Papers [VP]. Unless otherwise indicated, CS translations by Ken Woodgate.
2   Kaibel to CS, 6 August 1908, VP.
3   Leonhardi to CS, 10 September 1901.
4   Leonhardi to CS, 25 July 1907.
5   CS to Lohe, 23 June 1970, Lutheran Archives, Adelaide.

2   Clans

The Stoics[1] of Song

AMONG THE MANY important things said to me about Aranda people and their culture, statements made from deep, first-hand experience, perhaps the most important, and the one that took longest to sink in was this: *They feel it in their guts.* The 'it' was cultural damage of any sort, spiritual loss especially. The speaker was a fourth-generation Lutheran white man who spoke Aranda fluently and who had been working with Western Aranda people for most of his life. We were standing in the beautifully wooded country between the mission station and Gosses Bluff: the sun was going down behind the desert oaks, and the spinifex blond and shimmering.

At first I thought I was simply being told about the deep feeling of the Aranda people. About how much they cared for what they had lost, and so on. But it is better to say I was being enlightened about their structure of feeling. The emphasis was on how information of a certain kind is received, which is to say, not by intellectual channels, as we might call them, but straight into the body. Of course we too register emotions somatically: we ache, our bodies go cold, our hearts break, and we can in extreme circumstances become sick as a result. And I was being told more than that. In Aranda culture a set of identities thread thought and feeling inextricably into the whole body of the person, as if into the central nervous system, precisely because that knowledge involves a person's sense of self, their country, and the names of things, especially their ancestor being. That is to say the most important language that pertains to any of these dimensions of life—of selfhood and kinship, or home place or birth place, of origin and destiny—is integral to the health of the whole body. 'They feel it in their guts' is a way of saying that you can't separate these things out because they are by nature centrally, organically ingested and enacted.

The names, oneself, country: reverence for one imbued the other; they were at one with the other; and their common identity was sourced in genesis of the fecund ancestor creature. Perhaps the most vivid thing in Strehlow's *oeuvre*—and one that creates a leitmotiv for any study of him, as well as the people he enshrined in his texts—was the account he gave of the songmen in ceremony who call out the names of their ancestor beings, the names which are usually secret-sacred, and the calling of which constitutes a real re-enactment of how things began, how life was born and the country made. A real re-enactment for good reason: the names were not merely words in the air. Names constitute the ancestor beings themselves. And a man calling the name out—hurling it up in the song—was himself the ancestor. He was not acting out old times. He was dancing eternal spirit in present time.

Put this another way. In our culture we might think of living our lives in language. We are in it to varying degrees, and able at moments we are rather proud of choosing to contemplate the language apart from ourselves. Not so with the Aranda, who lived their language-in-life. In sacred matters no wedge could be driven between the language, its sacred performances, and life. As a result of this existential state of affairs, to appreciate the Aranda linguistically was to appreciate their essence. Nothing was more intimate than the sacred names; nothing truer, for all time. By virtue of the secret-sacred name a person had been woven into time. The linguist, one who interpretatively approaches the song, is one bearing witness to the eternity. Across Aboriginal country lies the net of language that *involves* the country in dance and makes the whole place glow with life, just as the songs themselves might be said to constitute the life.

To say 'they feel it in their guts' might also be understood as meaning: they feel it in the body of their country. To contemplate country is to gaze in a special way upon the self. Take the example of women dancing, splendidly described by Kimber and Smith. The women are painted up, they have white feathers on their foreheads, their breasts tasselled with white tail-tips of bandicoots, and possum fur strings as pubic aprons; and their dance goes sideways in short jumps, with hand claps and song. 'These women came from the west, where the Dancing Women Dreaming had travelled. In their land a mountain range held their dance, and at times they sat and looked at the distant lines of scarp faces that represented the ranked lines of the fringes and aprons, and they cried at the beauty of their country.'* The language of desire seeps into such accounts, even when we are not looking.

Among the twelve languages of Central Australia, the Aranda occupied the central position. At the centre of the region—if you think of Alice Springs as the navel, and the MacDonnell Ranges as the right and left arm of a green body—were the Aranda clan of the Caterpillar Totem. Their hunting ground, which served perhaps 100 people, ran along the range, and north and south of it for about five miles. Further out, other clans and skin groups had their totemic centres, and the whole region, linguistically speaking, shaded into five dialects of Aranda: Central, Southern, Eastern and Southern (with an Upper and Lower section), and Western. The mission station occupied one of the best spots in the homeland of the Western Aranda.

The Aranda speakers' immediate neighbours to the south and south-west spoke Martutjarra and Antakirinya, before meeting the Yankunytjatjara and Pitjantjatjara people further out. To the north-west and north there were the Anmatjarra, Ngaliya and Pintupi, and further out to the north and east, the Warlpiri, Kaytetye and Alyawarr.†

You might think, with this spread of Aranda speakers, that those in the rangelands were the Tuscans of the region, and those down south, in the desert, were the Ethiopians. Evidently not so. Certainly, the clans nearest the ranges had the pick of the hunting grounds; those further out had the toughest times in the ruggedly unpredictable periods of drought. In those times the water sources were still protected: they were, more often than not, the deeply important sacred sites, so by protecting them for religious ceremony the clan was doing both the culture and the habitat a service. In general, a range of food was often plentiful, and even in the south, life could be regarded as easy. The Aranda could call upon 140 species of plant food, 75 of which were

---

* This is vivid enough: even more so when you see the photograph of the tawny rock strata of the mountain range. See Kimber and Smith (1987: 232).

† These are the contemporary spellings: elsewhere I retain Strehlow's script.

exploited as seeds. And whatever the bounty of a season, the sparseness of material needs left much time for the cultivations of ceremony; for the aesthetics of a full spiritual life.

The dominant aesthetic principle was the one that organised the rituals. The songs that were sung, and the dances that went with them, the hours and days and nights of ceremony, were designed to commemorate the ancestor beings that had brought life onto the earth (and out of the earth, most commonly). The whole life of the region was, in a sense, conducted according to song, the secrets of which were central to the laws of the culture, so that existence was made to pivot on a stark contradiction: on the one hand a bare, elemental life; on the other, one that thrived on an elaborate use of language. The whole region was animated by song that gave almost everything—fauna, flora, much of the topography—meanings. The terrain was a narrative, and song, like rain, united the sky with the earth, and day with the stars of the night.

The songs were important among the deeds to the land. To sing the song was to transmit proprietorial responsibilities to others. A song served to locate men and women in totemic terms, and this in turn mapped individuals with regard to birth place and place of conception. A man or woman, and the clan to which they belonged, owned the song as they owned the land, rather in the spirit of copyright as it is understood today. They belonged to the song and its country, as much as the singer's voice belonged to his or her body. Everything in this scheme of things was vitally, metaphysically connected. Spirit animated earth: the ground of life was valued as spirit.

What had to be learnt by strangers to Aranda country was the extent to which everything had been imaginatively mapped. Discovering this was the saga Spencer and Gillen knew they had embarked upon, and which Pastor Strehlow knew he had tapped into, even though he did not travel much, or with an eye to Aboriginal country. A poignant, early bit of footslogging was done by the intrepid Olive Pink, who went 'walkabout' on the Burt plain with an 'Aboriginal headman' in 1931, moving about in the dry scrub, in rough, bare country fit for crows. When she wrote it up, *Oceania* published two photographs of a habitat that might have been a prototype stage set for a production of Samuel Beckett's *Waiting for Godot*. By contrast, Pink exclaimed that the sites 'retained a feeling of sanctity.' She was embracing the Aranda faith in the fecundity of ritual, and the beliefs that empowered them to not merely survive in an often hard place but to thrive there.

You do not need a notion of plenty to recognise the durability of Aboriginal wellbeing. Even though, by the turn of the century, the dislocations, disease and murder had reduced the region's population from 4,500 to less than 3,000, a vitality endured. It is manifest in the photographs of Spencer and Gillen: in the glossy vigour of the men, the warriors—'Knights of the Boomerang' as they were once called; and in the women so full of their bloom. The children are plump, cherubic. Of course these images are in part artefacts of the white imagination, but they are also proof, nonetheless, of the strength and grandeur of the desert people after 30 years of white contact. From them one can read backwards into something of the good life people had.

It is perhaps possible to say that their wellbeing was in part a result of their struggle for existence, the rigours of their skilled, hard life. Clans walked everywhere, ate food that did them good, and knew, as they went, that death walked with them. The mortality rate seems to have been high: reports of massacres amongst each other seem reliable.* The extent to which those sizeable, destructive battles were connected with the social dislocations generated by the white invasion is hard to say. The ethnology suggests a harsh culture with regard to the initiations of boys into men, even though very young children of both sexes were pampered. Infanticide was known: so was what we would call euthanasia. The country could not stomach those who were disabled, those unable to pull their weight in the communal round of hunting and gathering. The other absolute was the rule of patriarchy, and the initiations and kinship rules which enforced a regime of elders. Some of these men, perhaps the senior songmen, might be seen as priests, of sorts (although Strehlow did not agree with this): some were at least shamans in their techniques, or 'men of high degree.' The law, like the habitat, could be unforgiving, and as culturally conserving as rain.

Considering all of the above, it is difficult to find European terms that fully encompass the Aranda world. There is enough in most overviews of Aranda life to bring both Rousseau and Hobbes to mind. Young Theo, when he grew up, was going to say that Aranda reality was a unique combination of a sense of tragedy, strongly coupled with a capacity for joy. He also reported that the Aranda had in their mythology a concept of a Golden Age.[2]

---

* Most vividly recounted by Strehlow in *Journey to Horseshoe Bend* (1969: 36–42).

Servants of God

The other clan, the Lutherans, also had a belief in eternity, and a faith in sacraments and the Word. While they did not believe that nature was animated by spirit, they held that right belief could sustain a Holy Spirit in life. And while their bodies were deeply restrained in their religious ceremonies, their spirits were not: they could be at their freest and most believing in song. The pity was that they met the Aranda at a time in history when such affinities between pagan and Christian were not easily admitted.

They were a pious, stoical, industrious and culturally militant people, who had behind them what the Aranda had before them: a sense of persecution. They had arrived in Australia in 1838, religious exiles from their home country and therefore imbued with the feeling of right-eousness common to the collective memory of victims. In fact they were refugees from state intervention. King Frederick Wilhelm III of Prussia wanted to unify the various sects with a new liturgy. But defiant *Altlutherans*, Old Lutherans, protested on principle against state involve-ment in God's work, and took offence at the new interpretation of Holy Communion, holding to their belief that the bread and the wine actually become the body and blood of Christ. When their pastors resisted state demands they were imprisoned and their churches closed. When they had clandestine meetings in the forest, spies tracked them down.

With the help of a sympathetic London banker and shipowner, George Fife Angas, they sought refuge in Australia. In 1838 they bundled up their possessions, left their peasant holdings and travelled to Hamburg. When they sighted their vessel some cried out, 'O the ship is so black, just like a coffin.' But after the most patient of waits (caused by more state officialdom) they set sail for the other end of the world, where they would, God willing, make a joyous start anew. On the long voyage they comforted each other with hymns, the gusto of which impressed everyone who heard them. From their point of view the shipboard singing set them loose from every tie. 'Our psalms and hymns now seemed to sound much more delightful and majestic than they used to in man-made churches.'[3]

When they reached Adelaide they set to work—'with their hearts of oak and arms of steel'—like few immigrants before them. Indeed they were among the first to settle in the area after the Englishman, Colonel Light, had laid out his plans only three years before. They rushed to clear the best land, never pausing to consider the rights of native people in their areas, so assured were they of their rights to an agricultural inheritance. Soon they had fields marked out on the German model. Villages that sprang up in the hills east of Adelaide, and in the fertile Barossa Valley, each centred proudly around its church spire. The pastor and the schoolteacher, the blacksmith and the midwife—the medieval divisions of labour quickly produced prosperous, clannish settlements that did not pause to question the relevance of their faith in the modern world.

In this they were at one with the ferocious spiritual warrior who was their founder. Martin Luther's fervid doctrine of salvation through faith was born not only of his struggle with Rome's venal corruption of Christianity—principally the touting of indulgences by the sale of relics, so-called—but also his guilty sense of death: guilty because his consciousness was so riddled with the fear of death that his faith had to be revived, and then revived again, to overcome his sinful doubt in the Lord. His people, like his angry self, were people who would overcome, and whose will was inseparable from a faith in faith. And their faith, if they were to be secure against the intrusions of the modern state, was inseparable from the mission of preaching it.

The Lutherans ran the first school in Adelaide. They had mission stations outside Adelaide by the 1840s, at Port Lincoln in the west and Encounter Bay in the east. The men who led them, ministering to the heathen natives and to the white souls of the frontier at one and the same time, were strong in mind and body. So were their dutiful all-suffering wives. That did not mean that they accomplished their mission. The task they had set themselves—saving natives from their heathenisms and white souls from paganism—was never easy. In fact it was often insurmountably difficult, which seemed, according to their beliefs, to be a matter of God's willing it to be so. A life of struggle was ethnic to the Lutheran tribe. As dissenters they considered themselves purified by the fire of persecution. As believers they held to an orthodoxy steeled by will. They were that paradox of social change, fundamentalists who prided themselves on liberty.

As to the natives, their freedom would come when they had the Gospel. While the Prussian peasants were getting themselves established, the natives were not especially noticed, but when they were— around Adelaide in 1839—they were categorised in a way that put them in their place. 'They were lazy but good-natured, and lived by begging like gypsies. They went almost naked and wore only skins which they had tanned themselves and sewn together. The men wore long hair and beards like Jews. Fiedler expressed the curious view that perhaps they were descended from the Jews.'[4]

By 1866 Evangelical Lutherans had taken their mission as far inland as Cooper Creek near Lake Eyre. From the reports of those looking for the doomed Burke and Wills expedition the Lutherans had heard of the large numbers of natives in the area—souls calling out to be saved, for all the world like a lost tribe. 'The Lutheran Church has the oil and the wine for the wants of the poor heathen.'[5] The hope was that a mission far removed from other white settlements might have a better chance of becoming the ideal community they had in mind. Like the medieval monastery, it would be a hierarchical communal society based on agriculture, where the round of the day was determined by strict Christian tenets. This after all was the model that had inspired the founder of the seminary at Hermannsburg in northern Germany, as it had Carl Strehlow's seminary at Neuendettelsau in Bavaria. Such a community, it was assumed, would become an island of light in the surrounding darkness of modernity, from which others would go out to spread the Word, as still others from the pagan dark would want to come in.[6]

The mission was named Bethesda—Pool of Healing. The Bavarian-style church went up like a watchtower by the lake in 1877. When the Lutherans first arrived there was some water in the lake. More often than not it was a salt crust. The pastors who tried to make the mission work were to a man energetic and intelligent. A few were brilliant: men of some learning and skill in language, men of books as well as faith. But it often seemed that no amount of the good Word could contend with people who thrived in the dirt with the flies. They were savages who ate their children. They howled at night. They came and went in mysterious ways. Sometimes, admittedly, they seemed to follow what was required of them; but mostly they did not.

The stoical wives of these pastors were constantly appalled at the impossibility of keeping the natives clean. The impurity of their habits was at one with their nature and beliefs. This at least was the belief of the women of the mission who were themselves overwhelmed by the desert conditions. Soon enough, it seemed, the light and the dust had infected their eyes. They retired for days inside their shelter. Some went blind. Often the whole ordeal in the wilderness seemed designed to destroy their faith and that of their husbands. In the first 30 years of Bethesda the Lutheran authorities were chronically faced with the prospect of closure. Only the arrival of another new pastor, and the tenacity of a couple of old-timers, kept it on the map.

The natives must have noticed the white tribe's capacity for suffering. Perhaps that is what created a certain tolerance in them: a forgiveness, perhaps, of the rules and regulations they were subjected to. Still, they went on with their ceremonies, if at arm's length from the font where some had agreed to be baptised. They might be interrupted—as they were the night that Pastor Reuther came marching into the middle of their circle with his big book under his arm. In normal circumstances a man could be speared for that. But they sat the pastor out. He was not carrying a rifle. He was waving his book around, so they let him read from it, until he went away.[7]

At Bethesda the Lutherans learnt the Aboriginal language and translated it. Reuther excelled at this. His 1895 translation of the New Testament into Diyari was the first of its kind in Australia, and done with the collaboration of Carl Strehlow. He made dictionaries and grammars and wrote down myths and songs. The motive, of course, was to enable a Lutheran more easily to penetrate the heathen culture in order to change it, to convert it. The missionary assumption was that the intelligence of one tribe had to comprehend the other in order to save it. That was a tall order, linguistically, and a humanising, equalising one, potentially.

It seems not to have occurred to any Lutheran that there were certain affinities between their religious beliefs and those of the strangers they were among. The tribes had in common a sacramental culture. They subscribed absolutely to notions of eternity. They had rituals that enacted commitments to transubstantiation, where matter and spirit interpenetrated. They shared a culture where certain words and songs were sacred, and one that rested on the assumption that the ordering principle of reality was invisible because it was a spiritual one. The material world was there for all to see—and to share, as both tribes were uncommonly communal, at least in principle—but at the same time its meanings were located in spiritual history. As a result, the true believers in both tribes shared powerful characteristics: they did so *because* of their passion for converting the material into the spiritual. To this extent the religious teachers of both cultures were masters of metaphor, or poets of reality.

Because, perhaps, the Lutherans did not recognise their common ground with the natives they were bound to fail often in their spiritual endeavour. But lived metaphysics aside, they failed because it did not rain. And because daily life in the desert was so arduous; and because they had fraught relationships with other white men in the area who were only interested in transforming livestock and native labour into capital; and because the native's invisible life kept escaping them, even as they managed to do irreparable damage to it. To add to all this there was a lack of unity among themselves: one clan believed in the Second Coming, the other not. By 1877, the Lutheran movement had split, and a new start seemed possible further inland. This they did on the Finke River and called the place Hermannsburg, after the mission training centre near Hanover.

The Refuge of Rations

The mission had a lease on 1,200 square miles of land, some of the best land in the region—best in terms of the other white settlers who were hell-bent on making lives as pastoralists, and in the eyes of the Aranda whose land and best water places had been occupied by the invading cattle. The result was that for the first 30 years of its life the mission was cheek by jowl with frontier slaughter.

The scene was set, really, by the spearing of the two officers at the Barrow Creek telegraph station in 1874. As one of the dying men telegraphed his last words down the line to his wife, the word went out in the district, and overnight men were saddled up from a hundred miles away to get to the savages at Barrow Creek. Officially, two Aborigines were killed as a result: unofficially, the figure that emerged was between 50 and 90. The revenge party, taking their cue from Inspector Hamilton's advice that 'a close adherence to legal forms should not be insisted upon,' ranged far and wide, creating, eventually, a landmark called Skull Creek, where the remains of the Kaititja people could be detected for decades.[8]

For decades, too, the local white response to such frontier skirmishes was set. The popular outcry was that the natives had abused the generosity and trust of the white settlers, not that, as was so often the case when blood was spilt, the white settlers had raped an Aboriginal woman, or desecrated sacred sites, or taken the best water holes for their cattle (or all of these). After Barrow Creek, the Adelaide correspondent for the *Northern Territory Times* wanted to strike 'terror into the hearts of the natives' . . . 'wholesome terror' in fact. The same refrain was there in the paper's editorial ten years later, with the cry that the natives had 'no more trace of human feeling in their natures, than the Siberian wolves.' The result was the paper's call that 'the hand of every man be raised against a tribe of inhuman monsters, whose cowardly and murderous nature renders them unfit to live.'[9]

Hermannsburg had its ear to the ground as such murderous rumblings circulated through the district. Pastors could either block off or speak up. To its eternal credit it did the latter, especially as swaggering killers such as the Constables Wurmbrand and Willshire patrolled the district. Wurmbrand, a Prussian, disappeared from the territory as the race climate began to change. Willshire, whom Justice of the Peace Frank Gillen courageously brought to trial for murder in 1891, was a dandy who tried to persist, and who gloated.

Willshire was the kind of man who could make an ashtray of an Aboriginal skull. His most notorious statement—where he sang the praises of his 'Martini-Henry carbines talking English'—combines murderous glee at disposing of the virile Aboriginal men, and lechery towards their young women.[10] It is the kind of statement—a species of writing—that was designed to be the antithesis of any protective rhetoric by the missionaries.* His punitive patrols ranged far and wide from Alice Springs, and especially included the Hermannsburg area, after 1890, when he made his camp at Boggy Hole, a pretty place south of the mission on the Finke River. Naturally, the missionaries got wind

---

*   The notorious passage from *The Land of the Dawning: Being Facts Gleaned from Cannibals in the Australian Stone Age* (Willshire 1896: 40–43) runs: 'We came back and crossed the river at the same place, and again camped for the night. Next morning we went on, picked up another set of tracks on Black Gin Creek, followed them up, and at 3 p.m. came upon a large mob of natives camped amongst rocks of enormous magnitude and long dry grass, growing like a thick crop of wheat on the side of a mountain. They scattered in all directions, setting fire to the grass on each side of us, throwing occasional spears, and yelling at us. It's no use mincing matters—the Martini-Henry carbines at this critical moment were talking English in the silent majesty of those great eternal rocks. The mountain was swathed in a regal robe of fiery grandeur, and its ominous roar was close upon us. The weird, awful beauty of the scene held us spellbound for a few seconds. Out from between the rocks came a strapping young girl, with the agility of a mountain creature . . . this was the prettiest black girl I ever saw . . . a couple of imprisoned sun-beams seemed to be basking around her dimpled cheeks, and the grass beneath her feet shed tears of newly fallen dew. She was remarkably handsome, and every lineament of her face indicated a good disposition. One of my boys informed me that she wished to come in with us to the station. When I said she could if she liked a thrill of delight went to her heart and hope once more dawned.'

And then further on, an expression of compassion for cattle: 'The pioneer settlers in these wild parts have a lot to put up with. Cattle are so much afraid of these black demons on foot that they run and worry themselves to such an extent that they become poor, and are afraid to go in to water' (Headon 1990: 58–59).

of events in the backblocks, but Willshire found a way of discrediting native hearsay as well as the gullibly unhelpful mission people. 'The blacks,' he wrote, in his apologia for the unofficial policy of genocide, 'are extremely cunning in the way in which they enlist the sympathies of the inhabitants of the mission stations. If a white man happened to be out shooting emus or kangaroos, and blacks happened to be in the near vicinity, they would be likely to go to the missionaries and say that they had been shot at.' His 'emus and kangaroos' was a euphemism for his real quarry.[11]

The mission was privy to one atrocity when Mounted Constable Wurmbrand came through with his party of trackers. 'They caught three natives on the station, took them up to the MacDonnell Ranges, and shot them there,' Missionary Kempe reported to Adelaide. The dead men were still in their chains. 'With all the shooting that is taking place, it is hard to conceive that the native people have any kind of future,' Kempe reported, 'and our only hope is that they are rescued from this intolerable situation.' Kempe told the Minister of Education that 'the tribe at the mission station was not dying out, but our missionaries are convinced that if the Natives in other areas were treated more justly they would not be guilty of so many reprisals. The male population of the Natives has decreased alarmingly.'[12]

In fact, it seems, the native population of about 4,500 in 1860 had fallen by nearly 40 per cent in Central Australia by 1895, a loss of around 1,750 people. The loss was due to the white man's diseases, and to conflict between Aboriginal groups themselves, but the judicious finding of Dick Kimber has been that the dead included about 650 who had been shot, largely the victims of shooting parties never declared by official police reports, and mainly unrecorded by the white settlers who rode out with the police.[13] Willshire himself stated that on his trip after witnesses he did not keep journals.[14]

Willshire's regime came to its head in 1891 when he launched a 'terrorist raid' on Aborigines at Tempe Downs station just south of the mission. As Mulvaney reports: 'Using his native troopers to shoot two men, they cremated their bodies to conceal the evidence. It occurred so close to the station that Willshire callously adjourned there for breakfast.' It was the last straw for Gillen, who questioned the natives at the station and came on to Hermannsburg, where the wife of one of the murdered men had fled.[15]

Willshire's trial was much publicised. Fifty letters were written from the Territory in his support, his defence was funded by pastoralists, and he was found innocent by a partisan jury. It was a victory for the white frontiersmen, even though, in the eyes of Aborigines who had been terrorised for so long, Gillen emerged as their friend, as did, in other ways, the mission station. At the same time it involved a humiliation for the mission. Before his trial Willshire made complaints about its treatment of their natives and in 1890 an official board of inquiry was sent to the mission to look into matters. Fault was found on both sides—the police and the mission—but no one could say the missionaries had guns. The Lutherans felt persecuted. Kempe observed: 'It would probably be fair to say that the court was stacked. All available white cattlemen and station hands (about 50) were present to support the case for the police.'[16]

The police regime after Willshire's trial was more temperate. Mounted Constable Cowle, who began with Willshire and then replaced him, was stationed at Illamurta, 40 miles south of the mission, and was resigned to 'not advocating shooting,' in the 'so called good old style' and therefore had to find another way of dealing with cattle thieves. He thought 'the most salutary way' was the lash, which nonetheless was illegal. Although he could not get official permission to do so he carried on with it, notably in 1896, when he had captured five men for killing Hermannsburg stock. 'These I flogged and cautioned,' he reported, and at the same time rather worried that the missionaries might 'report me for wattling the deuce out of two of their blacks.'[17] What is remarkable about Cowle is the way the candour of his clannish talk does not run into the flamboyant sadism of Willshire. 'They should be made to respect the law of the Land that has been taken away from them,' Cowle declared of the natives, 'and it would be better for them.' He could say this while being quite genuine about forging a trust in communication that worked: he would be a decent employer, if 'they' believed in his personal honour.[18] All these permeations of voice, which filled the spaces once only inhabited by Aboriginal song, were to echo in the mind of young Theo. The manly frankness of the decent bushman was going to inhabit him as much as the lustful licence exuded by Willshire.

The simple truth was that missions, too, since it was historically integral to the white occupation, had to maintain their authority. As a refuge they were now essential to the natives, who came in for shelter, for food and for comforts as simple as a blanket, barely knowing, of course, the Christian faith that awaited them.

This was the state of things that Pastor Strehlow inherited. The respect that he earned among the tough men of the outback was a measure of his industry and strength of character. And so—as frontier time wore on—the essential gift-exchange at the mission station was more clearly entrenched. In return for refuge the natives had to cooperate as Christians. For some regular church-going, and the surrender of their children to the mission school, they could count on flour and sugar and tea, and on meat they could not be accused of having stolen. In addition, they were to wear clothes around the mission, and keep themselves and their clothes, especially their hymn-singing clothes, moderately clean. They were also to show an active interest in work around the station. And refrain from their sinful ceremonies. This was crucial, to Pastor Strehlow's mind. Even as he studied the beliefs of his natives he forbade their dancing and singing, and all that went with their bloody rites of initiation. For many years the mission laboured under the delusion that it had squashed the pagan ceremonies.

Thus the excruciating poignancy of the pastor's life, and the context he bequeathed to Theo. The mission was a place that gave to the natives with one hand, while militantly attempting to prevent and deprive them with the other. Its muscular Christianity would always have to contend with the worm in the wood of paternalism, because paternalism is so bound up with the authority of false love.[19]

---

1   My term, not theirs, naturally; and then not as Seneca would have it, as those who had freely eschewed the epicurean life, but rather those who could endure an existence of bare physical provisions and, out of that, celebrate life.

2   Apart from the classic texts by Spencer and Gillen and the Strehlows, the other main sources backgrounding these paragraphs are: Geza Roheim, *Children of the Desert: The Western Tribes of Central Australia* (New York: Basic Books, 1974) and *Children of the Desert II: Myths and Dreams of the Aborigines of Central Australia*, ed. Joan Morton and Werner Muensterberger (Sydney: Oceania Publications, University of Sydney, 1988); John Morton, 'Sustaining Desire' (PhD thesis, Australian National University, 1985) and other works including 'Singing Subjects and Sacred Objects' *Oceania* LVIII (1987), '"Secrets of the Aranda": T.G. H Strehlow and the Course of Revelation,' in *Politics of the Secret*, ed. Christopher Anderson, Oceania Monograph 45. (Sydney: University of Sydney, 1995) and 'The Effectiveness of Totemism: "Increase Ritual" and Resource Control in Central Australia,' *Man* 22 (1997). More generally on the desert peoples: M. Charlesworth, R.C. Kimber and Noel Wallace, *Ancestor Spirits* (Geelong: Deakin University Press, 1990); M.J. Meggitt, *The Desert People: A Study of the Walbiri Aborigines of Central Australia* (Sydney: Angus & Robertson, 1962); Fred R. Myers, *Pintupi Country, Pintupi Self: Sentiment, Place, and Politics Among Western Desert Aborigines* (Washington, DC: Smithsonian Institution Press, 1986); D. Bell, 1983 *Daughters of the Dreaming* (Melbourne: McPhee Gribble, 1983); A.P. Elkin, *The Australian Aborigine* (Sydney: Angus & Robertson, 1979) and *Aboriginal Men of High Degree*, 2nd ed. (St Lucia: University of Queensland

Press, 1980); Olive Pink, 'Spirit Ancestors in a Northern Aranda Horde
Country,' *Oceania* IV, no. 2 (1933); Deborah Bird Rose, *Nourishing Terrains:
Aboriginal Views of Landscape and Wilderness* (Canberra: Australian Heritage
Commisision,1996).

3   David Schubert, *Kavel's People: From Prussia to South Australia* (Adelaide:
Lutheran Publishing House, 1985), 22–27; Christine Stevens, *White Man's
Dreaming: Killalpaninna Mission, 1866–1915* (Melbourne: Oxford University
Press, 1994), 16–20.

4   Stevens, *White Man's Dreaming*, 16–20.

5   Schubert, *Kavel's People*, 96.

6   H.J. Schmiechen, 'The Hermannsburg Mission Society in Australia, 1866–1895'
(MA thesis, University of Adelaide, 1971), 1–5.

7   Stevens, 59–66, 119–28.

8   A vivid account of the event is in T.G.H. Strehlow, *Songs of Central Australia*
(Sydney: Angus & Robertson, 1971), xxxiii, 587–90, which in turn draws in
Spencer and Gillen's *Wanderings in Wild Australia* (London: Macmillan 1928),
401–04. See also R.G. Kimber, *Genocide or Not? The Situation in Central
Australia, 1860–1895*, Genocide Perspectives (Sydney: Centre for Comparative
Genocide Studies, 1997), 47–48, 54.

9   Quoted in David Headon, *North of the Ten Commandments* (Sydney: Hodder &
Stoughton, 1991), 53–54.

10   John Mulvaney, *So Much That Is New* (Melbourne: Melbourne University Press,
1985), 432, n. 27. And for Willshire's lust and blood lust see his *The Land of the
Dawning: Being Facts Gleaned from Cannibals in the Australian Stone Age* (Adelaide:
W.K. Thomas and Co., 1896). It should be obvious from Strehlow's account in
Journey to Horseshoe Bend (Sydney: Angus & Robertson, 1969), 7–12, that he
was to some extent vilifying Willshire while glorifying his father as a mission
defender of Aborigines. For a family defence of Willshire, see Austin Stapleton,
Willshire of Alice Springs (Melbourne: Hesperian Press, 1992). For a glib
recounting of Willshire's narratives, an exercise in literary relativism that
colludes with Willshire's colonialist rhetoric, see Sam D. Gill, S*tory Tracking:
Texts, Stories and Histories in Central Australia* (Melbourne: Oxford, 1997), 74–84.
For other details on Willshire, see John Mulvaney, *From the Frontier* (Sydney:
Allen & Unwin, 2000), 26–30.

11   Quoted in Kimber, *Genocide or Not?*, 44.

12   For mission responses see P.A. Scherer, *The Hermannsburg Chronicle* (Tanunda:
the author, 1995), 8; and Everard Leske, *Hermannsburg: A Vision and a Mission*
(Adelaide: Lutheran Publishing House, 1977), 17.

13   See Kimber, *Genocide or Not?*, passim and 60.

14   Quoted in Mulvaney, *From the Frontier*, 27.

15   Ibid., 28.

16   Leske, *Hermannsburg*, 17–18.

17   Mulvaney, *From the Frontier*, 33–36.

18   Ibid., 129–30.

19   The phrase is Richard Sennett's in *Authority* (New York: Knopf, 1980), 50–83,
where he argues not that love is impossible paternalistically, but that it is fraught
with the risk of pathos because it does not grasp its structural inability to
respect the freedom of others.

3   Missionswerke

Marriage and the Desert

CARL STREHLOW ARRIVED at Hermannsburg in 1894. He had come up from Bethesda at Lake Eyre, where Reuther, his fellow seminarian from Neuendettelsau, had found in him an excellent help in his translation work. It had become necessary, Strehlow wrote, to 'take our blacks further into the word of God and make them more acquainted with the New Testament.' But there was only so much you could do with words, despite the power of the Word. Progress with the instruction might be made and 'some youths could report in detail on the various miracles of the Lord and the journeys of the apostle Paul.' But these youths soon found the station's moral strictness not to their liking and would then 'leave the station of their own free will, one even leaving in secret.' 'Christianity is irreconcilable with the beliefs of the camp.'[1]

Reuther went with Strehlow to Hermannsburg, announcing when they met some natives that 'a teacher had come.' Pastor Reuther asked one of the young men, 'Do You know Dieri?'

'No,' said the Aranda man. They shook hands.

Pastor Reuther said, 'Your teacher is here. His name is Mr Strehlow.' He asked the young man, 'How many Christians are here?'

'We are fourteen Christians men here.'

'How many Christian children are there here?'

'Three boys. Hesekiel, Timotheus, and Abel, and one girl, Ruth,' was the reply.

The Germans were talking with a bright, willing man in his early twenties who was already a Christian and had taken the name of Moses. Moses remembered his parents running away at the first sight of white men because they feared spirits returned from the dead. From his own account, he seems to have been drawn to the mission after Pastors Schulze and Kempe had filled his belly with meat and given him a blanket when he was very cold and hungry. He had quickly taken to the Christian songs, and held the Commandments in his head after months out bush with his parents who were, in terms he had now adopted, still '*tjurunga* worshippers.' He remembered when the pastors grabbed the heads of his people during their ceremony, pulling the *tjurunga* out of their headpieces, and telling them that the *tjurunga* were bad and that they were lying and children of the devil. 'We are not heathens, we are iliara [initiates],' the others protested, but the battle continued through the years. By the time Moses was shaking hands with Reuther and Strehlow, he was a true believer in the word of Jesus. Whenever and wherever he could he told others about his faith in the eternal life rather than the *tjurunga*, which were man-made, and of wood which would perish. 'Old Man, don't do a lot of thinking. Put your faith in Jesus,' Moses said. His father coldly rejected him, and when he told his mother that he was happiest in school where he was taught God's word, she said, 'since you insist on staying here, you might as well die here.' From then on, even though he would be obliged to take part in the initiation ceremonies to be made a man, he was resolved to hold on to God's word and the Christian songs, more than on to the *tjurunga* and heathen songs.[2]

Despite the presence of Moses, whose depth of conviction was possibly not apparent, Strehlow found Hermannsburg in ruins. Eighteen years of toil by four successive pastors had failed to set a black Christian community on its feet, and the place had been abandoned. The droughts and the isolation, the cunning intractability of the heathens—all that had been bad enough. Pastors had worn themselves out, their wives had fallen ill, and in the case of Pastor Kempe, had died: some of their children, too, had died, as had those of white workers at the mission. So abandoned had the mission become that only a few months before, the eminent Professor Baldwin Spencer, travelling with the Horn Scientific Expedition to Central Australia, had thought it should be closed down or run by the government. In any case, Spencer, a secular scientific thinker who preferred Darwin to the deity, regarded the whole mission enterprise as futile:

> To attempt . . . to teach them ideas absolutely foreign to their minds and which they are *utterly incapable of grasping* simply results in destroying their faith in the precepts which they have been taught by their elders and in giving them in return nothing which they can understand. *In contact with the white man the aborigine is doomed to disappear:* it is far better that as much as possible he should be left in his native state and that *no attempt should be made* either to cause him to lose faith in the strict tribal rules, or to teach him abstract ideas which are utterly *beyond the comprehension of an aborigine.*[3]

Such reasoning was beyond the pale for a man of Strehlow's vocation, as well as being a nonsense to the mind of Moses. The pastor was not to know, either, as he looked about the mission that Spencer (as Protector of Aborigines in 1912, and then again in 1922) wanted to close the mission down. What he could see was that the roofs of the buildings had collapsed, and packs of playing cards lay about. Strehlow burnt the playing cards and set to work preaching and teaching, mending and rebuilding. More natives reappeared, heathens and baptised alike. Once their pastor had expelled the most corrupting white elements from the mission they began to settle again. A fence went round the vegetable garden: good rains that summer made the gardening worthwhile. Strehlow mended the old buildings, even though the rains washed away the clay between the stones. In eighteen months he had built an eating house for natives, as well as a school. In all this he had the help of a white builder and a stonemason, as well as the willing but unpaid native labour.[4]

He went back south to take possession of his betrothed, who had travelled from Germany to marry him. Frieda Keysser was the orphan daughter of a timber merchant in Upper Franconia. The *Register of German Nobility* indicates a minor German noble family with 'an attractive coat-of-arms.' She was better born than Carl (who was the seventh son of a schoolteacher in Brandenburg) and had been educated by tutors at home. Generations of her family had been formally educated. Carl's family had not. He went to his local school, where he was taught by his father; then to the seminary at Neuendettelsau, where he had received the solid missionary training of the day—in Scriptures and the Classics that would facilitate the teaching of Scripture. Against the wishes of his father he decided to be a pastor. He extended his education in the hands of a tutor, revealing something of his intellectual powers. Frieda's brother, Christian Keysser was to be a missionary too, a famous one, in New Guinea, and she had visions of a romantic life in Africa or America. Carl also wanted to go to America, from where the Lutherans on the frontier in Dakota were writing back vivid descriptions of the Indians, whose nobility and beauty they found ravishing. Reports from Australia were minimal, but that is where they would have to go, eventually, into the interior of a continent where life itself was an elemental prospect.

They met when Frieda was sixteen and Carl was twenty and passing through the Bavarian vicarage where she was a housekeeper, on his way to Australia. They spent a day walking in the woods together, and just as they were shaking hands to say goodbye, it passed through her mind 'that it would be nice to make my journey through life with him.' He wrote to her from Hergott Springs (now Marree), the nearest post office to Bethesda. Would she marry him? No, said her guardian aunt and uncle, she was far too young: the young man would have to wait three years. Further communications were forbidden. But he wrote again six months later: the mission authorities were urging him to marry and a wait of three years without any indication was impossible. The couple could write to each other but the marriage was put off, and it was not until three weeks short of her twentieth birthday that Frieda Keysser set off for Australia.[5]

At the Lutheran village of Point Pass in South Australia on 25 September 1895 Frieda Keysser married Carl Strehlow, thereby shouldering the stern duties the Lutherans gave their women, especially wives of missionaries. After a short honeymoon the couple trekked inland. From Oodnadatta they travelled by the mail buggy to Owen Springs, a journey of ten days, and then on to the mission by dray. Strehlow installed his wife in the mission house, freshly whitewashed. Her cases had been constructed to be used as wardrobes, and she had brought a chest of drawers, a sewing table and sewing machine, a reclining chair, pictures and curtains. She had the help of two native maids—two per missionary household was the rule. 'I like it here, and we are both so happy,' Frieda wrote back home in 1896. 'I would like to stay a long time, especially when the station is properly built.'[6]

By the middle of the following year a church was under way. 'We were again told to go and break stones,' Moses remembered, the 'again' referring to how he and other young men had prepared the house for the arrival of Mrs Strehlow. 'Then the young men dug the foundation, to build the wall. We worked outside . . . we worked with stones . . . The old men fetched water, to make mortar. Tobias did the sweeping. Samuel took the mortar up to . . . do the building. That is how they continued to work. We did a lot of work.'[7]

By December 1897 the church had been built. Admittedly, plans for a bell tower had to be abandoned, but it was dedicated on Christmas Day and Strehlow gave the service in Aranda, the tongue he had set about learning on arrival. From the start, Moses had been helping with the Aranda. Among a native community of about a hundred, 40 announced their desire to attend baptismal class. The early promise—the sweetness of their missionary beginning—is implicit in a moment Strehlow described:

Some time ago I went for a walk with my dear wife. When we returned, we heard in the distance a Christian with 2 men who attend the baptism lessons singing the melody Wie schön leucht uns der Morgenstern [How fair gleams the morning star]. At any rate, it was the song-: Wie schön ist's doch, Herr Jesu [How fair it is, Lord Jesus Christ], because one of the aforementioned came to me that evening and said that he wanted to marry. Whom? I asked. He gave the name of a girl of about 11 years who was attending the school. I replied that she was still a little girl and could not be a wife to him. Yet he felt that she was right for him; she had been intended for him since childhood. Well then, I said, take her as your wife: but you must never throw her out, you must keep her for ever. He replied that he wanted to do just that, and that I should give her away. Then bring her here tomorrow evening, I responded. On the following evening he returned, but alone. Where is your intended wife? I asked. He replied in a rather depressed, sad fashion that her mother did not want to let her go. I then pointed out to him that his bride was still very young, that he could easily wait, and thus I calmed him down.[8]

There would be many more poignant solicitous moments between the Strehlows and the blacks they were there to convert. Day by day—at the house, in the garden, and with all the duties attached to nourishing and maintaining the mission—one does not need to imagine the living patience extended to the native clan by the clan of zealous Germans. The practice of such patience was the Lord's will. But in practice, also, conditions were such as to try the patience sorely.

God's Rod

The year the church opened was the Strehlows' first disastrous drought. It lasted well into 1898. The garden died. The stock were dying. It became clear that there were chronic difficulties getting even basic provisions across vast distances. Strehlow's patience died on him one day in 1898 when 'a whole tribe' intercepted a dray of provisions at Ellery Creek, a few miles east of the mission on the track from Alice Springs. Fifteen horses were let loose and 100 pounds of provisions eaten—'no, gorged'—by black 'floosies' who had eaten seven stacks of flour even before getting to Ellery Creek. 'Eating is far too nice a word for such swinishness,' Strehlow railed. He wished his superiors back in Neuendettelsau could see the bad behaviour of the blacks at the mission, how dirty they were, how shameless and cheeky, running around. 'They think and even say: they don't have to work for meat alone; they find it in the creek!' One man bit his wife in the face out of hunger, he went on to say, because there was no soup. Others were still coming around begging for clothes. They were a very ungrateful people. They lacked real self-control. 'On the other hand they are taught, sometimes, by our whip, or rod. These Christians want to have a missionary who on the one hand has a whip, and the other the Bible.'[9]

In his early years at Hermannsburg Strehlow had given up on the 'old heathen.' Most were already impervious to the Gospel—'dulled,' he thought. There were fully grown men who had been baptised, 'but as far as I can tell Christianity is not a matter of the heart for them.' In contrast, there were those who had received instruction as children, serious, loyal, hard-working Christians—who sing religious songs at night of their own volition. The hope lay, then, in work with the children, but that required a certain amount of order in the community, where children could be expected to attend church and school with some regularity. If they disappeared according to the wanderlust of their parents, instruction was hopeless. If, as adolescents, they ran wild as young brides or paramours—indulging their heathen lusts casually, as was their wont—then that was hopeless also. It was not long before Strehlow thought it sensible to lock the native girls up at night. The success of the mission would depend on keeping Christians apart from heathens.[10]

But even at the mission there were savageries of the most disturbing kind. By the end of the ferocious summer of 1897 Frieda had given birth to her first son, Friedrich. She was worried about the catarrh and coughing that he shared with the blacks. She was shocked when one native mother was 'too lazy' to wash her sick child; the baby died. Then there were the cases when twins born to the black women were murdered and burnt. 'The blacks,' Frieda wrote to her homeland, 'said they had fish heads and the tails of kangaroos, that they were devils. No white person saw them. Such killings often take place, I know of others.'

She mentioned that an old heathen woman had died in the creek but the other women did not want to bury her: 'My dear man went down and found her.' And he himself had reached a lower point by then. Only weeks after the sacking of the dray at Ellery Creek he was writing: 'God alone knows when the mission will show a real upswing.' He had been dismayed when a woman hit another woman on the head over a piece of meat. And a man had left his wife with a bloody wound—just before church—because she had spoken to another man. He was upset at how the blacks looked at him. Blankly, or mockingly. He declared: 'It would be better if we hadn't occupied the place.'[11]

In the end the drought broke, more provisions got through, and the garden began to grow again. But in 1899 a measles epidemic 'snatched away very many, both young and old. During March alone twelve people died.' In 1900 it was dry again, 'so that many sheep and cattle starved to death.' In April that year there was the consolation of the baptism of heathen adults and one native child. But then several died of whooping cough. That year there were no Christmas gifts for the congregation because the camel train had not arrived.

The hard round of things was becoming clear and it would not change. The mission was an island of hope in a harsh desert of relent-less pressure, physical and social. From without, it had to contend with the waywardness and hostility of the white settlers. From within, it had to think and feel its way forward with the heathens who made a cult of their wanderlust. It was a trial, day after day, season after erratic season, of their faith and their missionaries' intelligence. It was all too easy for a pious Christian to indict the heathen and leave it at that. This had been the tendency at Bethesda as well as Hermannsburg before Strehlow arrived. Despite his wrathful outbursts, he was too intelligent to be summarily dismissive. Afraid that his missionary work was going the same way as it had at Bethesda, he had the powers of discrimination to see why, and to adjust his sights to what was possible:

> The people as a whole will doubtless not convert; only a small number will accept the Gospel. It is spiritually so difficult for the young Christians to follow the Lord's commandment to Abraham: leave the land of your fathers and your friends etc. and to remember the seriousness of Christ's demand: whosoever wishes to follow me must deny himself and take his cross on to himself. Having been preached the Gospel for over twenty years, they should confess their Christianity before their relations and their people.
>
> The hearts that the word of God must work on are particularly hard. Many heathen peoples regard lies, theft, fornication etc. as sins that incur the wrath of God. Not so here. Every first word that issues from the mouth of a Heathen is usually a lie. If one asks a Black a question regarding himself or his relatives, the answer is usually *juka* = I do not know. They do not see that this is incorrect and a lie. As regards property, they have common ownership of many things. The pipe is always passed around the circle. An article of clothing keeps on changing owner until it is completely in tatters. Whoever has a lot must give to him who has nothing; failing this, the latter often helps himself to his neighbour's property. Fornication per se is regarded as a permissible pleasure. Only infidelity is punished as a violation of the rights of another husband. The idea that God punishes sins is wholly foreign to them; their God does not care in the least about humans, just as they do not care about him. Thus the Christian faith must firstly awaken the consciousness of their sin and sharpen their conscience. That is why, when one asks the Christians at the confession time before Holy Communion whether they are sinners, one often receives the answer: No.[12]

Strong measures had to be taken. Firstly, those who did want to take up with the Gospel had to be kept apart as much as possible from their heathen relatives. Secondly, since a mass conversion was impossible, it made even more sense than before to focus on the language work—the translations of hymns and the Scriptures—for the benefit of the few. Thirdly, the ignorance of sin meant that wild or wicked behaviour must be punished. Officially, Lutheran history has it that 'Strehlow never once indulged in flogging or acute punishments: at all times he was the pastor.'

Strehlow himself might never have done any flogging, but two years before Theo was born a crisis of authority occurred that threatened both his language work and his regime at the mission.

Pastor Wettengel, who had been a welcome addition at first, complained to his superiors about Strehlow's translation of New Testament passages and the Catechism. He also accused Strehlow of not consulting him about the Catechism, even though he used it in the school. The matter was sufficiently acute for the Mission Committee to come to Hermannsburg to investigate. On the translation issue they found in Strehlow's favour, considering 'that Strehlow had been at Hermannsburg for eleven years, and had gained a thorough mastery of the Aranda tongue, and that his work on the Catechism was a revision of Kempe's earlier work'[13]

Wettengel also accused his pastor of mistreatment of the blacks. The Mission Committee cleared him of that charge too, but Strehlow's own remarks about his case reveal how entrenched the culture of corporal punishment had become.

It is clear that the treatment of the Aborigines, where love must be coupled with firmness, is a difficult problem, particularly with regard to the punishment of the guilty. The English government is guided by the following principle in their policy regarding the Blacks: let everything go its own way and avoid mixing in the Blacks' affairs, even if an Aborigine brutally murders his wife for some trifling matter. If a Black spears the cattle of a White, he receives 6 months gaol—not a punishment for the Black, since he does not regard gaol as a disgrace. He leads a life of sloth in good care and returns worse than he was before. What a black regards as punishment is labour, and, in particular, beating. This is why our predecessors beat poachers, because the livestock is necessary for the continuation of this mission. If a poacher is not punished, then he spears as many oxen as he can and leaves whole oxen lying untouched. Admittedly, the letter of the law does not allow the individual to carry out this punishment, because the law-making gentlemen do not have anything to do with the Blacks, even though beating is used on White criminals. Other missions have also resorted to this means ...

During my vacation in the south, while Miss[ionary] W was managing the station, several men who had speared oxen were beaten with Miss W's full knowledge. He did not protest to the white worker who carried out the punishment, nor did he speak out critically about it to the Committee. When some cattle were speared shamelessly close to the station soon after my return, our station's Blacks caught the offender and our stockman punished him with my consent. Miss W did not speak out critically about this, but behind my back sent such a hair-raising report to the Committee that P. Kaibel levelled the most serious reproaches at me in his initial agitation, and I was seriously considering whether it would not be better to hand in my resignation under the cir-cumstances . . . As Miss W has since told the Blacks that both he and the Committee object to beating, the notorious cattle thieves have now begun to increase the killing and in recent times have speared no less than 15 oxen; they left most of the meat behind. The commission vin-dicated me on the main issue and regretted that the law did not give us the right to punish cattle thieves in an appropriate fashion. In the future, we will be powerless in the face of these offenders.[14]

The resentment is clear, as is the weariness. Nothing had been solved.

Wettengel packed up and went back to Germany: he had a clutch of sacred objects with him and soon wrote up his observations of the native, as had Liebler and Reuther, joining the ranks of German mis-sionaries who had been drawn into rather competitive ventures into Australian ethnology. Wettengel sent his thoughts to the museum in Berlin, a development that prompted Strehlow's patron in Frankfurt to urge him on to do more with his own ethnology.

The Wettengel incident drained Strehlow and left him offended. The drought continued. Mr Hillier, who had been teaching at Bethesda, came to relieve him at the school, which was a good thing, but Strehlow was still the only missionary. When Theo was born, Frieda was again the only white woman at the mission.

Frieda's Regime

'At first I had to learn the language,' Frieda recalled years later:

That took me much longer than it took my husband, but eventually I could speak it after a fashion. There was an occasion when I wanted Rachel to do something; besides Pikepunta and Lukurta, she worked for me in the kitchen. She just stood there and laughed outright. I felt quite annoyed about that. So, when my husband came home from the school at midday, I told him my sad complaint. He said to me: 'How did you express yourself to Rachel?' When I repeated what I had told her, he remarked: 'No wonder! If you said it to her in that way, it was impossible for her to do it.' However, today I can no longer recall what it was.[15]

In due course Frieda learnt the native language, and her husband must have learnt to leave her alone with the domestic staff. At first she did not get along well with 'Christian women who were wilful and put on airs and graces.' She preferred the two 'heathen maids' who slept in their own huts. She let them do as much as possible, and she was pleased that they could sew their own clothes. 'They laughed a lot and were quite obedient.'[16]

When the children were little the domestic help was invaluable, especially in the summer. That was the case in Christmas 1898, when baby Friedrich had catarrh and a heat rash and was not sleeping. 'May God permit we have rain soon.' Still, that did not prevent a good Christmas for the Christians and heathens alike. Frieda decorated the Christmas tree and set up the crib and the manger. At first the people were speechless but tongues loosened when they saw the animals in the manger. On Christmas Eve all those who came to look at the display sang Luther's 'From Heaven High' and were given a piece of cake.

Martha was born in the summer of 1899. The birth was not as easy as expected but the baby was placid and made little trouble. This was just as well as 'Most of the time Friedrich lay weak and wretched in his cradle.'[17]

Frieda was also caught up with Aboriginal mothers and their children. Altogether, she estimated, there were 24 Christian women, not counting their children. Care also went, of course, to the heathens. As a nurse she would dispense belladonna or mercury. Frieda was struck by how quickly one of the native children had died: 'So quick!'

When domestic routines went wrong it was intensely frustrating. 'The blacks always seem to break everything, even what some families have kept for generations.' Nor did Frieda like the way the native men strutted around the station quite openly.

To her round of duties was added the garden. When the rains came it yielded lettuce and kohlrabi, and large leaves on the cauliflowers—all the more welcome when supplies did not get through. When it was especially dry only some of the asparagus came up. When they could not drink the water, their builder made lemonade instead. This was the pattern—one mishap after another, followed by a small or large event that brought relief. And all the times prayers were prayed and hymns sung: the Lord was their shepherd in the wilderness, and faith, while they kept it, would see them through.

The events that broke this chain of fretful effort were the Christian festivities, the dramas that beset her husband, or the occasional visitor from the outside world, as the mission was the most substantial settlement outside the little bush town called Stuart. Apart from that, the world that existed for her was the one she had left in Germany, to which she regularly sent her plainly written letters, and added footnotes to her husband's.

They were letters seeking sharp outlines in the face of the grind of mission life. The broken plate. The size of the cauliflowers. The behaviour of the natives. The sleepless son or daughter. The details hardly changed in the first decade of the century, during which she gave birth to four more sons: Rudolf in 1900, Karl in 1902, Hermann in 1905 and then Theo in 1908. As time went on the domestic help improved, as did Frieda's command of the language. In time she translated hymns into Aranda—joining, in her way, the Lutheran industry of translation. But for the most part it was the age-old female round of cooking, sewing, washing, mending and gardening that kept her busy and wore her out a little more, summer by summer.

Looking back, what she chronicles is durability rather than decline— how the first roofs they had were cane-grass from the Finke, very hot in summer, and the floors were clay, dusty in the heat unless they were sprinkled with the precious water; and how the natives helped themselves to the water, so that it did not last long in its iron tank:

Since I got stomach-pains from the well-water which was highly impregnated with magnesia, we arranged, week in week out, for the natives to bring water for drinking and cooking from the other side of the Finke, until it rained again and the floods came down and [sweetened] the well water. Later on, when we had more galvanised-iron roofs, we got more tanks installed, so that we had enough water for cooking, drinking, and washing our clothes.

Since we received only five gallons of kerosene a year, we had to use it very sparingly and hardly dared to light a lamp during the summer. For the kitchen, some fat was poured into a pannikin, a wick placed in the middle, and at night it was lit. We also made candles which burnt all right in winter, but in summer they melted and bent over. We generally received loads of provisions and necessary clothing twice a year. At first these were transported by teamsters; however, when 24 horses died [of feed poisoning] at Horseshoe Bend in 1896, the teamsters were dismissed and all loading was forwarded henceforth on camels.

It was always a great joy when the camels arrived, for in winter they brought potatoes and cheese. We were then able to live well for several months . . . especially when we could grow vegetables in the garden and had butter and eggs besides. Apples were about the only fresh fruit we could get and which could survive the transportation . . . Our order sheets were first scrutinised by the Mission committee in the South, and whatever those gentlemen considered superfluous was struck off the list, even when we had urgent need of such things as, for example, cutlery and swaddling material for my first baby.

One of those gentlemen once told me that they could not let us have any apples, as they hardly had sufficient to feed the pigs; besides, the freight costs were too high. That made me cry at the time, to think that we were only secondary to the pigs! Later on, however, things improved when we drew a salary: £75 for the manager, and £65 for other workers. Before that the missionaries got only £25 a year, and the Mission accepted responsibility for all other needs. But very often there was no money in the treasury, and so things had to be crossed off.

The mail came up the Finke every four weeks . . . If the Finke was in flood, you had to wait for days for the arrival of the mail, also for the loading which came by camels. It sometimes happened that when a camel was crossing a flooded creek, it stumbled and fell, so that the packing cases fell into the water. It so transpired, when we were unpacking a case of groceries that had been in the water, the caustic soda had spilt and was strewn all over our provisions. The sago was like a stone block, and the peas had begun to sprout.

It was a bad show when the camel didn't arrive on time and we were out of flour, tea and sugar supplies. We then had to borrow from our station neighbours. The 'blacks' received a serving of gruel every morning, at midday they had to search for their own food, while at evening they were given a piece of cooked meat. I had to cut up and count slices of bread, also for us whites. Most of the time two or three bullocks were killed every week. During winter, or on festive occasions, a sheep was sometimes slaughtered, mostly as a variation for the white people.

There was a time, too, when we planted orange and lemon trees in the garden, but they died from the bad [brackish] water. Also the grape vines didn't grow. At the same time the small almond trees were frost-bitten in winter and their roots were devoured by white ants. Very likely the winter of 1905 was the driest on record, so that we had to let the milking cows graze freely; for nine months we were without a drop of milk. Moreover, my baby developed a nasty rash.[18]

The baby was Hermann, the last before Theo, and his mother's chronicle speaks of a woman with a keen sense of her own story and an ambivalent attempt to sound uncomplaining. In 1910, eighteen months after Theo's birth, she fell ill. The precise ailments that slowed the Lutheran women are often vaguely named in the mission narratives: 'nervous condition' is the most common, and suggests that no amount of blessings, ceremonies, sayings and conventions could compensate for what was being asked of a woman. Frieda, like her husband, had had no real break for thirteen years. And for years at that time she suffered with toothache, and not once did she leave the mission: she never took respite in Stuart, the other white settlement that would be called, in 1933, Alice Springs.

The Strehlows were faced with the problem that beset all Germans in the colonies. How best to educate their children? The school at the mission was really for natives. Mr Hillier's tuition of their children was not a long-term solution. There was no school of any kind in Stuart until 1915. So in 1910 the ailing Frieda, and her very weary husband, at last had permission to take some leave of the mission. They travelled to Adelaide and left for Germany, where they arrived in 1911, resting there for nine months, ensconced among relatives.

Strehlow was pleased to give two lectures on the heathen beliefs of the Aranda. Frieda recuperated. Then, when the time came for them to return, the plan was to leave all of their children to be schooled in the German homeland and to return to the mission alone. The relatives were dismayed. It was customary to deposit children in Germany for a tertiary education, but not for the duration of schooling. The Strehlows' plan was surely extreme. And what of the youngest boy, who was barely four? Mother Frieda would be going back to the wilderness stripped of her brood.

Finally, the Strehlows relented. They would leave behind them only five children: Friedrich, Martha, Karl, Rudolf and Hermann, none of whom Frieda was to see for another twenty years, and whom Carl would never see again. The departure must have been an impoverishing moment for the Strehlows and the impact of their loss profound during the mission years that awaited them—yet another wearing test of faith. But with them, as they turned again towards Australia, they had their youngest and perhaps most sensitive boy, Theo. Back in the desert of Central Australia, he would be their only child.

Being Tamed

'Hold on to classical literature, or barbarism will come, and to the Bible, or paganism will come,' Carl Strehlow's teacher used to say.[19] On that principle, the pastor had given his older boys lessons in Latin and Greek, and instruction in the Gospel. Now that they were being educated in their homeland, the pedagogical focus was on his youngest son, who was expected to excel in everything. When he did not, he was beaten the way children in Europe had been beaten for centuries. The natives did nothing of the sort. Their children ran naked and free; they were brought to heel by scolding and shaming rather than physical assault, by the bogy of fear, rather than preaching or corporal punishment. When they saw one of their own boys, as a school monitor, beat the little children with a whip, he was 'nearly killed by the natives for doing so.' A slap was one thing, but not 'the sadistic pedagogy of the white man.'[20] When they saw whites preparing to punish their kin they thought murder was in the air.

The Lutherans had a long tradition of brutal parental authority. Luther himself was soundly beaten by his father, and, rather remarkably, by his mother. He famously confessed: 'for the sake of a nut my mother beat me until the blood flowed.' As if she knew how such treatment might bruise the self-esteem, she used to sing him a ditty: 'For me and you, no one cares / For that we are both guilty.'

'The German attitude,' as one historian has summarised, 'was that children were beasts to be tamed.' Medieval theologians were convinced that children were capable of sin at the age of six or seven. 'Some teachers are as cruel as hangmen,' Luther wrote. 'I was once beaten fifteen times before noon, without any fault of mine, because I was expected to decline and conjugate although I had not yet been taught this.' He sounds regretful, but that did not stop him recommending that for stealing a trifle one of his young relatives be beaten until the blood came.[21]

On this model God's will translated into the father's will. The father ruled at home and the teacher at school. In Theo's case two authorities—three if God was included—were rolled into one. In the infernal heat of his schoolroom at Hermannsburg Theo was subjected to them all. The Classics and the Gospel were drummed into him, even though he was obviously bright enough not to always displease his father with his performance. In his remarks about his father's teaching he did not emphasise the beatings, but years later, when he was a father himself, as he was preparing to beat his own children, often for minor offences, he would say that what they were about to receive was nothing, nothing compared to what he had received from his father.[22]

The model of good work—scholastically speaking—that arises from such teaching methods is bound to be of a certain type. It will be learning entrenched in the authority of the teacher, as distinct from the experience of the child. It will be learning based on rote memory at the expense of inductive explorations. Rules, record keeping, rigid habits will be the order of the day: duties rather than play. Pleasure—if there is any to be had in the intrinsic worth of the learning tasks—will tend to be deferred: the pleasure to be had will come from the satisfaction of having shown oneself, in the eyes of one's superiors, to have been virtuous after all, to have performed all one had to do. Under such an authoritarian regime, a brilliant student will excel at recitations, pedantry and mockery. The less brilliant will be dogged in the extreme, hopelessly thorough and unimaginative. Occasionally the system might produce a rebel. More often than not it brought about a grey repression in the student, a brooding, ambivalent inability to think—or be— outside narrow channels.

Strehlow has hardly written a line about his schooling at Hermannsburg. It is hard to know how he felt about it all: its effect lies hidden in his ambivalent recollections of his father. That Theo was good at his lessons was borne out by the skills he had by the time he arrived at Immanuel College in 1923. Latin and Greek were part of him by then, as was English. Bruce Chatwin, in one of his typical idealisations, exclaimed that Strehlow 'had grown up speaking Aranda, Classical Greek, German and English—in that order.'[23] It would be closer to the truth to say that along with English he was taught the Classics (Chatwin left out Latin) as a second language, taught formally, while his everyday talk from his earliest years was in German and Aranda. He would have been punished for making mistakes with the former. His free speech was in the latter. It was for German, and then Aranda, to draw him out.

German did it with its music. Hymns, and the great tradition of German song, were part of the air he breathed. The distance from the homeland might be closed by the right song. He could sing and play the organ as his mother had taught him. And the hymn-singing was, after all, part of the appeal the Gospel had for the natives; that was clear very early on in the experience of the mission. Hymns, along with stories, psalms and prayers, had gone into the native tongue as early as 1881, leaving aside those his mother had added later. Theo would have sung these with his schoolmates and had the strange experience of melodically transporting the pagan tongue spiritually towards Europe, of being the vehicle, linguistically, of a conversion. One imagines that he would not have been uncomfortable with that, as he lived so informally, acceptingly, in the house of both tongues. He could not, after all, sing the native songs, since they were forbidden by his father even to the natives themselves. But he could sing with his black friends the Aranda that was Christian, and that, in unison with them, was a belonging and freedom of a kind.

Black Juliets

What can be said about young Theo's life out there, along the river? One other photograph is suggestive. Here he is again on a donkey, this time in the company of Aboriginal friends on their donkeys. On a donkey you could get 30 kilometres from the mission in a day, away down river, or across country to fish and hunt and play—vigorous, chiacking, dangerous play, if we take some later accounts of growing up at the mission as a guide. When one historian of the mission speaks of it as a children's paradise, she has in mind the way the daily routines of the station—the devotions in the morning, the mealtimes and work times—framed a secure day for children which also allowed 'enormous latitude for enjoying oneself without the need for constant parental vigilance.' A boy who grew up at the time remembers the 'Strehlow time' and the fighting over the donkeys. Theo fought for the donkeys too—'he was like any other Aboriginal kid . . . Old Strehlow don't care, he didn't worry about fighting.'[24]

The gusto, the rumbustious activity of Aboriginal children, their physicality and ease in their own country, are the issue here. As a result of such running free—an education on the most progressive European model, learning from practical experience rather than formal instruction, where all the senses were constantly engaged in action rather than sedentary contemplation—he would surely shape a physical confidence and strength, becoming as much at home in the native bush as he was in his prayers. He would, if he could let himself go, have grown in that direction; if he had been brought up at a time when that sort of growth was valued for its own sake.[25]

Young Theo had Aboriginal friends. He names them in some of his later writings; Gustav, Christof, Lucas, James, were some of the boys at school when he was at school, or rather, when he was receiving instruction from his father and Mr Hillier. But when their names come up in his diaries and other contexts he does not enter into any reminiscences about growing up in a children's paradise. He does not cast himself back into an epoch of physical ease and kinship, of freedom and induction, or cultural privilege and wonder. And least of all does he celebrate the native foundations of any bushcraft. He had a donkey, but it might as well have been tethered.

The older he grew at the mission station, the greater his distance from his friends. 'He had always got on splendidly with them until the age of ten,' Strehlow later wrote of his young self. 'Even so, it has always been he who had been compelled to adopt the behaviour patterns of his dark playmates.' Is there resentment here, the white boy feeling that he should have had things more his own way? It seems so, even though it is hard to imagine how things could have been otherwise. In any event, he is emphasising the inevitable parting of the ways as the boys approached maturity. By the age of fourteen his friends were oriented towards their initiation rites of manhood, the secret-sacred ceremonies even his father had not been able to expunge from Aranda culture. At the same time he was being inducted into his 'entirely new interests.' At ten he started Latin; at twelve, Greek. 'These studies were interests that Theo could not share with his dark school friends,' any more than he could share their lives as novices ready for tribal initiation, or—he adds in a suggestive aside—be interested in the fourteen- and fifteen-year-old Aranda girls already regarded, 'like Shakespeare's Juliet as young women who were ripe for marriage.'[26]

It is as if Theo had absorbed Aranda life and language as a young child and the process had stopped of its own accord. Differences had to be accepted, if his own identity was to be protected and developed. Fundamental to this reasoning—it is implicit—are the strictures bound up with carnal and spiritual futures. He had made a precocious bond with Aranda language, but that was merely metaphoric of relationship, of intimacy. When meanings approached actuality—the bloody sexual initiation of boys, who were then to be trusted with sacred story and song, boys who would then be deserving of their 'Juliets'—he was not to be part of it. He might as well have been on the wrong side of the river, with them on the other bank. The Aranda culture was profoundly sexualised, and it was his fate to know this from the outside, as its student rather than its friend. Only in imagination could he live on both sides of the river.

During his last years at the mission, at the same period he was being inducted into his Greek and his Latin, he would have been more aware of what was at stake in his father's secular work, of the extent to which his father was caught up in his own dual life as a Pastor who would, even as he was conscience-bound to condemn the heathen, was being drawn step by step towards a deep regard for the depth of pagan spirituality.

On one momentous occasion his father drew him into the study to show him some *tjurunga*—the sacred boards with their inscriptions and the stones with their carvings, that were still puzzling the white ethnologists. Both the power of these objects and the power of that showing were clear to Theo at the time. In his father's study he was privy to things his Aranda playmates—still uninitiated—could not have seen on pain of death.

His father called the songs '*tjurunga* songs,' and he had been gathering them in the most intimate way. His informants, four Aranda men, came to his house, much to the chagrin of his wife. Pastor Carl took them into his study where they were allowed to sit on the floor. They sat on the rug and from time to time, between their snatches of song, and their accounts of legends, occasionally spat their native tobacco onto the rug. These men, it must be stressed were not Christians, necessarily, though it was the contention of Baldwin Spencer, and the particularly influential Sir James Frazer from his vantage point in Oxford, that Pastor Strehlow's information had been contaminated by Christianised natives. Of them only one, Tjalkabota (Moses), was the young convert of the group. The other Christian, Pmala, became one when he was 40, and so spoke to his pastor with many adult years as a well initiated pagan behind him. Talku, the main Loritja informant, who was in his thirties by the time he began to talk with the pastor, remained a pagan until he died in 1941, and he was happy to help very largely out of appreciation because the Strehlows had nursed the wounds after he had been shot by a police tracker.[27]

The principal informant, however, was the very senior man, Loatjira—'a medicine man of exceptionally keen intellect' to use Theo's subsequent words. Loatjira was the custodian of the Twins Dreaming, or the *Ratapa* (or Spirit) Boys from *Ntaria*, as the pagans called Hermannsburg. Loatjira's authority was known far and wide. He sat with Strehlow for years, and remained a staunch believer in his own traditions all the time the pastor was at the mission. He accepted baptism, however, only as an old and 'broken man' in November 1923, when he was well into his seventies. The life out of which he spoke during all of Strehlow's investigations was his own, and drawn out of him, obviously, by a white man who must have conveyed a regard that was sealed, eventually, by the photograph published on the front page of *Die Aranda*. There in the classic German ethnology, the four men stood, side by side with the country of *Ntaria* behind them, happy to have been helpful totemites. No such credit was paid to informants by the secular Spencer and Gillen.

Pastor Carl Strehlow had begun by preaching against native belief, but as his ethnographic studies continued he drew back from such militancy. He had, as his son was to write, a 'deep respect for aboriginal culture and for the creative aboriginal mind,' so much so that 'the sacred cave at Manangananga, two miles from Hermannsburg, was never permitted by him to be violated by any white intruders. When he visited it himself, he came as an honoured guest,' invited by Loatjira.[28] His father's regime, Strehlow was suggesting, was 'stern' and with 'strict discipline,' and yet by a strange process of respectful intimacy it was fostering a kind of quiet coexistence with the pagan culture.

Human Being Among Human Beings

It is important to say more about the quality of Pastor Strehlow's respect for the Aboriginal mind. Even though, as a Christian, he could not deny the heathen's evil ways, it was in the nature of the mission involvement itself to temper such judgments. Paul spoke of feeling 'a sort of universal obligation, I owe something to all men, from cultured Greek to ignorant savage' (Romans 5:14), and said 'though I am no man's slave, yet I have made myself everyone's slave' (Corinthians 9:19–22). The notion of going among people in this way was the basis of mission activity everywhere, and the seminarians from Neuendettelsau imbibed this creed which was reiterated as clearly as it could be by none other than Christian Keysser, Carl's brother-in-law, when he reflected on his way of working in New Guinea: 'When you work, you have to begin it as human being among human beings, not as master among servants, not as official among numbers, and not as preachers among listeners.'[29]

The phrase 'human beings among human beings' places mission intent squarely in the Enlightenment tradition.[30] It evokes Herder's exhortation to respect another culture in its own terms. That, Herder essayed, required 'sympathetic insight,' a capacity for *Einfühlung*, or empathy. Each nation, or culture, had its 'own centre of happiness,' 'its own centre of gravity,' which could never be exactly translated but, rather, interpreted with regard to its own incommensurable sense of what was True, or Good or Beautiful. Putting the matter linguistically, Herder thought of each culture as 'a harmonious lyre—one must merely have the ear to hear its melodies.' The Enlightenment man was committed to listening in ways that converged with the missionary.[31]

Keysser's project was to have an ear attuned to every nuance in the life of the other:

> The first prerequisite is the gaining of their confidence . . . in order to gain their confidence a profound knowledge is necessary. Knowledge of the individual! Therefore visit the villages, the homes. Talk in detail with the people and devote yourself to them. Never walk casually through the villages! Do not make any empty priestly noise. Rather show interest for the people, their work and their problems!—Make every effort to gain knowledge of the entities of the people, that is their villages, their tribes!—Indispensable is a knowledge of their manners and laws, their sins and weaknesses, of the good and evil.—Always place yourself on the ground of the laws of the natives!—Important is, furthermore, the knowledge of the language expressions, images, songs and myth.—All that is part of the soul of the people [*Volksseele*] and the cultural goods of the people [*Volksgut*] Disregard or even contempt shows lack of love and is detrimental. Love grows with the knowledge of the people.[32]

Keysser has in mind the Christian work, primarily. But by extension he is drawing a circle of toleration and imaginative entry that was just as applicable to Strehlow sitting with his informants in his study. The pastor was sitting down—human being with human beings—listening. That he was among them was entirely due to his empathy for their language. That he had a mind to do so was because he accepted the human existence of 'the soul of the people.'

Of course, this listening, this acceptance, was, from the Christian point of view, never entirely disinterested. The task in the long run was to show the pagan tribe their way from the folk lives that had affinities with the Old Testament, and to lead them to the New Testament, just as the nation of Israel came into nationhood. But having said that, the listening was at one with the others. It was a practice of knowing others, since 'Love grows with the knowledge of the people.'

This framework was crucially different from the one adopted by the British Darwinians, especially that of Baldwin Spencer, whose spell might one day be broken. By their own account they were scientists, not philologists or phenomenologists of religion, a field of inquiry that would get short shrift in Anglo Australia. To have something of the other's language was useful: pragmatically, it could be of some interest in sorting out the meanings of things, but it was not of the essence of cultural understanding. That could be best obtained scientifically—that is to say, as detached observers of native life, looking from the outside in, so to speak—by conducting oneself impersonally, and finding 'evidence' for behaviour that fitted theoretical notions impersonally constructed.[33] And so a distancing, a detachment, a shying off from any entry into the other inferior culture is the habit of mind that was opposed to the German ethnographic mode. From the British empiricist one tradition—a stark tendency to objectify the other as a specimen: from the European, a subjective encounter, albeit one perhaps marred by the ulterior designs,[34] but one conducive to relationship, and overall enhanced by an interest in listening *in the other's tongue*, and by a practised ability to hear their song, when song meant everything: the full innerness of the other's spirituality.

Theo, the silent presence, was there at his father's door, and sometimes, it seems, invited in. It must have been the counterweight to so much he heard from his father's pulpit.

Skirting the Dance

Despite all of the above, however—his father's intimate welcome of Aboriginal men, his close dialogues about native belief in the native language—there was an absolute barrier to the flow of contact. His

Christianity prevented him from going anywhere near the pagan ceremonies. The naked dances, the throbbing painted bodies of the ecstatic men in their initiation rituals, the spectacle of their celebration of totem, their union with nature, their simulations of procreation, their imaginative—no, their actual—entry into the erotic processes of the world at a celebratory level, without shame and with song, always with song—this he could not permit himself to face. He was compelled to withdraw, turn his back. More than that. He was doctrinally obliged to declare such ceremonies taboo. That was a condition for the privilege of settling at the mission and eating of its rations: that the pagan dances cease, that the pagan songs not be sung, on penalty of banishment from the mission refuge.

The sexual puritanism of the Christian was at the heart of the matter. Apostle Paul, Luther's favoured saint, and the man who had said most about the inseparability of faith from mission work, said as much about sins of the flesh. No sexuality was sacred out of wedlock: anything less was licentious.[35] Theo was acutely aware of his father's sense of sin in the sexual domain. It is never said by Theo, but the banning of the dances was part and parcel of this fear. The Lutheran regime at Hermannsburg was one conducted in apprehensive rejection of the native sexuality, their bodies, their nakedness. To admit the pagan ceremony into the culture of acceptance that they wanted to create in so many other ways was to admit the devil himself.[36]

There was another stark contrast to the Lutherans' prudery in the photographic work of Spencer and Gillen.[37] As the mission was campaigning for trousers and calico dresses for the natives, the rival ethnographers were dwelling on the splendid forms of the Aborigine. In Alice Springs, having observed the type of ceremonies Strehlow had forbidden himself to see, Spencer and Gillen gathered their Aranda friends into the clearings, brushed down the site and kept out the dogs, and posed the original people in all their glory: women by brush shelters, their shoulders and breasts gleaming; men standing and sitting and running, their thighs and chests as well formed in warriorship as any noble Greek on an ancient vase. Nowhere is this more evident than in photographs such as 'Welcome Dance' or a portrait Spencer called 'Dusky Venus.' Even as the Aranda were doomed like the kangaroo to extinction, they were there to be admired for the splendid physical specimens they were, to be appraised as objects of beauty. By contrast, a prudery and sexual trepidation kept Lutherans' eyes shut and lips sealed, for all the world as if they were as repelled by the bodies of the blacks as that other Protestant, William Dampier, when he came upon 'the miserablest people in the world.'*

It is a credit to Pastor Carl, however, that he could steady himself about the marriage business. It was quickly made known—even to the old men such as his informants—that they were living in sin with their polygamy, and especially with the custom of earmarking young girls as their brides to be. Pastor Carl campaigned; from all accounts he threatened and badgered: everyone, if they would be Christian, must get married. The exhortation went with the demand that clothes be worn, adultery and wife beating cease, and pagan dances end for ever. It was all part of seizing—laying hands upon without literally touching—the physicality of the pagan and putting him and her right.

When he grew up Theo told a story that illustrates the pragmatic nature of his father's zealotry. When the senior man Makarinja was undertaking instruction for baptism, Pastor Carl had to draw attention to the man's two wives: that could not continue if he were to become a Christian; he would have to give up one of the women. At which Makarinja protested: 'If he had two wives . . . he looked after them both. White men (whom he presumably thought were all Christians)

---

* The Lutheran trepidation about pagan beauty in Australia is even more striking when compared to their brethren in America, to whom Pastor Strehlow very much wanted to be posted. If he had been sent to America, and travelled west across the prairies to Wyoming, where Neuendettelsau preachers had lived intrepidly amongst the Crow, he might have had different eyes. Officially they were there because the seminary founder, the Reverend Wilhelm Loehe, had urged them to convert the 'lost sons of the wilderness,' which they attempted to do; but at the first glance of these 'lost' people their physical presence was almost overwhelming.

'Now they were very close. Beautiful view! How should I describe it,' exclaimed Missionary Schmidt: 'They came riding towards us as a front, these wild lords of the wild prairie on their courageous, mischievous horses . . . And behold! In front of that array of wildly beautiful riders walked proudly and dignified in their stately regalia two Indian chieftains.' These people, admittedly, were not naked, but that only further enabled an appreciation of the women, who were 'imposing and full of grace. No dirty blankets cover them but beautifully tanned, decorated hides adorned with eye-teeth. It looks most attractive when such a "daughter of the wilderness" is dressed in a tight leathery, clean garment [skirt], over which hangs a collar red as fire adorned with shiny white eye-teeth, reaching down to her waist, and when she mounts her beautiful horse and protects her brown face with a green branch from the burning rays of the sun. Yes, the Crows are attractive people. May they become the spoil of Christ, the Lord.' (Schmutter 1989: 128, 160.) Such appreciations are not common from the Australian frontier, least of all through missionary eyes.

had only one wife, officially, but unofficially they also had plenty of "other" wives on the side. What is more often they did not even look after one wife properly let alone the "others."'

'That was the end of Makarinja's interest in baptism.' And it was, Strehlow imagines, 'one of the few occasions when C. Strehlow would have been stuck for words.'[38]

The Aboriginal ways of love continued, as they would for the rest of the century. So did the dances and the songs, all out of Christian earshot. They would carry on side by side with the baptisms and the occasional Christian marriage. Deep down, the missionaries knew about pagan continuities, and it depressed them. For they liked many of these people, which meant that there must be limits to their militancy. At the same time, their *raison d'être* turned on being able to take matters in hand, which they would try to do in years to come, leaving them still depressed, and increasingly ambivalent. That is the aura so many mission photographs give off. There are the housemaids and congregation in heavy white cotton, freshly washed and their hair gleaming. And there too—though always in another photograph—are the young men, proud of their stockman's boots and belts. But it is a gloss, for the Aboriginal people posing for the camera had not lost touch with their naked, dancing, singing bodies.

Huns in the Desert

What the Lutherans were really trying to do in the Australian desert was make a medieval round of things. They had a passionate intensity they were trying to apply in ways Johan Huizinga describes in *The Autumn of the Middle Ages*:

> When the world was half a thousand years younger all events had much sharper outlines than now. The distance between sadness and joy, between good and bad fortune, seemed to be much greater than for us; every experience had that degree of directness and absoluteness that joy and sadness still have in the mind of a child. Every event, every deed, was defined in given and expressive forms and was in accord with the solemnity of a tight invariable lifestyle. The great events of human life—birth, marriage, death—by virtue of the sacraments, basked in the radiance of the divine mystery. But even the lesser events—a journey, labour, a visit—were accompanied by a multitude of blessings, ceremonies, sayings, and conventions.[39]

The Hermannsburg mission had its multitude of blessings. The ringing of the church bell was one. The singing of hymns was another. Prayers, births, baptisms, especially baptisms, these were events small and large to give form to the whole endeavour that could at times glow with the warmth of trust between congregation and pastor. These were what gave joy and the experience of good fortune: this and good rain, the arrival of provisions, letters from afar. They created the structure of feeling that was in a positive key. Equally though, and by stark contrast, misfortune was part of the same round. There was in the desert a chiaroscuro of feeling, for which no one in particular was to blame. What happened happened because the Lord had meant it to be. Freedom had little place in this world unless it was freedom to have faith. Faith would provide, or not. The round of mission life was a medieval mix of things fortified by the Puritan work ethic, but that was not to say that work would set anyone free.

We have to imagine the silent presence absorbing everything. Blessings one day; a kind of blight the next. Virtue rewarded one day; a kind of righteousness goaded the next. For the clan that had arrived in Australia hoping to be free, an atmosphere of grievance was not uncommon. This because they were a persecuted sect in a nation supposed to be free; and because some events did, it seem, conspire to rub salt into wounds. These events were real. Over Pastor Strehlow's last ten years, as their 'only son' was growing up, the mission had to contend with yet another humiliating state inspection; and then, when that was over, the serious threat of state persecution.

While they were in Germany the mission was in the hands of Missionary Liebler, a young man inept at human relationships, who had driven two valuable whites from the mission and estranged many natives with his discipline. In 1911, Liebler had received a visit from the explorer Captain Barclay, under instructions from the Federal government, to look into the treatment of Aborigines. Liebler told Barclay that the blacks at the mission had to buy all their food and clothing, that mission funds were diverted to other missions, and that the clothing given to the natives was rubbish. The news scandalised the Lutheran authorities and everyone else. Barclay also condemned the hygiene and lack of employment opportunities for the natives, and drew attention to the plight of the teenage girls, who were locked up at night. Their dormitory, in accordance with an earlier government specification, had a cement floor. Barclay, who was also reporting to

Baldwin Spencer, now acting as Protector of Aborigines in Darwin, did not go so far as to say that the mission should be closed; but he was of the opinion that the mission's land was the best in the region and could grow enough wheat to feed the natives in all of Central Australia.[40]

It was a devastating report and the mission authorities—still in Strehlow's absence—protested, laying the blame on Liebler. The Federal government was sufficiently sympathetic to ask for another report, this time by Sergeant Stott of Alice Springs, a man with local knowledge who liked and admired Pastor Strehlow. Stott's report was more favourable, drawing attention to the mission's isolation and shortage of staff. When the Strehlows returned in Easter 1912 they were 'welcomed by black and white alike' and 'the mission flag waved as the Aborigines sang the hymn "Abide O dearest Jesus, among us with Thy grace."' But much rebuilding—in morale and in other ways—had to be done.

By November 1913 they were ready for the state's follow-up visit. Dr Gilruth, the Administrator of the Northern Territory, came out with his private secretary and Sergeant Stott. Gilruth saw the improved sanitation and hygiene, but the girls were still locked up and many able-bodied men were sitting around the station. The food was satis-factory—two or three beasts were slaughtered for meat each week: twenty tons of flour, four tons of sugar, and 400 pounds of tea were supplied annually, as well as a lot of tobacco and medical supplies. 'He had a good look at everything and expressed his satisfaction at the work of the Mission,' Strehlow was able to write in his mission chronicle. The relief in these words does not express the humiliation to which the mission had been subjected, or the resentment it left in the hearts of the Strehlows, Theo included.[41]

At the beginning of 1914 'the Lord blessed us with lovely rains.' Later that year it was southern Australia that was ravaged by drought, as 'we heard of the outbreak of the dreadful European war.' The real horror, of course, lay in store for those in the trenches far away. The punish-ment for the Germans in Australia, especially in South Australia, where so many proud little communities had established themselves in villages replicating those of the homeland, was having Australian authorities turn on them as supporters of the Kaiser. In South Australia hundreds of Germans were interned; German newspapers were banned, as was the importing of German Bibles and prayer books; German schools were closed, and German place names were erased from the map. In this atmosphere of xenophobic reaction, the accusing gaze automatically turned towards the missions, especially the remote ones where German was still spoken and a 'Germanising of the Natives' might be taking place. One South Australian MP went so far as to exclaim that there was 'a Teuton Mission on the Overland Telegraph Line'—the mission was 90 miles from the line—'and these men could intercept messages from England.'[42]

In Central Australia a rumour went out that Strehlow 'had been lecturing and expounding to the Aborigines . . . that the Germans were their true Brothers . . . that the Germans were coming to take Australia.' Once again mission business fell into the lap of Sergeant Stott. In the summer of 1915 he made his way out from Alice Springs, taking it slowly and camping on the Finke about half a mile from the mission, where he interviewed several Aborigines. They had not heard the rumours. Stott then had a sociable dinner with Mr and Mrs Muchenburg who worked for the mission. In the roundabout way of policemen, he gathered that they supported the Allies. So he confided in them about the Strehlow rumours and was told there was not the slightest foundation to it. However: 'Mr and Mrs Strehlow are both very dispirited, rarely mention the War, both are very anxious to hear of their 5 children, who are in Germany.' He went on to the mission, where he told his friend Strehlow about the rumours and heard them emphatically denied. Strehlow told him he was a naturalised British subject and that as such, whilst in Australia, would always be a loyal subject. Stott wrote to his superiors that he knew nothing adverse about Strehlow: the man 'was devoted to his work and with no dangerous sentiments.' Besides, Strehlow 'could do no harm where he is.' The advice did not stop Gilruth officiously directing that 'all alien enemies on the staff of this mission to be interned at the mission without guard.'[43] The 'without guard' could hardly be expected to lessen the humiliation.

The rumours, the hostility, once again came from English-speaking settlers who had an axe to grind against German missionaries who had leases to land and the help of government subsidies for rations. As it happened, no subsidies were paid to the mission between the winters of 1917 and 1923, but that hardly mattered. It had yet another image to live down. This it did throughout the war by regularly demonstrating loyalty to King and country. The mission got a gramophone and Strehlow gathered them all to listen while the natives sang 'It's a Long Way to Tipperary.' Even the little children sang it, as they did the national anthem. The Strehlows must surely have resented the need to give such ostentatious proof of secular loyalties, when the desert wilderness could never be their homeland and, after all, their kingdom was not of this world: life hereafter was their hopeful bond with the natives, something beyond the realm of the secular state.

The year 1915 had the distinction, Strehlow recorded, 'of being the driest year we have ever experienced': 'There were severe drought and dust storms. The total rainfall for the year amounted to only 2¼ inches. The horses are too weak to work, whilst old cows and their calves collapse and die near the waterholes or are savaged by wild dogs. In Europe the dreadful war rages on and has implicated half the world in sympathy. May the Lord soon grant peace and good weather.'[44]

But the drought, like so many other obstacles, went on. The burdensome task of digging for water only came to an end in October, when 'God sent us beautiful rains and floods.' The war in Europe continued and there was renewed uncertainty about settler toleration of their presence. The other good news in October was that 'in spite of the strongest agitation by the enemies of our Mission in political newspapers and in Parliament, our Government has granted us the further use of our Mission land.' They soldiered on for another year.

In 1918 the new school year began after the heat of the summer. Four new boys and nine girls were admitted, so that 44 children were now on the roll: 45, counting Theo. The school had another teacher at last. Hillier had left in 1910, and the place was without a school until Mr H.A. Heinrich arrived in 1917 with the camels that brought the mail. Not that the camels always arrived with good tidings. For weeks that year the mission had no flour and sugar, and they had to send packhorses down to Henbury for basic provisions. That spring the mission got off 122 horses to market: they lost 30 along the way and those horses that got to market sold at a loss, yielding an average of £4 a head.

'On the 11th of November an armistice was declared between the warring [nations].' These were Strehlow's terms: they did not buy into German feelings about the massive defeat. 'We celebrated the Christmas festival as usual.' The year again ended in a big drought. 'May the Lord let us see better times again, after so much want and suffering.'[45]

1 'Moses' Story,' Albrecht version, unpublished, undated, 36. Translated by Pastor Paul Albrecht from the document in Aranda typed by his father, Pastor F.W. Albrecht, according to dictation by Moses. In the original document Paul Albrecht stresses that in places his translation may be unreliable, although 'the general thrust of Moses' story is clear.' My page references are to that 68-page document and are cited with Paul Albrecht's permission. Another 'Moses' Story' was dictated by Moses to an unnamed Aranda man in 1948 and T.G.H. Strehlow cites this almost in full in *Songs of Central Australia* (Sydney: Angus & Robertson, 1971), 347, the original of which has also been translated by Garry Stoll on 30 October 2000. Whereas the Albrecht version stresses Moses' embrace of Christianity, the unnamed version has strong things to say about early mission hostility to Aboriginal belief.
2 Moses' Story, 10, 53, 18, 40.
3 John Mulvaney, *So Much That Is New* (Melbourne: Melbourne University Press, 1985).
4 Everard Leske, *Hermannsburg: A Vision and a Mission* (Adelaide: Lutheran Publishing House, 1977), 17, 26–7.
5 John Strehlow, *Adelaide Review*, July 1995.
6 Frieda Strehlow [FS] to Frau Rechner, 3 March 1896, Walter Veit Papers [VP].
7 Moses' Story, 45.
8 Carl Strehlow [CS] to Keysser, 18 December 1896, VP.
9 CS to Richner, 2 February 1898, VP.
10 CS to Keysser, 11 November 1898, VP.
11 CS to Rechner, 3 September 1898, VP.
12 CS to Inspector, 30 May 1906, VP.
13 M. Lohe, 'The Modern Chapter,' in Leske, *Hermannsburg*, 28.
14 CS to Inspector, 30 May 1906, VP.
15 P.A. Scherer, *Select Letters From the Outback* (Tanunda: the author, 1994), 43.
16 Frieda Strehlow to Rechner, 3 March 1896, VP.
17 FS to Rechner, 9 February 1899, VP.
18 P.A. Scherer, *The Hermannsburg Chronicle* (Tanunda: the author, 1995), 44–45.
19 T.G.H. Strehlow, *Journey to Horseshoe Bend* [JHB] (Sydney: Angus & Robertson, 1969), 5.
20 Geza Roheim, *Children of the Desert: The Western Tribes of Central Australia* (New York: Basic Books, 1974), 75.
21 Richard Marius, *Martin Luther: The Christian Between God and Death* (Cambridge, Mass.: Harvard University Press, 1999), 22.
22 Mrs Shirley Crawley, personal conversation, July 1996.
23 Nicolas Shakespeare, *Bruce Chatwin* (London: Harvill. 1999), 409.
24 Barbara Henson, *A Straight-Out Man: F.W. Albrecht and Central Australian Aborigines* (Melbourne: Melbourne University Press, 1992), 1–2.
25 Peter Latz, personal conversation, 23 February 1997.
26 *JHB*, 27.
27 T.G.H. Strehlow, *Central Australian Religion: Personal Monototemism in a Polytotemic Community* (Adelaide: Australian Association for the Study of Religions, 1978), 58; *JHB*, 67.
28 *JHB*, 27.
29 Christine Keysser, *Eine Papuagameinde*, Neuendettelsauer Missionaschriften Nr 65 (Kassell: Barenreither-Verlag, 1929), 317, quoted by Walter Veit, 'In Search of Carl Strehlow: Lutheran Missionary and Australian Anthropologist,' in *From Berlin to the Burdekin: The German Contribution to the Development of Australian Science, Exploration and the Arts*, ed. David Wealker and Jurgen Tamke (Sydney: New South Wales University Press, 1991).
30 Veit, 'In Search of Carl Strehlow,' 130.

31 For this outline I have glossed Isaiah Berlin's *Vico and Herder* (London: Hogarth, 1976), 186–87, 209–10, 190.

32 Veit, 'In Search,' 130.

33 On Spencer's impersonal style see my 'Through Larapinta Land: Baldwin Spencer's Glass Case,' in *Exploring Central Australia*, ed. S. R. Morton and D.J. Mulvaney (Sydney: Surrey Beattie & Co., 1996).

34 It might be argued that the orientations cancel each other out once it is conceded that each had ulterior motives, one to gather specimens, the other to save souls and eclipse the pagan culture. My point is that the stagey insincerities of the former have been overlooked: viz. Gillen to Spencer in July 1901: 'In doing work such as we are engaged upon one has to be careful not to let the savage perceive that you disapprove of or disbelieve in his ideas for if he once gets that idea into his head he will shut up like an oyster and wild horses will not drag reliable information out of him' (D.J. Mulvaney, *My Dear Spencer* [Melbourne: Hyland House, 1997], 342). And on the methodological impoverishment that goes with not insisting on a full linguistic entry into the other culture, consider Spencer's praise of Parunda as an informant on the following basis: 'Though he could not write a word, he always had a paper and pencil…on which he made marks' (D.J. Mulvaney, *From the Frontier* [Sydney: Allen & Unwin, 2000], 194).

   Still, the British tradition can be too easily caricatured as overdetermined by theory and 'scientifically/objectively' removed from native belief. Even 'Frazer often said that the efforts of field workers would long outlast his own theoretical musings,' and when Darwinian anthropologist Tylor 'embellished his *Notes and Queries*' for fieldworkers, he advocated 'the collection of myth texts written down in the native languages, "translated by as skilled interpreter," as the most natural way to get at "beliefs and ideas"' (George Stocking, 'The Ethnographer's Magic,' in *Observers Observed* [Madison: University of Wisconsin Press, 1983], 80, 73). Nonetheless the general point stands: British methodology tended towards a behaviourism that regimented concepts of the field for some decades, when the problems were, very largely, a quest for a discourse that might encompass decent personal relationships with native 'subjects.'

35 In so far as the pastor equated savage sexuality with the promiscuous he was part of mainstream British anthropology, preoccupied if not titillated by the notion of 'group marriage,' along with the possible scandal of 'sexual communism.' See L.R. Hiatt, *Arguments About Aborigines: Australia and the Evolution of Social Anthropology* (Cambridge: Cambridge University Press, 1996), 36–77.

36 A contrast was the nakedness which was permitted at the Ernabella Mission in the Musgrave Ranges when it was set up for the other desert people, the Pitjantjatjara. There the children came and went to school naked, and they sat at the desks naked, while being encouraged to speak their own languages. Shaming was not an essential to Christian teaching.

37 Ron Vanderwal, *The Aboriginal Photographs of Baldwin Spencer* (Melbourne: Viking O'Neill and the National Museum of Victoria Council, 1987), passim.

38 T.G.H. Strehlow, *Christianity and the Australian Aborigine* [1960], 3.

39 Johan Huizinga, *The Autumn of the Middle Ages* (Chicago: University of Chicago Press, 1996), 1.

40 NAA MP 367/1. 512/1/1057 for Gilruth; and AA(ACT) A 3201/1 TE 1596 for Stott.

41 Lohe, 'The Modern Chapter,' 31.

42 Ibid., 31: for a vivid overview of anti-German policies during World War I, see D.F Hansen and I.V. Hansen, *With Wings: A Centenary History of Immanuel College* (Adelaide, Openbook, 1996), 77–90.

43 NAA MP 367/1. 512/1/1057 for Gilruth: and AA(ACT) A 3201/1 TE 1596 for Stott.

44 Scherer, *The Hermannsburg Chronicle*, 34.

45 Ibid., 39.

4   Death of the Father

Epic Journey

THEO'S FATHER WAS wearing himself out at the mission. This was clear by about 1920—after the internal mission strife, after the Great War, after another decade with hardly a week's rest. For years he had been seeking leave, asking his superiors for a replacement, but to no avail. He was a big man, overweight, and clearly in poor condition, and his health was failing. He soldiered on, but in 1922 he developed dropsy and pleurisy and his need for medical treatment became urgent. He telegraphed—via Alice Springs—the Mission Board, which made plans for a doctor to be sent up from Adelaide.

But there were delays, excruciating ones, and he was getting worse. The whole household was sweating on good news from the south, but it did not come. Young Theo—the silent presence—was recording the rising concern in the family, arousing himself to biblical injunctions. On 2 October 1922, while attempts were still being made to secure a car to take his father to a doctor, he wrote:

> our dear President, the Right Reverend Pastor Stolz, who is well to the front in all Church Committees, has also made no effort to look for a car. The men will experience one day what has been written in Matth.

XXX, 41–46. It is to be hoped that at least a 'place will come up' otherwise we will have to agree to undertake this uncomfortable and dangerous drive in a buggy. Pastor Stolz and the most worthy United Evangelical Lutheran Synod of Australia might also do well to read what is written in Luke, Chap, X 30–37, in James 11, 13, and in James 11, 15–16.[1]

A 'silent presence' Theo may have been, but here already, at the age of fourteen, a wrathful diarist is at work, a recorder hell-bent on judgment.

And at that time, in that moment when he was filled with dread for his father, before they had to set off on the buggy to Horseshoe Bend, the young diarist found himself describing another powerful experience. With regard to his father, he was looking inwards. Here, in the same passage, he is looking outward, observing the eclipse of the sun:

It was very beautiful to see. About ten minutes before 1.30 PM it started from the south west (from left to right) of the sun. Slowly the small black disc of the moon became wider. It was getting darker. Everything became still, the shadows became very clear and sharp. Every single leaf was outlined very clearly on the ground. All the air had a black and yellow tone. Jacob and I watched it through a sooty piece of glass. Suddenly it struck half past two. Then one could see the black disc of the moon clearly with your naked eye, and only a tiny piece of the sun was left. Suddenly rays of the sun—directly shining from north to south—frightened the sun to the east. To the east the darkness increased. And after a few seconds there was complete darkness. (When the blacks called out loud Jackia, Jackia . . . Others sang out of fear the song, 'You want to know what is my prize' . . .) Jacob and I went to the ponies and to the lovely longears [donkeys] which looked at us frightened with gleaming eyes. All the chickens flew quickly back to their roost on our arrival. After a few minutes we both went back.

Suddenly the rays of the sun hurried again towards the east and it became brighter. The disc of the moon moved again in the north east, and about ten minutes after half past three it was complete daylight again. The sun eclipse was over.[2]

And so too was the premonition that the sun had provided. The arrival of the black sun, an epiphany of the light going out in his life, came quickly, and then was gone. Since it was a gift for his unconscious, Theo could not be expected to remark upon it; but it is there—as the natives call out both in joy and in fear, and as fear gleams in the eyes of the warm animals that he loves—his sense of the heavens was about to change forever.

When he looked back on the ordeal of that moment years later it was with even sharper feeling. There are no bright rays in anything he had to say by then.

A few months earlier something might have been done. My father had then wired the Mission Board, asking them to approach one of the motor companies in Adelaide to send up a car to take him down; for during the previous years the first parties of people in cars had reached Hermannsburg. But the Mission Board made inquiries; and then they had a meeting, at which God's will was prayerfully ascertained. They then sent him a message in which they stated a) that they did not think a car would get through to Hbg; b) that the firm approached, Murray Aunger, wanted £500 for the journey, for they insisted on taking up two cars in case of one breaking down; c) that they thought he should muster up horses and come down in 'the good old way.' And of course they added a few Bible verses as well, urging him to rely on the dear Lord. My father's face fell when he received that letter. He actually broke down & cried. He had held out at Hbg for 28 years with only two holidays and now the Mission Board was weighing the £500 against his life, and dumping him because they thought that his useful-ness was over anyway. One of the laymen, however, was more merciful than the dedicated shepherds of the Lutheran flock. This was G. Wurst, who volunteered to drive his car up at his own expense, and to bring father down to Oodnadatta.[3]

The critical decision was taken: Carl Strehlow would travel south to Oodnadatta to meet Wurst's car. Thus began the legendary journey to Horseshoe Bend—a trek of 150 miles in an October heatwave, a journey by buggy; horse-drawn at first, and then by donkey—all the way down the river to the little bush hotel at the bend in the Finke on the edge of the Simpson Desert. The journey took time, with Theo and his mother in tow, along with the schoolteacher Heinrich and two Aborigines from the mission, Njitiaka and Jakobus.

Their leaving—the final farewell of the pastor who had won many hearts and minds after his decades at the mission, years when he had constructed something solid out of ruins—was deeply emotional. Pastor Carl had to be helped out to the buggy, and his bloated and swollen body lifted carefully onto it. They put him on an upholstered chair to try to ease the pain. A crowd had gathered round him and at first he could not speak to them. Then they surged forward, and, at the urging of Mr Heinrich, they rose with the hymn 'Karerai, wolambar-injai,' the Aranda translation of the Lutheran chorale 'Wachet auf, ruft uns die Stimme':

> 'Wake, awake!' proclaim with power
> The watchmen's voices from the tower,
> 'Awake, Jerusalem, arise!'[4]

They sang with fervour, and his father looked at them with tears running down his cheeks. The older men and women touched his legs and feet with their hands because he could not reach out to them, and he managed to say, in a 'strangely toneless,' tear-choked voice, 'May God bless you all, my friends' before the buggy had to move off. It gained speed quickly, and they saw their pastor—'the great rockplate upon which their community had been founded'—move off in a cloud of dust over the first sandridge to the east.

The convoy went down the Finke to Running Waters, then east to Henbury, where Bob Buck had his cattle station. Buck took them in and was kind to Theo. From Henbury they crossed the sand dunes to Alan Breaden's place at Idracowra, and from there they went south, cutting across one of the river's meanders, through country the natives called the Land of Death. It was hot all the way. At every jolt of the buggy Pastor Carl was in agony, his suffering plain to see. Frieda was by his side at all times, Theo less so; but save for the day and night he travelled alone with the Aboriginal escorts, he was with his father's suffering continually, listening to his moaning during the day and the night, bearing witness to the decline of the man and his crisis of faith.

His stricken father raged against those who had disparaged his work at the mission—'the tale bearers, calumniators, and spreaders of malicious gossip had always been the lowest kind of vermin in existence.' They were 'agents of the sinister Prince of Darkness.' He cried out at the injustice of the pain he was in, striving to learn the lesson of Job—the 'severe Old Testament lesson on punishment that awaits all self-righteous men.' He cried out to his God, the better to understand the futility of cries for God's mercy and the worth of a rock-like faith. He cried out to say that to protest against God was not only wrong but utterly futile, the result of man's insistence on envisaging God merely as a glorified and apotheosised human being. He cried out and he prayed the hardest, gravest, and darkest of all petitions in the Lord's Prayer—'Thy will be done.' He had prayed that many thousands of times in his life, in German, English, Deiri and Aranda, and he prayed it all of the way, and at each stop—at each of his stations of the cross—all the way down to the Bend.[5]

On the last leg, to avoid the searing heat, Theo's father was carted by night. Leading the way with the storm lanterns was Ruby Elliot, the wife of the bush publican at the Bend. She was not only a 'young and pretty' woman, but 'strong, athletic, vital, and courageous' (Theo's words for her knew no bounds, and for good reason, as we shall see). Ruby Elliot rode ahead of them all night, carrying the storm lanterns.[6] It was she who persuaded Pastor Carl to tackle the extra distance, because the hotel at least offered telephone contact with a doctor (who was still 600 miles away).

At last, guided by Ruby, they reached the hotel. The pastor was helped down from his buggy and taken inside, where for the next two days he lay in the oven of the iron-roofed hotel moaning unashamedly and crying out to his wife.

Theo came along later with the Aboriginal men, barely able to put one foot in front of the other. He had walked all night without a moon. It was so dark that he could hardly make out any objects and it seemed to him that neither the van nor the team were moving forward at all. 'In spite of all movement the travellers seemed to be marking time . . . from time to time Theo would ask how much further the station was, and Njitiaka would bark out gruffly in English that it was "close up now—little bit, long way yet."'

Like a sleepwalker he arrived. His van rolled slowly past the stock-yards gallows. His mother 'greeted her son briefly and then rushed back inside.' He had his supper with the party. 'Theo was bedded down on the iron stretcher placed on the hotel veranda outside the room in which his parents had been put up.'[7]

Inside the hotel his breathless father slept 'with a heavier dose of laudanum than ever before.' The next day, in his delirium, he asked about Wurst, who was supposed to be driving up. Wurst had in fact got twelve miles north of Oodnadatta but his local guide was too drunk to get him across the sandy Alberga Crossing. The car had to be hauled back to Oodnadatta for repairs. No one could bear to tell Strehlow.

But he knew he was near the end, and he called—not his wife, whom he asked to leave him a while—but Ruby Elliot to his bedside. He wanted to speak of what would happen to his wife and Australian son. 'I know that I am dying,' the pastor told the beautiful young woman. 'And I think you know too. And so does your husband. But my wife does not. And she must not be told.' He sought reassurance from Ruby that Frieda and Theo would have provisions to get to Adelaide, and would be cared for there. Then Ruby left the room and Frieda returned to sit by the bed, to listen to him, to sing him their hymns.

Pastor Stolz arrived: he had managed to come up from Oodnadatta with the camel mail and instantly went to the sick man. 'Brother Stolz,' the Pastor said slowly, 'I have been waiting for you for many years. You have come at last, but it is too late. I am too weak to say more than a few words to you today. I have been disappointed and very bitter during these last few weeks; but there must be no words of anger between us. We are both standing here in the sight of God. Let us do what He wants us to do.'

Strehlow wanted a reassurance from Stolz that he would not abandon the mission work at Hermannsburg, and tightly Stolz grasped Strehlow's tired hand. 'I make this promise before God,' he said. Strehlow returned the pressure of Stolz's hand, and then Stolz said a short prayer and slowly moved out of the sick room.

After he had gone Strehlow 'suddenly became a shaken and strangely quiet man.' He sat in his chair with closed eyes. 'Only eternity now remained to be faced.' Now he was waiting, like Christ in the garden at Gethsemane, for his own 'crown of righteousness.' His wife was singing to him:

Should dark doubts sometimes awaken
that God's folk are left forsaken
Then in faith I know for sure
God helps those who long endure.

Help he has today suspended
he has not forever ended
Though at times in vain we plead,
Help He gives in need.

At this point the sick man interrupted his wife's singing. 'Don't sing that hymn any more, Frieda,' he begged, in a strangely dull and strangled voice: 'God doesn't help!'

'O darling, please don't talk like that,' she pleaded tearfully, slipping down on her knees before him. 'God will help when His time has come. You have always said so. Perhaps His hour has come now.'

The sick man did not reply. His body shook, his lips quivered, the swollen veins in his purple face pulsed heavily; but he remained silent. He had, at long last, spoken what he knew to be the full truth—that his hour of death was at hand and that any further pleas to God were futile. God had said a final 'no' to all prayers—the communication line between God and the two people in the sick room had been severed inexorably.[8]

Pastor Carl Strehlow died at Horseshoe Bend on 20 October 1922. The news reached Theo outside, down at the Aboriginal camp. The wailing went up among the natives, and he ran to the hotel to comfort his mother. His father was buried two days later, in a coffin knocked up out of whisky cases.

Stolz conducted the service, most of it in English, but for the benefit of Frieda the benediction of the body was in German, and the service began with a German rendering of the hymn 'O Gott, Du frommer Gott,' with its final prayer:

Let me depart this life.
Confiding in my Saviour;
Do Thou my soul receive,
That it may live for ever . . .

Then, turning to 'the dark folk present,' the men who had come the journey from Hermannsburg and other natives settled around Horseshoe Bend, Pastor Stolz said that 'God and his Heaven existed not only for white people but also for the dark folk.'

Frieda was composed until the lumps of earth were falling on the coffin and Stolz was saying, 'earth to earth, ashes to ashes, dust to dust.' Finally, they sang the hymn that all could sing (carefully judged by Stolz after discussion with Mrs Elliot), the one most likely to be known by the bushmen present: 'Rock of Ages.' Stolz led it line by line until the end—'Wash me, Saviour, or I die.'

Theo's Baptism

Thus the death of the father—the bare bones of it at least—as told by the son forty-four years later. The passage above, and all the other details, come from *Journey to Horseshoe Bend,* the book Strehlow began to write in 1966 after his own brush with death, sitting up in his hospital bed and writing easily, as well he might: he had been brooding on the events all of his life, coming and going from Horseshoe Bend, and writing in his diaries since 1933.

There is no reason, at this stage of experiencing something of Strehlow's story, not to use his text as skeletal truth. Of course Strehlow must have relied on his memory for some details—his father's exact words in conversations, for instance. Some years before he first drafted the book he told his diary, 'What my father and Pastor Stolz said to each other on that last day no one will ever know. After their talk, father's condition suddenly grew worse. The agony of death was upon him.' The conversations reported above were imagined by Strehlow when he cast his mind back to Theo's world at the time—a world the silent presence seems to have taken in like a sponge, even when he was not writing everything down.

The narrative also rings true because of the way some personal incidents are told—naively, as a quiet Christian boy like Theo must have experienced them. We might bear in mind here that at fourteen as a Lutheran his Christianity had only recently been confirmed, a ceremony conducted by his father; and it was as the newly confirmed Christian son that he had an acute moment of disillusionment. They were staying at Idracowra, just sitting down at the hospitable table of Mr Breaden, when Theo did what he had been trained to do: say grace.

His teacher, Mr Heinrich, frowned him into silence, took him aside later and gave him a 'sharp rebuke.' Theo, 'full of indignation,' reported the incident to his mother. 'He had always been told by her never to disguise or hide his religious beliefs before outsiders, since such an action would amount to a denial of his Saviour; and he confidently expected her sympathy and approval. But she merely replied, "When you are eating at the table of people who don't believe in religion you must say grace silently to yourself"; and she refused to pass any comment on Heinrich's rebuke. Theo turned away bitterly offended.'

It is more than bitterness. It is pique and reaction, a retaliation. 'He had merely made a fool of himself. If this was the case why had not his religious training taken into account the sober realities of life? He felt that religious instruction should not merely serve to make people fit for living in their own homes but for conducting themselves appropriately in the outside world as well.' 'Deeply humiliated,' Theo made no reply to his mother. 'He left her in silence, but decided to be more circumspect in future in accepting religious advice from anyone, and to keep his most deeply felt convictions strictly to himself.' [9]

Theo's reaction is in keeping with a young boy's rigid expectations of a strict parent, especially a parent who had been living a sheltered, unworldly life at a mission. For the first time adrift in the world, miles from his home in the hut of a rough bushman, he naturally clung to his mother more than usual, but his response is also surely out of proportion, and a mark of his yearning and incipient loss of his father. His mother cannot succour him; she is by his father's side: he cannot be with his father, as the patriarch is too ill. Theo is suffering in isolation, bereft.

What also comes though is a more chronic distance from his father. There is no scene in Strehlow's reminiscence where the father addresses the son, or the son the father. And indeed the distance between father and son is as striking as Strehlow's narrative distance from himself. The device he uses is a strange one. He calls himself Theo throughout. Theo this, Theo that—as if the direct use of the first person was difficult for him, that it would have involved him, perhaps, in the ambivalences all sons feel towards fathers, especially towards one in whose hands they have been putty, having had to surrender over and over again to their moralisings, their disciplines. Love there might be between such a son and his father, but it must be, inevitably, a love laced with its negation, and a yearning for an embrace that is simultaneously a wish for escape.

Theo's idealisations of his father compound his distance from the actual man. 'The uncrowned king of Central Australia'—this from the much respected policeman of the region, Sergeant Stott. Strehlow reports this proudly, as he well might since it makes of him a prince. *Ingkata*, ceremonial chief—this according to the Aboriginal congregation at the mission. There are other epithets: 'fearless white champion,' 'great Aboriginal father figure,' 'great rockplate.' Then, as Pastor Carl faces death after forgiving Pastor Stolz of the Mission Board—a Christ-like act of absolution—he is the one who deserves 'that crown of righteousness' given to him by 'The Lord, the righteous Judge.'

Death, then, of the King, death of the Ceremonial Chief, the death of the fearless father figure, the blessed one. The percussion of primal homage and loss is Strehlow's, though his 'real life' father had been dead for nearly half a century, enough time for most sons to approach a more realistic account of their fathers. 'I shall always be what Horseshoe Bend made me,' Strehlow told his diary when he was a grown man.

What is it to live in the grievous shadow of an exalted, gifted father, one lost so early in an adolescent life? The opportunity for ritualistic acts of independence has been lost. The more one mourns one's father the greater the difficulty of becoming oneself: yet the more one becomes oneself in the absence of a father, the more his shadow looms. Each movement—the resolution of grief, the oedipal passage—thwarts the other, and the result is a self as clogged as the intersection of two rivers where the soul eddies, clouds, darkens in a complicated lack of momentum. Time slows, flow is lost, one might as well be going backwards as forwards. 'Sorrow,' as Oscar Wilde wrote in his noble letter of grief and remonstration, 'is one long moment.'[10]

Theo, even as he made the last walk into the Bend, had the feeling of time suspended: 'it often seemed as though neither the van nor the team was moving forward at all. In spite of all movement the travellers seemed to be marking time.'[11] And then, when his father died, time must have stopped. The one long moment began, which was him.

There is another way to couch the dark stasis of Theo's actual moment then—actual as distinct from what he would make of it as a middle aged man. With the death of his father the normal routines of initiation had been peremptorily cancelled. His Aranda friends were already on the edge of the ceremonial ground with their fathers. He, as the budding scholar, was sitting pretty in the lights of his father, but the light on his book had gone out. Lord, why me? What have I done to deserve this? The void here is the lack of ritual presence of the father to come, the one who would have seen him through to the dignified separations on the manly ground . . . Now he was as a silent presence suffering without prospect, and could only make the best of his grief.

'Suffering,' Wilde continued, 'is the means by which we exist, it is the only means by which we become conscious of existence, and the remembrance of suffering in the past is necessary to us as the warrant, the evidence of our continued identity.'[12] And so the writing begins.

After the burial, Strehlow tells us, Theo watched the buggy go back towards Henbury, the empty armchair on the top, as a present for Bob

Buck. He tells us he comforted his mother, which is more than likely true: it would have been his duty, in the eyes of the others, to behave in a manly way. And so by his own retrospective account, which is smothering his sorrow as much as it is expressing it, he then goes down along the river.

There, suddenly, he was full of 'an overwhelming sense of loss.' Strehlow: 'An uncertain future lay menacingly before him.' He had a 'deep distrust for the new white southern world into which he would soon be making his entry: would he find in it such things as friendship, kindness, decency and loyalty?' He thinks of the Lutheran Church which had let his father down so badly, and of his life at the mission where 'the only playmates he had ever known had been dark boys and girls'—when he should have at least mentioned having the company of four brothers and sisters when he was a baby.

'He wanted to be alone. And yet not alone—merely out in the open, somewhere by himself in the Finke bed.'

He walks down into the Finke, towards the painted cliffs. 'No matter what the future might bring, he would never cease to regard himself as one of the children of the Finke River.'

He quickens his steps, he is walking past the stockyard, the stench of blood and manure sickens him. He passes the killing pen and the gallows where 'squawking crows abused him.' He reaches the cliffs and lies down 'in the warm white sand for well over an hour, watching, reflecting, dreaming, before he felt calm enough to return to the station.' He'd have stayed longer, but the others might be missing him!

Then the storm.

He hears the roll of distant thunder, and thunderclaps above him. He hears them from two directions. Deafening rolls of thunder, lightning overhead, iron sheets of thunder, titanic cascades of sound, and then the first heavy drops of rain that are to break 'the unbearable tension in the air.' Then: 'A wild rain gale suddenly burst upon Horseshoe Bend in unbridled primal fury . . . Within minutes the two thunderstorms seemed to have joined their separate forces, and brilliant flashes of lightning began to writhe over Uralirburka as well. The landscape on all sides vanished behind dense white veils of pouring rain, it was as though the whole country around Horseshoe Bend was passing again through the mythical deluge of rain which had quenched the bush fires of Mbalka at the beginning of time.' The rain ancestors are fighting it out at the foot of the fire mountain. The storm was above him, thunder over one mountain answering thunder over another, 'the whole air resounding with the deafening noises of wind, rain and thunder' until, finally, after a half an hour, the violence faded away and 'only the sweet music of the quickening rain remained.'

'The heavy drops still fell in steady showers which the thirsty land drank up greedily. The rich scent of the rain soaked earth floated up from the cooled ground, and a delicious freshness spread through the fragrant air.'[13]

The handwritten first draft of *Journey to Horseshoe Bend* ended with these words:

As the dusk settled on the rain-drenched Finke valley and the rich smell of sodden brown earth filled the purified air, a sudden surge of joy hope surged through Theo, still gazing on the rapidly darkening cliffs and dune crests around him. It was true what Jakobus has suggested to him earlier that afternoon, that his father would sleep forever in Central Australia. No longer did he have to face life-long exile in that far away, foreign land from which his father had come and become part of the land that was Theo's home. He stood on the hotel verandah, still gazing on the rapidly darkening cliffs and dune crests around him. No longer did he have to dread a life-long exile in that far-away, foreign land from which his father had come. He felt certain that some day he would return to his own homeland and to those dark friends whose loyalty had brightened his whole boyhood.

In a few days from now green shoots of grass and herbage would be peeping out from the clay soil between the broken stones of the earth-mound [*sic*] under which the deceased man was sleeping his last sleep.

Death had claimed a human victim. But new life was returning to the earth with the rain. Men might die, but Nature never.

This was the Central Australia of aboriginal belief—it was the land of Altjira, the Land of Eternity.[14]

Not satisfied with this ending, Strehlow expanded his rain theme in the last three pages. He also needed it said that his father, and not merely a 'deceased man,' had been buried. And that this was 'foreign land' to his father, but land he had given the best of his life to, an Aranda land where 'the dead shared the land of the living in the company of their super-natural beings'—because, after all, his father had known the sacred myths and songs of the region, including much that was in 'top secrecy.'

The fuller music of Strehlow's final passage was a flood of revivifying rhetoric. Death could not triumph over 'the spirit of man':

Was not man superior to other living things only because of his spirit—because of his powers of speech and thought that enable him to probe deeply into the mysteries of the universe and the enigma of his own existence? Did man's personality survive death? His father had implicitly believed in the truth of the ancient words of the Preacher about the nature of death: 'Then shall the dust return to the earth as it was; and the spirit shall return unto God Who gave it.' Since the age of thirteen Theo had often been troubled by secret doubts about the absolute truth of many of the beliefs that had been inculcated into him by his parents from the earliest days of his childhood. The events of the past six weeks had shaken and shattered his faith to its very foundations. And yet he felt strangely reassured as he peered out into the deepening, wet gloom outside.

In a few days from now green shoots of grass and herbage would be peeping out from the clay soil between the broken stones of the mound under which his father was sleeping his last sleep. To the boy the rain that was falling on his father's grave had come to represent the symbol of life, the promise of life, the assurance of life, and the certainty of life. Life could not be finally conquered by death; for the power of life was greater than the destructiveness of death. Life was from eternity to eternity.[15]

Theo overcame. He was now baptised by the country, reborn in the moment of death. In *Journey to Horseshoe Bend* he wrote himself to the point of restoration from death, into a notion of resurrection according to the spirit and spirits of place.

The truth was, at another level, also more prosaic. Theo was also filled with a massive hostility towards the place. He may well have experienced the deluge of rain as a resurrection, of sorts, but at the same time he very soon resolved that he did not want to see the Centre again. This at least was what he wrote in an earlier version of his feelings at the time. 'I had always loathed the dust, the summer heat, the flies, the insects . . . The thought that I might have to return to my home country had always been a nightmare to me.'[16] The idea of going back filled him with dread. 'Dread' was the word he used more than once.

He never retracted this statement, which is made to carry the worst of the mission years on its shoulders. He put it in the draft of another volume of autobiography, 'Land of Altjira,' which he wrote in 1957 and never published. If it had been published, he would have been obliged to make sense of how he came to celebrate his place of birth and its native culture. He would have had to account for how he came—as reality, as myth—to baptise himself with an Aboriginal sense of country. The emergence of that transformation is the symphony to which we now turn.

---

1 T.G.H. Strehlow, diary [SD], cited to Lohe, 23 June 1970, Lutheran Archives, Adelaide.
2 SD, October 1922, translated by Simone Kaiser (April 2001), Strehlow Research Centre [SRC].
3 SD, 4 August 1953.
4 *JHB*, 23.
5 *JHB*, 174–75.
6 Ibid., 129.
7 Ibid., 142–43.
8 Ibid., 179.
9 Ibid., 102–03.
10 Wilde to Lord Alfred Douglas, January–March 1897, the letter that was to become, after substantial editorial fiddling, *De Profundis*. *The Complete Letters of Oscar Wilde*, ed. Merlin Holland and Rupert Hart-Davis (London: Fourth Estate, 2001), 720.
11 *JHB*, 142.
12 Wilde, letter, 696.
13 *JHB*, 216.
14 Handwritten MS, 1967, SRC.
15 *JHB*, 220.
16 'Land of Altjira,' unpublished MS, 1957, 17.

5   First Loves

HE STOOD THERE, in the doorway, a forlorn boy holding his mother's hand. This was the image of a lost fatherless boy that stayed in the mind of one German farmer who was there, in the Barossa Valley, when Theo arrived from the Bend.[1]

He did not go straight from the desert into the city. He and his grieving, exhausted mother were taken in by the Wurndt family at Tanunda, where the devout German community were thriving as farmers, inscribing themselves into the land with the passionate intensity of Aborigines. The Strehlows were welcomed onto the verandah, and into the house of the Wurndts. It was spring; they would be there for Christmas, the fatherless boy and the mother without a mission.

Then, in the hot summer of 1923, he was packed off to school, to Immanuel College and Seminary, the Lutheran coeducational boarding school on Jeffcott Street in North Adelaide. Some months later his mother joined him. As she had no widow's pension to speak of, and nothing approaching the funds she might need to return to the rest of her family in Germany (and to take her son with her), she worked for her board and lodgings, becoming, as the historians of the school have written, 'a wonderful matron of the College' who excelled in creating its 'family atmosphere.'[2]

He would have walked in under the Tudor clock tower of the school— the clock that was to ring for all boarders at 5.30 a.m., and at 9.30 p.m.

for lights out—into the small quad of the establishment, a building on the model of an English manor house. Then up the creaking wooden stairs to the landing and to the side where there was the boys' dormitory. His mother slept on the other side, where there was a room for the girls.

Contact with his mother was thereafter complicated, if he was not to compromise the school rules dividing the sexes, or be seen by other boys as sissy. Eventually, however, he came to visit his mother on that side of the staircase. He would go to her room and play her music on his gramophone. Schubert. Liszt. Bach. They were both—to an extent—orphaned by the death of the pastor, and sustained by the *Sehnsucht* of the German music that bound them.

Kissing Adelaide

He had come down to a smallish, Anglophile town that both breathed the air of the desert that seemed, on the hot days, to be the snap of a flywire door away, and which was on the cusp of modernity.

Charlie Chaplin's film, *The Idle Class*, the talk of New York, was playing at The Grand, a mere tram ride from the school. The stage show *Romance* was the biggest hit in town. A boy opening a newspaper could hardly have missed the brazen advertisement about 'an opera singer's love idyll.' It featured a kiss that brought forgetfulness to a minister of the church. 'Love had come quickly into the heart of the young minister . . . from the wonderful moment when his eyes had met those of Rita, the beautiful actress, he had been her willing slave. But the voice of conscience told him that such a love was shameful—impossible, and he vowed to forget. But the hour of parting, when her tear-dimmed eyes were raised in pleading to his, her tempting, alluring lips trembled ever so close, his senses reeled, and heeding not the bonds of convention . . . he pressed her to him.'

'Kiss me, he whispered. I am no longer a minister and you are no longer an actress. YOU ARE A WOMAN AND I AM A MAN.'

'What does a kiss?' asked a headline in the *Register* in January 1923. 'Have you ever stopped to consider what a dissected kiss is? Have you ever considered stripping the kiss of all sentimentality, reducing it to a more scientific rating, where it is weighed and measured, subdividing it into the point where it will give a rating in horsepower, and checking up its action on the heart and blood streams?' If you did, the story went on, you would attend to the use to which a Professor J.H. Krauss was putting his blood pressure machine.

This was science, after a fashion, a modernism that could be used satirically. But in other ways science had to be resisted. It could go too far, put things the wrong way round. Against a 'Dr Freud' the *Register* editorialised: 'the real self is the responsible self (and not the repressed self of the primitive unconscious).' And: 'One of the more amusing and least convincing of the doctrines . . . from psychoanalysis is that which insists that accidents never happen.'[3]

Adelaide was a city of churches. It had half a million souls, most of them Methodists and Anglicans. The Lutherans had the fifth-largest group of preachers. One historian called South Australia the Paradise of Dissent and spoke of Adelaide's 'noble, depressing, rectitude.'[4] The smugness was such that it had to be pricked by a scandalmonger calling herself Thistle Anderson (a retired actress and poet), whose scurrilous pamphlet claimed Adelaide had more brothels and opium dens per head than Melbourne, and declared the place a church village infested with 'Churchianity,' which was something different from spiritual endeavour.

The city fathers pressed on with developments that pertained to the spirit. 'Church on the Crest,' said a strong headline in the Adelaide *Register* in 1923. 'The Church is alive, active and energetic.' Good works persisted all round. The Adelaide Hospital was being remodelled; so was Yatala prison, which would instruct prisoners in trades so they could take their place as useful citizens when they were released. Admittedly, there was a shortage of teachers in the city as well as the arduous hinterland. Land settlement schemes on the Murray River promised much, but they were not yet the bedrock to prosperity; the members of the Irrigation Commission had just been appointed. What had happened (and the city was as proud of this as its war memorial) was the rail link from Port Augusta to Kalgoorlie. The first bitumen road was built in 1923, just as a drought relief scheme for outback farmers went into operation. The prospect of rural humiliation lived cheek by jowl with a proud urbanity, and Adelaide—then as now—would always be defining itself in relation to its arid interior, its desert prospect. Everything was moving and in flux, yet the official puritan ethos of the town was always able to unite its moral concerns in concrete ways. Among the Bills put to parliament in 1923 there was satisfaction expressed with regard to tighter control on liquor, the registration of stallions, the extension of the university (for better agricultural studies), and the upbringing and training of Aboriginal and half-caste children.

The parliamentary debate about Aborigines was hardly reported in the papers, but in the letter columns there was agitation about the kidnapping policy, and the way Adelaide might place Aborigines to be out of sight and possibly out of mind. At Immanuel College in 1923 there was no black or even half-caste student to be seen. However there was one Aboriginal in their midst, Rebecca, about 30, attached to the household of the college director, the Reverend J.P. Loehe. She was not unwelcomed by the boarders, but as one student recalled, 'her body emitted a very strong, and to us, very offensive odour.' 'Pooh!' one student exclaimed when she came out of the back entrance of the school. Rebecca took a metal bar and hit the lad across the thigh several times and very hard. Then she rushed inside and cried bitterly while telling Mrs Loehe all about it.[5]

Hamlet Rather Than Deutschtum

Immanuel College was essentially a boarding school for country teenagers of German stock. It was proud both of the family atmosphere it offered to its students away from home, and of the opportunity for them to shine with a syllabus that closely followed that of the University of Adelaide. It was thus their hearth, where their *Volkslieder* might be heard, and their vehicle for entry into the English professions, if a boy or girl was not wanted back on the farm. The school tended to be an enclave of mixed feelings.

Director Loehe spoke to the students in German, even when they did not understand the language, which was rarely. He thought students should always remember their German uniqueness—*Eigenart,* a peculiarity properly one's own. The school was run by the United Evangelical Lutheran Church in Australia, which was more liberal theologically and socially than the rival synod, the Evangelical-Lutheran Synod of Australia. The historians of Immanuel College stress how, in these early days, the college was fully in accord with the concept of *Deutschtum.* They explain that *Deutschtum* 'is an almost untranslatable word that takes in the conviction that: everything that is German is good: German depth, German strength, German culture, German thrift, and, above all, the German soul.'[6]

The school was, furthermore, still trembling from Australian xenophobia during the Great War: the internments, the Nomenclature Act, the prohibition of the importation of German Bibles and of the publication of German newspapers of any kind, and the closing of German schools—except, actually, Immanuel College, then located at Points Pass.

When Strehlow came to the school it was in its first year in Adelaide, opening on the former site of the seminary, Angas College, previously the North Adelaide Grammar School. And here was another historical split: the Lutheran college very much conducted itself as a British public school, on the Arnoldian model to train Christian gentleman, but it also operated in tandem with seminary training, the preparation of young men who might complete their studies in Neuendettelsau.

Strehlow started at the school along with 27 others, eight of them seminarians. Girls came into the school the following year. From the beginning, it was assumed that he would not—necessarily—follow in his father's footsteps. He was free to follow his own scholarly path, even if he did look like a bush boy, and as a result had to be held down in the dorm one night during his first week at school, and be shorn by his classmates. He acquiesced.

He was not to be one of the most vigorous boys in the school—who played football and cricket—but he played hockey well enough, and tennis. He did not have to withdraw into himself, as he could more than hold his own in class, and at music. Already he could play the organ and the piano, so he was the perfect student to join Director Loehe's Sunday afternoons after lunch when the family and staff gathered under his direction to sing hymns and spiritual songs for an hour or more. At school Theo joined the brass band, where he commanded the French horn.

By his third year he was helping edit the impressive little school magazine, *The Echo*, where he tried himself out as a writer. In 1925 he published in the magazine a story that revealed an inimitable tendency with regard to his narrative trajectory. It was called 'The Desert':

It was a hot day. The yellow desert sands were burning as though a fiery furnace were raging beneath the surface. The air itself was simmering with heat. No sound interrupted the solemn stillness of the great waste, save the occasional dismal cry of a kite circling above, in quest of food. The vast expanse of barren sandhills was stretching as far as human eye could see. The few trees that were able to defy the summer with its whirling sandstorms and months of drought were drooping their great needle shaped leaves. The only other signs of vegetation was the yellow and grey spinifex with its sharp spikes.

Out in the far dim distance you may behold a solitary pedestrian, wearily trudging along. A man, alone, all alone in this desert! He has lost his way and his strength is waning rapidly. His eyes are swimming, blinded by the hot glare of the sand. His head is unprotected against the fierce, merciless rays of the sun. His face is red and inflamed by the boiling heat. His feet are blistered from the long weary tramp, and scorched by the fire sands. And still he goes on, on, on! Parched with thirst, his tongue lolling out of his mouth, he has but one thought, one desire, one passion: Water! And it is this one last, all-devouring passion that enables him to bear up against the cruel heat, against the teasing, fiendish flies, against the endless waste which sternly threatens death to anyone seeking to penetrate the secrets of its kingdom. Mirages with their grey expanse of water and their cool, shady trees are mocking his agony. The birds of prey are greedily hovering around him, patiently awaiting their time. And still he goes on, on, on! Perhaps only one more hill to climb, only another few chains to go; if the fates are kind there may be water within reach after all, water, life-giving water! Alas! His steps become uncertain, tottering. A dreadful lightness seems to pervade his head, while his feet grow as heavy as lead. Wearily, hardly knowing why, hardly caring, he staggers on in an ever diminishing circle. Finally, with the last ounce of strength, he slowly drags himself into a meagre shade of a tree at the foot of a sandhill. And with a sigh he closes his weary eyes.

And on the other side of the same hill was a creek, deeply embedded in the sand, where green reeds and rushes grew on the brink of smiling blue lagoon, and where gum trees spread a sweet coolness in their deep shade![7]

All the exclamation marks prove that fate is a *very* bad thing. The tone is slightly tongue in cheek, hinting at a parody of Boy's Own adventures, but the shade that is 'mocking his agony'—mocking the futile tread of the solitary man in the desert—is close enough to the bone.

He was forging ahead at the school, a college now on the books of the state system as rival in academic success to the larger, more respectable Anglo colleges in Adelaide. The question before every bright chap at Immanuel was what the future would hold. Some might go back to the land, where their fathers awaited them. Most of the girls would certainly do so, if they did not seek employment in stenography. Strehlow was bright enough to play with his options. By the age of sixteen he was having fun with *Hamlet*:

To swot or not to swot: that is the question:
Whether 'tis better for a lad to go
Into the country and take farming on,
Or stay at Immanuel College still
And train his mental powers?
To plough: to sow
The grain: and by that very sowing say
That from decay will rise the golden corn
Heaven's priceless gift, and this in turn will fill
The purse with precious coin . . .

It goes on, wearing thin, as it must, and casting doubt on the scholarly alternative which could well include:

The failure at exams, and heading all
The loss of what seems perfect liberty.
When he himself might make an end of woes,
And run away? Subject himself to these
Who would, when only one from hundred doth.[8]

Run away? Well, he was joking. Besides, there was nowhere to run to: his life was now mapped out. In 1926 he was top of the State for his Leaving Examinations in Latin, Greek, and German, and in his honours year he was tenth in the State overall, which won him the government bursary into the University of Adelaide. He was off to the University of Adelaide the next year.

But he had not left the German fold yet: for the first two years at university he was teaching Classics and English at the Immanuel College, and still in the school orchestra. He boarded at the college until his last year. As a teacher at the school he was a taskmaster. He was not so surprised when his charges did well in Classics, but thought it worthy of note when he got a liking for English poetry into their heads.

They were, it seemed to him, excessively German heads due to the school's lamentable tendency to neglect the fact that all their peda-gogical activity was taking place in Adelaide, in an Anglophile society, and not somewhere else. He was upset at the lack of discipline in the school. When he saw some of the girls climbing halfway up the wall to talk with the boys he was 'disgusted.' He complained of student behaviour in the eating hall, and in the streets where the Lutherans were on show to the English. Through the eyes of the English, he found the Germanness of the school embarrassing.

A matter of discipline came to a head at a staff meeting in November 1930.

'I spoke of all the evils the head's methods had brought about in creating dissension and disorderliness in the College.' The headmaster understood Strehlow to be accusing him of a lack of personal support, and once again the German language, as Strehlow put it, rose to the ceiling. Another teacher spoke up for Strehlow and the head fell silent. After his outburst, Strehlow worried. That evening he went to the director's study where the older man 'made a long speech trembling with emotion': 'he said that he was often almost in despair at the end of his days: he was a German yet as Director had to give a hand in Anglicising Australian Germans . . . his own children were becoming English, and—German; this last was said as though there was something oppressing him, which no one knew. And now his whole system was undermined by one of his own pupils . . . referring I suppose to my 100 percent fail list in Latin last year.'

The director spoke at some length, and then invited Strehlow to do so. 'I said that I was sincerely sorry for having so deeply offended my dear old master by some hasty words . . . also that I always had the sincerest affection and esteem for him personally etc.'

It grew late. When Strehlow left, the older man had tears in his eyes and his voice was trembling. 'I went up into my study, and finished reading,' Strehlow recorded. 'I heard his step once more. He beckoned me out of the study, since Sieg. was there, and once more asked if there was anything else that I felt sore about . . . No, I replied. I am only too sorry it should ever have come to this between my esteemed teacher and myself; we once more warmly shook hands and he left; and I went to bed thoughtful but satisfied.'[9]

The young man was getting a sense of his own authority, while straining away from his German roots.

The English Fields

In Strehlow's first year on campus he excelled in Latin and Greek, winning the university prizes for the best student in each. In his second year he got first place in Latin, second in Greek. That year, he also took up the formal study of English and was fourth in the class. He was at that stage enrolled in a joint honours course in Classics and English, 'a feat,' as his old school magazine later reported, 'which practically no student attempts, no matter how brilliant.'[10] His brilliance aside, 'the pressure of work forced him to relinquish the Honours Classics course to concentrate on English.'

English, then, it was to be in 1929, the year the whole English culture of the university was receiving its shocks from the rest of the world. After the collapse on Wall Street there were soon humpies along the Torrens, at the back of the campus, and South Australia had the highest unemployment in the country. Mounted police would ride into a thousand demonstrators outside the Treasury Buildings in King William Street, the blood flowing freely. But for the young men—and women—who lay about on the summer lawns of the campus, a pastoral ease was hard to disturb. Admittedly, some students had only just returned from Europe, and wanted to opine in their newspaper about the state of affairs in the Soviet Union. A few had been to the future and seen it work. They might also have agreed with the fiery view of Katharine Susannah Prichard—reviewed in their newspaper's treatment of the third issue of *The Proletariat*—'that the Universities have been lethal chambers for the painless extraction of youthful vigour, enterprise and independent ability.' Then again they might not, as it was still a question of the day as to whether young women should be at the university at all. 'The present generation of women at the University is a happy race,' boomed the male vice of *On Dit*, 'they have a fine building of their own, and in pleasant weather they can sit in the cloisters and read in the sun, and live upon coffee, and hobnobs and bun.'[11]

In the years Strehlow was on campus, and as the world in Europe began to burn, the university was finishing its new facade 'in the Gothic mode.' This momentous social fact was applauded by one of its young dons at the time, a rising star in history, W.K. Hancock. 'In its academic tradition, Adelaide, like most other Australian Universities, had a Scottish stamp,' Hancock observed. It fostered considerable freedom in the professorate. Hancock felt Adelaide had about it an air of sedate churchiness. With regard to friendships, Hancock wrote:

> Sunday afternoons when four of us sat reading, reserving our talk till supper time; gramophone records and unsophisticated family bridge on winter evenings, tennis on the good grass of Saint Peter's College and expeditions to Victoria to fish for trout; the leisurely perambulations of

a garden at Mt Lofty, fresh shortbread cut into crisp golden oblongs—
the same that have so often since then been packed in layers between
sheets of greased paper, sealed in a tin and posted to London as an
easement of lean times. I also call to mind Saturday afternoon hockey
and the captains of the two teams with which I played, the University
team at first and later the Wanderers. Still more do I recall how hockey,
or rather the perpetual talks about it, began to become a bore and how
some of us seceded from THE Wanderers and invented Hunting the
Badger and other extraordinary games of chase which diversified our
Saturday runs in the Adelaide hills.[12]

Hancock's passage is redolent of the social ease of the Anglo establishment, and its blithe condescension to other people's 'lean times.' It speaks
of a culture light years away from Lutheran rural traditions. Scottish may
have been the university's academic tradition, but English was its social
one: a sedate Englishness at one with sedate churchiness . . . a little
attempt at a little Oxford. The atmosphere could not have failed to
impress itself upon the young German in Strehlow. He hurled himself
into the hockey and was never heard to express any boredom with it.

In Strehlow's last year on campus, power in Canberra shifted from
the Conservatives to Labor, the Depression deepened, and politics
everywhere became more serious, and confusing. He kept up, to some
extent, with events beyond the peaceful lawns of the campus. In his
diary—which he was writing all the time, inscribing himself as he transcribed some of the things that were important to him—he shows
himself to be an anti-militarist and democrat. He is not hostile to
Labor, but is not of the left, either. He was more intent on other things.
His studies, for one thing. Becoming successful—proving himself
worthy of the bursary, which might not be renewed if he fell short of
expectations—that was paramount. But it was intimately connected
with another facet of his future: the meanings to be drawn from the
first kisses he was able to win when he could, kisses that were, when it
came down to it, his most accurate barometer regarding the culture
from which he desired definitive embrace.

He turned 21 in his second year at university, and his celebrations
perfectly illustrate his two-sided life. He had the congratulations of Dr
Loehe, and a Bible and chocolates from his mother: some music books
were to come. From the Wursts at Laura arrived a kero case of cakes.
'What a blessing!' The night before he had taken a girl to the pictures

and noted: 'This is the first time that ever I took an English or Australian girl out to any show.' In bed that night he read psalms in his German Bible. 'After a prayer of thanksgiving for all help bestowed on me up at Hbg' he went to sleep. Thoughtful and satisfied again.

On his birthday he went down town and picked the rest of his equipment for his social ascent: a complete dinner suit—two stiff collars, the black bow tie, the studs, all of it costing him £3 7s. 3d.— 'all for my entry into "social life"!' In his excitement he forgot to collect the music his mother had ordered. The social life was still on his mind when he met a chap on the way back to the college: Strehlow wanted to know if he could go to the next dance without the formality of going to the next meeting of the University Dance Club.

Yes, he was relieved to learn.

Did he need cards? Yes, we supply them for all who wish, the kind chap said, thinking he meant playing cards.

No, Strehlow said.

Oh you mean programs for the dances!

No, no, Strehlow.

He meant cards used for introductions to the 'society' girls.

Those cards, he learnt, were not necessary. A great relief.

He went to hockey practice, the day of team selection. Ashley Cooper had missed out and Strehlow put in a good word for him 'since he was on the committee of the Varsity D.C. [Dance Club]. Also he is quite a fine player too.'

That was the English round: in the evening he was back with the German. A wonderful musical evening at the Bogners', 'the first place at which I stayed on coming down with mother from Central Australia in 1922': 'I opened the evening with Chopin's Polonaise in A Major, and a Waltz of his (both of my Chopin collections given to me by Anne-Marie Loehe), Mr Koch rendered several cello solos which I accompanied: Miss Koch sang the "Carnival," "To a Miniature" and two pieces from the "Quaker Girl" beautifully; and Miss Reidel also sang excellently.'

Outside the rain had stopped, and the shining lamps were reflected in the pools along the street. He and his best friend Bill Schneider walked back to the college chatting merrily, carrying the birthday cake with them. 'Arriving at the college at 5 past 1; I went to bed 15 minutes later.'

When he woke he did not feel well. He felt he did not have 'that superabundance of energy, vigour, spirits, jocularity and excitement of yesterday.' But his birthday was still not over. The teachers at the college had at last remembered him. Director Loehe gave him a book on Oxford University. That night Strehlow gave his birthday spree for his peers at the college. A dozen fellows ate his fruit and cake and toasted him, and joined him in hoping 'a much greater bond of fellowship would be established in the future.' After the Loyal Toast (to the King of England) they spent the rest of the evening 'singingly feelingly our old German Volkslieder': 'The songs we sang were . . .' and there follows, in Strehlow's animated diary of those days, the list of the songs that makes five lines, a kind of prose song of a list, rounding off his two days of coming of age in two cultures.[13]

In his surviving university diaries,* Strehlow says little about Classics and much about the English which consumed his later years. Despite his good start in English I, he felt unqualified success was as hard to achieve as it was with the English debutantes. When he read Kipling he 'felt quite jealous of his fine style. It only fills me with desire to strive after something like it.' He set to in his essays to write fluently, in long sentences that he hoped would come to him naturally. He is stopped in his tracks when a lecturer praised an essay but went on to say that he found signs 'that his first difficulties were the language itself.' That was bad enough. Worse was to come. The same teacher remarked that 'more than likely you will never write *quite* like an Englishman.'

When the idea that he was 'troubled' with the English was repeated by his Classics master, Professor J.A. Fitzherbert, Strehlow was furious. 'Why did they of the Eng. Dpt. not tell me this last year! I would have never thought of entering for a BA Honours in English. I feel like chucking up everything in my anguish. I am sick of working, sick of Latin and Greek, sick of teaching, sick of the English people and their dimmable language, sick of everything. And I suspect that many of these remarks of my Prof. are due to the fact that I am the owner of a German name, and that in their prejudiced minds they find fault with everything.'[14]

On this occasion his anger was partly with himself. As a class exercise he had been asked to write sonnets, the first he had tried, and he had found it damnable difficult. He looked at his efforts and reflected miserably on his hopeless metrics and phrasing. He wrote five over ten days, and copied them into his diary in order of composition.

---

* Only Strehlow's university diaries for 1929–31 seem to be extant at the Strehlow Research Centre.

The first was:

Fain would I rest my head 'neath cloudless skies
On desert sands untrod, and see again
Like silent sentinels the white cliffs rise
Majestic from the hushed moonspeckled plains;
Where now the mournful mopoke's weary lay
Drones through the balmy silence of the air
As if he sighs that Beauty's gone away
For ever from the desert once so fair
When in primeval glory first was born
A dew-young earth from raging chaos wild:
Alas! the even-cloud now hides thy moon,
Oh desert, and thy beauty has defiled:
Thou callest me come to thee, callest me to rest
And bidst me pour all cares into thy breasts.

'Desert' is one of the words he underlines, and it is the theme he works and reworks in his struggle with the diction of landscape, diction that might suit the landscape he actually knew, as distinct from the one a nineteenth-century English poet would have known. Desert and the notion of maternal comfort; desert and melancholia. In two drafts he manages to come out with a reference to 'a white cross'—the one from his father's grave. In one of the father poems—the third poem to be drafted—the last two lines run:

From sunken earth I hear the loved voice call,
'Forget not me that once for thee gave all!'

The white cross and the grave are not in the last poem, which ends:

But thy enchanting call I'll ever hear
Dear Desert, and thou shalt be ever near!

The literary critic in him was right; they were not good sonnets, and Fitzherbert told him so. The next day he was 'an absolute wash out in hockey practice.' And he broke out in eczema, which he often did in these years whenever he felt humiliated. The rash covered his hip and waist and went around to his back in red itching blotches. 'They are

gruesome devilish things that make my life a torture. It's just as if everything is rising up against me.'[15]

Hunting English Girls

But not everything was rising up against him—to repeat the incipiently
paranoid phrase that came to Theo's mind so easily. In his Greek exam
he had excelled: 'I was in my glory then; 2 of my partners were sure
that I was English.' And he was sailing along in Old English, which
could be learnt as a second language. And most important—or rather,
as a fundamental solace—his life in romance was looking up.

Loose in the folder of his diary was the image of what interested him
most. It is the pretty face of a girl; gamin, her hair like a boy's and her
eyes not, the heart-shaped chin tucked in as she looks, fetchingly, over
her shoulder. The flapper, the deb, the true love. Someone wrote 'From
Sweetheart' across her bare shoulder—Strehlow's diary does not
indicate whose pen it was.

He'd had no luck with sonnets, but he counted that he had made
another advance on 'paving the way' into 'society circles.' He went to
the Varsity Dance where he had the last dance with an English girl
called Isabel. He felt he 'broke the last crust of ice with her.' In addition
he met 'many pretty girls not all of whose names he knew.' He was
deliriously happy. 'When I did go home I felt like a victor, who has
overcome the last obstacle in the way of success—I have now made my
entry into social life at the 'Varsity. Now I do not have to fear any of
my old enemies anymore.'

There were many more dances, as well as English girls, with whom
he was happiest. At the theatre with one he feels 'immensely proud'
when spotted by some Immanuel College boys. They could see him at
last, out with an English girl. After three years of battling, he thought,
at last the ice was broken.

That night he is so excited he can't sleep, and reflects: 'I must take her
into my confidence, lay open to her all my heart, all my troubles, all my
disappointments: perhaps she will help me to get into society, help me
succeed in life, in the social world! I hope she will, dear old girl!'[16]

A few days later he pulls back from this swoon into helplessness—
never having confessed, in his diary, to what all his troubles consisted
of, exactly. He seems to be taking his grieving state for granted. No
matter, his next entries seem to imply. When the next debutante is
mentioned, when she has agreed to go out with him, he exclaims: 'Bliss

it was to be alive, but to be young was very heaven.' With this outburst of Wordsworth he leaps back into the fray of his social climbing, for all the world as if poetry might help. The highlight of the second year was the debutante ball, where he danced the night away with the English girls (even though he had gone with a German partner): 'a delirium of bliss . . . the most glorious night I have had in Adelaide.'[17]

He bought himself the complete works of Byron, of which he was particularly proud. He could not understand Browning at first, nor Shelley's *Defence of Poetry*; nor Arnold until he noticed there was that 'indefinable something that touches the inmost chords of the soul.'

The constant was the 'immortal' Shakespeare. In March 1930 he exclaimed, 'I have now read 31 plays by Shakespeare, eight of them this week: this is a real record!' The canon was not in doubt. The tragedies, it seems, were already so familiar to him as not to warrant comment, and he does not reflect on the downfall of kings and desolation of fathers or the treachery of wives and mothers. He makes notes on Hegel's theory of tragedy in the standard and most eminent text of the time, A.C. Bradley's *Shakespearean Tragedy*. But they are brief unreflective notes, indicative of his cast of mind: he would never take to philosophy, will never excel as a dialectician.

Rather, his bent is for the personal and the wistfully poignant. With *The Tempest* he was deeply affected by Prospero's last speech. 'Yes, truly we are such stuff as dreams are made of. In [a] hundred years time, what will remain of me? Just a handful of dust—common earth and ashes! Yes, all is vanity—my loves, my hopes, my ideals, my emotions, they shall all vanish, like dreams, as the shadow of a dream flutes (not floats!) away in the twilight.' Next day he revised the play and his opinion. 'Strange to say it is the play of Shakespeare so far which has best stuck in my memory after the first reading. I find the love scene between Ferdinand and Miranda very fine; I mean the one wherein she offers her help him carry the wood. Perhaps it's owing to my personal experiences in the holidays.' He was thinking of the German girls up in the Barossa Valley, and all their work in the house and the field.

The grind of term reading over, he was trying to catch up with the greats who were not English and more modern. Dostoyevsky, Russian short stories, Gide's *The Immoralist* which he thought 'glorified the lower animal passions in man a little unduly.'

The book that drew the most passionate outburst about events in the modern world was Erich Maria Remarque's *All Quiet on the Western Front,* which he read at the time when the Kaiser's sister Victoria had died. 'What a tragedy her marriage . . . must have been. Still, love comes even to an older woman.' Matters German were also on his mind because there was a debate in the parliament about restoring the German place names to the map of South Australia. He seems to have followed that without getting hot under the collar, one way or the other. Of Remarque's novel he proclaimed: 'It is the supreme expression of the modern cry against War—modern war where men are machines, where souls are blanks . . . The book tells in ever dying accents, the primitive emotions awakened by war, especially comradeship and lust for life: also the barrier it erects for ever between men and women and their acquaintances at home—between mother and son!'[18]

In 1931, he won an entrance scholarship to St Andrew's College. It was the realisation, he wrote, of the 'greatest ambition of his life so far,' especially since 'no German in the Synod was prepared to do a thing for me.' By that he meant that presumably no one in the German fold had fully understood his particular need to make the ascent into the university establishment. Moving from Immanuel to St Andrew's plunged him afresh into the social climbing and the quest for that English girl to whom he could, as he so nakedly expressed it, 'lay open all my heart, all my troubles, all my disappointments.' He was dismayed that the college had no piano—'Well, I never!'—but all was well when the dizzying dances resumed.[19]

After Mother

Frieda Strehlow was now aged 56. She had worked hard all of her life, and was still working—washing, cooking, cleaning—at the college. The widow had been treated affectionately and with respect by her Australian Lutheran community, but her future, everyone knew, lay elsewhere; in the greener lands of Germany, in the lush rolling countryside of Bavaria, near the seminary of Neuendettelsau, where her late husband had trained. Her daughter was living there and her sons were in reachable parts of the homeland.

She knew she was going, while continuing to mother her youngest son in the mission way. She would tell him, for instance, that all that dancing was nothing but a sin and a devilish temptation. She said so because she wished him to be saved on the last day. And she would be 'greatly' appeased if her son's account is to be trusted. 'I was hurt by her mistrust of me and tried to defend myself as best I could.' His defence, presumably, was to assure his mother that his intentions with the young women were honourable; that he was, in effect, looking for a wife.

Don't spend your money on my birthday presents, he said, but she insisted, telling him that it was the last of the birthdays she might be with him. A few weeks before his birthday in 1931 his body broke down, a sure sign of his anguish. He had a horrible night—'never have I suffered such a nightmare':

> When I woke up in the morning my right arm from the wrist to the shoulder was covered with ugly blotches . . . Mother—poor, good, old kindly soul—gave me one pound note and sent me to Berbilaque's Chemist shop in Prospect where I got a bottle of Sarsaparilla with Iodides. I was crying the whole day again in my grief at mother's impending departure, and my eyes were red with weeping. Dear old mother is making me plenty of greens and vegetable in order that my eczema may improve again. After tea we went up again into my old study and sat, in front of the radiator, and mother read out to me some of the reports in the Synod of 1912. And so time passed; and I must say that never since Xmas 1919 have I felt so mysteriously and tenderly connected to mother as I have yesterday and today; and it all came in a flash too. How I dread to go to bed tonight! I sat and sat in front of the red glow of the radiator, till my eyes closed in weariness and at last stumbled to bed.[20]

Frieda Strehlow retired from the college and went to live in Tanunda while her plans to leave for Germany finalised. Theo went up to see her, which meant that he then had to leave her again to go back to Adelaide. She was 'visibly affected' as he got on the train. 'Then the whistle sounded . . . it was 7.30 p.m.—and I went into the darkness and the quietness of the countryside . . . Then the relaxation set in. Suddenly I realised how tired I was. I was too tired to be sad.'

Too tired to be sad. Sadness and tiredness—they were constant companions in his mind and body, seldom more so it seems than when feelings of loss threatened to surface. It is a sense of loss—loss of his father, the imminent loss of his mother—that would have been poured into the lap of the Rosemarys of the world, if they had given him a chance. This mood—never fully articulated—seems to have reinforced his reading of Prospero's dream of futility, just as did the response to

Remarque that souls were blanks. The reasoning is that, beneath the pessimism, reason itself will not save the day. In the face of death—the death that has already occurred with the father, and the departure of the mother that might come to be a form of death—he did not pray, as Luther might have done. In his diary he names the psalms that he reads and he mentions praying, but the thrust of his account is not towards a spiritual solution to his melancholy. It is rather to resign himself to the weave of sadness and tiredness, especially when he has exhausted himself by massive exertions of will. 'Absolutely nothing interests me. I am dead.' This after his final exams, admittedly, but also, and more importantly, after his mother has finally left him to go back to Germany.

She went in July 1931, before Strehlow had sat for his exams, well before his deservedly proud graduation from the university with first class honours in Classics and English. In his diary he does not mention the day of her departure. He makes no mention of his loss at that time. He leaves five pages blank. For the first time in years, during term, he has nothing to say or cannot bring himself to speak.

Before Frieda's departure there had been all the farewells to her from the fold. There had been a service for her in Stolz's Hall at Tanunda. 'Command Whatever Grieves Thee' was sung in her honour and she cried all the way through it. Her son noted which verses in particular set her sobbing most. He does not say whether he was standing beside his mother or whether she had the comfort of his hand, or arm. We learn that she gave him a gold ring, 'so that I should not forget her.'[21] He seems not to have been able to tell her that he would not forget her.

After her departure he mentions Frieda for the first time on 27 July. She had sent him a note from Fremantle, as she was leaving Australian soil.

She is not mentioned for another fortnight. Then he has a dream, which he reports. 'I was much troubled last night by dreaming that mother had returned from the ship just to spend another day or so in Australia before leaving again and forever. I must have almost cried in my sleep when I saw her dear face again.'[22]

Thereafter Strehlow does not mention tears—his mother's or his own, that 'almost' came. For many years to come he spoke of letters to and from his mother, whom he did not see again until 1950. He had to live with her absence, and the fact that he had no family to bind him to his German past on Australian soil.

He buried himself in work. It was his final year: the exam preparation gave him a place of retreat. He kept dancing, but the social life was easing off: the tempo of English name-dropping seems to abate, the English sparklers fading in his night sky. When he looked up from his toiling at the end of the year it was not an English girl that he seized upon, but one of the German girls he had met in the previous summer round of holidays in the fecund Barossa Valley. 'What a fine sturdy type of womanhood those Schultz girls are,' he had reflected at the time, 'lithe, supple, strong, womanly, healthful, cheering, unspoilt maidens, unsophisticated yet clever and socially attractive.'

He had his eye on Doreen, who was a student at Immanuel College: 'She is the first German girl whom I could marry without any fear for the future as regards health, children, Church, and social life amongst the English.' He knew he was 'most seriously in love again.' When they stopped kissing he explained to her the difficulty, which arose from her age, clearly, and the fact that he was still a teacher at her school. She must promise not to mention the kiss to anyone. She was offended. How could he doubt the confidence of a German girl from Tanunda!

They wrote to each other. In his letter he said—as his responsibility demanded—that she should not take their kiss *too* seriously. He would understand if she did forget him after three months. He felt sick with 'agony' while waiting for her letter. While waiting he also kissed Dolly, one of Doreen's friends, and noted: 'She was not so satisfying as Doreen's had been, no, she doesn't give herself wholly, and it makes a difference.' In due course Doreen replied: she had the presence of mind to say that she did not share his feelings. It was the blow Strehlow had been waiting for, and he let it hurt him. He went out again with the English girls, including Bertha James, the girl he would marry.

Now, with his mother gone, and setting his eyes on Doreen again, she seems to have grown up even more. She is friendly and he shows her around the university and she chats with him in his rooms. 'Charming,' he thinks.

But with a pang a serious doubt struck me: could she ever remain true to me? Or was her loveliness to be defiled by the rude fingers and the slobbering mouths of Tanunda louts and larrikins after I had gone away? You see, she is still so young and girls demand excitement and we Germans have not yet learnt the art of using liberty in intercourse between the sexes with discretion. If only I could bind her to me with external bands of love.

In December 1931, he is in her arms, this time up at Tanunda again, at the onset of the summer. It was a warm night, and the moon had not yet risen.

> We spoke little but my heart was full to breaking of scores of things. I turned to tell her. For I want her to grow up into an 'English' lady— gracious, amiable, vivacious, charming and yet having reserve— being able to look after herself, capable of warding off spontaneously unnecessary intimacy on the part of boorish German males— a girl whom I can always trust to take care of herself never mind where she goes. I swung her in my arms, I held her a prisoner, I called her all terms of endearment.[23]

Then he had to go, back to Adelaide, wishing he hadn't.

Finding His Compass

Not only did Strehlow now have to work things out with Doreen. He had his compass to find for his career, and as was his wont, he chose to look back, the better to know if there was a way forward. What would be the outcome of 1931?

He had begun the year by declaring: '1931 is here at last—my long expected final year! And there is no light ray ahead. I am only hope; nothing so far is sure to me but darkness and doubt . . . no money, no help, no influential friends.' And early on he had a loss. 'My Prof has died; God wishes to lead me into the darkness of the abyss.'[24] The Prof had been Professor Strong, his supportive teacher of Classics.

Strehlow's lament at this loss of a father figure runs on to include the prospect of financial ruin coming for Australia, and then, doubling back on itself, considers that the previous year *had* been better than the previous one with regard to his studies and the varsity girls. But by the middle of 1931, when he turns 23, he feels that he has accomplished nothing yet, that he is on infirm ground and that it was 'my fault.' What *would* he do?

The obvious option was to continue with his studies, since despite all of his fretting he had graduated with a First in English. His results were good enough for Professor Fitzherbert to be taking an even livelier interest in him. Young Strehlow would go on to his MA.

It would be, to take the first of the proposals, on the ancient Nordic myths—more particularly on 'Primitive Elements in Old Icelandic Mythology and in Old English Heroic Verse, in the light of Aranda Myths and Legends.' With regard to *Beowulf*, he hoped 'to elucidate . . . the fundamental problem of the hero' in that poem and 'to explain primitive features which have been retained in it.' The whole project made sense. It sprang out of his studies in Old English, in which he had excelled; and it rooted him, once again, in some of his father's teachings, his father's penchant for the old German tales as well as his father's ethnography.

There was another idea, which came to replace the first. He might do his thesis on Bradley's essay on Shakespeare's tragedies. This topic was the logical culmination of his good work in English literature, as well as an indication of how far he had travelled towards overcoming the most obvious symptoms of English as an 'acquired language.' At the same time, if we consider his personal affinities with the topic, it is immensely suggestive. For events had already conspired to bring Strehlow closer than most young men to some of Shakespeare's primal themes: vengeance and parricide, adultery and the desire for matricide, the murder and mayhem of love and loss, and division of loyalties. For Bradley's position, put simply, and following Hegel's development of Aristotle, was that each of Shakespeare's tragic protagonists suffered his downfall because of some essential flaw in his character.

Due to the order of things, men do not achieve what they intend and the result so often is waste—'the central feeling'—as Bradley calls it. 'With Shakespeare the pity and fear which are stirred by the tragic story seem to unite with, and even to merge in, a profound sense of sadness and mystery, which is due to the impression of waste.' Tragedy was no more about justice than it was about good and evil. Double aspects could not be reconciled. The point was: 'tragedy would not be tragedy if it were not a painful mystery.' And: 'We remain confronted with the inexplicable fact, or the no less inexplicable appearance, of a world travailing for perfection, but bringing to birth, together with glorious good, an evil which it is able to overcome only by self-torture and self-waste. And this fact or appearance is tragedy.'

There was much psychological depth the young Strehlow could have explored. It would have been fascinating to see how well he fared in throwing off the chains of Lutheranism. Bradley himself was wrestling with the modernity of his position.

Meanwhile—amidst all the flirting, with girls, and with ideas he might make his own—he had Central Australia in the corner of his eye.

Two years earlier he had noted the momentous historical event for the Centre: 'The first official train to Alice Springs left Adelaide today. A party of scientists from the Adelaide University is leaving with it to study the blacks near Hermannsburg.' This is the first mention of Aborigines to be found in his student diary: it is as if they have disappeared from view in keeping with his social trajectory into the English society. The entry had, however, a double weighting: the blacks are those with whom he grew up; he is referring to the women who helped bring him up. Here they are referred to as colonial objects for scientific study, as part of nature rather than culture. At the same time he is registering the crucial geographic event. The rail link from Adelaide was to change everything. It would put an end to the first era of the frontier in Central Australia, when his old mission station and Alice Springs were completely determined by their isolation.

The Centre was also in his mind when his mother was staying with Herbert Basedow who showed her his photographs of the interior. The showing was 'more or less mother's farewell' and Strehlow asked Basedow for copies. He had seen Basedow give a lantern lecture at the Adelaide Town Hall, and it was all very interesting. The images were of Ayers Rock, which he was yet to visit, and of the Petermanns, which were even further west of the railway line. They had been taken on the Mackay expedition of 1926. 'After the lecture,' Strehlow noted, 'I felt quite different. *I felt that all the mental strain had disappeared,* and that indeed I had become quite hopeful again as far as my exams and my work is concerned' (emphasis added).[25]

This is a quiet entry. But a deep point is made. There might be solace to be found in the lap of the loving young girl, providing she was his and his alone. And there will be much satisfaction to be had in scholarly success, especially if it was esteemed in the English tradition. But here was the palliative of place in actuality, not merely in his poetic imagination. The prospect had not yet emerged but it was latent: that one day all three springs of love and security might flow together: his female love, his own loving pride of his mental achievements, and the love of place—an organic union that would make that 'mental strain' disappear.

Professor Fitzherbert had been nattering in his ear about thesis and future. In his early days as an undergraduate, when Strehlow was most worried as to whether he should continue with Classics Honours or not, Fitzherbert sometimes turned the conversation to the phonetics of native languages. It would be especially interesting, the professor opined, for a reliable book to be written on the language of the tribe before it became extinct. Fitzherbert also thought that there was an interesting connection to be heard by way of certain vowels in Aranda and Old English. It seems to be implied, in Strehlow's notes on these matters, that what was informing the professor's interests was the supposed linguistic connections between certain kinds of primitive languages, so-called. We might bear in mind here one of the historic roots of anthropology as a discipline: the move that some nineteenth-century classicists made, out of their philological reasoning, to consider the ancient world ethnographically. Another way of putting this is to say that a scholar in Fitzherbert's position, whose expertise was in the languages of ancient or Medieval Europe, was here applying himself as a mature anthropologist of people he had never met but whose culture he respected sufficiently to call a 'civilisation'—a rare term in this context at that time.[26] That a young man such as Strehlow had turned up at this time was fortuitous: here was one who knew the native language as a first language, who was in a perfect position to professionalise what was known, if he should so choose, or if he could be persuaded.

There is no hint, in the Strehlow of 1931, of excitement about the nature of Aranda, or any other language. He would, however, have been well informed by his professor that detailed studies of Aboriginal languages were scarce, and that none of the work that had been done to date had been done by someone who had grown up in the language. What he needed to do that was a grant from the Australian National Research Council. Fitzherbert was in touch with the colleagues who mattered, most significantly the Englishman and former Anglican cleric, Professor A.P. Elkin, who had not long been in the chair of anthropology at the University of Sydney. Meanwhile, in Adelaide he had the benevolent eye of the two scientists who had been travelling inland for the university and studying the Aborigines for nearly a decade: Professor John Cleland, the physiologist, and Norman Tindale, already a polymath. Only three years earlier Tindale had been at Hermannsburg, making some of the first ethnographic film.*

It was the prospect of such a grant that lay behind Strehlow referring to going away when he asked Doreen to wait for him. He would have to leave Adelaide for many months and travel the great distance to Central Australia—back to the heat and the flies and the dust that he dreaded, all those sonnets notwithstanding! In March he received news that the grant had come through.

Did he hesitate? It seems not. In 1931 there were no new positions at the university; no future for him in Norse myths or in theories of Shakespearean tragedy. His future lay in the direction of his past.

And still he had not heard back from Doreen. He was sweating on her reply. 'If only I could bind her to me with external bands of love.'[27] The letter comes—finally—and it is the bad news he more than half expects, as is his wont. For a few days he is full of bile and fretfulness about his solitary journey, and then he has to go.

---

* Norman Tindale (1900–93) was the author of several books and more than 200 scientific papers on entomology, ornithology and anthropology. Between 1922 and 1987 he wrote classic papers in each field and in anthropology he pioneered ethnographic film as well as, among other topics, studies in rock art and material culture, Aboriginal language and territories, genealogies and demographics. For most of his working life he was attached to the South Australian Museum, but he taught at American universities and was a research fellow at the Australian National University in 1973, which enabled him to refine his major work, *Aboriginal Tribes of Australia*, which had been first published in 1940. Until retirement to America Tindale was an avid fieldworker, probably spending on average two months in the field each year, often with limited public funds, about which he was not one to complain. His archive, the extent and accessible order of which is a model of its kind, expresses what Philip Jones at the museum calls 'an indefatigable commitment to making an enduring record of Aboriginal life before the transformations wrought by European contact' (Jones 1995: 176).

1 Personal conversations (February 1997) with Trudy Johannsen and T.G. Obst, former school friends of T.G.H. Strehlow, helped me with this chapter. Of invaluable assistance, also, is D.E. Hansen and I.V. Hansen's excellent history of Immanuel College, *With Wings* (Adelaide: Immanuel College, 1995).
2 Hansen and Hansen, *With Wings*, 149.
3 *The Register*, 1, 5, 6 January 1923.
4 Douglas Pike, *Paradise of Dissent*, 2nd ed. (Melbourne: Melbourne University Press, 1967).
5 T.G. Obst, *The Hands Move On: A Brief History and Recollections of Immanuel College, North Adelaide, 1922–1942* (Adelaide: Immanuel College, 1998), 38.
6 Hansen and Hansen, 23.
7 *The Echo*, December 1925, 28.
8 Ibid., December 1924, 12
9 T.G.H. Strehlow, diary [SD], 29 November 1930.
10 *The Echo*, November 1932.
11 *On Dit*, 16, 30 September 1932.
12 W.K. Hancock, *Country and Calling* (London: Faber, 1954), 117.
13 SD, 7–9 June 1929.
14 SD, 22 March 1929.
15 SD, 25 March 1929.
16 SD, 4 March 1930.
17 SD, 31 December 1931.
18 Remarks on Strehlow's reading are mainly from SD, January, August, October 1930 and January 1931.
19 Ibid.
20 SD, April–May 1931.
21 SD, 17 April 1931.
22 SD, 16 August 1931.
23 SD. References to Doreen are mainly 14 and 31 December 1931.
24 SD, January 1931.
25 SD, 23 April 1931.
26 'The work you can do collecting legends and other information about Aranda civilisation is very important' (Fitzherbert to Strehlow, 17 December 1931). Thanks to Philip Jones at the S.A. Museum for alerting me to this sentence.
27 SD, 23 December 1931.

PART II: NIGHTMARES

At this point we are confronted with our own problems:

What is essential in ourselves?

Bronislaw Malinowski

1   Homecomings

Pillow Talk

'SO YOU'VE COME back to your home country after all. Well, I'm glad to see you. I always used to think a lot of your people, you know.'

A stout elderly man with a bald head was offering Strehlow his weather-beaten hand.

They were rattling inland on the Ghan, on the way to Alice Springs.

'I always like to see young fellows coming back into the country they were born in instead of sticking around the big cities down south. And if you're taking after your dad at all—and after your mother too—well, you'll have the guts that a man needs who wants to live in this country.'

His blue eyes, Strehlow wrote, were keen and sharp but he was not unfriendly.* His carefully clipped moustache was of a reddish tinge, and his chronically red and sunburnt face betrayed that he was afflicted with one of those sensitive skins which even the fierce Central Australian summer never succeeds in tanning to the rich deep brown that is

---

*   In 'Land of Altjira' (1957) Strehlow's unpublished first volume of
    autobiography, from which I am both quoting and paraphrasing here,
    deliberately reflecting the content as well as the laboriousness of Strehlow's
    recollection, which also begins with the train ride, an event not recorded in his
    diary. Page references are to the handwritten manuscript. Strehlow finished the
    first draft in August 1957; the second and final revision by March 1959.

popularly believed to be the cover of the typical bushman of the outback.

His name was George Ballingall, a stockman and prospector who had lived in Central Australia since 1890.

It was only after they had shaken hands formally that George mentioned Strehlow's mother and father—to which, it seems, the son gave no reply. Nonetheless the man continued, praising the dedication and endurance and the good works of the mission. He greatly admired the missionary's knowledge of the Aborigines.

'When he talked about these niggers,' George told the pastor's son, 'I found out there was a lot about them and their customs that he knew and that I had never found out about. And I know lots about them myself, you know.' George smiled. 'Yes.' He stroked his moustache. 'I used to have a dark girl once, one from your tribe. I got to know the language pretty well. I used to understand the things she told me when she tried to teach me Aranda. And Bessie was a good girl—a decent loyal sort; the girls are always much better than the niggers. I suppose I had better start calling them "natives" when I'm talking to you: you've been down south and have got educated, a bushman like me knows how to behave himself when he meets educated people.'

Strehlow had been looking out the window. He was graphically conscious of coming back into his country. Across the gibber plain. Up into the terrain of the Finke, the great father river of the region, across land that had been ravaged by drought. But that was over for the time being. Rain had come. The country was in bloom.

'Yes, Bessie was a good sort.' The man laid it on about his black girl. 'She'd do my cooking and mend my clothes, come riding with me when I went out to muster the cattle, and she'd laugh and be full of fun all day long. She was a really good pal, was Bessie, and none of us bushmen would be living in these outback parts if it wasn't for good mates like Bessie. You can't get men to live anywhere if there are no women about. And Bessie was one of the best of them.'

He stopped for a moment, drew out his pipe and filled it with tobacco. He bit the tobacco slowly.

Strehlow was not entirely at ease with George's acclamation of his parents: honour bestowed upon parents can easily detract from the pride of their offspring. In addition, the bushman had, without necessarily realising it, highlighted another edge of self-consciousness when he spoke of Strehlow as a university man, a product of the cities. Little did he know—or perhaps he did, the wily old devil—that it was the city Strehlow had been obliged to leave behind in order to find something else. In the city he had got his degree, but the qualifications he was now anxious to acquire did not exist on paper. For how did you become a bushman without being a bushman like George?

There was another thing he couldn't say. He had had a dread of coming back. He might have romanticised his birth place at a distance, but dread was dread. 'I had few illusions,' he confessed later, ruminating about his first night back at Hermannsburg, 'as to the sacrifices I should have to make if I returned. I was too fond of music and the fine arts, of dancing and entertainment. I had always loathed the dust, the summer heat, the flies, the insects . . . The thought that I might have to return to my home country had always been a nightmare to me.'[1]

The train rattled away on its loose, noisy progress into the Centre.

Besides, there was that 'nigger' talk. It was George's native language. And his self-consciousness implied that the pastor's son had a different attitude, as indeed he did. Strehlow knew that you didn't shove piety about natives at bushmen who had found them to be lazy, ungrateful, sly and treacherous. That would underrate all the hard work the bushmen had done pioneering the godforsaken Outback. Nor could you comment on the arrangements bushmen made with the native women, with whom congress had been illegal since 1918.

George's smile hung in the air. I used to have a dark girl once, one from your tribe. His tribe. One of his girls. A girl to be had, by him? And there was the deeper assumption of his remark, the cultural epistemology he had going for him: that knowledge was to be gained though the language of his woman, the native woman. As if the bushman had claimed doctoral authority: I deeply understand by virtue of being intimate with a native woman.

We can imagine the old bushman's burnt presence, the warmth of his breath, pressing the idea into the lap of the mission boy.

Welcome

Claudia is the belle of Hermannsburg, at least in the estimation of all visiting tourists. Laughing eyes, light curly hair, lips that were made to smile, regular features almost European, graceful bearing, a slim yet rounded figure—she has been photographed over and over again by all visitors—yet she is as sweet and unspoiled as any girl of 18 could possibly be . . .

There is portly, faithful Marianna, who is now head-maid at Albrecht's house; and Christina, to whom smiles come seldom now, Christina who carried me to the baptismal font when I was less than twenty-four hours old . . . Then there are the two sisters, Maria and Agatha (the former is the wife of Nathaniel: I failed to recognise her when she first came to shake hands, and she burst into tears and rushed away)—both formerly faithful servants in my mother's kitchen; and old Lydia, Jakobus's wife, who nursed all my brothers and sisters in their infancy. There is Karma, Theodor's wife, with her fine eagle nose and her soft shining hair, now in the clutches of consumption; she has not much longer to live, but is peaceful now and happy like a little trusting child. She usually sits outside in the sun, drinking in warmth and comfort, before she will rest below in the dark, damp, cold grave. Her half-caste daughter, with her determined yet feminine face, her curved nose, her silky dark hair, her slender waist and soft, not full bosom, is a real Egyptian haughty type of beauty.[2]

On Tuesday 5 April 1932 Strehlow was back at Hermannsburg. He had last seen it on the day he left with his father and his mother on the buggy that carried his father downriver to his death. After that uprooting, he was back home: *Ntaria*, the place of the Twins Dreaming, where he was born.

In the passage above, which he worked up a few months later (in February 1933, actually, after he'd returned to the mission again), he does not focus entirely on the women, but there is a spark in it that George would have liked. In the full passage, the women are interspersed with the men, with the pretty ones half-hiding, like gins in the scrub, as George might have said. Then there were the men:

Old Jakobus is still faithfully riding up and down along the Ellery Creek, looking after the cattle; he has not visibly aged very much since he accompanied us down in October 1922. Nathaniel is the chief overseer of the shepherds, and is also camped permanently either at the Long Water Hole, or on the No. 4 Block. He is the only 'gentleman' amongst the natives at the Mission, a good-natured, jovial, open-hearted fellow, who, one feels, is superior by birth: one almost feels in him a sort of class-mate and school-mate of my father—indeed, his handshake and hearty 'Guten Tag' (he is the only native who knows one or two German phrases) is quite genteel . . . Old Moses with his silvery white beard looks just like one of the early pictures of one of the Disciples;

tall and erect, despite his blindness a sturdy walker,—a voice in the wilderness, whose resolute tones invite outsiders to submit to the New Way, which experience has taught him is better than the old: one child only, a daughter (Priscilla) remains, the other children he has all carried to the grave without bowing his fine head, even his two almost grown-up boys. Loneliness has no hold on him …

There is white-haired Abel, who assists the second missionary in the school; and his ageing half-caste wife Rosa, a daughter of old Mr Raggatt. Her son Christoph, who is about my age, has a huge flowing black beard, and possesses one of the finest organ bass voices in the Territory . . .

Julius and August look two real patriarchs with their magnificent flowing grey beards . . .

There is Jakob Kurka, cheerfulness personified, once my 'donkey man' ever-faithful companion, now a happy cow-herd; and his spouse Alma. Also old Margaret and Karolina, both effusive and sentimental, and M's son Lukas, who accompanied me back to Alice Springs, my tjoanana, now the owner of a thick, short black beard. And there are many other links with the past . . . And yet there is the rising flood of the new generation: perhaps the majority of the faces I saw were new and strange to me, after a lapse of a mere 10 years. Time flies—*tempora mutantur, nos et mutamur in illis.* The past is vanishing fast; soon I shall be a stranger in the land that bore me.[3]

A congregation of souls, a community of good feeling, his community, his village, after a fashion. They all came out to meet him. They all called out. They were pleased to see him taken in by Pastor F.W. Albrecht, the burly Pole who had come six years before, after the death of *ingkata* Carl Strehlow. Albrecht was a forthright, compassionate man—a 'straight out man,' as his congregation called him, and as his biographer, Barbara Henson, calls him in her most instructive book of that title.

Young Theo, the prodigal son of the mission station, was warmly fed by Mrs Albrecht in the main homestead And he went to bed there, under the roof where he had grown up. 'I slept little that night. I could hear only the whispering voices of the past crowding in upon me as I tossed sleeplessly.'[4]

This too was written much later, when he began to shape his auto-biographical account of the homecoming and what it meant to him. At the time it seems that the past was crowding in on him so much that he could not find his own voice in his diary. What he wrote on the spot was: 'Welcomed by the natives, but they were far more reserved and shy here.' He was comparing them to the reception party at Alice Springs, where he had, he told his diary, been 'proclaimed a *kalja* [older brother] of the tribe.'[5]

Tjurunga and the Golden Calf

He had come back to the mission at a historic moment. For four years the drought had been so bad that the corpses of rabbits and kangaroos lay in the forks of trees, where the animals had impaled themselves trying to reach edible growth. More children had died at the mission than were born; from measles, whooping cough, tuberculosis and scurvy, so many that the cemetery had to be extended. Moses told Albrecht that 'the Christians all die.' Moses lost four of his sons, and it was a major act of faith, Albrecht thought, that when they buried one of the boys—'a light in all the darkness'—Moses was able to thank the Lord his son had been 'saved.'[6]

The station had more mouths than it could possibly feed—closer to 400 than the manageable 250 to 300. The government had 'protectively' herded some of the half-castes from Alice Springs into the mission, as well as those who had been living along the new railway line. In from the drought-stricken west others had also come. Federal government subsidies were for Alice Springs people only, which bypassed mission provisions for all, especially the sick and needy. Resources were dangerously stretched.

Albrecht's strictures in the *Lutheran Herald* were designed to shame governments and public alike with the physical neglect of the people the mission could not and would not turn its back on. When scurvy was diagnosed by the Adelaide University party that visited the mission in 1929, the cry for help was heard. Supplies of brown rice and 132 cases of oranges arrived from the South. Oranges sliced into small pieces were fed to the sick until their mouths stopped bleeding. But nothing would ever be right unless the rain came and the general problem of water supply was addressed.

Good rain came at last in December 1929, and for the first time in five years the Finke flowed past the mission. By then, too, after years of campaigning, there was also the hope of a pipeline. At Kaporilja Springs, a traditional and sacred water source in the rocky hills about four miles south-west of the station, 15,000 gallons of good water ran to waste daily. With a pipeline, the water would flow down to the settlement and its gardens, putting an end to half a century of cyclic misery in times of drought, and making an oasis in the wilderness. It only remained for the mission to raise the funds to build the pipeline and the new era would begin. 'We therefore made a special appeal for funds for a water scheme,' Pastor Albrecht wrote in his annual report for 1932, 'as it is clear to everybody that the water is absolutely necessary for the Native.'[7]

There were other grounds for Christian optimism at the mission in 1932. Apart from the improvement in the children's health, there were now 79 of them in the school, and quite a number were progressing 'fairly well.' Albrecht valued the school as a general induction into the Christian society he was cultivating with festivals of one kind or another. There was a Bible Festival where all those who knew one to three verses of each chapter of St John off by heart met for an examination. And there was a mission festival, a triumphant one, held at the Manangananga cave.

The cave is in a tight little gully running south from the mission towards the back of Mount Hermannsburg. It is hard to see from the creek bed of huge boulders and shadowy saplings. Nearby is a beautiful oval pool. The pool is the water into which the two boys, the mythic twins of *Ntaria*, dived into on their journey from Palm Valley to Hermannsburg. The whole area was totemically charged, and to approach without permission or in the wrong way was to violate the sacred pool and trespass upon the approach to a major storehouse of *tjurunga*. But that is what Pastor Albrecht decided to do in these years of Christ militant.

One Saturday night, when a man's thigh had been cut to the bone with a butcher's knife, and the man looked like bleeding to death, Albrecht decided that the time had come to put God's word before tribal law. 'God cannot and will not bless you unless you are prepared to do that,' he told his people.[8]

On Pentecost Sunday 1930, he gathered the flock together—men, women and children. The cave had long been taboo to women and children on penalty and fear of death, but now the Christian soldiers walked the five kilometres to the cave, singing their hymns all the way. The Christian men were with them, including Nathaniel and Moses.

Outside the cave they lit a fire. This was for their picnic. They had cake and tea, and held the service designed to put an end to the spirits in the cave. Albrecht's biographer, whose perspective I am relying on here, quotes one of the natives who were there:

Before service, took stones out and put them on the ground. Everybody sat in big circle, and stones were put in the middle. Kids were scared! First time we bin see that stone. Old Man [Albrecht] start those opening words, In the name of the Father, the Son and the Holy Ghost, then everybody relax, we start to sing hymn. Then he preached about Moses and Aaron and the golden calf. *Tjurungas* were like the golden calf. Old man preach, and everybody look up, yes, that's really true. We bin think about God make this free. Yes, stones very frightening for Aboriginal people, that's why Pastor Albrecht go there, 'Come here, everybody, come near, sit down here.' People touched them, children, everybody. Moses preached too. People feel free altogether afterwards. Still tell stories, but never bin frightened.[9]

Thus Albrecht and his congregation conducted a triumphant Christian service, he himself preaching about the Golden Calf, and Moses sermonising under the rubric of 'Churinga or Christ?'

Later the *tjurunga* were displayed, like so many trophies of war, which they were, on the verandah of the homestead. And thereafter Pastor Albrecht was able to claim 'Mission Festivals' at the cave as a *fait accompli*, as proof of victory over the pagan site: gone the tribal business of *tjurunga* worship; now, with the emblem of the cross, the place had been universalised in significance, it was there for ever for everyone.*[10] Albrecht also thought it a victory over tribal fighting, 'a decisive victory of the Spirit over the lower instincts of their human nature.'[11]

As shocking as the raid on the cave was, it had been executed with the cooperation of the Aboriginal Christians, men and women who seem to have strongly turned against their old beliefs. A year before the sacking of the cave they had, for example, remonstrated with Albrecht because he had permitted their traditional dances in the vicinity of the

---

* And indeed for the next two generations even Lutherans strangely flirted with the powers credited to the place: In 1935 Dora Latz (née Pech) and others went to the 'sacred pool in the secret gully' where there was a 'fertility stone' that could be rubbed with another stone by those who dared (Latz 1996: 11, 61). Years later her son, Peter, felt as a boy he was tempting fate with other Aboriginal boys when they went into the gully because there 'was a rubbing stone together . . . that made sure you had a child.' The day he pressed on with three other white boys and swam in the sacred pool and then explored the cliff he stumbled upon 'the biggest snakes I've ever seen in Central Australia' and fled accordingly, as quick as the aboriginal kids had.' Peter Latz, interview, Northern Territory Archives Service Oral History Unit, March 1996, Tape 1 Side B: 17.

mission. Why, they demanded, had he done that? 'Here we praise God, not *tjurunga*.' Albrecht's lame answer at the time was because the musicologist Dr Harold Davies, director of the Conservatorium of Music in Adelaide, had come to study their songs so that people in the future would know what was sung. To which his faithful believers replied that nevertheless they had been shamed in the eyes of the more recent people to the mission, the 'wild ones' from out west. 'We understand the difference between corroboree singing and singing for Dr Davies. But these ignorant people from the west, they don't know the difference. Sing 'em daytime, sing 'em night time.' The congregation wanted a clear stop to any prospect of night-time singing, and Albrecht had to apologise to them.[12]

As to the 'so called wild ones,' as Albrecht called them, they had come in for special attention in recent years. During the drought they had suffered a great deal, and some had headed in to the mission. Some had come on the instigation of a rather remarkable white man who had come among them in 1929, Geza Roheim, the Hungarian Freudian who had learnt their language well enough to be recording, not their music, like Dr Davies, but their dreams. From these notations Roheim would construct cathedrals of illuminating European thought on the deep imaginings of the 'primitives,' mapping an inner life of the instincts that was the obverse of Christianity.[13]

Albrecht was of two rather contradictory opinions about the voluntary feelings of the desert people. He was convinced, on the one hand, that unless reserves were created in some of the remote areas, even the most self-sufficient people would be at risk of 'total extinction.' He also thought, however, that people were drifting towards the mission of their own free will, because, once their 'religious belief is shaken and their social life undermined' by contact with white men, the evidently superior life of the white man was a positive attraction. 'If a little tea and sugar is offered, he will gladly part with any of his sacred ceremonial objects, thus definitely giving up his old belief and there is even a possibility of never reviving it. And that usually means the end of their tribal life.' There is, noticeably, a reservation in this huge statement, which leaves open the possibility that native life would survive the entry into mission life. Nonetheless, it was Albrecht's working assumption that his teachings were to fill the vacuum left by the separation of people from the sacred objects of their fathers. The Word was there to help those who wanted to 'find a substitute for what they had lost in their inner life.'[14]

So in an optimistic vein Pastor Albrecht had been extending the parish. In February 1932 Titus, along with Rolf and his wife and mother, left the mission to go back to Potarti as evangelists. Albrecht expected a lot of Titus. He was the man 'who could satisfy their [the bush natives'] curiosity and answer all their questions in regard to the white man. He can show them how not everything that seems to be desirable to the natives is without its disadvantages.' That was one thing. He was also the man 'who drives fear away': 'He has a shot gun for his protection and to get some meat. They [the bush natives] are convinced that no enemy will come near his camp. Neither is he afraid of evil spirits.'[15]

Because Titus was to preach the Gospel, the life of the wild ones was 'being filled with new hope.' They would 'receive something definite that will carry them through life and death.' Albrecht was as affirmative as a man can be: 'The message of the Gospel, therefore, finds a ready response among those so called wild ones and has a most wonderful effect on their minds. Fear gradually disappears and the Natives once more see the happier side of life in this world.'[16]

There were other battles for Titus to fight out west, a glimpse of which Theo got from Mr Lewis the dingo scalper with whom he was yarning on 13 April. 'Two rascally whites, Kay and Krauss . . . who had been riding around with naked native girls' had robbed Titus's rations. When the natives tracked them they could see they had 'evidently walked to the box backwards, opened the lock, took the rations and returned to their horses, about a dozen in number, and then galloped off.' Lewis was 'deeply moved by the deep seriousness of Titus while conducting worship among the tribesmen.'

Angel and Snake

During his first days back home Theo walked around the 'vicinity,' as he called it, in a strangely unemotional way. He was brooding, taking it slowly. He had an evening with his old teacher Mr Heinrich, with whom he had travelled on that fateful journey to Horseshoe Bend ten years earlier: that evening passes without comment in his diary. He went to church. He talked with the Aboriginal men, one of whom wanted to show him a Central Australian mole—'a little sleek fat fellow . . . a beautiful silky coat.' On 14 April, he climbed Mount Hermannsburg under a beautiful cloudless sky, up to the flowers blossoming on the peak, 'but I did not risk picking them on any account in the heat of the windless valley.' They were 'just one creek west of Manangananga,' which he notes without comment. All this settling, this relocating, went on for some days. His diary is explicit about many things except his depth, or lack of depth, of feeling: expressions of that were to come later, when he had come back from nine months hard travelling out bush. His stronger feelings are reserved for one thing and one thing only, and this happened only five days after his return.

On 10 April he had opened up his father's work. He got out Pastor Carl's Aranda dictionary and compiled a list of Aranda names of plants and animals. 'I want to "get into" the Aranda tongue as quickly as possible,' he wrote that day.

This was the beginning. He had named the work before him. It was the getting into the Aranda language, the deep travelling into the language of the other, that would make a life in translation. Out of which he would construct, from his experience of English (and German, Greek and Latin), the poetic world and the poetics of the Aranda: the poetry, the thinking, the saying, each in the neighbourhood of each other, so they together constitute the way being dwells on this earth.[17] From this moment on, he was dwelling—inhabiting as he could—what it was to be Aranda, and what not: the yes and the no of their existence.

On that first day Moses paid a tribute to his father, and to the work of his father. Strehlow wrote it down in Aranda. 'I asked him the meaning of the old Kwatja Ceremony. I read to him the *tjurunga* words as given by my father, as he had "forgotten them a little." Whenever I halted, however, he continued on his own, and then gave the exact words as recorded by my father.'

The Kwatja was the rain ceremony; more specifically the lightning ceremony.

The son set it down in his diary. The phrases, which take up most of a typed page, fall down like lines of a poem, which indeed they are, and their inscription is the first of many—of scores, hundreds, by his final proud count—which would come to compose his life.

The next day he was with Moses again. They were still with the Kwatja myth, and by the end of their time together Strehlow was very pleased. For what they had been doing was scrutinising the work of Spencer and Gillen and 'substantiating my father's account that the soul is finally killed by lightning.'

As if sparked by that he asked Moses another question. This one went to the heart of the contest between the English scientists and the mission ethnologist, the men without fluency in Aranda and the man who had spent the best part of his life in their tongue. What was the meaning of *Altjira*? What did it mean before the missionaries arrived? Did it mean 'dream'?

A fundamental matter between Spencer and Carl Strehlow was the status of the Aranda terms that created the English-language concept of the Dreaming. *Alcheringa* was one, *Altjira* another. In translation where was the weighting to lie: in the realm of sleep rather than wakefulness, fantasy rather than reality, chimera rather than substance, the product of mind rather than of the world? Pastor Carl had been accused of imposing his monotheistic God on Aboriginal lore. At the mission Strehlow had open before him his father's passage that hinted at this:

> According to the tradition of the ancestors there is a being, called *Altjira*, who embodies the highest good (*mara*). This being is eternal (*ngambakala*), and is thought to be a tall, strong man with a red skin colour and long, fair hair (*gola*), which flows over his shoulders. *Altjira* has the feet of an emu (*ilia* = emu, *inka* = legs, feet) and is therefore called *Altjira iliinka*. His decoration consists of a white headband (*tjilara*), a necklace (*matara*) and an armband (*gultja*). He also wears a belt made of hair (*tjipa*) and a *worrabakana* (pubic covering). He has many wives, called *tnera* (the beautiful ones), who have legs like dogs (*knulja-inka*) and his own red skin colour. He has many sons and daughters, the former with emu feet and the latter with dog legs. Around him are many beautiful young men and girls . . .

The phrase 'highest good' certainly laid Pastor Strehlow open to the charge of importing Christian monotheism, even if the Aranda details did add up their own heavenly vision (T.G.H. Strehlow was later to speak of their 'Golden Age'). Then comes the crucial note:

> A linguistic derivation of the word *Altjira* has not yet been found. The natives now incorporate the concept of the Non-created One. Asked about the meaning of the word the natives repeatedly assured me that *Altjira* refers to him who has no beginning, who did not issue from another (*erina itja arbmanakala* = no one created him). Spencer and Gillen's claim ('Northern Tribes of Central Australia' p. 745) that 'the word *alcheri* means dream' is incorrect. *Altjirerama* means 'to dream' and is derived from *altjira* (god) and *rama* (to see), in other words 'to see god' . . . The Aranda language does not render the word 'dream' with *alcheri* but rather with *altjirrinja*, though this word is rarely used. The normal expression of the

1. The first missionaries at Hermannsburg: Pastors W.F. Schwarz (1877–89), L.G. Schulze (1878–91) and A.H. Kempe (1877–91).

2. Preacher 'Blind Moses' and his wife, Sophia, with Kamutu, a senior Pintubi man, c. 1920.

3. Mounted Constable Willshire taking directions from a 'tracker', 1898.

4. Baldwin Spencer and Frank Gillen looking their best in Victoria, 1899, photographed by J.W. Lindt.

5. Pastor Johann Reuther and wife Pauline in their desert cave of books at Killalpaninna, c. 1905.

6. Frieda and Pastor Carl Strehlow, recently married, at Point Pass, S.A., 1895.

7. Hermannsburg mission in the late 1890s, looking south.

8. Inside the mission church at Hermannsburg, c. 1900.

9. Theo and playmates, c. 1913.

10. Theo in the lap of his sister, Martha, c. 1908. His brothers, from left: Hermann, Rudolf, Friedrich, Karl.

11. 'Now an only child.' Theo and parents, 1913.

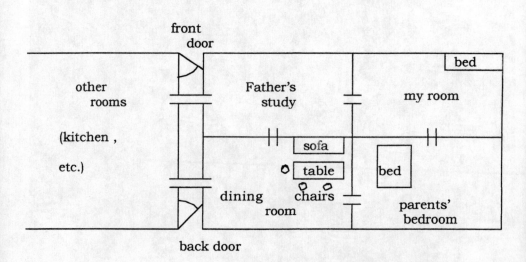

front
door

| other rooms | | Father's study | | my room |
bed

(kitchen ,

etc.)

sofa

table

chairs

dining
room

bed

parents'
bedroom

back door

12. Mission house floor plan, drawn by Strehlow to illustrate the childhood habitat of a 'silent presence.'

13. Strehlow the University Man,
c. 1928.

14. Strehlow with his mother Frieda,
who is embarking for Germany,
July 1931.

Diary 1932.
CENTRAL . AUSTRALIA.

Thursday March 31st   Left Adelaide by train at 9.20 a.m.

Sat. April 2nd   Arrived at Alice Springs about 10. p.m.

Sunday. Ap. 3rd   Met 'Mickey' at Mr. E. Kramer's. He comes from Bond
Springs, is an old native of about 60 or more. He belongs
to the 'Aranda Jorribra': these, he told me, say "jau", whereas
the A. aldolibra say 'awa'. He speaks English
quite well, + uses 'ana' a lot [±'and'], instead of his own
clumsy 'tula'.   Had a very enthusiastic reception at the
native camp this afternoon, where an old woman proclaimed
me as a 'kalja', + a 'tjia' of the tribe. All were then eager
to talk to me + to press my hand. I managed to understand
practically all they said to me; but I could hardly manage
a word myself.

Monday.   Wrote letters for tomorrow's mail.

Tuesday. 5th   Went to Hermannsburg by Wallis Fogarty's lorry. Welcomed by
the natives: but they were far more reserved + shy here: they
won't talk so readily, although again I was proclaimed
the 'tjia' of them all.

Thurs.   Took a rest + went for some walks in the vicinity.

Friday. Ap. 8th   A native brought me a specimen of the C.A. mole, which   from the west
he assured me lives in "ulttheia" and in sandhills. The little
fellow was about 9 inches long, + had a beautiful silky coat
light yellow golden in colour. He was very restless on the
little rag in which he had been brought. I let him go finally,
not knowing what to do with him. Acc. to the natives he was
fully grown; + he lived on sand "ana wara ilkuma", they
laughed. An old Kukatja native from Tempe Downs confirmed this;
they called the little mole "Itaratara."

Sunday Ap.10th   After Aranda service today Moses, Jacobus, Abel, Josef, + Martin came to
the verandah + revived some reminiscences of olden times. Moses
began by telling me, that "Loatjira, too" (do you remember L. don't you)
was baptized + died a Christian, under the name of Abraham. After your
father's death he too became a Christian + no longer left the station till
he died." This was interesting to me, in view of the fact that
considerable criticism has of late been raised ag. the accuracy of
my father's work on the Aranda + Loritja tribes of Central
Australia. The four natives in the picture given in Vol. I are (in that order)
Loatjira, Silas Lartjinaka, + Moses: L. was, perhaps, the last of the old

blacks is '*ta altjireraka*': = 'I have dreamed.' The word '*alcheringa*,' which according to Spencer and Gillen is supposed to mean 'dreamtime' is obviously a corruption of *altjirrinja*. The native knows nothing of 'dreamtime' as a designation of a certain period of their history. What his expression refers to is the time when the *Altjiranga mitjina* [*sic*] traversed the earth.[18]

Strehlow waited for Moses to reply. Did *Altjira* pertain to 'dream'?
'No,' Moses said.[19]

And Strehlow eagerly recorded, in Aranda, what the preacher had to say, blithely ignoring the fact that he was committing the error for which his father had been so condemned: using a Christian native to tell him about pre-contact meanings.

A few days later he was pleased with Moses again. The Blind Christian had given a sermon from the pulpit, in which he contradicted Spencer's idea that the Aranda people would go back to the beliefs of their forefathers. Spencer said that would happen in a week if there was no church, but it had not.

On 12 April, Strehlow was looking into the origin of children from *tjurunga*. The entry is typical of so many Strehlow was to make over the years, where what he writes seems to have a personal resonance of which he is oblivious. For here the Christian Gemini born of an Aboriginal place with Twins Dreaming, is puzzling over double spirits by birth and place:

I wished to get to the exact meaning of '*ngantja*.' This was not 'guruna' or 'spirit'; only a little like 'guruna.' It was 'spirit' and yet not 'spirit.' It was in this case like a tjilpa . . . (the native cat).

There were *two kinds of children*, distinguishable, however, (X Strehlow) only by reason of their birth, and therefore not separable in actual life—
(1) Those originating from the tjurungas which the tjilpa had lost on his wanderings . . .
(2) Those originating from the tjurunga inkana which was the transformed body of the tjilpa itself. After the death of the individual the tjilpa-ancestor could be reincarnated again, times without limit. This evidently applied to the other lost tjurungas as well.

And so on. All of this happened in a kind of rush of re-cognition. Young Strehlow was shadowing the hand of his father: defending; checking up; acknowledging—while at the same time amending and elaborating in his own manner as he worked his way back into the language, and progress in which he was soon able to report to Professor J.B. Cleland, back in Adelaide. 'After a fortnight, I found I was able to understand perfectly well all that they wished to say to me, even though I was still very unsure and halting in my speech. However the Natives had a lot of patience with me, and soon I felt quite at home again amongst them—*in conversation*'[20] (emphasis added). This was good to be able to report to a patron of his work.* Getting to be at home in the songs was the much harder work to come.

It was this intense and future-directed task that consumed him during his initial return to the mission; the business of recording what was remembered about origins, or stories of origins before—before anyone, or any white man like himself, had come *into* the country. It was a passionate act of recovery.

From the beginning, it was willed, anxious work. And work inseparable from the other tasks of writing, from the making of records, setting things down before they were lost—lost from himself, lost in time, lost for Eternity. An endless inscribing against the clock.[†] 'The past is vanishing fast; soon I shall be a stranger in the land that bore me.'

Towards the end of his stay, on 24 April, there was a moment that left

---

* Cleland, an anatomist, was one of several University of Adelaide scientists who went inland to study the people judged to be a vanishing race, and a key member of the local Board of Anthropological Studies which was the conduit for research funds from national research grants. Strehlow submitted his expenses to Cleland, including £50 for the purchase of Sir Douglas Mawson's rifle and 120 rounds of ammunition.

† Strehlow speaks, inimitably, for himself in these matters, which is the main reason for letting him dominate the narrative in this way. But it should also be said that at this time he was by no means alone as an elegist of the 'primitive native.' For ten years the scientists, Cleland included, of the Adelaide University parties had been hurrying inland precisely because they believed it was their last chance to gather information on a doomed race (Jones 1987: 71–92). At the same time, those who discoursed on these matters culturally rather than biologically had noted what Malinowski had in *Argonauts of the Western Pacific* called the 'sadly ludicrous not to say tragic position' of ethnology: 'at the very moment when it begins to put its workshop in order . . . the material of its study melts away with hopeless rapidity' (1922: xv). And, as Strehlow was reacquainting himself to the desert, Lévi-Strauss was about to encounter the tribes of Brazil, the record of which, *Tristes Tropiques*, was a sustained lament for elementary structures that were being lost even as they were being studied. 'I am a traveller in my own day,' Lévi-Strauss wrote, 'hastening in search of a vanishing reality.' (1974: 43). Before long Strehlow's recurring metaphor would be 'sunset,' a refrain as full of nostalgia and as expressive of the anthropological predicament as anything 'triste' written by Lévi-Strauss. For both Lévi-Strauss and Strehlow it was an anguished nostalgia for the disappearing subject of their ethnology which summonsed the political question: what must be done? And both, in different ways, stayed true to their pessimisms. For Lévi-Strauss' fatalistic resolution see his chapter, 'A Little Glass of Rum' (1974: 383–93); for Strehlow's, read on.

him rather speechless: 'An Aranda woman came to me yesterday and told me a dream: it contained some mention of snakes and also of an angel, but I had no chance to take it down. She also informed me that she often saw the Angel Gabriel in visions. I don't even know who she is.' It was not often he could let a remark rest like that.

His Father's Cave

His father's work before him was a treasure trove. It was nothing less than an overview of what the Germans called the *'intellectual* culture' of the tribes, a respectful phrase that would not easily have fallen from the lips of Darwinian Englishmen. In his first volume of *Die Aranda*, Carl Strehlow itemised at least 110 myths, and recounted them by reference to their Aboriginal names and sometimes the places to which the stories were connected. A short prose summary of the story was followed by the song. He provided an interlinear translation of the Aranda into German, then a smoother paraphrase as well. Sometimes the myth was accompanied by only a few verses; more often than not, however, up to a dozen verses were set down after those intimate liaisons with his Aboriginal friends in his parlour.

The key man, Loatjira, had been the subject of conversation as soon as Strehlow had returned to the mission. 'After Aranda service to-day,' Theo noted on 10 April:

> Moses, Jacobus [*sic*], Abel, Josef, and Martin came to the verandah and revived some reminiscences of olden times. Moses began by telling me without introduction, 'Loatjira even (you remember L[oatjira] don't you) was baptised and died a Christian too, under the name of Abraham. After your father's death he too became a Christian and no longer left the station till he died.' This was interesting to me, in view of the fact that considerable criticism has of late been raised against the accuracy of my father's work on the Aranda and Loritja tribes of Central Australia . . . L[oatjira] was, perhaps, the last of the old 'nankara' or witch-doctors of the Western Aranda, and a man of first importance in the tribe. He steadfastly used all his influence in the interests of the vanishing beliefs of the knaribata or old men till the death of my father. Furthermore, he was before then not a station native, but preferred to live the old ways of tradition.

And so yet another slur by Spencer and Gillen had been scotched: that his father's sources had been tainted with Christian belief. He also had reason to believe that Loatjira was a far better informant than Spencer and Gillen's Irrapmwe, who was known as King Charlie or Charlie Cooper. Strehlow had a friendly meeting with Cooper on 13 April and noted that he had a 'glib tongue, and speaks fluent and rather correct English' and the 'manner of an American business man.' He rather illogically concluded from this that Cooper's skill 'probably explains the attempt of Spencer to pose as master of the language.' Try as Strehlow might to pit his father's work victoriously over Spencer's, the two were to stand side by side, complementing each other as major ethnographic achievements of the time, and for posterity.[21]

Leaving the vindication of his father aside, Strehlow had before him crucial and correct foundational material on pagan secrets. At the end of Pastor Carl's second volume there is a lucid account of the *tjurunga*, the very meaning of which was 'one's own secret thing'; ('tju...is an antiquated word and means: hidden, concealed, secret; runga means: one's own, my own').[22] *Tjurunga* could be used as an adjective, as with one's *retna tjurunga* (one's secret name). It was also used substantively— as with the *tjurunga* rituals, and with regard to the decorated sacred objects. The latter were stored in secret-sacred places, the arknanaua (a word he considered for 'church' except that it was too pagan), and they originated from the ancestor beings in their 'eternal camps.'[23]

As for the sacred objects, Pastor Carl explained: 'the tjurunga passes as the common body of both a person and his totem ancestor.' He added that the *tjurunga* was 'not the habitation of a soul or of life itself.' It was, rather, as far as he could make out from the contradictions of belief, more in the nature of being a second body, the other body of the person.

The father made two other fundamental statements that were to resonate in the work of his son. The first was: 'One could not possibly understand the songs during the performances without an awareness of this union' (of the object with the person and the ancestor). The second seminal statement was about ownership of *tjurunga*. 'Although the *tjurunga* are the personal property of those related to it, they are nevertheless mostly stored in arknanaua and fetched only on festive occasions. Being personal property they are also inheritable.' There was an essential ambiguity here. In general the statement means the *tjurunga* were owned personally *and* collectively. With regard to the inheritance of the personal, the construction strongly suggests the inalienability of the *tjurunga* in that it could only be bequeathed to kin (that is, the collective). The son would have a lot to say about the 'personal.'

Finally, his third volume, on the 'Totemic Cults,' in which Pastor Carl itemised details of 59 such cults, advanced further observations that were to resonate through his son's life work. These were about the songs, and they were as crucial as what he had said about *tjurunga*.

The first observation concerned the difficulty of the songs, the aspect of them that made them so hard to translate. Their forms stemmed from earlier times. 'They contain quite a number of words which are no longer in use and therefore unintelligible to the younger men, and naturally even more so to the women and the children. These songs have been passed from generation to generation while the collo-quial speech has experienced quite a few changes.'[24] The son was to make much of the poetic diction, as we shall see: he prided himself in often cracking the code of the cryptic verses. His father added, however: 'During most of the cult rituals, old and new songs are sung side by side.' That is to say: not all the songs were arcane and impene-trable. Rituals carried on with newer songs, songs that were not so bound to the past, which suggested that the songs were not necessarily dying off. Theo, as he invested a life in translation, was going to empha-sise the cryptic and the archaic, rather than that which was accessible, and possibly the more enduring.

There was another, rather poetic observation by his father. It went to the heart of the sacred beliefs, and what was involved in the proper learning of a song. 'According to the views of the Aranda and Loritja, the learned men have been taught these *tjurunga* songs by the "hidden people" . . . living in the earth. These *rella ngantja* merge from their sub-terranean homes at night and go to the campfire of the sleeping person and impart these songs in him. A man who knows very many tjurunga songs is called *intarangalta*, i.e. very wise, and he also teaches (*beltama*) these tjurunga songs to the young men. This happens mostly at night.'[25]

This is a tale of sacred reception and transmission, the secret-sacred night work that was a mark of the trust involved by all in the song. These terms, and the obligations they summon, must have been noticed by the son. He inherited the texts of his father, and the question was whether he would address the semantic field of trust: 'intarangalta,' the wise man; 'beltama,' the teacher.

Only time would tell what Strehlow came to make of this. At that moment, in 1932, he was in any case harbouring his father's work as his own, rather as if he had come to it as an initiate, when of course he had not, not if initiation meant surrender to pagan ceremony. There seems to have been no murmur in him towards that. It was as out of the question as it had been to Baron Leonhardi in his father's time. Leonhardi had reeled back from the idea of initiation as it was flirted with in some ethnographic circles. He spoke of the trust with which Pastor Carl was obviously held as having nothing to do with 'any white man subjecting himself to the barbaric initiation rites of any Australian tribe. No researcher would undergo scarification, depilation, the ordeal by fire, the punctuating of the nose septum, the removal of a tooth, circumcision and subincision.' Conversely, Pastor Carl told Leonhardi that 'none of the blacks would regard me as a member of the tribe just because I had been an eye-witness to every ceremony.'[26]

Exactly the basis of the trust, then, remained undefined by Carl Strehlow. But it seemed to have come from his immersion in Aranda, as well as the relationships he formed as a Christian, *and* the exchanges he made as a preacher who ran a ration depot. The son would learn from that, too.

Pagans in the Saddlebag

His father's work, fortunately for Strehlow, was not the only thing in his head as he prepared to set off on his journeys. He was reading the latest things about the primitive. He had the new book by S.P. Porteus *The Psychology of a Primitive People*. Porteus was a well-meaning psychologist from the University of Hawaii, one of many scholars of the period drawn to native people in Central Australia, who made something of a base of the mission station. His work was intent on comparing the mental abilities of various indigenous groups, striving to do so objectively, according to 'culture free tests.' Porteus put the Aranda on the lower end of the mental scale along with the Bantu, and suspected that the Aborigine 'may become extinct before adaptation is possible.'[27]

'It is,' Strehlow told his diary on 13 April, 'an admirable and very convincing study of native mentality but too general.' What Porteus missed completely was the 'wonderful memory' of the Australian primitives, the ways in which they had no trouble holding hundreds of verses in their heads. That evening Pastor Albrecht told Strehlow such demands on the memory of white children would cause them considerable trouble.

There was another fellow who had used the mission station whose book Strehlow was reading: Geza Roheim's monumental *Australian Totemism*, which had been written out of his stay in the desert, and after his deep immersion in all the ethnography of Australia, especially the work of Carl Strehlow. Because of Roheim's skill with the ethnographic detail, not to mention the sweep of his psychological argument about the primitive mind, Strehlow never sought to argue much with him, neither in 1932 nor subsequently.

There was perhaps a quiet reason for this. For behind Roheim was another book, the one that had mainly brought him to Australia. This was Freud's *Totem and Taboo*, in which it is asserted, via reference to the ethnology of Aranda, that the foundations of culture are to be found in parricide: in the primal horde's murder of their rival for food and for women, namely their own fathers.

Strehlow had *Totem and Taboo* with him too. With this most pagan of texts in his saddlebag he would travel as far west as he could go, even though he did not write a word about the book in his diary.

---

1   T.G.H. Strehlow, 'Land of Altjira' [LOA], unpublished MS, 1957, 17–18.
2   T.G.H. Strehlow, diary [SD], 23 February 1933.
3   SD, 23 February 1933.
4   LOA, 12.
5   SD, 5 April 1932.
6   Barbara Henson, *A Straight-Out Man: F.W. Albrecht and Central Australian Aborigines* (Melbourne: Melbourne University Press, 1992), 50–75, for much of what follows below. Also, P.A. Scherer, *The Hermannsburg Chronicle* (Tanunda: the author, 1995).
7   F.W. Albrecht, Finke River Mission Station, *Annual Report*, 30 June 1932, 9–10.
8   Henson, *Straight-Out Man*, 53.
9   Ibid., 54.
10 For this account I have relied heavily on Henson; and also Philip Jones, 'Traveller Between Two Worlds' in *The Heritage of Namatjira*, ed. Jane Hardy, J.V.S. Megaw and H. Ruth Megaw (Melbourne: Heinemann, 1990), 122–23. See also Paul Carter, *The Lie of the Land* (London: Faber, 1996), 31–32.
11 Albrecht, *Annual Report*, 11–12.
12 Henson, *Straight-Out Man*, 47–48.
13 In 1925 Roheim published *Australian Totemism*, followed by other works which featured his Western Desert fieldwork: among them were *Animism and Religion* (1932), *Psycho-Analysis and Primitive Culture Types* (1932), *Women and Their Life in Central Australia* (1933) and *The Riddle of the Sphinx* (1934). *Children of the Desert*, which was not published until 1974, he regarded as his major work arising out of his first field report. For an overview of Roheim's work see Werner Muensterberger's introduction to *Children of the Desert* (New York: Basic Books, 1974) and John Morton (ed.) in *Children of the Desert II: Myths and Dreams of the Aborigines of Central Australia* (Sydney: Oceania Publications, University of Sydney, 1998).
14 Albrecht, *Annual Report*, 13–14.
15 Ibid., 15.
16 Ibid.
17 Martin Heidegger, '. . . Poetically Man Dwells . . .' in *Poetry, Language, Thought* (New York: Harper & Row, 1971), 211–29.

18 Carl Strehlow, 'The Aranda and Loritja Tribes of Central Australia', ed. M.F. von Leonhardi, trans. Hans D. Oberscheidt, 1907–1920 (unpublished), vol 1, pt 1, 1.
19 SD, 11 April 1932.
20 Strehlow to Cleland, 2 May 1932.
21 In his final three volumes, published between 1913 and 1920, Carl Strehlow described the social life and the material culture. Like the volumes on religion, these were replete with detail—descriptive, explanatory, speculative—that only an Aranda speaker could have gleaned. The passages on communal life, child rearing, hunting and gathering, on the lives of women as well as men, are vivid and *dispassionate*; he could write as an ethnologist *detached* from the missionary. His weaving of linguistic detail into the material fabric of the life composes, finally, a major work in the history of ethnography of equal worth to the achievements of Spencer and Gillen. John Morton, anthropologist for the 1997–9 Native Title Claim in Alice Springs, writes (personal communication, May 2000): 'In my opinion Carl Strehlow's work has stood the test of time every bit as much as Spencer and Gillen's. It is a highly authoritative study. The only thing that stopped it being as well known in the English-speaking world as S&G's work is that it was published in German. Although there were some key disputes between S&G and Carl Strehlow on a number of points, their respective volumes are mutually reinforcing in terms of giving us a picture of Aranda life. Those Arandic scholars who have followed them—TGHS, Roheim, me—haven't reserved higher criticism or praise for either S&G or Carl Strehlow. In the intellectual economy of mythical anthropological ancestors, both are out-and-out stars.'
22 C. Strehlow, pt II, 275.
23 Ibid., pt III, 309.
24 Ibid., 315.
25 Ibid.
26 Ibid., 295.
27 S.P. Porteus, *The Psychology of Primitive People: A Study of the Australian Aborigine* (New York: Longmans, 1931), 420.

2   Collecting

THE JOURNEYS STREHLOW made during 1932 were foundational. They set him up for his further travels in 1933–34 and then again in 1935, by which time he had covered more than 7,000 miles, over half of them by camel and often only in the company of Tom Ljonga.[1] They were gruelling, isolating journeys, demanding of body and mind, feats of tenacity, stoicism and a great deal of applied intelligence. He was justly proud of them. The upshot was that he gathered the basis of his final collection of some 300 songs, which he listed systematically, and of at least 1,200 sacred objects, which he did not.

Already by 1934 he was able to write back to Norman Tindale, his older colleague at the South Australian Museum.

Dear Tindale,

. . . During my two years stay in Central Australia I have collected an ample mass of material for the accurate delineation of the phonetic system of Aranda dialects, and also for a detailed recording of their grammatical structure. Over seventy full-length myths have been carefully noted down in phonetic script, and some 1,250 double-lined verses of native chants have been recorded with full notes concerning their tempo and their metrical structure. It is anticipated that it will take a very considerable time to work out a clear and detailed account of the

Aranda language from this supply of material probably twelve months would not be an exaggerated estimate.

The surviving groups of Aranda are scattered over an area of many thousands of square miles in extent. As a result a disproportionate amount of my time was spent travelling between haunts of these groups: in all 7,158 miles had to be travelled, 3,127 miles by train and car and 4,031 on camel back.[2]

By 1935, he calculated in another estimate, he had witnessed 166 totemic acts, which he also described as totemic ceremonies and complete totemic cycles,[3] and he was telling Tindale that he had recently gathered enough legends and chants to fill about 350 pages of *Oceania*. As early as 1933 he was writing up the material for that prestigious journal of anthropology, publishing a seminal essay on an Aranda myth. In 1934 and 1935 he delivered three brilliantly lucid talks on mythology and *tjurunga* ownership which were to become his first important book, *Aranda Traditions,* published in 1947. His travels between 1932 and 1935 were the fire and clay from which he made himself—for himself, and for the crucial eyes of others.

Over the Humps

'I think I'll soon feel quite at home on their fat humps,' Strehlow wrote optimistically, after sitting a while on his first camels.

They belonged to missionary Ernie Kramer who was employed by the Aborigines' Friends' Association in Adelaide. Kramer preached from a grass-roofed church near the railway station, basing himself in town for half the year and going bush for the rest. He travelled widely, spreading the Good Word, meeting with Aboriginal people on the distant cattle stations and beyond, trundling along with a van painted with the words 'BEHOLD I COME QUICKLY,' an announcement that amused many a stationary bushman. Behind the van tagged Faith and Charity, his two milking goats.

Kramer, a friendly man who supported Strehlow in Alice Springs for the next twenty years, pointed him in the direction of his own camel team. 'In the afternoon I saw the three camels, and I almost collapsed,' Strehlow told his diary when he had reached Bonnie Well in the company of another helpful churchman, the Methodist, Mr Lithgow. Strehlow had a bilious headache at the time, which he put down to eating too much of a fat wild turkey the day before, or perhaps the strength of the stewed tea.[4]

'I had not believed that camels could look so poor. As for humps, they seemed almost flatbacked. No saddle would fit them. One of them, in addition was blind in one eye, and had its nose peg pulled out when it was young. As a result part of its nose hung over its mouth like the wattle of a turkey: I was too shocked for words.' In due course, however, he roped them in as a team: Climax and Flossie were the ones to be ridden, Skipper would carry the boxes, Dot the blind one would be tied to Skipper, and behind Dot walked the other cow, Mulga.

It took a while to feel at home on the camels, even though Flossie was a camel in 'splendid nick.' Everything Strehlow learnt about camels came from the Aborigine who would be his solitary companion for the next two years, Tom Ljonga, Mr Kramer's 'camel boy.' Ljonga was an Aranda man who had grown up on the mission. He had worked as a 'police boy' for some years and knew a good deal of the country. He was only too pleased to come with him, Strehlow felt, and he would get 'the regulation wage—5 shillings a week, and keep, tobacco and clothing and blankets when he needed them.'[5]

That said, when they set off on 4 May 1932, the camels all packed up, Strehlow was anything but confident. He simply felt 'terrifyingly inadequate to the task' of going bush,[6] a feeling not helped by the weather that set in.

'Rain, rain rain, all day long.'

It was freezing cold on their first night, and there was little comfort to come as they moved north through 'a sea of mulga.'

'I am feeling very tired tonight,' he wrote a few days later. 'The first 181 miles are past; and I can sleep in tomorrow.' But then, the next morning:

'No good again! We had a warm night and the flies were up before sunrise . . .'

'My three new camels—well, the leader is first rate—sleek, glossy, and fat; but the other two haven't pick up a scrap yet.'[7] For they were trying to fatten the camels along the way: fattening them, as he was cutting his teeth on matters of bush craft.

He had by then learnt to make the damper for Tom: that was something.

Shocks to the System*

Strehlow's first trip in 1932 was north from Alice Springs as far as Barrow Creek, then west into the mulga scrub for some miles and home again to Alice. It was the country from which he gathered the myths and songs of the Northern Aranda, though at the time he was uncertain about his skills in any dialect but that of the Western Aranda people, whose country was around the mission. And it happened to be the area in which he had to contend with the feelings of the white settlers, which was another source of anxiety for him: he expected 'a large measure of personal ostracism' if he 'associated with the natives in the cattle station area.' And then: 'How would the natives themselves receive me?'[8]

He'd had a taste of what he was in for when he had gone north for the camel team. 'Camped overnight at Ryan's Well. Jack Kraft arrived from Barrow Creek, and Hughie Beale got drunk. Still we did manage to get some sleep finally.'[9]

Hughie Beale, who turned out to be an old boy of St Peter's school, was not too drunk to notice another city man. 'You're wearing a blazer with a magpie crest,' he said, 'an Adelaide Uni blazer. I know.' It was impossible to refuse Hughie's hospitality. Inside his hut 'a dark girl came in with some plates and cutlery, and looked around slyly.' 'My black servants' was Hughie's phrase, and he went on to talk a lot about his 'black maids.' Later he said that no one could drink out of his bottle, though no one had asked.

The next day it was warm again, and he travelled on past Tea Tree and on to Mount Peake station, owned by the Campbells. They all complained about the uncertainty created by the vicinity of the 'Myall niggers' and the wild tribes from the west. These would not work at all, though they sometimes passed through in large numbers. Only the 'gins' could sometimes be employed. The civilised natives from the telegraph line would not stay in this country out of terror. So Mr Campbell had

---

* The narrative in this chapter is constructed from Strehlow's Diaries from 1932 to 1935 (typed version) and 'Land of Altjira' (handwritten MS, 1957). In the text I usually but not always indicate whether Strehlow is speaking retrospectively or from his diary. When necessary, in other parts of this book I draw attention to discrepancies and ponder their significance. Here I am mainly interested in conveying the grain of his earliest journeys, which included: a northern trip in May–June, a trip north of the MacDonnell Ranges as far as Mount Liebig in July–August, another trip west and north of the ranges in November–December. In 1933 he went down the Finke to record Southern Aranda, and in 1935 to the east of Alice Springs to record Eastern Aranda. For a brief passage in this chapter I draw upon his camp experiences in 1935.

to do all his mustering with white labour, and do all his tracking himself. Only one old man, 'Jacky,' and his wife, with a baby boy whom she was still carrying about, was sometimes in the place. Mrs Campbell fed them well so that Jacky, who was evidently a chief of some sort, acted as a protection against the wild people from the west.[10]

Mrs Campbell moaned about the double standard. If the police could have gins any time they wanted, and they did, everyone knew that, what right did they have to interfere on the cattle stations when white men mistreated Aboriginal women? No right at all. It was because of this—the way the station fellers carried on, and the humbug of the police—that Mrs Campbell couldn't get the house girls she wanted.

Strehlow was biting his tongue. It was the first of many occasions when he would sit seething at the presumption that the natives were 'at best, cheap God-ordained servants or at worst sub-human vermin.'[11] But he was saying nothing. How could he? He was at the settlers' table enjoying their beef, produced at the cost of creating such havoc in the country. Piping up here would change nothing. It would only be taken for a mission boy's piety, or the pomposity of a university man, 'useless as an owl'; or worse, it would be seen as proof that he knew the bush no better than he knew his camels. So he held to his 'stony silence.' Later in the privacy of his swag when the others were asleep he had the muffled outlet of his diary.

The next day they were at Nugget Morton's camp. Morton, once a resident of Footscray in Melbourne, held forth from the top of an empty 44-gallon drum about having had more than his fair share of the 'dirty thieving, treacherous bastards.' He himself had been attacked in the area after the Coniston massacre in 1928, the most notorious of bloody incidents in Central Australia since the revenge killings at Barrow Creek.*

---

* Notorious because of the extent of official retaliation for the murder of 70-year-old dingo trapper Fred Brooks by Warramulla tribesmen on 7 August 1928, after which Mounted Constable W.G. Murray, formerly of the 4th Light Horse in Gallipoli and in France, rode out with a party to a native camp fourteen miles from Coniston where, according to the official inquiry that followed, seventeen natives were shot over four separate skirmishes while resisting arrest. The unofficial and subsequent estimate of dead ranges from 100 to 300 people, including women and children. At the official inquiry Murray could not say who shot 'two lubras' and the charge of 'general intent upon massacre' was dismissed by a carefully selected board that reported, in part, that the causes of the incident included white settlers 'making free with the natives and treating them as equals,' and denied 'evidence of any starvation among blacks in Central Australia.' The whitewash of Murray's revenge party resonated in the Territory for many years. See Read and Read (1991) and Kimber in *Northern Territory Dictionary of Biography* (1992:2:213–15).

Nugget had been sitting by his camp fire in the early hours when about 40 natives had approached along the creek and one had come asking for meat. When Nugget passed some over, the native had seized his hand, not the meat, and other natives had jumped on him. Someone hit him with a stick, someone else was hurling boomerangs. Nugget saw a tomahawk coming down on him, but managed to make it glance off his bare arm—there, see the scars. He knocked down the ringleader, a man he knew, and another native; he got to his gun and the rest fled. Must have been fifteen men in the attack, he had the scars to prove it. See—on both sides of his chin. A boomerang had cut him from below. The back of his head was uneven. But he had staggered to his horse and ridden back to the homestead fearing the natives would finish him off if they saw him collapse. He was groggy there for a few days on his own, and then he rode out to Harry Tilmouth, who was in a different spot with a big mob of cattle. Harry hadn't slept for days, having already shot a native.

Nugget had already squared the account with one of his attackers. He was still on the lookout for a big 'woolly-headed nigger' he knew. Strehlow wrote:

> I didn't quite know what to make of this, for Aranda and Loritja natives kill the man 'whom they want to get' in the last hours before dawn— about 3 or 4 o'clock . . . for they claim that at this time men sleep their deepest sleep. As a matter of fact, I had heard at the Campbells' that Nugget had been awakened by something that disturbed him one night; he woke up to see 6 or 7 spears above him. He felt under his blanket for his revolver only to remember he had left it somewhere else. But he leapt up, and being a strong man, managed to beat them off. Still the scars are genuine enough and date back to his early stay on the Lander. As a result he surrendered his lease, and moved back to the block next to Mt Peake Station. He had only set up a little bush wurly here last year; but he wishes to shift his camp to the Limestone Well, some 7 miles from here, where better water is to be found.[12]

Before long they reached Skull Creek, 'which had received its name from the bleaching skulls of the natives who had been shot here last century after being tracked down from Barrow Creek in revenge for the murder.' At Tea Tree Well Strehlow yarned with old Alec Ross, 'one of the oldest celebrities in the Territory,' who described the attack. Strehlow piped up, 'ventured to interpose' that a whole native camp had been wiped out at

Skull Creek, even though it was 50 miles south of where the white men Stapleton and Frank had been killed.

Old Alec looked at me with his steady, honest eyes. 'Many things have happened in this country that I have never liked, and I have kept my hand out of lots of things that others have done. I've believed in making the blacks respect me, but I have always treated them fair. I've never cheated them, nor knocked them about or stolen any lubra from her husband; and I've always got along with them splendidly myself. As for Skull Crk.,—well, of course nobody ever knew if any one who was shot there had ever had any hand in the attack on BC. They were just blacks sitting in their camp, and the party was looking around for blacks to shoot. Quite possibly some guilty ones were among them.'[13]

Strehlow nearly spoke up with old Mrs Price at Woola Downs station. The Prices had been warned by another settler not to set up there because of 'the white stones' near the soak, which the natives greatly valued. But the Prices refused to be afraid of the natives and 'tossed those white stones away.' According to Strehlow's diary, Mrs Price said, 'I think the niggers are a mean lot, don't you.'

'I hedged,' he wrote, 'and said that I thought the natives were very much like ourselves—there were mean ones amongst them as there were amongst ourselves.'

'Well, there might be a few ones down in the MacDonnells where you come from,' Mrs Price grudgingly admitted, but then went on about laziness and theft. Strehlow saw her 'motherly' face become 'set and hard.' She said: 'I met a lady in the Alice Springs once, who I asked whether she had ever seen the devil. "Yes," she said, "I see the devil every time I look a drunk in the face." "No," I told her, "you are wrong. When you see a drunk you see a poor misguided man who can't control himself. But I know when I see the devil. I see the devil every time I look in the face of a dirty, stinking nigger."'[14]

Again Strehlow fell into his 'usual, stony silence.'

From Barrow Creek he seems to have fled back to where he had come from. To their astonishment the Kramers saw him coming towards their house only two weeks after setting off. Strehlow did not confess to any quaking: the official reason was to organise more camels in order to go bush again. He had after all begun to manage the difficult beasts—the *sine qua non* of bushcraft in the Centre—so he had at least begun as a bushman. But not before a deeper disturbance.

He had gone to bed but could not sleep. He was overtired and apprehensive, 'overstirred' as he puts it:

Above all, I was feeling unutterably lonely. I longed for the city lights, for music, for halls whose floors resounded with the sound of dancing feet, for a well lit study with neat rows of books in orderly shelves. Here I was at the mercy of the bush and its inhabitants, Here a man relied on his own strength and force of character . . . In CA [Central Australia] only the man counted, not his rank or his paper authority.

Eventually I fell asleep from utter exhaustion . . . But I slept poorly, for memories of actual childhood experiences now closed in upon me and spread out their fingers to disturb my dreams.

I was a boy camped out in the open with my parents near Ljiltera Spring. The multitudinous bellowing of some six hundred cattle was resounding from the black moonlight cliffs at our back. Our swags were spread out beside the protection of the buggy, and a large fire was blazing in front of us. We could hear the feet of cattle running to the water at night. At least they ran until they came within a few feet of our camp fire—and then stopped suddenly, and in the sudden ghostly silence you seemed to feel the glare of their eyes often less than fifty feet away. For various reasons the cattle at Giltjera had been mustered so infrequently that they had almost ceased being tame; and now there were thought to be over a hundred wild bulls in that herd. Mustering had become a dangerous occupation, for the bulls would charge riders and horses if their way was blocked, and most of the Giltjera cattle had never seen the inside of a yard. We could hear the angry challenges of bulls tossing the dust high over their heads; and then would follow the sharp clash of their horns, the contact stopping only when one gored monster finally ran away, its shaggy hide flecked with blood. I was going again though all the boyhood terror of that night, for it seemed as though the hot breath of lowering cattle was hitting the camel boxes behind my head.

With an effort born of despair I sat up in my sleep. The moon was riding calmly in the sky overhead. A mopoke drowsily hooted in the midnight shadow of a silent gum. And then I heard the distant bellowing of a herd of cattle somewhere in the black ranges around me. They were probably a mile or more away. To judge from the occasional orchestral emission effect of the hundredfold high and low moaning it was a drover's herd which was camping out in the open, with stock-boys on night horses riding around the edge of the clearing . . .

How silly it had been to have a nightmare because of a common-place bellowing of a drover's herd! Once more a heavy sleep crashed down my tired eyelids.

But the same dream returned. The bulls were staring at me unflinch-ingly. Now they began to lower their heads—the greatest monster of them all, standing some nine feet away, was beginning to advance slowly. I had to move, to stir, from its fearful red-eyed stare, from the advancing avalanche of brute weight and horns. I felt as though I had become paralysed. At last with an agonised moan I wrenched myself from under the heavy weight of the camp sheet that was enveloping me tightly against the night air, which had suddenly turned very chilly. I sat up, bathed in perspiration.

The moon had begun his descent in the western sky. The multitudi-nous bellowing of the cattle even closer now. I could see Tom sitting up in his blankets, resetting his fire to prevent it going out, and I lay back once more, utterly exhausted by my dreams.[15]

He lay awake until dawn brought the fine call of the butcher bird, and the sight of Tom coming back with the camels. They had breakfast, and then there was the work of saddling and loading. Steadying work that did not call out for interpretation.*

---

* John Morton offers (personal communication, July 2001): 'Since Ted begins his account with the idea that "only the man counted, not his rank or his paper authority," I see this dream in terms of his coming face to face with his own manhood—and being rather frightened by it. The dream seems to be a classic combination of a powerful childhood memory (scary bulls and the oh-so-manly men who could deal with them—shades of the self/other dynamics of the matador?) and what Freud called the daytime residue . . .his [Ted's] encounters up north of Alice Springs which made him withdraw both mentally (into "stony silence") and geographically (to Alice Springs). Failing to "stand up" to the Prices seems to have "unmanned" him ("unmanning" was a word used by Schreber and has resonances throughout *Journey to Horseshoe Bend*). Note the reference to paralysis—the same experience he would have felt in being unable to stick up for the blacks up north. Note also the trivialisation of the dream experience—"how silly it had been to have a nightmare because of the commonplace bellowing of a drover's herd!" Well, maybe not so trivial if the bellowing is not so much that of cattle as the station owners who made him retreat and long for the orderly peace of the city, the dance hall and his study—where he could "talk up" the blacks without fear of bushy retribution. And here it seems the retribution has been symbolised by potential goring—a "shaggy hide flecked with blood."'

'Sell Their Tjurunga'

There were other nightmares and they belonged to the Aboriginal people. At every mile along the way in these early journeys Strehlow was conjuring those nightmares as he found himself collecting *tjurunga*—nightmares because, as he was to write, the *tjurunga* were the most treasured possessions. 'The ancestor regards the *tjurunga* which he owns as a portion of his own being; and he is very anxious lest strangers should come and rob him of those symbols of his very essence of life.'[16]

By virtue of his work in the language—his collection of myths and songs—Strehlow was inexorably involved with *tjurunga*. As he was to discover, the sacred chants were also referred to as *tjurunga*, as was some ceremonial headgear and ground-painting. The term covered much of what embodied the spiritual essence of Aranda being. To encounter *tjurunga* was to be face to face with the sacred. To receive, to collect, to solicit *tjurunga* was to be the recipient of gifts and trust, or, potentially, to be a sacrilegious thief, yet another white man come to plunder the culture. Everything depended, ultimately, on the moment of reception, the context of the gathering. In the metaphysical realm, *tjurunga* was the measure of relationship with the spiritual domain, just as, in earthly terms, contact with *tjurunga* was inseparable from relationship with their owners. The integrity and complexity of Strehlow's relationships with the Aranda hinge on this, on the evolving nature of his entanglement with the objects.[17]

In Tom Ljonga Strehlow had an eager scout for *tjurunga*, and they were only three days out when Strehlow made his first appreciative note. 'He [Tom] told me that *W. of Burt's Well* was a *sacred cave* guarded by "atua ntjara" [many men]; however, most men were now thinking of selling their tjurunga to the whites and giving up their old customs.'[18]

At Mrs Campbell's he made friends with a man guarding 'arknanauas'—collections of *tjurunga*—at three places. 'Somewhere near here, as I gathered,' Strehlow noted, but did not press the issue.

Tom enabled him to meet the old men who mattered, and one of them, for a stick of tobacco, told them about his wandering honey ant ancestors and the track they travelled. Pleased, Strehlow wrote it down, but later Tom expressed his disgust at that story. The old man, Tom said, had told *him* a different version. 'Many countries, many stories, many lies,' he exclaimed.

'Sell the *tjurunga*, I say, get rid of them. They won't make manna while they are lying in the caves; sell them to the whites and get some manna that way.'

> What was the use of men hanging on to the sacred objects of their forefathers? As long as the *tjurunga* rested in their caves, men felt that they had to go on yearly walkabout in order to inspect the *tjurunga*, sing the sacred chants over them and rub them with red ochre, and after that sacred ceremonies had to be performed in honour of the ancestors whose *tjurunga* were resting in the caves. Surely it was better to get rid of these objects by selling them to the whites, and thus being free from all religious restrictions as whites were. The latter had plenty of food to eat and plenty of tea and sugar to drink. They had liquor, and considered no one except themselves, they feared neither God nor the devil. Why should not dark men reach the same level of emancipation?[19]

Tom had, after all, been brought up on the mission and seemed to be mouthing a Lutheran rejection of pagan objects. His embrace of the white man's future set the terms of one aspect of Strehlow's relationship with the *tjurunga*: to a degree he was encouraged to feel, as had his father and Pastor Albrecht, that receiving them was a step towards Aranda progress.

It was one thing to listen to Tom's modern view, quite another to be face to face with the *tjurunga* when men were parting with them. Further on near Barrow Creek they camped with a couple of old men, one of whom, an Ilpara man, lay half-conscious by the fire, struggling for breath with a bad attack of the flu. 'He was a mere skeleton and I was dragged up there to have a look at him and give him some medicine etc.,' Strehlow noted:

> Then I had to boil meat and make two dampers in the evening. Then Tom came back from the camp and told me how the men everywhere wanted to *sell their tjurunga* to the whites, and to settle down like white men: the only reason for their walkabout was their duty to protect the sacred caves. Now they would sell not newly manufactured tjurunga but the really old treasures made by the erilknibata, so that they could change their old ways of living. He complained about the bad whites nowadays who lorded it over the natives, took their wives away from them, and threatened the men with their rifles; this was only bluff, of

course, but the men had no sense—'etnaka etalerinja kaputala itja'—else they would report the matter to the police and the Protectors. [20]

Men everywhere wanted to *sell their tjurunga*.[21] The emphasis is Strehlow's. It seems to register a certain satisfaction in the fact, at least in so much as they had found what they had been looking for. The other feeling in this entire process is sadness, Strehlow's as well as Tom's. It was a miserable cultural situation they were in: old men selling up their sacred inheritance, sick old men neglected by their white protectors, men making false *tjurunga*, men joining the white man's world at gunpoint, their wives stolen, and white drunks bribing natives outside the church—the scenes seem to have fed Strehlow's melancholy sense of where he was and what he was doing there.

There was some peace to be had the next night, when everything had settled down and all you could hear was 'the tinkle of camel bells, the chirping of crickets, the humming of a few beetles, and the distant croak of a mopoke . . . There is not a breath of wind stirring in the trees.'

They met another Ilpara man, Old Urartja, a wizened man who had lived through many years of drought. He was very shaken up by his camel ride when Tom brought him into the camp. He sat down with Strehlow and kept forgetting the words of his myth story. 'Tommy was annoyed that the story got all mixed up.' Strehlow had another go the next day, but when Urartja was 'trembling every limb with emotion,' the work had to stop.

It would be better, the old man said, they would be able to grasp the story more, if they could go to the place where the story belonged. They should go to the sacred cave and he would sing with the *tjurunga* which had the drawings on them:

We arrived at Urartja's cave just before sundown. It was among a pile of dark boulders which was linked by a thin line of rocks on a massive rockplate with a low complex of hills. There was a deep narrow cleft in the rockplate, and in the hollow, about seven or nine feet down, was a little black pool of water, into which a bushy dark green wild fig tree on the last side of the cliff might cast its shadow at noon. There had once sat a woman who owned a trantantja pole: this was represented by a bright stripe about an inch wide which was straight across the rock. The woman had been the sweetheart of the moon, who had here been united with her, and had then crept away to the west leaving the imprint of his fingers and his knee caps behind in the dark rockplate. She had kept the emblem of his manliness in token of their union. We gazed at the marks silently in the stillness of evening. The sun had set while Urartja was speaking; and above the deep crimson and yellow of the western sky could be seen the pale sickle of the sinking new moon. 'That was in the moon, who touched this rock,' says Urartja reverentially.

Eagerly he led the way to the cave where the tjurunga were resting. We climbed up some rocks, and then nimbly descended to another cleft. We waited expectantly . . . The old man searched and searched in the gloom of the cleft. The tjurunga had vanished. A round reddish stone as big as a pear, and an ant-eaten broken piece of wood with some drawings, were all that remained in the cave of the Moon's Sweetheart.

'Nothing, nothing,' murmured the old man. He suddenly looked old and broken. Perhaps some young native thief, or a wandering woman, or a white rogue had stolen them: Urartja had not been here since last winter.

We clambered down in silence. In the fading light we could just see the drawings on the rocks about us—drawings that were allegedly made by supernatural hands. The broken down old man whispered something about these stones being [——] apparently they have the seeds of life from which he hoped that his declining race would spring up once more. A few yards away, at the edge of the pile, was a heap of old coals: these were all that remained of the watch fires of his [——], his dead forefathers before white men arrived to rape and plunder without hindrance. Now he and his younger brother were the only two old men of any importance remaining in this part of the country.

On the way back Tom spotted tracks leading to and from the cave:

An overwhelming feeling of hatred and disgust swept over me when I thought of the white man who had stolen from an old native even the last and most precious things that still remained to him. I could of course say nothing to either Tom or Urartja about my informants. It could do no good. There was no law in the country to protect these sacred caves; it was not the first plundered storehouse. The Horn Expedition which contained . . . Sir Baldwin Spencer has similarly stolen from a cave in the far western Macdonnells and the young guide who had shown them these treasures was later on speared by his own relatives to atone for his crime. But it seemed incredible that on my first visit to a sacred cave I should be confronted with the inhumanity of men of my own race.[22]

This account in 'Land of Altjira,' written and coloured in 25 years after the event, is powerful enough, and in keeping with the diary. But in the diary, in its spareness, it is even more poignant.

'We ate tea in silence; and the old man wept quietly afterwards . . .

'He was planning and planning, but knew his helplessness . . .

'I made some damper and Tom cooked two wallabies.'[23]

That was the meal for 6 June 1932. Strehlow was getting better at damper. It was his birthday as well: he had turned 24.

Plunder

The plunder went a long way back, and Strehlow was right to name Baldwin Spencer as an early culprit. The Horn Scientific Expedition arrived in 1894 with the principal purpose of assembling all there was to know about the flora, fauna, and geography of the Centre. Their collecting came to include, under the lap of anthropological studies, the artefacts of the culture, the sacred objects becoming valuable on the white man's market.

Two members of the party, Charles Winnecke, explorer-surveyor, and Professor (Sir) Edward Stirling, anatomist, anthropologist and director of the South Australian Museum with a keen interest in Aboriginal 'artefacts,' heard about a major storehouse in a small cave east of Haasts Bluff. Before they could reach the place their guide took flight, but they pressed on to find 60 carved wooded boards and fifteen incised stones. They took all the sacred stones, and half the *tjurunga*, leaving in their place some steel axes and knives.

Baldwin Spencer was uneasy about such plunder. But Frank Gillen had already amassed over 100 *tjurunga*. Gillen was a friend of the Aborigines, but that did not prevent him recovering *tjurunga* buried with a dead man, or selling them to pay gambling debts. For several years after the expedition had returned south, Gillen, along with Mounted Constable Charles Cowle, who patrolled the area after the arrest of Willshire, shipped objects to the museum by the crate. In this 'museological era' all had struck it lucky in objects; there was a bonanza for merchants of the sacred, and a golden age for scientists to mount desacralised things in glass cases for collectors.[24]

Then, to their credit, they almost learnt a lesson. In 1897, Cowle wrote to Spencer that an old blackfellow had been killed for leading him to *tjurunga*. When Gillen heard this he wrote to Spencer: 'This upset me terribly. I would not have had it happen for £100 and I am going to write to Cowle about the Churinga business, there must be no more ertatulnga robberies. I bitterly regret ever having countenanced such a thing and can only say that I did so when in ignorance of what they meant to the natives—to fully realise this one requires to go as I did a few weeks ago . . . and watch them reverently handling their treasures.'[25]

By this time, Gillen was beginning to understand the place of the *tjurunga* in the culture. 'Yes,' he wrote to Spencer, 'the wandering of the totems is startlingly like the Children of Israel,' a remark that sported with the common analogy between ancient tribes. 'In the end we are not looking for "mathematical exactitude,"' Gillen went on, as if intuiting another modality of understanding. The *tjurunga* came in, he thought, 'to express the spiritual part of the *alcheringa* animal or man, the meaning of the term I take to be sacred—in the sense that the sacramental wafer is sacred to the Roman Catholic.'[26] And later: 'Sacred Churinga does not please me but I can offer no substitute for the word sacred.'[27]

Gillen sought to constrain Cowle. The constable did not warm to the suggestion and sent another hundred objects to Spencer in 1900. Spencer chose to accept Cowle's reassurance that they were not stolen but bartered in some way for tobacco, flour or tea on the open market. Cowle told Spencer about his strategy: 'I am standing off a while . . . by showing them I am not keen I will get the articles easier directly if they are worth securing.'[28]

There were others with even fewer scruples feverishly trading in objects. From the beginning, of course, settlers and prospectors and the men who worked on the Overland Telegraph line sold what they could get by way of *tjurunga*. One collector, the explorer and prospector R.T. Maurice, was a gleeful *tjurunga* hunter. Although he was 'bound to secrecy not to tell Gillen,' he wrote to Winnecke of his hopes of great success at Horseshoe Bend. For there was a big stone that 'Mr Gillen' had not yet heard of, 'the dream stone of all dream stones' said the hunter, who had become a romancer of stones. The trouble was: 'it's such a weight & kept so carefully guarded—a bag of flour won't buy it.'[29]

The mission had been dealing in *tjurunga* from the beginning. Pastor Schulze had declared that 'there was not a shred of evidence of a religious life among the people' but he went on to make vague references to 'the festival plates of slate or wood secreted in caves, unseen by women and children.' The term *secreted* is expressive, and it was perfectly in accord with the registration of the Horn Expedition which reported the *tjurunga* as 'objects of mystery and concealment.'[30] What the natives secreted, with their pagan ways in their dark places, had to be cleared by the light and Pastor Strehlow was one of the most energetic at doing it. Since *tjurunga* were the touchstones of the *Alcheringa* over which the Good Word had to triumph, he was keen to obtain them, gathering them from converts, trading them from others, then selling them to the Frankfurt museum, and putting the proceeds to better use for altar cloths and vestments for the chapel. Those not shipped to Germany went south to the museum in Adelaide (more than 90 by 1922). While Pastor Strehlow was on leave in Germany between 1910 and 1913, his stand-in Oscar Liebler gathered more than 2,000 artefacts and sold them to British and German museums as well as to Adelaide. Liebler's awkward English account is also redolent with a sense of things 'secreted': 'As never the blacks show ceremonial tjurunga marks,' he once observed, 'to white strangers nor their wives, they only in dark nights secretly bring those specimen articles to us to sell it for money or large amounts of rations.'[31] Liebler managed to observe, however, something that others had not: that the *tjurunga* did not so much belong to the Aranda men as the men belonged to the *tjurunga*.

The dark nights, the secret trade, the 'secreting' that men did, whites around the backs of blacks, and blacks and whites together: these transactions had a long history before T.G.H. Strehlow came on the scene. Throughout this period of crude colonial impositions the atmosphere around them was Faustian, in that it dawned, one way or the other on all parties, that they were dealing in powerful significations of foreign knowledge, for good and bad. The earliest mission dealers with them indicated as much when he called them 'wooden charms' and 'festival plates.' Throughout the period they were variously called 'sacred woods,' 'stone charm,' 'birth stones,' 'dream stones,' 'sacred emblems,' and 'soul stones.' The more scientific term, 'native religious specimens,' gave the clue to understandings that were most advanced by Gillen and Spencer, so that by 1927, all the insights developed in their letters could be expressed in the light of day in their two-volume *The Arunta*: 'The loss of the Charunga is the most significant evil that could befall any local group.'[32]

Strehlow, who arrived only five years after this history of colonial entanglements, was unavoidably in the path of the objects. He could not get out of their way, so to speak. Clearly, he was no plunderer. He was full of the solicitude that came from already knowing, in his bones, many of the secrets. We might ask, not, 'how he became such an avid collector?' but 'how could he not have been?' And since he was necessarily a collector, what 'permutations of debt' belonged to the situations he solicited and found himself in?

Songs out of Things

'After writing down the songs they asked me for—,' and he named the sacred Aboriginal word for the grease to oil the objects.

> They then took the tjurunga and rubbed them . . . for the last time, chanting in a wailing tone that went right through me, some of the verses I had noted down, one verse for each tjurunga . . . They started off from high pitched notes and dropped down to a solemn chant in the middle of each verse. Then as the stone glistened in the blazing shine of the noonday sun, they dropped into the lowest note of the base register, where the voice ceases to vibrate, and only a few poor broken accents then melted away into the silence.[33]

It was the silence—with its fullness of feeling—that moved Strehlow on another occasion the next year, when the men who had assembled to dance for him and to tell him their stories and songs, brought a load of *tjurunga* into the camp. Sign language fed the silence as a camp sheet was laid out. The men formed a half circle, moving their hands up and down—'palms up—in a pleading attitude, expressing longing for the tjurunga.'

The owners of *tjurunga* came up by name, and still not a word was said. Two of the men 'crouched together, walked fearfully and hurriedly, like guilty criminals, and sank on their knees on the camp sheet, breathing heavily. They put their bundles down before them. Still silence.' Then one of them said in a low voice, 'we have come without . . . For we are old men who cannot sight game properly.' In turn the men touched their bundles, the old men before the young men. 'Then all hugged it against their stomachs. Still tense silence.'

And then with some wailing the unwrapping began, the unwinding of the long string into a ball, and the bundles finding their owners again. 'Thereupon the . . . men broke out in . . . song and the others into the song, singing in competition as the long strings were unravelled.'

Four lines of verse Strehlow wrote down on that occasion. The men translated the lines. The *tjurunga* had been laid out on the sheet, and the song was sung again.

This time he had 54 lines.

And the song went on as, one *tjurunga* at a time, the men passed them to each other. 'All these hugged them tightly against their stomachs without saying a word.'[34]

The holding tight, the singing, the reverence and anxiety and mourning—how could these not penetrate the collector of the songs, who was receiving the words as a trustee, putting them down in his notebook as one would holy writ. Every one of Strehlow's sacred songs might be seen as such an acquisition: the result of deeply felt inscription at the font of Aboriginal belief—taken down on the ground, in the clearing, often near the sacred sites, words often given to him as the ancestor spirits themselves, embodied in their *tjurunga*, were handed over.

In his collecting of *tjurunga*, Strehlow was acting as a kind of under-taker, an embalmer of *tjurunga*. He was laying them to rest, as the men wanted him to do.

And yet if, on the one hand he was helping put things to sleep, on the other he was bringing them to life, or at least handling life in death. For as he stowed the *tjurunga* away, he kept the notebook out.

Onto his dusty pages went a line of verse. Then another, making the couplet. Then, if the men were helping him the way he wanted, another couplet after that, and so on until he had the song—not all of it in one sitting, since some song cycles might take days to sing, and they would only be sung at that length in ceremony, but a good run of it, enough to interrogate his informant about its meaning, about the events of which he sang. Those events became in due course the myth that belonged to the song, and this would be set down in a fairly straight-forward narrative prose, in Aranda, usually, a run of words on a foolscap page of the field diary that was to become, once he had filed it away, invaluable itself, also a sacred object of a kind.

The old men watched him do it. There is no record of what he told them at the time, as he transcribed for the page what had hitherto only ever been sung. They must have known that the young man sitting with them with his writing tools was engaged in a respectful activity; and they would have seen that the value he put on their words, his struggle to get their exact meaning in order to write the sounds down, had for him some kind of cultural significance, even if it was not spelt out by the custodian of the literate culture. As he took things in Strehlow may have been seen as an initiate, but it is hard to imagine his informants being able to imagine their songs in print many years after their deaths.

What was happening was momentous to anyone with a mind to the differences between cultures. An oral culture was being converted to a written one. After centuries of songs that had hitherto only travelled via the communal business of making music, mnemonic feats of great achievement, they were now being set down in words for private, solitary and relatively abstract contemplation. Once Homer was entirely in the lap of the bards. Before writing, villagers sang songs that were different strands before they came together in Homer. At a certain point in ancient history, Homer was written down. The full significance of that point is still a source of philosophic and poetic speculation.[35] Strehlow, like the first Greek scribes, was recording the components of native songs, not in order to create one song, as in Homer, but to set the record straight, with regard to all the sacred songs of a territory. If ever a Homer was going to come out of the oral tradition of the Aranda, then Strehlow was his herald.

Yet the verses he had written as Tom sang them were only snatches of song. Not only that: they belonged to many different *tjurunga*, and therefore many different men scattered far and wide, men who might or might not be able or willing to sit down with him and deliver more of their sacred songs. How could he get to them all? How to get around the station owners who banned the old ceremonies? How to negotiate the crown land? The task ahead could seem insoluble.

My nerves are not up to lasting this continual lonely travelling without companions, and with insufficient sleep and bad food . . . Last night for e.g., I went to bed about 8.30 dead tired. Cattle came in on all sides to water at the soak near by. About 11.30 I wake up, when one of the bulls comes in with a loud voice. I think he is right at the back of me as I lie between the boxes; but I rise and see he is well in front and walking along to the soak steadily. I tell myself that I am as safe here as in my Adelaide bedroom, but I only go to sleep again with difficulty. Hardly had I done so, when it seems to me that I hear the voice of the bull coming steadily towards me, and only a few feet away. I try to get awake quickly—every limb seems tied up in a fatal torpor—I moan loudly in order to keep the beast away—I hear my own last half-dream moans.[36]

Basic Exchanges

In that first year he tended to meet the knowledgeable men in ones and two, thanks mainly to Tom. Eventually he would be making camp with several, and sometimes many at a time. The deal would be simple: he would provide the damper and the tea, sugar and meat for the camp, and the knowledgeable men would sing and dance—literally, sing for their supper. That was the exchange at the crudest level. It went well when it went well. When it did not it is clear that in the exchange men had to put up with each other at many different levels.

'Gave neither tea, sugar nor tobacco to those men who had not chanted last night, or stolen away to the camp without singing. Dinner came and no speech stew was served out to them'—this when he was most peeved, when the camp was not working as he liked. In the first few years of collecting he developed the authority to do this, even when, as a result, one of the men 'broke down.'

The man who broke down was called Jim. He 'pleaded even more intently' for the men who were hungry:

> I said that I would speak to them in the evening, meanwhile only the rest could get served: the other half of the stew could remain till evening.
>
> Had a bath, but could not sleep in the afternoon; was too stirred up. I felt that I had to be firm with these men, but it hurt me terribly to be hard on such fine old men . . . yet I could not allow myself to make an exception of these merely because they were my own secret favourites.

He spoke to them later in the afternoon 'and they anticipated me in acknowledging their faults': 'I asked whether they were too tired of the whole business, in that case I could leave tomorrow. No, they were not, they said, and then eagerly added they would not let me go.' One of the men pressed his boot as they said that: it was to assure Strehlow that they still had many things to show him:

> So we had our little evening's reading as usual and then I gave them that withheld tobacco, and the flour, and the peach stew, and there was running about for Billy cans, and the silence of the day was broken by speech, and Jim who has just returned after tying up the camels broke into hysterical laughter in his joy and remarked—'Now they are all glad and will be able to talk again; that will teach them not to steal way again without telling you.'

'My own heart felt free again,' Strehlow added, 'and I was happy with my great old men.'[37]

For a few days things went well. The men were 'assiduous.' There was a particularly disruptive moment when a prospector came past their camp and saw Strehlow taking a photograph of the men in ceremonial mode. 'This upset everyone, including myself.' They waited until the man left, but still, 'I was so upset that I felt weak enough to collapse when reaching my tent: my nerves are in a fearful state.'

This condition, clearly, was due to the hard work, its relentlessness, and the emotional intensity of his dealings with the men. He had felt for his great old men when they felt their business had been exposed to the outsider.

The job was soon finished though, and he was happy and satisfied, only to find that he had to pull Jim back into line. Jim, who was there to help Tom Ljonga, had been getting slack about getting food and water for the old men; he had to be told to cut wood and then did not cut enough, and that morning he left the camp without permission. To punish him Strehlow packed him off.

When Jim showed up again, Strehlow gave him the cold shoulder.

'Good morning Ingkata,' Jim said.

'What do you want, Jim?'

'I am going away to work along gold—give us a hand shake before I go.'

It was said in a pleading tone of voice: and I did not know what to say; and as I am writing this tonight, something hurts within me, and my eyes are dim: that was what he had come for, after I had sent him away for punishment, without food yesterday and spoken to him in an unkind voice just now. We shook hands and his old wrinkled face lit up. Then he said, that he would go to work for gold for a few days, since I had told him to go; but he would then come back to me; would that please me? Of course it would—so he left, and I returned into my tent, with my knowledge of the human heart enriched beyond measure. For this is Jim, who has no illusions about white men; Jim who has talked back to others when spoken to . . . Human heart, human soul,—there is no man living who can fathom its innermost depths, neither in his fellow beings nor in his own self.[38]

Strehlow is, at one level, in the wilderness with these men. The Jims of the camp might want to go off mining. Some of the other men, especially the older ones, might be seen to belong to the neighbouring cattle stations, which meant that pressure on Strehlow came from that direction.

In one camp, a pastoralist rode down and told him he had 'all the niggers in the country at his camp, that some of those here had left their jobs; that people were beginning to get annoyed.' Another once wrote to Strehlow, paying 'all due respects to his work,' but said that his camp was 'making our working boys very discontented.' Strehlow was 'hurt' by the letter, and protested: he had never enticed any working boys away, and he had always sent men away from his camp when he heard that their employers wanted them. That was probably true, but it was also the case that once such exchanges between himself and a pastoralist took place, his days in an area were numbered.[39]

Apart from that, he felt that his camp was a place to which the men should be free to chose to come. He was offering the men a balance. 'Is it quite playing the game,' he wrote, with a touch of the English gentleman abroad in the colonies, 'to refuse working men from coming here sometimes? It's one of the few chances—if not the only one—that these men have of seeing the ceremonies of their forefathers about which they have heard so much. What would white men do, if they were barred from ever attending national festivals and great meetings of people, Centenary celebrations, the recitals of foreign artists etc.; and for these natives their age-old ceremonies have quite as deep a significance or an even deeper one.'[40]

That was their reward, just as it was his, when a camp was going well. 'The old men started chanting tonight . . . they sang lustily. It was wonderful to hear the chanting again . . . their heads and bodies shaking rhythmically, chanting with the enthusiasm that made then forget age and weakness and become young again . . . a break wind of boughs, a moon dipping through white fleecy clouds, a rising and falling of the chant melody like the breathing that gives us life.'[41]

And that was the paradox right through: the old men were certainly giving to Strehlow, and he had the upper hand in pleasant and unpleasant ways, and yet he was giving back to them, facilitating the songs that created their life, even if the time was coming when their breath might stop. Meanwhile, he would keep at it: for himself, for them, for both parties.

The physical task day by day of the writing—the verses, the myths, the diary—was gruelling. That he could so deny what he called 'the weariness of the flesh' was a mark of his most Protestant virtue: his capacity for work. He would not be overcome in his physical task or defeated in his mental one.

> I hardly had any appetite tonight, I only wanted to sleep and forget—and yet there are diaries to be kept, and there is meat to be laid out etc. I ought to cook a damper, but there is no wood, and anyhow the soil is too hard; I ought to boil meat—but we haven't got sufficient water for that, unless we strike water tomorrow. This is wonderful moonlight tonight, and the crickets are chirping about me; but I am in no mood for romance.[42]

But in a way he was. In that first year the lusty and active young man might well lie in his swag dreaming of dance halls and wondering if anyone in Adelaide was missing him—as he did in September, thinking particularly that it was a year since the Women's Union Dance—but there was also romance where he was. It was in the stories he was writing down, in their power and antiquity. 'Their myths are altogether rooted in the past . . . [with] many elements that are *relics* of an earlier and more primitive order than that which is found in the Aranda tribe of today' (emphasis added).[43] He was setting himself up as an archaeologist of song, an excavator of myth.

Most myths and verses were hard won. In one day he might not be able to get anything down because he could not get a man to 'talk slowly and coherently . . . They all break down under the mental effort involved.'[44] On another day an old man who was also reluctant to speak slowly said his ears were no good, and that his head was 'cranky' because the wind was blowing too much in his ears.

Some myths and many verses would not emerge in their entirety for years. Strehlow had to keep coming back to the place, where the same man might be there to pick it up where they left off, or another man might take over the telling. The wind blew in the ears of the teller and around the pages of Strehlow's notebooks. 'If only my work would progress more rapidly and successfully; but work among the Aranda at present seems like love's labour lost—the old vein is exhausted, and what remains is so broken and shattered that it is almost too expensive and unprofitable and unsatisfying to recover the broken remnants of it.'[45] Writing this in 1932 he felt that the shards might never be reassembled, the relics never be recovered, that the whole Homeric project might vanish under the wind-blown sand.

His own notes, too, were something to contend with. Strehlow called them his 'foul papers' and sat down with them night after night when he was out bush, cleaning them up for his diary.

Living Recitals

Writing to his teacher Fitzherbert back in Adelaide Strehlow noted how even a 'specimen of dialect'—the language alone—shows 'exceptionally well how a few broken words make into a real living recital a tale conveyed mainly by gestures and by drawing in the sand.'

Broken words, gestures, drawing—*a living recital*. All of these signs that did not pertain to written language, all of them embodying, in different ways, what was meant. Strehlow's method, his kind of interest, did not accommodate the full implications of this variation that was being performed by his informants. He was aware of the sacred nature of the content transmitted to him, and to that extent he knew its connection with being. But his literary agenda, to get the song or the myth onto the page, gave him little pause to try and convey what was actually happening in the process of his transcribing the language. That would have involved the use of an awareness that only recent writers have wanted to articulate.*

---

* The best account of this kind is James Bardon's protagonist in *Revolution by Night* (1991: 23), a novel that gets to grip with the Aborigines' fullness of gesture and their embodiment of signs. 'I transcribe and I itemise,' the fictional Professor Jack Terrence Dutruck says, 'the signs upon my notebook and ask how the relationship between signs made the story talk. Billy Titus-Mindah is sort of growling and wheezing at once about how each sign can mean this, then mean that, it can have two or three meanings depending on where everything else speaks. When it speaks here, he whispers, when it speaks there, when I come and add this place to that. No time in the story, I try to say, yet he won't talk about time, he doesn't want to know where it's at, spreading out more spaces before me so as to say what the story said. I am trying again, marking in my note book the story-lines which he is singing, uiri, the names of, because it means name "Same work," he trickles his fingers about in the shape of the cave he has told me of and seems to waste his thumb upon the incising now. The water-man emerges out of his song, he says, like this, "You see," this, and he dabs his thumb into the direction he is singing, where the track went in the story he has brought to me this afternoon, and I understand there is no time in the story, only space, time can only be known by the names of the places over which the song goes, talking so softly you can only gradually catch their words, they are sliding their fingers upon the paper, closing their eyes as they do, and suddenly I am thinking of how I, of all the people, have brought myself here to watch them put the lie to what McDouall Stuart and Sturt thought.'

James Bardon, brother of Geoffrey, created a protagonist who shadowed the situation out of which the painting at Papunya arose in 1972, an illustration par excellence of multiple transcriptions (G. Bardon 1991: 23).

Strehlow often used a word that disguised the context from which he derived his versions of a myth: 'condensed.' Writing to Fitzherbert in October 1932, he described how his extremely condensed piece was partly due to the story not having been related to himself in the first place, but rather to 'my camel boy who knew the *omitted* portion of the tale well enough because the scene there had been placed in his own former part of the tribal territory' (emphasis added). Even so, he went on to say:

> the extreme condensation tends to obscure the meaning of the story. As a result a drawing (included above) was started in the sand and completed gradually as the story advanced. I have added the points of the compass to the drawing, but these were never ever mentioned in the original tale: the speaker sat facing south, and the listeners all knew, from the drawing, in what direction the snake men wandered . . .
>
> The *proper names* of the ancestors are never mentioned. These stories are usually told to the very young men when the tjurunga representing the transformed bodies of these 'heroes' are shown to them. These tjurunga are then pointed at when there is doubt about the identity of any personage in a tale in which a multitude of characters figure. In addition, the totem, to which these personages had belonged, is usually only expressed in sign language . . . The listeners sit around in a circle in tense silence . . . only broken by certain *clicks*—to be described at a latter date—denoting assent or admiration: actions of totemic ancestors cannot call for censure.

There is rich material here. Strehlow has tabled matters of symbols and a range of considerations about their uses in different contexts, and most of what he has to say implies that his own translations of meaning may have been complicated by them all. But he is not writing to Fitzherbert to account for his difficulties, least of all to imply that the results of his research may be open to sceptical inquiry. Rather he is trying to show how language, narrowly defined, fits into the larger scheme. Having mentioned all the above complexities he adds: 'Most interesting to me was the fact that this piece is composed partly in a kind of sustained direct speech: "kamerila," "albila" and the rest of the verbs ending in —la, are not finite verbs but participles.' The focus of the linguist takes precedence over the anthropologist.

But he had two very important things to say on the language front, which he was keen to point out to his teacher. The first was the strange thing that happened when words were sung, as distinct from spoken. There was what he called the 'sound-law.' This was the changing of the quality of vowels—the adding or dropping of letters before vowels. 'A further feature of those *tjurunga* songs is the remarkable fact that they invariably falsify the natural accent of the words they contain. This falsification is quite deliberate . . . It was a practice that made the 'incredible rapidity' with which the lines were chanted—phrases that became 'sentence-words'—even more difficult to apprehend and write down. Strehlow told Fitzherbert that the men up at Napperby, where he was intensifying his study of Northern Aranda for the purposes of his report, were 'rapturously delighted' when he could chant their words accurately.

All of this was in Strehlow's preliminary report on Aranda phonetics which he sent down in October 1932. Fitzherbert was pleased with it, and encouraged Strehlow not to forget the 'linguistic side' by getting sidetracked with the 'literature, history and antiquities, religion and philosophy.' Though they were 'more important: but we want both sides: and we do want the foundation.'

The other linguistic matter was the meaning of *Altjira*. 'A native's powers of explaining new words to a white man are very poor,' Strehlow informed Fitzherbert, 'he has never seen a dictionary or learnt a new language from a teacher or a printed course.' As a result, it was only usage in different contexts that helped the native make meanings clear: a case in point was *Altjira*,

> which I have met invariably in the form of 'altjerira' or 'altjirana' (both of these forms are dialectical variants of the 'ablative case'), and very frequently the word nambakala (= always, ever) is added to it. Often it is used in a parallel phrase for 'kutanga kutata' (= 'always from always,' 'ever of old'). I have found that in most examples that I have ever collected 'altjirana nambakala' means 'ever since eternity,' 'always from the very beginnings' (= semper ex aete aeternitate); it is often applied to customs which the forefathers have been practicing up to the present day 'ever for eternity'; or a tjurunga is shown representing the body of some man in the form of which it has reposed in the sacred cave 'ever from the beginning.' Perhaps this subject has not been exhausted as yet: it is possible that the native may attach other meanings to the word. But so far I have found no instances where it has meant either 'God' or 'dream' or 'dream-time.' If the common meaning of 'altjira' then is 'eternity' (i.e. something that is

always existent, is uncreated), the *derived* meanings of the words in com-
pounds may be explained with a certain measure of ease.[46]

To this, which shows him more provisional than usual in his thinking, he
added: 'The *original* meaning of "altjira" is linked up with the *original*
meaning of "nambakala": I am not quite satisfied with the usual rendering "eternal."' He was satisfied enough, however. His posture was that he
had set Spencer and Gillen right and gone beyond his father.

But he had done neither. Apart from the possible roots of the term
Altjira. Strehlow was ignoring the serious depths to which Spencer and
Gillen had gone only five years earlier in *The Arunta*. Sorting out the
history of the term, they noted what Strehlow had not, that the first to
use *Altjira* was Pastor Schulze in 1891, defining it as 'past times' and
(with regard to *tjurunga*) 'not made.' They noted that Krichauf in 1890
has used *altgiva* to mean 'everlasting existence.' As for Pastor Carl, he had
referred to 'the good God of the *Altjira*,' a meaning reinforced by
mission work that had grasped onto the native word for eternity, a fact
they confirmed in their own communications with Pastor Kempe.

With regard to their own meanings for *Alchera* and *Alcheringa*,
Spencer and Gillen took it as referring to 'the far past ancestors and the
mythic times in which they lived.' They brought in the concept of
dream meaning *Alchera* from 'ordinary language,' since 'to dream' is
alcherama. They explained: 'As indicating a past period of a very vague
and, it seemed to us, "dreamy" nature we adopted, to express as nearly
as possible the meaning of the word *alcheringa* (*alchera*, a dream, and
ringa, a suffix meaning "of" or "belonging to") the term "dream times."'
In other words they were transparent about their extended usage. Their
case comes home to rest when they cite a letter by Pastor Strehlow in
1901, conceding that : 'It is remarkable the way this word *Altjira* greatly
resembles to dream (*altjirerama*).'[47] Strehlow never seems to have been
able to acknowledge this utterance by his father, and later, when he
started his Aranda dictionary, he avoided any comment on even the
similarity between the terms.

There was another insight sent down to Fitzherbert and it is an
astonishing one. It is a revelation that suggests that despite all the
sophistication of the above, a basic understanding was still only taking
shape in Strehlow. Only in this period would he come 'to see how the
old legends fit in with the general geography of the tribal territory. It
is only after a trip such as this that the old legends—which are usually

told in an extremely terse style, an intimate knowledge of the locality described on the part of the listeners being presupposed by the story teller—really begins to live in one's mind.'

The remark suggests that Strehlow did not know this as a boy, any more than he gained the truth from his father's ethnographic understanding. There are resonant ramifications here. We have to say that so successful was the mission work during his boyhood that he grew up in a Lutheran landscape rather than a totemic one. There was the Manangananga cave, he knew that, as his father did when he protected it from plunder, but that was a long way from first-hand experience with the resonance of country pulsating with sacred sites. Despite Strehlow's intimacy with the Aranda language, and his occasional journeys out from the mission, neither he nor his father had experienced the topography in the Aboriginal way. Nor had such understanding been gained from their reading of Spencer and Gillen, even though the British work had important things to say about how ceremonies belonged to special places. To really get this knowledge, Strehlow was slowly gleaning in 1932, does not come from reading at all, but only from travelling and from ground-level listening. He was for the first time intuiting the experiential power of being there.*

In general, what Strehlow was contending with—all along—was not the death of things, the *tjurunga*, so much as cryptic and various forms of living knowledge. Gesture, song, whispers, drawing, silence, shifts of sound and sense, the named and the unnameable, tacit presuppositions, signs that only sang in the right place, signs that lived in music not in nests of other words alone—all this not to mention dance and elaborate ritual. What he was writing down was one thing, the thing that he would put out wonderfully in his fullness of time. But what he was also conscious of as he started out was the embodied nature of Aboriginal signs, and how close he needed to be to their lived and felt context before they could 'really begin to live in one's mind.'[48]

'My First Corroboree'[49]

In August 1932 Strehlow saw—confronted—his first sacred ceremony. 'Today I saw my first corroboree.' It was a Pintubi kangaroo ceremony

---

* Dick Kimber, who knew every word of Spencer and Gillen before he came to the Centre and travelled with knowledgeable Walpiri and Pintubi men, writes: 'In essence, to make an analogy, I have had Christmas cards every year of my life depicting snow, and I have seen films with snow, but I do not believe I knew what snow was like' (personal communication, March 2002).

near Mount Liebig. He had trekked out there to meet a team of scientists from the University of Adelaide, among them his patron Professor John Cleland, who was the leader of the party.

Strehlow's job was to round up natives for the university men to study—'mustering' them, as he said at one point. He had been honoured to be asked, to be part of the team at a distance, as it were. But gathering in the family groups was easier said than done. The Aboriginal groups were few and far between, and he had some trouble getting the message through that it would be good for them to meet the 'doctor mob.' There was an important, and immensely frustrating, incident when one Aboriginal man they met near Mount Liebig, who spoke English 'rather fluently' would not help them at all. Strehlow wanted to find Titus' camp, but the English-speaking man just eyed him suspiciously and gave noncommittal answers, as a result of which Strehlow had to wander around for a day in the heat, quite off the track. 'Here I was doing the dirty work, without knowing the country or the natives,' Strehlow muttered into his diary. 'I felt like hitting him over the head with my rifle.'[50] It was a communication that left a lasting impression on Strehlow and of which he would make much later.

It was his most arduous journey. He had Mr Kramer with him, but in the dry, bony country he felt that he was walking in the 'Valley of Death,' that it was a country of 'Death and Horror,' and had to round up people against the clock. Often he found little groups in a miserable condition. His heart only lifted when he met a group of 50 people who were 'all bright, light hearted, homely confiding children of Nature: no rags amongst them. Only a string around the waist, and sometimes an ornament fastened on front. Even the women did not wear the usual covering. I gave them wheat and lexia, and the old chief touched my back, requesting me to stop in my munificence.'[51]

Finally, when he did meet up with the university men, he was delighted and had 'most interesting and stimulating talks with many members of the party.'

It was one of numerous excursions organised by the Board for Anthropological Research which had since the mid-twenties been coming inland to inspect the dying race: the feeling among the scientists was one of urgency, that they record the splendid 'human material' before it was too late. Numerous tests of native body and mind were done, all of it with the cooperation of natives who were being well fed, and much amused by the white men's caravan of technology. Their cooperation on touchy matters—the taking of a blood sample, for instance—required some tact, or special skills in communication. Cleland had a trick of explaining to the natives in pidgin that they wanted to see if 'the blackfellow's blood was more like the white man's than that of a Chinaman or an Afghan.'[52] Trust was established.

This university party filmed the natives walking, running, spear-throwing and hunting, and, though this film was rather filed away, copulating. Happy native subjects were thoroughly assessed as objects, and where possible, medical attention was given. Such visits tied in with Albrecht's rescue efforts with remote Christian ration stations. It was important, unifying work for Strehlow.

But then, after only three days, rather than the three weeks he was expecting, they all went on their way leaving him 'most disappointed, inexpressibly so': 'I have been hurrying, hurrying, hurrying, ever since the middle of June in order to be able to get things ready for their arrival, and when I look back I can only say that I have accomplished almost nothing despite all my efforts . . . Tonight I feel as though there is little left worth living for—why all this vain effort!'[53]

What is striking about this separation, perhaps, is that it underlined the way in which Strehlow would continue to be in the field: alone apart from his native companions, not one of a team, his own man making his own way in the language. But there were consolations about the rendezvous: he had met up with Tindale and climbed Mount Liebig to look at the sunrise lighting a magnificent view over the country (Tindale alone got to the peak). And he had been able to see his first sacred ceremony.

In his diary Strehlow wrote graphically of what followed, and the description he included in the draft of his 'Land of Altjira.' He wrote out the details of the blood-letting, as would an anthropologist, but also because it was an object of horror to him. He had to sit down. He found a spot where he could still see, away from 'the reek of hot human blood.' When it was over he told his diary he was 'not keen on the sight of blood at the best of times.'

Yet he'd sat it out, and then slowly walked back to his camp, relieved that he had managed to watch 'without disgracing my rising reputation as *inkata* by fainting at my first ceremony.' He hastened to add, for the reader who might be as aghast as he was at the blood: 'Gods everywhere at all times have been honoured and appeased by gifts of blood.'

There was even a Christian hymn that began with an image he found 'nauseating': 'There Is a Fountain Filled With Blood.' In Scandinavia in 1067 a 'doom-ring' existed where men had been held for sacrifice and had their heads smashed in on the stone of Thor. 'And the English word "blessing," which dates back to pagan times, is thought by many to refer to an original sprinkling of the worshippers with blood at the end of their heathen worship. In Central Australia the totemites at least offered their own blood, their own life, in these sacred ceremonies.'[54]

Last Cave

The collecting of the songs, the searching for the *tjurunga* (by the end of the year he could call it *hunting*[55]) went on.* Collecting the songs was frequently entangled with receiving the *tjurunga*, and when it was not, the *tjurunga* could be sought in any case.

I decided to look for the cave myself. At last I lit upon a large rock, cleft in two, whose cracks had been stopped up with little stones. I took these

---

*   At the usage of the term hunting in this sentence Brett Galt-Smith, research director of the Strehlow Research Centre in Alice Springs, took pains to write to me that Strehlow only uses the words 'hunt' or 'hunting' three times over the three days when looking for the *tjurunga* of the Ulamba cave. The Strehlow Research Centre was most concerned that the word not be taken in a 'pejorative sense' because 'it is a loaded word in relation to cultural material given that its common European usage implies chasing and killing in a hostile and forceful manner.' Galt-Smith suggests that Strehlow might have been shadowing Ljonga's language for what they were doing together and that, in any case, 'hunt' was also used when they were looking for a cave and for 'big-water.'
    The possibility that Strehlow's language usage echoes his dialogue with Ljonga is an attractive one in terms of relationship, and is an illustration of what Elkin was to call Strehlow's benefit of 'linguistic liaisons' with the Aranda men (see below for Elkin's 1947 review of *Aranda Traditions*). These contextual details do not, however, negate the plain fact that Strehlow and Ljonga were looking for *tjurunga* for important stretches of time: in that sense I use the term 'hunt' simply meaning 'eagerly search.' Something of Strehlow's keenness is clear from his diary entry for 12 October 1933. 'Unfortunately N and N stuck to their own tjurunga . . . held them tight . . . as a result I failed to get the N tjurunga, the only one that had any markings from N and above all the tjurunga from N' (the 'N's here refer to proper, place and totem names). Strehlow added: 'Still, the rest are just as interesting in their own way and I am well satisfied. Only the price remains to be discussed.' This is not to say, either, that Strehlow was exclusively interested in *tjurunga*. Far from it, but it is to assert, as historian Dick Kimber has remarked, 'He [Strehlow] was *really* going after them' (personal conversation, November 1999), and to agree with John Morton's general observation that, 'Strehlow was an avaricious collector, casting the net widely' (1995: 54).

out, and to my surprise a little smooth edge was sticking out in the cavity below, half smothered with soil. It was an engraved stone tjurunga, the cave contained two more. Tom was highly elated at this. Tomorrow we can start on our hunt for the other tjurunga: 1) some are hidden on the plain North or North West from here—an open space is to be found there, with a group of inkuta bushes in the middle, and here the tjurunga are to be found; 2) others are hidden in a cave on a . . . in the Northern range; only Tom can't think which pass it is; 3) others are hidden at the foot of a bloodwood and at the foot of a dead-finish bush respectively, both standing at the end of a little—or rather two little—creeks issuing from the North range onto the plain.[56]

The hidden cave was the main thing. They had heard about it a few months before when they were on the great trek towards Mount Liebig, near the Western Australian border, but had not been able to find it. In November, very excited, they went looking again, and found the place on 26 November.

This was Ulamba, an important kangaroo site, an isolated mountain formation several miles north-east of the highest peaks in the Western MacDonnells. It was the place of the Eater of Dead Men, who had sprung to life on the slope of the main peak. The Eater of Dead Men hunted men down, raiding camps for bodies and roasting them until their body fats poured out on the ground. From the body fats and the bones of the dead there rose the Bird of Death, which flew in the night sky, screaming so that men would know their murderers.

Strehlow and Tom had to climb up through dangerous rocky ground, flinging handfuls of sticks and pine needles to give 'the grim ancestor' notice of their approach. When they reached the cave, Tom had to climb further up and remove the stones that blocked its mouth. He sang as he did and passed down the *tjurunga* bundles to Strehlow, still chanting as he unwrapped the hairstring.

The cave held many *tjurunga* that belonged to men from far afield. Of those that did belong to him, Tom gave four to Strehlow and kept one for himself, the one that was the Eater of Dead Men. Then he said, 'I have given you all my tjurunga now. I have no further tjurunga left—only this Old Man and those other tjurunga which I can't find. I can leave this country forever now: I have nothing left in it that I have to guard.'

They prepared to go. They bundled ten of the *tjurunga* back into the cave, and resealed the entrance with stones. Then made their way back down. That night they camped four miles off, where there was good feed for the camels.

> This is the last original cave with tjurunga in the Western MacDonnells. When those last 10 that are now reposing at KS will have been sold (or stolen), this last arknanaua will soon be a memory for the old men only, and in a few years time this once renowned cave will be forgotten, and perhaps no one will ever see it again. Then a spot whither men only last century approached only in fear and trembling, will have died to this world for ever, and Ulamba will be no more.
>
> I can see to-night peaks around me everywhere; once their names were familiar to every child in the Aranda tribe, and there were sacred caves wherever you looked—at Ulaterka, at Ulamba, at Rabuntja. There still are a few Rabuntja tjurunga; but these have long ago been hidden in the sandhills E. of the mountain, to escape being stolen. Only Ulamba now remains, and its ten tjurunga; and when Ulamba passes, another chapter in the history of the Aranda tribe will have closed. Another step nearer the grave. For the black man is one with the soil he inhabits, and now all this vast and once populous territory is silent as the grave. Men have died and some have drifted to the centres of the white man's civilisation and there degenerated . . . Once there were firelight processions and chants and dance and song in these parts; now even the white squatter forsakes them. That last cave—it is as though Time had halted for a second and turned back and cast a pitying glance upon the dust of its sons; for these men were once a Great Race. And now—long live the White Man's Civilisation! Welcome chaos in the world of today; for that is the modern youth's heritage from his own civilisation.[57]

The hard travelling, and the elegiac note: the elegiac note and then more hard travelling—physically and emotionally, in unforgiving country, in the heat, with the dust and the flies during the day and mosquitoes at night. There was, the further he went, an increasing pride and confidence in himself as a bushman, along with an affection for Flossie, and for Ranji, the other healthy camel they had acquired by the middle of the year; he was very pleased with all of this, and could at the end of a day sit quietly and love the sound of camel bells tinkling, and the repose of himself and Ljonga at the camp fire, even if he did, when he finally bedded down after writing up his journals, think of the girls in Adelaide and whether they *were* missing him at the college dance. This was the point: blessings and curses were constantly intermingled in these lonely treks; even though his notebooks were filling with myths and songs, ambivalence was the order of the day.

'I had to weep tonight when I thought of all this depopulated country. But, of course, superior Civilisation must go on!'[58]

Home Again

At the end of that first year Strehlow came back to the mission again on 'a prostratingly hot day' in December. He had been on the move for months, travelling hard on the admirable, stoical journeys that would make his name. All the way he had been collecting songs and *tjurunga*, and so he returned with songs in his notebook and *tjurunga* in his saddlebags, with camel-loads of eternity. But was not entirely happy with what he had or what was before him.

He was one day out from the mission when he sat down in the heat of the evening to reflect. We have read a fragment of this reflection before, but here it is worth contemplating in full because of its context, and its characteristic nature: his integration of references to the country, the movement of the sun from morning into night, and his melancholic sense of achievement. On 4 December 1932 he was camping on the 'bed of the Finke, The Father of Centralian Rivers.' In 'Land of Altjira,' he wrote:

> Slowly the long day has passed, from the first hot glare of the sun at dawn to the burning stinging heat of noon, and again to the dying, faltering warmth of a red sunset—and another day has passed into the vast gulf of Time to be swallowed there forever, just as the waters of the mighty Finke lose themselves at last in the barren sands of the dead heart of this Continent.
>
> Five weeks ago I was still dreading this last trip in the seat and the heat of the summer, and today I am near the end of my trip. Soon the year will be rung in by bells in the far off South, and I shall still be here, hoping, dreaming, waiting—for what? If only my work would progress more rapidly and successfully; but work among the Arandas at present seems like love's labour lost—the old vein of gold is exhausted, and what remains is so broken and shattered that it is almost too expensive and unprofitable and unsatisfying to recover the broken remnants of it.

Then he was back at the mission, well in time for Christmas.

'Now I am home.'

He was to make much of that homecoming later on, when he sat down to write his autobiography: how the children ran out to meet him, how the number of children at the mission gave him hope, because it meant that here, at least, at the mission station, the tribes were not dying off: there was hope, there was not the 'mute despair' he had seen among people at the cattle stations. 'Little devils,' he might have thought before; now he could see 'sunny faces, sunny minded gifts of God.'

Pastor Albrecht loomed. 'Welcome home, Mr Strehlow.'

'And I felt that he meant, the "home." '59

He stayed for all the festivities. He was one of the congregation preparing for Christmas. He returned to playing the organ, since the men's choir had to learn their four-part arrangements of Lutheran liturgy as well as hymns.

From early December to the New Year was a brief rest for him. He collected and pressed some wild flowers, caught up on his correspondence, and worried, as always, whether his grant would come through to allow him to continue his research (it would). For he was, despite his feeling that the vein of gold had been exhausted, the culture broken, still pleased with himself, still collecting, and, crucially, had positioned himself somewhat with regard to his father's work, the archive with which he had started out. 'After New Year, I began to collect linguistic information again, and made splendid headway. The names of my informants are all given in the respective entries of the myths and the songs . . . I was gratified beyond all expectations with the results. *I was careful to avoid ground touched upon by my father*' (emphasis added).[60]

He had in fact already surpassed the work of his father. What his father had bequeathed him, apart from the seminal insights into how the songs worked, and the *tjurunga* were owned, was the linguistic ground: the lists of myths and songs, the framework of the religious culture, along with many summaries of the myths. Without that foundation Strehlow's first year out bush would have been consumed with tabulating these fundamentals. But with his father's work under his belt, he could go further, and quickly. As a result, in the volumes referred to above he had long narratives of the myth stories, 'a connected, well-told story' was what he was after, rather than a 'few, brief explanatory remarks'[61] which was all his father often had; and he had pages of verse couplets, when at the most his father's songs stretched to fifteen verses. It was to be not uncommon for Strehlow to get down 50 verses, and sometimes more.

The pages Strehlow created in the field were themselves indicative of how far he had come. On the left hand is his meticulous record of his informants' comments about a detail of a story or myth. The man's manner of speaking, his state of knowledge, his doubts and certainties, and Strehlow's reflections on these are there on this page, along with biographical information about the man: his country, skin group, age, as well as his willingness or unwillingness to go beyond a certain point with a story or a song if it was not, strictly speaking, his own. The writing here, by Strehlow, is some of his best: it is him at work; unself-conscious, all of his brightness at a stretch.

Then, on the right-hand side of the page is the song or the myth story written out usually in Aranda, sometimes with paragraphs in English. Here the writing—as in penmanship—is striking: perfect cop-perplate down the page, inscriptions devoted to the accuracy of the song that once lived only in the air. The left hand doing the process work, the right hand crafting the song for the page, immaculately forming each letter, and the runs of letters in the agglutinating lines, with the diacritics for each letter the entirely scientific adornment, the finest feathers for words that once were danced. The pages were to be often beautiful, and the journals themselves were becoming, as Strehlow was sensing, works of art. His father would have been proud of him.

Strehlow was due to return to Alice Springs by the end of February, when, one night, some of the senior Aranda men wanted to talk with him. He did not know what it was about, only that it might have some-thing to do with a disagreement between Pastor Albrecht and Mr Heinrich.

The men came to him on Albrecht's verandah and he waited until they were ready to speak. One of the 'old churchmen' was first. 'We have not been very happy at Hermannsburg since your father left,' the man said gravely:

When your father was with us we were well looked after. We were happy. We had good health. Since then the whites at *Ntaria* have always been quarrelling amongst themselves. That is not the right thing for Christians to do—and they are moreover our teachers. If we native

Christians are committing a sin when we quarrel, then our white inkata here are also committing a sin when they quarrel. And in that time far too many of our people have died. In that time men women and children at *Ntaria* have died like cattle in a drought. Perhaps it was because the whites made our women and children go to the sacred cave of our forefathers at Manangananga, perhaps it was because God was angry with our inkatas for always quarrelling among themselves. We are Christians and we have no more tjurunga left at Manangananga, but why not leave Manangananga alone. Our fathers always told us that epidemics would come upon us if we desecrated our totemic sites—and that our enemies would kill us if we revealed our secrets to women and children. Why are not the whites content with preaching to us the word of God? Why must they force us to desecrate our sacred caves as well? It is we who must die when our epidemics come upon us or our enemies come to attack us. After they took our women, our children, to Manangananga—to our sacred cave, a great drought came upon us which killed our animals everywhere—then came a terrible disease such as we have never known before. Perhaps our old men were right when they warned us . . .

'Inkata,' he said, 'why don't you stay with us?' Your father was our father, too, and under him we were well and happy. Like your father, you respect our tjurunga. You belong to us. Your home is Ntaria: you are akarmara, you are one of the ratape ancestors of Manangananga. It is here that you have become reincarnated. You are a white man but you are also a full Aranda. You speak our language as we do. Your understanding is like our own. We have come to ask you to do one thing— here he paused and looked at the others and asked them, 'Am I right?' They all nodded and he continued:–

'We have come to ask you to stay with us and be our inkata. We shall then be happy and well, just as we were when your father was our inkata.'

'The request,' Strehlow wrote, 'came so suddenly and was so unexpected that I could say nothing . . . I felt a sickening wave of helplessness coming over me.'

Pastor Albrecht, he told them, was a good man. He would stay with them forever. And he himself was not merely the son of a missionary father, but a person who had developed his own personality. Part of him belonged to the bush but the other part to the cities.

Silently the men rose and shook hands. Strehlow judged that they did not understand his attitude, yet they accepted his refusal with dignity.[62]

He leaves it at that: he rests the account of this remarkable event there. For in a sense, a circle had been completed. He had started the year by ingesting the work of his father: becoming at one with the spiritual life of the Aranda, and working his way into their language sufficiently to surpass his father in penetration of sacred song. Now, at the end of the year, senior Aranda men want him to step into his father's shoes. Those shoes, admittedly, are the shoes of a pastor, and it is as a Christian *ingkata* that the old men seem to have been imagining him.

Was he Christian enough? Aranda enough? Could a man, twin-like, be sufficiently both?

Strehlow does not meditate on the circle that has been completed, or the complications of the compliment. The passage above is how he chose to recall it in his autobiography many years later. The event is not mentioned at all in his diary at the time. If it happened, it would appear that the power of the event was perhaps too complex for him to process at that moment. Perhaps, too, he was acutely aware that the ghost of his father also awaited him elsewhere. He was yet to return to Horseshoe Bend.

---

1   T.G.H. Strehlow 1971, *Songs of Central Australia* [*SCA*] (Sydney: Angus & Robertson, 1971), xviii.
2   Strehlow to Tindale, March 1934, South Australian Museum.
3   *SCA*, xviii.
4   T.G.H. Strehlow, diary [SD],11 May 1932.
5   Strehlow to Cleland, 2 May 1911.
6   T.G.H. Strehlow, Land of Altjira [LOA], unpublished MS, 1957, 17.
7   SD, 20–23 May 1932.
8   LOA, 53.
9   SD, 4 May 1932.
10 SD, 6 May 1932.
11 LOA, 53.
12 SD, 7 May 1932.
13 LOA, 30–31.
14 Ibid., 66–68.
15 Ibid., 53–54.
16 T.G.H. Strehlow, *Aranda Traditions* (Melbourne: Melbourne University Press, 1947), 18.
17 'Entanglements' is the operative work in Nicholas Thomas, *Entangled Objects: Exchange, Material Culture, and Colonialism in the Pacific* (Cambridge, Mass.: Harvard University Press, 1991), 14–21. Thomas' intricate insistence is that the formal model of gift exchange famously advanced by Marcel Mauss in 1925 must be seen in specific historical contexts, and that those contexts evolve in

time, from frontier situations, where dualist models of appropriation apply, to others where the agency of indigenous peoples and complex involvements by colonisers determine the system of exchange. Put simply, the gift objects take 'different historical paths'; those paths may or may not convert an 'inalienable gift' into a 'commodity'; what Mauss called 'archaic gifts' may point to the thing and/or the act of giving, and that with both what is involved through time with regard to debt may or may not be constructed in colonialist 'us/them' terms, although this distinction is necessary in order to narrate the history of exchange. In general Thomas' point that most pertains to Strehlow's context is the connection between artefact and relationship, and the way in which the valuable object comes to be signified at the historical moment of exchange. Take, for example, the giving of an engagement ring, 'an exemplary sign' until the moment when Madame Bovary says 'Qu'importe?' This is the adulterous moment, when it becomes a 'false engagement ring.' Analogously, Strehlow was collecting objects that signalled a kind of betrothal to the worth of Aranda belief: he would not have been engaged for their safekeeping otherwise. But later, years later, when the culture has, arguably, died and the giver also is deceased, what becomes of that marriage? Is divorce from the 'eternal' possible? Of what value the artefact then? And who is to value it: the descendants of the giver or the receiver? What are, to use Thomas' phrase, 'the permutations of debt'?

18 SD, 21 May 1932.
19 SD, 24 May 1932; LOA, 57–58.
20 SD 28 May 1932.
21 Ibid.
22 LOA, 59–60.
23 SD, 8 June 1932.
24 Philip Jones, 'Objects of Mystery and Concealment: A History of Tjurunga Collecting,' in *Politics of the Secret*, ed. Christopher Anderson, Oceania Monograph 45 (Sydney: University of Sydney, 1995), 68 and passim.; John Mulvaney, *So Much That Is New* (Melbourne: Melbourne University Press,1985), 125–28, *My Dear Spencer: The Letters of F.J. Gillen to Baldwin Spencer* (Melbourne: Hyland House, 1997), especially 173–93, *From the Frontier: Outback Letters to Baldwin Spencer* (Sydney: Allen & Unwin, 2000), passim and especially 76–7, 81, 96–7, 158–60, 165; John Morton, '"Secrets of the Aranda": T.G.H. Strehlow and the Course of Revelation,' in *Politics of the Secret*.
25 Mulvaney, *My Dear Spencer*, 179.
26 Ibid.
27 Gillen to Spencer, 10 September 1897, in Mulvaney, *My Dear Spencer*, 188.
28 Cowle to Spencer, 20 September 1902, in Mulvaney, *From the Frontier*, 165.
29 Jones, 'Objects of Mystery,' 81.
30 *Report on the Work of the Horn Scientific Expedition . . .* ed. Baldwin Spencer (Melbourne: Melville, Mullen and Slade, 1896), pt 4,76.
31 Jones, 'Objects of Mystery,' 83–84.
32 Baldwin Spencer and Frank Gillen, *The Arunta* (London: Macmillan, 1927), 2:111.
33 SD, 19 June 1932.
34 SD, 20 May 1933.
35 G.S. Kirk, *Homer and the Epic* (Cambridge: Cambridge University Press, 1965), 1985.
36 SD, 28 September 1932.
37 SD, 18 August 1935.
38 SD, 7 September 1935.
39 SD, 30 September, 1 October 1935.

40 SD, 30 September, 1 October 1935.
41 SD, 16 April 1935.
42 SD, 8 September 1932.
43 Strehlow, *Aranda Traditions*, 6.
44 SD, 30 August 1932.
45 SD, 4 December 1932.
46 Strehlow to Fitzherbert, 2 March 1933.
47 Spencer and Gillen, *The Arunta*, vol. 2:589–96.
48 A more formal account confirming this picture was offered to me by Peter Sutton when he read the above. It is one that allows us to say, apropos my previous remarks about the 'British' and the 'German' traditions, that when Strehlow sat with the Aranda men he was interacting with phenomenologists not positivists. The men were helping him map things, but their maps were not 'formal' so much as spiritually felt, place by place, scene by scene (for more on maps, see Part V, 'Finders Keepers,' below). Under the heading 'Performance Versus Information' Sutton has written:

'A key reason for being cautious about identifying painted and sculpted Aboriginal icons of country as "kinds of map," is that they arise principally as display or performance rather than as explanation or record . . . No doubt Aboriginal ceremonial performances, particularly where novices become inducted into new knowledge, involved and still involve the transmission of information, but even under a tutor the decoding of classical Aboriginal iconographies by a novice is typically dependent on some foreknowledge, both of the depicted landscape and of the conventions of its showing, especially since "explanation" in an Aboriginal ritual context is often highly cryptic and places the onus on the subject to generate his (or her) own understanding on the basis of somewhat fragmentary pieces of verbal guidance. The process of information transmission generally, in Aboriginal culture, is more like natural language acquisition than formal instruction in the industrial academy, although at times it may resemble both.

'That is, novices learn, not so much by absorbing pre-existing facts under programmed instruction, as by generating a model of aspects of the world out of a mixture of explicit statements and a scatter of explanatory shreds and patches, under a general prohibition on the asking of questions . . . They thus have to literally create their world of knowledge anew, in a sense that justifies the contention that theirs is a particularly phenomenologically based understanding of the constitution of knowledge . . . As an Aboriginal man said to me during field work in the north-west Simpson Desert in 1995, a propos of his then small knowledge of the meanings of some sacred rock engravings: "Old people only give you hint. You gotta pick it outa the puzzle yourself." In Aboriginal tradition, sacred knowledge is not a fixed and "complete" canon, and it is thus not beyond debate and logical extension. The epistemological conditions of positivism are alien. This practice proceeds, however, under a stated ideology of changelessness in sacred knowledge. Such stability is constantly regenerated, rather than merely cloned.

'Aboriginal revelatory ceremonies, such as the different levels of initiation of male youths and men, typically involve the exposure of novices to designs they have not previously seen, but it takes place within a framework of geographical knowledge and under a generally well understood range of visual conventions that the novice must already possess if the "new information" is to be of any intelligibility, let alone of any emotional significance. This is as true in the 1990s in remote Central and northern Australia as it was in the now heavily impacted south-eastern Australia in the nineteenth century—the novices of nineteenth century initiations were covered in blankets for much of their "exposure" to sacred designs such as earth sculptures . . .

'The question of emotional significance is not ungermane to our purpose here. One of the salient differences between Aboriginal icons and the kind of Aboriginal maps drawn to explain political geography to ethnologists, perhaps until very recently when such ethnological maps have been used in land claims contested by rival groups . . . has been their difference of emotional temperature. The icons carry the baggage of highly charged local inter-group relations, the sentiment of attachment to home country . . . and the profound emotional meanings that mythic events have for the unconscious. Ethnological maps, whether drawn by Aborigines or others, tend to be less multidimensional and their emotional connotations tend to be more political than spiritual.'
[Sutton was citing his own article, 'Icons of Country' (1998), from which I have removed the internal references.]

49 SD, 17 July 1932.
50 SD, 20 July 1932.
51 SD, 30 July 1932.
52 Cited in Philip Jones' vivid account of this and other expeditions in 'South Australian Anthropological History: The Board for Anthropological Research and its early Expeditions,' *Records of the South Australian Museum* 20 (1987): 71–92.
53 SD, 20 August 1932.
54 LOA, 134–35.
55 SD, 9 November 1932.
56 SD, 7 November 1932.
57 SD, 6 November 1932.
58 SD, 20 September 1932.
59 LOA, 218–19.
60 SD, 4 March 1933.
61 SD, 13 May 1935.
62 LOA, 232–33.

3   Heartbreak and Prowess

His Own Sacred Object

THERE IS A whole other side to Strehlow that has hardly seen the light of day in this narrative. If, due to the gravitas of his diaries, and the remorseless metronome that seems to be his heartbeat, the impression has been created of a joyless young man, it has to be corrected. By 1933, after the first year in the bush, he was not that. He was lean and brown, trimmed back, springy and fit. He was a bright, gay man to be with: talkative, humorous, interested and interesting. He was the kind of chap whose very presence would hinder a girl from finishing a letter she happened to be writing at the time.[1] He could be the life of a party, especially when he stepped up to the piano, and he loved the piano.

He loved tennis. He loved picnics, walking by rivers, and visiting waterholes. He loved going to Mr Kramer's church in Alice Springs, because almost certainly, afterwards, there was a young woman he might amuse and be amused by.

There was a glow about his young manhood of which he was proud, having done so much already out bush. One of his former school friends, the daughter of an Alice Springs settler, took a photograph of him during this period. There he is, sunburnt and smiling into the camera while sitting on a pile of bricks outside a shed. He is a light spirit: a Puck of the Bush. This shot is reminiscent of the black-and-white film taken out at

Mount Liebig, where, to see him among the smiling Pintubi, as they stand by the camel he has by the nose rope, a laughing scene full of friskiness on all sides, is to be struck by his zest for life. He is as happily full of himself, all feather and head crest, as a spinifex pigeon.

The other side was there, too, of course. There is a companion portrait to Theo sitting on the bricks. He has moved back to the shed and is sitting on the ground in the doorway. He has tilted his head back, along with his hat, and he is looking into the camera, or the light, or into the eyes of his photographer, with a dreamy, naked expression of unadulterated yearning [see Plate 16]. 'The spirit is willing, but the flesh is weak.'*

Then, one imagines, he opened his mouth again and began to speak: once again the bright voice, the quick speech, the gaiety sprang up. Against this, only the diary he has left us catches him out. One of Strehlow's sons is of the opinion that the endemic melancholia of the diaries is a fiction, something Theo put on for himself.[2] We will come to that. For the moment, though, the social reality of the man was sunny, outgoing, generous, optimistic. He was the talented university chap who had every reason to tread lightly, as if he had the world at his feet.

And out bush he would have been treading lightly, or at least less heavily, but for one thing: his pining for the melody of female company. When he came back into Alice Springs, his eye was sharp, his energy keen. And there, one Sunday night at church after a splendid sermon by Canon Nash, there she was, his 'desert maiden.'[3]

He was smitten at a glance. Her name was Sheila Elliot and she was none other than the daughter of Mr and Mrs Elliot of the Hotel at Horseshoe Bend. That is to say, she was the daughter of Ruby, the beauty who rode all night with the storm lanterns ahead of his father's buggy. Theo declared Sheila even more beautiful than her mother, and in his mind he named her then as his desert maiden because she had, like him, been born of the Territory.

On that first meeting he spoke a few words to her, but that was all until the following Sunday when he met her again, with Mary Roper. He walked and laughed and held both girls' arms, and it was the gentle

---

*   Strehlow's words to his photographer, the young Trudy Johannsen, in 1932 as he 'collapsed' in the doorway of their cellar in Alice Springs. 'He was getting ready to go bush again, but just couldn't bring himself to go downstairs and carry up the stores' (Trudy Johannsen, personal conversation, June 2002).

answer of Sheila's fingers as he pressed her hand that stayed with him. 'I had repressed my feelings to such an extent,' he wrote, 'I almost lost my head. For the first time since over thirteen and a half moons ago I was with girls on my own,' and he imagines himself offering to kiss her there on the spot, his fierce hot kisses overwhelming her with his love, and her returning his with 'a yielding embrace in which she might cling to him as a bride does to bridegroom. Bliss indeed that would have been, a feast of love.'

'Mother desert should smile for a brief moment on her two happy children.'[4]

The next day Sheila had to go back to the Bend. Sheila and Mary wanted him to go to the ball but he said no. He went and played the piano and wrote letters to 'smother his grief.' Then he went bush again, which helped take his mind off her, and in still another way deepened his sense of where and what he was in Central Australia.

When he was back in Alice Springs that June, an event that was unique took place. He was camping near Kramer's 'Goat Camp' just out of town to the north, which was one of his local spots for gathering men together to show him their ceremonies, and presented with the birthday present of his life.

The men were all dressed up for the dancing, in black and white down, and 'much fire was flying around.' 'The singing was as spirited as I have ever heard it,' and it finished, after a substantial performance, with verses sung around the fire.' Then: 'For the first time I saw *my own* tjurunga.' He underlined 'my own.'

The men explained to whom the *tjurunga* once belonged.

'Now I could be chief if I wanted to.'

Strehlow does not say what he said in reply. Did he reply that he could not be, since he was a man from the cities, as he says he said on Albrecht's verandah? That was written years later. Here, in this situation, and out bush, was he able to be more inclusive? Did he convey any notion that the idea was in some way tangible because, having entered their language and learnt their songs, he had a deep and silent affinity with the idea: no, more than an idea; that he was in himself akin to their feeling? Out of courtesy and possibly affinity did he then hold the *tjurunga* against the pit of his stomach where true feelings of belonging lived?

He does not say. The diary entry is noticeably brief, considering the gravity of the moment when the white custodian of *Ntaria*, the Twins Dreaming, was presented with his inheritance: the Aranda's essential birthday gift to him.

Strangely, he reported to himself the next morning that he was 'dog tired' from all the singing that night, and that he did not wake on his birthday with any 'pleasant feelings.' The men were still dressed up to perform for him and they did, but he 'had a dull head and was rather touchy, and hence had to fight a hard battle all day long to attend to my work and keep from getting "catty." I was really glad when I could stop with decency.'[5]

He was back in Alice Springs soon after that: after what, perhaps, was a misery generated by inner conflict—that 'hard battle all day long'—after his invitation to be chief if he wanted to.

In Alice he was bright again, more his outer social self. More walking with Mary and Sheila and he was pleased with this until, after supper, a man called Tom Barrett arrived back from a party. To Strehlow's horror, he came straight across and embraced Sheila, burying his face in her hair and pressing his mouth on her head, and she had exclaimed languidly. 'Oh Tom, so this is the first bit of love I have had tonight!'

'So I had nothing more to say,' Strehlow told his private diary (the one he kept beside his field diary and the log he had for the *tjurunga*), 'my feelings were squashed to nothingness . . . no man wants a girl who has been everybody's darling.'

It was ten days after that he arrived at Horseshoe Bend, to which the desert maiden had by then returned. The week that followed was momentous, and he was compelled to begin 'venting' himself in his diary. It was a cold day in May, 'almost a new moon,' and although what he was going to write was painful, he told himself, and it was quite strange recording a personal memoir instead of being 'the mechanical mouthpiece' of the songs and the legends, he was resigned to the necessity. 'I can only say that I am still unchanged and indeed incorrigible. It is woman again—strange word in this land of masculine harshness.'

He recounts—speaking to himself in the diary, modulating his voice as if to a friendly stranger in the fire light—how he's come all the way with Tom Ljonga and camel team, pitched camp in the high dune outside the hotel, with 'the red dunes falling ominously over the white cliffs,' where he was in 'the shadow of a death's land in a land of ruin.' Tired from a broken sleep the night before, hungry from the poor breakfast, he finally went up to the hotel where his father had died.

'Sheila held out her hand.'

He meets her in the kitchen, in the presence of her mother and father. 'They said come in.'

It was welcome enough in that he was invited for dinner. But over the meal his ready talk died down and his laughter, it seemed to him, was unnatural. 'They were tired.' And Sheila went to bed.

Back in his camp, he turned in and shivered. 'So this was the warm welcome that I had dreamed about.' Next morning, no one called him for breakfast. 'So I went hungry.'

'I visited my father's grave, and thought of the change of things. He at least was happy; life held no more disappointments in store for him. When I last stood here the body of a strong man was laid to its rest; now only the dust remained—I wrote letters in one of the hotel rooms today;—and being on the premises all day long was allowed to share in the dinner and the tea. More letter writing at night. All day long it was cloudy—bleak and windy; but as I went to bed the sky was brightening up.'

There was no invitation to breakfast next morning either. He could bear it no longer. He went to Mrs Elliot and asked could he have meals if he paid for them. Yes. So Sheila made the breakfast for him and later they went out in the truck into the 'bare and barren and arid Godforsaken country that made your heart sick to look at the Rumbalara.' Strehlow tried to photograph the flat-topped mountain but it was shrouded in a haze. They went to meet the mail train and on the way back Sheila drove the truck, 'treating me with contemptuous silence.'

But later she was in his room. He stretched out his hands. No, no, she said, and went out. Victoria, 'a half-caste maid,' brought him tea and he did not see Sheila until the next day.

The piano, he said, show me the piano.

He played some pieces, but no one seemed to appreciate them, and the piano was out of tune. 'I closed the piano in disgust.'

Days passed. Dust storms. Cards at night—sevens—with her parents. 'I taught her casino, and that was a little more exciting.'

More dust storms until, one day in the dining room, he called her a fraud.

Why? she asked.

You know why, he said.

He stroked her black poodle. 'Banker, you at least are not a fraud like your mistress.'

No cards that night. And he was not allowed to go near the dog.

The storm abated and she was talking to him the next day—chat about the people in Alice that she liked, and those that she didn't. She looked lovely as she spoke, her skin was velvet, her slim form alluring and her bosom was one where a man might rest his head and never again wake from his sleep.

'I placed my hand on her shoulders, they fell down and encircled her, and my lips drew down upon her. She shrank from me.'

"'Don't Theo," she said, "oh, please don't"—and she tried to free herself. So I let her go.'

He does not tell us how long it took him to let her go, but afterward he followed her into the kitchen and said sorry. Would she forgive him? Yes, she would, she said, without emotion.

But why wouldn't you kiss me, he pleaded, the prettiest girl in Central Australia, it would not have hurt you.

I don't suppose it would have hurt, she said calmly.

You have often been kissed before?

I suppose I have been.

Are you sure you could not give me just one kiss, Sheila?

But there was no kiss, she was never to kiss him, and although he was sick with pain he forced himself to speak 'unconcernedly.' They had arranged to take photographs of him at his father's grave, so they did that, and then he went to write letters.

In the next few days they were still talking about Alice and friendships and she would sit with him, he felt, a little more intimately. She asked him to play the piano for her again and he did. After a while she sat beside him on the stool.

So.

Had she changed her mind about that kiss?

No.

But why Sheila? Is it because you like someone else?

Yes, she whispered.

'Gone were all my dreams and hopes. This was the end of a perfect day. Das Lied ist aus, die Melodie verklungen; nichts bleibt von der Musik zurück (the song is finished, the melody has died away; nothing remains of the music).'

Who was the other man?

Play me some more, she requested.

But he couldn't. He'd been playing Dvorak's Humoresque—'where the master had tried to wed the spirit of sadness with the rhythm of the dance . . . My grief grew wild and Sheila could not do anything to stop me. "Oh Theo," she said warmly, and touched my shoulders, "I so hate hurting you." "It's all right girl," I replied, "you can't help your feelings and I can't help mine.""

He wanted to rush back to his camp there and then. But she soothed his tear, brought him to sit by the fire where he gazed at the burning coals of the tree that was burning to ash.

'Tomorrow,' he mused, 'nothing will remain, only the dead ashes,— the wind will scatter them—such—so little is the life of a tree.'

'Don't,' she said. 'But I couldn't be stopped . . . I told her of my father's death, how he died like a worm and not a man, despite the inscription on his tombstone; how her mother brought him here to this last resting place . . . "Don't Theo," she pleaded, and enfolded my head in her arms; "you are only hurting yourself." "What does it matter about me?" I asked, while the tears ran down her cheeks.'

He walked back to his camp in bright moonlight.

It was becoming clear that, even as a ladies' man, or the ladies' man who was so wanting to be with Sheila Elliot, that grief for his father kept breaking through. The long and short of it was: if a girl was to fall for him she would have to deal with his loss of his father, which he would be compelled to bring to her, just as he had brought himself in such a powerfully fated way to Horseshoe Bend. His thread on this was like a heavy leather lace in a boot.

He had come all the way to the Bend in elegiac mode. When he stopped at Idracowra, where he had had that breakfast with Mr Breaden, and 'my father rested on his last journey' he looked in on the 'two bush beds with bullock hide with their legs let on through the stone floor. Another broken bed lay outside. The door was open when I looked in; the walls had once been covered with illustrations from the weekly papers, but it was too dark to see what these were.'

He walked around the other buildings, the kitchen, the meat house, and the block harness house, empty except for a few broken bits of leather and chains, and wandered around outside that, where a few hides still hung. A cold wind blew from the NE. He walked back to his camp past the old yard.

'Such is the death of a station.'

He was at the Bend two days later.

He slept on the wet ground, and the next day had visited his father's grave.

'All is as I still remember it—bare—desolate and without hope. A few newer mounds are near by, I don't know who was sleeping their final sleep under these.' It was 25 July 1933, eleven years since his father's death.

It is a note as bare as the grave.

A couple of days later he goes a little further south, as far as Crown Point, where there is no feed for his camels. 'We are certainly travelling in a land that is in the shadow of death. Time is, Time was, Time has been.'[6]

This was the masochistic overture. Masochistic and yet—as he had hopefully found a safe lap, a sanctuary, in which to speak of the death of his father, to speak of his troubles, doing what he had dreamed of doing back in Adelaide, when he had yearned for a future with an English girl—it was solace of sorts. After this episode he went off for about ten days, travelling as far south as Macumba, and came back in rain, in freezing cold, in anticipation of a warm fireside at the hotel. With fingers too stiff to strike a match he pitched camp. At a quarter to eight in the evening of 12 August, he walked up to the house that was dark from the outside and knocked once more.

'Come in.'

A blazing fire and a warm look from Sheila, and Act Two begins. For she tells him her dream.

It is about three men. A very nice boy about 5 feet 8, whose face she could not recall, and an older man built like Nugget Morton. The nice boy is called Jack Bailey and he is in the room with her, trying to put his arms around her. 'Leave her alone,' says the older man. Then Jack disappears, and later, in the street, she finds that he has fallen down, his face all blotched with blood. She wanted to help but then saw Tony Lynch there. He had a cut on his chin—and he pointed to the ring on Jack's hand, the ring that had cut him. She smiled at Tony, and forgot all about Jack . . .

The Jack was me, Strehlow exclaimed, merely a substitution for me!

He offered to interpret her dream. He told her it was merely a realisation of her subconscious primal feminine wish to see her two rivals fight for her love, and to see the man whom she preferred killing the other.

O Theo I'll never tell you another of my dreams! Never! Never!

But she had admitted that Tony was the man she actually preferred.

Tony Lynch was the man Sheila would marry. He was Irish and he was a policeman. For the moment he was away in Charlotte Waters, but

Strehlow did not know that. Nor could he know that Lynch, as policeman in different parts of the Territory, would in years to come keep
crossing his own path as a patrol officer. 'I had guessed this and told her
that he would have to be a big tall man, strongly built. Why? But I could
not tell her of the Oedipus complex. So I played the piano for a while.'

Next day, however, he did: he told her the story of King Oedipus. I
can't believe, she protested, that my unconscious mind should be such
a wicked, horrible, cruel thing:

> I was overcome with emotion. For I felt that Sheila, if my interpreta-
> tion of her dream was correct, would never be my love. I was miserable
> and wretched. I would have gladly freed myself of all cares: only one
> pull of a trigger and—But here was one thing—was there a beyond?
> She asked me, 'what would your mother think?' I said, 'at this moment,
> even my mother means nothing to me.'
>
> I had to go out. So I went up the creek to the Potta Intjinja, and my
> heart was heavy, and my eyes were full of tears, and I rebelled against
> God, who holds all happiness in the palm of His hand and yet crushes
> people into the dust. So He had laid low my father and my mother, as
> though He had laid a curse upon our house; now he had created a
> woman for me—a woman who understood me and whom I under-
> stood; both of us felt at first sight that we were soul mates—and then
> he allowed false hopes to spring up into my heart merely in order to
> humble me the lower. Yet if I ended this insufferable pain His anger
> would crush me for all eternity. My thoughts grew more and more
> wild. Then I wept—and prayed the Lord's Prayer—the only prayer I
> could utter . . . I walked home, and had a little tea, and then I read the
> paper a little, and sat at the fireside in silence. The sky was threatening
> rain, and Mrs Elliot kindly asked me to sleep at the house tonight.[7]

Where to draw the line in the recounting of a young man's misery? If
Acts One and Two in his domestic drama tilted towards drawing-room
comedy, his development of it was something else. In the days that
followed the interpretation of the dream, where he had suggested that
Sheila was insufficiently aware of displacements about her father
(a stark displacement on his part), he was inconsolable, and kept telling
his diary so. He was sleepless, 'mad with anguish,' and kept up the Lord's
Prayer to no avail.

'Why shall I go out and work? What does success mean to me

without Sheila? Strange word, success!' . . . 'With Sheila I shall be prepared to give up my life to Central Australia, to use all my faculties and talents for the work that they are destined to do. Without Sheila I can do naught. She alone can make a man of me.'[8]

'For two days I sulked on the camels and my heart was restless.'

He cried again to the Lord, and heard a voice say 'Child' and he replied, 'My Lord.'*

Nothing helped, but he hung on, annoying her and being unable to take hold of the fact that she was not his to have. 'If only I could possess her warm sympathetic womanly love,' he moaned. 'You hurt yourself,' she told him, but he could not stop himself.

Don't let us quarrel, Sheila, let me take your photo.

No, she replied, icily.

Is that your last word?

Yes.

But they were not the last words, not really. She let him take the photo, and she took his. Then there was a decent enough goodbye when she went off to Alice Springs, leaving him there to get on with his research. He had had an encouraging letter from Fitzherbert saying that they were pleased with his work. Write an article, Fitzherbert said, it is good to publish. Success, he mocked, what was success if he did not have Sheila, if he did not have his 'life's mate!' He did not want success. He wanted happiness!

'Ashes of hopes and fears! the wind shall soon scatter them away and I . . . *must* I live on?'

When she received a letter from Lynch he swept it off the piano. 'Sheila was taken aback at my fury.'

Alone, he cried, and despaired at the glory of His name. He thought of his mother's 'doomed family'—'the Keyssers; the old stock fell when the mine that had centuries ago gave out. Ever since then disappointment, want, death, unhappiness, unfaithfulness, sorrow had followed

---

*   The poem in his mind was George Herbert's 'The Collar,' which begins:
     I struck the board, and cry'd, No More.
     I will abroad?
     What? shall I ever sigh and pine? . . .
  and ends:
     But as I have rav'ed and grew more fierce and wilde
     At every word,
     Me thoughts I heard one calling, Child!
     And I reply'd, My Lord.

mercilessly the last children of the unhappy old house, till it was almost extinguishable by now. And I was my mother's son.'[9]

'Better be dead than be unhappy: He might in his mercy have let me die on that day that I was born. But I was the clay.'

He went bush again, but when he came back he was still breaking down, sobbing 'bitterly, unrestrainedly, like a little child.' One day he fell to his knees on the ground, and was prostrate on the carpet. 'I cannot describe that agony, it was like unendurable pain infinitely prolonged. Only the viii chaps of Luke kept ringing in my ears—"fear not, believe only . . . weep not: she is not dead, but sleepeth? O Lord let me go hence in peace, helped by my faith."'

He went bush once more. He was clay. It was his insufficient prayer, surely, that created his misfortune: so he would pray more. He would lose her for eternity if he did not pray, if he did not have Faith. 'My book religion, learnt parrot-like as a child, my shallow light-hearted world philosophy, my pride of learning as a source of power, particularly in the applications of psycho analysis—all these have gone now, never to return . . . Now I shall pray that Sheila and I may be united for ever in the love of Christ.'[10]

This—his abandonment of Freud in favour of Christ—was written on Sunday 10 September. He had been in this misery since late July. How much longer could it last, how could he endure?

He was drawing nearer to God as father: the Bible was no longer a closed book. It was his only book, a never-ending source of comfort and assurance. 'Sheila and I will yet meet.' Again he thinks of 'the loveliness of suicide'[11] but then after weeping he prays again and is comforted. 'O ye of little faith!' he exclaims and cites his Bible in German. 'Tonight I am facing the greatest crisis of my life' and he prays again, for his new faith demands that his 'sinful weak doubting heart' and 'the talents which it has pleased him to lend me' would do His will alone. Then he felt at last that he had changed, that he had been converted to the Lord, and that Sheila might recognise this. But when she came back from Alice and had not changed towards him it was agony all over again and he almost broke down 'completely.'[12]

New doubts now: 'Did the Lord *frown* upon my prayer?' Sleepless, wretched nights, headaches from what he himself calls 'self torture.' And was this his punishment for treating the Lord as Sheila had been treating him?—'getting everything out of me without giving anything in return.' Another fierce sand blast outside his tent! When it stopped, the following day, it was a real pleasure to be alive, but there was still the question beneath the last doubt. Had his requests of the Lord been 'spiritual adultery?' Might she not be destined to be his? The heat was ferocious, the heat and dust. He woke in his tent at 2 a.m. with the storm howling again.

He was waiting for 'the signs.' 'The Lord has kept silent up to now. I have prayed to him, like a bride that has been unfaithful and has come back to her wronged bridegroom, and asked him about Sheila—as a sign that he has forgiven me my wrongs; but He has listened to all my confessions of trust in silence and has not yet spoken, even as the wronged bridegroom waits a moment before he lifts up his eyes and looks into those of the repentant bride, and tells her what is on his mind.'

For a while he is sleeping better and dreaming 'normal dreams.' He dreamt of Sheila on a verandah, and in the glory of her beauty she leaned over him and kissed him.[13]

'So I have decided to ask the Lord to be gracious unto me again.'

The furnace continued. After days in it he thinks of leaving, of breaking out of his infernal circles. The Lord might have helped him get some distance from his capricious love object, since he found himself writing: 'She was too selfish to love anyone but herself.' And he did not like her racist remarks about the blacks either. So he started to get ready to ship out, only to see her beauty all over again, and to wish once more that she was his—'MINE.'[14] He is possessed. Possessive. And possessed of possession.

His Goethe and Luther

There is no escaping the actuality of Strehlow's suffering; equally, it would seem, the literary model shaping it. Young Strehlow as Werther. Goethe's hero must have been an inescapable presence to the mind of a boy who sang German songs at Immanuel College. It is an assumption with which the historians of the college concur but which cannot be precisely documented as Strehlow's German library is not in the possession of the Strehlow Research Centre.

The Sorrows of Young Werther is a story of unrequited love and excess of feeling that lead to the hero's suicide. It is an epistolary novel, a halfway house between monologue and dialogue, which exuded private feeling after the fashion of a diary. *Werther* was not so much a love story as a story of 'the self-destruction of the feeling heart' and a study of 'the pathology and the crisis of contemporary Sentimentality.' The pathology was, essentially, the product of the hero's solipsisms—the monodrama—and his anguish at the fact that no specific thing, least of all the object of his love, 'would accommodate itself perfectly to his feeling.' As a result, 'the only alternative for his heart is to subside into impotence,' Goethe has his tragic creation proclaim, in the florid prose that has trickled down through generations of romantics, including Strehlow: 'And the heart is now dead, no ecstasies flow from it any more . . . I have lost that which was the only bliss in my life, the sacred life-giving power with which I created worlds all around me: it is gone . . . oh, when this glorious Nature stands frozen before me like an enamelled miniature and none of this bliss can pump a single drop of happiness up from my heart into my brain.'

Goethe's biographer tells us that Werther's contemporaries found Werther's sensibility distasteful because of 'his habit of appropriating everything about him by means of the possessive adjective ("my forest," "my Homer"). Yet that very act of appropriation indicates a discrepancy between the heart and its object'—which happens when the 'feeling does not *quite* reach out and embrace the appearances.' The appearances are what is before the acutely subjective—exclusively subjective, really—mind of the hero. For this reason alone they are never attainable. And so Werther's is a story 'in which excessive demands on the capacity for feeling lead with irresistible logic to a loss of all contact with the objects of feeling.' Or, to put this another way: in the mind of the quintessential romantic, possessiveness is a project yielding its own lost cause.

For Goethe, writing *Werther* was an act of religious emancipation. His hero used religious vocabulary not in order to provide meaning to his story, but rather to give his own story meaning. Goethe had Werther die as Christ is born, and in his letters to his own love at the time he was using the Lutheran language of consubstantiation in a way that gave sacramental significance to himself and his love, to his heroes. The analogy was blasphemous, and the novel's indulgence of suicide was seen so at the time. Such excess of feeling—sentimentality itself—pointed away from God.[15]

All this young Strehlow seems to have known in his bones. He was a victim of sentiment and sentimentality (in the modern sense of the term). He was hysterically writing—as a diarist, *acting* ('venting' he said)—things out. But because he was still a Christian he was all the time winching his anguish towards the heavens, striving to write his ego into an eternal scheme of things.

Cycles, eternal cycles—these too Strehlow was trying to surmount. To no avail, because they are the time-bound Lutheran oscillations—'why me, Lord?'—and then the channelling of the self into justification by further suffering: the Lord has chosen *me* in order that I might vindicate *my* faith. And then the round of doubts once more. Strehlow's wheel of fire at the Fire Dreaming place of Horseshoe Bend. A purgatory from which there was no escape unless it was, finally, a full vindication of faith in the Lord. What hope though if doubt squats too, like the devil himself, at the heart of the prayer? Strehlow was praying not for the Lord but for her, his desert maiden, for a 'her' to be 'MINE.' He knew this every minute of the day and the nights at Horseshoe Bend: hence the guilty question—was he committing 'spiritual adultery' in the eyes of the Lord? In Luther there was no end to prayer because a fear of death goaded him into doubt, the fear of death that was living proof of lack of faith. With Strehlow, whose anguish was expressed in the language of a religious crisis, his prayers that *she* would save him, that she would make his success worthwhile, was also tantamount to a lack of faith. Strehlow's extra burden is his compulsion to find a woman as complete saviour: she would, if she was the one, carry the grief of his lost father; she would take on the burden of his loss and anger. Deep down, such a one would be kin to the one his father loved—his mother, whom he had also lost, not to mention the 'other woman,' the one who rode all night to save his father . . . Desert Maiden, Mother, Bride, Salvation. All this only the Lord knew; and all of it could not be said at once but only felt by the Christian romantic who had flirted with his 'psycho analysis' and found it wanting. So he continued to wait for the signs. The Lord withheld. Only time would tell. Time on this earth, and time Eternal.

At last he was making real plans to leave. He was loaded up. Strehlow's diary tries to slip into another key as the curtain is drawn.

Ta-ta, and good luck, they said, and all shook hands.

Sheila, he asked, what's the time?

She told him. Ta-ta, she said, good luck.

It was still an inferno.

The plan was to travel in the cool of the night. As his father had arrived, so he would depart, in the hope of respite in the night.

He had said to himself: 'I shall cast a last look at my father's grave, touch the piano keys once more, and say good bye to Mr and Mrs Elliot and to Sheila: who knows whether I shall ever see them again.' Sheila was all kindness and forgiveness, and more beautiful than ever, and still he did not know what 'Father had decided.' He could not help but note, as well, that all that time the piano he had been playing was in the room in which his father had died. Music that had come to nothing.

The goodbyes were at dusk. Mrs Elliot gave him apples and cakes and bread and all the meat she could spare. Together they had tea in silence.

It was a quarter to eight when they stepped outside with the five camels—Snowy, Possum, Dot, Mulga, and Flossie—all loaded.

'Ta-ta, good luck.'

'Ta-ta, good luck.'

In the dimness of the early moon the camels moved off.

'And the camel bells tinkled, and their feet broke through the heavy sand—the wind blew at our backs and the dark gums sounded dreamy into the night. Soon we had left the Finke, and ascended though the pass and reached the sandhills. There were no more lights to be seen behind us. Horseshoe Bend and all it held for me was no more. The Lord had withheld His answer.'[16]

He walked off into the furnace of the night.

The Outside Work

Yet all the work at the Bend—despite his romantic agonies—was paying off. If, indoors by the piano, Strehlow could not like Werther get 'a single drop of happiness up from my heart into my brain,' outdoors he could put his brain and his body to work and experience something else. Outside, on the ground with the old Aboriginal men, there was the manly work that invited a classic mode. The native legends of the area were made of much sterner stuff than the solitary ego's pining for a Dream Woman. Fire, rain, death, primal punishments and revenge— themes inhabiting the landscape he would describe years later in *Journey to Horseshoe Bend*—put him up against the forces of Nature itself: a world outside himself, that was not himself. Up and down the Finke he travelled with Ljonga and all the old men he could round up.

It took some time getting into the country, just as it had getting into the language. A good sign was meeting the old stockman Charlie McLeod near Crown Point. 'He welcomed me heartily enough for my father's sake, and shared what little meat he had with me.' But then he had to go 150 miles down the Finke to Macumba before hearing the good news that some Aranda men would come up to meet him. The longer he was in the area of the Finke, the more men gathered, camping at different places with him over the months. There were some camps where he was very pleased with his informants—with how they dressed up, danced vigorously near the camp fires, spilling coals about, and disregarded 'all burns with amazing fortitude.'[17]

There were others where he had to scold Tom for running out of food, and Tom walked away saying. 'If you talk like that I leavem job':

> So I told him that if he wanted to leave he could. He ought to just sit down quietly now and tell me for breakfast if he wanted to leave. After breakfast he came up, penitently enough, and told me that he had realised it was all his own fault—that he had been a 'bloody fool'—that this was not the way to talk to his ingkata . . . So all was all right again.

But what was not quite right—still, was the invasion of their camp by Alice Springs men, rather than the Southern Aranda men he wanted. They were 'a real nuisance.'

> They arrive here in the morning, lie down in Tom L's camp till dinner, laughing and talking, and then get a good share of the soup and damper provided for the workers before they drawl off again towards evening. This must be stopped. I cannot keep on increasing the rations issue if the workers do not get the benefit . . .
>
> I'll probably have to dish out the portions at each meal myself in future.[18]

That winter and spring along the Finke he was working in the wind and rain. Blankets were sometimes too wet to sleep in, and when he got up the sugar for the tea was wet as well. In the spring, he had the dust and the heat. In dry country they had to go looking for herbage for the camels. The meat got flyblown. Their water had the disgusting taste of tannin from the waterbags. His moods—as anybody's would in this situation—oscillated. Gloom one day, joy in the bright morning the next. The work always went on.

It slowed momentarily when a telegram at Charlotte Waters told him that his research grant had been reduced by £50: from £175 to £125. He wrote anxiously to Fitzherbert who replied to him in Latin, and, to keep their communication from the eyes of the Outback, Strehlow wrote back in Latin. The grant would be sorted out: the work would go on.

As did the collecting, as the men sang their songs and danced for him. There were more caves, some of them with the last collections. In one place he noted 'these 38 articles, then, represent, all the *tjurunga* that once rested at various points on the Finke River between Horseshoe Bend and Idracowra.' He did not always collect the *tjurunga*, a point he was rather to emphasise in years to come, when he reproduced a long extract from his diary at this time.[19] He might, for instance, buy some while leaving others there, which was satisfying to the old owner. 'Now the two tjurunga will rest in the cave till the old man does die, when they are to descend upon me.'[20]

From his diaries it is clear that the *tjurunga* were often handed over after the men had performed elaborate ceremonies for him, sharing with him the main rituals and myths of which he was to make so much when he came to write *Journey to Horseshoe Bend*. There was the passion of gift-giving in their performances, and he registers the excitement. Then, when all was done, he went through the quieter civilities involved with the exchange of objects:

W and P sorted out the tjurunga which had lost their owners through death; they were nearly all in pairs. As each pair was handed to me, either W or P would call out to the assembled men, 'If any man opposed me, let him speak now, & let him hate me alone.' The men then would give their consent unanimously. Only A once ventured to oppose P when the latter showed the two altentinja of Lalkara; but P. insisted, 'I am giving them away, they are my fathers', no other man has any right to them,' until A., too, gave way. The tjurunga so secured will be described & listed later on. U was at my side, all excitement & eagerness: for were not he and I countrymen, and was not therefore this gift of tjurunga to me to be rejoiced at by him? Tom, too, was just so pleased. U kept saying 'Thank you,' every time a pair was handed to me. Then everything was wrapped up in emu feathers and hairstring. My lot was put separately, & their tjurunga were left in my tent till a more convenient time can be found for transferring them to the cave. Unfortunately both W & P stuck to their own tjurunga, i.e. the tjurunga from near their homes 'held them tight' . . . as a result I failed to get the altjatia tjurunga, the only ones that had any markings from P, and above all the antja (from W). Still, the rest are just as interesting in their way, & I am well satisfied.[21]

There was no end to the arduous detail of his life out along the river. But he soldiered on nonetheless, even as he came and went from his heartbreak hotel. Finally, at the end of this first stint as a researcher in the land of the Southern Aranda, he was able to report to Tindale:

> During my stay at Horseshoe Bend I collected sixteen myths and over 300 double line verses of native chants. This, of course, does not exhaust all the available material; indeed, I am afraid that it represents only a small portion of what might have been collected ever from the present few survivors of the Southern Aranda group; but it is quite sufficient for a generally linguistic survey of the dialect. I am quoting here one of those myths and the chant connected with it; and in my comments upon the myth and its chant I shall attempt to set out briefly the differences between the Southern Aranda groups in regard to thought and language; and a brief summary will also be given of some of the more striking linguistic characteristics of Southern speech.

What followed was called 'The Two intjira women of Potta Arugutja' (a hill near Horseshoe Bend). The account, which includes a 'very free' translation of four verses, linguistic notes and footnotes about the myth, runs for five typed pages, single-spaced. It was an expansive entry, obviously designed to impress. And Strehlow's choice of story to spell out was symptomatic of the forces at work in the turbulent shaping of his identity.

The myth is about a mother, two mothers, actually: the intjira woman, a kind of butterfly and her companion urula, a mulga parrot. And it tells of a lost son, a fatherless boy, who is exchanged for a kind of twin. No great stretch of the imagination is required—or even anything of what Strehlow was then calling 'psycho analysis'—to see what might have drawn him to it at Horseshoe Bend.

The women were always gathering the seed, and the boy, when he enters the story is ready for initiation. He is sent away for this—200 miles off to Rabuntja. When the men had finished with him and the ceremonies they did not want to send him back: they kept him and sent another boy back to the mother instead, one with a lighter skin colour. When the wrong boy comes back and stands before her the mother looks around, and exclaimed 'He is lost to me forever.'

So the mother threw the meal away and only gave water—or what looked like water—to the initiates. It was a magic poison . . . The old men who were at the rear died first, the younger ones surviving a little longer . . . No one escaped. They all died to a man . . . The two women watched them die, and rejoiced greatly in their death. ''Tis well done: embrace me, sister; come and sit down on my lap.'

In the end the women—'after their embraces were done'—gathered up their chattels and left, flying east and scattering seed, then south, before getting tired and sinking to rest at Jitutna where the scattered rocks there may be rubbed in order to create intjira grass seed.

Strehlow lets his narration sink to rest here too. The five verses of chant, he goes on to tell Tindale, do not reveal the full myth story. Nor do they name all the actors in the drama. 'It should be noted that in the song—which is the only unchangeable "authority" on which the myth is based—there are no verses relating either to the women or to the boy or to the visitors from Rubuntja.' He goes on to speak of the links and changes between totems. He suggests that the butterfly women formerly belonged to the grass seed totem; which was to say it was once the embodiment of all the fertility of that particular grass seed. 'Such a change of totem amongst totem ancestors almost approximates to a kind of transmigration of souls.'

He refers Tindale to his photographs of the ceremonies performed in connection with this totem. And then speculates on what was old, what was new, about ceremonial links between places. Again it was a matter of making more of the song than the song told:

Since the song does not include any mention of the main facts of the myth, it seems probable that the myth is only a fabrication of later ages, intended to link up Potta Arugutja with Rubuntja. For Rubuntja (about 200 miles from Horseshoe Bend), is the great Northern centre of the Fire-Rukuta totem, and it seems that there was a local fire-totem centre very close to Potta Arugutja, in fact on the very site now occupied by the buildings of Horseshoe Bend Station. This southern fire-myth has been lost; but a few of the southern fire chants have survived. Hence the intjira myth, as it stands, is probably merely a later elaboration of the link invented by one of the old story tellers to connect up the fire myths, those of Rubuntja and that of Potta Arugutja.[22]

It is hard to say what Tindale felt about this report from the budding anthropologist in the field—hardly budding now, Strehlow's speculative fertility is an explosion of grass seeds. He has things to say with regard to the meaning and origin and even the verisimilitude of the myth stories. He has managed in a few pages to evoke a world of myths lost, myths refound, or rather, 'fabricated' by the old storytellers. Of myths written down by other storytellers—by men such as himself, who knew the map of the fire centres, and could see how it was natural to link them up. Myths recounted on the basis of reconstruction from other stories that are an elaboration of whatever was in the song, the cryptic chants that were linked to ceremony. Of myths therefore at least three times removed from their ritual meaning: first by the business of informants telling what was deeply in or behind the song; by the business of recording their oral account; and by its shaping into another language, not to mention all the shadings that go into the record-keeper's disposition in that language. Myths coloured—finally—by what might be called the narrator's relationship with the material of the story, its manifest if not its latent content.

Most of all though, in the above passage Strehlow seems to assert the priority of songs over everything. The song takes precedence over narrative. In the beginning, he hints to Tindale, was the song: poetry as genesis.

This chain of concerns was not obviously, or fully, spelt out by Strehlow. Such intellectual self-consciousness was still uncommon in anthropology, which was still in its classic stage[23]: Strehlow in the field was very much a man of his times; imperialistically focused on the products he would be able to bring back to his peers rather than the processes of their acquisition. His tone with Tindale was that of a pioneer and prospector who would press on intrepidly. 'After the departure of this mail train,' he wrote when he was back in Alice Springs, 'I intend to set out for Hermannsburg, where I expect to meet again one or two of my southern informants. I shall stay there till after New Year, and then leave for the East, to carry out investigations into the Eastern Aranda dialect. My base camp has not been fixed definitely as yet. It will probably be either Love's Creek or Ambalindum.'

There, he was saying to Tindale, see what I can do: I have as much stamina as any scientist in the field. He was both fitting into the scientific mode and flaunting his literariness, trying hard to make an impression on Tindale, as well he might. Even by 1933, Tindale, only 34 himself, had 31 scientific papers to his credit, in entomology and ornithology as well as archaeology and ethnography. By 1935 he had made films among desert peoples in seven locations, including sound recordings of ceremonies and song cycles, and by 1937 he was lucidly and rather beautifully writing up some songs from the Yorke Peninsula. Fortunately for Strehlow's sensitivities Tindale had not recorded anything at Hermannsburg since 1929, where the Aranda had thought well enough of him to declare his totem to be the brown hawk: much of Tindale's desert work would be with the Pitjantjatjara. What he was generally advancing was new work on the mapping of Aboriginal languages, along with extensive genealogies designed to show connections between individuals, sites and their Dreamings. In this period Strehlow could not have been anything but awed by Tindale's industry, just as he must have had his own feelings about another aspect of the man: the mentorship of Baldwin Spencer. It was from Spencer in Melbourne that Tindale learnt how to keep his extensive field notes, and from whom he adopted the famous 'Notes and Queries,' the guide for anthropologists in the field that had been drawn up at Oxford. From Spencer, too, Tindale adopted a method of language transcription designed to make comparisons across language, and which was to enable the first tribal map of Australia to be published in 1940.[24] Strehlow had his own reasons for not having any of that, just as he had no inclination for adopting a method of language transcription that did less than justice to his sense of the complexity of his Aranda.

In any case, well before the end of the decade by which time the authority and compass of Tindale's work was even more evident, Strehlow had no personal political reason to be reporting to him at all. He would drift from this mentor, just as he would from Fitzherbert. He had less need for father figures now that he was toiling in the complex shadow of his own father.

The Brilliant Debut

The story of the 'wrong boy'—the one who never returned to his mother in the fire country of Horseshoe Bend—was not published until 1969, when Strehlow gave it a key position in his own Aboriginal rendering of landscape in *Journey to Horseshoe Bend*. It was, romantically speaking, too close to his lonely heart to publish in another place. But that was not the case with the myth he did write for publication, and with which he made his precocious debut as an anthropologist.

By October 1933 he had done what Fitzherbert suggested: written an article—a firm-minded, sophisticated article written in the classic mode about the ancient culture. It was published that year in the prestigious *Oceania*, confirming the faith others had in him.

It was the story of Ankotarinja, the dingo ancestor at Ankota, a dreaming site on Burt Plain, about 20 miles north-west of Alice Springs. Strehlow had been told the story during his travels in 1932. His main informant was an old man called Ankota, named after the ancestor creature himself: Ankota lived in Alice Springs when Strehlow met him. The tale begins:

> In the beginning there was living in Ankota a man who had sprung from the earth without father or mother. He had been lying asleep in the bosom of the earth, and the white ants had eaten his body hollow while the soil rested on him like a white coverlet. As he was lying in the ground a thought arose in his mind: 'Perhaps it would be pleasant to arise.' He lay there, deep in thought. Then he arose, out of the soft soil of a little watercourse.
>
> He looks around himself, still half asleep. Around him he sees great *tnatantjas* waving against the sky, *tnatantjas* belonging to other men and women who have originated in the same way in which he has. He hesitates—'Where shall I go to?' He stands, on legs as yet weak and tottering; his body is like a skeleton, for the white ants have been feeding on him for a long while. He stands there listlessly. Then he goes to a swamp nearby, and sits down on the edge of the water. Thoughts and wishes form in his mind. He begins to decorate himself with red down. A great *tnatantja* stands on his head: he has arisen out of the ground with this *tnatantja* on his head, and it has shot up until it hit the vault of the sky. He begins to breathe heavily, and he sniffs around into the four winds: a cold breeze is blowing from the north . . . a cold breeze is blowing from the south . . . a cold breeze is blowing from the east . . . but there! a warm breeze is coming from the west. He draws warm scent in eagerly—'from the west comes the breeze that warms my heart.' He returns to the spot where he first issued forth. But his heart is now burning with anger against the west. The great *tjurunga* on his head falls down to the ground, and he rises and leaves it behind and sets out on his journey westward.[25]

It is a fine beginning by any standards, full of mystery and power. Strehlow goes on to say that his prose translation is 'very free.' It has been particularly so in its use of an Old Testament phrasing and tone. And its beauty—especially in the first paragraph—comes from the elegant simplicity with which the translator sets the scene. We might baulk at the slight quaintness of terms like 'coverlet' and 'arise,' but there is no escaping the force of its clarity. We meet a story as primal as Genesis.

As the story unfolds, other features of Strehlow's telling emerge. First of all he is prepared to let the events speak for themselves, even when the meaning of some are not exactly clear. 'The white ants had eaten his body hollow.' We are not told why. 'Thoughts and wishes form in his mind.' What thoughts? 'But his heart is now burning with anger against the west.' The pull of the west is never explained, except for the fact that, as the story goes on, it is clear that we are being inducted into certain features of Aboriginal culture as much as this particular creation story. Tnatantjas—a word used by Strehlow in his own incantatory way—is Aranda for the men's decorated ceremonial pole that was often worn on the head. *Tjurunga,* a term suddenly used to replace tnatantjas, is the generic term for a sacred object, often considered to be the spirit body of an ancestor. But Strehlow does not tell us this. His technique is to withhold this information, just as the story itself (assuming Strehlow has not come between us and the story itself) is oiled by secrets. It is hard to know, at this point, whether these features reflect aspects of the Aboriginal culture or Strehlow's wish to enhance his own controlling power as storyteller.

What is clear is the very literary nature of his enterprise. Strehlow calls it prose, even though Aboriginal culture has no writing. And he renders it in a most literary way, even though the story has been told to him over many sittings and quite a bit of question and answer. That is to say, it has been recounted by the custodians of the story in their terms, in speech patterns that bear no relationship to sentences meant for the page. Exactly how the story was told we do not know, as Strehlow, for all his diligence as a diarist, did not keep verbatim notes of his conversations: he was always more concerned to keep a thorough record of the results of his inquiries. And yet we now know that the Aboriginal way of telling a story—with its pauses, silences and circumlocutions—may well be more expressive of its nature than the 'higher quality of English' to which Strehlow always aspired.*

---

* It is important, in the light of Strehlow's purist commitment to English in the Stuart Case (see 'Saving Caliban,' below) to compare this version with the following, the start of the same story written down some years later:
'Ungortarenga is the name of the place. What the white man calls Burt Well, where there is a well for cattle, lies close to this place. An old man there has a shield and a boomerang. All the winds that blow, blow back to this one place where that old man stays. The old man lies down and the winds from all

Strehlow sustains the myth for some pages, communicating its richness and power. Ankotarinja disappears into the ground, and proceeds on his journey underneath. He emerges and sees footprints of women. Hungrily he sees where they have been digging for frogs in the creek. When he catches up with them they are sitting there helpless, and cannot eat any longer: they gaze away into the far distance. But the man has already hidden himself. While they are still gazing into the distance with their eyes lifted up high, he comes upon them, crouching flat to the ground in the long grass. 'His teeth pierce deeply into the waists of the two women. He crushes them and then goes on: for he has now espied his real quarry.'

The real quarry are the 'Tjilpa men of Parr' Eruyltja. *Tjilpa* is native cat, though Strehlow does not tell us that. He comes over the rise, sees them all in a clear space, and pounces on them. 'Like a whirlwind he rakes them together, snatches them up fiercely, and swallows them down, one and all. Full to bursting, he now stretches himself out at the foot of the tnatantja. Then he falls asleep.'

Another man approaches. He wonders what has happened to the native cat men. He wonders what has caused the wind to cease. Then he sees 'the monster.' He approaches, his anger kindled. He hurls a *tjurunga* and hits the monster in the nape of the neck.

The head of the monster rolls away, and the swallowed men are all disgorged again: they are being spilled out like water. At once they climb up on the rocky hills again, swing the bullroarers merrily, and decorate their heads with green twigs and wallaby tails.

---

directions come and cover him up with dust and sand. When a bird calls out from a tree that old man sits up out of the dust and sand and looks out everywhere. He thinks, he looks round, then lies down again. The winds blow from all directions and cover him up again with dust and sand. The wind blew from the south. First the nose of the old man came up out of the dust, then his head and shoulders. He rose on his hands and knees with the dust and the sand sliding off him. On his hands and knees he stretched forward, smelling the wind and looking out in its direction. As the old man smelled the wind and stretched forward he changed into the big devil dog Erintja Ngoolya.'

The speaker here is Albert Namatjira and he is talking to the poet Roland Robinson. They were sitting down at Haasts Bluff in 1954. When Robinson came to write it up in his book, *The Feathered Serpent* (1956), Strehlow, who wrote a foreword, thought Robinson had 'on the whole successfully preserved the style of the original myths.' But Strehlow added: 'Whether he has always been successful in blending certain pidgin English expressions with the *higher quality English* used normally in his final versions, I must leave to the artistic judgment of each reader. But his personal sympathetic attitude towards the native way of thinking is undeniable, and can be felt throughout his book' (vii, emphasis added).

The dead body of the monster is lying on the ground, but the severed head is still alive. The head reflects: 'My home is not far away; let me return to it for my last rest.' And so the head rolled back, underneath the ground, and emerged finally out of a little watercourse near Ankota. And there it remained and passed again into the earth forever.[26]

Thus Strehlow ends the prose version of the myth (which he sometimes calls a legend). Later, in his commentary, he tells us that Ankotarinja, the 'hero' of this myth, is always imagined as a man decorated with the traditional designs illustrated by the *Oceania* photographs. The hero is a dog, but decorated in the manner of the *tjilpa* men, whose sites are the most numerous in the area.

In what follows Strehlow tells us about the place of the *tjurunga* in story and song; the dance that went with the song from which the prose story is derived; details of the headgear illustrated in the photographs; the nature of the verse, and something of the ownership of the story. That is to say he uses the story to introduce the reader to a range of general considerations about the place of the myth in Aranda culture. He does not say any more about the possible meaning of the story. Indeed, he confesses to avoiding such issues, except to remark that murderous detail surrounding the hero 'was not very different from the primitive horde as pictured by psychoanalysis.' The reference here is to the primitive horde in Freud's *Totem and Taboo*. But despite the intellectual enticement, Strehlow does not spell this out. He also goes on to say that 'a consideration of native symbolism is beyond the scope of the present brief treatise.' We might well experience some frustration at these deflections, as they avoid two major strands of approach to the whole field of mythology. To put this another way: Strehlow's intellectual debut in anthropology shows a keenness to step aside from the intellectual currents of his time. He would no more openly engage with depth psychology and social anthropology than he would with the cultural problem of meaning. Instead, he marked out the terrain he wanted to claim as his own. For the purpose of his short treatise was, he concludes, to show: 'the deep and essential unity between myth and drama, *tjurunga* worship, and "poetry" in its most primitive stage. As amongst the old white races, so amongst the natives of the great Central Australian spaces the first faltering beginnings of "religion" are the fountain from which spring poetry and drama and the making of decorative and artistic objects: native art, literature and religion, in the widest sense of these terms, form one indissoluble and splendidly complete unity.'[27]

The Main Connection

The absolutely distinguishing feature of the Ankotarinja article was in Strehlow's presentation of the verse chants. No one had before done this as thoroughly, or with as much authority. In his introductory note, J.A. Fitzherbert told readers that at a time when many of the native languages had disappeared completely, and when few attempts had been made to give an account of native languages, Strehlow was 'exceptionally qualified to do so because he had been familiar with the Aranda language from his earliest years.' The Ankotarinja article was 'a specimen of the linguistic material which he is collecting, and shows some of the difficulties involved in interpreting the ceremonial songs.'

So it did. Immediately following his prose elaboration of the myth, Strehlow presented the extraordinarily beautiful and cryptic phrases that encoded the story. This was his first version of Aboriginal chant into English poetry.

1. No: madau'e: 're: rlando'pa: i (Bauerela 'nopa'nama
   'No: majatin: 'tje: Lano'pa:i 'Ja:tinti'jala 'nopa'nama.)

   Red is the down which is covering me;
   Red I am as though I was burning in a fire.

2. 'No: mabau'e: 're: lano'pai:i (Bauerela nopanama
   No: maal'ba: 'tji: njano' pa'i 'Alba'ti: nja nopanama.)

   Red I am as though I was burning in a fire,
   Bright red gleams the ochre with which I have rubbed my body. *

Without the Aranda, which Strehlow retained throughout, it runs:

3. *Red I am as though I was burning in a fire,*
   Red, too, is the hollow in which I am lying.

4. *Red I am like the heart of a flame of fire,*
   Red, too, is the hollow in which I am lying.

---

* Strehlow's diacritics are retained here, as far as possible in keeping with his 1933 article in *Oceania*. For the rest of the book no such replication is attempted as it would be of technical interest only to linguists.

5. *The red tjurunga is resting upon my head,*
   Red, too is the hollow in which I am lying.[28]

The verses describe how the great *tnatantja* stands on his head and shoots up to the sky: the country around Ankota; the scent of an underground pathway that opens before Ankotarinja, and his following up the scent. When he devours the *tjilpa* men, the verse goes:

Irresistible and foaming with rage,—
Like a whirlwind he rakes them together.

Then after being struck down, he sees his home at Ankota, and returns by the underground pathway:

Out yonder, not far from me, lies Ankota;
The underground hollow is gaping open before me.

Two more verses hold to this underground journey before Ankotarinja is once more back in his old home:

Red I am, like the heart of the flame of fire,
Red, too, is the hollow in which I am resting.

In all, Strehlow presented eighteen verses of the Ankotarinja chant. It was a short run compared to the passages he would display 30 years later in his *Songs of Central Australia*, and especially considering that some song cycles can run for days, even weeks. It did not invite any entry to the processes or problems of translation. But it was enough to begin the kind of commentary with which he would make his name, and which would be extended in his great book.

With Ankotarinja, Strehlow focused on three aspects of the verse, each laid out most lucidly, while displaying the special nature of his knowledge, his touch with the language, his intimacy with the sacred material.

He highlighted the special linguistic features of the chant, one being the chant's relationship to the spoken language. The words of everyday speech were dismembered and rearranged according to formal and traditional verse patterns, at the same time as speech accents gave way to verse accents, with the addition of additional syllables, or a shift of stress with the vowels. The two verses that Strehlow set out above the English translation give some idea of how the spoken line related to the line chanted in ceremony. In Ankotarinja Strehlow stressed the ways in which all this facilitated the chant as a chant. Later on, in *Songs*, he says much more about this differential.

He showed the inseparable link between poetry and the sacred in another way. The link was the *tjurunga*—the sacred object. The Anko-tarinja myth performed a chant of the hero and his *tjurunga* in such a way that the *tjurunga* itself—the embodiment of its essential spirit—was named in the song. This relationship between the naming of the spirit, the *tjurunga* and their owners, and the chant's self-naming is what Strehlow brilliantly laid out:

> the old man who recently died in Alice Springs, and who was the rein-carnated form of Ankotarinja, regarded the two stone *tjurunga* as his own body, which had thus been kept alive through the ages: but he also regarded the wooden *tjurunga* as forming part of this supernatural deathless body. Perhaps this reasoning may be made clearer and easier to follow if one compares the different *tjurunga* which form one body with different phases of the moon: each night between the dates of first quarter and last the moon offered a slightly different picture to the observer; yet all these different 'moons' are one and the same heavenly body. In the same way, the different *tjurunga* depict Ankotarinja at dif-ferent stages or 'phases' of his life; but they all *are* the one body of this man, and hence taken together form the one body which has under-gone all these varied experiences.
>
> In view of the slight differences between these *tjurunga* it becomes quite clear that they must have different 'names,' that is, that they claimed different verses of the same song as belonging to them exclu-sively. Incidentally, the native term for the ceremonial chants is '*tjurunga retnja*,' which means, literally, 'names of *tjurunga*.'[29]

From all this Strehlow helps the reader understand something quite won-derful about the Aboriginal chant. Not only was it sacred in its origins: its form embodied what was sacred; and all of it was sung under the rubric of sacred naming. Strehlow had written a definitive paper about primal generative unities, the spirit and the substance of which made up the poetics of Aboriginal song. He had, well before his time, dem-onstrated that the Dreaming was the 'poetic key to reality' (the phrase is W.H. Stanner's 30 years later) and that the poetry in performance was the seed bed of everything. Later on he constructed an argument that went close to giving the poetry the priority, as if to say that 'in the beginning was the Word.' But for now he had tabled the unities, and in so doing had projected the moon of his own life's work into the sky—up there, *out* there—shining for all to see.

In Goethe's terms, a Werther could only drown in the light of his moon, whereas a man in touch with sacred knowledge beyond himself—directly so—was like Faust, stalking the boardwalk of power in the world.

Where did all this leave the head and heart of the mission boy? Strehlow was yet to reveal the amplitude of his cultural ambivalence: but in 1933 his profound intimacy with Aboriginal knowledge was manifold, and it meant that he had to contend with its welter of responsibilities. What would guide him? By what authority would he work it out?

---

1 Dora Latz, *A Hermannsburg Love Story: Dora's 1935 Journal*, ed. Eric and Ruth Fiebig (Fulham, S.A.: photocopy, Abbotts Copy Centre, 1996), 3.
2 John Strehlow, personal communication, April 2001.
3 T.G.H. Strehlow, diaries [SD], 1933, 1–3. Because Strehlow wrote these diary entries after the event, many of them are undated.
4 SD, 1933, 3. The precise date of the first meeting with Sheila is not clear from Strehlow's diary because his account of the event starts on 'a cold day in May' at Horseshoe Bend. His ordeal with her lasted until November that year. In the account that follows I have paraphrased freely, but the direct speech is verbatim.
5 SD, 5, 6 June 1933.
6 SD, 4 August 1933.
7 SD, 1933, 15–17.
8 SD, 1933, 29, 33.
9 SD, 1933, 37.
10 SD, 1933, 43.
11 SD, 1933, 49.
12 SD, 1933, 52.
13 SD, 1933, 61.
14 SD, 1933, 75.
15 Nicholas Boyle, *Goethe: The Poet and the Age*, vol. 1: *The Poetry of Desire* (Oxford: Clarendon Press, 1991), 168–75.
16 SD, 1933, 79.
17 SD, 19 August 1933.
18 SD, 7 September 1933.
19 See T.G.H. Strehlow, *Songs of Central Australia* (Sydney: Angus & Robertson, 1971), 446–47.
20 Ibid., 73.
21 SD, 20 August 1933.
22 Strehlow to Tindale, December 1933.
23 George Stocking, *After Tylor: British Social Anthropology, 1888–1951* (Madison: University of Wisconsin Press, 1992), passim, and *Observers Observed: Essays on*

Ethnographic Field Work, History of Anthropology, vol. 1 (Madison: University of Wisconsin Press, 1983).

24   P.G. Jones, 'Norman B. Tindale; An Obituary,' *Records of the South Australian Museum*, December 1995, 159–76; N.B. Tindale, 1937 'Native Songs of the South East of South Australia,' *Transactions of the Royal Society of South Australia*, 6 (1937): 107–20.

25   T.G.H. Strehlow, 'Ankotarinja, an Aranda Myth,' *Oceania* IV, no. 2 (1933): 187–200.

26   Ibid., 189.

27   Strehlow, 'Ankotarinja,' 200.

28   Ibid., 190.

29   Ibid., 194.

4   Primal Journeys

Destroying Fathers

DURING 1934—back in Adelaide—Strehlow wrote the papers that
consolidated his reputation. With them he not only demonstrated
his authority in the field, but displayed material that was close to the
personal themes of his life, or which resonated there, in ways he could
hardly account for himself but which permeated him. The papers were
not about language or linguistics. They were about myth and ownership—the network of beliefs involving the *tjurunga*. The first paper,
'Northern Aranda Myths,' which he read to the English Association in
August, focused on the Great Father and his *tjurunga*. It was about the
death of mythic fathers, and the succession of sons. In Freudian terms,
Strehlow was talking about parricide, the deeds of the primal horde.
Freud's famous and ethnographically dubious tract, *Totem and Taboo*, was
published in Vienna in 1913 and Strehlow had a German edition of it
in his swag when he was at Mount Liebig watching the blood-letting
of his first sacred ceremony. Freud's central thesis was that at some stage
of prehistory—in psychic and actual time—sons had to kill their fathers
in order to assert their sexual dominance and their possession of power.
In Strehlow's papers Freud is not mentioned by name.[1] As was to be so
often the case, Strehlow avoided any indication of the source of his
main ideas. But he used the term 'horde' after Freud, as well as 'primal,'

and in the Freudian way asserts that the mythmakers 'have been irresponsible for veiling the more revolting features of a crude but striking picture of life in an early primitive society.'[2]

To make his lurid point about the Great Father, Strehlow relishes the details of the great sire Karora of the Ilbalintja or bandicoot myth. 'My account,' he began by saying, 'had been considerably compressed from the myth as related by my native informants in Aranda; but in translation I have followed the working of the original as faithfully as possible.' Then, having sidestepped the precise nature of his native accounts, his literary version begins: 'In the very beginning everything was resting in perpetual darkness: night oppressed all the earth like an impenetrable thicket. The *gurra* ancestor—his name was Karora—was lying asleep, in everlasting night, at the very bottom of the soak of Ilbalintja.'

It is a creation story, related with biblical overtones, but with pagan intent. Or to put this another way: it once more demonstrates how Strehlow was so at home in the allegoric mode, having chosen, with Freud, the pseudo-scientific fable of origins.[3] His ethnography happily served two purposes: it recounted actual events while at the same time satisfying a deeper structure of feeling in him. It enabled him to enact elective affinities between himself and 'them,' displaying in the process what has always been the case in ethnology: that it is a vaguely theoretical practice (sometimes dressed up as theory) which has always more or less applied European subjectivities to the culture of others; a projection, if you like, of 'personal values.'[4]

The Ilbalintja story is about the father's giving birth to his sons out of a hole in the ground: 'the gaping hole that he left behind became the Ilbalintja soak, filled with the sweet dark juice of the honeysuckle buds.' When the father opens his eyes 'he feels a moving mass of bandicoots all around him. He is now standing more firmly on his feet. He thinks, he desires.'[5]

The father eats the first of his offspring. Later in the story, however, the father gives birth to the first of his 'sons.' Soon he has others, who hunt for him, while each night he continues to give birth to more sons. In this story the sons do not turn on the father by name. Rather, they wound a bandicoot who turns out to be a man—an ancestor creature that is, Strehlow tells us, the symbolic substitute for the bandicoot chief.

The Karora story is Strehlow's first example of 'the primal sire' who is 'mutilated or disabled by his sons.' It is vivid enough, but with a keen dramatic sense Strehlow saves his strongest example till last, when he cites the climax of the *tjilpa* or native cat story. '[N] is left behind deprived of sight, a pitiful half-wit, whose strength has been broken for ever: his eldest son, after breaking through the earth-mound, had chanted magic spells and destroyed the sight of his father, *because the latter had not taken him to his side as his equal,* so that father and son could both have sat at the foot of the tnatantja.'[6]

The italics are Strehlow's and he puts them into his 'condensed' paragraph without explanation. What Strehlow was going on to talk about, really, were the rites according to which the young men were initiated into their patriarchal powers. He refers to 'the veil of secrecy with which the *tjurunga* are invested by their anxious fathers' and how this was used to arouse the curiosity of the adolescent boys. Thereafter, with a detail that prompts one to wonder whether he might have envied the initiates' ordeals of sacred trust, he described the ceremonial ground where the boys 'receive the final stamp of citizenship which entitles them to a recognised place in the social and cultural sphere of their people.'[7] Pride, solemnity, these are the feelings the Aranda ceremonies arouse in the males as they partake in their acts of belonging. All of this, as well as a great deal of suffering—as the boys must endure the rituals of the ceremonial ground for some months. It is there they are circumcised, and confined; there where they are bled, profusely; and where they are burnt by firebrands and made to wait for food.

At this point in his exposition, Strehlow makes the most of one of his main informants during these years—Gurra, a Northern Aranda man whose totem was the bandicoot ancestor of Ilbalintja. Strehlow had met Gurra through the Kramers, as he had met Tom Ljonga. But Gurra, unlike Ljonga, still had loyalties to the traditional ways, and thus becomes a standard reference in Strehlow's expositions. Gurra's memory of this boyhood experience gave him a primal claim on isolation and suffering:

> We used to wait wearily, our stomachs aching with hunger. We did not dare to approach too closely before we had been called. We lived in great terror of our fathers when they were assembled on the inkura ground. At last they would call us. We used to run forward, lay the killed game at the feet of the chief, and join in the dance. Our elders roasted the meat. We could see, from the down still adhering to their bodies, that they had been engaged in other ceremonies during out absence. We

said: 'They must have fashioned great *tjurunga* today.' They would not show them to us; they were too sacred for us; we could not bear their power. We did not dare to question our fathers: our fear was too great.[8]

Strehlow's exposition is charged with detail, for all the world as if he knew very well what it was for a son to suffer at the hands of his father. It was probably the most vivid, best informed description of sacred ceremony for its time, a promise of many more things to come. And it was striking for the coherent way in which myth fitted ritual in the sacred scheme of fathers and sons. For as in the myth, where the father is destroyed, when the son 'breaks through the earth mound' so in the ritual. The earth mound which has been broken through is an allusion to the inkura ceremony where the initiates stage their most triumphant scene with the rala parra (earth penis), 'the greatest of all sacred *tjurunga*, which has tormented them during the weary months of their toil on the inkura ground.' For in that time they have endured fire, hunger, exhaustion over weeks designed to prove themselves deserving of the sacred knowledge of their fathers. Now, with all that done, 'They seize the pole in a body, move it up and down horizontally in front of their chests, and dance savagely around the earth mound with the pole placed on their shoulders. They "weary it and exhaust their strength" before "rudely" stripping its decorations, and throwing it away. They dance this success in single file . . . The great *tjurunga* has been shattered; its spell has been broken; its power is no more.'[9]

Freud himself could not have dreamed a text more thematically expressive of his grand thesis. It is as if Strehlow had so assimilated *Totem and Taboo* that his material could speak no language other than Freud's. There is one pause in his application of Freudian misanthropy however. Strehlow constructs an antidote to the dark story. He was drawn to composing two exceptional pages on what he calls 'The Golden Age.' He builds this up, he says, 'from *descriptive touches* found in these Northern Aranda legends and their chant verses' (emphasis added). The picture adds up to a 'highly idealised picture' of a time when the totemic ancestors lived a life of idleness in a land of plenty, when honeysuckle not only flowed from trees, and gleamed from foliage like blood, but dripped like sweat from the arms of an ancestor. Strehlow cites one myth about mulga parrots and kangaroos and feasting and waking, where 'the kangaroos drink the water which is brought to them by mulga parrots in the shape of women.'

So much for the native's own desire for happiness, Strehlow writes, and declares his totemic world to be 'the unattainable Golden world of the native himself; the age in which they live is the Golden Age of his dreams.'[10]

This is said with the minimum of ethnographic detail, and it seems designed not only to compensate for the unmitigated 'theft, robbery and murder' that dominate the myths,[11] but to make it even clearer to his readers that he is writing allegorically. He is telling their story, and bringing to it his own, both culturally and perhaps personally. Culturally, there is almost no end to echoes for Strehlow. One might start with Schiller: 'All people that have a history have a paradise, a state of innocence, a golden age. Moreover, every single man has his paradise, his golden age, which he recollects with more or less rapture according to his more or less poetic nature.' From the Romantics the line of thought goes back through time and space, from the here and now to Arcadia, Eden, Heaven, according to one's golden thread of discourse. Strehlow's honeyed terms sound closer to his sense of the Classics, his dreamers closer to pagan hedonisms than any sense of God, but the general location of his thought is clear. He is speaking in the long tradition of allegory which idealises primitivism, locates it in the pastoral tradition and, as we shall see, sets up the major paradigm of 'the discontent of the civilised with civilisation' which was to be central to Strehlow's later thought.[12]

All that said, however, and in only two pages, Strehlow returns with a kind of backlash at his own dualism, to speak again of primitive modes of conduct, and of death. Here again is the personal pull of the primal story. That the mythic son took a wife after his disposal of his father is an irresistible interpretation. As in ritual so, it would appear, in Strehlow's life, since he had by then taken a wife. He had completed the Freudian trajectory, having disposed of his father.* Strehlow's Freudianism shapes the content and the movement of his narrative.

More prosaically, in these early talks, and also when they were later published as a book, Strehlow conspicuously avoids any substantial reference to the work of his father. A Great Father of Australian ethnology in Germany barely rates a footnote. Strehlow might have said,

---

* Conjecture 'irresistible' to John Morton, who writes (personal communication, October 2000): 'Once Ted symbolically kills his father, he claims for himself a wife . . . Now this not only reproduced the whole "primal" scenario—the father is killed to gain access to females, it is also exactly what happens in the ceremonial round. After circumcision, the circumciser (ideally the boy's father-in-law) "repays" the boy for "killing him" with his wife (his daughter).'

by way of defensive explanation, that he was reporting on Northern Aranda myth, not the Western Aranda that was the subject of his father's studies. But that is half my point: he chose the area that led him away from his father; and, even in the more general discussion of myths and *tjurunga*, avoided almost all mention of the earlier foundational thinking. Strehlow's whole, precocious exposition of the Aranda's Great Father served the purpose of demonstrating his usurpation of his own father.

And, as chance had it, an opportunity arose in this period for Strehlow to help his father's work be published for the first time in English. Fitzherbert wrote to him about publishing the handwritten translation done by Charles Chewings and held at the University of Adelaide.* Tindale thought it a good idea, and wanted to illustrate it with some of Gillen's photographs. 'He also wants me,' Fitzherbert went on, obviously oblivious to Strehlow's twitching at the Gillen idea, 'to revise the theology in the direction of the ideas of some modern anthropologists; but as I am not an anthropologist I am not prepared to do that: in any case it would, I think, be a totally unjustifiable action.'[13]

The idea got barely a murmur from Strehlow. Fitzherbert brought it up again in May 1938, with the Clarendon Press in the wings. Nothing came of that. Strehlow was as still as a spear. He said hardly a word to indicate he would put anything into seeing his father's work into English. He had, for the moment, danced around and beyond his father, having initiated himself to the point of being able to command the ceremonial ground.†

---

*   Explorer, geologist and anthropologist, Adelaide-educated Charles Chewings (1859–1937) polished his German at the University of Heidelberg in 1891, when he was continuing his studies in geology. He knew Central Australia and its people well, having explored much of the region by camel in an unsuccessful effort to discover lucrative mineral deposits. In retirement after the Great War he published *Back to the Stone Age* (1936), completed a manuscript of an Aranda grammar, and translated the work of Carl Strehlow, the manuscripts of which he left with the University of Adelaide.

†   The loaded question arises about the unacknowledged uses to which Strehlow put his father's work. Dick Kimber in his biographical entry (Northern Territory Dictionary of Biography 1992: 2:205) says that Strehlow 'did not substantially plagiarise.' Kimber seems to be implying substantial overlaps, reworkings and assimilation of the father's in the son's work, not unlike the processes involved in some of my narrative with its dependence on Strehlow's diaries. In any case, as already suggested, Strehlow's own work had substantially gone beyond his father's. If, perchance, an English edition of Pastor Carl's work stood side by side with *Aranda Traditions* and *Songs of Central Australia* the texts would be in conversation with each other, complementing each other in dialogue rather than stealing each other's fire. Upon his father's foundations Strehlow built his mansion, which he then lit in his own ambivalent terms.

Inheritance of Sons

When Strehlow turned to *tjurunga* ownership, about which he spoke at the ANZAAS conference in Melbourne in January 1935, he had a wider brief. What the first talk did to fathers, this one did for mothers: considerable attention is given to the ways in which *tjurunga* ownership was determined by a man's conception site, the place and psychological state that pertained to the mother on her travels through the country. 'A woman,' Strehlow said, somewhat ahead of his time, 'by reason of her conception site, may be entitled to a position of supreme authority in her own community, she may be the owner of the most sacred tjurunga treasured by her clan, but all knowledge of them is carefully hidden away from her.'[14] In myth the deathless body of the woman—the *tjurunga*—might be revered, and in mythology the men sometimes lived in constant terror of the magical powers of female ancestors; and indeed in the rituals themselves much seems to have been designed to appropriate the powers of women. But in life, 'Aranda men look down upon women with a certain measure of pitying contempt.'[15]

Strehlow began with a very wide definition of *tjurunga*, since the Aranda might use the term to encompass, not just their carved boards and stones but their ceremonial pole, the ceremonial headgear, ground painting and the earth mound, as well as the sacred chants and the whole ceremony itself. To speak of *tjurunga* ownership was therefore to speak of ownership of the ritual itself: the secret-sacred ritual that initiated men into religious belief. Ownership in this context was a truism: it was by virtue of belonging to the culture that ownership was established. Ownership was a matter of inalienable identity (my terms, not Strehlow's). But at the same time *tjurunga* did specifically refer to the objects that Strehlow had been so avidly collecting—though he did not mention this activity in his talk, or indeed in *Aranda Traditions* when it was published many years later. Ownership in this context went to the heart of the question of legitimacy of his collecting. For if objects were collectively owned, could they be given away, even in trust?

Strehlow was adamant. 'These sacred stone and wooden objects, myths, ceremonies and chants, are amongst the few forms of property which may be owned legitimately by individual persons in Central Australia.'[16] There would be problems (to put it mildly) in years to come about this proposition. But from where Strehlow stood in 1935 the situation was clear. The 'regulations' which governed ownership were 'intricate' but they were regulations that he understood, and which validated his collecting. He did not say this outright, because he did not have to, having not mentioned his collecting per se. In his paper he went to some lengths explaining the ancestral claims his main informants—Gurra (from northern area), Njitia and Makarinja (from country near Horseshoe Bend)—had on their *tjurunga*. The point was to show how individualised such claims were, and how subject they might be to disagreement between men. A man knew that a *tjurunga* was his by exhaustive reference to lineage to the ancestor creature, his own ancestors, his clan, a site, a song—and so on. To put this another way: his property claim was inseparable from a profound knowledge claim, so that any decision, say, to give a *tjurunga* to someone else was a deeply considered, responsible act of freedom on the part of its owner.

Again, these were not Strehlow's terms at the time. In 1935 circumstances had not yet rendered him a defensive recipient of sacred goods. But they were the purport of his talk. It was as if, in one paper, he had tabled the tragic downfall of fathers, at least at the mythic level: now he had sketched the rightful basis of a son's inheritance, even if the 'son' in this case was himself, insofar as he had been trusted with the *tjurunga*. It went without saying in this paper that only extreme circumstances—tragic ones, in fact—led to such a state of affairs. The *tjurunga* were freely given because their owners had clearly seen that the white man's culture had broken the continuity of their own. Once broken—so Strehlow argued from the many things the senior Aranda men said—broken for ever: that was tragedy at another level. Aboriginal freedom, so eloquently expressed by Tom Ljonga, was the sad recognition of this necessity.

In manifold ways, then, as early as 1935 reality for Strehlow already had different layers of tragedy written into it. Not simply because of his romantic sensibility and romantic experiences, or because the young man unresolvedly grieved for his father, but also because there was an aspect of Aranda culture which accentuated tragedy that was, in turn, compounded by colonial history. A double emphasis was on ill-fatedness.

Not long after his experience at Ulamba, Strehlow expressed his considered opinion that the Aranda were 'not so much a primitive as a decadent race.' He was holding forth to the English Association in Adelaide, speaking 'from a fullness of fresh knowledge.'[17] By that he meant that they were tied by the 'rigid bonds of tradition' which 'firmly fettered' chant, myth and ceremony to landscape and had been so thoroughly preconceived by 'the absolute authority of the old men' that there was no room for the imagination. Thus: 'We can readily

understand the attitude of utter apathy and the general mental stagnation that exist amongst the present generation of the natives as far as
literary efforts of any kind whatsoever are concerned.'[18]

This is now a contentious statement, in the light of some of the
continuities of Aboriginal culture. It is also a puzzling one, in that
Strehlow's field diaries, as well as his autobiography, do not really
demonstrate 'utter apathy' and 'general mental stagnation.' What they
demonstrate is the grief and desperation of the men parting with their
tjurunga. Once their songs were activated they 'sang lustily' and became
'young again.'

On the Aborigines' own tragic sense, no one has put it better than
W.H. Stanner when he wrote of the Murinbata, the people around Port
Keats, that through their myths they saw reality 'as a joyous thing with
maggots at the centre.' Stanner, perhaps influenced by *Aranda Traditions*,
was speaking of the poetic unities in Aboriginal culture, of the ways in
which 'mythopoetic thought is probably a continuous function of
Aboriginal mentality.' In the rite he was examining he was struck by
how the poetic mode could embody both celebration and 'continuing
tragedy in human affairs.'[19]

Stanner drew back from big generalities about Aboriginal religion
and tragedy, and indeed about religion itself and tragedy. But these were
necessary academic reservations. His own poetic choice of metaphor—
reality was a joyous thing with maggots at the centre—carried the weight. A
similar weight belonged to Strehlow's intellectual structures by 1934;
his discourse on the Aranda was permeated with his own tragic sense,
and the shapes of his own thought were continuously mythopoetic. He
was both agent and captive of the elegaic, allegorical mode.

A Joyous Thing

In his own life there came a joyous thing. According to Ward McNally,
the biographer who had the complicated benefit of being able to speak
with Strehlow towards the end of Strehlow's life, it happened on the
dance floor at the university—an occasion sponsored by his old hockey
team. 'He went and was surprised to see Bertha there.'

Bertha James had been at university when Strehlow was in hot
pursuit of the 'English' debutantes. He had met her then, and liked her:
he had been impressed with her intelligence and level of interest in his
work, especially when he got the news that he would be going to
Central Australia to conduct research. From the Centre they had

written each other letters: in fact, he had been pleased to get a letter from Bertha when he was at Horseshoe Bend, and had to tuck the letter away when Sheila walked into the room.

While dancing with Bertha, Strehlow learnt that his first love, Sheila, had married.

'You must remember him,' Bertha said, The young policeman—the man with the black curly hair.'

'She married him!' Strehlow spluttered. 'That damn ignorant Irishman!'

'He isn't ignorant, Ted. He's a very nice man, and he has a wonderful sense of humour.'

'I found him ignorant,' Strehlow repeated. As they circled the dance floor, he castigated himself for being stupid, admitting to himself that he had taken too much for granted, and that, anyway, he had little in common with city girls.

'I should have known better. My place is back in the desert with the aborigines. I was a fool to think I could interest a girl like Sheila, a sophisticated city-bred girl,' he said.

'Don't be silly, Ted!' Bertha replied. 'You're a very nice man. Lots of girls would be proud to have you as their boyfriend. Besides, your work is fascinating . . . You've got courage, real courage.' She was silent for a moment, then looked up at him and continued: 'As a matter of fact, I think Sheila was foolish letting you slip through her fingers.'

Strehlow looked down at Bertha as though seeing her as a beautiful young woman for the first time. His grip around her waist tightened a little and he asked, 'What about you, Bertha? Would you have let me slip though your fingers?'

'No, Ted. I don't think I would have.'[20]

McNally, who seems to have based his debonair sketch on Bertha's information, reports that that evening 'Strehlow courted Bertha with a fervour that surprised friends.' As well he might: he had not only fibbed to her about the nature and significance of Sheila his 'desert maiden' now denied as a city girl, he had, potentially, insulted the chances of city-bred Bertha. But then Bertha had reassured him of her interests and in his lovelessness that seems to have been more than enough for him.

Bertha told McNally that Strehlow seemed shy and self-effacing at first. (Competitive and a touch arrogant, too, she might have felt after his outburst on the dance floor.) It was when he showed her some of his diaries and photographs from the Centre that her positive opinion consolidated. 'I was fascinated. I learnt from Ted's diaries the hardships he had often had to endure to perform his work. And I began seeing him in a different light—as a man of courage and compassion, with a great depth of understanding of, and love for, his Aboriginal friends.'

In her he had a find. She was touched by his compassion because she was, herself, a naturally generous, warm-hearted woman. She was one of the University of Adelaide's first female graduates, had done well at her studies, and had chosen to make a life of teaching. She was comfortably at home in Adelaide's 'English' establishment: she had been educated at St Peter's school and her father was a successful accountant. Her mother had died when she was eight and the woman her father had then married was mentally unstable and at times institutionalised. That experience, it seemed, developed skills in Bertha that few women of her age had: of coping with the highly strung and sick of heart.

And she could sing. This was another gift for Strehlow. Bertha's grandfather, Charles Pugh James, staged amateur performances of Gilbert and Sullivan in towns such as Mount Gambier and Broken Hill, and her uncle Arnold James sang solo for the Belgian King when he visited Australian troops during the Great War. In a way, Bertha was already launched on a singing career: she was giving concerts in the Adelaide Town Hall and getting good reviews.*

For the rest of the year she was his steady partner and the following year they became engaged to be married. 'When he asked me to marry him,' Bertha told McNally, 'and I said I would, he told me he was delighted that I was agreeable to go to the Outback with him. I think he honestly thought he was going to have to give up the work he loved so much.'[21]

They were married at Prospect on 21 December 1935. Three weeks later they were on the Ghan, rattling north.

---

* In addition, John Strehlow informs me (personal communication, April 2001): 'She and TG performed (in private) all manner of songs together . . . One such was I think called "Wagon Wheels." TG and B also loved Gilbert and Sullivan operas and had operas such as the Mikado, The Yeomen of the Guard, etc. . . . They also—during the 30s—liked the Blues and used to dance to records from their collection while at the tent at Jay Creek. TG's favourite song was apparently "Nobody Knows What Troubles I've Seen," though I never heard him play it.'

Farce of an Inquiry

By the time Strehlow returned to the Centre as a married man his dealings with Aborigines had gained another dimension. He had been a member of a commission of inquiry into police misconduct, an experience that inspired him to a rather cynical analysis of communications on the frontier.

In 1934 a Pitjantjatjara man called Jokanana was shot by a police party at Ayers Rock. Jokanana and three others were on the run from Constable William McKinnon, who had arrested them and two others for murder at Mount Connor four days before. McKinnon, a keen 32-year-old already with a reputation for brutality towards Aborigines, hunted them down with resolve.

The murdered man was Kai-Umen, from the Olgas, and he was killed, McKinnon was told, because he had told sacred secrets to white men. No other weapons but sticks and stones were used, his captives said. The constable dug up the body and cut off its head—the better to have identification back in Alice Springs. There the matter might have rested except that later, when examining the skull, McKinnon heard the rattle of a bullet inside. One of his men still in chains, Numberlin, made the crucial admission that brought the white man's law into full play.

The rifle belonged to a white man, Robert Hughes, a dingo scalper. The 'dogger' had lent Numberlin his gun when they were camping together at Mount Connor. Numberlin said he wanted to shoot kangaroo, and Hughes let him go off with two cartridges. When Numberlin came back with one cartridge and no kangaroo, Hughes was uneasy; when Kai-Umen's body was found, suspicion turned to alarm. That a white man's weapon had been used now made it imperative that the other offenders be brought in.

Jokanana was wounded while escaping but had made his way across country to the shelter of the Rock. But when he heard the police coming his wounds prevented him from crawling as far into the cave as the others. The men inside heard the footsteps. 'Then someone called something from outside. The man in the cave called out, "Wait, I'll finish this bastard." Shots were fired. After that more shots were fired into the cave, but none of the police party would go right inside into the darkness.' Jokanana was dead but the other others lay low until the police left. Then they buried him, hid their *tjurunga* that were too heavy to carry, and ran south, far south to Mimili station in South Australia.[22]

The incident was instant bad news for the Northern Territory authorities. Only seven years earlier the region had been scandalised by the Coniston massacre, and the official cover-up that followed. Political reality of 1935 demanded that any inquiry now conducted be seen to be authentic. Already McKinnon was in the bad books for allegedly beating natives at Hermannsburg, so that the shooting at the Rock invited a double investigation. The chairman was the Adelaide professor of pathology, John Cleland. The others included Vin White, a respected public servant from the Northern Territory, and, to appease the troublesome humanitarian lobby down south, the Reverend John Sexton from the Aborigines' Friends' Association in Adelaide. A young man, a postman by profession and amateur anthropologist in the making, Charles Mountford, was to be secretary. Strehlow agreed to be translator and to become, in Cleland's words, 'a guide to native mentality and understanding.'[23]

It was the job of the inquiry to tour the area taking evidence, all the while presenting what might be called the kinder face of white man's law. In an atmosphere of affable forbearance—hearty bushmen together—Constable McKinnon went with them. On their camels and in their stop-start motor vehicle they made their slow way through the sandhill country to the Rock, stopping at places where they could talk to Aboriginal men. In the wobbly black-and-white film taken at the time—Strehlow's first home movie—the men can been seen in a huddle with the flies, enduring the heat and the dust as well as the often circuitous ways of Aboriginal communication.

Strehlow's initial feelings are clear from his journal entry for early June, when his Romantic reflexes had to contend with some gruesome reality.

> The Rock was reached at last, the goal of my boyhood dreams—the shadow of a great rock in a weary land, and how welcome it was. All hushed tonight, only the moon is shining down upon the great black walls of the rock—and one feels that the Land of God is indeed near. It is like the great silence of eternity. And nearby lies the body of the dead man; and that body has brought us hither to this vast pile that shall endure long after our own bodies will be only dim scattered dust, known to no man, forgotten by all save God alone who moulded them first even as He fashioned this great Rock, that sleeps tonight in a still moon dream.

Next day he was obliged to face unpleasant facts more directly:

> The body of Jokanana was exhumed by McKinnon, White and the Pro-
> fessor this morning, and will be taken back by the Professor.
>
> The camels strayed last night, and Walker and Carbine brought them
> back only about 3 p.m. So no inquiry was held in the afternoon, the
> party having already dispersed in order to view the Rock.
>
> Saw the scene of the final tragedy today. I was greatly shocked by the
> way in which poor Jokanana met his death—a poor, hunted creature, shot
> callously at least twice in the cave, without being able to defend his life or
> to escape. And now he is being taken back—his bones and head wrapped
> up in a calico parcel; his vitals, lungs, blood, entrails, liquefying flesh in a
> large billy can. And that is permitted by our white man's civilisation.[24]

It was a brutal killing at the Rock, and Strehlow's note to himself makes
no bones about it as he sat on his swag under the great black walls of the
Rock in the moonlight and the silence of eternity. After the exhumation
Mountford was also registering his private horror. 'Cleland did not wish
to take more evidence. I wonder why he accepted this position. He is
much more interested in the disappearance of the mulga than that of the
native.' Mountford was 'savage at J. Cleland's attempt to shield
McKinnon, when White had him cornered,' and even more disillusioned
when Cleland called him over to his camp to take dictation. 'He,
however, dictated to me, the whole report relating to the shooting
(without consulting either of the members of the board).'[25]

Both young men were writing their indictments into their diaries as
McKinnon was sitting in friendly fashion nearby. Only six days earlier
Strehlow had turned 27 and had been delighted to record in his private
journal that McKinnon had 'smilingly given me some of our boiled
sweets as a birthday present.' On the way back, McKinnon had a
birthday and the party treated him to a special dinner of the last of the
plum pudding and radishes.

When they reached Alice Springs the camaraderie of the white
investigators held firm. Here they are at the prison, conducting the last
stages of their inquiry in a bleak tin shed, as an icy wind chilled
everyone's bones, despite overcoats. Strehlow wrote:

> Numberlin, Nantji [Nangee], Panna, Saltpetre, Munty, and a few of
> others were re-examined, without results. There was, however, one great

dramatic moment in the bleak tin shed, when Numberlin alleged that McKinnon had come to his cell before the arrival of the Board, and persuaded him to give false evidence—to tell the Board that McKinnon had never hit him, and had always been kind to him etc. Old Panna caused some mirth in the court room later on. Mr White asked him why he had told Dr Kirkland a lie about his broken arm. Panna then told the interpreter [Syd Walker] how it had happened. Dr Kirkland had come to him and had said to him (here Panna cleverly imitated the agitated tones of the Doctor), 'Tell the truth, tell the truth, tell the truth.' At this Panna got such a fright that he told him a whole lot of lies. This must have happened to most of the witnesses whom the Board interviewed.[26]

Throughout, the white man's bantering mirth—an atmosphere of winks and nods about police brutality—is implicit. Strehlow was glad when it was all over and told his diary that the whole inquiry was a farce.

Numberlin and Nangee were both sentenced to ten years' imprisonment by Judge Wells on 21 February 1936, a savage punishment in the circumstances.

The other official outcome was equivocating. On the Hermannsburg incident, Cleland reported that 'at the request of Mr Mattner, a responsible officer at the Hermannsburg Mission station, Constable W. McKinnon, after hesitation, inflicted corporal punishment on certain Aborigines . . . These boys had been reported to have been troublesome. Nevertheless, the infliction of such corporal punishment is illegal, being an assault if not done with magisterial authority. Constable McKinnon denied that he struck these natives, stating that he simply held the rope in his hands, but did not apply it to them.'[27] After this perfunctory summary, Cleland added: 'White witnesses on oath and many native witnesses spoke highly of Constable McKinnon's general humane treatment of natives.'

As to the murder of Jokanana, Cleland found that the shooting was legally justified, though not warranted under the circumstances. Shooting 'should be resorted to only when all other possible methods of recapture have been exhausted.' No charges were to be laid. Submitting the report to the Commonwealth Department of the Interior, Cleland opined that 'the Northern Territory has progressed further than any part of Australia towards the solution to the native problem.' It was, all things considered, a whitewash.

But the recommendations of the Cleland Inquiry were another

matter: they implied that something did have to be done about disorder on the frontier, that Aborigines had to be protected from white assaults, and that their plight on what was once their home lands called for ration stations to be established west of Alice Springs so as to 'stem the tide of migration of the outback natives to the civilised areas where they become detribalised.'

With all this in mind the committee had a proposal—one that was to have a definitive impact on Strehlow's life. Rather than have a policeman patrol the area of 15,000 square miles with a resident white population of less than 30, there should be 'an officer belonging to the Department of the Protector of Aborigines.' Such an officer would be 'specially selected for his knowledge of native languages and customs, and knowledge of bush craft. If such an officer were a special magistrate, most of the trouble arising from the natives might be settled.' The committee wanted the officer to be empowered 'to authorise a reasonable whipping, which would be carried out under his supervision with the old men of the tribe,' and that might be supervised by a 'special police officer,' also to be appointed.[28]

This new position—patrol officer—was both pivotal and potentially impotent. But this was not clear to its proponents at the time. Immediately the right man for the job was canvassed, and, as must have been obvious when Cleland was drafting the report after his weeks in the field with a young man already well versed in native language and bushcraft, the first choice was Strehlow.

Born Actors

Strehlow had done something else before going inland with his bride. In *Oceania*, he tabled his views about communications on the frontier. He called it, as if to place it as supplementary alternative equal in status to the Cleland report, 'Notes on Native Evidence and its Value.'[29] It is a firmly written anecdotal piece that begins: 'The value of native evidence is difficult to assess without full consideration of the circumstances in which it was given' . . .

> If a native is examined by a white man whom he regards for any reason as being either unsympathetic or antagonistic to his cause, he will normally give evasive or even untrue replies to the questions of his interrogator. The native, if he senses any approaching trouble, will try to escape it by protesting his ignorance in the most innocent manner or

by denying emphatically all charges and accusing questions directed against him. The native's first and strongest reaction will be to extricate himself at all costs from any approaching embarrassment or future serious consequences. If lies will achieve his purpose, he will not hesitate to resort to them. Dissimulation comes naturally to him; for he is a born actor of a very high order. He can assume an air of surprised ignorance or injured innocence with a perfection that would impress the minds of the most sophisticated of his questioners.

Drawing on several of his own earlier experiences with natives, Strehlow says that when it came to telling the truth, or giving evidence, what a native says depended on the trustworthiness of the white person, the relative stranger asking the questions. If the stranger is held in esteem or respect, well and good, the native will be candidly informative. If not, then it makes common kin-sense for the native to lie, to dissemble or evade, especially since 'the natives are naturally suspicious of the good intentions of strange white men because they have been frequently deceived and exploited and robbed by unscrupulous whites.'

One story Strehlow told against himself. It concerned the moment out near Mount Liebig, when he felt like hitting a native over the head with a rifle (a temptation he passes over in *Oceania*), preferring to say that he was 'getting furious' with the English speaking man who would not point him towards Titus' camp. But there was reason in the man's method. He was stalling, treating Strehlow as a stranger until he found out who he was, because two other white men, complete strangers, had recently plundered Titus' camp. The man, who turned out to have grown up at Hermannsburg, and was a few years older than Strehlow, then 'recognised' him. 'He brought me some emu eggs and asked me if I wanted them. He was all politeness and contrition.' And Strehlow adds that the man's replies, 'it will be noted, were merely evasive and misleading, not actually untrue; he was a Christianised native, and was careful not to tell lies openly.'[30]

Furthermore, Strehlow spoke unambiguously about the most sensitive area of social reality in the Territory, on the sexual relations between the races:

The white man takes away his women and lives with them; but he does not fulfil any of the traditional obligations towards the native relatives of those women. White scientists, under the promise of deepest secrecy towards all women, obtain the sacred objects of the black man and are admitted to his sacred ceremonies; but the native soon sees his treasured sacred objects in the hands of white women, and hears the scoffs of other whites about his ceremonies. These experiences embitter the natives; and, just as the average white settler commonly classes all natives together when speaking about them, so the native regards all white persons as members of *one* people—of a people whose main character- istics are greed and deceitfulness and immorality.[31]

White men, black women, sacred objects, white women, bitterness . . . this bead chain about trust, articulated when he was a young, unmarried collector in the field of the traditional, was to resonate throughout Strehlow's life. Few people but Strehlow could have written this at the time. Many a settler, including his own father, had labelled the natives as untrustworthy and whatnot—treacherous, ungrateful, lazy were the key words of deprecation, all proof that much was lacking in the communi- cation between the races. On the face of things each group acting according to different values and rules of communication might remain a mystery to the other. So at one level Strehlow was confirming the obvious—but with a difference. He was writing closer to the Aboriginal understanding of social encounters, and was doing so with a keen sense of the imbalances of power in colonial history. Against uncomprehend- ing social distance, he was implying another option; a notion of delicately grounded trust, trust that might be described as a notion of civility.[32]

Officially, the authorities had no reason but to be pleased with the idea of their appointment of T.G.H. Strehlow as their first patrol officer in Central Australia. But reading between the lines of this deceptively academic paper they might well have taken pause. They had appointed a linguistically proficient young bushman all right: there was none better. But they would have on their hands someone as internally com- plicated, really, as the whole business of translating on the colonial frontier.

Maggots at the Centre
In February 1936 Strehlow took Bertha out to Hermannsburg where they made house at the mission. The Albrechts and the natives took her in. 'My wife has Ruth as helper in house and kitchen,' the proud husband reported. They went walking along the Finke, one day going as far as the bend it takes towards Palm Valley, and on another glorious

day they strolled upstream towards the gift of water at Kaporilja.

'Lovely' was a word that entered Strehlow's diary for the first time. It became a refrain. He might write late and was able to report: 'Very tired but still very happy.' He took her camping for the first time and they were there after good rains—lovely rains—when the Finke was in glorious flow. 'My wife and I walked down and saw the flood in the silver gleam of moonlight.'[33] It was romance become real. He had never been happier, and possibly extremely happy for the first time in his life.

News then came of his appointment as Patrol Officer for Central Australia, which lightened his spirits even more. 'I should be very glad indeed if I could get a position which would enable me to put my life at the service of the interests of the natives of my old home.'

Bertha was learning to type, and Strehlow was busy with some of the old men, who gave him a large collection of *tjurunga*. Then, in May, they heard that he had got the job. The Melbourne *Herald* had reported it under the heading, 'Playmate of Blacks Becomes Protector,' and its news story was a prophetic, if crude, version of the heroic script Strehlow cultivated for the rest of his life.* Congratulatory telegrams from his parents-in-law. Another from Mountford: 'Heartiest congratulations the Aborigine of Central Australia is indeed lucky.' Soon he would be told what to do in his first job as a patrol officer. Meanwhile he had his research work to finish, and that would involve another journey to Horseshoe Bend, and beyond.

They left on 5 June, packed on the five camels, along with three Aboriginal men: Ljonga and Witchetty and George Tjinapatala. He was elated with the loveliness of the country, 'as in a dream,' its glow and its lushness as they made their way down the Finke to Irbmanjkara, or Running Waters, the most reliable of watering places in the whole region. They camped there and he reflected on the number of times the ancient songs of 'the ancestors re-echoed from the cliffs [and how]

---

* 'Mr Strehlow's appointment comes at a time when he is engaged in Central Australia on a most important scientific task—recording the passing of one of the last surviving stone age races. Sitting down with the oldest men of the tribes around camp fires and wurlies Mr Strehlow has been gathering the secrets and lore of the Arandas. It will be scientifically recorded. / Perhaps the greatest accomplishment has been the mastering of the Aranda language. He can speak the dialect as well as the natives themselves, and he writes the language. / During the recent trial of two natives at Alice Springs the Court was unable to understand phrases used by one of the witnesses despite the presence of native interpreters. Mr Strehlow from the body of the Court was able to explain what the native meant' (Melbourne *Herald*, 30 April 1936).

many times have the slim, quick feet . . . walked quietly through the dense thickets of gums and reeds that are the glory of Running Waters; the last great rally of the Northern, Southern, and Western Aranda took place within a view of the stony ridge where the river takes a plunge to the south; all is stillness now,—silence, oblivion, the beauty of death brood over the clear waters of Irbmanjkara.'[34]

Death was not with them, however, at least not yet. They remain light hearted and happy, even though their pet euro, Wendy, is playing up terribly. She will not walk with them, and fusses in the direction of the camels, so they have to put her back in a bag, which was not the best way for the cuddly thing to travel. The country remains lovely. Even the parched, barren stretch towards the Bend cannot affect their spirits. From camp site to camp site the newlyweds moved south, revelling, it would seem, in the adventure. There is a lovely minute or two of black-and-white footage Strehlow took of them about this time, the camera doting on a laughing Bertha sitting up in her swag, the man behind the camera obviously her source of delight, the new bride gaily rising to his attentions [see Plate 35]. He always refers to her through these diaries as his wife or 'my wife,' sometimes 'my dear wife'—never as Bertha. She is denoted as an act of possession.

Even when they reach the Bend, all remains well. No diary entries about his father, or Sheila, his other great loss.

Mrs Elliot was full of welcome. The only sad thing was that Wendy had been re-named Hoppety, and is the subject of a harsh decision. She will have to be left behind as she was so unmanageable and a risk to the camels. Much love had been shed on her by both husband and wife, but for her it would be 'Journey's End.'

Strehlow wants to meet up with some of the old men of three years earlier but none were around, so after a few days resting at the Bend they go further south. Now a certain weariness began to set in; the realities of travelling with camels, breaking camp each morning, the loading and the unloading, the mending of camel boxes and saddles, begin to take their toll. 'Very tiring for my wife and myself,' he notes but without indicating that there might be anything wrong with his wife but tiredness.

They reach Macumba. There they must wait for a few days, still in search of the knowledgeable Aranda men. Impatiently he waits for the old men to make contact with him when an urgent word comes from his new authorities. A telegram—delivered via the railway station at

Charlotte Waters—instructs him to look into reports that a German prospector near Lasseter's Reef has been shooting natives. Strehlow's instructions are to follow tracks as far as he must, and the site of the offence is supposed to be 400 miles off at Piltardi Rockhole in the Petermanns, far to the west of Ayers Rock, well into the Commonwealth's Aboriginal reserve: an expedition away, a major trek, for which they will get government supplies up by train to Charlotte Waters. More waiting.

Bertha's weakness has set in. She will have good days, which her husband celebrates, but by the time they set off he is recording the naked truth about her condition. She is pregnant. He writes out of worry for her, and the possible loss of his 'heir.'

Even before they set off from Macumba he records, 'My wife cried in bed tonight.'[35] Next night, 'I am weary and my wife is asleep in bed. Poor dear, it's too strenuous for her,—the toil never ceases, she is not used to it as I am.'

Finally—though the horrors have barely begun—they set off, across rough country, unforgiving country. Maggots must be dug out of the backs of one camel. Crows had dug into the flesh of another. Off the back of one camel 'the boys' shot one crow, but that is hardly enough to scare the flock. They would have to watch over the others more efficiently. Another of their camels has a hole bitten out of it by a travelling companion and there are maggots in that, too: Strehlow takes to the wound with Condy's crystals.

Then, in a spasm of movement, they might come into greener country—'lovely' again—and that lifted the spirits. Bertha sometimes comes good. 'My wife had a splendid day today,' he tells himself on 28 June, but when she stepped off Ranji, at sunset, 'she suddenly felt sick and then she had to go to bed at once.' Strehlow rose early and gave her breakfast in bed. They have many miles to go even before reaching Mount Connor. After that they have to get through the sand-dune country and then way beyond that, where no one could guarantee water. From here they are joined by another helpful Aboriginal guide, an old man called Tjutjunana.

Strehlow is beginning to talk to his diary about gloom and failure. His wife is bleeding. His Aboriginal men are nervous about going into new country and express fears about the dangers of some white men. Strehlow shows them the scorn he thinks they deserve.

He is wishing that he was bearing up better for his wife's sake. It is

8 July by then. His spirits rise when he makes bread, but late at night around midnight—after he had been walking all day, and yet holding to his diary entries with religious regularity—they plummet.

'Lord, help.'

'My wife heard her first dingo howling last night, and shuddered at its sickening, wailing cry.'[36]

They had come, Strehlow assesses the next day, 500 miles since Macumba. In effect, he is saying that they have come 500 miles since his wife fell ill and fear set in. Still, there are hopeful days. 'My wife washed . . .' 'My wife cut my hair today, and I cut hers.' And then, the next day, 'Bertha was up to ironing.' One of the boys shot a rabbit and they had their first fresh meat for many days. 'She has been improving since the last week,' he tells himself. There is some hope at that moment, even though they had been on the track for ten weeks and were still weeks away from tracking their German quarry.

On 28 August, the twelfth week of her pregnancy, Bertha tells him that her trouble had come again. 'The blow had staggered us. Cruel blow, it came after we thought all danger was past. Our only hope is in the mercy of God. Surely He will not forsake us in the wilderness. Our faith has been sorely shaken; but we know that he can spare us. Lord, help!'

Strehlow's fear, his 'cold terror,' is that they will have to trek so far west they will not have the water to get back. 'It was too awful, I could not bear to think about these things; and yet I could not turn my thoughts away from death and thirst.'[37]

'I PRAY? to God, but my prayers gave me little comfort at first. Gradually I regained some of my faith, and went to sleep like a tired little boy.' Next day was a wonderful day and they picked up the German's tracks. They followed these tracks—of three men—until they found the remains of a camp. It was about two months old, although the tracks were more recent. They headed into the granite hills to the north, but, given their supplies, it was too dangerous to go further in that direction. Strehlow decided to give up the chase on 31 August. They were now at Pitalda, and decided at last to turn back, tackling the spinifex and dune country in the direction of the Olgas. Oh Lord, help, Strehlow wrote, not knowing that the worst for Bertha was still to come.

September 4, after they had gone to bed, was 'a night of horror.'

He woke up to hear his wife groaning loudly, fierce pains in her lower abdomen; she was tortured for hours before rising to vomit, gaining some relief, and then again gripped by pain. 'It was horrible. She was calm and courageous, clear-headed, though the pains immediately set in again . . . I got out of bed. It was bitterly cold. The moon was shining high in the sky and its dim light was poured over our agony in the dark mulga scrub.' Then again, another round of agony for her, with him mopping up her blood—'blood, blood. And pain.'

'My wife finally told me to sit down. She had her moments of slight relief now between wild pangs of pain.'

It was after 4 a.m. when she slept again, and Strehlow saw the cold dawn in. 'Then the sky lightened, the boys stirred, and there was the ever-present tinkling of the camel bell.'

'I gave breakfast to the boys. They spoke in whispers.'

Bertha told him she had no more pain, but she was utterly exhausted. Strehlow went off into the sandhills. He fell down onto the ground, sobbing and crying out. 'Lord Have mercy O Lord, help! O Bertha darling, sweetheart, wife, my crown my treasure, my glory,— O Lord, help! My crown has been stripped off my head, my glory lies shattered and broken,—O lord, Help. My wife is very ill, my sweetheart has come close to the gates of death,—O Lord Jesus help! She is lying in bed so still and quiet, death is brooding grimly in the distance, O Lord Jesus, Thou who has conquered Death, help! . . . Father be merciful upon us; Father heal us.'

He wrote the prayer—much longer than the above—into his diary. He had made a small white tent over Bertha. 'My little wife is sleeping,' he wrote, and cites Scripture in German.

But the next night her pains return again, she slept between spasms and he hardly slept at all. Fear gripped his throat, he could hardly gulp. 'I foresaw the death of my young wife, my disgrace upon my return to civilisations—whenever that might be—for having caused the death of my wife; the pain of my friends, the scorn of my acquaintances, the sorrow of her two lone old parents; my position as Patrol Officer would be lost; I would be left, a name to be remembered with spitting and detestation.'

There were more days and nights to go.

On one of those days Strehlow made bread.

And he washed what he had to wash. 'It was a horrible job, but I received the courage to do it,' he wrote, barely repressing his genuine phobia of blood—'O Lord, help. The starlit heavens proclaim Thy glory.

Lord of Hosts, Father almighty . . . Lord give me faith to trust in thee, and to hope upon thee, while there is life in either of us—my wife or me.'

He built a stretcher for Bertha, so they could travel out of their hell on the back of Flossie, the most biddable of the camels. But Bertha had lost so much blood and was so weak they could not leave immediately. 'She is reading our Bible now.' It was in this state of naked dependence on each other that an extraordinary event between them took place. Strehlow called it their 'confessions.'

He had written: 'The sun is low in the west. My wife's condition is still unchanged. O Lord, thy will be done!'—and then he had gone to her as she was still in pain.

I had a confession to make about my past life: I was certain now that I had brought my wife into this fiery ordeal though my past sins. I had not finished my recital, when she, too, came out with a confession about her own past mistakes: and she confessed that all through her agony a voice had been calling to her telling to confess it all; she had not had the courage then, but now that I had begun, she could speak also. And so we sat, and confessed our past sins without reserve; and the pain left her, and we grew calmer. Tonight we feel that we are humbled before the Lord; we have sinned, and are weeping some of the wages of sin. So we prayed tonight for forgiveness of sins, and asked the Lord to let His will be done: what right have we to ask for more?

Eventually they slept. Next morning they felt more peaceful together than they had for many months. And Strehlow wrote: 'This morning my wife delivered what was apparently the dead foetus . . . Oh Lord, spare Thou my wife, and grant that she and I may yet reform our lives with Thy aid and become fit instruments for Thy divine purposes.'

Deliverance

Gingerly, still struggling, relieved somewhat, but with Bertha in the stretcher, they moved east, back to Ayers Rock. From there to the Liddles' station at Angas Downs, because God, it seemed to Strehlow, 'has helped us along wonderfully.' 'It was glorious'—when Liddle gave them freshly roasted mutton and chops for tea, and Strehlow could that night of 15 September make yeast and tell himself that 'Everything has moved so smoothly since we made our confessions . . . Never before have my dear wife and I been so conscious of being helped by God. Difficulties have been smoothed over, mighty obstructions have been rolled out of our way. Truly God's wonderful right hand has been with us. Praise him and any soul, and forget not his benefits. Praise him in eternity. Amen.' All these acclamations were written on 15 September.

Then they could turn south towards the mission station, and come into Palm Valley where, five days later, they made camp. Bliss. They were almost home. From their rest point in the beautiful valley, they wrote notes to Hermannsburg and sent them off with Tom and Witchetty. It was Saturday. Tom and Witchetty had been instructed to return on Monday. They had Sunday in the valley that Strehlow remembered from September 1921 when he was camping with his parents.

'My wife walked a little today without assistance.' In the next few days he would make bread, they would cut each other's hair again, and he would rest and write his report on the German suspect. Then on their fourth day of rest—he was counting the days Edenically—they walked in the valley with its lovely dense groves of palms and its rock pools. They walked for about two miles, and Bertha was strong. On the way back they bathed in one of the rock pools. 'We were happy and joyous and light hearted.'

And he wrote a poem about their release from the wilderness. It is the only poem to be found in his diaries which are so full of the Aboriginal poetics.

At the water of Piltardi we sat and mourned:
  Our hearts were filled with fear O Lord
The cry of the curlew in the cliffs rang in our ears;
  Thou alone didst watch over us in the moondark nights
We cried unto Thee, O Lord, how long?
  O help us Lord of Hosts, and save our souls in the valley of death.

We came over the sandhills, grim and red
  Through the eternal lisp of the desert oaks;
The silence of death lay upon our souls;
  Our lips were parched, our hearts were beating in sore distress.
A mulga flat, yawning like the abyss of night, greeted our eyes:
  There didst Thou come to judgment over us, O Lord.

Death came and laughed at us, his grim cold hands he shook at us;

In fear and blank despair we fell at Thy feet, Lord of life and death.
Thy anger was kindled; Thy terror fell upon us;
  Our tears were dried in the fire of Thy fury, O Lord of Justice
Then did we remember our sins;
  Then did the memory of old hidden trespass oppress our souls.

In the fireglow of Thy anger did we confess our shame:
  Our sins, long-hidden, did we lay bare before Thy all-seeing eyes.
Then did Thou foregivest our sins;
  Thou spakest unto our souls like a loving, kindly Father.
Death fed; Life and Love and Peace returned to our hearts.
  Then were we united in heaven as we had been on earth before.

There were twelve more stanzas and the poem ends as a psalm of deliverance: 'Honour and Glory, and Praise be to thee for ever and ever.'[38]

Then they walked down the Finke back into Hermannsburg. It was 25 September. They had been away for four months and twenty days. They had travelled more than 1,000 miles, a great deal of it on foot, walking the exhausted camels.*

By What Authority?

Strehlow's first job as a patrol officer was to chase a German whom he failed to find. His second—though he called it his 'first case'—was to give a beating to a Hermannsburg Aborigine with whom he had gone to school. The culprit was Lukas—'my former favourite playmate when I was a little boy here.'

---

*   Bertha wrote her account of the journey inland in 1940 and again in 1945. Not unnaturally, neither account has any suggestion of inner trauma, and the second concludes that 'our trip had been a great adventure and a complete success.' The only clue a reader might get about the nightmare aspect of the journey is her tense account of water supplies, and of the suffering of the Aborigines in the reserve that seemed to be depleted of game. She and her husband found their rockholes, she stresses, because of their 'collaboration with the natives,' the 'dark people [who] proved themselves our faithful and willing friends.' She went on: 'Over and over again these people help the white man, either in his daily work or when he undertakes some exceptional travels, as in this case, and yet they receive so little in return. Seldom does a native's faithfulness result in some permanent good for his race as a whole. The natives as a community are indispensable to the Territory . . . yet they have no guarantee that they will be cared for when they grow old and sick.' The article, which she published rather against the wishes of her husband, began as a travelogue and became a case for reserves upon which natives might survive. 'It is not good enough to give the natives land that no one else wants because it is unproductive. They do not want it either' (1940:46).

Lukas had 'because of his baseless suspicions cruelly belaboured his wife Elvida—with tomahawk, boot and stick. So brutal a behaviour had to be punished. So, after a long talk in order to convince Lukas as well as the others of the shocking brutality of his action, I told him to choose between two punishments: (1) I would send for the police to take him to AS [Alice Springs] and lock him up (2) he could receive a whipping here. He chose the latter.'[39]

Two relatives of Lukas were shown the stockwhip. They gave Lukas five strokes each as he held onto the gum tree near the storage tank. The blows of the second relative were much more severe than the first. 'I had to stand by—a horrible sight,' Strehlow wrote. 'Such was my first case.'

Horrible though it was, he felt that there was no alternative. As he was not a policeman, what else could he do? After the flogging he sat down and wrote to Canberra, making out a case for the introduction of corporal punishment. 'I can't see how one can get on without it under present conditions.' The next day, his treatment seemed to have paid off when Lukas and Elvida came to see him.

He [Lukas] is deeply repentant; she said at first that she was too afraid of him, but later agreed to live with him once more, provided he would not beat her again. He promised in future to go to Rev. Albrecht as soon as the first jealous thought came into his mind . . . they agreed to make another fresh stand in their married life . . . Lukas wishes to come with his wife out west with me: he wants to forget all that happened here,—and be at ease with his wife (as he said to her—'we never have any quarrels when we are wandering about; it is only when we sit about in the camp here and have much time to think that all these jealous thoughts come into my head.)'

So Lukas wanted the shelter, so to speak, of the white man's moral authority. Yet Strehlow was not merely anxious about his authority over offenders. There was also the issue of his 'own' boys, the natives he would rely on, one way or the other, in his new job. After justice had been administered to Lukas, he had to travel to Haasts Bluff—a splendid journey, 'wonderful to be alive'—and they made a fine camp on the river within sight of the magnificent range. Strehlow was filled with hope about his new job. 'A number of men and women are camped about a mile down from here. They all came and shook hands with . . . my wife and myself. They looked so nice and eager and trusting. Some of the women were very young—pretty,—and some of the children the dearest sweet chubby things. One longs to help them do something . . . that will preserve this race, and give them happiness in the new environment that has begun.'[40]

Later, he made an effort to explain to them his office of patrol officer. 'I would have been so pleased had I been able to promise them as well some Government help and assistance in the form of a medical service and payment for dingo scalps and an additional area of better-class game country to be included in the present Reserve. But it would have been bad to have aroused . . . hopes that may never be fulfilled. They listened attentively and promised to do as I had told them, and bring their troubles before me instead of taking the law into their own hands.'[41]

Back at the mission, he took stock of the men who might help him in his work. He turned to two Hermannsburg men, Rolf and Henock, who had just been out with him. Would they like to come with him to Jay Creek? Jay Creek was the settlement—35 miles west of Alice Springs—where he would set up his administration as patrol officer. Would they like, he asked the men, to live there and be his assistants? The men hesitated, then said no: they would prefer to stay at the mission.

'I was thunderstruck: such disloyalty after only twelve days of service!' Strehlow dismissed the men, said he would speak to them tomorrow, and then fulminated in his diary: 'was it worthwhile doing anything for a race of people, who did not care for your efforts, who were weak, selfish, unreliable, and often even disloyal. It was a bitter draught to swallow: these two men came from Hbg, and have grown up with me, and should be my particular devoted followers; and that is what happens after they have only been with me for twelve days.'[42]

Still, Rolf, like Lukas, came to him the next day: he said that he had been very sorry as soon as he had said no. (That morning Strehlow had asked Albrecht to speak with Rolf, which he had done.) Rolf's message to Strehlow was: 'I had always been such a great friend to the natives, and it was wrong to leave me.' Rolf was 'ashamed' and now keen to come with him. 'Now that I wanted a man to go with me, amongst these other heathen people, he felt that he should come and work with me, and also do his duty among them.'

So Strehlow said yes, Rolf could come with his wife and children to

Jay Creek; and that he should suggest that Henock do the same. 'Henock, of course, quite fell in with the idea: he always does as Rolf does.'

That settled, the men set off with him to Jay Creek, to all intents and purposes resigned to be his loyal helpers in the administration of justice and welfare in Central Australia for the next five years. Some ground-level matters had been settled, but no sooner had they started out than Strehlow was telling himself: 'There is no other authority except from God: have I got this authority? This question haunted me.'[43]

Diary and Embarrassment

By what authority indeed? It is chastening to be so close to a man's diary, and Strehlow is consternating to be with over any length of time.

Strehlow's own authority here is as problematic as anything he had described in his paper, 'Notes on Native Evidence and Their Value.' His paternalism seems to blind him from the pitfalls of thinking of people as 'devoted followers': the manipulative remonstration with Henock could hardly be expected to cultivate adult trust. That is precisely why paternalism is, when all is said and done, the authority of false love: under the plea of doing good for people, it denies them their freedom. Strehlow seems to know this only sufficiently to be guiltily 'haunted' by the standing of his own authority. To his credit he has asked the right question for readers who might flinch at such a priggish outburst with the natives; just as they might at first have squirmed at various other naked episodes laid out in such exhaustive and exhausting detail in other moments in his diary, upon which we have been heavily relying to suggest his inner life.

The authority here, for Strehlow as well as anyone travelling with him in this way, is not God but the diary, with its cunning ability to seduce the diarist into a strange double life. The doubleness for the diarist consists of the phenomenon of writing for oneself directly, sensately, cathartically (or any of the terms that indicate a minimum of self-consciousness) while at the same time cultivating a second reader at one's elbow. The latter is the other private reader of one's diary: it is the means by which one writes so theatrically, so confessionally, thus making an echo chamber of the deceptively solitary inner citadel of the self. No diarist, starting with Rousseau, has ever sat alone.

For the self in the first instance Strehlow said of his diary that it was a 'venting': that is what he as a writer wished the reader to endure when he was pouring himself out at Horseshoe Bend, and when he was contending with the sufferings of Bertha at the Piltardi Rockhole. For the self in the second instance, the double at his elbow, he was calling out to the Lord, and in that moment opening the pages of his diary to others. Thus, after one's initial embarrassment at the ventings, perhaps in the same instant, the voice on Strehlow's pages is strangely outwardly directed, energised, not by the possibility of silence, which is the natural tendency of the self in the first instance, but rather by the need to make an appeal, the compulsion to remonstrate and justify, to reason and be reasoned with—which is what the diary, with Strehlow, is almost always seeking to do. We are, thank goodness, not intruding as much as we thought.

Some entries are naked exposures, there is no question about that; and it is a humbling privilege to read them, as with many diaries. But at the same time they are the work of a silent presence who more than anything else wishes to be heard. Even at this youthful point in time— before he goes into the world with the political authority of a patrol officer—he is placing his private self in a public realm: where the sources of his private authority might require justification. 'There is no other authority except from God: have I got this authority? This question haunted me.' It is a statement that seeks to wave the pages of the diary in daylight.

It might have been different—the diaries may well have taken a genuinely private turn—if, back at Horseshoe Bend with Sheila, Strehlow had found 'psycho analysis' more help than it was to him. If he had experienced some kind of insight into his suffering—the connection, for example, between the weight of his father complex, his sense of abandonment by his mother, and his yearnings for a desert bride—if he had seen the dynamic of that, some kind of path of self-analysis may have opened for him. That path may or may not have involved psychoanalysis in the long run; but then, when Freud's steely option was so present, and Strehlow chose instead to call and to call again outwards to the authority of the Lord, that constituted a turning point in his career as a diarist. Thereafter he is writing private thoughts seeking to be read by others.

And, if he had agonised over that choice he had then, that too might have turned the diaries deeply, idiosyncratically inward in ways that truly privatised them, as well as deepening him. If, for example, he was as an intellectual contending with Freud's challenge to religious faith; if he had been, as Hans Kung puts it, combating 'projection theory, opium theory or illusion theory,'[44] in order to get him and his father *clear*, then an inner citadel demanding exceptional treatment might have been the work of his diaries. But that did not happen: so the diaries are simply what they are in all their sorrowful, wretched, constricted, historically revealing, and ordinary worth.

To say this is not to use the diaries against the man. Bear in mind the remark Freud made when he received the Goethe Prize for literature. Speaking of biographers, and their desire to help us 'acquire affective relations' with considerable men, 'fathers, teachers, exemplars,' Freud worried the issue as to whether the biographer might, by 'reducing the distance' between him and his subject, 'tend in effect towards degradation.' Intimacy was not the issue, Freud said, so much as the ambivalence that we have towards authority figures in the first place. Similarly with the intimacy solicited by psychoanalysis, which did not seek to degrade but 'demonstrate new connecting threads in the "weaver's" masterpiece.'[45] As with Freud's tender trust with psychoanalysis, so with Strehlow's diaries, which he was writing as a long-term offering to anyone who might eventually wish to connect the threads.

'You have noticed,' he wrote years later, 'how very detailed my diary is—I know.' He was informing members of his department at the University of Adelaide. 'Today I know that I am recording *the sunset of an age* that will never return—every act that I see is being performed for the last time, and the men who are with me have no successors. When they die, they will take all their knowledge to the grave with them—except that part of which I have recorded. Hence I am writing down everything in full detail, so as to give the clearest picture of an age and of a culture that no one else but I have been privileged to witness.'[46] Admittedly, he simply appears to be offering his diary as evidence of his ethnographic work for posterity: this rather than his private self. But the more he wrote over the years the more that distinction blurred, as the heroic tone of his entry suggests.

The appeal, 'by what authority,' was both heartfelt in its sincerity and gestural, both private and publicly intended. It was as studied as his remarks about 'Native Evidence and Their Value.' He was simply pointing to the lived, ongoing consequences of operating out of the mission tradition when, already, he was officially accountable to secular authority. He was taking for granted that his diary was not a diary in the strict sense of the term, and that if we choose, for instance, to look unkindly upon his manipulation of Henock, or to remind him of the moment he felt like hitting the Pintubi man over the head with his rifle, then we miss the full trajectory of his address. He was speaking out about the moral dilemma of being with natives who were, or had been, complete strangers. He was trying to position himself in the company of beloved strangers.

Still, such outbursts in Strehlow's diaries produce a surface shock akin to the one delivered by the lively Malinowski when his *A Diary in the Strict Sense of the Term* was published many years after his work with his natives. The notorious remark was: 'On the whole my feelings towards the natives are decidedly tending to *"Exterminate the Brutes."*'[47] The italics were the diarist's and the posthumous publication of the line, and others like it, scandalised a profession which had by then made a myth of their fieldwork as one involving an exemplary poise in human relationships. Malinowski's diary was 'in the strict sense' because his entries did issue from the self in the first instance: they were never meant for publication, and so it seemed scandalous to some to come face to face with the anthropologist's rages, lusts, depressions, his boredom and his condescension towards the 'savage.' The famous author of the *Sexual Life of Savages* and the *Argonauts of the Pacific*—calm texts sailing on carefully constructed intellectual superstructures—was exposed as a feverish, narcissistic, self-centred, Dostoyevskian figure, hardly an authority on anything worth having. As it happens, Malinowski, like Strehlow, struggled with a mercurial mix of loneliness, yearning, nostalgia, nervous panic and ambition; he had hypochondriacal tendencies and was regularly stricken with bouts of homesickness for his mother, who was as far away from New Guinea as Strehlow's was from Central Australia. 'At last I begin to feel a deep strong longing for [mother] in my innermost being. I have resolved to keep a day to day account.'[48]

Tossing and turning on sultry nights, with Casanova memories about former loves and worries about the spiritual nature (or otherwise) of his love for his fiancée in Melbourne (a respectable young woman whose safety Baldwin Spencer feared for), Malinowski was, in his prose style, lighter, wittier, more morally engaging and self-analytical than Strehlow, and much of this was due, not simply to the vitality of his lapsed Catholicism, but to his keen literary sense. This is the crucial thing: he could not help himself writing so well. His is a diary in the strict sense of the term, the work of the self in the first instance, but its brilliant literariness brings the double in: it is finally a diary with its ear attuned for admirers, literary listeners.

After all, the notorious phrase 'Exterminate the Brutes,' which the profession hardly knew how to stomach, was a quotation from Conrad's *Heart of Darkness*. Malinowski was parodying Kurtz. In literary terms, Malinowski knew where he was. He knew and did not like the 'sahib' feeling. He was reading his Kipling, and his James Fenimore Cooper. He might get fed up with the savages, but he was also 'disgusted' with white superiority. [49]

Malinowski arrived in the tropics acutely conscious of not knowing the language, or the people. He was chronically disoriented by the exotic depth of things around him. His consciousness swam—floated— on the heat and the light, on the shimmering seas, and his writing was an attempt to keep himself straight for the interpretative ethnographic work. It was a way of disciplining himself for the disciplined work and telling himself where he was, where he had found himself and whether he was finding himself. Hence the confident assertions (as well as confessions), including the offensive assertions, because their function—it is clear from the flickering desperation of so many entries—is to try to integrate the writerly self with the world and the work. All the detail of Malinowski's narcissism, so-called, arose out of two noble realisations. He knew that to ask questions about others was to lead to questions about the self, to be 'confronted with our own problems.'[50] And he was acutely conscious that the ethnography was connected with how he was in himself in the whole situation. 'Feeling of ownership: it is I who will describe them or create them.'[51]

'This morning I decided to exert all my strength to master *feverishness*,' Malinowski told himself.[52] The diary is feverish. But that is less important than the ventings and revelations of bad form. He is as a diarist promoting an enlightenment project ('I am trying to "deepen" my diary'[53]), even as he was nervously contending with thoughts that would 'pull him down.'[54] He was a stranger to himself because everything was so exotic, and his diary was a stocktaking so that he could think, and feel, straight. It took twenty years for his fellow anthropologists to grant him the right to so expose himself as human, all too human, and to accommodate the idiosyncratic anguish of a Pole who would have been a poet, an artist, a metaphysician—anything but let his soul languish in the company of others whose lives might be more fully lived.[55] 'To what extent am I living in the starlit darkness—like Swinburne's Tiresias?'[56] This is not the refrain supposed to become a professional in the field of wild strangers.

Strehlow? Strehlow by stark contrast was in a familiar place. He was among those he knew. He was all too familiar with himself, and this, unfortunately, was one of the reasons he wrote in his diary. That is the real shame of the entries where he rails at his natives. He was being entirely himself, rather as if the fate of his diary was to discover the same self, over and over again. With Malinowski, the diary moves with the dragonflies across shimmering water; with Strehlow it arises from his 'foul papers' to move from rock to rock.*

---

*   Gregory Bateson, like Malinowski, knew how to enlighten the constructions of his identity in the field. On board ship to sail to New Guinea, in the footsteps of his Cambridge mentor A.C. Haddon, he won a prize for fancy dress. 'I appeared as a naturalist under the title of "myself" and got the prize for realistic acting the part.' He was also asked to preach the Sunday sermon, and thought he might 'give them . . . black–white culture contact' (Lipset 1982: especially 126–125). It is hard to imagine the fancy dress to fit Strehlow's double as naturalist and missionary's son: hence his heavy tread.

1   Freud was even less visible in 1947 when the paper became part of *Aranda Traditions* [*AT*] (Melbourne: Melbourne University Press, 1947), the introduction of which cited, not material on the savage resolution of the oedipal complex, but rather the more diffuse psychoanalyst Carl Jung on 'universally human symbols' as well as the psychologist McDougall on 'the uniformity of the human mind' (xv). If Strehlow had been as open about his Freud as Ruth Benedict had been about her Nietzsche, his work might have taken a very interesting turn. Benedict was claiming only a few years earlier, in 1930, that her Pueblo Indians arrived at their values of existence via the Apollonian type ('Psychological Types in the Cultures of the Southwest,' [1930] in *Writings of Ruth Benedict: An Anthropologist at Work*, ed. Margaret Mead [New York: Atherton Press, 1959], 248–61). That Nietzsche named and described his Dionysian and Apollonian types under the rubric of Greek Tragedy may also have appealed to Strehlow, if he could have withstood the company of the philosopher who declared God dead. As it was, his Freud served to smuggle nature through the back door of his text; this rather than join the contemporary debate about culture.

2   *AT*, 13. For the sharpest Australian remarks on Freud's incorrect use of Australian anthropology, and how 'parricide, blood guilt, fear and hate' were premises rather than findings, and expressions of Freud's 'vision' of the religion of Australia's 'poor naked cannibals,' see W.E.H Stanner, 'On Freud's Totem and Taboo,' written 1953–5, *Canberra Anthropologist* 5, no. 1 (1982). For a friendlier treatment of Freud, see L.R. Hiatt, 'Freud and Anthropology,' in *Creating Culture: Profiles in the Study of Culture*, ed. D.J. Austin-Broos (Sydney: Allen & Unwin, 1987).

3   See James Clifford, 'On Ethnographic Allegory,' in James Clifford, *Writing Culture: The Poetics and Politics of Ethnography* (Berkeley and Los Angeles: University of California Press, 1986), 98–121.

4   The point can be put in numerous ways. Suffice to say here my key term is 'elective affinities,' and it is by way of stressing symmetries that are imaginatively persuasive, as distinct from any explanatory model of the relationship between personal values and cultural currents at any historical moment. 'Personal values' is George Stocking's term in his most stimulating overview of one moment in the 1920s in American anthropology when anthropologists such as Benedict and Mead can be seen as members of the literary intelligentsia romantically enamoured of the 'primitive,' this as expressive of a constellation of personal and political attitudes to themselves and their own culture as well as what they might find in others. Benedict is the exemplary case, as Judith Modell has so vividly shown (*Ruth Benedict: Patterns of a Life* [London: Chatto Windus, 1984]). Cultural anthropology might be seen as an alternative to Darwin, Marx and Freud played out by young scholars of poetic disposition in a spirit of quest. Stocking was writing in particular of the idealised construction of the primitive which he called 'Apollonian Ethnography': Benedict on the Pueblo Indians, Redfield on the Mexicans in Tepoztlan and Mead on the Samoans were as expressive of the discontent of the civilised with civilisation as of anything ethnographic. In due course each of the above was subject to their historical moment of demystification, the most violent of those being Freeman's 'desecration' of the 'holy woman' Mead had become for American anthropology. Each 'biography' here differs in its encounter with the field, and there is no easy frame in which to put 'personal values' and see them applied. That makes it, Stocking argues, hard to say which ethnology—the original and transparently needful romantic constructions, or the supposedly objectifying corrective—is true. Stocking is inclined to suggest that the Apollonians tended to spend less time in the field, had less linguistic

competence and fewer informants than other workers. Having said that, however, he is also keen to add that critics, too, have their historic moments, which are as hard to characterise as the cultural moment of the romantic. For example, was Derek Freeman's assault on Mead driven by a revival of scientific positivism and Darwinian biology as a reaction to the cultural relativism of the Boasins? In which case, how does one frame the frame for a judicious anti-anti-relativism? (See Clifford Geertz, 'Anti Anti-Relativism?' *American Anthropology*, 86 [1994].) The eternal return of some issues in anthropology ends up as one of Stocking's final points. But then, looping up and out of this infinite and conceptually evasive prospect, he posits the distinction beautifully explored by Boas many years ago: the contrast of the physicist with the cosmographer/historian: the former who would fragment phenomena into their objective elements, all the better to find unities and verifiable general laws; the latter who, in the interests of a holistic study, would rest with 'a merely subjective unity' whose 'elements seem to be connected only in the mind of the observer.' In Stocking's paraphrase of Boas: 'Motivated by the personal feeling of man towards the world,' such study required the observer 'lovingly' to 'penetrate' into the secrets of the phenomena until their 'truth' could be affectively apprehended—without concern for 'the laws which it corroborates or which may be deduced from it.' See George Stocking, 'The Ethnographic Sensibility of the 1920s and the Dualism of the Anthropological Tradition,' in his *Romantic Motives: Essays on the Anthropological Sensibility*, History of Anthropology vol. 6 (Madison: University of Wisconsin Press, 1989).

Apprehend is the key term. We are back to the elective affinities, which in this context is an expression akin to the Boas sense of apprehension. Strehlow was apprehending Aranda myth as if it was his own.

The reader might at this point wonder why my examples are American rather than Australian. The general answer is that with the exception of Patrick Wolfe's *Settler Colonisation and The Transformation of Anthropology* (London Continuum, 1999) the general history of Australian anthropology has yet to be written, and in some cases has been thwarted, as Annette Hamilton has argued on Elkin ('L.R. Hiatt: Life, Thought and Misunderstanding,' in *Scholar and Sceptic: Australian Aboriginal Studies in honour of L.R. Hiatt*, ed Francesa Merlan, John Morton and Alan Ramsey [Canberra: Aboriginal Studies Press, 1997]). The overviews that exist have not fully attempted to put the individual lives of anthropologists into the field of cultural history. Mulvaney on Spencer is the grand exception, along with Patrick Wolfe on Spencer ('On Being Woken Up: The Dreamtime in Anthropology and in Australian Settler Culture,' *Comparative Studies in Society and History* 32, no. 2 [1991]). In the best overview of Australian anthropology so far, by Les Hiatt (*Arguments About Aborigines: Australia and the Evolution of Social Anthropology* [Cambridge: Cambridge University Press, 1996]), the content of Australian studies is located in the long history of dualistic perplexity about the 'primitive,' but that is all. Kenneth Maddock has in turn written an incisive intellectual portrait of Hiatt ('The Temptation of Paris Resisted: An Intellectual Portrait of a Sydney Anthropologist,' in *Scholar and Sceptic*) and there are moments in Tiger Wise's biography of Elkin when one can glimpse the personal meeting the object of study to shape it. I am thinking particularly of Elkin's spiritual epiphanies (*The Self-Made Anthropologist: A Life of A.P. Elkin* [Sydney: Allen & Unwin, 1985). Radcliffe-Brown, Stanner, the Berndts, Thompson, the power of their elective affinities had yet to be explored, as well as their historical 'moments.' Only the beginnings have been made in the various festschriften. As to the historic moment of the next wave of anthropologists crucial to the modern shape of Aboriginal political identities (Bell, Bird-Rose, Keen, Morphy, Maddock, Morton, Peterson, Sutton, to name the most obvious) their historical moment, which we are still in, arguably pivots around the cultural uncertainties and methodological dilemmas similar to and different from those in the 1920s in America: similar in their intellectual roots, different with regard to relationships, or lack of them. 'Relationships' has a new meaning in the post-colonial era; 'indigenous' is a post-colonial world away from 'primitive,' but the structures of feeling with regard to the passing of time, political process, social attachments, intimacy and distance, optimism and pessimism, aversion, love, dialogue, inter-relationships, interdependence, the place of the oral and the written—these as aspects of biography await the general historian of the present who will deal with the ongoing mix of thoughts inhabiting the chemical affinities of people who have them.

5   *AT*, 7–8.
6   Ibid., 14.
7   Ibid., 100.
8   Ibid., 106.
9   Ibid., 111.
10 Ibid., 37.
11 Ibid., 38.
12 Schiller is cited by Harry Levin, *The Myth of the Golden Age in the Renaissance* (London: Faber, 1970), xv, and the connection with the primitivist childhood of man is clearly made at 3–7 and passim. See also Clifford, *Writing Culture*, especially 112–16.
13 Fitzherbert to Strehlow, 27 August 1937.
14 *AT*, 93.
15 Ibid., 94. On the rival connections between male and female power, see L.R. Hiatt ('Freud and Anthropology,' in *Creating Culture: Profiles in the Study of Culture*, ed. D.J. Austin-Broos [Sydney: Allen & Unwin, 1987] Sydney); Annette Hamilton ('Dual Social Systems: Technology, Labour and Women's Secret Rites in the Eastern Western Desert of Australia,' *Oceania* LI [1980]) and John Morton ('Sustaining Desire' [PhD thesis, Australian National University, 1985], 507–58).
16 *AT*, 120.
17 Strehlow to James at Melbourne University Press, 9 June 1944, MUP Archives.
18 *AT*, 6.
19 W.H. Stanner, 1989, *On Aboriginal Religion,* Oceania Monograph 36 (Sydney: University of Sydney, 1989), 37, 85, 100.
20 Ward McNally, *Aborigines, Artefacts and Anguish* (Adelaide: Lutheran Publishing House, 1981), 42–43.
21 Ibid., 44.
22 For a fuller account of this episode see Barry Hill, *The Rock: Travelling to Uluru* (Sydney: Allen & Unwin, 1994), 117–20; and the sources for the above: Robert Layton, *Uluru: An Aboriginal History of Ayers Rock* (Canberra: Aboriginal Studies Press, 1999), 69, 72; and Jim Dowling, *Ngurra Walytja: Country for My Spirit* (Casuarina, N.T.: Northern Australia Research Unit, 1988), 9, 11.
23 J.B. Cleland, V.J. White and J.H Sexton, 'Report of the Board of Inquiry . . .' 8 May 1935. AA CRS FI Item 1938/636, 4.
24 T.G.H. Strehlow, diary [SD], 11, 12 June 1935.
25 Charles Mountford, diary, 13, 14 June 1935, H.L. Sheard Collection, State Library of South Australia.
26 Ibid., 22 June 1935.
27 'Report of the Board of Inquiry . . .' 5.
28 Ibid., 6–7.
29 T.G.H. Strehlow, 'Notes on Native Evidence and its Value,' *Oceania* VI, no. 3 (March 1936): 323–35.

30 Ibid., 330.
31 Ibid., 331.
32 On the basis of which, it might be argued, the firmest knowledge can be gained: see Steven Shapin's account of the growth of scientific knowledge as a manifestation of codes of trust between gentlemen (*A Social History of Truth, Civility and Science in Seventeenth-Century England* [Chicago: University of Chicago Press, 1994]).
33 SD, 10 May 1936.
34 SD, 8 June 1936,
35 SD, 22 June 1936.
36 SD, 19 August 1936.
37 SD, 30 August 1936.
38 SD, 14 September 1936.
39 SD, 15 October 1936.
40 SD, 23 October 1936.
41 SD, 28 October 1936.
42 SD, 1 November 1936.
43 SD, 3 November 1936.
44 Hans Kung, *Freud and the Problem of God* (New Haven, Conn.:Yale University Press, 1990), cited in W.W. Meissner, *Ignatius of Loyola: The Psychology of a Saint* (New Haven, Conn.:Yale University Press, 1992), xxvi.
45 Meissner, *Ignatius*, xxix.
46 Strehlow to members of his department at the University of Adelaide, received 14 July 1964.
47 Bronislaw Malinowski, *A Diary in the Strict Sense of the Term* (Stanford, Ca.: Stanford University Press, 1967), 69.
48 Ibid., 28.
49 Ibid., 16.
50 Ibid., 119.
51 Ibid., 140.
52 Ibid., 133.
53 Ibid., 172.
54 Ibid., 131.
55 Clifford Geertz (*New York Review of Books*, 14 September 1967) excelled in the personal attack on the 'crabbed, self-preoccupied, hypochondriacally narcissist' Malinowski whose 'embarrassing example is that, if one takes it seriously, it makes it difficult to defend the sentimental view of rapport as depending on the unfolding of anthropologist and informant into a single moral and emotional universe.' Other early responses, for example by Audrey Richards (*The Cambridge Review*, 19 January 1968), were less censorious and tried to assimilate Malinowski's brutal honesty as an 'anti-hero.' Of the positive response the leading historian of anthropology, George Stocking (*Journal of the History of Behavioral Sciences* 4, no. 2 [1968]) took up Malinowski's knowing usage of Conrad as a template for a European self-knowing encounter with the savage, a view that seemed to have influenced Geertz when he had a second, more appreciative, bite at the cherry, embracing the diary as a literary text which was 'a backstage masterpiece of anthropology, our The Double Helix' (*Works and Lives: The Anthropologist as Author* [Stanford, Ca.: Stanford University Press, 1988]). Raymond Firth gives an overview of responses in his introduction to the 1989 edition of Malinowski's diary.
56 Malinowski, *Diary*, 173.

PART III: PATROLLING

Whatever the past hides, the present of the unfortunate Aborigine is sufficiently miserable, native food of any description is almost non-existent, and under the circumstances, the rations issued to the old natives are insufficient. But for the earnings of the younger men, who buy food, and the kindness of some of the older residents, the old blacks would be semi-starved. All these old people have been accustomed to clothes and tobacco, and, now, the amount supplied to them is absurdly small. In addition, our missionaries undermine their authority, and ridicule their traditions, we take from them everything that makes life worth living, work them until they can work no longer, and then hand them over to the police, whose main endeavour is to work things as cheaply as possible, and thus please a gov't that has neither knowledge nor conscience. It is a despicable crime.

Paddo Byrne to Baldwin Spencer, 1925

1   Crime Scenes

The High Road to Extinction?

STREHLOW TOOK OFFICE as patrol officer at a crucial time in Australia's colonial history, the moment when, after nearly a century and a half of white settlement, a brutal fact could no longer be avoided. In 150 years of white settlement the indigenous Australians had been almost wiped out, 'a rate equivalent to the death every year since 1788 of two large tribes totalling 1,700 souls.'[1] Now they were at risk of final extinction. Whites had to face the question: had this happened wilfully, or somehow by default on their part? If that could be faced squarely, there were other questions. What must be done about it? Could anything be done? Should anything be done? The last question was often subtextual, but it went to the heart of the social Darwinian assumption that had bled into so much policy for several generations: that the survival of the strong and the demise of the weak was the natural order of things. And here thought and feeling was riddled in the Christian, humanitarian and increasingly 'anthropological' conscience.

The dying, or the killing, of a people in eastern and southern Australia a century before had not gone unnoticed. As the 'Australian Correspondent' for the London *Times* told its readers in 1937, in parts of Australia 'one could travel for thousands of miles . . . which has no sound or echo of native life.' There were now up to 50,000 'blackfellows' left on the continent, in 'the half-way house of the sparsely peopled sheep, cattle and mining country,'[2] and the issue was whether the forces at work would keep the numbers dwindling to the point of extinction. *Need* they die out?[3]—that was the desperate question.

On 25 November 1937 *The Times* editorialised, choosing terms designed to arouse. It referred to a petition that had just been signed by '1,800 blackfellows' and addressed to the King. It developed the theme of extinction mentioned by their Australian correspondent. The causes of decline varied from district to district, said the leader, but the pattern was all too clear: the restless drift to the white settlements, diseases brought by Europeans, the vulnerable people; 'many seem simply not to possess power to adapt themselves to change and to be dying out partly through their inability to understand their real interests.' The newspaper listed the material distress of Aborigines, and puzzled that Australian administrators had not shown 'the skill and humanity' they had shown in their mandated New Guinea.

The next passage pointed the bone in the most uncompromising way. 'The immediate cause of this deplorable state of affairs has been both the lack of trained administrators and of the funds which any comprehensive scheme of native administration requires. Professor Wood-Jones, an eminent scientist, recently ascribed its ultimate cause to official and popular indifference. In his opinion neither the Australian Governments nor the Australian people had ever desired to preserve the natives.'

Wood-Jones was a professor of anthropology in Hawaii; he had once been the curator of the South Australian Museum. *The Times* cited him because he was someone in the world of anthropology, whereas their Australian correspondent, who more than likely helped them shape the actual editorial, was not. His name was W.H. Stanner, a young Australian anthropologist in London, a research assistant to the famous Malinowski at the London School of Economics.

The article and the leader caused 'quite a stir,' as Stanner recalled much later. The article, reprinted as a pamphlet and widely distributed by the influential Anti-Slavery and Aborigines Protection Society, was in the long tradition—or in the long revolution—of humanitarian resistance to the excesses of colonisation. In London the pamphlet had the immediate support of A.R. Radcliffe-Brown, the South African dandy at All Souls College, Oxford, who had, only a few years before, resigned from Australia's first chair of anthropology in Sydney. Radcliffe-Brown wrote to *The Times* rebuking Australia's Agent General for Western

Australia who had defensively reasoned the Aboriginal people were an 'already decaying people.'[4]

'This,' wrote Radcliffe-Brown, 'is an idea that one often meets in Australia, and it is sometimes offered as an excuse for not being more concerned over the fate of an unfortunate people. But there is nothing that a scientist could accept as evidence for this belief.' The 'stir' was the creation of anthropologists in London—Stanner among others—connected with the Royal Anthropological Institute. Its wellspring was twofold: a reaction to the newspaper publicity about poor diet, health, housing, and employment conditions of Australian Aborigines; and an expression of a professional pitch to convince others that their 'scientific' knowledge of native peoples should be put to use in the colonial administrations. They wanted to practise 'applied anthropology' so that the rapid social change produced by empires might be better managed for the benefit of indigenous communities. This idea—that scientific knowledge could be usefully brought to bear in a way that would please both colonial administration and the 'natives'—was naturally problematic: the conflicts of interests and sympathies were predictable.* Such a conflict had led to Radcliffe-Brown's self-catapulting from Sydney, when his scientific approach was seen as provocation by Sir Hubert Murray, Lieutenant Governor of Papua. Radcliffe-Brown was more willing than most to speak of the natural tendency of applied anthropology to side with the colonised. 'How long the peoples of India and Africa will permit us to exercise control over their destiny, or how long we shall continue to think we have a right to do so, I do not know,' he told an ANZAAS conference, when Sir Hubert was in the audience.[5]

The wider, post-colonial trajectory is the right frame, ultimately, to place upon the situation in Central Australia in the 1930s. It was

---

*   Raymond Firth, a secular social anthropologist destined to be involved in Strehlow's life, was even more expressive of ambivalent colonial evaluations in his 1932 overview of anthropology in Australia for Elkin's *Oceania*. He referred to 'the materials for study, the aborigines' and to 'rich fields of investigations,' expressions fit for a mining manual. When it came to the destructive impact of colonisation, his language was similarly mechanistic: the Aborigine had been 'rudely thrown out of gear by the impact of an alien civilisation—he mutely dies.' But he also reproached white regimes for their 'mixed motives' that thwarted 'humanitarianism and ideals of justice,' namely, the 'purely practical economic considerations': 'We are genuinely concerned for the welfare of the natives, but not at too great a cost to ourselves.' After this glimmer of human involvement in native affairs, he pulled back to a plea for studying the natives 'dispassionately' (Firth 1932: 3, 6, 9, 10–11, 12).

glimpsed more clearly by some than others. My emphasis here is on the sense of existential crisis: of a common ground on the matter of the living death of Aboriginal people. One pat figure was that Aborigines were dying off at a rate of 5,000 a year.[6] To those scientifically inclined, the depopulation meant a rapid loss of 'data.' This had been the view of the anthropological expeditions in South Australia, the university men such as Cleland and Tindale who had been trekking inland from Adelaide since the mid-twenties. But the plight of Aborigines was also seen in humanitarian terms that were plainly used by men such as A.P. Elkin, Sydney's new professor of anthropology, when he addressed the budding profession in Australia. Aborigines, Elkin wanted to stress, were individuals, men and women with 'their desires, loves, fears, hates, delights and so on.'[7] The human face of the tragedy—not just the loss to 'science'—was the point: 'the woman's life, and that of the man's life which is passed with the women and children, reveal the essential and natural humanity of the aboriginals.'[8]

Elkin was still an Anglican deacon when he took the chair. His Christian conscience agonised at the prospect of Aborigines being on 'the high road to extinction.'[9] In addition, he felt connected to the people and their land after some deeply personal experiences in the Musgrave Ranges of South Australia. There, in 1931, where he had gone to do his first fieldwork, he had been ravished by the blossoming of the desert after rain and by camping under the stars on the secret-sacred ceremonial ground of the Pitjantjatjara people. After waiting several days he was finally witness to the kangaroo dance, and was greatly moved. It was the beginning of Elkin's special study in the 'cult lodges.' It was also the site of an epiphany. 'If you be an anthropologist, you realise that those dark skinned men have felt as you feel. Those stars at which you gaze, why they are the metamorphosed heroes of old; the Milky Way, a great road along which the souls of men must travel . . . But surely queries puzzled the soul, those Aborigines are not religious. Aye, they are, and they are so because they can sit quiet, meditating in a receptive mood, "be still and know."'[10]

This was not, of course, how the new 'science' wanted to see itself; as co-participants in the spiritual endeavour of a primitive people. And yet a philanthropic tendency to value an indigenous culture for its own sake, even as it was valued for science, was also endemic in the anthro-pological endeavour,[11] and Elkin's own religious disposition helped to emphasise the fact. His argument was that the perishing people might be Stone Age—'Palaeolithic'—in their material culture, but that did not mean they lacked a spiritual life worth speaking of. 'This phenomena warn us that we must not judge the human book by its material cover. Real knowledge of the Aborigines can come only from an understanding of their living, pulsating, social organisation, and, even more, of their cult life.' Elkin was already well known for his public lectures that advocated a greater 'understanding' of Aborigines. In this he was supported by the heartfelt activism of organisations determined to be friends of Aborigines: each state had its lobby group for speaking up for them when they were blighted and mistreated, and for spotlighting those on the frontier who were violating natural justice.[*]

In London, where, much to the *chagrin* of Australian officials and politicians, the lobby groups had a good press, violations were the point. Stanner and colleagues achieved the publicity they wanted. Their objective was to get the Commonwealth government to do something concrete and urgent for Aborigines. The Scullin Government of 1931 had listened to the anthropologists in London but said it could do nothing because the States had the power. In 1938 the Royal Institute for Anthropology sent their memorandum on the conditions of Australian Aborigines (the basis of Stanner's pamphlet) to the Australian High Commissioner in London, S.M. Bruce; to the Prime Minister, Joseph Lyons, and to all State premiers. The applied anthropologists wanted a conference of premiers. In April, the Commonwealth told the Institute that a Conference of Commonwealth and State Ministers would discuss Aboriginal welfare 'at an early date.' 'In fact,' as Stanner recorded bitterly, 'no meeting of officers was held until 1948 and the Ministers did not meet until 1951.'[12]

It was not that the Commonwealth did not have any policy objectives at all. They were noted in the first paragraph of the anthropologists' memorandum as including: 'the protection of the nomadic tribes;

---

[*]   The humanitarian lobby included: the South Australian Aborigines' Friends' Association formed in 1868; the Association for the Protection of Native Races, which was based in Sydney; and in Victoria the Victorian Aboriginal Group formed in 1929, the Aboriginal Fellowship Group (1932) and the Aborigines' Uplift Society (1939). Degrees of activism and campaign focus varied from time to time, but in the thirties to them must be added the assemblies and leadership of the Protestant churches; women's organisations such as the Australian Federation of Women Voters, the Trades and Labour Councils in New South Wales and Victoria, and the Communist Party. The political left at the time supported Aboriginal republics and land rights (Marcus 1990: 158–59).

the establishment and maintenance of inviolable reserves; the protection of native women from moral abuses; the adequate feeding and
medical supervision of broken down tribes; the economic protection of
Aboriginal employees; the assembly, education and training of mixed-
bloods to allow them to take a place in the life of the Australian community.'[13]

The objectives had been clearly defined by the Prime Minister in
1931. But they remained very largely intentions on paper. Stanner
thought the whole round of policy utterance and inaction, or action
half-baked or underfunded, added up to a 'tragi-comedy.'[14]

'Damned Dirty Niggers'

'I was,' said Charles Duguid when he visited Alice Springs in 1934,
'appalled by the physical condition of the Aborigines.'

Duguid had come up from Adelaide, where he was a practising
doctor. He was a member of the Aboriginal Advancement League and
had helped found the Presbyterian mission station among the Pitjantjatjara people at Ernabella. He went on: 'Its most dastardly aspect was
the spread of venereal disease, through pregnancies forced upon Aboriginal women by infected white men. The eyes of all the babies born
to those infected women were damaged by gonorrhoea, often with
serious impairment of vision. I saw one baby with an eye so damaged
that it was likely to be sightless.'

Equally shocking to Duguid was the callous racism of the whites,
including his own Christian colleagues. The padre of the Australian
Inland Mission greeted him with, 'I believe you are interested in the
niggers.'

'To hear this from the local leader of the mission maintained by
my own church was staggering, but I asked only, "do you mean the
Aborigines?"'

'You can call them what you like. They've never been any good and
never will be. The best they've any right to expect is a decent funeral.'

In 1934 a hospital was finally built for Aborigines. It was a galvanised
iron shed with room for two patients. The Inland Mission had banned
Aborigines from their hospital: 'The AIM is only for white people,' the
padre told him. 'You are only wasting your time among so many
damned dirty niggers.'

'All the Aboriginal women children and unemployed men whom I
saw in 1934,' Duguid wrote, 'were undernourished and listless.'[15]

One word could summarise the deadly picture in the mid-thirties. Hunger. Aborigines were half-starving. Stanner's considered report could not have been clearer:

If a corps of impartial and internationally accredited experts were to make a tour of Australia, inspecting every native camp, every station where black fellows work, every town where there is an encampment of detribalised remnants, the facts which would come to light would make disturbing reading.

Most of the detribalised and semi-civilised natives would be shown to be badly under-nourished, and to be living precariously from hand to mouth on what in many cases is a wretchedly inferior diet. Many of them are short of essential proteins, fats, mineral salts, and vitamins. The number of Aborigines just over the threshold of scurvy, beri-beri, and other deficiency diseases must be very great. For instance, out of fifty-one children born on a station in central Australia from 1925 to 1929, only ten survived. Why? The others died from the effects of an unbalanced diet, principally from lack of vitamin C. This was in time of drought, and over a great area of native Australia drought conditions recur time and again . . . Official rations are issued in some of these areas to aged and infirm blacks, but the food received in this way is a mockery of an adequate level of diet. The rations were originally intended only to supplement the food gathered by natives in their traditional hunting way. But, unfortunately, in so many outback areas these official rations, which are inferior in quality and insufficient in quantity, have become almost the only food some natives receive. The rations thus given consist of a little white flour, and small quantities of polished rice, tea, sugar, and tobacco. There is no official meat ration. The quantity is often just sufficient to encourage the natives to stay around the ration depot, but not sufficient to give them all one square meal a day. In most cases the old, tired natives are obliged by tribal custom to share the food out with other members of the tribe. Thus, what in itself is insufficient to feed the old people themselves becomes part of the tribal foodstuffs as a whole. On this meagre standard of living, supplementing the poor and inferior official rations as best they can, many a tribe lives from ration day to ration day. A generous and sensible official gesture has thus been perverted in the course of a few years into a thoroughly ruinous principle.

Nor can it be said that the rations given by many private employers are much better. The fresh meat ration is invariably too small, the use of white flour and polished rice too common, and the physiological inadequacy of the diet in other respects far too obvious. A great many white men in the same areas are living on food which is very little better, because of the poverty of the pastoral and farming properties over so much of native Australia. But can it really be held that this white poverty is a sufficient reason for the ruinous under-nourishment of native employees and dependents, or that the restricted budgets of the native administrations are a sufficient reason for the under-feeding of detribalised Aborigines who are otherwise left unprovided for?[16]

And so on. Stanner's remarks imply that the Territory was most representative of this general picture. They were also made with an emphasis on what was an 'intricate and difficult problem,'* one demanding accurate local information and focused policies that would, in the sharp parlance of a *Times* leader writer, 'bite.'

What Stanner might have said, too—it was implicit in his argument—was that even as the Aborigines were not being adequately fed, their dependence on white rations deepened: they were paupers in the making, people fed without the dignity of work, hopeless prospects as citizens. Their humbling and their powerlessness was intimately connected with their dependence on rations, just as white authority was contingent on their labour. The colonial nexus was, as one historian has so definitively argued, a matter of 'white flour' constituting 'white power.'[17] Strehlow, of course, knew this from his mission days. As patrol officer he found his authority bound up with the equation all over again.

The Protection of Protection
As a patrol officer Strehlow was an employee of the Chief Protector of Aborigines, a title that history had by then underlined with a bitter irony. It was an office invented for the southern colonies a century before as a Christian, humanitarian response to the dispossession of native people, and then, on the frontier, their violent mistreatment by the 'dregs' of British society.[18] The protector was to ameliorate the dis-

---

* On health Stanner went on to say: 'the factors involved are rather different from those responsible for the poverty of native nutrition. The blacks themselves make the control and treatment of disease doubly difficult by their fear, ignorance, and misunderstanidng of attempts made to help them. They live in unhygienic camps, they actively help to spread disease among themselves, and often refuse treatment.'

possession by becoming a buffer between ruthless vested interests and the state's obligation towards justice and charity. That was the theory, but the story of the early protectors is mostly a sorry one: what they could not do by way of civilising white settlers towards natives they compounded by poorly financed regimes of coercive paternalism. Hence, in the Northern Territory from 1911 (the year the Commonwealth government relieved the South Australian government of its colonial responsibilities), the regime of ordinances made of the protector a puritan patriarch of a special kind.

The Territory's first chief protector was Herbert Basedow, an Adelaide doctor, geologist and anthropologist, who thought it essential that each native have 'some ready means of permanent individual identification' that would be registered in government records. The best way to do this was 'a slight lesion of the superficial skin' which could be done 'in an absolutely painless way and without disfigurement. The . . . mark need not exceed one or two square inches and would be chosen in quite an inconspicuous position.'[19] The federal minister, to whom the protector was accountable, did not approve of branding. As it turned out, Basedow lasted 45 days in the job, which was then occupied by the eminent Baldwin Spencer.

The powers of the Territory's protector evolved from Spencer's report on Aborigines in 1913, when Spencer was Acting Chief Protector for a short time. Spencer thought the protection natives needed was from 'a civilisation that they do not understand.'[20] The symptoms of that incomprehension were the most licentious offences visible in Darwin's torrid zone—drink, prostitution, domestic disorder. It went almost without saying that all the above were inseparable from the twin evils of venereal disease and interracial sexual activity. Darwin was so pox-ridden, it was said, that no decent woman from the south would consider living there. The worst elements of white society were at liberty with Aboriginal women, and increasingly breeding a generation of half-castes about whom no one yet had a clear social policy. Apart from the native women themselves, the chief offenders, in Spencer's opinion, were the lustful Asians who addicted native women to opium and took advantage of them. And so there was further miscegenation: not just 'half-castes,' but half-caste Asiatics would increasingly populate the colony unless actions were taken.[21] Spencer's thinking was fervently married to the White Australia policy.

Spencer spoke well, however, of the 'preservation' of Aborigines. For a man who once declared the Aborigines to be as doomed to extinction as the platypus, this was his humanism winning over his biology. While Aborigines had a child-like mentality, and 'no sense of responsibility, and . . . no initiative,' they could, if a national policy was adopted, be 'uplifted' to a higher stage of civilisation. Education should be the cornerstone.[22]

Spencer had in mind some instruction on the reserves as well as in the white settlements—but that never happened. From 1911 to well into the thirties the Commonwealth was in practice a passive protector, letting the social trends take their fatal course. A complacency about the fate of Aborigines seemed to feed social policy—as if to express, without saying so, that 'if you leave 'em alone, they will die out.'

The Chief Protector in the Territory, however, was meant to be the permeating presence in the cultural politics of the whole region. Spencer revelled in it—he liked 'the power to order any police officer to arrest a native and do with him or her what I think best. At the same time I can take any native from under the control of a white man if I think that the latter is not treating him properly.'[23] The implication was, of course, that the affairs of white men were similarly manageable, especially the white men abusing their labourers, or consorting with Aboriginal women, or both.

By 1930 in the Northern Territory there were at least 68 ordinances—regulations designed, at least on paper, to control all aspects of a native's life, his or her freedom of movement, terms of employment, sexual conduct, parenting, health care. All of this because, as Queensland's Protector, J. W. Bleakley, reasoned at the time, 'The aborigines are a child race, requiring parental control and protection.'[24]

Bleakley's landmark 1928 report on the conditions of Aborigines in the Territory revealed some naked home truths about the domain of the protector. 'The pastoral industry,' Bleakley wrote, 'is absolutely dependent on the blacks for the labour, domestic and field, necessary to successfully carry on. If they were removed, most of the holdings, especially the smaller ones, would have to be abandoned.' That was one truth: the raw economic fact. The other, more intimate, had even more profound social ramifications for the white man's ability to deal with reality: it concerned Aboriginal women. Bleakley: 'a lubra is one of the greatest pioneers of the Territories, for without her it would have been impossible for the white man to have carried on.'[25] Capital and Carnality: under these two headings *together* the race history of the

Northern Territory has yet to be fully written, even though the sexual vicissitudes of white authority, white *investments*, were from the beginning bound up with the convolutions of philanthropic policies founded on nineteenth-century racist premises.

When Strehlow took up his post, the Chief Protector was C.E.A. Cook. Cook was a doctor, a medical researcher by training, an expert in yaws and leprosy, and had been in the post for ten years. He was both Protector and Chief Medical Officer, and saw their administrative link as essential to native policy. Bleakley had been graphic on health (his report had a page of ugly photographs showing 'Sores, Granuloma, Syphilis and Yaws from Infection by Flies'; four of these six specimen pictures were of children) and Cook sought to act accordingly. But his health policies were checked by the Commonwealth's meagre funding: the Protector was already managing a legacy of neglect,* but in some ways Bleakley had moved the focus of the protector's control from policing to health. Outback police were labelled protectors, and ordered to carry a medical kit and be responsible for the health of Aborigines. The impact of his policy shift was dubious. Tuberculosis was already known to be a serious problem in the centre: four people died of it at Hermannsburg in 1934, but no quarantine policy had been shaped; a case diagnosed in Alice Springs in 1931 remained untreated. Curable eye diseases were endemic in the Territory.

Cook had been moved, in part, by the poor record of mission stations such as Hermannsburg, where children had died of scurvy in 1929. He wanted the state to do more of the welfare work and for the missions, if they had to continue, to stick to their religion. In 1931 he reduced mission subsidies by 20 per cent and refused funds to new missions. In 1934 he stopped the supply of medical kits and blankets to aged and infirm Aborigines.[26]

Arguably, this was policy progress, of sorts: it advanced the cause of active *government* responsibility for the victims of white invasion. The state could not pass the buck. It had to take seriously the report of Professor F. Wood-Jones from the University of Melbourne who had been to Alice Springs in 1937 and reported back with horror that 'easily cured diseases

---

* Northern Territory expenditure had increased from £3,000 to £14,000, a pittance considering the governor-general at the time was paid £19,000 and Vestey's had spent £900,000 on an abattoir. 'The Commonwealth estimated that it spent £212,368 on Aborigines from 1911 to 1939—less than a quarter of the cost of the meatworks' (Marcus 1990: 9–10).

were untreated . . . the Government medical officers never got near the great body of the aborigines.' The professor gained the 'most harrowing stories' of Aborigines afflicted with yaws being left to suffer and die.[27]

As a doctor, Cook was speaking Hippocratically about those in his charge: as the medical officer he was tangibly their protector. But as a policy maker, Cook placed medical thinking in the political domain, arguing for medical policy as an aid to white colonisation of the tropics. Here all philanthropy converted into racist thinking. As he explained to his federal minister in September 1938, the Northern Territory Medical Service was 'charged with safeguarding' the White Australia policy, which was in turn 'the keynote of Australian nationalism' and this it did by protecting the whites against the tropical diseases to which the natives were host. He named leprosy, hookworm, malaria, and to these added tuberculosis, not because he did not know that it was a disease introduced by whites, but because natives had less resistance to it, 'an infected native is an infinitely greater menace than an average infected white.'

But the greatest menace of all was venereal disease—'of much greater importance in a country of mixed races than elsewhere.' As if the plight of native women did not count at all, Cook declared VD to be of 'utmost importance as a threat to the health of the white(s) [sic] in this region,' and concluded that since 'legal prohibitions of intercourse are ineffective, no matter how large the penalties' it had to be tackled as a medical problem by officers with 'complete liberty to physically examine the native, to regulate his behaviour and his migrations, to impound him, restrain him, or otherwise isolate him, and to treat him without the delays attendant upon compliance with legal formalities appertaining to the prerogative of one department or another or the rights of the individual.'[28]

Cook seems to be on the edge of saying that diseased white men should be put away, but does not. Whereas wayward native women were in fact put in the Darwin camp called the Compound—a refuge that no more protected them from pregnancy than a walking path to the beach. Cook's main point was brutally clear: native health was essential if the region was to 'be settled and successfully exploited by a white population.' And to do this the notion of 'full powers' was his refrain, an unapologetic case for a totalitarian social order.[29]

On matters of carnal control, he had the wit to declare that 'sexual passion after prolonged repression [he was talking about the "White males in remote localities . . . deprived of all female society"] is unlikely to be influenced by academic legal enactments . . . it is not too much to say that cohabitation could not be effectively prevented unless a white guard were in constant attendance upon every lubra and even then it would be necessary to provide additional staff to keep the guard under observation.'[30]

Cook looked to a eugenicist solution to the rapid increase of half-castes who threatened to outnumber whites, a prospect that not only aroused sexual phobias but the political one of breeding a 'left-wing revolutionary element in Australia.'[31] Cook first wanted to 'breed him white' by encouraging marriages of the right sort, and during his office he managed to do so on seven occasions. Secondly, he wanted to remove boys whose fathers were white and apprentice them to the pastoral industry, and to train girls to 'a white standard' in domestic work. These women were acceptable for breeding purposes as 'a large proportion of the half-caste female population is derived from the best white stock in the country.'[32] This framework raised an obvious question: what of the sexual future for half-caste men? With whom would they breed? Again this was too hard to say—without contemplating that they would not merely mate with girls of their kind, but perhaps become prospects for willing white women. But such mixed race future was both messy, and too sexy, to articulate fully: a matter of steamy irresolution.

The cloying official term at the 1937 interstate conference of protectors was 'absorption.' After all, the Bleakley inquiry had been set up partly to squash the idea of 'a native state with self-government.' That idea was completely out of the question because, in the end, the numbers in the black state would be greater than the whites. The half-castes were multiplying—'breeding' was the panicky biological term—at an alarming rate. Again the root cause was the absence of white women on the frontier: Bleakley wanted passionately to encourage the immigration of white women into the Territory. 'One good white woman in a district will have more restraining influence than all the Acts and Regulations.' In the absence of that, though, 'the evils of miscegenation' demanded that half-caste children 'be rescued as early as possible.'[33]

The method of absorption was the systematic removal of children from their parents into institutions for 'care and training.' The lighter the children's skin, the further away from their families they should be moved: and the better their chances of absorption. Darker children might be educated with more of their kind, but even with such children, 'to avoid the dangers of the blood call, employment should be found where they will not come into contact with Aboriginals or Aboriginal half-castes.'[34]

'Check in every way possible,' Bleakley said with a summary flourish, 'the breeding of half-castes.'[35] The recommendation was, among others, that all 'cross-breeds' had to be 'rescued from camps' so that they could be educated in institutions. 'Separate the quadroon and octoroon types, at an early age, from the Aboriginal, and give special care to training for the future reception into the white races.'[36]

Here Bleakley ratified past policies and confirmed the thinking Cook was to apply when he dumped half-caste children in the Compound in Darwin, and in the Bungalow, as it was called, in Alice Springs. The Bungalow, set up in 1914, was notorious by the time Baldwin Spencer set eyes on it, and it was moved out of town to Jay Creek in 1927, away from its proximity to the Stuart Arms, then back into town in 1932, when it was planted near the telegraph station and where it continued to be the dumping ground of 'illegitimate' half-caste children removed from their parents, young children with their mothers, and pregnant mothers who were children themselves. Few of these children, as Cook seems to have admitted by 1938, were systematically getting the job training planned for them, let alone anything that could be called education.[*37] Under Cook's administration during the 1930s removal of children to 'homes' increased by more than 70 per cent.[38]

In some ways Bleakley's approach was simply philanthropic. His recommendations were especially designed to improve the lot of those on the pastoral stations where, for a licence fee of 10 shillings an employer was entitled to work an unlimited number of Aborigines without payment, as long as they were clothed and fed and reasonably sheltered. Of Aborigines with jobs in the Territory, eight out of ten were on cattle stations. Bleakley went some way towards exposing the erratic way the cattle stations kept their side of the bargain, and recommended a definite scale of wages for permanent workers (paid, as far as possible, in goods rather than cash, with a percentage of native earnings deducted for compulsory savings).

Bleakley wanted shelters to become better than uninhabitable iron huts, or 'mere kennels.' As for the camp dependants on the stations, it called for immediate relief measures to prevent the 'semi-starvation' that led to the prostitution of women and reports of what he called 'gin sprees' where 'car loads of men from bush townships and construction

---

*   The benefits to be had from life at the Bungalow seemed to depend on the personal care and industry of the town's first teacher, Ida Standley, and the industry of Sergeant Robert Stott, the protector who established it (Donovan 1988: 111, 127–31, 139).

camps . . . had given trouble on stations even 100 miles distant.' And there was the plight of the old people, many of whom had helped pioneer the station, and whose 'whole life is bound up in the totemic associations of their tribal habitat.' Bleakley wrote of 'fair entitlements' and the 'moral abuse of these people,' just as he noted that the station owners saw no point at all in offering any education to its charges, even though they were the 'machinery,' because 'education spoils them, making them cunning and cheeky.' Bleakley added: 'The trouble probably is that they become enlightened, and as a result, dissatisfied with conditions.'[39]

The Bleakley report might be seen as the genesis of a modern social justice policy for outback Aborigines—even though, when the report was tabled, the federal minister did his best to leave the details out of account. It was crucial to Bleakley's scheme that the protector be more present out bush: he proposed that telegraph officers be declared protectors, and the idea of a roaming patrol officer with the responsibilities of a protector was in the air.

So, in keeping with a total policy that destroyed lives on the one hand while trying to 'breed' them with the other, further ordinances in 1933 and 1936 tightened the laws against miscegenation outside marriage, 'maintaining the same heavy penalties that had already proved ineffective.' It was 'the high tide of control and protection, with the other effect of restricting Aboriginal rights.'[40]

Meanwhile, Cook was forthright about the pastoralists. While he was of the opinion that the territory 'must be governed as a white man's country, by the white man for the white man,' after the Bleakley report he went so far as to say that in their proprietorial attitudes pastoralists leaned towards the 'principles of slavery.'[41] Cook advocated a minimum wage for half-caste stockmen, including half-caste boys. The idea was revolutionary, and immediately declared by the Pastoral Lessees' Association to be against the natural order of things. It might work in Queensland, where some wages were paid, but to apply it in the Territory would risk an exodus of pastoralists across the border. For a brief period some payments were required by law, as they were in Queensland, but then Cook had to back down.

Frank Democrats

There was a mocking term for the colonial administration of the Northern Territory. *Khaki gentry*. It was a term used by the swaggering, angry, lusty satirist of the Territory's domestic politics, Xavier Herbert.

The force of it can be gleaned from an image in *Governing Savages,* the excellent study of Northern Territory politics in the 1930s by Andrew Marcus. There are two photographs, one above the other. The top one shows a group of 'the white upper class male, immaculately dressed and groomed.' Most of them are tanned, stern and plump: they are in whites that might as well be safari suits, with a Kiplingesque shadow like a pith helmet over their heads. The lower image is a group of young Aboriginal men: to a man they are almost naked, strappingly healthy, glossy in their virility, or as the caption puts it: 'lean and muscular men in the prime of their life.' It is one of those Baldwin Spencer shots that captured the native not too long after he had surrendered his hunting grounds to white invaders.

Sexual rivalry between white and black men has no literature in Australia: this very largely because the Australian frontier was so short of white women that a black paramour was automatically sidelined. But still the juxtaposition of the two sets of men is powerful, a stark reminder of certain elementals. The white authority with guns had physically conquered the black warriors. And it was the women of these native men (and of older men not in the picture) who were coveted by the white colonist, and the interplay of that—its sexuality and its range of affections—created a world that had to be officially beyond the ken of the khaki gentry, politically obliged though they were to meddle with it.

Take the case of Administrator C.A.E. Abbott, the Commonwealth government's officer in the Territory, to whom the protector was responsible. Abbott believed axiomatically in the ascendant economic rights of those who would develop a country. His conviction was that the pastoral interests of the Territory held the key to the best interests of the native in the long run.[42] Abbott had himself been a pastoralist in New South Wales, and had won the Federal seat of Gwydir for the Country Party in 1925. Prior to that he'd been a mounted policeman, and served in the 12th Light Horse, and with the AIF at Gallipoli and the Middle East (he entered the forces as a corporal and came out as an officer). He was educated at the King's School, Parramatta. He had been the Minister for Home and Territories in the 1928 Bruce–Page Government, and he was still a successful minister in 1937 when he resigned his seat to take the post of administrator. He was, according to his biographer, a 'thoroughly' conservative figure. In the democratic parlance, he was khaki gentry to a 'T.'[43]

Abbott's attitude towards the native was 'ambivalent.'[44] When it came to the sexual politics of policy, the same term, I think, might apply. He worried about the black girls in a rather worrying way. He wrote that he had been 'watching' the sexual problem of the half-caste women 'from all angles.' Abbott thought that 'half-caste' men should be helped towards employment, and the inculcation of 'responsibility and independence,' but declared the 'Females' in need of confinement.

He began with some suspect avuncular warmth: 'The female half-caste's life history is generally a sad one. She herself has many assets. She is good tempered, comparatively intelligent, is fond of domestic work and responds very much to kind treatment.' He went on to say: 'Most unfortunately from the age of puberty she is prey of the degenerate white and strangely enough, but to a lesser degree, of the black. As a rule she is not so much immoral as unmoral, and does not appear to have any powers of resistance. The result is that practically every female half-caste in the Darwin area has become the mother of at least one illegitimate child and very often more than one. For the last year, since I have been here, the Quarantine Station has been used for the purpose of treating VD women, all of whom have been half-castes and some of whom are married women.'

Abbott thought the real dangers to the women were heightened once they went into employment, because the class of employer varied so much. 'In studying this matter, watching it from all angles, I have come to the conclusion that the main trouble arises from lack of moral fibre,— from not possessing the moral power to resist. It appears to me that this moral strength of character can only be firmly grafted on during childhood and I think that can only come from a steady and definitely religious training. Without any religious bias whatsoever, I am bound to say that for a steady religious training for girls nothing can compare with a Roman Catholic Convent.' And it was to convents that many girls were sent, because they were 'the responsibility of the Government.'[45]

Abbott is blind here to brutal facts. For many Aboriginal women, to say no would have incited violence in much of the Outback company they kept, not to mention the fact that starvation produced prostitution, creating the conditions ripe for the 'gin sprees' Bleakley had documented. Abbott's combination of neglect of white atrocities and vaguely salacious solicitude towards the 'unmoral' girls was the shocking thing. It warranted the scorn of white men who had the courage to be open about consorting with Aboriginal women.

The sharpest, eagle eye for the sexual tendencies of white males in the Northern Territory was Olive Pink's. Hobart-born, an art teacher by training, Pink came to Central Australia to sketch, but was waylaid for the rest of her life by the mysteries and plight of the Aborigines. In 1933 and 1936 she wrote two scholarly articles for *Oceania* on secret men's business,[46] but her scholarship gradually gave way to the cause of trying to save the 'full-bloods' from extinction—speaking out for 'him' because 'religious persecution' and 'economic oppression and exploitation' prevented 'him' from speaking for himself. At the 1935 Melbourne Science Congress she gave a paper called 'Camouflage' in which she spoke of a 'sex solidarity' among men which kept them silent about the true situation of Aborigines. After some years in the Centre, and much observation of life on the ground, she was herself of the opinion that the matter of sex was 'the root of most native problems, or in unjust economic dealings with them.' She proclaimed this in the *Canberra Times* in 1938. Writing for newspapers in ways designed to prick the gentry, whom she was to devote twenty years of her life informing, correcting, badgering and exposing, she indicted 'the two codes of morality' and went on: 'Why should there (in the Northern Territory of all places) be such an hysterical and hypocritical outcry about protecting our wives when there is no similar feeling when full bloods try to protect theirs? If a white wife is sacrosanct, so is a black one.'[47]

The man who did most to alert others to the heat and the humbug of the situation was the novelist Xavier Herbert whose graphic novel, *Capricornia*, published in 1938, was based on his Darwin days in the early twenties. Herbert was as keen as Henry Miller to get inside the whale of sexual politics; and he had Orwell's sharp eye for the discomforts of colonial authority. Here he is reminding readers that the white man who loved (leaving definitions aside) an Aboriginal woman was more likely to value his 'housekeeper' as 'comely' than mistreat her as a domestic slave. Herbert is talking about the 'combo,' the white man who openly, or more or less openly, shared his life with an Aboriginal woman. 'A true combo,' Herbert wrote, 'would have thought her even beautiful. One who was observant and aesthetic would have gloated over the perfect symmetry expressed in the curves of the wide mobile nostrils and arched septum of her fleshy nose, would have delighted in her peculiar pouting mouth with thick puckered lips of colour reddish black like withered rose, in the lustrous irises and fleckless white-of-egg whites of her large black slightly-tilted eyes, in her long luxuriant bronzy lashes, in the curves of her neck and back, in the coppery black colour of her velvet skin and its fascinating musky odour . . .'[48]

And so on. Herbert's account is more than a corrective to prim social policy; it romances Aboriginal carnality rather to its own stylistic detriment. But its fullness of utterance is a reminder of feelings omitted in policy documents that repressed sexual and racial anxieties. The redolent phrase 'black velvet' was coined by white men to suggest that what they desired they might also fear in earnest. It even suggested an unknown future—'dark' in that sense where Aboriginal potency was something in its own right, and where a life would have to be made *with* Aborigines, rather than *for* them. But canvassing any of that at the time was beyond the pale. Because open, serious inter-racial intimacies could not be fully contemplated, the whole melting pot of the Territory turned on a sexual momentum that had to die as it was being born. This was indeed a love that could not speak its name. As a result a certain kind of future was treated as stillborn, or was aborted in concept. Colonial thinking made a pact of love and death.

Herbert was passionate about the hope an inter-racial Territory might hold for a decent Australian nationalism, and it was that passion— egocentric, quirky, irreverent—that helped disqualify him as a patrol officer. Administrator Abbott judged Herbert to be lacking a sense of the necessary 'loyalty and certain standards to adhere to.'[49] By contrast, W.E. Harney—Bill Harney—was embraced by officialdom as the most useful and stable of bushmen suited to the job, even though Harney's earthy view of life in the Territory, including his working man's, nonpuritanical acceptance of the combo life, was full of a libertarian gusto that implicitly mocked the khaki gentry. In 1941 Harney showed Elkin a set of short stories: Elkin helped edit them, and wrote the introduction to the book published two years later as *Taboo*. Harney called them stories of 'A Culture Clash, with the victory always in favour of the superior race' (by 'race' he meant superior white power). 'Clash' was not quite the right word either. They were stories—about Aboriginal elders, crooked lawyers, doctors, black stockmen, Chinamen and Aboriginal women, that featured the meeting of cultures and its impact on lives, on *relationships*. Those relationships, their humanity as much as their dislocations, were Harney's theme. Harney was no great writer and his sentiments were as raw as a socialist realist but the ground-level, melting-pot message was clear from his story 'The Doctor,' which ends: 'Pity, that knows no boundary of colour or creed, is always right. It is an emotion that does not spring from duty to a member of a society, but forms the tie that binds forever the human race, and must continue when hatred of class and colour is gone and the human race stands forth as one, and wars and all such viciousness have faded away.'[50]

The other value driving Harney's stories was the relativity of knowledge, which revealed the silliness of one culture *thinking* it could lord it over another. By the end of the story 'Mumba,' which is about the death spirits that inhabit the daily life of natives, Harney was able to write:

> You civilised man, you savage native, though your ideas are as one, they are really apart. Each sneers at the other, and each thinks he is right, while I think of the Procurator who asked Christ that ancient question, 'What is truth?' Though he was unanswered then, nevertheless the native is right and we are right. The customs and beliefs of a people, built up by ages of experience, are the answer—'they are the truth.' But because civilised man thinks he knows, he causes the customs of primitive man to be trampled underfoot, with the result that the ties and the people fade away.[51]

In *Taboo* there are two photographs of young Aboriginal women that are remarkable for two reasons: they neither feature native beauty in a salacious way, nor convey any need for pity. The young women are there as individuals. One is captioned 'light caste Aboriginal woman,' rather than 'half-caste'; the other, 'young Aboriginal woman.' A poignant story is about a young woman, Nance, a girl shoved from pillar to post as the 'wife' of various men, black and white, all the time trying to find her feet. The punch line is that after all this 'she has only reached the threshold of life—for she has just turned sixteen years old.' Harney had pity, but the story does not turn on pity. It has too much respect for the girl in it. And the sorrow in it derives from the girl's hapless social plight between cultures. In general Harney's stories at their best weave a web of the spiritual and the carnal, a weave that is bound to elude the machinations of any bureaucracy.

Harney himself was a 'combo.' He married a mixed-blood woman, Linda (her Aboriginal mother's name Harney avoided giving, as he did her white father's). He first saw her with a 'team of girls straining on a rope hauling logs to the mission saw mill,'[52] courted her in the respectable way and married her. Thereafter he lost the hospitality of many station owners, and he had to camp down on the river, away from the homestead, even when Linda was dying of tuberculosis, and to move from station to station with their two young children. After Linda died at the Katherine hospital in 1932 Harney had bitter memories as to who had helped them out and who not, and when he was patrol officer he 'never ate at the table of the cattle bosses.'[53] Harney could sing, in the way of the lustful bushman, of gin-shepherding—

The bushman's gin, a very fine thing
A very fine thing to have.
Twinkling eyes and gleaming teeth,
Eyes to shock an Irish priest . . .

but it was with a note of irony as well as unjudgmental acceptance of love lives in the Outback, and an interest in the 'depth of romance behind the veil.'[54] 'To me the best stories in the bush are those which cannot be printed,' he wrote in one of his later books, and the ones most stately against the grain of the official culture of the Territory.

Harney's writings were, really, a setting down of what could not be written in the official records, a laconic revelation of the hidden life of the Territory that placed white secrets in the open as much as the anthropologists were prone to place black secrets. He was simply always speaking—'so I talked and talked, becoming milder all the while'[55]—with narrative cunning and bush tact about complex realities Darwin could never control. His actual life of intermingling in the Territory—his fluency of friendship with whites and blacks—enabled him to sense the cant of official policy. Yet his administrative superiors relied on him because his grasp of fluid social realities was truer than their own.

The fatal flaw of the khaki gentry's thinking was classification. The racial categories designed to solve a racist problem—that of the 'half-caste'—involved the extinction of individuality, the death of relationships. No one put this better than another democratic writer out of the Territory, Ion Idriess, when he raged in the letter columns of the *Sydney Morning Herald*. A news report had mentioned a Harvard–Adelaide research expedition to 'ascertain whether half-castes can be adjusted to modern civilisation, or must remain a group apart' and that, Idriess wrote, 'gives a nasty jar to old half-caste mates of mine, and adds to the bitter grudge that all unfortunate "thinking" half-castes bear the whites throughout this continent':

I remember so often riding in from the far bush with mates who had worked happily together for twelve months at a time under conditions of hardship. In town our half-caste mate would have to stand outside: we could ask him in for a drink but he would not be served. Should we move out of the district and go further south, our half-caste mate dare not come, knowing only too well that the further south he went the less chance he would have of even being allowed to sit at table for his meals with white men. Imagine the immeasurably more miserable plight of the educated half-caste girl . . .

I have had some splendid mates among the half-castes, men who were as well educated as I and as mentally alert. As to having 'guts,' well, a half-caste mate has saved my life more than once. In war I have fought beside him, and seen him die with a smile on his face. And yet we won't give him a chance to make good. If he is trained to good honest work, then he responds to that training as we all do. If he is decently educated, then his mental powers are developed for a responsible job, just as ours are. City folk have no idea of the bitterness with which the half-caste regards the whites.[56]

Each of these frank democrats—Herbert, Harney, Idriess—spoke from their various trusting intimacies with Aboriginal people, which Strehlow could never fully share. He was a mission boy. The taboos against consorting with Aboriginal women, even though he knew their beauty, and as a boy had known their touch, were obviously too great. This would have been the case even if he had not been married. Furthermore, as a patrol officer he was now himself member—at least nominally—of the khaki gentry. He had his authority to uphold, which was not to say, however, that he could not share one fundamental truth with them: that everything they said about their dark friends (their mates, as Idriess said, a term that Strehlow could never have used) underlined them as victims of white colonisation. Khaki gentry or not, Strehlow came to share that.

Taking Office

By early 1937 Strehlow had some of the formal authority he wanted. Cook had memoed all concerned that he was to carry out the duties of a protector in all districts. He was to inspect all books or records about Aborigines or Aboriginal affairs at police stations; he could issue instructions or advice to any rural protectors; and they were to cooperate with him in all matters. You will note, Cook told his staff, that 'the Patrol

Officer has been definitely charged with the responsibility of supervising the employment of Aboriginals on stations and their welfare generally.'[57] Cook also made another thing clear, for those who had any 'misapprehension.' Strehlow's patrol should not be limited to the south-western reserve. Reading between the lines, the point of this was clear: pastoralists and mining interests north of Alice Springs had been warned. It was the duty of the new patrol officer to see what they were up to.

But Strehlow was also lacking powers he needed, namely to take action where some kind of corporal punishment was called for. The police had been able to exercise that power in certain circumstances. He had 'vestiges' of power. He told himself on 31 May, after about nine months in the job: 'I am left as a "PO" without power in my own district: I am not even a police officer, and could only appear in the capacity of a Patrol Officer advertising crimes perpetrated in his own district by native offenders.' The rights to corporal punishment were never to come either, officially: try though he would to get authorities to realise that he was, if anyone was to be, especially capable of implementing both laws in Aranda territory.

Strehlow's domain stretched from Tennant Creek to the South Australian border, and from about 100 miles east of Alice Springs to the Western Australian border, an area the size of England and where there were about 4,600 Aborigines. Most—3,217—of these people were still classified as 'nomads' despite the so-called drift towards settlements (the numbers in the Petermann Ranges, Strehlow's 'south-west patrol,' had actually increased between 1930 to 1935). In 1935 those in supervised camps numbered 696; those in regular employment 529.*

In the beginning he was stationed in Alice Springs, now 'the Capital of Central Australia' as distinct from the quiet little telegraph station of Stuart. The town got its new name in 1933, after, as one droll administrator remarked, 'the Australian Government turned in its sleep and decided at last that something must be done for the Northern Territory.' Henceforth public servants would be stationed in the town, even if, for some time, they had no place of their own to stay. After the railway link was made from Adelaide the white population in the

---

*   The figures are rubbery, but they were at least the result of Cook putting the police to work on a census, the better to get a bearing on the needs of policy. Bleakley, after all, had wanted to increase provisions on the reserves hoping that missionaries could 'provide a sanctuary for the natives, exercise a steadying influence and relieve distress' (Rowse 1989: 49–56).

region grew steadily (from 400 in 1928 to 590 in 1930).

Alice was a town comfortably spreadeagled on either side of the Todd River, once the home country of the Central Aranda people. Further out from the town's precincts were the early pastoral holdings, Undoolya to the east of the town, Owen Springs to the north. To a visiting geologist, the Oxford-educated Cecil Madigan, the whole place was still rather raw—the Stuart Arms had an outdoor shower, where you stepped carefully 'between the old boots and trousers left behind by travellers coming in,' and at Foggarty and Wallis' store you could buy anything from fly nets to camels' nosepegs. It was a town with one foot in the 'bad old days' of the frontier, as Dick Kimber referred to them,[58] and the other in the beginning of modernity. The first bank had opened, and various aircraft had been seen in the skies, not just those looking for Kingsford Smith in his *Southern Cross*. Airplanes were beginning to fly doctors and mail across country, and the town would have garages for motor cars, some electric light and paving in the streets. Other mission outfits had arrived: Methodists, Catholics and Anglicans had churches in town. Alice was a place to which the pastoralists came and reaffirmed their occupation of the land, miners arrived with the lust of optimistic prospects, and public servants settled with some trepidation.[59]

The Aboriginal population had been growing steadily since the turn of the century, with different language groups drifting towards what the white settlement might have to offer. The white man's idea was to keep most Aborigines out of the town for most of the time. But the truth was that Aborigines were needed in town for their cheap labour: the men disposed of sanitary waste, and odd-jobbed with livestock; Aboriginal women were domestic help. A little way out of town were the camps where people were encouraged to stay, and to survive on government rations if they had no jobs. Strehlow had only been in his job a few months when he told Cook what was what:

> The living conditions of natives in the various camps . . . are deplorable, and probably cannot be improved to any appreciable extent. The present gazetted area is barren and rocky, devoid of shade and firewood. The huts and tin shacks are disgraceful structures, the surrounding district is practically devoid of any form of game with which the natives could eke out their present rations.
>
> Employment can be found by only a small percentage of the natives in the camp. The rest receive scanty Government rations, and rely for

their living very largely on begging, gambling and the proceeds of various forms of immorality and procuring. At the same time the presence of the ration depot at Alice Springs continues to attract into this undesirable centre scores of natives from all parts of Central Australia . . . They have come from places hundred of miles southeast, east and northeast of Alice Springs, and are at present useless drifting wreckage.

I have indicated in two previous reports the degrading influence which is exercised by such Government ration depots as Alice Springs and Charlotte Waters upon the young native immigrants. It is my opinion that the majority of these natives rapidly degenerate and turn into a band of unemployable hooligans, beggars, and wasters.[60]

Strehlow wanted most of the Alice Springs natives to be repatriated to their homelands. More particularly, he wanted a settlement re-established at Jay Creek, a watering place in the rocky hills 35 miles west of Alice Springs, on the road out to Hermannsburg. There was enough water there in most seasons, Strehlow argued, provided the stock from the Owens Springs station were kept out! He urged Darwin to base him at Jay Creek. 'The total result would be an attractive native camp, in which the survivors of the original inhabitants of the country could get a decent living in return for a reasonable measure of work.'

Six months later Strehlow was even more impatient, still emphasising 'the sordid precincts of Alice Springs native camps' with their 'infamous trade in Aboriginal women.' He worked himself up to a huge statement, one that presumed to table a complete overview of native policy in Central Australia. 'Now is the time to act,' he told the Chief Protector:

If the present opportunity for helping the natives is frittered away, future incurable disease and undertaker's measures will be of little value: it is the present young generation of natives that must be assisted and tided over the present crisis brought about by the dissolution of their tribal life. It was the dishonest 'leave 'em alone' policy sponsored by such pompous professional misrepresenters of native thought and culture as Sir Baldwin Spencer and H. Basedow that led to the betrayal by the Aboriginals Department of such vigorous tribes as the Aranda and Loritja tribes of Central Australia. However, time has proved how impracticable and devastating such a policy has been even though backed by the *bubble reputations* which these degreed men enjoyed among people of their own generations. Even if the less well-informed people in Australia still believe faithfully in the outworn and useless tenets of the 'leave 'em alone' creed, surely the Aboriginals Department of the Northern Territory, which has no longer the excuse of ignorance, will stand by its responsibilities and duties firmly and courageously; and excise all cancerous growths from the body of the Central Australian native community before it is too late to save the patient . . .

If the natives of Central Australia ever die out, posterity will justly place the blame where it belongs,—on an Aboriginals Department which adopted and clung on to a 'leave 'em alone' policy. (emphasis added)[61]

It is hard to imagine a more trenchant set of remarks coming from a new public servant. With a depth of personal passion he is asserting his authority, and in the upright manner that would often unsettle those in authority. To some extent he was on firm ground. Few knew better than Strehlow what the doomed-race theory might mean in practice: how social Darwinism became a self-fulfilling prophecy. The mission work he had seen for much of his life demonstrated what needed to be done when the dispossessed were in physical need. But his outburst revealed other things. The fact that he completely misrepresented Baldwin Spencer's policy (which was not a 'leave 'em alone' one at all), is something that might have given Cook pause, especially if he detected a touch of personal malice in Strehlow against the man who had wanted to close his father's mission. Here there was personal compulsion about Strehlow's claims to authority.*

There is another aspect of Strehlow's forthrightness that deserves attention. He was speaking up as if he was alone, a solitary voice in the

---

*   Then there was that Shakespearean reference to 'bubble reputations,' an allusion to the speech in *As You Like It* that most fully expands upon the notion that 'all the world's a stage, And all the men and women merely players.' It was a window into young Strehlow's hostility toward 'parental authority' and his tendency to confuse that with his own claims to maturity. The bubble reputation is the soldier's who is 'jealous in honour, sudden and quick in quarrel.' The passage includes the most mocking description of infantile dependence, 'mewling and puking in the nurse's arms. And then the whining schoolboy.' The seven ages of man is the arc Shakespeare is describing: from childhood to the shrinking of man back to 'childish treble,' to 'second childishness, and mere oblivion, Sans teeth, sans eyes, sans taste, sans everything.' Futility right down the line, you might say, an emotion Strehlow had a tendency to indulge.

wilderness. You would never know that his own senior patron and editor A.P. Elkin was well known for his policy statements on the 'native problem' and had been publishing the most enlightened thinking of the day. As early as 1932, the year Strehlow returned inland, Elkin had written about 'the secret life' of Aborigines as worthy of respect; and of initiation ceremonies that 'sanctify hope for the future both in this life and life after death.' 'Secret life should not be interfered with,' Elkin wrote, and worried about the creation of a 'dichotomy' in young men's minds. Admittedly, Elkin had gone on to say things about mission work that would have displeased Strehlow: remarks to the effect that despite all the efforts of the missionary to be the 'civilising agent' and break down tribal authority, 'The Old Men and the glamour of the secret life win.' Elkin painted a picture of the missionary duped by the outward appearances of 'the young fellow advancing along the secret path, and in his heart getting further and further away from the white man's doctrines and view of life.'

'Yes,' wrote Elkin, as if to fully affirm all the old ways, 'see him there and you will know where he finds his meaning for life, sanction for conduct and hope for the future. And unless the tribe breaks down, or is broken down, he will sooner or later spend a great deal of his time wandering over haunts sanctified by the wanderings of the great heroes of old, and performing the sacred rites on which the life of the tribe and nature depend.'[62]

Strehlow could not have liked these remarks because they boldly declared much mission work to be damaging to Aboriginal welfare and a failure. They also advanced the idea that the culture was not as broken as it might seem. If true, this would have applied to the young men drifting about in Alice Springs, not just those on the mission stations. The point was that there was still power left in the secret life, that some old men still had the 'glamour' to 'win.' Quite apart from the ethnographic facts of the matter in different contexts across the Territory, Strehlow was already rather personally invested in them not winning.

And yet Elkin blended compassion with social analysis—an analysis that included, as we have seen, a non-doctrinal embrace of Aboriginal spirituality. And he was vociferous about the need to understand Aborigines, and to support their 'uplift' through education.

But Strehlow does not summon Elkin's expertise, or anyone else's if it comes to that. Why?

The simple answer is that he did not feel the need. He knew enough himself. He knew because of his mission background, and of course from his recent travelling in Central Australia. His ally in understanding was, if anyone, Pastor Albrecht, whose work also gave him personal authority to speak. That was the point: *personal* authority. Strehlow's command of Aranda and his fieldwork, including his brilliant article in *Oceania*, gave him the authority, if he wanted to use it, as an academic 'anthropologist.' But he chose not to speak in that way because, I think, he would have regarded most academic understanding as paper thin. Radcliffe-Brown, when he was calling for governments to employ the expertise of the 'applied anthropologist,' was of the opinion that 'a thoroughly trained and competent anthropologist can learn more about a native tribe in a few weeks than an untrained person can do in several years.'[63]

Such an assertion of professional prowess would already have been anathema to Strehlow. He was already standing on his biographical ground, upon which his claims to knowledge were inseparable from his grasp of the native tongue and his mission-based moral relationships with Aboriginal people. The mortal time *he* had spent with 'them' was what mattered most. That's what he was already implicitly claiming: a kind of exclusivity, of time passed, of his time being invested, of himself having a kind of natural authority.

The Whole Immensity of the Problem

In June 1937 Strehlow set out to show his colleague Sergeant Koop the 'whole immensity of the "contact" problem.'[64]

They went back over the track Strehlow had been on in 1932: north from Alice Springs, up towards Barrow Creek and Tea Tree, as well as the tin field at Aningie, a district which had been settled in the most callous way, where waterholes had been commandeered from Aboriginal country, *tjurunga* storehouses raided, and scores of people shot. Strehlow's diary account is rather bantering at first, and then shades into a terrible seriousness.

They were not long on the track when they met Don Campbell, the owner of Mount Peake station. 'He told me,' Strehlow wrote in his diary, 'about happenings.' These included Nugget Morton keeping a Western Australian lubra there for his stockwork: she had tried to run away but Morton had got her back each time and inflicted a severe hiding as a deterrent against further attempts to run away. Strehlow recorded that Nugget was now employing as 'stockmen' one or two other little native girls, nine or ten years of age, whom he had raped. Another little girl he had given to his nephew, who was about seventeen years of age. Ben Nicker, who was working for Nugget, was also using a little girl, and both Ben and the girl were suffering from gonorrhoea.

'Campbell added that he had given this information to Muldoon, the Constable at Barrow Creek and now Acting Sergeant at Alice Springs; but the latter had declined to act, saying that it would be impossible to get the necessary evidence for a court prosecution. Campbell added that he himself would not give evidence in court in support of these charges, as then he would be liable to have his stock interfered with by Morton and Co.'

'Probably,' Strehlow concluded, 'the story is true, other station owners have hinted at the same thing previously.'[65]

So they were on the lookout for Morton, who had merely seemed a flamboyant bush character when Strehlow first met him in 1932. The challenge was to find where Morton had his main camp. On their first trip north Strehlow and Koop could not find him. In May, they went backwards and forwards to the Aningie tin field—looking again but to no avail. They met Mrs Davis, Morton's sister, who wanted permission to keep a young girl called Kitty as her domestic help. But Kitty's story, when she was interviewed by Koop, created more complications.

Strehlow wrote in his diary: 'According to Koop she left Mount Peake because of hidings received from Mr and Mrs Campbell. She went and stayed with Lil (the W.A. lubra) at "Nugget" Morton's camp. Kitty has lived with Morton, is Morton's missus. She usually stayed with Lil. Kitty had a baby which lived for some days,—then "died itself,"—i.e. from natural causes. She had this baby some time ago, "when there was small rain."'

'Kitty, to us,' Strehlow observed, 'looked very mature. She had the figure and the full breasts of a woman, also a full set of teeth. Probably child bearing had made her look older. She could have been 17 years of age.' According to Mrs Campbell, Strehlow noted, Morton had taken Kitty when she was only nine or ten. Evidently Morton also claimed that he was the 'guardian' of Lil because she had been in his care as a child.[66]

After this news from Mrs Campbell, they set off once more. This time they went towards Mount Brown. The reason for this destination was horrible. 'Mrs Campbell told us that some time ago a little native girl aged *three* [Strehlow's emphasis] had been raped somewhere here and had died of her injuries a few days later.'[67]

For his reported offences with Aboriginal girls Morton was never brought to account by Strehlow: the evidence was evidently too difficult to gather. Nor was the death of the little girl fully investigated. By the end of those early trips Strehlow seems to have felt that he had given Koop a fair introduction to the 'contact' problem.

In 1937 Strehlow had a visit from his secular masters, the Federal Minister of the Interior, T. Paterson, and the influential permanent head of the department, J.A. Carrodus. Paterson, a member of the Bruce Government, had come to the Centre as the site of recent controversies. He wanted to see for himself, the better to appease the pressure groups when they banged on his door about the plight of Aborigines.

Carrodus was in principle a reformer along the lines of Cook, but he believed that the education of natives was a waste of time, and he failed to help Cook improve medical facilities. Carrodus was also sufficiently defensive about government policy to breach public service etiquette that year by writing to the press that 'everything that is humanly possible is being done to preserve the race and attend to the welfare of the native populations.'[68]

Strehlow and Koop went into town to meet them. After one and a half hours with the Canberra officials Strehlow told his diary that points raised were:

1) Protest against a permit being granted to Hummerston to trespass upon S.W. Reserve.* Minister stated that this had been granted, not to H, but to the honourable Sydney business man who had financed the expedition. However M for Interior had been so troubled about it all that he got Cabinet's approval first. No local officials were consulted.

     My protest stands, even if ineffective.

2) Mentioned my action in the case Lukas V Elvida at Hbg in Oct last year. Minister and Sec. strongly approved of my action, and suggested that I should be given the power to authorise corporal punishment which would then have to be carried out by the proper tribal authorities. They promised to have this granted to me,—if it would not cause the govt. any 'embarrassment.'

---

* Hummerston was the German Strehlow had unsuccessfully pursued in 1935 (see 'Primal Journeys').

3) They approved of my suggestion that tribal murderers be sent into exile, e.g., the new Darwin compound when this is finished.

4) Approved, in principle, of Sgt Koop's and my proposed campaign against illicit relationships between blacks, whites and half-castes.

5) They concurred in my suggestion that, if there were *old, longstanding* irregular alliances between lubras and whites should be permitted to be changed into normal legal marriages, if the white man wished to make such amends to his lubra. They suggested that a definite time limit be fixed, so as to prevent younger new comers from living with and marrying lubras.

6) Approved in principle of my suggested scheme of scalp depots within Native Reserve, when I explained that the necessary staff should be provided by the principal Australian Churches, each of whom would then be allowed a diplomatic sphere of action. The Minister and the Secretary asked me to get into touch directly and unofficially with the Churches in question on this matter.[69]

It would appear that Strehlow had a good audience with his superiors—although the note of protest and the tendency to speak of his protests as 'ineffective' colour his report and, I suspect, crept into his face-to-face dealings. He often knew that what he was talking about acutely required the approval of authorities, and would always be piqued when he did not get it.

What also comes through is his compliance with the conventional colonial imposition of corporal punishment, the most brutal demonstration of paternalism at work; the white authority unashamedly acting in loco parentis. This policy might seem justifiable, as it was with Lukas, as 'better' than sending a native to gaol. But there was no getting away from its physical reality as a gross expression of racist power on a colonial frontier, and that, naturally, was why the government men spoke to him quietly about 'embarrassment.' The bind Strehlow was then in was also acute: the direction of his thought and feeling was closer to those humanitarian campaigners down south, those who would kick up a fuss at such treatment, but here he was as an advocate of floggings. Yet he was so with a crucial difference from previous practice.

'I should be given the power to authorise corporal punishment which would then have to be carried out by *the proper tribal authorities*' (emphasis added). This was crucial. It moved white authority into the camp of customary Aboriginal law. It was not Strehlow's idea. It had been recommended by the Cleland report, and it had the support of Elkin. But it was an idea that looked into the future, by way of saying 'this is a better way to conceive of justice than imposing laws that natives cannot be expected to understand.' It raised other difficulties, of course, the most obvious being the political implications of having a whole people and therefore territories governed by laws other than those of the sovereign colonial powers. But that issue was not pressing. The urgent issue was to settle conflicts out bush in ways that were both more effective—more meaningful and less obviously brutal in white terms—than whites flogging blacks. To apply this concept required someone who knew 'the proper tribal authorities.' Who better than a man who had grown up among 'them,' who spoke 'their' language?

Strehlow obviously felt it was the most natural thing to take this authority upon himself: the authority to delegate, transferring his proper judgment to their proper authorities, placing the white whip into black hands. Overall, any appraisal of the justice of this logic would depend on who were to be the 'the proper tribal authorities.' By what criteria would proper be judged? And in what kind of context—for what offences exactly, judged by whose cultural values—were they to be involved? Would proper tribal authorities have flogged Lukas for beating Elvida? That event had left him worried, his guilt unresolved. Would they want to beat their kin for spearing cattle? For a payback killing after a man had sold another's *tjurunga*? In 1937, Strehlow was not considering political spaces for any Aboriginal self-government. His stance on corporal punishment was enlightened enough, but on balance it was mainly a pragmatic corrective of the grosser colonialisms; a translation of power that made no structural difference.

On sexual order he was looking for a middle way. Yes to liaisons that were the 'old, longstanding' ones: a white man should be allowed to marry his Aboriginal woman, 'if the white man wished to make such amends.' No to the others, the 'illicit' ones he wanted to track down with the help of Sergeant Koop. Strehlow was fitting into official policy, including, it would seem, the policy of removing some illegitimate or neglected children from their parents. He was more attentive to the sexual adulthood of Aboriginal girls than their youth, and thereby gave something of a moral fillip to official policy. Here the mission boy was keen to be on the trail of the sexual offenders—the likes of whom he had spotted many times in his previous travels. Neither the minister nor the secretary chose to remark on the potential futility of that quest: they were overlooking Cook's realistic drollery about guarding the guard.

Soon enough—the next day—Strehlow and Koop were out on the track. They drove down to Linda Vale to see what the station owner Pearce was up to. Pearce had once had a licence to employ female Aboriginal labour, but had lost it when he admitted that three of the children in the half-caste institution were his by his Aboriginal companion Fanny. They reached the property before midnight and roused Pearce so that Koop could flash his torch around the premises. 'No lubra; only the two half-caste apprentices were there,' Strehlow noted.

But Pearce lived suspiciously close to his camp of Aboriginal shepherds—the bough shelters were only 80 yards from his house rather than the regulation five chains (110 yards). In a shelter they found Fanny with a half-caste child: what they had to establish was whether she still shared her boss's bed.

They camped the night between the shelters and the house so that Pearce could not talk to his other native workers. They 'interrogated' Fanny, who told them she did not do 'housework' for Pearce and that the child was hers by an unknown white man she had slept with in Alice Springs. They questioned the others, who told them Fanny did do housework but did not sleep with Pearce.

'We were checkmate now,' Strehlow thought.[70]

Pearce had been standing around anxiously. Koop told him he had a bad reputation, reminded him of his previous offspring, and said that he and Strehlow had plans to make the 1918 ordinance work, even if it never had before.

'Pearce squirmed; he had been here and there all his life,—he had been rover here, stockman there, had been recommended once for the position of head manager of Victoria River Downs Station, etc, and now, after all the battling of a hard life—54 years old he is now—all was to be nought. Koop replied that this showed that Pearce had the opportunities to rear a white family and be a decent married man, instead of wasting his money and years on lubras. Now [Pearce] had nothing to live for. Also, this thing had to be stopped, lest other young men follow the same bad example.'

Koop put the question to Pearce. Did he want to marry Fanny or not?

'No,' Pearce said. 'I have disgraced my poor old mother enough, already.'

But the next day when Strehlow and Koop were getting ready to go,

Pearce changed his mind. 'Pearce now expressed his desire to marry Fanny! Koop said that he would support P's request, and suggest[ed] that P get my support also. P then thanked us both very heartily, assuring us that now at least he felt a free honest man again, after having been all of a tremor since midnight last night. P later assured me that Fanny had said that it was a good job that they had refrained from intercourse for so many months now—else they might both have gone to gaol now.'[71]

From Strehlow's account it is not clear whether Fanny was consulted about the marriage. In any case, 'Pearce loaded up Fanny'—put her in the car with her 'dresses, soap, stockings, shoes etc.' for transportation back to Jay Creek. There she was to live out of harm's way until permission to marry was granted. 'Both looked happy,—were all smiles now.' Back at Jay Creek Fanny was to wait for many months for news from Darwin, in the meantime helping Bertha with her chores.

From Linda Vale they went down to Angas Downs, owned by Billy Liddle. It was a similar story—making a raid where they had to do their private investigating of a station owner's life, and then as gently as possible cross-questioning the owner about the sexual state of play. On the way towards the homestead they met two female shepherds. One 'admitted' to having a child by Liddle, which was now in the Half-Caste Institution, but said she had not lived with Liddle recently. Nor, said the other, had she. But the women gave 'quite a number of names' of girls who had been 'shepherds' for Liddle.

The point was—or half the point—that Liddle only had a licence to employ Aboriginal men. Arriving at the station, the patrol officer and the policeman observed Liddle had four men working for him and fifteen females, eleven of whom were single and aged between eleven and 35. They found that Liddle had not paid any money into the trust account of his two half-caste apprentices, claiming he was paying them in stock.

Koop took Liddle's licence so that he could prosecute later. But, Strehlow recorded, it was impossible to arrest Liddle because he would have lost all his sheep. And it was equally difficult to take all the single girls and women away—too difficult, apparently, because there was nowhere to take them. So Koop did some 'straight talking,' to which Liddle protested that he had tried to employ men but they would not stay to work. His natives kept coming and going. He reported sheep killings and the theft of a pair of trousers. The culprits were from the reserve out at the Petermann, as were the women.

Strehlow chipped in:

I remarked that it was strange that all the young women here were
'single' as in every central Australian tribe the girls are normally
promised by their parents to men when they are still quite young, often
soon after birth. Liddle knew this custom, and weakly expressed his
'surprise' that the groups of natives at his place apparently had not
promised their girls away(!) I remarked that young native women
normally refused to live with black husbands only when they had associated too freely with whites previously; & Sgt Koop remarked that the
same thing was probably the case here too, even though Liddle had
claimed not to have had intercourse since about 5 or 6 years.[72]

Everyone was losing in this conversation. Liddle was on the mat, and the
government men thought he could not be trusted. But Strehlow's
sarcastic reminder of ethnographic practice was two-timing as well. It
was one thing to protect the young girls; another, perhaps, to indict the
Aboriginal women who had chosen to go with the white man. And if
it was true as he had told Liddle that once they had done so regularly
they were estranged from their 'black husbands,' why sheet home the
trend to Liddle? What Liddle was getting was an earful of the chief
protector's unpoliceable law, rather coloured by the 'anthropologist'
sounding like a missionary's son. Liddle was also listening to the man
who had once descended upon him in need: Angas Downs had been
Strehlow and Bertha's port of call on their return from their tragic
ordeal out west, less than two years before.

All this had an element of burlesque, nonetheless. Strehlow sometimes wrote up his trips in the idiom of the bush yarn, for all the world
as if he had digested something of Tom Collins' *Such Is Life*. After this
outing—which had taken him 595 miles and left him almost dizzy
with weariness when he got back to Jay Creek, he felt it was all worthwhile, 'most successful' and 'a wonderful encouragement for continuing
with my work.'[73] Pearce would be obliged to marry Fanny, once the
chief protector granted permission. Liddle would be fined for not
paying his apprentices. And Koop had had another lesson on 'the
immensity of the contact problem.'

The euphoria of return in 1937 did not, however, fit the adjustments
Strehlow made the following year. For example, he went back to see
Billy Liddle and found that, as he wrote to Cook, the 'book keeping

was greatly improved.' And, 'No females were to be found at the station itself.'

Cook knew what that phrasing meant. It indicated that Strehlow had decided that prosecuting Liddle for cohabitation was useless. Strehlow was honest enough to go on: 'It is, of course, not necessary to suppose that Liddle had reformed his way of living . . . last year's females have now turned into "dependants" and last year's aged fathers and mothers of the female employees have been booked down now as "employees." However the natives at Liddle's place are well-trained; and no grounds could be found for taking any action. It is even possible that Liddle, who is rapidly getting an old man and is not in good health, may be tiring somewhat of his old-time band of lubras.'[74]

The whole issue of Aboriginal girls would fester for the rest of his term as a patrol officer. Sometimes the situations were relatively benign, as they seem to have been at Linda Vale and Angas Downs. At other places this was far from being so. As late as 1940 Strehlow was reporting on gruesome details of miners near Mount Doreen who were involved with seven girls between the ages of eleven and sixteen, and he reported to Darwin that 'each one stated that she visited the miners' camps for food after dark, the miner asked her into his camp, had intercourse with her, then gave her food and sent her back to camp. The girls stated that their only reason for visiting the miners' camps was because they were hungry and the miners gave them food.'[75]

1   W.E.H. Stanner, 'The Aborigines' [1938], in *White Man Got no Dreaming* (Canberra: Australian National University Press, 1979), 1.
2   W.E.H. Stanner, 'Not by Eastern Windows Only: Anthropological Advice to Australian Governments in 1938,' *Aboriginal History* 3, no. 1 (1979): 41.
3   Ibid.
4   Stanner, 'The Aborigines,' 100.
5   Tigger Wise, *The Self-Made Anthropologist: A Life of A.P. Elkin,* (Sydney: Allen & Unwin. Sydney, 1985), 100.
6   Ibid., 119.
7   Ibid., 105.
8   A.P. Elkin, *Anthropology in Australia, Past and Present: Report of the Presidential Address to Australian and New Zealand Association for the Advancement of Science. Melbourne Meeting January 1935* (Sydney: the association, 1935), 197.
9   Wise, *Self-Made Anthropologist,* 95
10 Ibid., 95.
11 Kenelm Burridge, *Encountering Aborigines: A Case Study: Anthropology and the Australian Aboriginal* (New York: Pergamon, 1973), 6–38, 197.
12 Stanner, 'Not by Eastern Windows Only,' 37–61.
13 Ibid., 55.

14 Stanner, 'The Aborigines,' 17.
15 Charles Duguid, *Doctor and the Aborigines* (Adelaide: Rigby, 1972), 93–104.
16 Stanner, 'The Aborigines,' 8–9.
17 Tim Rowse, *White Flour, White Power* (Melbourne: Cambridge University Press, 1988), passim.
18 *Historical Records of Victoria*. vol. 2A, 62
19 Russell McGregor, *Imagined Destinies: Aboriginal Australians and the Doomed Race Theory, 1880–1939* (Melbourne: Melbourne University Press, 1998), 69.
20 Ibid., 75.
21 Ibid., 78.
22 Ibid., 83–86; John Mulvaney, *So Much That Is New* (Melbourne: Melbourne University Press, 1985), 280–85.
23 McGregor, *Imagined Destinies*, 75.
24 Julie Marcus, *First in Their Field* (Melbourne: Melbourne University Press, 1993), 6.
25 J.W. Bleakley, *The Aboriginals and the Half-Castes of Central Australia and North Australia* (Canberra: Commonwealth Government Printer, 1929), 7.
26 *National Territory Dictionary of Biography*, vol. 1, 60.
27 Marcus, *First in their Field*, 17.
28 Cook to Patterson, 2 September 1938, AA452/1 Item 52/541.
29 Cook to Patterson, September 1938, AA452/1 Item 52/541.
30 Cited in Andrew Marcus, *Governing Savages* (Sydney: Allen & Unwin, 1990), 94, as something of a refrain by Cook between 1929 and 1936.
31 Cited in Anna Haebich, *Broken Circles: Fragmenting Indigenous Families* (Fremantle: Fremantle Arts Centre Press, 2001), 195.
32 Marcus, *First in Their Field*, 92–94.
33 Bleakley, *The Aboriginals and the Half-Castes*, 27–30.
34 Ibid., 29.
35 Ibid., 40.
36 Ibid., 40.
37 See, for example, the exchange between District Officer V.G. Carrington and Cook, 27 April and 19 May 1938, AA F1/42/70A.
38 Cited in Haebich, *Broken Circles*, 195.
39 Bleakley, *The Aboriginals and the Half-Castes*, 6–10.
40 C.D. Rowley, *The Remote Aborigines* (Ringwood: Penguin, 1972), 280.
41 Marcus, *First in their Field*, 57, 90.
42 Jeremy Long, *The Go-Betweens. Patrol Officers in Aboriginal Affairs Administration in the Northern Territories* (Casuarina, N.T.: North Australian Research Unit, Australian National University Press, 1992), 56.
43 *Northern Territory Dictionary of Biography*, vol. 1, 2.
44 Ibid., 3.
45 Abbott to Patterson, 28 April 1938, AA452/1 Item 52/541.
46 Olive Pink, 'Spirit Ancestors in a Northern Aranda Horde Country,' *Oceania* IV, no. 2 (1933); 'The Landowners in the Northern Division of the Aranda Tribe,' *Oceania* VI, no. 2 (1936).
47 *Canberra Times*, 6 November 1938.
48 Xavier Herbert, *Capricornia* (Sydney: Angus and Robertson, 1938), 15.
49 Abbott to Patterson, 28 April 1938, AA 452/1 Item 52/541.
50 W.E. Harney, *Taboo* (Sydney: Australasian Publishing Company, 1943), 69.
51 Ibid., 152.
52 W.E. Harney, *Grief, Gaiety and Aborigines* (London: Hale, 1961), 15.
53 Ibid., 66.
54 W.E. Harney, *North of 23* (Sydney: Australasian Publishing Company, 1946), 85.
55 Ibid., 44.

56 *Sydney Morning Herald*, 6 April 1938.
57 Cook Memorandum, 7 March 1937, AI/15 31/2597.
58 R.G. Kimber, *The End of the Bad Old Days: European Settlement in Central Australia, 1871-1894* (Darwin. State Library of the Northern Territory, 1991).
59 Peter Donovan, *Alice Springs: Its History and the People who Made It* (Alice Springs: Alice Springs Town Council, 1988), 136–38.
60 AA (NT) CRS F126 Item 27.
61 Strehlow's memorandums to Cook, 20 August and 23 September 1937, AA CRS: F126/19.
62 A.P. Elkin, 'The Secret Life of the Australian Aborigines,' *Oceania* III, no. 2 (December 1932): 125, 134, 121–23.
63 Stanner, 'Not by Eastern Windows Only,' 45.
64 T.G.H. Strehlow, diary [SD], 19 May 1937.
65 SD, 28 April 1937.
66 SD, 20 May 1937.
67 SD, 20 May 1937.
68 Marcus, *First in Their Field*, 124–27.
69 SD, 14 July 1937.
70 SD, 14 July 1937.
71 SD, 13–16 July 1937.
72 SD, 16 July 1937.
73 SD, 18 July 1937.
74 Report on the trip to S.W. Station Area, December 1938, CRS F 126 Item 37.
75 AA 431/1. Item 46/164.

2   Labour of Love

Not Only for Our Masters

EARLY IN 1937 the Strehlows moved out of Alice Springs to make Jay Creek their official settlement. 'My only early worries,' Bertha recalled, 'were the snakes . . . I was cooking dinner late one afternoon when I heard a rustling sound behind me, and I looked around to see a large snake slithering under a camel box near the tent flap. Ted had just arrived home, so I called to him to come and get rid of the intruder. He tried getting it out with a broom handle, but couldn't, so he waded across the creek which was running high and brought back two trackers from the camp on the other side. They soon caught and killed the snake and took it back to camp to eat.'[1]

The natives came to the rescue with snakes; natives helped set up the camp; and natives helped Bertha keep house, as they had done back at Hermannsburg. They were, as Strehlow put it, 'servants' in whom complete trustworthiness was assumed.[2]

'It was assumed, as a matter of course,' Bertha wrote, 'that Maria would help me, and I soon came to value her very highly, as she was capable and clean and quick to learn anything new, such as the art of baking yeast and bread. Occasionally, she would go for a walkabout for the day and then she would gather grass seeds and yelka or gum tree sugar.' The assumption, it must be said, was the mission station's, not the

Commonwealth government's. From first to last the Jay Creek settlement lived in the spiritual shelter of Hermannsburg.

Maria was the wife of Tom Ljonga, and the future grandmother of Rupert Max Stuart, who was to play a dramatic part in Strehlow's later life. 'After three or four months' work in the house, Maria would feel the need of a holiday, so she and Thomas gather together all their pots and set off for a month or longer to visit friends who were camped at distant places. Once the rations were finished they would have to live as primitive natives and seek their food daily, but this held no problems for them. In spite of their sophistication they never lost their art of living off the land.'

The Strehlows' relationships with Aborigines at Jay Creek could be warmly personal, but they were founded absolutely on a shouldering of their sense of Kipling's white man's burden towards 'your new-caught, sullen peoples, half-devil and half-child.' They were there to attend to what Strehlow called 'natives' wants' and therefore had to maintain a community in order.

Early on, Strehlow had to explain to Tom that his behaviour was not up to scratch.

I told him that I could find no use for a 'boy' who gambled with cards,—who was discourteous in speech to me (forgot to say 'please' and 'thank you' and 'good morning,' and shouted to me from a long distance away when he wanted something): I did not wish the uncivilised natives in the Reserve to learn bad things from my boys. Tommy was very crushed and said he wanted to reform; he wanted to be allowed to work for me in the future; he was content to stop in A.S. [Alice Springs] now, if I had no immediate use for him; but perhaps he could come on long trips with me. So I gave him £4, and the old campsheet for his services; I added that I would not leave him in the lurch now since he had been very loyal to me for years.

Strehlow thought that Tom went away 'pleased and contented.'[3] Eventually Tom settled with his wife at Jay Creek, and Bertha observed that while everyone was going about their duties, 'he preferred to lie down in the shade when he was at home.'

Rolf and Henock worked away at laying the foundations for the settlement—sinking the posts, putting up the tents, constructing the brush cover that would keep the tents cool, planting the garden, piping the

16. Strehlow, 1932, back in town with 'a dreamy, naked expression of unadulterated yearning.'

17. A.P. Elkin, 1929, ready for 'the field': anthropologist à la mode.

18. Strehlow at Mt Liebig, October 1932, where 'relationship' might contrast with formal problems of 'being in the field.'

19. 'Tom Ljonga at my Inirintinga camp ("Paddy's Hole"), 1935.' Paddy's Hole was at Altunga.

20. Strehlow's shot of 'Gura (Tjentermana), the last ingkata of the Northern Aranda gura pmara kutata of Ilbalintja, at the Buljabulja waterhole, some four miles north-west of Alice Springs, on 26th April, 1932. He had taken me for a picnic walk to show me some langgua country.'

21. The Manangananga cave in the beautiful gully a few miles from the mission, once a secret-sacred storehouse of *tjurunga*.

22. The Christian congregation gathered for a triumphant service outside the once 'pagan' cave, October 1930.

23. Evangelist Titus with congregation at Haasts Bluff, c. 1938.

24. Mission party setting off to holiday in Palm Valley, c. 1929. Mrs Minna Albrecht holding baby Ted, and Marianna holding baby Helene. Marianna was one of the Aboriginal women who nursed T.G.H. Strehlow.

25. Pastor F.W. Albrecht with Dr Charles Duguid and the Reverend David Munro: back at the mission after their 1936 journey west, to the proposed reserve at Haasts Bluff.

26. Bertha Strehlow's photograph of, perhaps, Flossie, Mulga and Ranji, c. 1933.

27. Aboriginal group, c. 1933, probably near Mount Liebig.

28. The 'Puck of the bush' sitting on a drum, 1934.

29. Strehlow at Mount Liebig, 1932, with Pintubi boys, Reverend Kramer, and camel.

30. Strehlow at his father's grave, Horseshoe Bend, 1936.

31. The Elliot family at their hotel, Horseshoe Bend. Gus, Martin, Ruby and Sheila, c. 1933.

32. The swag, the night, Strehlow, 1934.

33. Strehlow photographed by Sheila Elliot, 1933.

34. Sheila Elliot ('desert maiden') taken by Strehlow, 1933.

35. Bertha Strehlow at Goyder Springs: on the track to Horseshoe Bend and beyond, 1936.

36. Newlyweds Ted and Bertha Strehlow, ready for their thousand-mile trek by camel, 1936.

37. Karinja, Central Mount Wedge, with camels passing over salt lake at its base, August 1932.

38. The stretcher made for Bertha's painful return journey from Mount Olga, 1936.

39. On the track with the Cleland Inquiry into the shooting of an Aborigine at Ayers Rock, 1935.

40. Henock, Tom and Rolf labouring for the Strehlows at Jay Creek, 1937.

41. The house that Ted built at Jay Creek, 1938.

42. Strehlow and Billy Liddle at Angas Downs, 1935.

43. Strehlow's translation committee, 1938. From left: Strehlow, Conrad, Zacharias, Jakobus, Nathaniel and Moses.

water, tending the goats [see Plate 40]. Then they needed a talking to as well. They were working too slowly for Strehlow's liking, and he was irked when Rolf said it was because Strehlow was not hurrying them along enough. Then Henock said he had sore shoulders, that he wanted to go back to the mission and have lighter duties.

'I was most disgusted,' Strehlow wrote in his diary. 'What a soft bellied generation is being turned out now by Hbg! Men who will leave their employers in the lurch after working only a week or two. They have been cared for too well, have had all their food found for them ever since they were babies. Now Henock . . . wants to go back to Hbg and loaf on mission tucker. He will get disillusioned, if he leaves me, he will not get free rations at Hbg. I merely said to him however, that I would speak to him tomorrow about his proposed departure.'

The next morning Strehlow gave his speech:

I told him how the old Aranda forefathers used to train their young men to 'work' at the Urumbula festivals: make them go hunting for the whole camp during the day, give them only a little of the total game for the day at daylight, and then keep them awake with ceremonies and chanting at night. Also, they trained their young men to stand pain. Yet here were the young men of the present native generation: they were 'knocked up' immediately they worked a little, and moaned about every little ache and pain they had. Henock was moaning about a 'sore shoulder' after a little over a week's work. I had been trained to work down south by Mr Wurst (who was up at Hbg last year): I used to study during winter and then go to work at Xmas time for about eight weeks: the first time I worked at securing wheat bags. I got first blistered then raw hands; but I kept on working: I would have been ashamed to admit that I was a 'cry-baby.' I stuck at the job, and my hands were cured by work. What did they think Hbg was going to do with its present soft and lazy young generation? The only thing to do was to tell the Christian folk down south who earned their living by work and gave their surplus earnings into the mission treasury that they might as well cease giving such donations and have Hbg closed: the young people were lazy and did not want to work. — As Christians we all worked not only for our masters, but for God.[4]

Henock said nothing. It is hard to imagine what he could have said to this mixture of shaming and bribery.

Strehlow was sounding off as the most imperialistic of missionaries in full flight—compounding Christian manipulation with cultural insult. That Rolf and Henock were disappointments to their own fathers was not at all clear, and there is no reason to think, on Strehlow's evidence, that they had not been through the trials of Aboriginal initiations. It was an outburst that foreshadowed a key to his thinking about Aboriginal culture. It expressed the deep exasperation he had for the generations of young men who would depart from the rigours of their traditional tribal life, an exasperation that would consolidate as intolerance in years to come, as he froze that life in time, and nostalgically mourned its passing.

Rolf and Henock stayed on to finish the work that Strehlow wanted, and after the labours of November and December 1936 the camp at Jay Creek was ready for Christmas.

Hessian walls were built between the tents so that they shaded the Christmas tree. Tom, who was visiting from Alice Springs, caught the fish for the Christmas table, and Strehlow gathered the wood to bake the cake. On Christmas eve Strehlow undid the boxes that contained his parents' decorations. 'It had not been opened since 1921 Xmas. Then father and mother had rejoiced in the light of Xmas candles.' Memories brought tears to his eyes. Sand was brought up from the creek by Flossie and spread all over the boxes so that the 'old beautiful figures that tell the Xmas story were set up.' Nothing had altered, it was Christmas 1921 again.

Bertha's parents had come up from Adelaide. On Christmas Day the natives came to rejoice over the tree and the figures. 'All got presents and went home smiling and happy.' That night Strehlow and Bertha sat up late and read Luke. 'Our first Xmas tree together.'

It was this happiness they hoped to replicate in 1937, and each year beyond that now that Jay Creek was their official quarters. Admittedly, they only lived in tents—which Strehlow called their 'island'—and their waterhole was still invaded by the cattle on the Owen Springs station to the immediate north; and their supply of rations and medical supplies was inadequate, as were the means by which Strehlow could cover the vast territory that was his responsibility as patrol officer. But they had made a settlement in the right way, the Christian way. As Strehlow had told Henock: 'As Christians we all worked not only for our masters, but for God.'

That first Christmas at Jay Creek in 1936 had moments of happiness.

The job was ahead of Strehlow and he permitted himself some optimism. But the happiness was not to last. By May 1937 Bertha had had another miscarriage: after bouts of sickness and the 'agony of waiting' they lost an unborn boy. In the middle of the year Strehlow had to do some hard travelling, with Bertha always on his mind. By November he was writing: 'It is a year ago since my wife and I arrived here at Jay Creek, after many weary months of wanderings. And here we are,—no house, no home, no ration depot, no medical station, nothing for the natives anywhere in C.A. [Central Australia], and the department talking gloomily about "abandoning" all projects.'[5]

At Christmas 1937 they managed festivities for the 56 adults and 26 children dependent on their rations. Albrecht added to their gifts for the natives. They gave out lollies, and meat and cake, bath soap, combs, coloured handkerchiefs and bush biscuits, and clay pipes—'a pleasing store.' A Christmas tree was erected in the high tent, and decorated with the Strehlows' family ornaments from Hermannsburg. The figures of Mary, Joseph and Child were at the foot of the tree, along with ox, ass, sheep and watchdog. And, as Strehlow wrote for the *Lutheran Herald*: 'The shepherds listened with devotion to the message of the angel. From a different corner came the three wise men from the East, with their retinue.' He went on:

> After all gifts had been issued and the tree decorated, evening had set in. The whole population eagerly assembled outside our big tent. Rolf had spent a few nights previously in practising some Christmas hymns with them. These they sang vigorously and joyously, gazing intently at the decorated Christmas tree within. I read the Christmas story to them in Aranda. It was a strangely moving experience to see their happy faces; and it was a deep joy to us both to feel that we had been enabled to render a small service to these people on the night when Love and Light came into a broken dark and disillusioned world.[6]

On the last, humid night of the year it was trying hard to rain and the cattle were coming to 'our dying water hole in swarms eager to lap it up altogether . . . It's the end of a hard year. The year has brought little except hardships and disappointments, as far as we can see now. Or can it be that the year 1937 did lay the foundation stones upon our efforts for the natives will at last succeed in raising an adequate sheltering edifice? . . . Time alone would tell.'[7]

The devil was in the detail, the grind, the round, the unrelenting charity of the work at Jay Creek. 'Much trouble,' Strehlow told Cook in the summer of 1938, 'was experienced during the past month with coughs colds and influenza.' The camp had 82 persons in all, 56 adults (24 men, 32 men), and 26 children. The number would rise and then hover around 150 persons, with more in 1941, when the logistics of war in Alice Springs involved an extra injection of the aged and infirm, almost doubling the numbers and creating a crisis in the meat supply.

Throughout Strehlow's term at least half of the usual population were on rations and he was very proud, when he looked back on his term, to say that he had improved the amount and quality of the rations. He reported that he had added wholemeal flour and rice to the ration, and had widened the eligibility for rations from the aged and infirm to include all mothers with babies, and all disabled men.[8] He introduced cattle to the reserve, thus improving the supply of fresh meat, and the reserve itself was doubled in size, due to his recommendation. And none of this, of course, was separable from the ongoing need for water, battles for which he fought all along.

Jay Creek needed more than its well as its main water source. There was a watercourse on Jay Creek, but that, as Strehlow forewarned from the start, would only do if the cattle from the adjacent Owen Springs station could be kept at bay. 'The Owen Springs cattle are still raiding it heavily,' he told Cook in the summer of 1938, and by October the manager, Mr E. Hayes, was using a lawyer to tell the government that he wished to cooperate, but that nothing short of a cattle-proof fence would work. The fence never arrived.

In good seasons there was clearly enough water in the main waterhole at Jay Creek. When the country dried up, Strehlow was always afraid that the hole would become a manure heap, or a sight like Gall Springs, Hayes' other watering place: one summer it was filled with the stench of dead beasts, and it 'looked like a series of black, evil smelling septic tanks, connected by dark streams of putrescent filth.'[9]

There were, in a way, dark streams in everything: something of the relentless mix of concerns that consumed the Strehlows might be gained from his diary entry for 10 October 1938:

> Moses arrived here yesterday afternoon. He has brought his goats with him—about 26 in number—& he is going to leave them here as there is no feed for them in A.S. Rolf told me this morning that word has

come of a big fight among the Ngalia men at Jack Miller's sheep camp—evidently on the Ormiston, Nth of Glen Helen; one man is said to have been killed out there. I am in doubts as to what should be done: the murderer should be removed, but whither? I can't very well have any more cases to look after here at the Jay until the Govt. makes provision for them by putting up a store room and some shacks, & by appointing a permanent white observer to take charge of them.

We are having many native patients here in the mornings: Maggie gets her heart medicine, Larry, Tom and some women come for cough mixture; Papitjultura comes for Epsom salts (and so have several others recently); Palierana swallows his Stovarsol tablets; Polly Kumia has her foot bandaged and Bates's Salve stuck on to draw out a stick that is said to be in it; Kugnuna has inflamed eyelids and comes for an application of Morris's eye ointment; and Rolf's three children have sores all over their bodies,—what is causing them I don't know.

With any one of these individuals one could develop a case history, of sorts, from Strehlow's records. When the social history of Central Australia is fully written that will be done, as well as some sense made of the lives lived out bush, where Strehlow did not want to exercise his authority, as well as those already far from being Caliban or the Noble Savage, to use Stanner's terms here, and who had become one of several other types produced by colonisation—the Orphan, or the Ward of Chancery.[10]

Strehlow's own terms are closer to the recognition of individuals than most reports of the period. Maggie, one of those mentioned above by Strehlow, was a half-caste girl from Mount Cavenagh station. She was nineteen, with tuberculosis in the larynx. She had been diagnosed in Alice Springs as sufficiently infectious to need the sanctuary of Jay Creek. But she was short of blankets. Strehlow wanted to pitch her camp clear of the others where she could warm herself with a generous fire, but she was too afraid to be far from his and Bertha's tents. What she needed, he told Cook, was a plate, pannikin and quartpot, two woollen singlets, a woollen cardigan, basin, knife and fork, and a waterproof campsheet.

Strehlow asked for the campsheet because 'the District Officer did not think it could be justified. In the end my wife and I made a straw mattress for Maggie and rigged up a little hut out of flour bags for her. We experienced 234 points of rain during June at Jay Creek. Fortunately for

Maggie the rain fell very steadily, and the bag shelter managed to keep her dry.'

She still needed meat, milk and fresh vegetables in her diet. 'I was prepared to feed her from my own supplies at the ordinary departmental rate of 1s. per meal,' Strehlow reported, but 'the District Officer declined to sanction my proposal since there was no precedent for it and in the end, after consultation with Dr Reilly, he agreed that I should supply one pint of milk and 1/2 lb of meat to Maggie daily.' The Strehlows added fresh vegetables from their garden.[11]

Visitors passing through Jay Creek gave Maggie sweets. 'We have little reason for pride in respect of the facilities available for Aboriginal patients at present.' Strehlow, more tactful than usual, was quietly trying to shame Cook.

Eventually Maggie was taken to Alice Springs for treatment. and nine months later Strehlow was able to report that her TB 'had definitely been arrested.' By that time welfare agencies such as the Uplift Society in Melbourne were helping with blankets and the like. When they gave two bags of clothes, mainly for women and children, Strehlow noted that 'it was just as well that no die-hard anthropologists were present on this occasion: the wild joy of those of the younger women who received the prettiest of those clothes would, no doubt, have hurt their scientific feelings greatly.'

For the children at Jay Creek there was no school, no built shelters. In one dispatch, where Strehlow reported the deaths of three children all under four (two from influenza and one from measles), he was compelled to say that 'we had seven or eight times that number ill with measles, coughs and influenza during the past three months . . . The boy who died of measles when visited by us looked listless, but had no temperature, and was not lying down.' The baby boy who died of influenza 'had no parents here; his foster parents brought him up for the first time on the morning of the day when he died; it was then too late to call any help.' The other influenza victim, a little girl, 'appeared to have the same illness as did the children of two other "penal cases": the latter did not. In her case, it must not be forgotten that she came from Mount Doreen, where vegetable foods have been scarce for at least 2 years.'[12]

'I do not pretend,' Strehlow told Cook, 'to possess any medical training, or knowledge whatsoever. I must emphasise that all illness treated at Jay Creek is attended to out of mere good will: it is purely a labour of love.'[13]

Making House, Keeping Terror at Bay

It was a labour of love together. The hardships at Jay Creek were shared absolutely between the Strehlows. Bertha was in effect the patrol officer's unpaid assistant. She helped her husband in every way, especially with the children, the elderly and the sick. She was matron, nurse, housekeeper and wife—though not, as yet, a mother herself. The precariousness of her health was still a mystery to them, but they shared the romance of their bush isolation, of what had become their own little mission station.

Uncomplaining herself, Bertha had a keen eye for the forbearance of the native women. When she had been out bush she had been struck by how it was 'the duty of the wife to fall in behind her husband and bear all the household effects.' She went on:

> the husband meanwhile walked ahead with no burdens to bear except a handful of spears. This mode of progress is accepted as correct by the natives. In theory the man must be free to use his spears quickly when he sees game or catches sight of an enemy, and he cannot be distracted from his duties as protector of the family, yet in practice this often means that the native woman has a very hard time. While her husband walks along, swinging his arms freely, she is weighed down with heavy burdens and has to pause periodically to dig rabbits out of their burrows with her digging stick, collect grass seeds, and gather edible roots. At sun down, when camp is made, it is the husband who has first taste of the food and first drink of water. If the supply is small, it is the wife who goes supperless to bed.[14]

It was Bertha's opinion that it made sense for Aboriginal women to seek out white men as protectors, lovers and possibly husbands: they might be better treated than they were by Aboriginal men.

Strehlow, whose tone with Bertha had not impressed his parents-in-law when they stayed that Christmas, was nonetheless fretful and solicitous about her. The nightmare out at Piltardi Rockhole was something to which they still referred—uniting them, he felt, on their nights alone in their tent, on their 'island.' But it was also something that could return with a vengeance. Early in 1938 he had to go down to Tempe Downs with Sergeant Koop to attend to the burial of a white woman who had died suddenly. By the time they arrived the body was already liquefying in the heat, and it became clear that she had died from a self-inflicted abortion. After the burial his 'thoughts were heavy like nightmares.' It was the isolated fate of the woman, the newly-dug grave nearby, and the parched country all around, 'the cruel waves of a boundless sea of sand' that triggered his panic.

'Would I never be able to escape for good from the Red Centre? My thoughts tormented and haunted me. I was weary, very, very weary, and felt unfitted for my job. It haunted me to think that now I was even investing money in a house at the Jay, when I was so terrified to move about in this country of my own patrol.'[15]

Strehlow was right to be afraid, because Bertha was ill—and, it seems, possibly pregnant again. When he was out bush a few weeks later Albrecht handed him an urgent telegram. Bertha was in the hands of an Alice Springs doctor who recommended an operation. 'It is like a last blow in a losing battle for me.' But a second opinion forestalled that decision. Remote, alone, worried sick about Bertha, Strehlow could sink into despair.

The money that he was investing was to build their house. He had pressed his superiors for months, in vain. He made the outlay on materials and set to on the day they arrived, much impressing Bertha. 'He quickly got into the swing of things and had the foundations poured. With the help of three Aboriginal friends, he made 2,600 bricks for the cottage. He used a professional builder from Alice Springs, but also did some of the work himself as often as his normal duties allowed. I helped him with the painting. And the end product was excellent.'[16]

When she said 2,600 bricks, Bertha was wrong. Brick by brick, Strehlow tallied 2,699 as the 'Grand Total.' The difference would have been important to her husband who counted everything. He added them up through May and June 1938, itemising them as small and large and then in turn according to whether they were 'bricks, both ends hollow' or 'divisible into halves,' or 'one end square' or 'both ends hollow.' The grand total of 2,699 was 'if all half bricks are counted separately': if not it was 2,603 minus '1 broken brick.' The tally page also had an 'NB' which said, 'About 58 bricks (i.e., counting 1/2 bricks as singles) remained over after the building had been completed.'[17]

No doubt his superiors would not have been impressed by the pride that went into this tally—the nervous energy channelled into its establishment.

When it was done they were both very pleased. They had a long low building with a closed verandah, not unlike the long houses at

Hermannsburg. It was going to be cooler than the tents, they hoped, and certainly was more like a permanent home. And it was a much better place to be than out bush, when he could be 'terrified' about Bertha.

Protecting the Sacred

It was the opinion of Administrator Abbott that Strehlow tended to stay back at Jay Creek rather than go on his patrols. Either that, Abbott thought, or he would visit Hermannsburg, where most of his duties did not lie either, any more than they did in Alice Springs where he could not have had that much work to do. Abbot sneered at the way Strehlow had 'gleefully' reported starting work on his private house, the existence of which tended to keep him at home. Against the charge of avoiding the longer, difficult patrols (which was never levelled at Strehlow officially), Strehlow had the support of the then Director of Native Affairs, E.W.P. Chinnery. But it was as if Abbott had intuited a truth: Strehlow was doing work that had little to do with patrolling.

When he could, he was still translating songs. He could be sufficiently focused on that research task to be doing the unusual thing of referring to the work of others in his diary. The sound recordings of Davies were the object of his attention early in 1937, when he compared the recordings to what was known by his own informants.[18] He seems to have gone on collecting the 'legends' whenever possible.

In November 1937 he was typing up his MA thesis, 'Aranda Phonetics and Grammar.' Sound off as he might as the colonial master, he was nevertheless thinking well of the native language and its dignifying virtues. He would, as we shall see, write glowingly of the intelligence and adaptability of the primitive language, so-called. He would lay out its grammar in a way that invited a non-colonial mind to enter the nature of its understandings, and to appreciate the activities that were the foundation of its song and mythology.

He had more than one reason to go out to Hermannsburg whenever he could. He was going back home. He could sit down and refine a linguistic point or two with men like Moses. It was where he could fraternise with Pastor Albrecht, who was happily collecting things such as grinding stones for him, telling him that the natives were very pleased to be passing over a good one because, as they said, 'Mr Strehlow had been growing up with this stone'—'another link,' as Albrecht put it, 'that binds your childhood with this country.'[19]

Albrecht had been a friend of Jay Creek from the start—calling in from time to time, leaving provisions for Christmas gifts to the natives, mending the wireless, dispensing advice on what the mission and Jay Creek basically had in common: welfare work, the routines of feeding and healing. Going out to reconnoitre at Hermannsburg must have been a solace to Strehlow, and in due course Albrecht asked him to return to a job partially done by his father: the translation of the New Testament into Aranda. Strehlow did not hesitate. He would do so as an expression of his support for mission work. He would carry it out as the professional linguist that he had become. And he would do so because, as with most of his work, it involved a continuation of, and a corrective to, the footsteps of his father. Albrecht approached Strehlow in 1938, and from this time on the translation of Scripture into Aranda was a central part of Strehlow's life, albeit part time work, another labour of love. He had his government duties by day; the Scriptures were his night work.

Albrecht spoke to Strehlow in the Lutheran way about the battles he would have against the world, especially as he was trying to break 'new ground' in fighting 'for every step you wish to take in the interests of the Natives.' 'We shall remember you in our prayers,' Albrecht went on, as if speaking to a young knight of the church. 'As soon as some quarters will feel that your presence makes things uncomfortable they will do their very best to discredit you even under the most feeble pretexts. On the other side I am convinced that what the Lord wants you to carry out, will be put into your way in such a way as to make it entirely impossible to get around them. And then I am sure you will not be found wanting.'[20]

This was said—prophetically—in Strehlow's first few months of office, when his struggles and the discrediting of his work had barely begun.

His good works included a precocious defence of the Aranda's own religious rights. In June 1937, Cook sought Strehlow's advice on the 'protection of relics of prehistoric value in Australia.'[21] The Australian and New Zealand Association for the Advancement of Science had recently moved a resolution expressing 'grave concern' about the 'unchecked destruction of relics of prehistoric value in Australia.'

Strehlow was 'fully in accord' with the idea. For Cook he listed what he knew about sacred places in Central Australia, the places where there were rock paintings and carvings, and storehouses of *tjurunga*. He then made an all-encompassing policy statement as to how such a heritage could be protected. Rather than protect them by gazetting them, thus projecting them into the public arena where they might be 'attacked by local inhabitants, tourists, souvenir-hunters, and certain types of anthropologists, who could carry off anything that could be moved,' he suggested that:

A better way of protecting these sacred sites, store-houses and memorials would be to pass adequate legislation giving natives legal property rights over them. Such legislation could specify that no white person suddenly coming upon a sacred cave or tree store replete with ceremonial stores was entitled to plunder its contents; also that no white person coming upon rock paintings or rock structures that had obviously been made by native hands, was permitted to deface or destroy them: severe penalties should be provided for any breaches . . . The purpose of such legislation then would be to instruct the white man about forbidden native property, and to give the natives legal rights over such property. To give such legislation a general character instead of limiting Government protection to a few specified areas would seem to be the best solution to the whole difficulty. After all, our laws, for instance, guarantee a certain measure of protection to every church, public building, and private house in the land instead of limiting such protection only to a small number of structures named specifically in an Act. Why the natives of Australia should be denied any property rights to their own sacred places and assembly sites merely because they do not consist of buildings seems to lie in the past iniquitous policy of all Australian Governments to allow neither property nor land rights to the aboriginals of the country and to treat them legally more like animals than humans,—on the excuse apparently, that they did not build houses for themselves. It is to be hoped that a more enlightened attitude be adopted in this matter by our future Governments.[22]

It is a remarkable statement for its time. In one formulation Strehlow had linked property rights, religious freedom and land rights. It would be decades before these connections were fully addressed by white authorities claiming to care for Aboriginal interests. To do so in 1937 was to have thrown down the gauntlet in the face of colonial ideology—so much so, perhaps, that Strehlow was not to make such a clear statement himself for another twenty years. It was a statement that also implied that Aboriginal religion was worthy of respect in its own right, an idea hardly compatible with the Lutheran mission project. That implication seems by Strehlow to have been left aside as well—and yet he had, as if inspired by the poetics of his contact with the secret-sacred life of the Aranda, spoken up for Caliban rather than Luther.

Receiving the Sacred

All this time Strehlow was collecting the *tjurunga*, a fact that he seems to have kept from his employers. Stationed at Jay Creek as he was, he was no longer energetically pursuing them—as in 'hunting'—but he was actively receiving. By 1935 he had 78 *tjurunga*. Between 1935 and 1939 he acquired another 125. Most seem to have come to him at Jay Creek, and when he was staying at Hermannsburg rather than when he was out on patrol, and his record of them went, somewhat erratically, into his book under the heading, 'Tjurunga, Sacred Objects, Native Goods.' That is to say, he was collecting generally, and not always the *tjurunga*, but the *tjurunga* were the main thing, the objects of greatest worth to the givers and to their receiver. In return Strehlow often paid rations—especially when he had been camping with the men and recording their myths and songs, as well as cash. There would be ten shillings here, another five shillings there, for a clutch of *tjurunga*, and there is no suggestion in the records that there was any haggling about the price. This was because, with Strehlow, the *tjurunga* were also a gift, and the exchange was one saturated with solicitude.[23]

Strehlow's diaries are replete with descriptions of what it meant to the men when they were speaking of, or handling, or handing over the objects that contained the spirits of their ancestors, and which were sometimes collectively owned, though often their 'most personal private property' to use the terms that Strehlow used in a 1935 talk to a science conference in Melbourne. The message from the old men to Strehlow is that the times had tragically changed, there was no future for the secret-sacred tradition, that the really knowledgeable songmen were the last of the songmen. Always, with Strehlow, he was collecting at a time of sunset, when the light was fading on all that had been.

His perspective at the time is hard to challenge, especially with regard to the Aranda men. Albrecht's militancy was undoubtedly a serious blow to traditions, and the men had told Strehlow so. Strehlow had arrived, as a collector, at a time when the release of *tjurunga* was not so much a matter of adjustment to the white presence as a 'capitulation.' As Albrecht wrote in a letter to the press in 1936: 'the white man's teaching is shaking their religious beliefs, and undermining their social organisation. Their unbounded faith in magic is being shattered by the *ridicule* that the whites pour into them. The native has arrived at the stage when he willingly parts with his most sacred *tjurunga* and other ceremonial objects to the whites for a little tea or sugar, flour or clothing, and having done so means the end of his old beliefs and of ever reviving them again.'[24]

It is possible to say, in this context, that some kind of 'corporate decision' had been made by the senior Aranda men,[25] and that as with corporate decisions today, Strehlow did not have much choice but to go along with it. When he was living in Central Australia and pouring his life into the practical matters of native welfare, it is hard to imagine him being able to say no to what was brought to him, even if he had, in so many ways, been soliciting the 'gifts.' The truth was they were gifts that he wanted, and gifts that he could not refuse without —without what, exactly? Well, he never goes into that. He seems to take it for granted that to reject the *tjurunga* in any way would have been a matter of callous disrespect.

The poignancy of his position is clear from his response to an unexpected incident that came at the end of his stay at Jay Creek. Without warning, and 'during the stresses and confusion' of his last week, a bundle of about 40 *tjurunga* were handed to him. 'I took these objects in the end only because of the pleading of my dark friends to do so, and I was unable to give much more than my gratitude and appreciation in return for them; they were parting gifts which I valued all the more because I knew that my term of living among my dark friends had been brought to a sudden stop by our common white ill-wishers. The tjurunga were accepted and a few words relating to them hastily written on a sheet of paper.'[26]

His collecting was, among other things, an extension of his welfare work, another way of looking after people.

Policing the Mine

Abbott's complaint about Strehlow wanting to stay back at Jay Creek had a focus: the Granites, the mining camp about 300 miles to the north-west of Alice Springs, in the hard, dry Tanami Desert. Strehlow's records revealed to the Administrator that the place had been checked only three times in his five years; he claimed that 'there had never been any supervision exercised by Strehlow over the employment of the natives there.'[27]

The rush to the Granites started in 1932 when a gold strike was made by C.H. Chapman, who was funded by a Queensland finance company. Investors flocked: Australia was looking for a new Kalgoorlie. Scores of excited miners, prospectors and adventurers rattled inland by rail to Alice Springs. Big rains had flooded the plains and it was too boggy to travel north so the town crowded with impatient, zestful men. The pubs seemed to be open all night and two-up was played on the roads. Cecil Madigan, the English geologist who went up to report on the substance of the strike, found that hop-beer shops made a brew with more kick than the standard beer at a lower price. 'The wife of one of the brokers had sent up a case of champagne, and the mining experts and leading citizens, including the Administrator, the police sergeant, the postal officials, the member for the Northern Territory, and myself, all spent a very merry evening, at which everyone made a speech. It was clear that no one at that meeting had much faith in the discovery. I told them I would say nothing till I had seen for myself.'[28]

The sceptics were right. When Madigan got there—after a laborious journey on an 'execrable' track, across dehydrated country 'saturated with heat and light,' past native soaks that had been drained by travellers—he found a small settlement of men who had found some gold on a rich little quartz vein that had run out. The country had been pegged out for miles, but many profitless leases were already called 'spinifex farms.' Within hours of Madigan's report to the papers down south, the bubble had burst. The drift back to Alice began.

Chapman, a gritty man, stayed on at his Golden Shoe mine in the most inhospitable of country: a spinifex and rocky surface as far as the eye could see, temperatures as high as 110°F for days on end in summer. The only shade was the shade a man could make for himself. The food was what could be lugged up from Alice, and the men in Chapman's camp subsisted on flour, tea and tinned meat. They distilled water from the well the government had already dug to help prospecting in the district. It was to this camp, which always employed a few white people including Chapman's son, that Strehlow had to trek as a patrol officer in April 1937.

His job was to take the camp by surprise—the better to get the real picture of their lubra dealings. He had to inspect the Aboriginal workforce, to check their payments and conditions. Chapman employed fifteen to twenty half-castes at the mine and was legally obliged to pay wages in the form of rations and clothing. Strehlow also had to consider the welfare of the people—the bush people, the 'myalls,' the 'full-bloods' who had come in from the desert to the white man's bore. Those from the west came from country that dried up very quickly in times of drought. Those from the south had been dispossessed of their best country by the Mount Doreen station, and the mines in its area.

It was a hard journey up for Strehlow, too 'monotonous and tiresome,' he told Cook. 'Ruts, gutters, the low clearance of the car, and a radiator choked with spinifex seeds.' The rough ride smashed the battery and they had to walk the last two miles to the Granites—an arrival which must have made the surprise somewhat less dramatic than it might have been.[29]

Strehlow found Jack Lewis outside his low house made of ironstone and ant bed, the roof rigged with galvanised iron tied to lengths of pipe. 'He had two lubras washing his clothes just outside the verandah.' At Chapman's house, 'There were three or four lubras there, doing more washing.' Chapman claimed that he had engaged them for only one or two days each week, on Sunday and Monday, for this special purpose, and hence was of the opinion that he was not actually employing them.

At the bore, Strehlow found 'a number' of myall natives clad only in loincloths. One had been speared through the leg and had a cut wrist that had been bandaged the day before by Chapman. There were three other Aboriginal workers—Alfie, Mick and Sambo—who were fully clad and could speak pidgin.

There was no native camp at the Granites, but from the smoke in the distance Strehlow could see the family groups. There was no firewood nearer the mine. All of these wanderers, Chapman told Strehlow, came in periodically. They got some food, tea, and sugar for odd jobs such as removing sand from the mine.

A key question for the patrol officer was whether the Granites was a prohibited area for natives. The trouble was, no records existed to clarify this. Constable Hamilton in Alice Springs told Strehlow that he remembered it had been prohibited, but Chapman told him that he'd received a licence to employ Aborigines about six months after the gold boom had subsided. On balance, Strehlow thought, Chapman was acting legally, since it did not make sense that natives would have been prohibited after the rush.

Having established this bureaucratic clarity, Strehlow thought 'that was no real reason for withholding from Chapman a Licence to Employ Aborigines,' especially since it was such a small operation. 'The Granites field is being controlled in much the same fashion as a cattle station, with one white manager being responsible for the actions of his white employees.'

Strehlow gave Chapman the benefit of the doubt on other matters. He listed the white people at the mine, taking special care to note their marital status. With the exception of Chapman's son, four were married and one was about to be. Admittedly, only one of these men had his wife with him, and Chapman himself was 'living separately from his wife.' But Strehlow concluded: 'While marriage in Central Australia does not necessarily preclude irregular relationships with lubras, the above list does suggest that men living at the Granites may be trusted to keep their relations with the natives at a higher level than is usual on a large mining field.'

As to the full-bloods, Strehlow was satisfied that they were not doing the dangerous skilled work. At the mine shaft, Strehlow found Ben and Harry Palmer, half-castes who did 'most of the developmental work in this section of the field.' Harry and Ben Palmer were apprenticed, and paid accordingly. They got £4 a week for a 44-hour week. That was Chapman's figure; the men told Strehlow in private that they thought it was £3 but were not sure because they were taking out most of their wages in stores. Strehlow was rather impressed with Harry and Ben. He found them in their shack reading magazines containing useful mechanical information. They spent most of their money on rations and lived 'quite as liberally as the whites.' They told Strehlow they were satisfied with their work at the mine.

Strehlow wanted to give the settlement at the Granites a clean bill of health. It should not be gazetted as a prohibited area. He thought only that Chapman should be warned not to breach the Aboriginal Ordinance ('He is not the only man in Central Australia who has been guilty of a breach'). And he recommended that Chapman's promises be accepted. 'An occasional surprise visit should reveal whether . . . [he was] genuine or not.'

If Chapman was to get an Aboriginal Employment Licence, Strehlow noted, he promised to keep proper books in the future so that all rations and clothing could be checked. It was also reasonable to grant him medical supplies—iodine, Condy's crystals, eyedrops, bandages, etc.[30]

In all, Strehlow clearly wanted to make life easier for Chapman, as far as the law and the special remote circumstances demanded. On one matter, though, he held strictly to regulations. 'As regards lubras, Chapman has been informed that their employment is to be discontinued immediately on pain of prosecution. No licence to employ them can or will be issued to him.'

Chapman and Lewis had to do their own washing. Native women who came to the bore for water would have to stop coming so close to the white men's quarters: their men would have to come in and get it for them. Strehlow said there was no evidence of cohabitation with lubras 'at present' and again recommended 'a second surprise visit . . . at some future date.' An official in Darwin emphasised 'at present' by underlining it.

Chapman made it his business to get on side with the authorities. His communiqués are little studies in local pragmatisms. 'I can assure you,' he wrote to 'T.G. Strehlow Esq / Abo Protector' after the first visit, 'that the Abos have always had a fair spin with me & they show their appreciation by always returning & asking for work.' He went on with the charm: 'I have written to the deputy protector about this & suggest that I keep a book showing how the money is spent and prices charged . . . New clothes have been supplied and some dresses have been sent for on account of Mick, Bill and Sambo.'[31]

Dealing with foxes, Strehlow had to be at least two things himself: firm, and not without a sense of humour. A lapse in one or the other would open him to the charge of incompetence.

More of the Granites, and Bush Gothic

Strehlow had to go back to the Granites in 1939. February. The worst of the heat. Again he travelled with Sergeant Koop, and again, en route, they had the business of tracking the bushmen with Aboriginal women. Strehlow's official report is replete with the details of these matters, as distinct from the conditions at the Granites. His writing for his superiors takes a new turn at this time: he is beginning to lace his accounts with a mix of caricature, farce and black comedy, simulating the genre of the bush yarn. It is writing in search of 'the elasticity of irony' and may well have been his way of staving off the deeply personal fear he could have in the remote, dry country, the panic and despair when the repetition of nightmare was upon him.

Just past Rabbit Flat on the other side of the Tanami, they met 'the Apparition': 'It was Goodall, a Tanamite, who had been engaged by Mr Morley Cutlack of Sydney, together with the camel team—for about £10 a week. However, Cutlack had gone to Sydney, and Goodall still had only promises and no money. The Apparition proposed to go to Alice Springs to seek legal redress; but Sergeant Koop heartlessly pointed out that the Alice Springs solicitor would probably be found to be Cutlack's solicitor also. A myall youth and male piccaninny brought up the rear. We left the Apparition to his own thoughts, and drove on.'

Down the track, however, the natives told them the truth. Goodall was yet another offender: he had been living with an Aboriginal woman. But another man—a white man—had taken her away from him, which was much to his benefit.

Just before meeting the Apparition, they had come across an old Ford pulled up in the shade of a tree. Ted Bolton, wanted by the Western Australian police for the abduction of the lubra Nellie from the Moolabulla station, was camped there. Unlike the Apparition, Bolton was prepared to confess. 'He admitted having been associated with the lubra Nellie and said that he had been rearing her half-caste child and feeding her. He expressed surprise that the police were after him, claiming that he knew Tony Jones, the Constable at Hall's Creek, and no one had ever troubled him because of the lubra; in fact, he had talked with Father Francis of Moolabulla station about the half-caste child, and he was quite prepared to pay Francis £35 per year for its education. He claimed that he had left lubra Nellie and her child that morning at Tanami.'

As Bolton was 'the very soul of frankness,' patrol officer and police-man 'did not trouble to search in the bush around the well.' While talking to Bolton they watched the antics of their native guide, Albert. From his perch on the back of the car, Albert had a good view over the tall grass, and he had spotted a small child and the head of a lubra. He did not call out because he had been travelling in the back of the car and was unacquainted with what the white men were looking for.

Bolton is apprehended: Koop calls him a liar, and the bushman is offended. He protests that the four years of companionship with Nellie had been 'Platonic love'! 'His oath was not worth a hiss,' Strehlow snorts. 'Bolton was arrested and told to cook his final meal and get his belongings together for his trip to Alice Springs.'

And Nugget Hunter was apprehended near the Mount Stafford tin field. Nugget tried to sneak away 'to his own show' so they called him back and insisted on driving him home to his camp.

Koop and I were sitting in the cabin, and Hunter was directing us from the back of the utility. We could see his afternoon shadow quite plainly, however, and noticed how he was trying to chase the aboriginals at his camp away into the bush by frantically waving his hat about. It was too late. An elderly full blooded couple and a young native woman were at the camp. The latter was very obtuse and staunchly denied any relations with Nugget, but the latter himself after a while confessed to having lived with the lubra for the past twelve months. The officials 'removed' the lubra, told Hunter to meet them at Coniston on their way back, and to make sure he did, took his bags of tin.

And so on. Drolleries pile up, and all in an official report for a bureaucracy, or rather two bureaucracies, a small one in Darwin and the much larger one in Canberra. It is hard to know what Strehlow was thinking of his readership. For once, the moralist takes a back seat and the joke, to some extent, is on him. He seems to have felt as if he was doing himself a favour when he was not.

Finally, at the Granites, he has tea with Chapman, and goes though the 1938 labour records. About these he makes no comment at the time, but will later say that the 'muddled entries' were not intentional.[32] Then he and Koop arrest Barney, who has broken into Chapman's store. Chasing the native boy gets the yarning treatment given to the Apparition and the others. And so it seems, reading between the lines of Strehlow's 1939 report on the Granites, that other aspects of Chapman's camp take priority.

With that, Koop and Strehlow were then on their long way back home, the narrative of which was to incense Abbott as much as Strehlow's soft focus on Chapman. For now the tragi-comedy of the bush genre gives way to some stock poeticising of the landscape (they have similarly sentimental roots). In his joy to be going home and in his relief, we can say, in the knowledge of his fears, the prose of the patrol officer hit its straps during the night scenes—'When tattered clouds hid the moon in the east,' and he is moving through 'the freshness of the sleeping landscape,' with the car purring 'contentedly despite the anthills and the snake-like twists in the road.'

Strehlow's phrases become a kind of chant— 'Soon the pale light of the moon was gleaming on the desolated, stark boulders—and break into a song of 'the safety of the midnight journey':

we were winding our way among the giant anthills that guarded the passage into the desert. Stark, sombre, silent, haughty, they ignored the hurrying humans in their flight through the age-old undisputed domain. Sixty miles. Curves, bends, occasionally jolts, racing on; the moon soaring higher over the bleak landscape, sombre and stark in the gloom; the swish of a tree against the mudguards, a sudden jar as the brakes slowed down the car to lessen a particularly heavy bump; in the vast silence we seemed the only living beings [but for] the sleepy breath of the wind and the contented purr of our car alone echoed through the midnight desert . . . At last I sighted a tree bearing a white shield labelled '100 miles.' I stopped the car. It was 3 o'clock a.m. Heavy lidded passengers staggered off the car. Everyman hurriedly spread out his blanket. And then—sleep.[33]

Sleep, the traveller, the desert stars. The moon, antiquity and contentment. Heaven it could be to be patrolling the 'age-old undisputed domain.' Bliss it was for Strehlow to indulge his Wordsworthian tendencies, even if he was to pay a price.

He had to go back again in December 1940. The drought had deepened. Chapman had sent an SOS to the administration: 'ALL WATER DRIED GRANITES DISTRICT, OVER 100 ABORIGINALS STARVING STEALING FOOD FROM MINES SHOP.' Chapman went on to say that he was willing to assist the Department of Native Affairs but he would need immediate 'food relief.'[34]

Strehlow had to investigate and act promptly. And he had to inspect the 'severe fighting amongst the natives' and 'to inquire about the allegations made by "Bluey" Connell that Mr Chapman was feeding his own aboriginal employees with flour from the Government store.'

It turned out that the brawl had indeed badly wounded two people. A woman had numerous scars from spear wounds, and the man had a knife wound in his chest from a fortnight before: 'the stench of his wound could be compared only to the foul odour of a corpse.' He was lying in Chapman's truck shed. Strehlow had him flown out by Eddie Connellan's plane, straight to the Alice Springs hospital. Strehlow's report makes no mention of Chapman's neglect.

As to the flour, Strehlow told his department, 'we got very poor and disappointing results.' Again, Chapman's records were almost impossible to check—partly because the European names of his fifteen Aboriginal employees were confusing to all, even the natives themselves, Strehlow claimed, as was their erratic employment and therefore their entitlements to Chapman's rations as distinct from government flour. Strehlow referred to the 'callous practice' of Chapman not issuing the government flour when his men were out of work, even though there was no native food for miles around. But there is no record of a reprimand of Chapman.

A new three-ton lot of flour arrived when Strehlow was there. It went into Chapman's shed because there was nowhere else to store it. Chapman was put on trust to continue to feed the natives their rations every second day—at least for the duration of the drought. Chapman's records were to be sent down to Alice Springs by air mail. 'So long as the number remains constant, the chances are that no flour is being misappropriated.'

There Strehlow left the matter in 1940, and it might be unfairly suggested, as Abbott did in retrospect, that Strehlow was soft, or soft minded, on Chapman. But Strehlow's counsel was pragmatic. After all the years of bureaucratic minutiae concerning the white man's sloppy record-keeping, and the obvious understanding the white men had reached with Aboriginal women, and the fighting among the natives, he was telling Cook that 'Chapman's place is the only centre for hundreds of miles where these natives can be fed, and the aboriginals are dependent for their water on Chapman's bore.' Strehlow was speaking of at least 124 natives. If they were added to the people near the mining settlements at Tanami and around Mount Doreen that would be sufficient to justify a reserve. But that in effect would have been to overlook the contribution of the mines. Strehlow found the natives who worked at the mines 'well fed and well looked after.' There was, he conceded, the question of what they should be paid. Since most of them were 'pure myall,' and were 'apt to leave their job at a moment's notice'—a definite wage scale would mean that their employers would want an end to walkabouts. Low wages were the trade-off in terms of cultural tolerance. Furthermore:

The ability of their employers to pay wages must also be borne in mind. High wages would probably force some of these employers to discontinue mining altogether. The poorness of these three districts for mining may be gauged by the fact that up-to-date almost all mining activities have been carried on by one white man and his family in each instance. This shows that the employment of white labour, or of native labour at award rates, would have meant closing down mining activities at the Granites, Tanami and Mt Doreen.

On the other hand, while mining is being carried on in these three districts, myall natives are enabled to improve their conditions of living.

If these three districts were to close down these natives would drift into the cattle stations closer to the telegraph line. And eventually become a charge upon our Department.[35]

Here speaks Strehlow the practical patrol officer. He could weigh things up, he was not driven by any automatic anti-colonial agenda; he could see the implications of simple economic reforms. A reserve—which had been proposed for the Granites—might look good on paper but not be that good in practice. Here was a man who could think through the complex ecology of native affairs. When a patrol officer reported like this he could not help but be valued by his superiors. It was only hindsight about the Granites that made Strehlow look bad.

Settlement of Hard Times

By the Christmas of 1938, Strehlow and Bertha were in the house he had built. That was progress; 'the foundations for a permanent establishment had been laid.' But still his question was: 'will such an establishment ever come into being, or will the discordant hoots and jeers of other Government officials prevail at Canberra and destroy all our strivings, toil, labours, and aspirations that we have ever entertained at Jay Creek? 1939 will show the issue.'[36]

In the same breath he was able to mention one sign of progress: 'The health of the natives has been splendid. There has been no serious illness during the year.'[37] That was indeed something to report: from it we can probably assume that Jay Creek as a ration depot with medical resources had been stabilised. The stability was also very much due to the Strehlows' dogged sense of responsibility for individuals in need, the personal realities of their labours of love.

On Christmas Day 1938, a particularly hot day under heavy clouds, after helping Moses hold a Christmas service under the gum trees below the garden, Strehlow had to meet Dr Reilly, who had come out from Alice Springs to check on Elvida, who had just given birth, and on Maggie, who seemed to be recovering from her tuberculosis. Only then did Strehlow and Bertha go into Alice Springs for their own Christmas tea—'the first leisurely meal for days.'

The Jay Creek duties were relentless. They demanded the writing of reports, and Strehlow's monthly reports are studies in social detail, some of it routine, some of it crisis management, all of it ongoing, and involving a constant negotiation of his own authority.

When, for example, he was up around Newcastle Waters in October 1938, Darwin wanted him to go ever further afield and scout out the conditions of Aborigines on Vestey's stations. Strehlow gesticulated into his diary on 10 October; he had no warning of this extra travelling, he was ill-equipped with petrol and provisions, he was not in a fit physical condition to take on the tropics, and he did not want to get stranded when the rains came. Also: 'All my reports here have been ignored so far, and not one of my investigations has ever borne any fruit. After all my toil to do my job in my own district, Darwin has consistently failed to acknowledge even receipt of these reports. The lot of abos. has been improved no whit though any laborious investigations of mine. Neither have I had hope left that any such trip undertaken now would yield anything of value for the natives.'

At this low ebb he was faced with the prospect of disobeying an instruction to go north. But he received a telegram: 'RETURN TO ALICE SPRINGS.' Before turning back he called at Dunmara station to check out the usual things and found himself having to make a decision about Trickler, 'a lad about 12.' Trickler had been talking with Tom Ljonga and expressed a wish to go back to Jay Creek with Strehlow and 'go to Moses' school & learn Aranda.' Strehlow consulted with the boy's mother and father, 'and they said yes,—as long as I would come back again this way next year. So I accepted the lad, and gave flour, tea, sugar and tobacco to his mother.'[38]

Further south, with Trickler on board, Strehlow was astonished to get a telegram from his authorities. 'POSTMASTER DALY WATERS COMPLAINS YOU REMOVED ABORIGINAL CHILD TRICKLER PLEASE ADVISE.' Strehlow rang Medser the postmaster and explained, only to find his word doubted, and the word 'abducted' used by the sceptical Medser. The story that had reached the postmaster was that Strehlow had 'bought the boy' and wanted to take his sister too, and that the whole camp was upset: they felt that if Strehlow could come and take a boy like that, anything could happen. Medser doubted Strehlow's word that Trickler was to be returned next year.

'I was annoyed beyond measure,' Strehlow wrote, and handed the boy back. He reasoned that the boy's parents must be now grieving for him. Trickler was to stay at Newcastle Waters until the local constable, Edwards, could take him back to camp. Strehlow travelled on, back to

Alice Springs, patrolling the stations along the way, and finally, on 16 October, riding 'on and on' in the darkness, he 'reached Alice Springs at midnight . . . with burning eyes, aching with weariness.'

With this kind of work it is hard to imagine, really, what would have constituted satisfaction. The attempt to help Trickler was a metaphor for the hopeless predicaments that could arise: a decision based on local knowledge could so easily backfire, even though his own sympathies were against removing children from their parents. All decisions, fur-thermore, had to be taken on the basis of individual needs in the context of poor provisions.

Strehlow's monthly report for April 1939 is as vivid as any with regard to intractable human detail:

Much of this month's activities centre around the disciplinary cases now held at Jay Creek. On Feb 28th Saltpetre (held here since December last year) caused a disturbance. He had, without reason, assaulted his wife on the previous day with a stone, and had then slept with Jessie, the mental case from Tempe Downs. Thinking that his wife might resent such conduct, Saltpetre become convinced that in order to prevent her from leaving him, he should administer another beating to her. He accordingly pursued her right on to the verandah of the Patrol Officer, who however stopped him and took him in to Alice Springs. On the way in, Saltpetre was rather carsick, and even though he took off his trousers, did not feel much better for it. In Alice Springs he pretended to be violently ill . . . he was committed to gaol for two months. His wife has been kept at Jay Creek meanwhile.

Jessie the mental case, kept on running away from the Reserve. Finally, she was caught in Alice Springs only a day earlier, she had already obtained the sum of One Shilling for lending herself out to a white man. She was gaoled for one month for having run away from an aboriginal reserve. (She has since been returned to Jay Creek, and appears to be sitting down at last, her mother has been at Jay Creek for several months now.)

Archie, the lad from Hatche's Creek, likewise absconded. He was picked up by the police in Alice Springs, and held in one of the disused cells at the Police Station until I could collect him. As he is a lad spoiled exceedingly by contact with miners, I gave him a few a cuts with a strap when I got him back to Jay Creek. Since then he seems to be quite happy with the other children here. Evelyn, a full blooded aboriginal woman, who had served a sentence in gaol for partaking in a drunken orgy with white men was brought out to Jay Creek on March 7th. She had several previous convictions.

On March 27th two young aboriginal women were brought out to Jay Creek. Both of them have young half-caste infants, who are still too young to be admitted to the Halfcaste Institution. They are to remain here until their infants are old enough to be admitted to the Halfcaste Institution.

Since Archie's return, no further trouble has been experienced with the disciplinary cases here. They are free to roam about within the precincts of the Aboriginal Reserve, and they have made no attempts to abscond since realising that flights from the Reserve merely lead them into the Alice Springs gaol.

On March 9th I took a woman of about 40 years to the Alice Springs Hospital. She was Kekimana, and she died on the following day. A post-mortem examination revealed the cause of death to have been T.B. in the kidneys. Reticence on the part of her relatives about what they imagined to have been a female complaint led to the seriousness of her condition not being revealed earlier.[39]

Strehlow's reports interweave. They thread details of Aboriginal lives—the full resonance of which, in the absence of Aboriginal narratives, can only be intimated—with the anecdotal stresses of a colonial bureaucrat. The reference to removing children to the Half-Caste Institution—the Bungalow, in Alice Springs—is straightforward. It was government policy, and Strehlow is dutifully fitting in with it, despite his antipathies.* In this context he did so because he would have thought the young Aboriginal women incapable of giving their

---

*   'Dutifully' because I have not turned up any policy statement by Strehlow to the contrary. Nor has the historian of child removal in Central Australia, Tony Austin (1987, 1992, 1993). 'Fitting in' rather than carrying it out since there is no mention in his diaries of actually transporting children to the Bungalow: he must have left that to the police. In quietly opposing such policies Strehlow was in accord with Albrecht's policy at the mission which on at least one occasion had received a mother and child Strehlow had prevented a local policeman from separating (Henson 1992: 171). Out at Arltunga in April 1935 he was pleased to meet 'Jim and his half-caste wife' and noted how Jim 'proudly showed me his two fat boys, one aged about 5, and the other about 3—they were his *own* sons, he repeated several times, & not the offspring of whites. His half-caste wife had never been to the bungalow, but she could wash gold . . . [she] looked happier than those unfortunate girls of the bungalow

children reasonable care: this most likely because they were the kind of women most easily abused and used by the white men he found so hard to prosecute, and who would never marry any of them. When he put the matter more censoriously, these were women who resented protection as an infringement of their liberty, and had decided to 'go to Hell in their own way.'[40]

In general, reading these reports on the social matrix at Jay Creek, grim detail piles on grim detail in a Dickensian manner. Strehlow tries to lighten some things—fancying his own drolleries—but more often he veers towards intimations of doom for many of the characters involved. What is striking, overall, is the *fatedness* that imbues his reports. This happens, then that; that is how things have worked out. Strehlow had begun his job as patrol officer by urgently reproaching his superiors, but within a few years of the grind at Jay Creek his reports exude a heavy, bitter sense of resignation. Jay Creek was a settlement made for hard times.

At the same time, he is playing his part in people's lives—intensely so. That is perhaps the dominating aspect of Strehlow's years as a patrol officer. He was inseparably bound up with the lives of individuals. Each was a separate case but it is the uniqueness of the person that also shows through in the reports, and in that can be detected something of the Christian way of seeing things.

Whatever their personal details as 'cases,' the people in Strehlow's charge at Jay Creek were crying out to be treated as dislocated people, for an application of anthropological understanding. They were people now trying to live in two places on a number of fronts: in two laws, in two or more places, in two generations, one closer to their cultural roots than the other. In his plea to Cook, Strehlow had used the word 'drifting' to suggest the plight of such people, a term also used by Elkin: terms of loss and abandonment came easily to the mind of these key participant observers of colonial history. And the drifting made inevitable the notion of such people as 'driftwood'—as the debris of an historical process, the final upshot of personal and social ruin—history's wreckage. Still, such understanding is absent from his reporting at this time. We have to ask why.

---

who have grown up without mother love who fall an easy use of prey to syphilitic ruffians as soon as they leave....What's the earthly use of education to them without home or affection or kinship while they are yet children! Better let them be happy among the blacks, & rear babies whom they can fondle and bring up themselves.'

The answer lies in Strehlow's complicated feelings about the moral basis of authority. As the Christian doing the social work of a missionary, he could speak of each individual as a person. He knows their country, their parents, often their genealogy; he knows their ancestry, and the land of belief from which they have drifted. But at this point there is a complication in Strehlow's thought and feeling. As people who had drifted—they are driftwood now, the object—they are so because *they have forsaken the ways of their fathers.* Strehlow knows that as individuals they have had no choice in the matter: it has been their fate as colonised people. But he is also inclined to feel very strongly that their departure from the old ways has been their responsibility as well, and that they could, if they would only listen, take something worthwhile from even the remnants of that culture. That Strehlow believed this is clear from the kind of lecture he gave Henock, who seemed to be soft on work and oblivious to the disciplines of his fathers and uncles. Exasperated, Strehlow passed judgment. His intolerance of generational change is striking. And yet so is his great sadness—expressed as a kind of oceanic nostalgia when he is collecting the broken songs—that the old ways have gone. It is as if Strehlow carried within him two competing structures of feeling on the native problem; one thriving on paternalistic coercion, the other on a romanticisation of the past. They find it hard to meet with regard to the psychological plight of any one individual. The moralism of the Christian case worker thwarted his willingness to offer an analysis of the complexities of social rift.

A better way to make the point—rather than appear to carp about what Strehlow was not, or could not adequately be—is to pause with a contrast. Elkin on generational change was instructively different from Strehlow. Elkin set the scene for Bill Harney's *Taboo*, stories about ambiguities in time and space, in a way that was not an invitation to moral judgment. Referring to the young folk and the elders, Elkin wrote:

The former are attracted to the apparently superior ways and goods of the white man, whether or not the latter shows his disdain for the traditions and customs maintained by the old members of the tribe, the young men adopt an attitude of superiority to those old ways. The elders, however, realise that the white man's manner of life and beliefs are not for the black folk, at least, not yet, and they believe that only by adherence to the old way can their future be assured. As a result they are greatly perturbed, for they do not feel justified in handing on to these 'irreverent' and disdainful youths a knowledge of the life-giving secrets (myths, and rites) of which they are the custodians, and so, apart from a few exceptions, they die knowing that the old life dies with them, believing that the race is doomed, but satisfied that they themselves have been loyal to their dream-time tenets and obligations.

But that is not all. As the years pass by, and the young men reach middle-age, they realise that the old men were right, that entry into white life (social, economic and religious) is for the most part denied them, and that they are but hangers-on. Then they would return to the old ways, the old rites and beliefs, and from these draw strength and comfort. But the link has been broken. Their initiation, if it occurred at all, was a mere outline of the real thing. The old faith has been lost and the old knowledge forgotten. Unless, then, the white man steps into the breach and, on the basis of knowledge and understanding, helps these men to win a new faith and fresh intellectual confidence and moral strength, their future is indeed black.

Such is the *psychological damage* which is done to the aborigines in the clash with ourselves. It does not, however, remain in the mind. It results in a weakening or loss of the will to live, to overcome illness and to bear children. The feeling of inferiority, hopelessness and uselessness is manifested in a fatalistic acceptance of the disappearance of the race. Therefore, those who would save this people must, by action and word, help them to a fresh out-look on life and see that they are allotted a definite part in Australian life. (emphasis added)[41]

The key term is 'psychological damage.' It is both a pointer for care and for social policy. Elkin's formulation allows a go-between such as a patrol officer to weave his way into the lives of men and women trying to live through their dislocations, to garner understandings and help individuals find their feet with their old country as well as their new. As much as Strehlow's melancholic imagination lived in the past, he was not consistently thinking in terms that might help others recover theirs.

The New Deal?

While Neville Chamberlain was meeting Hitler in Munich, a 'new deal' for Australian Aborigines was being hatched. By the time Hitler invaded Poland, in September 1939, and war with Germany was declared by Britain and therefore the Commonwealth of Australia, that new deal had seen the light of day even if it could not, at such a historic moment, warrant much political attention. By the time it had been aired—June 1940—conscription had been declared in Australia, and in Central Australia the working lives of many Aborigines had been transformed. By that time, too, Strehlow had been named in the House of Representatives as a Nazi, a slur that compounded many perceptions and misperceptions at once.

It was not a new deal, anyway. It was more another version of Cook's policy that had been shaped five years earlier but not officially broadcast: an emphasis on the idea of resourcing the reserves and training the half-castes for employment. But policy—or the new script of what Stanner called the 'tragi-comedy'—was now the political property of the new Minister of Territories, John McEwen, who was responding largely to the swell of public opinion about the Territory, and into whose ear Elkin had been injecting his anthropological thinking. There was to be a new department, the Department of Native Affairs. It was to replace the Aborigine Unit under the wing of Cook, who was combined Medical Officer and Protector. Cook protested vigorously (this was the occasion of his *Realpolitik* case for native health) but he lost the battle with Elkin and J.A. Carrodus, who were seeking to expand the role of the Federal government in Aboriginal policy.

The Director of the Department of Native Affairs, E.W.P. Chinnery, was fresh from another Native Affairs directorship in the mandated territory of New Guinea. Elkin's ideas here were intellectually central: they expressed the advanced view of the time that Australian policy with its natives could benefit from the wider view of administration built up in other colonies. With this went the idea of increasing the number of competent district officers who would impart education to natives; men with some training in anthropology. Chinnery, who had studied anthropology at Cambridge, arrived from New Guinea aware, as were Elkin and others, that the strength of local village life had enabled natives to negotiate a new reality with the colonisers. Settling Aborigines to new things was the fresh hope. The *Sydney Morning Herald* reported Chinnery's arrival under the heading 'New Policy for Aborigines. Conversion to Food Producers,' and had Chinnery opine:

There have been many statements in recent years that the Australian aborigines are a dying race, beyond redemption. I do not believe that. We should be able not only to stop their decrease, but to train the younger generation for useful work on the stations, and in the towns of Central and Northern Australia. I think it is possible and I am going to do my utmost to bring it about.

To me, the Australian aboriginal is little different from the New Guinea native in many ways. There is, of course, one fundamental difference—the New Guinea native is a food producer; the Australian native is a food gatherer.

The Australian aboriginal is a nomad, following the food with the seasons. He is where the kangaroo is one month, living on native roots the next, and chasing the wild geese at some far distant lake the next. Our task will be to educate him to be a food producer.

The paper said that Chinnery added: 'with subsidised mission stations, central Government stations, and district services of trained men similar to that set up in New Guinea, a definite policy aimed at the spiritual and physical welfare of the natives could be put into practice. The Native Affairs Branch would not be completely separated from other Departments of the Ministry of the Interior.'[42]

Australian natives growing food was pie in the sky and most people knew it. No extra funds emerged for mission stations; no central government stations were set up—though Jay Creek, if only it could secure its water, remained a candidate. Nor were extra full-time officers appointed, although Bill Harney was set to work patrolling the outskirts of Darwin and Melville Island. Before the big announcement, Strehlow was considered for an appointment, which would have been a promotion from his grind in the field. He had written to Chinnery in April, telling the new director that he had been offered a lectureship at the University of Adelaide: he wanted advice and reassurance about the prospects of doing useful work where he was. He felt that he was more or less an 'untrained manual worker' at Jay Creek, and did not want to become one of the 'undertakers' of the Aboriginal people.[43]

This was an interesting moment for Native Affairs. Here they had a man as knowledgeable as Elkin seeking a post where some clear thinking tied to local knowledge was very much needed. If Strehlow had been appointed by Chinnery, he might well have come to see himself as fully valued for his intelligence and understanding: he might have found his feet as a policy maker, and not felt he was wasting so much of his youthful energy in thankless toil. But Administrator Abbott had other ideas for Strehlow, none of them good. Abbott told Chinnery that Mr Strehlow was 'a most earnest and enthusiastic but temperamental officer who requires a certain amount of tactful handling. Another point which strikes me about Mr Strehlow is that although he has a very profound knowledge of the habits, customs, and language of the Central Australian Aboriginals, he is singularly lacking in bush-craft and is a shockingly bad car driver. I am not impugning his value by way of saying this, but they are certainly points which make his work quite difficult.'[44]

Abbott also discounted Xavier Herbert on the grounds of lacking 'loyalty and certain standards,' a view that would have been reinforced by reading *Capricornia*, then about to be published. A young anthropologist, W.H. Stanner—'a tactful type,' Elkin thought—was also considered, but he was in London or Africa. So the new department was set up without any new talent to speak of; it was hardly blessed with funds either, especially after the Country Party–UAP coalition, of which McEwen was a part, lost office; and once the war started in Europe, and then Northern Australia began to prepare for a Japanese invasion, all the fanfare could be safely forgotten. The new deal died as the white administration moved south to Alice Springs and all human and natural resources were diverted into the war effort.

Meanwhile, however, Chinnery had to make himself acquainted with reality on the ground. He reached out to Strehlow. In the winter of 1939 they travelled extensively together—down to the Presbyterian mission at Ernabella, to Hermannsburg, and out to the new ration depot at Haasts Bluff, and to the mining areas of the north-east, Harts Range and Hatches Creek. Chinnery found Strehlow was 'not liked—unjustly so.' He also thought him 'a good fellow' and was 'lifting him in every way possible.' Chinnery, from Strehlow's point of view, prompted no miseries in the diary: it seems that he then felt that he had an ally in the new director.

In July and August 1939 Strehlow made his long journey back to Piltardi Rockhole in the Petermann Range. He seems to have had his nightmare under control. There he met up with an eight-man camel team he had despatched earlier from Hermannsburg, as well as Dr Duguid and others from the Ernabella mission. Strehlow went down by truck with Albrecht, along with the superintendent and the mechanic from Hermannsburg. It was a journey that confirmed fears about the plight of the remote natives and the dire need to set up a ration station in the drought-stricken ranges—a station from which the natives could trade dingo scalps, and run some cattle. Only this could stop the drift to Alice Springs and the cattle stations in the area. In saying this he was saying little that had not been said as general policy since Baldwin Spencer and, even more starkly, what had been called for by the Bleakley Report ten years earlier.

The recommendation was set down in the six pages of conclusions in Strehlow's sixteen-page report on the journey. They were wordy, lacking policy precision, and Chinnery told him so. 'Chinnery had to ask him for a more business-like set of recommendations setting out the essential facts and estimating the likely costs of sinking wells, improving the track and establishing a depot.'[45] By the time Strehlow got around to this, war had broken out and it was even clearer that funds were to be short.

Strehlow travelled extensively in the winter of 1939, and he showed the strain. Duguid seemed to think he might be running the risk of a breakdown. 'I do not know,' the doctor wrote in August, 'what your wife thought about you on your return, but I came to the conclusion that at the end of the patrol, you were, both mentally and physically, weary. My diagnosis may be incorrect, and my reference to you may appear "darned cheek," but you are far too valuable a man to get thoroughly run down. You mentioned when we were together, that you had not had a holiday for several years, isn't it just about time you knocked off?'[46]

Whose Reserves?

Strehlow's chronic worries can be simply listed. Bertha's recurring sickness. Lack of reliable water at Jay Creek and its consequent vulnerability as a long-term settlement, its handicap as a candidate for being gazetted as a reserve. His recalcitrant administration. Racist station owners. Barbaric bushmen. Sick or disorderly natives. His own lack of authority or knowledge (or both) as a doctor and as a magistrate. His doubt about doing good in the long run, as distinct from being an 'undertaker.' All this gnawed away at him.

And then there was the endemic problem of the whole region: the reserves, or rather the idea of reserves. The problem of the reserves—where most of the Aboriginal population still lived, or might live, if safe ones could be established—was a life-and-death matter. The Petermann journey had highlighted that. Reserves were pressure points in more ways than one.

To speak of reserves at all was to have to speak of social and economic priorities, of history, of living and dying people and peoples. A reserve raised the issue of previous generations and those to come: was a reserve to secure the traditional lives of native peoples, to protect them absolutely from modernity? Or a mere framework for a ration depot? Or a political strategy, a measure of sovereignty over native title to land? These terms are the modern ones, but they were in the air, and almost grounded as concepts, once a reserve was conceived as a sanctuary.

One pressure point was around Haasts Bluff, where the Hermannsburg mission had set up a ration station manned by its Aboriginal preacher, Titus, in 1931. For some years it had been remote enough from pastoral activity to have functioned as a reserve without being called one. The nearest station to the Haasts depot was at Glen Helen, and mission organisers managed to keep their myalls from wandering in that direction. But in 1937 a Mr Holt bought land at Haasts Bluff, with a licence to graze there. Pastor Albrecht was the first to ring the alarm bell on behalf of the natives who would 'be denied the very simplest form of subsistence.' If sheep were allowed, he told the native administration, 'about 200 natives will be forced the first step to total extinction, and all this just in order to provide the means of livelihood for one white man. History in Central Australia will once more repeat itself in its most dreadful aspects.'[47]

Albrecht predicted that once the sheep got the waterholes, and the native supply of berries and grasses, the natives would be bound to interfere with the flocks. 'Frontier conflict would be revived. The heads of families and groups will be brought into the Alice Springs gaol. Then when they got out of gaol, they would find their tribal organisation broken up without the slightest hope of having it re-established again.' Albrecht described how other desert people—the Ngalia and the Pintubi—had lost their best hunting areas. Haasts Bluff was the last place of refuge in the area. The only solution was all too clear if their 'death warrant' was not to be signed. 'On behalf of these poor unfortunates who have no voice in our public life I plead with your Honour not to allow the restocking of Haasts Bluff, but rather declare the whole area a permanent Reserve for Natives.'

Strehlow supported Albrecht, but for some years the plea fell on deaf ears. When Haasts Bluff was gazetted as a reserve it was a hard-won victory for them both.

In the meantime, a strong case could be made for natives in another area—the district south of the Granites and north of Mount Doreen station. Dispossessed Walpiri people, many of them still haunted by the slaughter at Coniston, eked out a dependent living from the white settlements and wandered across pastoral estates, to the chagrin of their owners. A reserve had been urged upon the government since 1935. It had the backing of Professor Cleland and Dr Fry from Adelaide, but the Northern Territory authorities had rejected the idea because it might interfere with a proposed stock route from the Tanami to Alice Springs.

No one was more vociferous in advocacy than Olive Pink. Pink knew the Granites area herself because she had helped Charles Mountford make a film there in 1936, footage of Aboriginal ceremony and ground painting. Pink was dismayed when she heard that Mountford had shown the secret-sacred material in Britain and America. To Pink it was irrelevant that the film was shown in universities—'another world,' as it was called. She thought it an abuse of Aboriginal trust. For this peppery protest she got short shrift from her anthropological colleagues, and in 1937 the ANRC actually recalled her from the field to put a stop to her research work. Embattled with Elkin, she left Central Australia for a time. She decided that the details of her own world would not go anywhere, that she would withhold access to her research data for 50 years, and that none of her papers would ever return to the Territory. With this she withdrew from academic anthropology, defeated by the budding Australian establishment. But she was not yet defeated in the Aboriginal cause.[48]

When she made her 1938 *Canberra Times* statement about sex being at the root of problems she had her case for a reserve at Mount Doreen in mind. She called for a secular sanctuary. Secular, because she held the missions in contempt for their persecution of Aborigines. She spoke of 'freedoms of conscience' for the 'full-bloods.' And in any case she judged the mission project to have been a failure, to have produced 'artificial conversion' and 'a resentful conformity only' among the natives: 'a putting up with forms and ceremonies and prohibitions (and quite uncongenial occupations in which their labour is exploited), and with injustices so that food and clothes may be obtained.' As if this was not bad enough for secular officials who had been using the missions as welfare agencies, she went on to rub salt into the wound of all Christian endeavour: 'I have discussed converts' beliefs with them without them knowing my views, of course.' Bought over 'with better food and better (second hand) clothes, they could be reconverted to Mohammedanism (or any other "ism") tomorrow outwardly and still remain the Totemites they originally were at heart through it all. I am interested in getting freedom of conscience for Totemites just as I want it for ourselves.'

Pink wanted authority to run the reserve. The case for a woman holding such a position was linked to the need for that person to be neither an official nor anyone bent on religious conversion—a person who would have no objection to their initiation and totemic cere-monies. Pink had her own passionate reasons for proposing herself, but she might, too, have had in mind that Baldwin Spencer thought of women as honorary protectors.[49] More radical, though, was her political reasoning. The reserve had to be a sanctuary to protect the tribal ways, and that could best be done by respecting 'an inalienable area in each tribe for full bloods.' It was only in places that absolutely excluded 'missionaries and their black preachers and all mission endeavours' that 'we shall then, and only then, be attempting to give them a fair deal and something of value to themselves.'

All this was ahead of its time. It was the kind of utterance hell-bent on alienating all manner of persons in Central Australia: the official for neglect (and sexual humbug); the station owner for rapacity and inhumanity; the missionary for bigotry. For some years Pink had the sympathy of southern philanthropists like Cleland and Fry and Duguid, but in the Territory itself, and before long in Canberra, where her energetically large handwriting was to be seen often on the desk of Secretary Carrodus, she had installed herself as Public Nuisance Number One. Her modus operandi put her colleagues off side, and at the 1930 science conference she was sidelined from giving a paper on her secular sanctuary.

Strehlow agreed with the idea of a sanctuary: he too thought that the tribal people should be properly protected from white intrusion. He spoke of an 'absolute reserve,' although hedging about whether it should be 'secular' or not. He looked favourably on the idea of a reserve roughly in the area proposed by Pink. But he did not, it goes almost without saying, go along with her anti-mission diatribe: how could he even countenance men like Titus and Moses being described as 'artificial' converts. It would have demolished the ground of his own history, his father's whole life's work, as well as his living faith in the Christian authority of his daily work. On the other hand he was already championing the religious rights of Aborigines with regard to their sacred objects and the land to which they belonged. He might well have agreed with the idea if it had not come from Pink, a woman who had already become a nuisance to him.

As early as 1933, Strehlow had complained to Elkin that Pink had taken one of his Aranda informants, the indispensable Mickey Gurra, the man who had given him the great song and story of Ilbalintja, the Bandicoot Sire. Pink had been on Strehlow's territory doing a 'walk-about,' as she called it, with three Aranda men, to the oldest one of whom (Gurra) she was deeply and almost entirely indebted. Gurra took her, in the ritually right way, to his totem site, and explained 'it was done for all time, and I could take my friends there now without harm to me.' Gurra, in his sophisticated way, also had a joke with Pink: the place to which they had gone was 'like government-man's office' ('the Deputy Administrator's,' Pink exclaimed, when she wrote up her account). She was shown other places along the way, including kangaroo sites, and places where ancestral kangaroo had eaten, and was greatly moved by how the country still had its 'feeling of sanctity' despite being 'desecrated by people of our own culture.'[50]

Pink's article, which is striking for the tentative way her knowledge is advanced, and the respect she accorded the men who had taken her into their trust ('It taught me that if you trust a native, then trust him absolutely') was guaranteed to unsettle the more conventional worker, especially one with Strehlow's proprietorial instincts. Elkin had to remind him that Pink had not 'taken' Gurra away, and that Gurra 'was really quite ready to help her again.' Elkin went along with Strehlow's other worry: that a woman was on dangerous ground inquiring into the secret-sacred men's business. 'I could not imagine her endeavouring to force her way into aboriginal secret matters,' Elkin wrote. 'If she does go out I will have a talk to her about the problems.'[51] Both Elkin and Strehlow blithely overlooked Gurra and company's capacity for deciding such matters for themselves.

When it came to Pink and the sanctuary at Mount Doreen (where Pink had even mapped an area with the necessary waterholes), Strehlow was able to speak with conviction at several levels. There was the past: Pink trespassing on the secret-sacred Aranda ground upon which he was already building his career. Then there was his present: why support her reserve when his own at Jay Creek had not yet been gazetted as a reserve, and where he was still waiting for his own boundaries to be extended, and the water supply secured from the cattle run at Owen Springs? If anything, he thought there was a 'crying need' for a mission in the area, something he did not really express until somewhat later.[52] For the moment he seems to have stalled in reply for a while.

Then in August 1939, Eddie Ward, MHR, put his probing parliamentary question to Prime Minister Menzies. Ward's question, obviously informed by Pink and others, was (in part):

Will the Prime Minister confirm or otherwise the statement of an official that a tin-mining field has been recently opened up near the Coniston Station. Will the Prime Minster state what has been done to make the law respected in regard to white men who are co-habiting with the full-blood women of that tribe? . . . What has been done to give effect to a recommendations from the Science Congress in Melbourne in 1935 that a secular Reserve be proclaimed? . . . What were the reports of:
  a) The Patrol Officer, Mr T.G.H. Strehlow?
  b) The Deputy Chief Protector of Aboriginals, Dr P.J. Reilly
  on that Sanctuary's-
    1) urgency
    2) need
    3) site?

Chinnery had to find the answers and turned to Strehlow who spoke up. He told Chinnery the proposal was 'quite impracticable and undesirable.' 'Miss Pink herself,' he told Chinnery,

is not by constitution fitted for long and continuous stays in the outback portions of the interior. She mentions in her letter to the Minister that on one occasion Mr Braitling (of Mt Doreen station) had to come out and bring some meat for her by car fifty miles across the desert; and on another occasion had to rescue her by car,—saving her life when she fell ill by taking her to the Alice Springs Hospital. It is to be anticipated that Miss Pink would not be able to get along on her own in her Secular Reserve without outside assistance: her provisions would have to be sent to her; she would require police assistance to keep out any white prospectors, in fact in order to remove white prospectors from this area; she would find that medical supplies for the aboriginals and later on rations for the old people or for the sick people would be necessary, unless she had sufficient private funds to minister to the wants of the aboriginals out of her own pockets. With her delicate constitution it is doubtful how long she would last in the hard, hot desolation of the area in suggestion. And what would become of the Secular Reserve after she had left? Some anthropologists have so far failed to remain at their post and minister to the wants of natives for a continuous period of say over ten years. It is probable that after Miss Pink's departure the only person who would be prepared to go into the Secular Reserve would be some missionary.

That was not all Strehlow had to say about Miss Pink. He went on:

She cannot speak the language of the myalls of that area, and she would need to be very firm and understanding and patient in order to achieve any success in her endeavours. Miss Pink, moreover, has the habit of interviewing the old men of the tribe in order to give her information about their religious ideas; and quite a few of the old men resent this, and either turn from her or else are forced to utter falsehoods in order to put her off the trail when discussing some of the things that may not be told to a woman.[53]

Strehlow's tone is one he came to adopt on many occasions in the future: it is that of a man who regards himself as superior to anyone who might appear to be encroaching on his domain. His judgment is scathing: his motive territorial.[54] It is hard to say how much his superiors took the personal edge of his advice into account, but politically, Strehlow's advice was what they wanted to hear. No one wanted a troublemaker like Pink installed and a few months later, when she applied for a permit to travel into the reserves to do more of her own research, she played into the authorities' hands.

Strehlow granted her the permit with a humiliating proviso: that she apply to the local government or the mission authorities in order to 'obviate all unnecessary friction.' Pink applied for a 'general permit,' and Strehlow obliged her to give more details of her research. It was 'independent sociological research' Pink replied—and it was at this point Strehlow sought to discredit her credentials and questioned her stance against the missions. He expressed the general-prejudice view about the elderly single spinster: that she had an unhealthy interest in sex, and that her anthropological work would lead to 'bitter attacks on the persons in charge.'

Together, Strehlow, Chinnery and Abbott concurred that Pink was an undesirable presence in Central Australia and that her permit should be refused. Strehlow was instructed to tell her so and he did so in person, handing her the official letter as a policeman would a summons. Pink was scandalised, and rightly felt persecuted, but to no avail, officially. Her idea of the secular sanctuary died with that, even though she came back to camp at Thompson's Rockhole, about 40 miles from the Granites, in 1942, and for two years was a flea in the ear of officialdom—which she then continued to be for the next three decades, from a hut in Alice Springs. She campaigned relentlessly: for the health of natives, and for their land rights as well as mining rights. After 1939 she had no more dealings with Strehlow as an official, and had to accept that her work as an anthropologist was over. When he saw her in Alice Springs one day he thought her a wizened hag.

The case for a reserve near Mount Doreen would not go away either. In December 1940 Strehlow had to visit the Braitling property again, looking into the usual thing—the secret combo lives, and the health of all concerned. When they got to the 'homestead'— tents under brush shelters, and a couple of galvanised-iron structures—they went on to the new bore where the Aborigines were camped. What they found there confirmed their worst suspicions of venereal disease.

Dr Reilly took the swabs from all the likely men; then the women. In the afternoon the doctor and Strehlow inspected the slides. The results were most unsatisfactory. 'Out of 33 adult persons tested there were: 16 positive cases of gonorrhoea, 4 doubtful cases, and only 13 negative cases.'[55]

Braitling tried to explain. He named two roving prospectors who had come through the camp a few months back. They had infected three young girls (the youngest was fifteen) who had spread it through the rest of the camp. Braitling himself denied any intimacy with lubras. Strehlow was dubious. (When Sergeant Koop had camped there one night 'two abo girls' had offered themselves to him.)

Strehlow: 'The low morale of the native community here may be assessed from the fact that one old hag had contracted gonorrhoea from her own mentally deficient son—and apparently the tribe did not feel outraged thereby! In other groups such incest would have been punished by death.'[56]

1 Ward McNally, *Aborigines, Artefacts and Anguish* (Adelaide: Lutheran Publishing House, 1981), 57.
2 T.G.H. Strehlow, diary [SD], 26 October 1937.
3 SD, 9 November 1936.
4 SD, 19 November 1936.
5 SD, 5 November 1937.
6 *Lutheran Herald*, 28 February 1938, 77.
7 Ibid., 71.
8 Strehlow to Wentworth, 7 July 1971.
9 Strehlow to Cook, 26 February 1939, AA CRS.
10 W.E.H. Stanner, 'Caliban Discovered,' in *White Man Got no Dreaming* (Canberra: Australian National University Press, 1979), 151.
11 'Report re Half-Caste Maggie from Mount Cavenagh Station,' 2 August 1938, AA CRS F126 Item 37.
12 'Sickness and Death at Jay Creek Reserve,' February 1941, Strehlow Research Centre.
13 Ibid.
14 Bertha Strehlow, 'Glimpses of Lubra Life in Central Australia,' *AFA Annual Report*, 1949, 34.
15 SD, 17 March 1938.
16 McNally, *Aborigines, Artefacts and Anguish*, 64.
17 Ibid., 99.
18 Dr Harold Davies, director of the Elder Conservatorium of Music in Adelaide, recorded traditional songs from the area of the mission in 1929, in the process upsetting the Christian converts. Barbara Henson, *A Straight-Out Man: F.W. Albrecht and Central Australian Aborigines* (Melbourne: Melbourne University Press, 1992), 47: E. Harold Davies, 'Aboriginal Songs of Central and Southern Australia,' *Oceania*, II, no. 1 (September 1931).
19 Albrecht to Strehlow, 24 February 1937.
20 Ibid.
21 Cook to Strehlow, 14 July 1937, AA(NT) CRTS F126 Item 51.
22 Strehlow to Cook, 14 July 1937, AA(NT) CRTS F126 Item 51.
23 The records of the Strehlow Research Centre are scattered (as Strehlow had left them), but prices and exchanges were documented clearly enough to make these observations.
24 P.G. Jones, 'South Australian Anthropological History: The Board for Anthropological Research and its Early Expeditions,' *Records of the South Australian Museum* 20 (1995): 71–92.
25 Ibid., 74.
26 SD, 31 August 1941.
27 AA CRS F 126/ 44
28 C.T. Madigan, *Central Australia* (London: Oxford University Press, 1936), 234.
29 The reports on the trip to the Granites, 1937, 1939 and 1940, are at AA CRS F126 Item 29: my narrative draws freely on each of them.
30 Report on the trip to the Granites, 1937.
31 Chapman to Strehlow, 24 September 1937, AA CRS F126 Item 29.
32 Strehlow to Chinnery, 16 October 1941, AA CRS F126 Item 29.
33 Report on trip to Granites, February 1939, AA CRS F126 Item 29.
34 Ibid.
35 Strehlow to Cook, 16 October 1941, AA CRS F126 Item 29.
36 SD, 31 December 1938.
37 SD, 31 December 1938.
38 SD, 10 October 1938.

39 AA CRS F126 Item 29.
40 Strehlow to Braille, 25 April 1941, AA(NT) F126/12.
41 Bill Harney, *Taboo* (Sydney: Australasian Publishing House, 1943), 10.
42 *Sydney Morning Herald*, 25 March 1939.
43 Jeremy Long, *The Go-Betweens: Patrol Officers in Aboriginal Affairs Administration in the Northern Territory* (Casuarina, N.T.: North Australian Research Unit, 1992), 32.
44 Abbott to Carrodus, 28 April 1938, AA 452/1 Item 52 541.
45 Long, *Go-Betweens*, 45.
46 Duguid to Strehlow, 30 August 1939.
47 Albrecht to Deputy Administrator, 28 January 1937.
48 Julie Marcus, *First in Their Field* (Melbourne: Melbourne University Press, 1993), 114.
49 Ibid., 123.
50 Olive Pink, 'Spirit Ancestors in a Northern Aranda Horde Country,' *Oceania* IV, no. 2 (1933):, 76, 183, 184, 185.
51 Elkin to Strehlow, 19 July 1933.
52 Strehlow to Carrodus, 1942, AA 659/1 Item 41.
53 Strehlow to Cook, 15 September 1939, AA 659/ I Item 41.
54 Still, the 'my people' ethic was not confined to Strehlow in anthropology. It was there at the beginning, and was still there four decades later: 'Given the sense of urgency that characterised ethnographic endeavour since the early nineteenth century, and the consequent commitment to the importance of "salvaging" the presumed pristine human variety facing obliteration by the march of European civilisation . . . it is scarcely surprising that the ethnography of academic anthropologists tended to follow a "one ethnographer/one tribe" pattern.' George Stocking. 'The Ethnographic Sensibility of the 1920s and the Dualism of the Anthropological Tradition,' in *Romantic Motives: Essays on the Anthropological Sensibility*, History of Anthropology, vol. 6 (Madison: University of Wisconsin Press, 1989), 210.
55 SD, 4 December 1940.
56 Report on trip to Mount Doreen, December 1940, passim.

3   Punishing Strehlow

To a Literary Fault

IN STREHLOW'S REPORTS as a patrol officer there were several personas riding side by side. There was the diligent official in native affairs, the valuable man who could give such useful pragmatic details: the man he was paid to be. There was the opinionated university man, the know-all fellow who went on as if he knew the whole history of native policy first-hand. This was the fellow they might put up with. There was the fervent friend of the native, who could sound for all the world like a missionary. This was the one who could be a pain in the neck, even though the administration needed the missions (for who else would run the ration stations?).

Then there were the other two personas alive and well in Strehlow that had nothing to do with his official line of work, but which he indulged, as a writer will, when he hits his straps. There was the bush humorist. This was the Strehlow who laid it on thick when he was reporting on the Outback villains of the world, on the bush characters, on the farcical business of them making tracks, and the officers of the law making tracks after them and often losing out. Strehlow the yarning Australian bushman, a parodic Henry Lawson or a kind of Outback anecdotist, rather like Bill Harney was to become. Either way: Strehlow the mimic of Australiana.

And there was Strehlow the lyricist, the rhapsodist of midnight desert rides, and romancer of landscape. As the bush parodist he was indulging his black humour, flirting with the Gothic element of the bush genre. As the lyricist, he showed the opposite face: he sang like Wordsworth of affirmations of place, of home and the Sublime.

In the Petermanns he had rather excelled himself:

Foster's Cliff was a forsaken peak sitting in the silence of sinister wastes of sand, a sentinel still watching over a land whose soul had passed away. Still he was staring into the glare of the sand-reflected sunlight. Still the moon shone down uneasily upon his stern furrowed brow. The howling desert storms might beat upon him by day, and the curlews would shriek at the base in the eerie dead of the night. But Foster's Cliff would stand unmoved—a monument defying time, looming up into eternity.

At last we reached the top of a very high hill from which we obtained an unforgettable view of the western Petermann. To the east Ruined Ramparts burned like red fire, its magnificent red rocks challenging the ravaging hand of time to destroy them. Kekinkura's sheer cliffs—hundreds of feet of sheer crag rising into the cloudy sky—threw out their challenge to all passers by. Behind us the blue ridges of Tjintirintira swept away into the dim distance of Kekinkura; and through this gap could be seen the outlines of a faint blue mountain range, probably Blood's Range. It was a scene of colossal grandeur, an age-old symphony of rock, a vision of wild cliffs towering over a chaos of tumbled-down boulders whose crash had re-echoed like thunder from the sheer faces of the mountains.[1]

On a trip to Mount Doreen he let himself out again:

We now headed northwest. The country was flat, and covered with mulga, Grevillia, bare-stemmed poplars, and spinifex. Then came some limestone country, where tea-tree bushes and some stunted eucalypts showed that these parts were occasionally flooded by the creeks from the Napperby holding. A well. A halt. An orange or two, and some water to drink. Water in the engine, which was beginning to warm up. It was 4 p.m. Then along dusty tracks, cut up to powder by the hooves of hungry roving cattle to a well on the sandy banks of the Napperby Creek. Multitudinous bellows of gaunt cattle filling their hollow stomachs with luke warm water.

We were close to the Stuart Bluff Range. We struck northwest, now on a surveyed, straight, fire-ploughed road, passed through a gap in the Range, and headed north. The bush at long last grew luxuriant; it consisted of mulga, witchetty bush, Petermann wattle, and much spinifex. At sunset we caught a glimpse of far-off Central Mt Wedge, looming up greyish-blue against the orange western sky. Soon afterwards we passed a new Government bore. We now got back into thick mulga country, and the straight road was replaced by the usual crooked, narrow, aimless car tracks, whose curves recalled some of the Humerstonian efforts at their best. We spun forward into the night and the darkening forest of mulga and witchetty bush, curve upon curve, and bend upon bend. At long last the spinifex clearing. A light. Some tents. Then giant uprights of the boring plant. We were at Gorey's new Government bore, already in granite at 30 feet, without having struck water. We had come 200 miles, and it was a quarter to nine p.m. Some food. Then bed.[2]

Those 'multitudinous bellows'—as we know from his own boyhood nightmare—were more to him than cattle on the edge of drought. He speeds on in the car, and to the satisfaction of having arrived—across relentless, unyielding country—in to camp, and to bed. The rhythms of the passage hark for a glimpse of the sublime, and after that, rest of the most profound kind. From the peaks to sleep, and to his own deeper dreaming of country.

In his reports, the intense focus on the sex problem of native girls feeds into the dark side of the bush parodist. In the lyrical passage, all Aboriginal presence is buried in the landscape. Yet the Romantic sense of landscape is meant to unite all; the country called up the poet. And it was the poet in Strehlow that was starting to get under people's skin.

The Administrator, C.A.E. Abbott, who had been in his job since Strehlow's arrival in 1937, was particularly irritated, taking exception to these 'excursions into literary heights.' Abbott told Chinnery that he did not need to know about the multitudinous bellows, or the number of oranges consumed. 'While Mr Strehlow's report is interesting it appears to me that it could be very much curtailed and would save, not only his own typing, but that of your staff.'[3]

But that was a matter of bureaucratic opinion. Chinnery defended Strehlow. He thought that patrolling officers should be instructed and encouraged to describe their journeys fully. He wanted the descriptive detail 'in order that a comprehensive picture of conditions existing in the districts visited and the experience gained by the patrols may be available in the records of the Branch for future guidance. A great deal of valuable data relating to outlying places are observed and experiences in conditions of travel are gained by patrolling officers.'[4]

Abbott remained unhappy. He made another directive about Strehlow's 'phraseology.' Chinnery should 'see that the official reports which come to me are couched in concise and official language . . . I insist that reports to me, which may go to the Minister or may even be tabled in Parliament, are so written that they are understandable and will not bring ridicule upon the Administration.' As it happened, ridicule would be brought upon the Administration by Abbott himself when he scandalously mismanaged Darwin as it was bombed by the Japanese.

True Feelings

This tussle between two bureaucrats on matters of style hid more than it said. Chinnery was an educated man versed in some anthropology and colonial administration: he was trying to evolve a policy for the natives which did not fit, necessarily, into all vested interests in the territory. Chinnery was a man who could sincerely use the phrase 'common humanity,' and who was prepared to say 'that there has always been a strong anti-aboriginal and anti-half caste opinion throughout the Territory which has increased the burden of officials, complicating even the simplest humanitarian work.'[5]

Abbott did not have Chinnery's hopes about Aboriginal policy. 'I am intensely sympathetic towards the Australian aboriginal,' he declared in a policy paper, 'but I am doubtful whether he is receptive enough to hope that he can be brought to such a high standard as to entitle him to full rights and privileges of citizenship . . . the difficulty will always be whether the foundation of the structure of the Australian aboriginal is sufficiently strong to sustain a new edifice . . . in other words will a few years of training and schooling so alter the aboriginal that he will not revert periodically?'[6]

Abbott was writing confidentially. It is important to notice this, as Territory policy, the 'tragi-comedy' of it was as much a product of what could not be publicly uttered as what had to be written down in the welfare policy scheme of things. Officially, a philanthropic optimism had to show through. Privately, pessimism lurked in the old feelings that went with the doomed race theory. And privately, too, there was the simple fact that any welfare policy brought acute frustrations, and paternalism in general was an invitation to the most bitter, arrogant judgments. On this front Strehlow's private thoughts—expressed at such length in his cathartic diaries—could no more be officially quoted than Abbott's confidential memos.

When Strehlow was fed up, as he was heartily towards the end of 1937, when he felt that he had given up so much for so little, he could exclaim: 'And if the natives themselves have no desire to be helped and to be helped into a strong race once more, what can I do? If God does not help, I may as well give up now and leave this place as a man would do who departs from the grave of his deepest hopes. Let God decide what it is to be.'[7]

If the natives themselves have no desire to be helped. It was a feeling that had, potentially, serious implications for policy making. It went to the heart of the problem that is today called welfare dependence. If a people did not want help, what was the use? Much depends, of course, on where the line on hope is to be drawn, and whether situations allow for those who are receiving help to draw it themselves. Strehlow's exasperation could run him into statements that echoed the worst of colonial history. Out at Haasts Bluff in early 1941, for example, he discovered that for the 'first time natives have thieved from me.' He had found the remains of a goat. He lamented that this was his 'reward' — despite the battle he and Albrecht had waged for a reserve. The culprits said it all belonged to them. Strehlow: 'No doubt the goat killing was merely a prelude to the killing of cattle held here, so much for charity to the lazy parasites—they refuse to work, but want to eat while lying down idly in the camp. Hence "all belong to aboriginals!" The wives of these lazy brutes, of course, have been fed here for many months.'

Parasites. Lazy. Brutes. Even in a diary half-meant for others, this was as unpublishable as Abbott's reservations. Yet he was expressing no more than righteous indignation common to Lutheran mission history. It was paternalism fuelled, you might say, by an unpleasant mix of personal spleen, the racist vernacular of the region, and an obvious suspension of the sociological imagination.

Jay Creek had really become a co-station of the Hermannsburg Mission. Not in the sense that it was a centre for religious conversion (Strehlow made this officially clear to Carrodus) but as a welfare depot with an aura of Christian congregation.[8] Strehlow and Albrecht were in regular touch about the kind of cases one place would take rather than the other. The people they were dealing with often moved from one place to another. And most importantly, those Aranda people among them, the largest language group, had mission histories, which meant that it made perfect sense to help them celebrate Christmas each year, drawing people together on the basis of faith as much as pauperism. Consequently, 7 December 1941, the day of the bombing of Pearl Harbor, was nonetheless a great day for the settlement.

Jay Creek's church was opened. It was quite possibly the first church built without consultation on Commonwealth property. I have not been able to find any documentation of Strehlow asking permission to set up his chapel. It seems from the files that it just happened, a result of some tacit compliance on the part of the Chief Protector. If Strehlow had built the church contrary to government policy, his offence would surely have created conflict, especially with Abbott. No one complained at the patrol officer's Christian initiative.

Albrecht gave the first service in the Jay Creek church. About 400 natives came, including many half-castes, Strehlow reported. They were half in and half outside the church standing under the trees—'a very impressive gathering'. The church was full again on Christmas Day, when Albrecht's service was conducted in Aranda. At the New Year Strehlow took the service himself—'Moses having been taken away by Rev. Albrecht last week.'[9]

There was one other truth by this stage of Strehlow's career as a patrol officer. Despite all his feelings of futility, he had become Deputy Director of Native Affairs for the Territory, a small measure of his worth in the eyes of Darwin. Circumstances now entrenched him in the job. He had, it seemed, considered a lectureship in German at the University of Adelaide: Fitzherbert had drawn his attention to it as a job meant for him since so many Jews had been applying for it.* Strehlow passed that up. With the war in high gear he seems to have thought that his best service to the nation would be among the Aborigines in Alice Springs.

Strehlow the Nazi

On 23 May 1940, as Hitler secured the invasion of Belgium and Holland, Adair Macallister Blain, the popular and populist member for

---

*   'During the last couple of years there have been numerous applications for such a post from incredibly qualified German Jews. The Vice-Chancellor has asked me to find out whether you would be a candidate for this post. Would you please let me know as soon as you can? Of course he is not promising anything: but he wants to know whether you would like to get the post.' (Fitzherbert to Strehlow, 17 April 1939.)

the Northern Territory, was on his feet in Federal parliament. He had been holding forth about how Bolsheviks and Communists were not to blame for labour problems on the Darwin wharves, fulminating about stock levels in the tropics, and saying that in the region of Alice Springs, the mining of wolfram, essential for the war economy, was not at full capacity, and this was perhaps due to the interference of foreign interests. Blain wanted to ensure that the mineral did not get to Italy or Germany, and he suspected that 'foreign controllers' might be determined to leave it in the ground if it could not reach Germany.

After rambling about minerals and mining, his mind went again to 'the Alice Springs area, 1,000 miles south of Darwin,' and from there he fell into a stream of remarks that became a little river of paranoia:

I ask the honourable members to remember that Mr Greenfell, the British member of parliament, told them in unmistakable terms, at the dinner that was given for him at Parliament House, not at the private lecture, which was confidential, that he had seen a coloured map published by the Nazi Hitler, showing Central Australia as a Nazi area. What are we to do about this 'fifth column'? In his inimitable way the honourable member for Wannon (Mr Schofield) today attempted to stir honourable members and Ministers from their apparent apathy about his enemy within. I now give him my support. Hermannsburg mission. Can honourable members spell it? Is it Norwegian? Is it Czechoslovak or Rumanian? Does it spell anything but 'Nazi'? This Nazi mission is only 40 miles west of Alice Springs.

Mr MARTENS.—The Nazis have friends in this Parliament.

Mr BLAIN.—I am surprised at the honourable gentleman's statement. I do not believe it. This mission is the headquarters of nazi-ism in Central Australia. In 1933 I met, when I was surveying the Granites, three Nazis who went back to Germany from the mission. One was a geologist and another a miner. The royal mail contractor from Alice Springs to Darwin is a Nazi. Our own Commonwealth Anthropologist, Dr Strehlow, who is on the exempt list is another Nazi. He is the man engaged to teach the natives. Why, there are swastikas on the rocks at Alice Springs! I could make another charge, but I shall reserve it for the Minister. The returned soldiers at Alice Springs do not treat this matter as a joke. I am surprised that the honourable members paid such scant heed to what the honourable member for Wannon told them earlier. The 'fifth column' is here, right in the centre of Australia . . . I hope the

Opposition will realise that it is its duty to get its teeth into this matter and to support the Minister for the Navy, the member for Wannon and myself in what we are doing to awaken Australia, because 1,000 Australian lives may be lost as a result of the activities of each one of the Central Australian Nazis.[10]

Blain was a politician with a flair for the sensational. A veteran of the Great War, a surveyor by training (he was the first to survey the Granites gold-field on the eve of its boom), he had been elected in 1933 on a promise to win for the Territory the right of its member to vote in the House of Representatives or resign in six months. By 1940 the Territory still had no vote in the Federal parliament, and Blain was still the member. A hesitant public figure at first, he was now a loud advocate of Territory development, a defendant of mining and pastoral interests, a man who travelled a lot and kept in touch with his Outback electorate.[11]

As for the native problem, Blain thought it would never be solved until white people were 'kind to the aborigines, not white people living sheltered lives in Sydney or Melbourne, but station owners, managers and their wives . . . A kind, firm hand was what the native appreciated,' as long as it was applied 'actually by those people who knew natives.' It was Blain who coined the slogan 'The Territory for the Territorians.'[12]

Strehlow first got news four days later when he collected his mail in Alice Springs. His Anglophile father-in-law had sent him a clipping from the *Adelaide Advertiser* 'in which accusations are lodged against the Hermannsburg authorities and myself as being Nazi agents.' Strehlow noted the event as calmly as he could. The next day he focused on the 'little gratitude' the Aboriginal workers at Jay Creek were showing him. Should I have taken the job at all? he reflected. 'Now it's difficult if not impossible to change; very little or nothing has been done, but the abo [*sic*] problem has become very much more menacing now and much more difficult to solve.'[13] At no stage, it seems, did Carrodus and his department suspect their patrol officer of treason, and the report that they produced on 14 June for the Attorney-General, a one-page résumé of his CV, stated unambiguously that 'there should be no doubt as to Mr Strehlow's loyalty.' But they had to go through the process of despatching Captain Balfe, from Army Intelligence in Darwin, to Alice Springs. Balfe arrived at Jay Creek on 15 June, three days after Italy had entered the war.

'He was a thorough gentleman,' Strehlow wrote in his diary for the next day, 'and very considerate to us on this painful inquiry. Some allegations against me were—I had said to Const. McKinnon in Nov. 1938 (while on a trip to Tempe Downs): "I am a Nazi, and am proud of it"; I had given German names to the children at Jay Creek, etc. I am completely weary & exhausted & despondent tonight.'

If he had known everything that had been said behind the scenes he'd have been even more despondent. He was on the Australian government's security files in both farcical and grave ways. The first he was somewhat familiar with as a result of a wild goose chase for swastikas in Central Australia.[14]

The second matter was a file of deadly gossip on his conversations with white settlers of the district. Part of it was generated by H.V.C. Thorby, MP, who had written to William Morris Hughes, Federal Attorney-General: 'I understand that Dr Strehlow, the Anthropologist, at Alice Springs, is a German with strong Nazi tendencies. It appears that he has absolute freedom of action amongst the native population and has travelled extensively in Central Australia, maintaining contact with other Germans who are scattered through that territory.'

The Department of the Attorney-General had no choice but to seek a report from J.A. Carrodus. On top of this, the Commonwealth Investigation Branch had the testimony of a 'well-known Adelaide professional man who [has] an extensive knowledge of the Northern Territory' and knew Strehlow. He said that in 1937 Strehlow was 'in a high state of nervous tension,' overworked and 'all nerves.' 'Strehlow told me that he was terribly worried over his people being in Germany. He said that they were all caught up with the Nazi movement.' The informant had 'been on patrol with Strehlow and [he had] never heard him say anything that could be construed as disloyal, but I know that he does speak very foolishly in defence of Germany but I will not say in defence of Hitler. Strehlow is very argumentative but harmless.'

Also on file was a much sharper view of Strehlow's bluster from 'the wife of a well-known pastoralist of the Territory' who had lived there for eighteen years and 'knew Ted Strehlow well.' 'Last Winter,' she told the spycatchers, 'he called at our home and absolutely amazed me with his remarks in regard to Germany. He openly sided with Hitler and I remonstrated with him. I said to him, "I knew your dear old father and Hitler has shown himself totally opposed to your late father's beliefs and teachings." Strehlow replied, "My mother is in Germany and she can attend her Church. All that Hitler did was to take the revenue of the Church." I cannot remember all the conversation but I do know that Strehlow openly expressed admiration for Hitler.'

The slurs in the security file were implicitly abusive of Strehlow's rights as an Australian citizen with German kin. It was no fault of his that his parents were German, that his brothers and sister had been in Germany since 1911, that his father had been unjustly interned at the mission during the Great War, or that his mother had returned to her homeland in 1931. His heart was still with his mother. They had been writing to each other since she had left. Frieda Strehlow had been unsettled by the rise of Hitler, and had been telling her son since she arrived back in Germany. Strehlow had been, in those early years of Hitler's rise, appalled at what was happening to Germany and what might become of the nation. These were matters he had shared with his mother, along with her general sense of dislocation when she was trying to find her feet among a family she had not seen for so long, and who had little sense of the Australian life she had left.

Strehlow had been in touch with his mother right up until 1939, when war was declared and censorship put an end to the flow of letters between Germany and Allied countries. She was then reporting to him the fate of her oldest sons, Karl and Rudolf, who had been drafted into the German Army. The blackouts had begun. Germany was looking to war with Russia, and his mother remembered that in 1914 some people thought the war would be over in four to six weeks. Karl marched into Poland with the army, and wrote to his mother about all that had been burnt and destroyed. He mouthed German propaganda about Poles mistreating Germans, mocked the Poles for believing support was coming, and noted the establishment of camps for the Jews. 'All the Poles go to Heaven, and all the Germans go to hell,' Frederick wrote ironically to his mother on 20 October 1939, which his mother put into her diary, along with reports of new babies born, socks darned, rations and blackouts. The British had not yet begun to fight, she noted, but a British plane had flown overhead, dropping leaflets into the Bavarian villages. This time, his mother thought, the Germans would not be so stupid as to put the Führer away when he was most needed.[15]

The above communication probably did not get to Strehlow, though at the time his mother hoped it might be smuggled via a friend in America. Her unposted letters became a diary, to be read by her son six years after the war. From the above, however, something can be gleaned of the emotional ambivalence generated in Strehlow. His mother, an unsophisticated political intelligence, was writing from a German village as she feared for her sons in Hitler's army. She was writing as a German nationalist, and without the benefit of hindsight of the atrocities the war would bring. Having, in the early years of Hitler, expressed dismay at her country's political turbulence, she was, now that the war had broken out, on the side of Germany rather than Germany's enemies. In Germany, public opposition to Hitler no longer existed, and the tide of public opinion, of which she was a part, had flowed with Hitler's aggressive expansion. Now it was poised, as indeed many in the West were poised, in the hope that Nazism might put an end to the evil of Communism. In this flux, how could a son on the other side of the world not experience a deep range of feelings, not all of them as cut and dried as Churchill was yet to encourage? At no stage did Strehlow have Nazi sympathies, but in the build-up to the war his Germanness was sufficient for him to want to sound off, one way or the other. For this, and for what he had been doing in Central Australia, he was paying the price. Not so long back he had asked himself: 'How can I do my job if I depend for my progress upon the good graces of the persons whom I am to question and pester?' The answer had arrived, accelerated by the xenophobia of another war with Germany.

Having to meet up with Army Intelligence was bad enough. Worse was the ordeal Abbott required of him, which was to officially respond to his nameless accusers. Thus their loyal patrol officer had to essay upon his 'own personal attitude to the present international conflagration.'

'My parents,' Strehlow began in his defence, 'were German-born naturalised Australian citizens' and he went on to explain the context of his brothers' and his sister's return to Germany in 1911, when Central Australia was extremely isolated and 'the Great War could not be foreseen'; and of his mother's return there in 1931, when he could not provide a home for her in Australia. He told Abbott he had 'never really known' his brothers and sister: 'The hard fact of a separation for almost thirty years naturally cannot be overcome by mere correspondence. Also, none of this correspondence has ever been of a political nature: my family realises that I have been brought up in a British community and that I form part of it.'

He documented his own education, and his marriage to 'an Australian of purely British descent' (a fact that interested his superiors, who had sometimes wondered about the wife).

What then—the loaded questions smoked from the fire of his defensive rhetoric—*were* his feelings towards Germany? As he pointed out:

The Prime Minister of Great Britain had declared in 1939 when the war started that there was 'no bitter enmity on the side of the British people towards the German people.' Your Honour will appreciate the fact then, that, owing to my German origin, I cannot entertain feelings of hatred toward the members of my own family whom cruel circumstances have placed in the opposite camp. If I held that all the music, all the art, all the literature, all the science produced in Germany in the past was now merely beastly, and that everyone of German blood was a monster of cruelty and treachery; then I should have to condemn myself as someone equally sinister and abominable.

However, in the present conflict my duty is perfectly clear. My country is Australia. I have been born in this country, in fact, have known no other home. In a material sense, Australia has given me my living and my income. Spiritually, owing to my training, I can claim that I am more deeply steeped into the cultural heritage of the British race than most of my present unknown detractors. I have owed my advancements in life almost wholly to the interest, the help, and the loyalty of English friends and superiors . . .

Further: 'Whatever my faults, may be, I claim that I am no traitor. Whatever help Australia may require from me in her hour of need I am prepared to give, faithfully and loyally. I am not dead to gratitude; nor would I repay friendship, help, and generosity with betrayal.'

As for the swastika, he had never seen any on the rocks at Alice Springs. And the natives? 'I have not even mentioned the present war to any native up to date. In my belief, it would be better for the aboriginal not to know much about the war; it undermines his belief in the solidarity of the white race, and it has an unfortunate tendency to justify to the untrained native the legality of his own personal feuds. Of course, the natives must know a great deal of the present war; they can see the news reels for themselves in the Alice Springs Picture show. From the same source, they should also be familiar with the swastika.'

The next paragraph was angry, defiant: 'Of course, I have never been under any illusions concerning my personal unpopularity amongst residents of Central Australia by virtue of my official position. Any officer, whose duty leads him to carry out the provisions of the Aboriginals Ordinance, or who has constant dealings with the native populations, is ostracised by a very large section of the local white community. It is this section, too, that never fails to give vent loudly to its private grudges,—usually behind the back of the person criticised.'

As to the rumour that he and his wife had been shadowed the last time they were down south, he looked for a trump card. 'However, I did not notice any "shadows" when my wife and I were privileged to pay a visit to the Governor-General's residence, Canberra, at the gracious invitation of Her Excellency, Lady Gowrie. My wife also had the honour of being entertained in Canberra by Dame Mary Hughes and Mrs J. McEwen, wife of the Minister of Foreign Affairs.'[16]

Strehlow signed off. His anger and anguish were clear. His letter exudes a meticulous indignation, written in the teeth of anonymous scuttlebutt. It was a justified self-righteousness, and he had gone on at some length. Indeed his remarks to Abbott about Germany were the kind of thing that had led his accusers to think he could speak very foolishly about Germany. There were bound to be some listeners who would misunderstand his emphasis; he might be argumentative and harmless, and yet harm himself. But did he have to say so much?

The answer might be found in the slight dissembling with Abbott: 'I cannot entertain feelings of hatred toward the members of my own family whom cruel circumstances have placed in the opposite camp.' This was a half-truth. Strehlow's brothers were ardent Nazis.* Strehlow had no intimate contact with them after they arrived in Germany in 1911, but they were Hitler's men and by the end of the war two of them had died for Hitler. The mix of family allegiances was not easily accommodated in a letter intended for Australian security. After the war, when the full extent of Nazi crimes came into view, Strehlow ceased to brag about German culture and stressed his Australian roots even more.

---

* 'Ardent': the term is Wilhelm Fuggman's (personal conversation, Freiburg, July 1997). He was speaking of the degree to which the Strehlow brothers would have supported Hitler's cause. Fuggman, who married Frieda Keysser's sister, was a businessman responsible for the coffee collectives owned by the Lutheran missions. He worked with missionary Pastor Christian Keysser (Frieda's brother) in the 1930s and was interned in Victoria for the duration of the war.

As to his attempt to have the last word—his jaunty remark about 'shadows'—it was as illogical as it was proudly petty. Not only did many a spy—there were to be some notorious British ones—make it their business to be guests of the establishment, they were *of* the establishment. Strehlow was revealing his snobbery rather than scoring a political point.

Yet it was also a brave, defiant letter, politically speaking. He explained that he had never had any illusions about his 'personal unpopularity among residents of Central Australia' since it was his job to enforce the Aboriginal Ordinance, and to have 'constant dealings with the native population'—enough to make 'any officer ostracised by a very large section of the local white community.'

Strehlow was in no position to name his accusers, and Abbott, to judge from the confidential files, did not know them either. The Commonwealth Investigation Branch file does not link Blain's public assault with any of the informants or any particular interest group in the Territory. Evidently Blain's own papers offer no link to miners or pastoralists who had it in for the dogged Strehlow.[17] But after the parliamentary attack Blain was receiving mail from R.H. Purvis, the owner of Wood Green station, a man who had been pestering Strehlow to help him get a half-caste girl as a domestic. The minister would be well advised to inquire into Mr Strehlow, Purvis wrote, 'as with his broken German lingo the average Britisher is at a loss to understand him.'[18]

Overall, Strehlow was probably right to feel that, as explanations go, the Nazi slander was just that: a manifestation of malicious rumour that expressed in a diffuse way the displacement of colonialist antagonisms to policies of Aboriginal 'protection.' No conspiracy is needed to account for the momentum of slur, especially when his job had been to pry into the domestic lives of pastoralists. In the parlance of the Chief Protector, himself and Sergeant Koop's many visits to the cattle stations had been 'raids.' They were therefore easily construed as meddling, going beyond the call of duty. Ward McNally conveys the edge the industrious puritan was on:

> On one occasion, while out on investigation, Strehlow was enjoying the hospitality one weekend of a station owner. While he was walking to the homestead from a shed with his host, he unknowingly dropped his diary. One of the Aboriginal housegirls (who could not read or write)

found it the day after Strehlow had left, and handed it to her employer.

He turned the leaves casually, but soon his anger began to rise as he digested some of the contents. He was personally mentioned. So were other station owners and managers well known to the man. Nothing written about them was complimentary. Strehlow had recorded everything they had said in his presence that he regarded as being anti-Aboriginal, and it was obvious that many of the things he had mentioned had been said over the dinner table, and should have been confidential. The station owner sent the diary to McCaffrey [Strehlow's immediate superior] with a bluntly-worded complaint against Strehlow.

The next time Strehlow was in Alice Springs, McCaffrey called him to his office and challenged him on his comments. 'How could you record such things about people who make you welcome at their table, Ted?' he asked. 'Don't you think you owe them loyalty? Some mutual trust?'

'My loyalty is to the Aborigines, not to white men who misuse them, or exploit them. That material might be valuable some day. That's why I wrote it,' Strehlow replied.

'But some of the things you've written here are defamatory, Ted. You couldn't sustain some of this stuff in court if you had to. How could you?' McCaffrey argued, shaking the diary at his patrol officer.

'I don't know. Perhaps I couldn't. But when a man, irrespective of whether he gives me hospitality or not, boasts to me about the way he keeps his "abos in line," and makes no secret of the fact that he condones his station-hands raping Aboriginal girls of eleven and twelve, I think some record of his conversation is a necessary thing.'

'Rape? Who said rape, Ted? Only you. What was probably said was that he (naming the station owner) knew his white station-hands were having sexual relations with some Aboriginal girls. Nothing more. And that happens all the time. You know that. Men will be men. There's a shortage of white women, you know. I don't call having a bit of nookie with an Aboriginal girl rape, Ted.'

'I call taking a girl of eleven or twelve to bed rape. They're under the age of consent, and they have been made to believe that it is obligatory on them to satisfy white men's sexual demands. In my viewpoint that amounts to rape,' Strehlow replied.[19]

Going by this account, which there is no reason to doubt, Strehlow was indeed doing some spying, though not for the Germans.

Finally Strehlow was cleared, at least officially and by his immediate superiors. No one in Native Affairs, not even the exasperated Abbott, took the spy charges seriously. As they advised the Attorney-General, who wrote to Thorby in September, 'Investigation had failed to disclose any substantiation of the allegations of disloyalty made against him.'[20]

But by May 1942 Strehlow was in the army—as was, incidentally, his loudest slanderer, Blain. In a fit of chauvinism Blain had volunteered in 1940, lying about his age in order to enlist, and sailed off with the 8th Division Engineers to be captured in Singapore in February 1942, the only serving Member of Parliament to be a prisoner-of-war. Upon his repatriation he received a standing ovation when he re-entered the House. Strehlow was to endure his war without much distinction, all the time battling for the Aborigines of Central Australia. He got little applause for that.

Banning Kitto

Ironically, it was Strehlow's stand over the death of a native at Mount Cavenagh station that would have crystallised all the Nazi slander, if it had happened at the right time: for those who hated the patrol officer, it would have just gone to show. In March 1941 the owner of the station, Herbert Kitto, had liberally applied the notion of corporal punishment. He and his partner Owen D'Conlay had savagely beaten an Aboriginal man, and then tied a wire around his neck and dragged him along behind their truck.

Even before their arrest, Strehlow cancelled their pastoral licence. He sustained his decision after the trial, even though they were acquitted. The whole case was a scandal down south, and an acute source of embarrassment for Native Affairs in the Territory. For Strehlow it was a last-ditch battle as patrol officer against racist brutality in the Territory.

The native was Lilliliki, otherwise known as Lollylegs. He was a Pitjantjatjara man from Ernabella Mission in South Australia, who sometimes worked for Kitto. The story Strehlow heard from Aboriginal witnesses was that Lilliliki, who was visiting his relatives at the station, had been ordered away, but instead of doing as Kitto said he had hung around and accepted rations from other workers. A sister of one of the shepherds gave him a damper; Lilliliki ate part of it and hid the rest in the fork of a tree. When D'Conlay spotted the damper he rode back to the house and came back with Kitto in their truck. The beating began.

As Lilliliki was knocked about he was told, 'You are the man who is always hanging around the workers in order to take their rations from them.'[21]

Kitto and D'Conlay were brought to trial in Alice Springs in April 1941 and charged with murder. The presiding judge was the Sydney silk, D.G. Bathgate, new to the Territory and without the partisan reputation of Judge Wells. The accused told the judge that they had loosely put the wire around the man's neck, and that he could have removed it at any time as they slowly drove their truck. But the stronger testimony was that the native was 'forced to run behind the moving motor car and the fella was dragged a considerable portion of the 600 yards.' This was the evidence of none other than Strehlow's former colleague in investigations of brutality, Constable McKinnon.

It was Constable McKinnon, Strehlow's travelling companion on the murder inquiry at the Rock six years before, who had exhumed the body of Lilliliki for the coroner and, finding it rather decomposed, had taken only the head as evidence back to Alice Springs. But that head, as the judge wrote later, 'was as smooth as the proverbial billiard ball' and showed no sign of the 'heavy swinging blows' by a revolver and a rifle allegedly wielded by Kitto and D'Conlay.[22] Nor had the head been severed—until, that is, McKinnon did so. Doubt was cast on the identity of the skull, which meant that the actual whereabouts of the body that had been dragged by wire was unknown. Kitto was on record as having said, when he was arrested by McKinnon, 'If Lollylegs is dead, it is news to me.'[23]

There was still another difficulty with the evidence. By the time the trial began two of the essential Aboriginal witnesses had absconded. They had been with Sergeant Koop coming back from Mount Cavenagh when the police truck got bogged and the party had to camp for the night. Next morning, the witnesses had gone. 'Their reason for running away is a mystery,' Koop reported. 'Ever since they have been in hand they have been extremely docile and settled and have given no trouble whatever. It is my opinion that the fact that I was carrying portions of the dead man in the car may have upset them.'[24]

With the material evidence inadequate, and key witnesses gone bush, the prosecution case collapsed. Judge Bathgate acquitted the accused. The major implication of the judgment was that somehow Kitto and D'Conlay had been framed by the natives. Alternatively, it might seem that the conduct of the investigation left much to be desired, perhaps deliberately. Over both possibilities unanswered questions hung in the air. Whose head was it? Where was Lilliliki? Was he dead or alive?

Strehlow had been clear in his mind. 'I have no doubt personally,' he had told Chinnery before the trial,

> that De Conlay and Kitto did murder aboriginal Lalliliki in the manner described by the aboriginal witnesses. The very manner of the murder—dragging the aboriginal by means of a wire noose around his neck behind a car—is something so foreign to the mentality of semi-nomadic natives, that it is very difficult to believe that the Mount Cavenagh witnesses (who are still semi-Myalls) could possibly have thought up such an event. I don't know of any cases of strangling ever having occurred among the natives of the Centre . . . It is unfortunate that McKinnon's exhumations probably destroyed the only means of ascertaining the correctness of the aboriginal witness's story, viz., that the dead man was dragged to death by means of a wire noose around his neck.[25]

The acquittal pleased many Territorians, but dismayed activists down south. It was what friends of the Aborigine most feared; a jury sympathetic to white pastoralists had had its way. Before the trial, public meetings in Sydney expressed alarm at the slack nature of the investigation. Several organisations concerned with the welfare of Aborigines had tried to urge Native Affairs authorities to secure a southern barrister for the trial: neither Canberra nor Darwin thought that would do.*

After the trial, with the station owners apparently off the hook, it might have seemed a straightforward matter for normal affairs at Mount Cavenagh to resume. But no: the licence would not be renewed, Strehlow told Abbott. It was out of the question after what the accused had owned up to in court. In their defence they had admitted to the row, to their arrival at the shepherds' camp with firearms, and to having overpowered Lollylegs and put a fourteen-foot length of wire doubled and fastened round his neck. Strehlow went on with his list:

---

*   The organisations included the Aboriginal Fellowship Group, the Aboriginal Uplift Society, the Church Missionary Society, Australian Board of Missions, YWCA of Australia and the Women's Christian Temperance Union.

(4) they then attached the loose end of this doubled wire to the back of Kitto's truck and so hauled Lollylegs to Kitto's residence, a distance of several hundred yards.

(5) Kitto drove this truck in third gear while doing so (the truck has a four speed transmission gear box);

(6) that in the opinion of Messrs Kitto & de Conlay, such an action was justified by their need to be 'firm with aboriginals' on their station property.

Strehlow was phrasing things carefully, in accord with the transcript of the trial. Later he was to ground the social context even more strongly. He held to the cancellation of the licence because Kitto and D'Conlay 'had employed natives without paying them any wages. When a relative of their employees came into the camp, and—in full accordance with native custom—successfully begged food off them Messrs Kitto and De Conlay went down to him.' Hence they had forfeited all further 'rights to exploit native labour.' 'Since the white settlers have money and influence to plead their cause, it is absolutely essential that the natives should have strong Protectors to safeguard their interests.'[26]

Plead their cause the white settlers did. Against the patrol officer's intransigence, they were soon writing to officials and seeking to make deputations to Darwin. Abbott was under pressure and casting about for policy. In May he took the trouble to write to the trial judge Bathgate. Should the Kittos get their licence back? What did the judge think of the Kittos? Were there any extenuating circumstances?

Bathgate replied at length, and rather passionately. 'There is nothing in the evidence suggesting a ground for any revocation. On the contrary there was direct evidence in their favour of being of good character and of their humane treatment of aboriginals which I accepted and believed.' 'Some of that evidence,' Bathgate added, 'came from a Reverend gentleman' whose name he could not recall. But he mentioned it to Abbott as 'evidence of the fact that both Kitto's and De Conlay's treatment of the natives was very good indeed. In fact better than many other station owners.'

Abbott was also writing to the father of one of the accused, James Kitto who lived in New South Wales. Kitto senior was grateful for this attention and his reply perfectly expresses the ethos of pastoralists determined to have their own way with the natives. 'My son has been a long time in the Territory,' he wrote, and he had created a 'national asset.' 'The struggle was severe. Men with less ability or of faint heart would have abandoned the project at an early stage.' To refuse his son native labour, Kitto went on, would 'drive him out of the country', and be 'a drastic penalty for an occurrence so simple in its facts that he had no necessity nor desire to conceal it.'[27]

The letter from Kitto senior was followed by another to Abbott, a tear-jerker from the acquitted. He implored Abbott to let his wife have the licence. They needed 'a cow shepherd or a gin to help her in the house': 'To deny my wife the opportunity to get milk for herself and the kiddie [was] the height of spite and victimisation.' The next day Mrs Kitto herself wrote to Strehlow about 'the kiddie and myself': 'I must have someone to shepherd the cows as I have no goats. As we have no regular means of getting mail, I would like a reply by radio to Kulgera radio.'

The last part of the request served two purposes. It advertised the acute isolation of the pioneering family. And, potentially, it drew Strehlow on to the bush telegraph, where all and sundry could hear him officiating against the interests of hardy Territorians. When Chinnery came down from Darwin to visit Mount Cavenagh in August, numerous open telegrams were received at various points in the district, each deploring Strehlow's undue harshness towards the Kittos. By then Strehlow had replied to Mrs Kitto, making a suggestion about their labour problem: 'Your difficulty might be met by employing either white labour or else adult male half-castes over the age of 21 who can be employed without a licence.'[28]

It was now an acute situation for Strehlow's superiors. The Secretary of Native Affairs in Darwin, V.J. White, wanted to give the licence to Mrs Kitto—'an ingenious way of evading the law, which I refused to adopt,' Strehlow recorded.[29] Abbott was waiting on his superior—Carrodus in Canberra—for guidance. By September Carrodus was also hearing from Judge Bathgate, who was of the firm opinion that 'the administration of Justice in the Northern Territory is on a sound footing.' The judge was writing with a mind to those critical of the ways of Territorians, notably the residents of southern states and like-minded people in London. 'It is quite apparent . . . that people in London do not seem to understand that Central Australia is a vast territory of very great distances . . . I do not know when the alleged death was reported, but knowing the competency of the officer in charge of Police in Alice Springs, I would find it hard to believe that there was any unnecessary delay in endeavouring to bring an accused to Justice.'[30]

The politics of the situation were now adrift, with Strehlow potentially stranded. The nature of the political moment can perhaps be detected in the airy postscript of Bathgate's letter to Carrodus. Although the judge had forgotten the name of the officer stationed at a reserve about twenty miles from Alice Springs, he recalled that he was 'a graduate with honours of the South Australian University, and is I believe, a son of the deceased missioner lately in charge of the Hermannsburg Mission.' Bathgate went on: 'he is a gentleman saturated with the law, custom and legends of the aborigines' whose researches might one day be of 'worldwide value.' Then Bathgate wondered if the services of this unnamed gentleman 'could be utilised in a broader way by the Department of the Interior.' [31] That is to say: could Strehlow be moved on?

For Abbott, Bathgate's sly remarks were a nice reminder that Strehlow's skills might well lie elsewhere, that he was not entirely suited to his office, that he had best go. When Carrodus drew Abbott's attention to the postscript, Abbott wrote: 'I personally think that the qualities and knowledge possessed by Mr Strehlow fit him rather for an academic position than the rough and tumble life of a Patrol Officer.'[32]

Even so, this time Strehlow won the rough and tumble. For another year and a half the Kitto case was unresolved. The events of the war, and the logistical activities in the Territory, had a tendency to concentrate the bureaucratic mind. Finally Native Affairs had to give a cut-and-dried answer to the Kittos. The cancellation would stand. Despite all his reservations, Abbott finally backed up his stubborn official. By then Strehlow was in the Australian Army, and stationed in Canberra.

He may well have left the Centre, but on this issue he was still a moralist at large.

Private Nuisance

Strehlow did not want to go into the army. He told his superiors that he felt he could be more useful if he stayed in Central Australia, continuing to work in native affairs, carrying on with the people whose lives were even more dislocated now that the region had become an army encampment. His cry fell on deaf ears. With the Nazi slur still in the air, it was decided that he was excess labour in the Territory—this because he was a married man but without children, and a government employee who might be better used elsewhere.

He felt that Native Affairs could hardly wait to get rid of him. When he was called up in April 1941, he was given three days to leave Jay Creek. Bertha's health was frail and Strehlow appealed to extend the time by three months. The government man said he could do nothing: he would have to forsake his community at Jay Creek. Strehlow told his diary: 'I have failed . . . Thus God has delivered my work to the hands of my enemies.'[33]

Only when Professor Fitzherbert and the Chancellor of the University of Adelaide wrote to the base commandant was the extra time granted. By then the Strehlows had already been moved out of their house at Jay Creek and had to find a place in Alice Springs. Strehlow: 'After the place had been built up to a certain degree, however, and looked like being a success after all, they showed their appreciation by using the excuse of a military call-up in order to push me out at three days notice. Thus my wife was forced to come back to Jay Creek in order to assist in selecting her most necessary belongings, and packing them before she was turned out of her house by the Administration.'[34]

In May 1942—'a day of great joy for us'—the Strehlows' first son was born, 'full of life and vigour.' They called him Theo. 'We had almost become reconciled to a childless marriage.' Strehlow wrote, and said it was 'the lifting of the shadow of Ayers Rock,' the nightmare at Piltardi Rockhole.[35] There had been three other miscarriages before the birth of Theo. The sicknesses that accompanied them, not to mention the grief, was a dark current running through all of Strehlow's years as patrol officer. Bertha's demoralisation seems to have been profound: by the end of their stay she had been blaming herself as an inadequate wife and thinking she might need psychological help. She had managed to go full term by acting on medical advice to have a six-month program of vitamins, drugs and bed rest. No sooner had Theo arrived than the Strehlows had to part—for a 'homeless future': Bertha to Adelaide, Strehlow to Canberra where he was installed in the barracks at Duntroon. There was an understanding, at least in Strehlow's mind, that his post at Jay Creek might be still open to him after the war—that technically he was on leave.

The army did not make him an officer. He was Private Strehlow. That such an educated, competent man with his authority and field experience should be so instantly 'demoted' was itself shocking. Was this the result of Nazi slander infecting the top brass of the Australian defence forces? It was certainly the case that infection lingered after he had been cleared. In September 1942 the Investigation Branch was still filing reports from the Centre that he was a man who spoke in glowing terms of Hitler and the effect of Hitler's administration on the people of Germany. Army Command in Central Australia decided that the Hermannsburg Mission would only continue on condition it had a resident inspector (Rex Battarbee). Two years later it had come to the notice of Air Force Headquarters in Melbourne that the airstrip at Hermannsburg had increased in size and was stocking up on food. Then the searchlight fell on Jay Creek, where 'a German named Strehlow had constructed an aerodrome and laid in stores . . . Strehlow was looked upon as pro-Nazi with considerable suspicion.' Some rumour is as persistent as spinifex.

'They seem to think,' Strehlow told a friend, 'I'm some sort of dirty German. The fools. Don't they understand?'

He could not put such thoughts into his letters, as they were now censored. But he was deeply, personally, affronted: wounded to the point of despair, and according to one member of his family on the point of contemplating suicide. Whether that is true or not, the despair fed his anger. From his army headquarters he looked back to the Centre ferociously, and mounted his attack, a sustained assault on the management of Native Affairs.

His successor as a patrol officer at Jay Creek was the 47-year-old police officer, Vic Hall, who had received depositions about atrocious misconduct by C.H. Chapman at the Granites, allegations of starvation, and cruel neglect.* Hall's reports were tabled with Abbott while Strehlow was still on deck in Alice Springs, and Abbott had kept them from Strehlow. Hall wanted a full inquiry, which had the backing of organisations such as the Aborigines' Friends' Association in Adelaide, as well as the South Australian Anthropological Society. Hall, whose title was *acting* patrol officer (confirming Strehlow's hope that he might go back to the position after the war), kept in touch with Strehlow when he went off to the army.

---

* Francis Glastonbury, a mechanic, reported: 'Some of the old lubras and piccaninnies used to beg for food for [*sic*] me as a regular thing' and in the absence of blankets 'even my grease rags they used to take to try to cover themselves.' Berthold Altmann, blacksmith, reported workers' exhaustion because of 'hard labour on the diet of flour only,' as well as 'no pay.' When he appealed to Chapman to help save the life of an Aboriginal woman who had been lying for two days in the open with a wound to her back, Chapman allegedly said, 'Blow her,—she is only a nigger.' (AA CRS F3 Item 21/59.)

Dear Ted,

I received your letter and was most glad to hear from you. Needless to say I was sorry to hear about your illness, and congratulate you on your recovery. That southern climate is probably not good for you.

Well, I most cordially agree with your remarks. I put up exactly these arguments to His Dishonour while he was ranting about you. Exactly. I was (I told him) in my estimate acting for an officer absent on leave, and who had a right to be kept informed of the trend of events. This was the line I took. In the second phase of the attack he harped on Mr Chapman's long struggle and the fact that he had had at last 'a fortune within his grasp.' 'And how much of this fortune will have been made out [of] the blood and lives of these natives?'—I asked him. He turned loose a glare, or rather a fishy stare intended for a glare and literally hissed 'I can get that sort of talk from the Missionaries!'[36]

Abbott had by now brought his office of the administrator from Darwin to Alice Springs, a massive move that came in the wake of the Japanese bombing of Darwin, for which, under Abbott's patrician administration, the town had been astonishingly unprepared. There was to be a Royal Commission into his neglect of civil defence, an inquiry from which his reputation never recovered.[37] From Alice Springs he was set on running a tight ship with Native Affairs, struggling against staff shortages and the local army commander. Hall's report on the Granites drove Abbott back to the Strehlow file and the conclusion that the administration had been 'badly served by this officer, who, in my opinion, has shown no spirit of service or loyalty or of co-operation.' Abbott was even more incensed at the disloyalty when the disgruntled Private Strehlow wrote on Hall's behalf to Carrodus. Abbott hoped Strehlow would not return to Central Australia.[38]

Abbott did not reject the contents of Hall's report on the Granites, but he did not want to remove Chapman's licence either. Rather than conduct an inquiry he instructed Hall to set up his patrol at the Granites, where he would remain until a permanent police station could follow. Hall was not silly; he would not be banished into the desert. His protests within the administration were futile, even though he had, thanks to the confidential lobbying of Bertha Strehlow in Adelaide, the backing of Duguid, Mountford, and the Women's Christian Temperance Union, each seeking to be heard in Canberra. 'In an issue such as this,' Hall had written to Strehlow, 'it is just a case of accept humiliation and injustice or fight.' Hall tried to fight and lost: he was out of the job by the end of 1942 and in later years found an outlet writing novels about the frontier life of a policeman, a man set against the racist face of pastoralism.

Strehlow supported Hall. The Jay Creek Reserve itself was at risk: the government, under pressures of cost-cutting in time of war, was considering turning it over to be a mission station. The idea was, in the parlance of those who already thought too much was being spent on Aborigines, 'weaning natives off Government rations and turning them out into the bush.'

Strehlow: 'Not content with merely evicting me, they [the Native Affairs department] are now seeking to undo every bit of work that I have done during the last six years. They handed over last year all the N.T. half-caste children to the care of the missions; and then left the missions to evacuate these children as best they could when the Japanese war began—the result being that these unfortunate half-castes have been scattered to the four winds and are now to be found in exile in N.S.W., Victoria, and S.A.'[39]

The point was, Strehlow insisted, there was indeed 'a crying need' for another mission station in the district, and the best place was around Barrow Creek. The military had conscripted all the able-bodied native men into labour gangs and sent them down to Alice Springs, leaving the women and children without protection. Two pastoral holdings in the district (Woolla Downs and Harpers Springs) had changed hands twice in recent years and could well be the place for a new mission. 'Surely the interests of several hundred natives should be more worthy of consideration than the selfish interests of one white man.' Meanwhile, 'Jay Creek, on the other hand, should be retained solely as a Government Station.'

To prove his point Strehlow reached for the report of Patrol Officer Hall of Napperby Station District, which included Mount Doreen station where Strehlow had found so many cases of venereal disease in 1938. It was from Mount Doreen to Jay Creek that Strehlow had once removed blind people who 'had been abandoned to die, unwanted old people, and young lads who were going wrong under the bad influence of mining camps.' Hall had camped the night among many children and women, and found them all naked and in a 'deplorable condition.' Strehlow thrust Hall's words at Carrodus: 'The semi-starvation in which they wage their consistent battle against a hostile milieu was apparent in their thin limbs and haggard faces. A constant chorus of coughing, spitting and the crying of hungry children arose. My cook worked half the night making johnny cakes from our slender stock, and we did what we could for them.'[40]

The Native Affairs department was increasingly aware of the crisis as the war effort gained momentum. Chinnery thought natives should be given the opportunity to help in the war work, and supported the recruitment of adult males from the ration centres, including the mission at Hermannsburg, where, incidentally, the wireless was to be removed just in case of German treason. Chinnery went along with its removal on the condition that, as a 'health precaution,' an army medical officer visited the mission once a week. In general, and like Strehlow, he was dismayed at the idea of the military logistics ruling over the plight of the helpless and sick natives at the Half-Caste Institution in Alice Springs. He urged the government to request the army to do everything possible to safeguard the welfare of the Aborigines. He was afraid that 'the strong anti-aboriginal and anti-halfcaste opinion in the Territory,' which had long increased the burden of official work and complicated even the simplest humanitarian work, might 'infect' the military personnel and their judgment on Aboriginal welfare. 'The aboriginals are Australian citizens,' Chinnery reminded Canberra, 'entitled to the fullest possible consideration. They form the backbone of the great stock raising interests and other phases of the Territory's economic activities, so that apart altogether from questions of common humanity it is sound policy to prevent anything being done which might cause disruption, discontent and distress amongst the aboriginal population.'

Despite Chinnery's sincerity—he was particularly incensed at the *Bulletin* article of 29 January headed 'An Expensive Abo,' which sought to discredit what he felt to be 'the bare essentials of a welfare policy'—many of these 'Australian citizens' were half-starved. Hall's official reference to this was the first of many acknowledgments of the food shortage between 1942 and 1945. Chinnery's documentation of the period drew attention to the Reverend Sexton in 1943 for a Royal Commission on the food position of the natives in the western areas of Central Australia. No such commission was established.

In 1942 Strehlow made an extraordinary proposal. The natives needed urgent protection. His vision was that comprehensive powers be vested in a special military employment officer 'not a civilian anthropologist who had no standing with the military authorities.' That person would be given complete control over the movements, welfare and activities of all natives living along the military transport routes north of the South Australian border. For native men not working, they and their dependants would be removed to certain specified districts, to be looked after by civilians or missionaries, providing the special military employment officer, assisted by military police, was in full control.[41]

Strehlow suggested a name for the new post: Controlling Military Officer. He nominated himself for the position.

Remarkably, Chinnery reported Strehlow's idea sympathetically: he knew his former patrol officer well enough not to mock the man. Chinnery seemed to be drawing attention to the bizarre aspect of the proposal when he noted: 'After the outbreak of the war, Mr Strehlow, who is of German descent, became the victim of severe criticism which, unfortunately, continued acutely until he was called up for military service. This undoubtedly hampered his movements and in other ways restricted his usefulness as an official. It also caused him profound personal distress.' How much more distress—for him and others—if he had returned to the colonial frontier with military authority! A suspected Nazi with military authority and the aid of Australian military police would have made a powerful impression on the minds of some pastoralists.[42]

Abbott was outraged. Private Strehlow should not be meddling in affairs he had left behind. But as Strehlow pointed out, technically he was on leave: the understanding he had extracted from his department was that his position as patrol officer would be left open for him until after the war. Constable Hall had initiated the communication about events in the Centre. Besides, as he told Carrodus, 'having lived for nine years in the Alice Springs district, I have other sources of information.'[43]

Abbott instructed Hall not to send Strehlow any more information, and no more reports. Strehlow was goaded into an even more explicit attack. Again writing to Carrodus—apparently on the naive political assumption that Carrodus would side with a fervent patrol officer against his whole department in Darwin and Alice Springs—Strehlow railed against 'the sympathies' of the Northern Territory administration. He was referring to its relative inability to protect the natives against 'white settlers [who] have money and influence and the ability to write direct to Canberra, whereas the natives need our help to plead their case.'

Strehlow displayed his flair for political suicide. Scornfully referring to White and Abbott's attempts to restore Kitto's licence, defending Hall's fearlessness, he went on to accuse Chinnery of condoning the sexual exploitation of native girls:

> This firmness I have not found in the personnel of the Native Affairs Department of the N.T., who are too apt to look around for formulae in order to excuse their inaction. Thus, the Aboriginals Ordinance contains a stringent prohibition against the employment of native girls on licensed premises; but the Director of Native Affairs, when seeing such girls openly employed on the Hotel premises at Birdum and Daly Waters, merely remarked that in his opinion the prohibition was absurd and that he would not consider enforcing it. In the same way a sugges-tion made by Const. E. Morey (of Newcastle Waters), Mr V. J. White, and myself that the native girls employed in the house by single white men at Dunmara Station be removed from there was countered by a telegram from the Director in which he stated that 'caution' was neces-sary since it was a 'question affecting station management.'[44]

Chinnery now had to defend himself, which he did in a credible memo to Abbott. To Abbott, Strehlow's attacks were the nail in the coffin, absolutely confirming that he was unsuited to be a patrol officer in the first place. 'No spirit of service, or loyalty, or of co-operation,' was his final judgment on Strehlow. To which Strehlow, equally inevitably, told Carrodus that he resented Abbott's remarks deeply. 'They mean either that I am unfit to receive such information because I am in uniform, or else that I am unfit to receive it because of my character. They are either a slur on the uniform that I am wearing, or else a libellous insinuation against my character.'

'Here I stand,' said Strehlow, in Luther's footsteps. Then, it seems, he fell into a silence.

Character Versus Racism

Time passed in the army. Being a private was hellish, but after eight months he was made a second lieutenant. 'All his talk of suicide evap-orated,' his son Theo is on record as saying. 'Once he had a smart uniform to wear and an officer's mess to dine and wine in, the war assumed a rosy hue for him, and he was happy enough.'[45] The claim seems true enough if Strehlow's army photographs are a guide. He took numerous shots of the female officers, some in their smiling group, others singly in their bathing suit by the pool, prettily reflecting, it would appear, the 'rosy hue' of the man behind the camera.

He was sent to Enoggera in Brisbane to head an intelligence unit. Several months later he returned to Duntroon to head up the preparation of army cadets for service in New Guinea because, as he told his first biographer; 'my knowledge of Aborigines was supposed to serve as a platform between the cadets and their relationship with the New Guinea natives . . . When I pointed out that there's really no similarity between the two peoples, I was told to teach the cadets the best I could how to get along with the natives. There was some very woolly headed thinking among army top-brass, I soon learnt.'[46]

Lieutenant Strehlow served out the war in Australia, which is what he wanted. 'He said that, apart from the spy label hurting him and disturbing Bertha, he was worried that if he had to join the Australian Army and fight overseas, he could fire the shot that might kill one of his brothers, as they served in the German Army.'[47] At each leave he was back home in Adelaide to be with his new family. By 1944, the Strehlows had a daughter, Shirley; and in 1946 a second son, John.

Meanwhile, events in the Centre vindicated Strehlow. After Hall, Gordon Sweeney was patrol officer, and he too communicated with Strehlow. Chapman was in touch with Sweeney. Writing as if the new patrol officer knew nothing about the natives, which was far from the truth, Chapman said, 'I have been in Stations and various other business employing Abos for 50 years & must admit that they still puzzle me in many ways & all old hands will tell you the same story.' He thought the natives were 'much like grown up children with advanced Socialist tendencies.' He gave Sweeney a bantering description about the joy of the lubras when they received handouts of new clothes, since, as with their 'white sisters', the 'new gaudy clothes' were 'everything'.[48]

'Grown up children with advanced socialist tendencies' did not quite gel with another description Chapman had given of the natives he knew. 'I have got to admire the way in which the abo carries out his tribal duties and avoids at the same time serious intertribal wars. The chiefs (Tugermurras) are wise old men.'[49] Children, wise old men—whatever: Chapman had the gift of the gab, and the test of his rhetoric could only be in his actual conduct at the Granites. Sweeney had flown into the place in December 1943 and found nothing out of order. This was six months after Hall's damning report. For the rest of the war Chapman was regularly inspected, and just as regularly avoided official reprimand.

Another Territorian prominent during Strehlow's regime was the owner of the Mount Doreen station, W.W. Braitling. Sweeney, as if drawn by the shadow of Strehlow's worst suspicions, was soon back at the station looking into reports that natives had been forbidden to use water protected for the cattle. On three occasions, Sweeney was told, Braitling had tied up natives and flogged them. Braitling was charged with assault and his case heard in the Supreme Court in Alice Springs in August 1945. Judge Wells, back in action again, acquitted the pastoralist, ruling that the evidence of the Aboriginal witnesses did not stand up to cross-examination.

There was much more to the case, and what unfolded helps frame the scene that Strehlow had left, the nature of the struggle that had ensnared him. For at the trial it was not just the Aboriginal witnesses who had been discredited. So too was the word of the patrol officer. In the words of the historian of these patrol officers, Jeremy Long, 'defence counsel made allegations that the charges had been trumped up in an effort to justify cancellation of Braitling's pastoral leases so that a mission could be established at Vaughan Springs. It was suggested that Sweeney had used improper methods to secure evidence against Braitling.' Long's account is worth reading in full because of the ground it retrospectively creates for Strehlow:

> Judge T.A. Wells . . . seemed to give credence to the allegations and plainly the government could not afford to ignore them. In due course a special inquiry was ordered and a Judge of the Supreme Court of the ACI, Mr Justice W.B. Simpson, was appointed in April 1946 to investigate. Simpson had been a Sydney barrister who had served in the 1914–18 war and later as a citizen-soldier . . . The outcome of Simpson's inquiry was a complete dismissal of the allegations made at the trial and a vindication of Sweeney. At the inquiry his superiors had opportunities to give the Commissioner their views on his character. Chinnery, whose time as director was at its end, declared that Sweeney was 'one of the most honourable men I have ever met, and as a Native Affairs officer, one of the best.'[50]

> Victor Carrington, a long-serving officer of the administration who had been acting as director in Alice Springs, described Sweeney as 'very energetic, capable, conscientious, honest and reliable.' Simpson, not

satisfied that negative findings on the allegations were adequate in the circumstances, went out of his way to clear Sweeney's name: 'It would be doing a great deal less than justice to Mr Sweeney to leave the matter in so short a finding. I am satisfied that Mr Sweeney's accounts of how he got the statements are substantially true and I am quite satisfied that Wilson's accounts of how the statement was allegedly obtained from him by trickery are completely false.'[51]

Commenting to Carrodus on the outcome of the case against Braitling, Chinnery had noted that the failure of the Aboriginal witnesses to stick to their stories had 'exposed one of [his] best officers, Sweeney, to the kind of treatment which an honourable man doing an honourable duty in an honourable way should be protected from.'[52] At considerable cost to Sweeney, the case and the inquiry had served to demonstrate that there was a need for officers like him who could investigate complaints of mistreatment and see that laws designed to protect the interests of Aboriginal people living on pastoral leases were observed. They had also shown that those who took on this work might need to have *considerable strength of character.* (emphasis added)[53]

Strehlow had had that strength of character. He was punished for having it. The situations that unfolded for his successors, Hall and Sweeney, even when recounted without polemic and with full sympathy for the tasks of the administration in the Territory at that time, which is the manner of Jeremy Long, once a patrol officer himself, reveal a political struggle that was stark: the interests of the economic development of the frontier were chronically pitted against those who wanted to philanthropically regulate the conditions of Aboriginal labour. Those conditions were conceived of very broadly by the vested interests: they included rights over all aspects of Aboriginal life. Wages and rations, food and shelter, water and territorial placement, freedom of movement, sexual freedom, or rather, the tacit sexual freedoms claimed by pastoralists, the carnal uses to which they put the female bodies of their labour force—all these considerations channelled into each other in the spoken and unspoken ideology of the most chauvinistic Territorians. It was an ideology that hinged on notions of property rights, writ large.

Strehlow had spent six years of his life up against the membrane of Northern Territory racism. It would have been too much for any man and it was too much for him, partly because he was, in some of his most paternalistic and priggish ways, himself part of the organism which he abhorred; and also because he met the opposition which I have been recounting. What he felt to have been the success of that opposition, and of the failure of native policy in general, prompted in him a kind of disgusted silence. After Hall's demise, he felt that all his work at Jay Creek had been 'contemptuously wiped out.' And he did not wish to talk or write about the years he had, he felt, wasted there. He simply continued to think of the natives each Christmas, and 'endeavoured to let them know that my heart had not lost its old love for them or for the land of my birth.'

He was writing this to Albrecht in February 1945

Indeed, rarely does a day pass when I do not think back with longing upon all that I have lost—for even if I never return to the Centre, my heart will always belong to it, and to the folk whom I was willing to dedicate my whole life. But God willed otherwise—& who would ever think of returning to work under people like Chinnery and White: their plans for native development are not mine, and after my experiences at their hands I would never again have any confidence on return to the Centre. When the personal malice & spite of men such as these was vented upon me, there was no one to gainsay them, neither could my devotion to duty and to the ideals of the office that had been entrusted to me avail me in the slightest. I had always been prepared for the venom of the people whom I had offended by standing up for the rights of the natives; but I did not expect that so many of my friends would abandon me as well when the blow came. And God remained silent.

You know, my experiences of C.A. have included three particularly terrible emotional catastrophes: there was the terrifying journey of my father to his lonely & tortured death at Horseshoe Bend when I was fourteen; there was that nightmare experience for me at Mt Olga in 1936, when I was on my honeymoon trip with my wife, & had, to bring her back 240 miles over the desert waste in a mulga 'carriage' tied to the side of a camel; and then there was that last experience. I don't know what sort of an uplifting, reassuring, guarantee would now be given to me that would really induce me to return to the Centre of my own free will. I was willing to dedicate my life to the natives, but I ended up by becoming a plain fool in the eyes of everyone. There may be people willing to become martyrs for lost causes: but nobody wants to be turned into a mere fool whom even his friends shun.

Please pardon my bitterness—I should not have brought up the Centre: for when I do I have to think of Chinnery, White, Abbott & the rest, who flourish like green bay trees. However, God alone is the judge over all that has happened.[54]

Albrecht pardoned the bitterness, and kept to himself any thoughts he might have had about the pattern of Strehlow's thought and feeling, its grave and leaden tendency to link one item of sadness to another, which can be enough to drag a man down to self-fulfilling prophecy. But Strehlow's refrains about how everything had been a waste of time seem to have continued. In September 1946, Strehlow was discharged from the army and back in Adelaide, about to take up a position as a lecturer in English Literature and Linguistics. Albrecht wrote to him saying that he 'heartily disagreed' that those six years of official life had been wasted.

'The Dpt's policy has been very largely influenced by your work.' Albrecht cited the reserve at Haasts Bluff, and the one at Areyonga, which had recently been gazetted (near the South West reserve that Strehlow had alerted people to). He went on:

Still, if the little you have done so far has meant the saving of many lives, it still has been abundantly worth while. And then, we have to remember that the best part of our service very seldom becomes evident to ourselves, in fact it remains hidden. Looking upon it from that angle, I am sure you will come to a different conclusion. I think there is so very much you may look upon with a feeling of deep gratitude to God; perhaps the time will come when even to others, and your self, the results will become more apparent and give you that measure of satisfaction which you so richly deserve after those years of self sacrificing work.[55]

Strehlow was now 38 years old. He was in the middle of his journey, and speaking out of his dark wood. In the time to come he would, as he had threatened, never again put himself at the mercy of good works and the administrations of others. He would toil in the field of language.

1   Report on the trip to the Petermann Ranges, 14 August 1939, AA CRS: FI 38/414.
2   Report on trip to Mt Doreen, 9 December 1940, AA CRS F3, 5.
3   Abbott to Chinnery, 13 December 1940, AA CRS F3 Item 32/3.
4   Chinnery to Abbott, 17 December 1940, AA CRS F3 Item 32/3.
5   Chinnery to Carrodus, 21 May 1942, AA 452/1 52/5 41.
6   Abbott to Carrodus, 28 April 1938, AA 452/1 52/5 41.
7   T.G.H. Strehlow, diary [SD], 7 October 1937.
8   Strehlow to Carrodus, 1942, AA 659/1 Item 41.
9   SD, 29 December 1941.
10   *Hansard*, 23 May 1940.
11   See entry on Blain by Murray Maynard in *Northern Territory Dictionary of Biography*, vol. 1. The authority on the Blain papers, Professor David Carment, describes Blain as a 'bit of a sensationalist' (personal conversation, 22 April 1999).
12   *Northern Standard*, 16 May, 1939.
13   SD, 17 May 1940.
14   A swastika, drawn in charcoal, had been sighted in the Petermann Range early in 1940. News came to the Australian security police and Inspector Williams in Adelaide received a letter from a Mr Browne. That letter contained a reference to a footnote in a private letter written by a 'Dr Dugod' to Mr Holloway, MLA. Apparently Duguid had said to Holloway there was 'a huge swastika painted in black with a German signature underneath. One hardly looked for that in the very heart of the continent.' And that, in the opinion of Browne, warranted investigation. Browne suspected a German actor called Stolling, who had recently been released from a detention camp in Victoria. Stolling had been to remote areas and written a book. Williams shot off a letter to Victor Carrington in Darwin. Maybe, Williams suggested, your patrol officer at Jay Creek would know? He hastened to add: 'It is not desired or suggested for a moment that any special inquiries should be made but only requested that if either you or Mr Strehlow should be possessed of any information on the matter, it would be appreciated.'
    It turned out that Patrol Officer Strehlow did have information. Carrington was able to write back to Williams: Yes, there was a large swastika in charcoal on the cliff face at Piltardi Rockhole. It dated from the Foy party in 1936, and was drawn by one Gus Schwaller. His name was in full below, with the initials of several others. Schwaller had been to Germany in recent times but had returned to Australia and worked at Holden's in Victoria.
    Williams wrote back to Browne and closed the file. Soon afterwards, however, there was another swastika sighting, this time on the face of Ayers Rock. There was another investigation which drew a blank. All was clear at the face of the rock (AA367/1 Item C71358). The Williams correspondence including the letters from Thorby, Carrodus, the anonymous informants, and from Strehlow to Abbott, are in 'Strehlow T.G.H.': AA 367/1 Item C71358.
15   John Strehlow, personal communication, April 2001; and a free translation of Frieda Strehlow's diary for September/October 1939 by Simone Kaiser at the Strehlow Research Centre, April 2001.
16   Strehlow to Abbott, 14 June 1940, A367/I Item C71358.
17   David Carment, personal conversation, 22 April 1999.
18   Purvis to Blain, 2 June 1940, AA NT CRS F 126 Item 33.
19   Ward McNally, *Aborigines, Artefacts and Anguish* (Adelaide: Lutheran Publishing House, 1981), 70, 72.
20   AA 367/1 Item C71358.
21   Strehlow to Chinnery, 15, 17 March 1941, AA659/1 Item 41/1/101.

22 Bathgate to Abbott, 23 May 1941 AA 659/1 Item 41/1/101, and for all other citations from Bathgate.
23 W.S. Flynn, Acting Crown Law Officer, to Carrodus, 14 March 1941, AA 659/1 Item 41/1/101.
24 Koop to A.V. Stretton, 19 April 1941, AA 659/1 Item 41/1/101.
25 Strehlow to Chinnery, 17 March 1941, AA 659/1 Item 41/1/101.
26 Ibid.
27 Kitto to Abbott, 12 May 1941, AA 659/1 Item 41/1/101.
28 Ibid.
29 Strehlow to Carrodus, 18 October 1942, AA 659/1 Item 41.
30 D.G. Bathgate to Carrodus, 4 September 1941, AA 659/1 Item 41.
31 Ibid.
32 Carrodus to Abbott, 22 September 1941; Abbott to Carrodus, 3 October 1941, AA 659/1 Item 41.
33 SD, 23 April 1941.
34 Strehlow to Carrodus, undated, 1942 AA 659/1 Item 41.
35 SD, 14 May 1942.
36 Hall to Strehlow, 15 October 1942.
37 *Northern Territory Dictionary of Biography*, vol. 1, 3.
38 Jeremy Long, *The Go-Betweens: Patrol Officers in Aboriginal Affairs Administration in the Northern Territories* (Casuarina, N.T.: North Australian Research Unit, 1992), 48–50.
39 Strehlow to Carrodus, undated, AA 659/1 Item 41.
40 Ibid., 3.
41 Strehlow's notions as reported by Chinnery to Abbott, 14 August 1942, AA 659/1 Item 41.
42 Chinnery to Abbott, 14 August 1942, AA 659/1 Item 41.
43 Strehlow to Carrodus, 18 October 1942, AA 659/1 Item 41.
44 Ibid.
45 McNally, *Aborigines, Artefacts and Anguish*, 73.
46 Ibid., 73.
47 Ibid., 69.
48 Chapman to Sweeney, May 1943, AA CRS F 3 21–59.
49 Chapman to Reverend Sexton, 31 December 1938, AA CRS F126 Item 29.
50 Transcript of evidence, AA CRS A431 46/3011.
51 Inquiry Report, 21 October 1946, AA CRS A431 461164.
52 Memorandum, 7 August 1945, AA CRS F3 20/164.
53 Long, *Go-Betweens*, 54–55.
54 Strehlow to Albrecht, 18 February 1945.
55 Albrecht to Strehlow, 21 September 1946.

PART IV:
LUTHER'S CALIBAN

I feel an urge to reach

For the original, the sacred text, appealing

To simple honesty of feeling,

To render it in my dear German speech.

   He opens a tome and sets forth.

'In the beginning was the Word'—thus runs the

    text.

Who helps me on? Already I'm perplexed!

I cannot grant the word such sovereign merit,

I must translate it in a different way

If I'm indeed illumined by the Spirit.

'In the beginning was the Sense.' But stay!

Reflect on this first sentence well and truly

Lest the light pen be hurrying unduly!

Is sense in fact all action's spur and source?

It should read: 'In the beginning was the Force!'

Yet as I write it down, some warning sense

Alerts me that it, too, will give offense.

The spirit speaks! And lo, the way is freed,

I calmly write: 'In the beginning was the Deed!'

    Goethe, Faust

1   Native Languages

as if talk's spirit could ever be tracked down anywhere
but in its linguistic body . . .

Martin Buber

Against Babel

POETRY IS WHAT gets lost in translation.[1] To translate is to traduce. Two of the grand aphorisms in the forest of paradoxes called translation, one of them, actually, a mistranslation.* And from the aphorism on betrayal the question has to be asked: 'Translator of what messages / Betrayer of what values?[2]—the asking of which also tends to deepen pessimism. To couch the pessimistic view in summary: it is all too difficult to make a good version of the original; there must be, by virtue of its unique properties and the nature of different languages, a shortfall, a gap, an inadequacy. It is firmer to speak of untranslatability in poetry.[3] Translation is the domain where fools of a certain kind—those who must by definition settle for inaccuracy, inadequacy—do not, alas,

---

*   'An error or misreading initiates the modern history of our subject. Romance languages derive their terms for "translation" from *traducere* because Leonardo Bruni misinterpreted a sentence in the *Noctes of Aulus Gellius* in which the Latin actually signifies "to introduce, to lead into." The point is trivial but symbolic. Often, in the records of translation, a fortunate misreading is the source of new life' (Steiner 1975: 295).

fear to tread. Well, if not fools, the scholars of various kinds, and lesser poets. Translation as the arena of noble endeavour, divine reach, and failure. Translation as the proof, if proof be needed, of some unbridgeable distances between cultures, and souls. We can no more perfectly translate a foreign tongue than we can perfectly understand each other, or even, if it comes to that, ourselves. Translation as a utopian project, bound to produce misery.[4] And so on: the counsel of communicative despair.

The argument can be turned on its head. 'That poetry cannot be translated is a cliché begotten by romantic poetics, nourished by bad translations, and chiefly serviceable in apostrophes to ineffable poesy.'[5] Rather than what is lost in translation, consider what is gained at the interface of the original and its host language. Two languages meet, the better to comprehend each other, to enrich and enliven each other. No matter how difficult translation is in theory, we do translate all the time, as speakers, hearers, readers. Language, after all, is the means of communication. Languages are not strangers to one another.[6] The meeting of two languages itself, with their powers at full stretch, must of necessity be a cultural moment worthy of acclamation, a possible love match in the intensity of its comprehension, its incorporation, and mutual respect of differences because each is intrinsically valuable.[7] The act of translation is the model, *par excellence*, of universal *communitas*, even tolerance among nations,[8] made possible by *the form of life* that is a given,[9] just as figures of speech are commonly grounded in translation of non-verbal signs.[10] Translation is then the deepest level of measured exchange, solemnly if not sacredly valued; translation as definitive understanding, a dialogic act as natural as breathing.[11] All this is to put translation on the model of speech acts imbued with energised, intentional, trust,[12] in faith well grounded. Translation as the domain of fidelity, as well as freedom.

It is possible to have it both ways. We have had it so. The fidelity/ freedom debate in translation has produced splendour as well as misery and its history is a history of complex realisations about consciousness and language, of sophisticated achievements, not futilities. Recognition of the difficulty of translation has never resulted in the abandonment of the project whether the stakes pertain to poetry or, to raise them to the highest degree, Scripture. We speak, we read, we worship, we sing across cultures as an expression of being language creatures with multifarious interests. The care we take with translation is a mark of good faith in the transport of beauty and meaning across space and time. Each lived moment of understanding, as with each text-based achievement in translation, is a sign that language is not hermetic, and that the Tower of Babel is not our prison: indeed, once we grant the variety of languages we can be easier with the multiple possibilities in translation, not just in terms of texts as a whole but of interpretations themselves. We might happily welcome the twists and turns of indebtedness that languages have to each other, with no one language (or act of translating) being able to dominate.[13]

But the anxiety—transcultural, intra-linguistic, perhaps existential—is still there. It is hard to say whether this anxiety is part of a dream of a possible perfect language that might be implied by the activity of translation, or of a mythic time when there was only one language.[14] Equally, the strain might be sadness rather than angst: that poetic truths require a language at all, when it is possible to imagine—well, almost—the world revealed without words. And then, above all these possibilities, the habit of translation, its compulsion and necessity, is an expression of all of these intuitions at once. Translation is the house in which we worship what has never been satisfactorily understood: the intimacy of language with our being, the marriage language makes of the world and our consciousness from day to day and from eternity to eternity. Translations attune us to the spirit of the infinite in all language, and all poetry.[15] Translation becomes the model of transcendence in the *Logos* . . .

At this junction then, even a short refrain on translation opens another window: out of it shines a light on the world that might have existed before language, and might exist yet, if we were to understand translation well enough. Translation as the microscope of mind, a telescope into the universe, a necessary bondage to what is freely native to us.

The Tropics of Translation

Strehlow spent his life in translation. He was a go-between on the field of language. He was a traveller there, a journeyman, as distinct from an artist, but his artistry, and his inclinations towards being an artist, also play their part in his life on that field. The unexamined—by him, by others—nature of that work places him in a potential wilderness of issues with regard to translation. First of all there is the task of accounting for his great book on the songs of Central Australia—his translations from the black man's to the white man's tongue. He would restore the broken songs, set them down right again, as they were in their native tongues. That was his day work, basically done by 1950 and published in 1971, and in the last line of which he expressed the hope that 'when the strong web of future Australian verse comes to be woven, probably some of its strands will be found to be poetic threads spun on the Stone Age hair-spindles of Central Australia.' In other words, he ended by compounding the act of translation: having carried the songs over from Aranda into English, they were then meant to go their way in the native language of English-speaking Australian poets.

His night work—after hours, his labour of love—was the translation of European language, biblical German and English, into Aranda. This was his work on the New Testament, done by 1949 and published in 1956. When it was done he was proud of it, as it represented his then private sense of it being the complement to the work on the Aboriginal songs. But again, he did not say much about what he was doing with this work. Did his left hand—he had used it with the Aranda songs—know what the right was doing? Yes, because he was a twin, born of *Ntaria*, the Twins Dreaming. What this meant, however, for the Aranda, was another matter, which needs to be told.

Then there is, further along the troubled track of his life, his famous legal battle on behalf of a black man called Rupert Max Stuart, Tom Ljonga's grandson, who was tried and convicted for the brutal murder and rape of a nine-year-old white girl in 1959. Strehlow played a central part in the attempted defence of Stuart, and he did so on the grounds of language. To look at that incident is to look again at Strehlow's view of language: his need for pure models, and his absolutism in translation. The outcome was a calamity for Strehlow.

Strehlow devoted a life to moving language both ways, but in all that life he hardly paused to reflect on his antecedents in that domain, or the criteria by which his own work might be judged. The dogged translator was himself silent on the matter most salient to his own vocation: the ways in which both the content and form of his work might be best appreciated, appraised.

Despite Strehlow's characteristic lack of intellectual self-consciousness as a linguist, his work remains a rich, rough country calling for some elucidation from the vast literature on translation. That perhaps is the measure of his achievement: the fire in his work with tongues is still there, demanding attention. The Lutheran German boy born on Pentecost Sunday, the boy versed in Latin and Greek, the lad who ran with the native boys in Aranda, the collector of sacred songs, the translator of mission Scripture, the university teacher of English language and literature—all of his language work covers ground that has to be traversed, even though he left few maps of his own, and showed even less inclination to refer to maps made by others.

The terrain might be described geometrically. The country called Translation has three sides. On the first side there is the original language, or the 'native' language to its users, whether they be speakers of Aranda or Latin. Conceptions of the original, degrees of respect or condescension, are variable. On the second side there is the host language, which must be employed in right measure, and the idioms of which are subject to many pressures—historical, cultural, social, aesthetic. On the third side there are the beleaguered tropics of translation, the realm of *what happens in between*. This is the place where all the tropes of translation literature are played out, where translation turns on notions of equivalence, on what is thought possible and impossible with regard to the liaison between the original and the host languages. It is a tropical zone where the translator must please two masters at once—an impossible task. The movement of one towards or away from the other has to be negotiated, the merger or lack of merger, the interpenetrations and possible transformations; and the speech and hearing of each weighed up in terms of relationship, a matter further complicated according to whether the voice of that speech is personally present or not.

The literature of translation worries each of these sides in various ways according to the convictions and affections of scholar/critic/poet.[*] Some of these figures, occasionally, offer guidance into Strehlow's country, his *oeuvre*, his labours of love and justification. Strehlow is best approached by various coordinates, all the better to enter what he achieved so innocently.

Love's Body

'No two languages cover each other fully,' Strehlow said in 1947, speaking to the ANZAAS conference in Perth, 'and the natural corollary is that the two worlds of ideas influence the thinking of the speakers of

---

[*]   In English the seminal figures are Dryden, Arnold and Pound, in whom all three functions are embodied. In the German tradition, where the translation of Scripture, as well as poetry, has affected every turn of translation, the definitive figures are Luther, Goethe, Schleiermacher, Buber, and, in the twentieth century, Benjamin and Steiner.

two different languages are also dissimilar at many points. It is an old truism that people cannot think deeply or utter a prayer or make love in a language other than their mother tongue. In addition it takes even a good linguist a long time before he ceases translating his thoughts from his own childhood speech into an acquired foreign language, and begins to form his thoughts in terms of that acquired language itself.'[16]

A messy statement. It speaks of the differences between languages (no two languages cover each other fully) and confuses that with what can and cannot be done in the mother tongue (thinking, praying, lovemaking), and then with a further assertion about how a new language is learnt (by translating one into another). But there is a focal point: Strehlow is talking about the need for anthropologists to involve themselves in an 'intimate knowledge of the language' of the culture they seek to study and comprehend. Indeed the key terminology—the covering, the praying and lovemaking, and the gestation out of childhood speech from the mother tongue—exudes the language of intimacy, the somatic foundation of language.[17] Strehlow's language for language pertains to the language of love or, to be more precise, love's body.

Thus: 'The human body cannot function for long unless the beating of the heart circulates a steady stream of blood through the arteries; similarly, language is the very life-blood of the human mind.' It is by language, the understanding of the language of the other, that we 'probe ever more deeply into the hidden recesses of the human mind, conscious and sub-conscious mind.' And not just a penetration of the sub-conscious, obviously, but of the intelligence and mentality of so-called primitive peoples as well—their intelligence. 'What is intelligence?' is as difficult to answer accurately as the question, 'What is electricity?' Strehlow goes on, but language, its workings, will still give the clue because it is that 'life-blood.' And even more generally, it betokens us, as members of 'one large, indivisible family,' to fully value the power and richness of all language, even though past anthropologists have not made sufficient allowance for the 'elasticity and adaptive power' inherent in a 'primitive' language. The vital necessity of so doing is nowhere more apparent than in the activity of appreciating sacred ceremony, for there, if the words are not understood nor is its sacred or magical character. 'It is the word which quickens dead symbolism into life.'[18]

Such rhetoric composes, in effect, a love song to language. In its sustained physicality of imagery pertaining to the commitment and affiliations of the body's life blood; it is tantamount to an eroticisation of language. You can feel Strehlow getting carried away with his imagery, spelling out a deep part of himself as he goes. For in general, at a certain point talk about language phases into talk about sexuality, an intimate connection because, 'Eros and language mesh at every point.'*

'In the highly articulate individual,' George Steiner says, when he is elaborating on the connection between Eros and language, 'the current of verbal-psychic energy flows inward.' But we should also say, because the acquisition of language is so social, so rooted in time and place, that the current flows outwards. Strehlow felt this to be so with regard to the native tongue of Aranda. When he finished his study of the language he felt that it 'harmonises strikingly with the country which was once occupied by the people who spoke this tongue.' He went on to describe the ranges and the valleys, 'the dark mulga of the plains and the red-crested, spinifex-covered sandhills':

The total impression of the landscape is one of the stern beauty and rugged majesty of slumbering wrinkled old age; it would seem foolish to look around for the light and pretty sweetness or the boisterous strength and glory of an inexperienced young country in the sombre, colourful landscape which is Central Australia.

As the country, so the language spoken in that country by the original inhabitants. Aranda is an old language—it is plain, levelled down by analogy, and often lacking in the lighter graces. But it has a vigour and a ruggedness all of its own. It is not incapable of grandeur or of beauty. It can stir the imagination and the heart of the jaded mind of the disillusioned twentieth century student. As a medium for the legends and traditions of the Central Australian tribesmen, Aranda cannot be excelled.[19]

---

* Steiner goes on (1975: 38): 'Intercourse and discourse, copula and copulation, are sub-classes of the dominant fact of communication. They arise from the life-need of the ego to reach out and comprehend, in the two vital senses of "understanding" and "containment," another human being. Sex is a profoundly semantic act. Like language, it is subject to the shaping force of social convention, rules of proceeding, and accumulated precedent. To speak and to make love is to enact a distinctive twofold universality: both forms of communication are universals of human physiology as well as of social evolution. It is likely that human sexuality and speech developed in close-knit reciprocity. Together they generate the history of self-consciousness, the process, presumably millenary and marked by innumerable regressions, whereby we have hammered out the notion of self and otherness.'

This is a fine passage, intuitively brilliant in its suggestion—a poetic suggestion rather than an academic thesis—that the language was by analogy an expression of relationship to place, and that at a fundamental level, consciousness of country was tantamount to consciousness of being. Today it is rather commonplace to be able to spell out Aboriginal thinking in terms of the Dreamings, with particular references to secret sites. Strehlow stated the existential connection more generally. It implied a precocious and useful metaphor of the language being the country, and the country being, in its own way, the body of the language. In one amorous embrace the commitment to both is expressed.

Strehlow manages his ambivalence reasonably. The harmonies are not perfect. The country, as he knows too well from his years of hard travelling, has 'featureless plains and barren sandhills.' The mountains have that 'lonely, rugged grandeur' while the creeks have 'lovely waterholes and clear springs in hidden valleys.' One sentence captures Strehlow's blend of misery and exaltation perfectly: 'It [the landscape] is not incapable of grandeur or of beauty.'

So much that Strehlow says about the country called language rounds out the internal and the external under the heading of desire. The mother tongue is not merely the one intimately learnt from the nurturing woman. It is the one acquired in the lap of the place to which mother, and the father, belong. It is the language of the hearth. It is the tongue warmed by fire and cooled by the waters that flow like language through a place. The hills and the valleys, the rocky outcrops and the plains named by the mother tongue become, in effect, the topographic perimeters of that tongue. And then, as the new speaker moves about in that place—eating, sleeping, hunting, thinking, lovemaking in that place—the land itself becomes of his language. Out of love's body is born love of the home country.

To say that Strehlow translated is to say that in complicated ways he travelled amorously.

Native Being (in English)

In 1935, when he was back in Central Australia, hot and tired and lonely again, Strehlow had a brief, warm encounter with the work of a young poet who wanted to do something new with his native Australian/English language. His name was Rex Ingamells, an Adelaide school teacher who had grown up in Orroroo, in the north of the State, on the track to Central Australia. Ingamells was soon to be famous as the founder of the Jindyworobak movement which wanted to free Australian art from European literariness and root it in an indigenous sense of place.* He reached out to Strehlow as a teacher of English, and the man who had written so memorably about Aboriginal myth.

At the time Strehlow's sense of Adelaide poetry would have been confined to another literary impulse entirely, one that would make it hard for Australian poetry to become at ease with itself.

An exemplary case was the Adelaide-born poet and playwright Charles Rischbieth Jury, who had taught Strehlow Greek at university. Jury was educated in Greats at Oxford. In 1922 he was offered the chair of English at the University of Adelaide which had been endowed by his mother. He declined the offer. His father wished him to be a poet and had provided him with a full-time income to do so. Poems, plays and a popular school anthology of translations from the Classics were to follow. In 1929, when Strehlow was an undergraduate in English and Classics Jury put out his verse play, *Love and the Virgins*. It is a flowery work: its diction is playful, ornate and archaic. Allusions to classical figures do the creative work.

Nevertheless, Jury very much considered himself to be an Australian poet. 'Encomium of Adelaide' is an ode to the particulars of the lived place as much as it is a literary homage to Apollo.

City sweet,
Mead-built, with thy morning in the hills;
Whose land is dry, and dry the air,
And when summer hath parched thy pastures bare
Thou sittest by waterless rills
And criest for rain, like a swallow . . .

---

* Rex Ingamells put out the Jindyworobak manifesto in 1938. '"Jindyworobak" is an Aboriginal word meaning "to annex, to join," and I propose to coin it for a particular use. The Jindyworobaks, I say, are those individuals who are endeavouring to free Australian art from whatever alien influences trammel it, that is, bring it into proper contact with its material. They are the few who seriously realise that an Australian culture depends on the fulfilment and sublimation of certain definite conditions, namely:
'1 A clear recognition of environmental values.
'2 The debunking of much nonsense.
'3 An understanding of Australia's history and traditions, primaeval, colonial and modern.'
   As Brian Elliott observes (1979: xxvii, xxx), the manifesto might have been more precise, but as it stands the first point simply affirms poetry's link with the landscape; the second is a breezy embrace of the vernacular. What united Aboriginal thinking and that of the Jindyworobaks was the notion of 'site magic.'

These lines are locally earthed enough, until perhaps the reader comes to the poet's urgent, classicist hope:

> That from secret earth, who hath once given birth
> Such a city as thou might rise, and bear
> A race whose spirits lusty and fair
> Should build again on a virgin plain
> Athens, the splendour of thought.[20]

Adelaide as a new Athens. Nothing could be further from this than the song the Jindyworobaks wanted to sing.

The manuscript that Ingamells sent to Strehlow was called 'Gumtops,' a title that signalled more than it could say. It was an allusion to the lines of the nationalist Bernard O'Dowd, whose most famous and possible best poem was 'The Bush,' published in 1912.

> When, now I say the 'The Bush,' I see the top
> Delicate amber leafings of the gum
> Flutter, or flocks of screaming greenleeks drop
> Silent . . .

O'Dowd, a democrat who corresponded with Walt Whitman, made a didactic virtue of the Australian landscape and its peoples locally described. He was alive to the presence of Aborigines and their songs. He was the first poet to indicate in his work that he had read Spencer and Gillen's *Native Tribes of Central Australia,* and it was from that work that the terms *Alchera* and *Alcheringa* slipped into poeticising (the spellings of which were Spencer's and not Strehlow's *Altjira*). Brian Elliott notes that 'It was Bernard O Dowd who first rationalised the Dreamtime for white Australian consumption.' O'Dowd made reference to the 'Golden Age of the Alchera,' and composed such lines as

> And Spencer sails from Alcheringa bringing
> Intaglios totems and Books of the Dead.

The 'intaglios' might have been meant to indicate the *tjurunga*. In any case, the touch of exotic or esoteric, if we take 'Books of the Dead' to allude to Egypt or even Tibet, is grounded locally by topographic references recognisably Australian, as well as the use of 'Alchera.' It was the *symbolic* placement of 'Alchera' that placed the lyric in the European tradition of pastoral poetry, a political and a 'pastoral simplification.'[21]

Ingamells' 'Gumtops' was not didactic, but its thrust was to reflect upon and perhaps even incorporate, not the splendours of the Greeks but the sacred purport of an Australian landscape imbued by the still more ancient culture. 'Boomerang,' the first poem in the collection, was iconic enough, but it had to clear away some Victoriana before the local could stand up:

> *This piece of hardwood, cunningly shaped,*
> *Was curved so evenly while piccaninnies gaped*
> *At a warrior who chipped at it with pieces of flint,*
> *And formed it by meticulous dint upon dint*
> *Outside his wurly he sat beside a tree*
> *And chipped at it patiently for hours—not for me,*
> *But for to kill the wallaby in the rocky pass,*
> *For to kill the wild-turkey hiding in the grass.*[22]

The manuscript was a swag of poems that advertised their celebrations of inland Australia: 'The Old Telegraph Station, Strangeways,' 'The Afghans,' 'Camels' and so on. Others rendered the landscape in diction a Jury might have liked:

> *O I have seen one flaming peak at dawn*
> *Across a sea of sand, Alone it stood,*
> *And bare of all but colour: no great wood*
> *Had up its side a shaggy mantle drawn . . .*
> ('Forlorn Beauty')[23]

and so on, in a more English vein than any mature Jindyworobak would ever want.

Ingamells was more at home, and coming into his own voice, with the most traditional of bush topics. 'Bullocky' begins:

> *A bullocky came at noon,*
> *With his lumbering team and low*
> *Leaving behind a heavy cloud*
> *Of red-dust hanging low.*[24]

In Australian terms—diction, ease with country, localness of perception, its intrinsic aboriginality—'Gumtops' was a modest start but an important one: it displayed all the branches if not the leaves of the program to come.

Strehlow wrote back to Ingamells from Alice Springs on 28 February. Apologising for his inability to read the poems when he had been in Adelaide, he went on to some detailed criticism, and began by praising some of the most flowery writing: 'Of the poems in the copy that I am returning to you the best seem to be "Forlorn Beauty?" with its fine picture of the flaming desert peak in the desolation of a grim dawn; "The Fire Behind the Hills" with its mysterious and striking, yet true account of a blood-red moon rise; "Sea-Things" with its rapid succession of clear-cut clearly imagined pictures; and a few other poems, which I shall now discuss in more detail.'

So much for Strehlow's critical sense. As he went on it becomes clear that he is not so much moved by Ingamells' rudimentary poetic skills as the subject matter made for his own heart.

> To my mind the finest single poem in the copy I am returning is the piece entitled 'Camels.' Your picture of a fierce sunrise in the desert is the finest that I have yet read in Australian verse–
>
> And when the gloomy vastness
> of sandy solitude
> Is smitten bright with morning light
> When, fiery and imbued
> With strength, the sun has risen,
> And scorches everywhere,
> The camel trains go stringing
> Amid the blinding glare.
>
> (By the way do you think that '*Into* the blinding glare' would be just as effective?)
>
> The poem is full of happy effects. No simile could be more apt than that in which the 'strings of slow brown camels' moving over the sand hills are likened to 'dull gigantic pythons.'
>
> Very fine, too, is the stanza describing sunset. It combines high natural beauty with scrupulous accuracy of observation on a deeply poetical insight into nature as revealed to us in the barren waste lands of Central Australia—

When range, purple, crimson
Creeps o'er the sandhills bare,
Ere night encroach with swift approach
And star-fires in her hair;
Then the red sandhills, gilded,
Burn up with copper fire,
While westward sparks and smolders
The daylight's brilliant pyre.

The spirit of Central Australia, cruel, beautiful, alluring & menacing, broods over such lines. They present successfully the paradox of the barren wastes of Australia—a landscape full of weariness and hardness and cruelty which takes on at times a loveliness and a strange fascination that haunts the passing traveller and holds the lifelong affections of the man or woman who was born in such a land.

Clearly, the company of 'Gumtops' was a godsend to Strehlow, alone in the Centre. But there was another poem in the collection that was, potentially, even closer to his heart, and perhaps Ingamells knew this. It was 'The Bandicoot-God,' which tried to do nothing less than address itself to the place and the myth about which Strehlow already knew so much: the story Gurra had told him at Ilbalintja, the story of the Great Father, which was the subject of his first public talk, on Myths of the Northern Aranda. Whether Ingamells heard that talk does not emerge from their correspondence, and is unknown to the Jindyworobaks' historian. In any case, sufficient essentials had been absorbed by Ingamells. His poem begins:

The Bandicoot-god
In sacred deeps
'Neath the plain's thick crust,
Though all time sleeps.

Undreaming he lies
Long nights and days
From stars far hidden
And the sun's hot blaze.

Yet each time's night
Since even the first,
His armpits have swollen,
His navel has burst.[25]

The timeless aspect of the myth is there, and the simple echo of a chant; but so is the jingle of the nursery rhyme. Entirely missing is the savage meat of the story, the primal horde's killing of the father. Strehlow was not going to let the outsider get any closer, either. He wrote to Ingamells:

> [It] is a promising poem; but perhaps it has not quite recaptured the spirit of the aboriginal legend on which it is based. Rigid economy of diction would add enormously to its dignity. It contains a few loose lines which add little to the interest of the poem—e.g.
> And soon—ah, soon,
> The bandicoots scamper
> About and about . . .
> If every single adjective contained in the poem were indispensable and conveyed a new and striking idea, the poem, which is written in a severely simple, economic meter, would gain much greater power and terseness.

Ingamells asked Strehlow to write an introduction* for the book, but Strehlow missed the post from Alice Springs and on 7 April sent instead what he accurately described as 'altogether inadequate criticism . . . a weak effort . . . written in a wild hurry.' The *Mail*'s editor made it, in Strehlow's opinion, 'a little less wearisome than it was in its original form.' Under the heading 'Praise for Young South Australian Poet,' the review read:

> Central Australia is, to most Australian city dwellers, a land of mystery which they know mainly from sensational reports and unpleasant rumours. Its people and its scenery have been ludicrously misrepresented within recent years. But as one who has been born and bred in Central Australia I can truthfully say I have derived much pleasure from reading 'Gumtops.' This slender volume contains some of the best lines of Australian verse that have been written, and the young poet has succeeded in recapturing much of the spirit of this enigmatical country in some of its multitudinous and ever-changing moods.

---

* In the introduction L.F. Giblin said that 'Our Australian poetry . . . needs a new Adam.' Ingamells was not declared to be Adam but one of the 'pioneers' among the Australian poets who 'have a long, hard journey before them' (Ingamells 1935: 1–2).

When Strehlow came to the poem 'Camels,' he exclaimed: '"Smitten" is a master stroke. It suggests, in one hammer blow, as it were, the whole anguish of the day that is to follow, with its toil and vexation and scorching blaze from which there can be no escape.' Quite apart from Ingamells, 'smitten' must have thrown Strehlow back to Sheila at Horseshoe Bend.

The egocentricity of Strehlow's review is so striking that it hardly needs more labouring than Strehlow applied. He embraces the efforts of the young Ingamells as they pertain to what he, the critic, so well recognises. In general it is praise for Ingamells' 'close personal observation and sympathetic understanding.' There is, however, a rider. 'The Bandicoot-God' still did not please the critic. Of this direct Aboriginal reference, Strehlow declared that it 'does not rise to quite the same level of the very best verse, but it gives, adequately enough, a metrical version of the beginning of an Aranda native legend. In that, perhaps, lies its main interest.' But it was not 'interest' enough for Strehlow to carry on his literary affair with the new poet.*

Strehlow's literary criticism was barely conscious of modernism's attempt to clear up Edwardian diction, to get rid of what Pound admirably called emotional slither or of the obstacles facing Australian poets trying to shape an Australian voice. Instead he sent homilies to Ingamells about 'hard work, an infinite capacity for taking pains, and unfailing honesty towards one's own work,' and being 'prepared at all times to sacrifice work that is not up to the standard of the remainder' because: 'Writing poetry, like every other art, requires much hard toil at times; & it often needs a very large amount of will-power & enthusiasm to put down on paper the fruits of one's inspiration, & then to smooth over all the little edges that it still may have in its original form.' It was puritan advice through and through: he might have been talking about woodwork.

He was at the same time sitting with ants and snakes on rocky ground out at Arltunga, not the right place to draw upon the letters of

---

*   Strehlow remained in contact with Ingamells until the latter's death in 1955, but this correspondence between them is all that is extant at the Strehlow Research Centre and the State Library of Victoria. Strehlow's continuity of interest in matters Jindyworobak is more visible with regard to his support for another Jindyworobak poet, Roland Robinson, writing a preface for his The Feathered Serpent (1956) which drew on Namatjira's telling of the Ankotarinja myth; and he was for decades an avid supporter of the work of the sculptor William Ricketts, who had also made trusted contact with Namatjira and other Western Aranda men, and whose work is a translation of Jindyworobak ideas into clay.

Keats. It was a chunky letter to Ingamells saying how tired he was. But he was still in camp with his Aboriginal men, and still writing down the songs and the myths. That process, as we know from our travels with him, had poetry enough in it, if he had had the wherewithal to translate his poetic sympathies into poems. But he had not, which is probably a good thing, considering his critical sense. What he had, however, was what he was able to draw Ingamells' attention to: 'With all its toil and weariness, one gets so much inspiring material noted down, that in the end all the labour will seem insignificant when compared to the collected wealth of ancient legends and chants. One only wishes that White Australia would soon wake up to the richness of its heritage, & preserve it and honour it, instead of treading it down ignorantly under its feet.'[26]

I am not a poet, he was saying. But I am becoming the collector upon whom poets might draw. All they will have to do is translate in their way, as I am bound to translate, hard for all of my life.

Dwelling in Paraphrase

Strehlow was translating himself—in English—to another speaker in English, and they seem to have been in a different key. There is nothing wrong with Strehlow's English, and his admiration for Kipling, when he was polishing himself as an undergraduate, comes to mind. He has not become a Kipling, whose light, supple prose was startling, and who would not have tolerated laborious sentences committed to noun phrases. Kipling was keeping faith, not just with the white man's burden, but with a tradition of English prose that could keep the object of a man's attention at a witty distance. Strehlow, it seems, was keeping faith with his German, the inner authority of which seemed to weigh him down. We get a sense, reading Strehlow, that his English is often a kind of paraphrase of German, that somehow, somewhere inside himself, he was affected by the genetic presence of that original.

To return to the geometry of the problem: there is (a) the original language calling up the translator, (b) the host language, which the translator must call upon, and (c) the tropical zone of what happens in between. It is with regard to the host language that we have been commenting on Strehlow's qualities. Whatever transpires in between for Strehlow will always be marked by his lack of genius for English—this at a point in the history of translation when it had become a given to insist that a translator must have that *genius*, must be an artistic talent of a very high order.

John Dryden said so most effectively three centuries ago, when he had seminally essayed on the right kind of 'latitude' the translator could exercise while respecting the sense of the original which must be 'sacred and inviolable'[27]; Matthew Arnold modernised the point with regard to translating Homer when he said that the task of rendering the nobility of the style 'most depends on the individual personality of the artists'[28]; and Ezra Pound illustrated this view in action with his many daring imitations from many languages. Fidelity to the original became, with Pound's aesthetic genius, compatible with doing violence to the original and speaking well of 'atrocities,' providing they were committed 'with the aim of driving the readers' perception further into the original' than before.[29]

Each of these critics/poets was driven by a need to keep a special faith with the host language as much as the original: they wanted the English to excel as well as it might in a poem composed in English. The translation would be, inevitably, a paraphrase, but it would be *a poem*—if the vital linguistic energy of the translator was fine, bold, and free enough.

Inside himself Strehlow had many tongues from which to choose: German as his mother tongue; Aranda that of his youth; English running between them. And then, as he entered adolescence, the formalities of Latin and Greek. Before he left Central Australia he was something of a polyglot, a language being of some depth and complexity. By the time he came back to the Centre this was even more the case and, to deepen the matter further, he chose to 'get back into' the native language all over again. The 'into' is important. We are speaking of grounding here, of the psycholinguistics of an identity driven to define itself in terms of language.

All this he had within him when he came to the tropical zone.

He had the gift of tongues and yet was not liberated by them; he did not seem to be able to let one enlighten—or lighten—the other.

He was *heavy* with language.

There is hardly a playful word in the corpus of Strehlow.

A congestion of tongues? Was there a complication of some kind between them?

In the passage when he speaks of not being able to think or pray or make love in anything but one's mother tongue, a fundamental assumption is at work. It is that there, in the polylingual mind, there is a dominant root tongue, a unitary, unifying single root. That root, for Strehlow, was German, the impact of which is palpable, as I have said.

Is he also implying that his thinking and praying and lovemaking—him in his most intimate being—has thus been severed from that root? That for all the languages on the tip of his tongue he is not easily operating from the quick of himself? If so, then what happens in between his original and the translated language must be already thwarted, a stilted affair. Much must have depended on how Strehlow carried the languages within him.

Two of the languages were double layered from the start. The German, of course, was not simply his: it was the German of his father and his mother. When he read his father's work it was written in the old German. The incorporation of what his father had written about the Aranda was already a textual translation, even before it was the dialogic one of a young man understanding what a father had written. Then, in conjunction with that, there was his father's Aranda, which was partly derived from the hard lessons of earlier missionaries. At first Strehlow pored over his father's work as a student; later he knew more about the language than his father ever knew. But that process had its echoes as well, since his own early Aranda was the diction spoken by women and children, not the cultivated senior men. He had to develop that understanding to enter the songs, the culture. Already, through these strata, there is room for much complicated feeling, as Strehlow's usage of German and Aranda interpenetrate in the business of 'getting the songs right.'

He had to dig, so to speak, through two lines of his father's speech, before shaping his own. Once he had shaped his own speech, the result must have felt hard won. Right down the line it is possible that Strehlow felt the best he could do was paraphrase.

The actual place of the Aranda—in the original—is suddenly hard to locate in this schema. Where is it now? In Carl Strehlow's translation? In his son's? Somewhere in between? The internal linguistic stresses of a translator get caught up in the definition of the original.

George Steiner has a vivid account of the phenomenology of the polyglot. 'What is certain is that the immediacy, the irretrievability of different tongues in the speech acts of the polyglot is, in crucial part, a function of the environment. Different moods, different social settings, different locations strongly modify the sense of linguistic priority.' In the language layers of the polyglot brain analogies between languages are formally linguistic, and also unique to the individual, 'wholly personal and interlingual':

Thus one of the 'languages' inside me, probably the richest, is an eclectic cross-weave whose patterns are unique to myself though the fabric is quite palpably drawn from the public means and rule-governed realities of English, French, German, and Italian. Moving 'between' languages, moreover, in which I obscurely apprehend as a complex, highly energised zone of modulation and *indeterminacy*, I register contiguities, correspondences, short-cuts, which are based not only on speech-sounds, on patterns of meaning, on associations particular to my own life, but on word shapes and tactile-values. The implicit phenomenon is general but little understood. Words have their 'edge,' their angularities, their concavities and force of tectonic suggestion. These features operate at a level deeper, less definable than that of either sound or semantics. They can, in a multilingual matrix, extend across and between languages. When we learn a new language, it may be that these modes of evocative congruence are the most helpful. Often, as we shall see, great translation moves by touch, finding the matching shape, the corresponding rugosity, even before it looks for counterpart of meaning. (emphasis added)[30]

Strehlow never formally spoke of his own language use in such tactile terms, of its 'rugosity,' its sensual truths. But he did rather unwittingly hit upon symbols that give a clue to his phenomenology. German was the black square. English was the circle with a dotted line. Aranda was the black circle. And his own movement, when he was contending with vowels, was from the German square through the open English circle to the point of arrival in the black circle of the black language.

In this way he laid things out in a diagram of his MA thesis, 'Aranda Phonetics and Grammar', which he finished in 1938. While the exposition is largely technical, one gathers a tangible personal sense of Strehlow's sensate listening, hearing, straining to travel the right way in his polyglot system. It is his zone of indeterminacy. Throughout his thesis he is acutely personal in his responses to his position in the traffic of sounds. For instance, he thought the rolling *r*'s of the Aranda (which is one of the sounds that gives the language its vibrant energy, especially when arising from barrel-chested men) might be exaggerated in the recording, and felt obliged to announce: 'Personally I am acquainted with some people of German and Swiss origin whose pronunciation of *r* is far more noisy than that in use amongst average Aranda speakers.'[31] On the topic of 'nasal twang' he opined that it was sometimes due to Aranda 'laziness,' and that sometimes with the older

men it was sometimes 'very difficult to record the words at all.'[32] 'Phonetics,' with its grainy display of sensate activity of language, exudes
Strehlow's early struggles getting back into the language.

Linguistically, he was breathing heavily, trying to keep faith with
more than one original, and with a host language that he had learnt in
translation.

Strangely, however, his vitality was released when he turned to speak
about the grammar of the native tongue.

Hamlet Versus Kangaroo Eating

Strehlow's 'Aranda Phonetics and Grammar,' made a pioneering case
for an Australian Aboriginal language that was unique. It was unique for
two reasons: it was, as Elkin wrote in the introduction to the published
version, 'the first complete phonetic and grammatical study of an Australian Aboriginal language to appear'*; and because it was the first full
study of a native language by one who had spoken it from birth.[33]
It was pioneering because it was the first detailed study designed, at
least in part, to overthrow two colonial prejudices about the native
tongue: that it was hardly a language worthy of the name, so 'primitive'
was its system, and that as a language it was of little value compared to
those from the European stock.[34]

Elkin valued the arrival of Strehlow's publication exactly because it
could be put before those who 'timidly or even cynically ask: "Have
Aboriginal languages anything like a grammar or rules?" It may even
convince them that a people who use and hand on such a language are
after all not so inferior to us or lacking in intelligence.' It was a case
Elkin himself had made convincingly in his lucid overview of
Australian linguistics.[†] The furphy Elkin wanted to squash was that
Aboriginal languages were 'primitive,' crude tools of Stone Age

---

*   Peter Sutton comments (personal communication, 7 July 2001): 'certainly the
     first "comprehensive"—perhaps no grammar is very complete as one can
     always go on peeling off onion skins.'
†   In 1937, the same year Strehlow was writing up his *Grammar* at Jay Creek,
     Elkin looked back on the mission studies of language as valuable but
     'atomistic' because they failed to give 'living pictures of the languages.' Elkin
     meant, particularly, that so intent were missionaries in seeking literal
     equivalents for 'Western and Christian ideals of justice, mercy, faith and
     brotherhood, sacrifice, atonement, eternal life et cetera,' that they mistakenly
     concluded that 'the native mind did not possess such ideas and could only
     with very great difficulty be made to appreciate them.' Elkin's alternative,
     which he plainly called the cultural approach, and which was about

peoples, because of their low-level powers of abstraction, an argument that turned on the relative absence of abstract nouns, generic terms, and arithmetic.[35] The counter view, at least in part, Strehlow delivered in his *Grammar*.

It is important to say 'in part.' For he only made his counter-case after some convoluted and typically ambivalent reasoning. He had to say, first of all, that Aranda, 'like all other primitive languages is very weak in its stock of abstract nouns.'[36] However, it was also true to say that the 'principle of analogy' allowed Aranda to form 'such abstract nouns from almost every verb that the language possesses.'[37] The 'genius' of the language was its 'elasticity,' which had enabled it to take in what the missions had to teach. Strehlow passionately illustrated this by scathing refutation of Daisy Bates, who said that the Lord's Prayer could not be translated into an Australian language.[38] And yet following these equalising acclamations, Strehlow adds: 'Of course the Aranda abstract nouns will not be sufficient to express all the abstract ideas which are current in any modern European language. *But* it may be noted that even Old English is extremely poor in abstract nouns' (emphasis added).[39] This is going around the bush. It is as if Strehlow does not know how to value one square or circle while talking about the other.

He breaks into his clearing when he comes to the Aranda verbs, the elasticity of which allows him to revisit the Aranda's powers of abstraction. And again, his is a negative thesis followed by a counter thesis. Verbs in all languages, are 'used for two main reasons: (1) to express attitudes of the mind, and (2) to describe physical actions.' Aranda was weak on the first, and not on the second. The contrast was with 'the flexion of the verb in modern European languages, where the use of

---

forms of life in Wittgenstein's sense, was to affirm: 'The deeper a student penetrates into such aspects of Aboriginal life, the nearer he gets to an appreciation of its ideas and ideals, and of the way in which these are represented linguistically.' The living picture that followed covered what was known about many Aboriginal languages, and demonstrated that in ordinary speech, and especially 'the secret life' with its myths and chants, use was made of 'abstract terms, metaphorical expression, poetic form, delicate shades of meaning and dramatic presentation, resulting in literature which is an inspiration and a source of life to the initiated.' Ironically, Elkin's focus on the secret life referred to the language work at Hermannsburg, including Pastor Strehlow's observations about how expressions kept cropping up for things for which it was thought the natives had no words. All mission translation, then, was not atomistic. In this grand post-colonial case for Aboriginal language Elkin diplomatically embraced the background of his protégé, T.G.H. Strehlow.

auxiliary verbs has been developed to the highest degree possible in order to assist in the expression of ideas peculiar to the modern cultured mind':

> For the educated white person tends to be introspective, argumentative, hesitant, analytical, bent on abstract ideas and suppositions. He lives largely in a world of abstractions, imaginary ills or benefits, elaborate systems and theories, and abstruse reasoning generally. He broods over what might have been, what could have been, or what should have been; over what would have happened, what should have happened, what might have happened; over what might be done in the future or at the present moment; and over many other similar suppositions . . .
>
> Such Hamlet-like thoughts are foreign to the mind of the Australian native, and are always difficult to express in his language.[40]

Hamlet-like thoughts indeed. It is hard not to hear the translator speaking of himself in this passage, even as he makes an objective linguistic point. Strehlow's being is as present here as it was in his presentation of the bond between language and landscape. With that he evoked the history of his body in transit in the landscape: with Hamlet he locates the anguish of his mind in the same place. And at the same time he is invoking a stereotype of the native as a 'primitive': as a people bound to the concrete, whose limited linguistic powers of conjecture blurred the distinction between the imaginary and the real, who inhabited a world where there might be no difference between dreaming and real experience.[41]

Now, though, Strehlow is ready to show Aranda in the most positive light. The most striking passage in *Aranda Grammar* is where he illustrates the way a verb could be made to do so much descriptive work in the context of tribal life: how the verb could *perform*, we might say, in a way that elucidated a life where understandings were as vital as any particularly 'abstract' thought. Strehlow:

> Let us in mind follow the native hunter in his daily task of tracking an animal, say a mountain kangaroo. Let us assume that he contents himself by using various forms derived from the one verb, '*ilkuma*' (= to eat) in order to explain to us the movements of the animal which he is tracking up. The mountain kangaroo comes down in the waning afternoon in

order to feed on the more luxuriant grass on the plain below. Our guide will point to a trail leading down from the mountain slope, with nibbled-off grass on both sides of it; and he will remark; '*Nala* (= here) *era* (= it) *ilkutjakalaka* (= descended-eating).' If much grass had been nibbled off, this would show a long and slow descent, and the verb in the preceding sentence would be altered to '*ilkulb-ilkutjakalanaka*' (= 'descended-slowly-eating-all-the-while'); here the reduplication and the longer derived form indicate both the slow progress of the animal and its long-continued bout of munching grass.

   The trail now has reached the plain. '*Nala* (here) *era* (it) *ilkuetnalalbuka*,' will be the next remark—*ilkuenalalbuka* meaning: 'wandered-on-away-from-us-eating-on-its-way.' After a few more steps a cross track cuts the trail: the kangaroo, after going on a few yards further, had circled around and come back to where its pursuers are now—'*nala era ilkup-ilkuentjal-buka*' (= 'here-it-came-back-towards-us-eating-ravenously-the-whole-time'). After a while a particularly good patch of grass is reached: the tracks show that the animal feasted here for a long while, browsing about leisurely in big circles—'*nala era ilkup-ilkulanaka*' (= 'here it kept on browsing and browsing').[42]

This is Strehlow at his best, tracking sound, tracking the live culture, alive to the movements of individuals and their sounds, and the meaning of the sounds as they go. At last the tracks lead upwards and the guide exclaims, '*Nala era ilkutjintjka* (here-it-browsed-on-its-way-up)'. One senses, reading this, Strehlow on the way up: into the language and onto the lived plateau of it: into the animations of speech acts that constitute the full understandings of Aboriginal life, including abstract understandings. The categories of the kangaroo behaviour might well lack generic terms. But the language is working well enough; the verb 'to eat' is at large in the world in a way that makes 'abstract' speculation redundant.

   This is one's sense of the Strehlow passage; and the sense of its sense is intended by Strehlow: the kangaroo passage points us to what is vivid and concrete about the use of Aranda. In common parlance we might say that such concrete particulars are poetic. They are so in our modern aesthetic: they are graphic and particular. In their *immediacy* they sing. The pulse quickens as we read it, just as Strehlow's must have when he wrote it. No one could have written this passage who did not have a sense of the poetry that could inform the activities of native life. The passage suggests the unity of thought and action to which so much poetry aspires.

Elkin and others had reason to be pleased with Strehlow's achievement: it was his intimate detail that gave his account such authority. Acknowledgement of authority went rather one way. Strehlow does not substantially mention other work in the field, explaining that 'the earlier grammars of the language were not available to me at the time of writing this Grammar in Central Australia.' He was referring to the work of Pastor Kempe and his own father, and couching his reason as if he had been in prison in Central Australia, and unfamiliar with his father's work.[43] Even more peculiar is silence about other work in German, though he takes a moment to put Basedow right on a small point.[44] Elkin gets no acknowledgement for his framing work, either, nor any other Australian linguists, arid though they were, and funded in the field under his auspices.[45]

The authority Strehlow did acknowledge was the much published Otto Jespersen, from the University of Copenhagen. He cited Jespersen's technical book, *Lehrbuch der Phonetik* (1926). But what he did not openly indicate was his reliance on Jespersen's more general perspective laid out in his earlier *Language: Its Nature, Development and Origin*.[46] This was the book that Strehlow had in his saddlebag in Central Australia in 1935, and from it he seems to have derived his key statements about the primitive and the abstract,* and even more, evocatively, imbued his thesis with something of a German spirit towards the poetic origins of language.

Jespersen, after Rousseau and Herder, had a golden link to make.

---

* Modern linguistics, Jespersen was at pains to point out, had to be grounded in ethnography. This is by way of saying that the languages of other peoples could not be judged as complex or simple (civilised or not) according to the written language of Latin. Rather, the scientific appreciation of language involved the natural development of living speech, which should not be judged in any terms but its own, according to the 'relative value of languages from the point of view of their users.' Still, the notion of the primitive did have some application. 'The more advanced a language is, the more developed its power of expressing abstract or general ideas,' Jespersen wrote. This was the conventional wisdom about 'savage languages.' Jespersen mentions the natives of Tasmania, the Mohicans, Zulus, and the Bakaair of Central Brazil, along with the Bushmen of the Kalahari: all tribes which lacked abstract nouns (as well as any developed arithmetic). This did not mean that the native tongues were poor languages; they were indeed rich in their descriptive powers. But they 'lacked names for a great number of ideas that were outside the sphere of interest of uncivilised people.' Jespersen 1921: 26, 320, 431.

It was between the notion of the origin of languages and the poetic nature of primitive tongues. The matter went to the heart of the generic Romantic literature about language, the modern version of which began with Rousseau's questions about the sad gap between consciousness and speech, and which Herder turned around on itself, finding happy, organic unities between language and being. It became a debate that could frame both *Hamlet* as the alienated subject of language and the language model of the kangaroo eating, where a unified living world was present in language.[47] The tradition discoursed about being, rather than the mechanics of language; and about the origins of being arising in language, as distinct from a rationalistic account of language as an objective entity. It was a tradition that was entirely against the grain of the English empiricist brief for Australia at this time: their call was for secular technics, not soul or Babel talk.[48]

Jespersen was most conscious of the poetic qualities of the less abstract languages, and how each language is not only the instrument for literature but is itself literature and poetry.[49] 'A nation speaks its soul in the words it uses,' was Jespersen's gloss on Herder. Jespersen wanted to say that from the earliest times 'sound systems' evolved where primitive man, thanks to his 'graphic concrete words,' 'was constantly reduced to using words and phrases figuratively; he was forced to express his thoughts in the language of poetry'[50]

Indeed the genesis of language was not to be sought in the prosaic, but in the poetic side of life:

> The source of speech is not gloomy seriousness, but merry play, and youthful hilarity. And among the emotions which were most powerful in eliciting outbursts of music and of song, love must be placed in the front rank. To the feeling of love, which has left traces of its vast influences on countless points in the evolution of organic nature, are due not only, as Darwin has shown, the magnificent colours of birds and flowers, but also many of the things that fill us with joy in human life; it inspired many of the first songs, and through them was instrumental in bringing about human primitive speech. I hear laughing cries of exultation when lads and lasses vied with one another to attract the attention of the other sex, when everybody sang his merriest and danced his bravest to lure a pair of eyes to throw admiring glances in his direction. *Language was born in the courting days of mankind.* (emphasis added)[51]

There is no 'romanticism' in such a view of language, Jespersen insisted (he was defending his book about the progress in language, the book in which he had put his view about the original place of primitive love songs). But it was Romanticism as it asserted an organic link between the genesis of language, poetry and music. How to say the whole at once, Herder wondered, when he was essaying upon the ancient tongue of Hebrew, which was dominated by verbs, and 'animated with living spirit'? And his answer was, rhapsodically, in terms of 'entire performances for a going out toward other creatures' by virtue of the music of sound that was in language. On Herder's model there was no original sin of abstraction. The deed of the word, with its inner music, and its commingling with other senses, ran deep. The simplest crying out, one might say, showed that 'nature did not merely "ring it out," she "rang it in, deep into the soul."'[52]

In *Aranda Grammar* Strehlow makes no comment about ancient poetry, or love song. That would have been to go beyond his academic, scientific brief, and to have been speaking a language that Elkin did not want. He would save that for another place. Perhaps, too, Jespersen's celebratory pitch was too far from his melancholic cast of mind. Yet Jespersen, in the glow of his Romanticisms, is surely present in the last entry of *Aranda Grammar* where Strehlow writes about the various uses of one sound, one crying out, an exclamation. Out of the blue he gives a page and a half to a word that is as heartfelt and as unifying of body and mind, spirit and speech, as any word in the language; and one rooted in it from the beginning, and central to its whole music of being. *Jakai.*

An expression of surprise, of excitement, wonder, warning, fear, and joy.

Jakai is also the sound emitted by the native when he makes a grieving reference to his conception site.

Here is Strehlow dwelling on the doubleness of a simple sound, conveying what it might be to listen more closely, more systematically, with a mind to all the branches and the roots. 'It is not unfitting, then, that *jakai* should be the interjection chosen to denote this kind of joy which is, both outwardly and inwardly, mingled with sincere sorrow. The use of the interjection of deepest sorrow and pain to denote the highest and truest joy of which the native is capable, is typical of a language whose term for consuming love is the verb "erarerama"—"to long for that which has been lost."'[53]

This statement on joy-in-loss was the final thing Strehlow had to say in his thesis. He had closed with words most designed to re-fuse its speakers to the world, words that could make a speaker, or translator, the apotheosis of Romanticism.

Purity and Penetration

If, by 1938, Strehlow was dualistically amorous about the original native language, by 1947 he was proprietarily assertive. 'The Aranda and archaic language of the chants, is an instrument of great strength and beauty, which can rise to great heights of feeling.' Along with this praise went a corollary: Strehlow's indictment of what he called pidgin English. The reputation of the Aranda dialect suffered because too many people had a false idea of Aboriginal speakers amongst whom pidgin was fostered as 'the medium of intercourse between the natives and the whites . . . Northern Territory pidgin English is not English perverted and mangled by the natives; it is English perverted and mangled by ignorant whites, who have in turn taught this ridiculous gibberish to the natives and who then affect to be amused by the childish babbling of these "savages."'

Strehlow rendered some *Macbeth* in pidgin—'Long time ago old feller Donkey him bin big fella boss longa country. Alright. By an' by another feller—him name ole Muckbet—bin hearmen longa three feller debbil-debbil woman'—labouring the obvious so the result becomes 'utterly childish' and 'a malicious character of a great story.'[54]

Strehlow is saying that the same burlesque would be made of Aranda myth in pidgin. His teaching seems to be that both languages, the original and the host language, should at all times be kept pure; that they should never be allowed to mingle. The need is for a pure language, a mutual respect for the otherness of each tongue, rather than an indulgence of a mongrel tongue. On language grounds, the motivation is clear enough. Languages, since they are spoken by people of comparable worth and culture, warrant parity of esteem.

But of course on social grounds, considering the pragmatic need for clear communication when neither speaker has the other's tongue, the purist call is an imperialism. Then there is an even more fundamental consideration about social life: all communication, in whatever tongue, takes place in social contexts that have a history, and in which the issue is not so much language as trust. Strehlow himself expounded on this truth in 1936, in his 'Notes on Native Evidence in Value.'[55] There he was facing a practical reality: that in the real world not everyone from cultures foreign to each other can bridge the communication by speaking the same language. They are obliged, in their speech *acts*, to find other common ground. The creole that arises is the result, and its value and status as a new native tongue, are by no means cut and dried. That it is not as cut and dried as makers of traditional dictionaries might like—but is fluid, demotic, colloquial and original—may be its human, not to mention poetic, joy.

But Strehlow did not want to explore contemporary freedom in language, and the cultural respect it could generate. He preferred to hold up the traditional culture and defend it, far more than he did in his *Grammar,* against the label of 'primitive.' 'Like other human beings the natives of Australia reveal one of the signs of the intelligent mind— the ability of thinking abstractly; and to that end they have shaped for themselves a language capable of expressing such metaphysical concerns.' He goes on to say there were terms for 'deceit' and 'theft,' 'right' and 'wrong,' 'excellence,' 'beauty'; and that there were many other 'expressive-factual' or 'coloured' words in the legends which indicated that the living storytellers lived in a world of ideas and moral concepts. 'We must not fall into the old mistake of undervaluing the power and richness of any language.' And as to number, the concept of which was so undeveloped in Aboriginal culture, Strehlow reminds his audience that hunters and gatherers, as distinct from shepherds and grain growers, had little need for arithmetic. Furthermore, what was in the language did not limit what was in the mind. A footnote said: 'The Australian natives, who rank intellectually as thorough primitives, possess a mathematical instinct (or what comes to the same thing, a power of thinking in numbers which is not yet communicable by signs or words) that as regards the interpretation of pure space is far superior to that of the Greeks.' The author of that note was Otto Spengler, the German, par excellence, who had much to say about the decline and fall of civilisations.

What *was* 'primitive,' however, was the material culture of Aborigines. Few could deny that. Aboriginal languages were not subhuman, but their poverty could appear so. Yet their rudimentary means were most adaptive to their harsh circumstances, just as their language, which, even though it had developed in geographical isolation when compared to Indo-European tongues, had 'the elasticity and adaptive power' (the terms were Jespersen's) inherent in 'primitive' languages.

With the Aborigine there was even a 'separate language for use in his sacred chants, and this language is of an elaboration which is difficult to describe except by extensive quotation':

> It is a sign of the good intelligence of the average native that he is able to speak his intricate language without faltering and without grammatical mistakes, whereas in our own white society only a relatively small section of the population achieves any real measure of fluency, correctness and assurance, when discussing philosophical, religious, or literary themes in the mother tongue. The average native's superior command over his language is undoubtedly due to the absence of written records in his society. Every aboriginal tribesman had to learn by heart large portions of the tribal myths and totemic chants in order to ensure their accurate transmission to succeeding generations. In so doing he acquires a power of speech we cannot but admire.[56]

Here speaks the scholar and the meritocratic, German mission boy: he was saying, in effect, that the Aranda spoke their language better than most of the white men around them spoke their English. And he was also saying, as he stood before his gathering of colleagues at the Science Conference in Perth, that there was only one way for authors to study the culture of such people. That was through having 'a *thorough* [Strehlow's emphasis] knowledge of any of the languages spoken by their native informants.' That was essential if serious mistakes in translation were to be avoided, if anthropological fieldwork data were to be of 'unimpeachable accuracy.'

'I am the one,' Strehlow was telling his colleagues, 'I am, perhaps, the only one.' For who else had the Aboriginal language as the mother tongue? The tone, even today, is somewhat insufferable, despite the speaker having good reason to be pleased with his own work to date: the printing of his excellent thesis in *Oceania* in 1942–44, and, in the year of his ANZAAS talk, the publication of his first book, *Aranda Traditions*. Strehlow is 39 and well entitled, at one level, to give advice to his profession, if only, some would have understandably felt, it could be done without such intense subtraction from the work of others. But there he was casting himself against many colleagues, taking a stance that would in years to come entrench him in claims for purity and ownership.

The force of his injection of his solitary self is even more obvious because the anthropologist must grasp 'the spiritual and psychological significance' of the sacred performances; the thoroughly grounded linguist needed to *penetrate* the chants. 'If the ceremony seeks to increase the totem animal or plant, the native would regard the mere symbolism of the action as inadequate to produce the desired result unless accompanied by the intonation of the appropriate chant verses. In other words, a ceremony is useless and magically inoperative unless validated by the spoken or chanted word; it is this which gives it either a sacred or magical character. It is the word which quickens dead symbolism into life.'[57]

There is urgency here (not to mention a Christian gloss on the primacy of the Word). It echoes Jespersen on the origins of language, and sings of all that poetry might absolutely be: words that quicken a ritual, words that dance in their own right on the sacred ground of song. Strehlow's note is absolutely reminiscent of the last words of his *Grammar*: he is upholding the exclamatory, performative power of Aranda, its unity with being.

And—his 1947 paper seems to have no end, because there is no end with regard to the Romantic unities of this theme—all this has little to do with science, Strehlow says, to the scientists. No. Not even that science meant to penetrate 'ever more deeply into the hidden recesses of the human sub-conscious mind.' He was glancing across at his old flame, the one he had never really taken up—psychoanalysis. No, not that. The right direction was one that approaches, via 'the key of language,' through the 'quickening, elevating power of the spoken word' of living men and women, who were part of 'the one, large, indivisible family.' And here—it is Strehlow's final point, which he makes by reference to Malinowski—what is required is not more science, but a 'fuller measure of artistic and intuitive talent . . . Here the anthropologist may have to cease to be a mere analytic man of science. He may have to become almost an artist.'

In his 1938 thesis Strehlow had been happy to sound like a man of science, keeping his romanticisms off stage. Now he is espousing a sympathetic entry into the sacred activities of a tribal tongue. Hamlet fades, Caliban is invoked.

---

1   Robert Frost, whose exact phrasing I cannot find even in the Library of America edition any more than could Douglas Hoffstadter, who has seen it quoted in print in the following manner: 'Poetry is what disappears in translation.' Douglas R. Hofstadter, *Le Ton Beau de Marot* (New York: Basic Books, 1997), 138.

2 Eric Jacobson, 'On Linguistic Aspects of Translation,' in *Theories of Translation*, ed. Rainer Schulte and John Biguenet (Chicago; University of Chicago Press, 1992), 152.

3 Ezra Pound's technical term was *Logopoeia*, which he thought the least translatable aspect of poetry, after the unique music of the original, the *Melopoeia*, and the images, *Phanopoeia*, which was the only aspect that could be fully translated.

4 José Ortega Y Gasset, 'The Misery and Splendor of Translation,' in Schulte and Biguenet, *Theories of Translation*, 93–111.

5 *Princeton Encyclopedia of Poetry and Poetics*, ed. Alex Preminger (Princeton, N.J.: Princeton University Press, 1974. Kenner's is an ironical assertion, considering he was the most reverent disciple of Pound, who so seminally described poetry in terms of its untranslatability.

6 Walter Benjamin, 'The Task of the Translator,' in *Illuminations* (New York: Schocken, 1969), 72.

7 Extracts from Herder's 'Fragmente' (1766–67), in Andre Lefevere, *Translating Literature: A German Tradition: From Luther to Rosenzweig* (Assen/Amsterdam: Van Gorcum, 1977), 32.

8 Johann Wolfgang van Goethe, 'West–East Divan' (1819), in Lefevere, *Translating Literature*, 35.

9 Ludwig Wittgenstein, *Philosophical Investigations* (Oxford: Blackwell, 1953).

10 Octavio Paz, 'Translation: Literature and Letters,' in Schulte and Biguenet, *Theories of Translation*, 152ff.

11 Martin Buber and Franz Rosenzweig, *Scripture and Translation* (Bloomington: Indiana University Press, 1994), passim.

12 John Searle, *Mind, Language and Society* (London: Weidenfeld & Nicolson, 1999), 139–45. For Bakhtin's 'speech energy' see Douglas Robinson, *The Translator's Turn* (Baltimore: The Johns Hopkins University Press, 1991), 279, n15.

13 Jacques Derrida, from 'Tours de Babel,' in Schulte and Biguenet, *Theories of Translation*, 228–30.

14 Umberto Eco, *The Search for the Perfect Language* (Oxford: Blackwell, 1997); George Steiner, *After Babel* (Oxford: Oxford University Press, 1975).

15 Lefevere, *Translating Literature*, 30; Benjamin, 82; Buber and Rosenzweig 20–21.

16 T.G.H. Strehlow. 'Anthropology and the Study of Languages,' in *Report of 26th Meeting of ANZAAS*, Perth, 1947, 167–78.

17 Robinson, *Translator's Turn*, 3–63.

18 Strehlow, 'Anthropology and the Study of Languages,' 28, 13–14, 29, 25, 8.

19 T.G.H. Strehlow, *Aranda Phonetics and Grammar* Oceania Monograph 7 (Sydney: University of Sydney, 1944), 56.

20 C.R. Jury, *The Sun in Servitude and other Plays* (Melbourne: F.W. Cheshire, 1961).

21 Brian Elliott, *The Jindyworobaks* (St Lucia: University of Queensland Press, 1979), xxii–xxiii.

22 Rex Ingamells, 1935, *Gumtops* (Adelaide: F.W. Preece & Sons, 1935), 3.

23 Ibid., 5.

24 Ibid., 22.

25 Ibid., 17–18.

26 Strehlow to Ingamells, September 1935.

27 After 'Metaphrase,' the word-for-word translation that invited pedantry, Dryden warned against 'Imitation' because it fostered 'libertine' ways and did the 'greatest wrong to the Memory and Reputation of the Dead.' Dryden favoured a middle way he called Paraphrase, or 'Translation with Latitude, where the Author is kept in view by the Translator, so as never to be lost.' Dryden's remarks on paraphrase have become the benchmark in terms of keeping faith

with the original, a task that requires a genius and is a test of character:

'No man is capable of Translating Poetry, who besides a Genius to that Art, is not a Master both of his Authour's Language, and of his own: Nor must we understand the Language only of the Poet, but his particular turn of Thoughts, and of Expression, which are the Characters that distinguish, and as it were individuate him from all other writers. When we are come thus far, 'tis time to look into our selves, to conform our Genius to his, to give his thought either the same turn if our tongue will bear it, or if not, to vary but the dress, not to alter or destroy the substance. The like Care must be taken of the more outward Ornaments, the Words: when they appear (which is but seldom) literally graceful, it were an injury to the Authour that they should be chang'd: But since every Language is so full of its own proprieties, that what is Beautiful in one, is often Barbarous, nay sometimes Nonsence in another, it would be unreasonable to limit a Translator to the narrow compass of his Authour's words: 'tis enough if he choose out some Expression which does not vitiate the Sense . . . for thought, if it be Translated truly, cannot be lost in another Language, but the words that convey it to our apprehension . . . . may be so ill chosen as to make it appear in an unhandsome dress, and rob it of its native Lustre. There is therefore a Liberty to be allow'd for the Expression, neither is it necessary that Words and Lines should be confin'd to the measure of their Original. The sense of an Authour, generally speaking, is to be Sacred and inviolable.' John Dryden, Preface to Ovid's Epistles, *The Works of John Dryden*, vol. 1 (Berkeley and Los Angeles: University of California Press, 1961), 118.

28 Matthew Arnold, 'On Translating Homer,' in *Poetry and Prose* (London: Rupert Hart-Davis, 1954), 315.

29 Ezra Pound, 'Cavalcanti,' in *Literary Essays* (London: Faber, 1931), 168–69.

30 Steiner, *After Babel*, 292–93.

31 Strehlow, *Aranda Phonetics and Grammar*, 23.

32 Ibid., 46.

33 In *Aranda Phonetics* Elkin took pains to list the other studies of the time, notably those promoted by the Australian National Research Council. None of these studies made the case for the native language in the way that Strehlow did.

34 Most noticeably in the remarks by Stirling, who wrote more about 'sign language' than the language of social life and the songs. *Report on the Work of the Horn Scientific Expedition* . . . ed. Baldwin Spencer (Melbourne: Melville, Mullen and Slade, 1896), part 4, 37–39, 111–23.

35 The issue does not sit very clearly today, especially with regard to abstract concepts. R. W. Dixon, in his authoritative *The Languages of Australia* (Cambridge: Cambridge University Press, 1980), 4–5, rejects the usefulness of 'primitive' altogether: 'Every known language has about the same degree of complexity and richness as every other,' which seems to ignore the substantial differences in grammatical complexity between, say, Nunggubuyu and Anindilyakwa in Northern Australia compared to the Western Desert languages. Dixon goes on to deny 'that Aboriginal Australians lack the facility for general or abstract thought' and refers his reader to his chapter on songs which, however, does not really canvass that issue beyond the more specific linguistic matter: the role, or relative absence, of abstract nouns.

36 T. G. H. Strehlow, *Aranda Traditions* (Melbourne: Melbourne University Press, 1947), 61.

37 Ibid., 62.

38 Ibid.

39 Ibid., 63.

40 Strehlow, *Aranda Phonetics and Grammar*, 107.
41 Ibid., 196.
42 Ibid., 108–9.
43 Kempe had published his 'A Grammar Vocabulary of the Language of the Aborigines of the MacDonnell Ranges' in *Transactions of the Royal Society of South Australia* 14 (1888), which was hardly out of Strehlow's reach when he was in Adelaide.
44 Notably, W. Planert, 'Australische Frschungen. I, Aranda–Grammatik,' *Zeitschrift fur Ethnologie*, XXXIX, 557; and Teichelmann and Schuermann, 'Outlines of Grammar, Vocabulary and Phraseology of the Aborigines of South Australia'; H. Basedow, 'Vergleichende Vokabularein der Aluridja-und Arundta-Dielecte Zentral Australiens,' *Zeitscrift fur Ethnologie*, XL, 210.
45 That is, assisted in various ways by the Australian National Research Council. When he published Strehlow Elkin included references to others: viz. the Rev. J.R.B. Love, Ernest Worms, Dr Nekes, and Mr R.M. Trudinaer in Oceania Monograph No. 3 (1937), *Studies in Australian Linguistics*, and in 'Grammar of the Pitjantjara Dialect, Central Australia,' *Oceania*, XIII, no. 3, 205–23; also by Dr Capell's fieldwork and publications 'The Classification of Languages in North and North-West Australia,' *Oceania*, X, no. 3, 241–72, and no. 4, 404–33; 'Notes on the Wunambal Language,' *Oceania* XI, no. 3, 295–308, and XII, no. 4, 364–92; and 'Languages of Arnhem Land, North Australia,' *Oceania* XIII, no. 1, 24–50. I said 'arid' because none of the above went beyond technical accounts of limited aspects of the language, and only one—Worms on onomatopoeia—touches on the poetic.
46 Otto Jespersen, *Language: Its Nature, Development and Origin* (London: Allen & Unwin, 1921).
47 For an expansive account of the long romantic tradition concerned with speaking and being, see Thomas de Zengotita, 1989, 'Speakers of Being: Romantic Refusion and Cultural Anthropology,' in George Stocking, *Romantic Motives: Essays on the Anthropological Sensibility*, History of Anthropology, vol. 6 (Madison: University of Wisconsin Press, 1989), 75–123.
48 The set against speculation about ancient origins was sharply expressed by Fitzherbert in 1931 in a draft letter to his MA student, the Rev. J.R.B. Love, who was working on a grammar of Worrora. Love had expressed pleasure in 'reducing the language to order,' only to be told: 'There is no reason why the Worrora language should be any nearer to the primitive speech of earliest man than is English. Each represents the same number of years of development from the speech of the Garden of Eden or the Tower of Babel, or whatever you wish to make your starting point.' Fitzherbert Papers, Special Collection, Barr Smith Library, MS 0030.
49 Elkin noticed this when he wrote: 'the language being a part of that life, is sacred . . . not just . . . a tool, but is itself filled with "virtue."' A.P. Elkin, 'The Nature of Australian Languages,' *Oceania* VIII, no. 3 (1937): 169.
50 Jespersen, *Language*, 431, 432. The language of the first men, he said, was not like 'the tongues of geometers' but like the 'tongues of poets': Zengotita, 'Speakers of Being,' 82, citing Rousseau's essay, 'The Origin of Language.'
51 Jespersen, *Language*, 431, 432, 433.
52 I am glossing in the extreme Zengotita's own encompassing of Herder, especially Herder's essay on 'The Origin of Language' (1769). Zengotita, 'Speakers of Being,' 88–93.
53 Strehlow, *Aranda Phonetics and Grammar*, 26.
54 Strehlow, *Aranda Traditions*, xviii–xix.
55 *Oceania*, VI, no. 3 (1936).
56 Strehlow, *Aranda Traditions*, 24–25.
57 Ibid., 8.

2   Day Work for Caliban

National Stakes
Elkin's Boot

THE MANUSCRIPT OF *Songs* evolved from 1945 to 1953, a time for Strehlow that consolidated his sense of being as an Australian, and an Australian whose fate it had been to acquire Aboriginal possessions. The initial shaping of the text, and his sense of its value, was embedded in a complex of personal feelings about his sense of the old world and the new, as well as his manly desires as a wayward, middle-aged husband. It is bound up, too, with his sense of himself as a scholar, a unique student, not only of the music and the words of the Aranda, but also of native ceremony which he was recording on film and with sound recordings, an enterprise that placed him on the cutting edge of ethnology. All these things pressed in on the writing, making the book acutely the product of its time, even as it was becoming a kind of scripture for all time, and even though another two decades would elapse before it appeared in print.

The publication of *Aranda Traditions* by Melbourne University Press in 1947 formalised his position on the map. It too was slow to arrive. Elkin would have published it before the war in *Oceania* because he though it 'of a very good standard,' but he did not because 'Strehlow preferred to wait until certain old natives had died.'[1] The publisher had been a little shy of some aspects of the book, however. They noticed Strehlow had changed 'The All-Father' (in Aranda mythology) to 'The Great Father,' and expressed anxiety about the connotations that had provoked 'rather violent controversies as to whether such a conception really exists in the mind of the native.'[2] Strehlow reassured them that that was why he had made the change in the first place: 'too many readers would have regarded "All-Father" as a synonym for "God."'[3]

The other early worry was Strehlow's lack of acknowledgment of other scholars. 'It might therefore be advisable to add occasional annotation to make it quite clear where the view of previous investigators such as Baldwin Spencer are confirmed, where they are modified and where they are rejected.'[4] Strehlow, who was still in the army at the time, did not disagree. But he defended his omission by saying that he had 'studiously avoided other than passing references to Spencer and Gillen and other anthropologists,' having decided to do so at a later date. Besides, he had no books to hand in his army camp, and, as he said later on, it was a book based on papers written 'from a fullness of fresh knowledge' and he wanted it to be published as it stood as a 'curtain raiser' to the major work he would one day do on the 'thousands' of songs he had collected.[5]

Publisher and author saw the book through the press after a gruelling three years. The spelling of the Aranda names with Strehlow's diacritics were a publisher's nightmare. Galleys arrived at Duntroon only to show that some of Strehlow's inserts had not been included. And when the book was printed there was a major typographical error on the kinship table, a fact pointed out to Strehlow by the anthropologist Raymond Firth, and which prompted Strehlow to write a very embarrassed letter apologising for his careless proofreading, an error that he shared with the publisher. By the time the book was in the hands of reviewers Strehlow was out of the army and looking forward to some plain sailing in his academic career. Alas.

The first scholarly review was Elkin's, writing as he so often did in his own journal, *Oceania*, and setting the climate for discussion of the latest, potentially important book in anthropology. That was not surprising, considering Elkin's early patronage of Strehlow's fieldwork and his praise of the manuscript three years earlier; but the damningly faint praise was. 'An interesting book,' Elkin began, 'but somewhat difficult to read, both because of the arguments and of the constant use of native words.'

Elkin acknowledged Strehlow's linguistic work, and in the same breath made a heavy point about Strehlow's backing by the Australian National Research Council, of which Elkin was chair. He said, with deceptive respect, that it was the work of a 'literary scholar' but went on to say: 'Those conversant with the anthropological research carried out amongst the Aranda and adjacent tribes during the past fifty or more years will find little in the book that is new in principle with regard either to the meaning or to the social aspects of the myths or other sacred possession. But it does not detract from its value, for Mr Strehlow's presentation is based on a linguistic liaison with his informants, which no other workers in the region possessed.'

Elkin lists the other researchers—Carl Strehlow, Spencer and Gillen, Olive Pink, Geza Roheim and H.K. Fry as well as himself—and laments again: 'Mr Strehlow seldom relates his findings to those of other workers.' And then the jab: 'I have come from a careful study of Mr Strehlow's book with an added respect for Spencer and Gillen's *Native Tribes of Central Australia*,' which is followed by a kind of pat: 'Of course, Spencer could not give the poetry of the chants, nor the vividness of their expression. But this is just what Mr Strehlow can do. In the course of his analysis of the mythological themes, he gives some translations of parts of the myths. These are beautifully rendered.' Then the full attack.

Elkin listed at least five weaknesses in the book's 'social anthropology' because it was 'fundamentally literary' on the 'scientific side.' Several pertain to Strehlow's terminology. Others pinpointed his argument by allusion: 'because of a similarity in a couple of mythological traits, some cultural or racial relationship between the Aborigines and the Norse is suggested, but no real grounds for this inference is given. The use of the terms "sire" and "totemic hero" suggests a Freudian interpretation of totemism, but it is not examined.' And so on, with the list becoming more technical, and more designed to tell Strehlow that he should have paid more attention to the work of his colleagues, to 'the scientific side.'

Up until this point Elkin seems to be respecting what he calls Strehlow's special 'linguistic liaison' with the Aranda. But not really, not in the end. The attack finally comes home in terms of Strehlow's careless writing, including his thinking that the Aranda culture was doomed. 'Incidentally,' Elkin writes, when he is clearly not being incidental at all, some of the poetic-prose in the text could be pruned to advantage. 'Red-flaming fires' (p. 94) and 'red-flaming torches' (p. 79), 'red coals' (p. 106) and 'glimmering coals glow dimly, casting a reddish half-light,' become tiring, are unnecessary, and probably not exact. Grey streaks of dawn become boring when repeated. Moreover, the search for such expressions leads to inconsistency. Thus, 'The confusion . . . endures for many hours, and night moves on rapidly.' And in the urge of writing, inconsistency of interpretation appears. In the first chapter, pp. 6 and 35, the tyranny of tradition and of the old men 'stifles all creative impulse' and even prevents the improvement of weapons. Indeed, Mr Strehlow speaks of the 'utter apathy and the general mental stagnation' of the natives, who are a 'decadent race,' although the myths reflect a 'more primitive order of society' than that of the Aranda of 1930. But on p.160, he says, 'the sacred traditions are not the hastily invented productions of primitive savages, but the amazing heritage of an age-old native culture of no mean order.' Moreover, Spencer and Gillen pointed out how customs change through the councils of the old men, and indeed were changing in the 1890s. Nor were the Aranda slow to use the superior materials brought in by the white man.[6]

Strehlow's deflation can only be imagined. He seems to have said nothing about this review in his diary. All a man could do in his position was trust that the book would be well received elsewhere, in places, perhaps, where the literary approach, and the specialness of his own 'linguistic liaisons,' were better appreciated. He could only press on.

Utopian Sharing
In 1948 Strehlow made a fertile connection with the fledgling Australian National University (ANU), the institution that aspired to be the country's permanent research centre in many schools of thought, including anthropology and linguistics. He had applied for a two-year Research Fellowship in Social Science in order to complete the manuscript that would become *Songs of Central Australia*. In November 1948 he told the selection committee he had written two of its four parts: Part I on 'Rhythms and Musical Structure,' and Part II, 'Language and Structure of the Chants.' He wanted to finish Part III, 'The Themes Treated in the Native Chants,' and Part IV, which would deal 'with the various conclusions drawn from a comparison of the material given in the first three parts with "primitive" verse in other

parts of the world.' To do all of this fully, he claimed, he needed to go back to Central Australia. He wanted to fill in some gaps in his knowledge. He wanted to record and film some of the old chants and ceremonies that he had only in note form. 'Many of the ceremonies that are described could be appreciated properly only if modern colour film movies were made of them . . . the full implications of many recorded facts were not realised by me twelve years ago.' Furthermore, 'there are old informants in the areas traversed earlier who can supply an amazing amount of good information for filling in some of the gaps.' After this consolidation work in the Centre he wished to spend a year in England, preferably at the University of London, to discuss his work with linguists and cultural and social anthropologists. Here he had the support of the linguist J.R. Firth of the University of London.[7]

Strehlow was successful on both counts. Altogether, the ANU would outlay about £3,600 on his ventures, full of confidence that they were supporting research that was unique and well informed and in the national interest. Strehlow would go back to the Centre in 1949 and 1950, and in 1951 he would be in London and Europe trying to make a name for himself as linguist and anthropologist. In the process, however, the seed would be sown for his first major dispute with authorities about the issue that would plague his life. Who was to own what he collected?

In the beginning of Strehlow's dealings with the ANU it looked simple. The terms of the fellowship were 'on the understanding that the equipment provided, including exposed films, will remain the property of the University.' In 1949 Strehlow showed no sign of disagreement. On the contrary, the ANU had reason to think that the researcher had a vision of sharing a great deal with them. In two long letters written in February 1950 Strehlow had a rather grand plan, providing the ANU shared his sense of the national interest. He told the registrar:

> As you know, I have a very large collection of manuscripts, sacred native objects, photos, negatives and various documents relating to the early history of the missions and native reserves in Central Australia in my private possession. This material is at present scattered about in various places, such as my room at the Adelaide University, in the vaults of the Adelaide Museum, in boxes stored in my home, and elsewhere. I have found it impossible to keep this in any semblance of order: permanent secretarial assistance of a special type would be required to sort this

material out under my supervision, to get it typed out, and to get the native records into shape where they could be readily translated. All the myths and chants, and most of the notes to the sacred objects, are in the form in which I obtained them, i.e. they have been written down in the various Aranda and Loritja dialects. Since I know these dialects— including the ceremonial languages—thoroughly, only the minimum of English explanations has been inserted, and most of my records would be therefore unintelligible to anyone else but myself. Even the younger natives in the mission stations and reserves of Central Australia (Hermannsburg, Haasts Bluff, Areyonga, and Jay Creek) would find difficulty in understanding the language of these traditions, since they are no longer being instructed in this traditional lore by their tribal elders.[8]

Strehlow's conditions for sharing his already considerable collection were extensive. He was asking for a full-time assistant to help him order his collection, as well as to complete the diacritics on the native texts. He envisaged that he and the assistant would compile 'the first complete native dictionary ever made of any Australian language.' Thereafter, the texts would be typed out, along with 'several copies to ensure their preservation.' He went on: 'With the texts put into proper shape, and after the compilation of a complete dictionary, the future translation of my collected texts would be assured even if I could not complete this task personally. The necessary apparatus would then have been created for other scholars, if necessary, to carry on this task. They would be enabled to check my own translations for accuracy.'[9]

Furthermore, the university might consider a permanent research station in Central Australia—a place where anthropological research workers would have their headquarters, the better to make the most of 'the old men ready to part with even their last tribal secrets to trusted outsiders who have learnt to speak their languages.' Other research workers—in botany, zoology and geology—could use the centre, all of them working with 'the aid of the Australian natives whose bush lore and knowledge of the Australian fauna and flora is, of course, unrivalled.'

The grand plan was remarkably collaborative for a man like Strehlow—a bid for a sociable research life based on a good deal of sharing, and one directed at students in the field as distinct from collectors. It is hard to imagine him sharing fieldwork in ways suggested by the plan. But still, looking back, we can see that a national university with its wits about it should have seized this offer with both hands. The registrar was indeed interested. He said as much to Professor Raymond Firth in London, and went on to say that the National Library had expressed interest in the preservation of Strehlow's material. But it was early days for the ANU. Funds were short, and as W.H. Stanner remarked five years later, when the row over ownership fully erupted, policy in such matters had been made ad hoc.[10] More to the point, perhaps, the ANU's anthropological focus was directed more towards Pacific studies than Central Australia. The ANU continued to support Strehlow, but not to the remarkable extent of fulfilling the dream of something called a permanent research station. And in any case, had not Strehlow just come back from the Centre, where, to all intents and purposes, he had done much good work as the solitary, self-sufficient individual he was? He had indeed.

Natural Goodness, Living Spirits

Strehlow was in Central Australia benefiting from his first year of the ANU fellowship between July 1949 and 14 February 1950. He went back in March 1950 and returned in June in order to leave for London in July. Both trips to the Centre were invaluable, as he was, in a limited way, to report to Canberra. But they were not without their difficulties. Indeed, anyone following his tracks is bound to be left with the impression that he was compelled to collect frustrations as much as he was collecting *tjurunga*, and that the further he went on his journey the more culturally complex his situation became, demanding more of a man's peace of mind, if he had it, to cope with reality.

There was the basic matter of transport in the Centre. The ANU had found him a rather special vehicle—a second-hand Ford motor ambulance, no less. The plan was to get it across from Canberra to Adelaide so he could set off about March. The coal strike, which had thrown the Australian labour movement into its own native turmoil, disrupted that plan. Then, when the ambulance reached Adelaide, it proved to be in such ill-repair that Strehlow had to attend to it. As he wrote to his patron:

> I have just spent several days hunting around in Adelaide at the various motor firms for the fan belts, motor tubes, etc. mentioned in your last letter; I have also taken the ambulance for a trial run, and cleaned it up and checked over the tools etc. in its cupboards.
>
> So far I have been unable to procure any spare fan belts; but several

city firms advised me to try at the country garages on my way to
Quorn, as some of these might have in stock the size that I require . . .
The ambulance possessed no tyre pump or gauge, no patches or vul-
canising outfit, and no grease gun; also its rear vision mirror is ineffective and broken. I would, therefore, recommend that the following
items be purchased from the firms from whom I was able to get the following quotes.[11]

A list followed. Strehlow's habit of listing the detail of all matters that
frustrated him is compulsive. He seems to be saying over and over again
that the world, including the material world and intractable things like
motor cars, is against him. Some puritans in these circumstances would
pray to Providence. Not Strehlow. To add to his misery he proudly does
not express any trust in chance. He grits his teeth, mutters and moans,
and then stoically perseveres until he gets his way or matters improve of
their own accord, or almost. Anyway, by August he was able to drive the
ambulance, loaded with camping and recording gear, from Adelaide to
Quorn, where it was put on the train to Alice Springs. Strehlow arrived
there on 27 August.

His hope then was to set to with the filming work. But no. The Bell
and Howell camera did not arrive from the ANU until the end of
November; the filming of ceremonies had to wait until he returned in
the middle of the following year. He decided to concentrate on his
written records of chants and myths, and to set to work with sound
recordings, putting to use the ANU's Pyros wire recorder. With this in
mind he set off to Hermannsburg, where, as he was to proudly report
to the university, he located 'the last old man from the Western Aranda
group, who had still received the full training in the ritual and traditions of the district. He was a man aged approximately 78 years and was
gifted with an excellent memory.'

The old man had been one of Pastor Carl's informants. By the time
he was through he had given Strehlow ten hours of playing time and
500 pages of native text—'if,' Strehlow dourly told the university, 'all of
it was ever translated.' Of the 'Honey-Ant Song' the old man could rec-
ollect 88 couplets—an offering which delighted Strehlow, if only
because his father, who collected the song from the Ellery Creek area
in 1900, had not obtained so many. Strehlow explained his good
fortune to the university:

Fifty years ago the honey ant totemic clan of Ellery Creek was still intact; and no single member of his class would have dared divulge more than a few verses of the secret honey ant song to an outsider without the consent of his fellows. Even if all members of the clan had been assembled, there would still have been a number of special secret couplets that could not have been divulged to any but the clan heads without committing sacrilege. My informant, however, being the last old man who knew the complete chant, could do with it what he liked. He could take all his knowledge with him into oblivion or he could divulge it to a trusted and interested outsider to preserve it for posterity. In this way I was able to obtain not only a full version of the honey ant song, but also of various healing charms and other verses which are normally known only to the medicine men: my informant had originally been destined to become of the latter. [12]

So trusting was the old man that he even revealed his real name to Strehlow. It was masked in one of the sacred chants about the two carpet snake ancestors. A couple of weeks after writing the song down, Strehlow realised that he had not noticed any verse containing the man's real name. He pointed this out, and the old man smiled. As it had been his property, he had withheld it; normally he would have only given it to some trusted man who was keen to possess it after his death. But since the Western Aranda had been Christianised, and none of the younger men were interested in sacred verses, and because he was pleased that Strehlow 'correctly guessed that he possessed a special secret,' he chanted his verse. He said: 'Now you know my real name is Rauwiraka: remember it when I am no more.'

Strehlow withheld the name from the ANU at the time. But when *Songs* was published in 1971, Rauwiraka (and other key informants) had died and the name is spelt out. In *Songs*, where he tells the Rauwiraka story, he reflects on the pride of the young men when they were shown their personal *tjurunga*—the object that was their name, in effect. It was that name that must have given them an emotional satisfaction much deeper than any of their new Christian names, Strehlow thought, especially when they were prompted by the verse in Revelation: 'To him who conquers I will give some of the hidden manna, and I will give him a white stone, with a new name written on the stone which no one knows except him who receives it.'[13]

Rauwiraka pointed Strehlow towards a great deal of manna. The old man's resonance as an informant is clear from the many passages in which he is mentioned in *Songs*. Not only could Rauwiraka recount the numerous love charms, spells and rain-making charms, demonstrate the relationship between chant and music, and expound upon the grim tradition of avenger battles, he was a most instructive guide to more interpretative matters of Aboriginal religious belief. Strehlow had more thoughts about the 'other self' or the 'spirit-double,' the notion that every man had two souls, one of which was mortal, one not. The latter was the soul that derived in part from the totemic ancestor—in part because the totemic ancestor was still present at all times in the rock, or tree, or *tjurunga* of the special site. The mortal soul (his *garuna*) was the one that left his sleeping body at night when he was dreaming, and which he might be aware of during the day, as his spirit double. Before speaking with Rauwiraka, Strehlow thought that after death the *garuna* died: if not after a period of lingering about the grave, then eventually by lightning. After Rauwiraka, Strehlow was prepared to think that there was no such death: the soul returned to the *tjurunga* object. A man returned to the thing from which it had originally issued in order to become reincarnated.[14]

Strehlow often spoke with Rauwiraka in the company of two other old men, Utnadata and Namatjira (father of Albert). From one long, discursive conversation, during which he let the men expound in their natural way, Strehlow was given more to reflect on about life everlasting. Human creatures, like their ancestors, did die; and when they did their souls returned to the earth from which they had originally been born. They were earth-born and earth-bound. But there were also the sky creatures, who lived eternally and untroubled in the realm of the Milky Way. The principal being in the sky was the Giant Emu being, which was male, and had a female companion in the form of a dingo, subservient to it. Utnadata captured the quality of Ilinka's life when he said: 'Eternally he lives, he lives above, he lives in the green land, with a great store of fresh fish and green plants. Most certainly he lives above in a land that is always green.'

Strehlow wanted to stress an absolute gulf between the eternal divine sky dwellers and the earthbound. One possessed eternal life: the others knew death, a death that was final. Its finality was the thing. All such concepts were to be found in pagan religions elsewhere, Strehlow argued, but probably nowhere outside Australia was there such an absolute barrier between the two realms. Admittedly, Strehlow hastened to add, as if he sensed a rashly sweeping remark, there were differences of belief even in Central Australia. Gurra, for example, who is referred to as 'my Northern Aranda informant,' had hardly heard of the sky creatures spoken of by Rauwiraka and the others who spoke of Western Aranda traditions. And there were, in different parts of the country, myth stories of a vital link, the promising link that once existed between earth and sky in a time before death had its victory. To the south-east, near the Simpson Desert, there was once a great casuarina tree. And on the Lower Finke near Horseshoe Bend there was, as we have seen, the story of the Ntjikantja brothers, who had once been able to use their spear to climb into the sky. But not around Hermannsburg. Indeed, in conclusion Strehlow sums up as if Hermannsburg was the centre of Aranda religion. The sky creatures were remote and irrelevant to earthly concerns: the death-born and earth-bound creatures knew a death that was everlasting, and from which there was no consolation. 'Hence the sight of the starlit Central Australian sky brought no consolations of immortality to the dark folk who gazed at the full glory of its brilliant magnificence. For mortal men no bridge remained that might have linked the earth with the sky.'[15]

Strehlow was sitting down with Rauwiraka, Utnadata and Namatjira just before Christmas 1949. The paradox—of so valuing their proud paganism at such a moment in the history of a mission—seems to have struck him. For these old men were like those who had resisted the first Christian attempts to disparage and displace their beliefs. The simple fact was, as Strehlow pointed out, that they believed in natural goodness. From that came a proud dignity. No better expression of this could have been made than that of Moses the year before when, without the mediation of a white man, he dictated what he had to say to a young Aranda man:

> The preachers preached sermons year after year; but they would not believe . . . You are utter heathens, said the preachers to them, 'you are utterly ignorant and can perceive nothing.' The old men asked, 'What are heathens?' The preachers replied to them—'*You* are heathens.' 'We are not heathens; we are iliara men and not heathens—we are men who have been initiated at injura festivals; we have followed in the footsteps of Kulurba . . .'
>
> The preachers said—'Malbunka is not God: this is where you are telling great lies. You heathen folk have wrong beliefs, your thoughts are

utterly senseless and wrong. The true God is in the sky' . . . Then the old men replied—'We are good and morally blameless people. We cannot imagine what your God is like. We are upright, we are altogether different and better—we children of the tjibulkara (brightness). When we gaze upon the tjilpa (totemic ancestor) on his own ground, then this is altogether virtuous.'[16]

'Natural goodness' is the term Strehlow used in *Songs*, and one which managed simultaneously to echo his earlier references to the Classicists' Golden Age and, perhaps, the Garden of Eden. We might also suspect Strehlow of having slipped into a Rousseauistic notion of the Noble Savage but for our knowledge that, in another context, he would have been the first to recount the savagery of their deeds. The point here is that Strehlow wants us to see the contrast between what the old men once had, in the past, and what they now had, on the mission. Once they had their virtuous ceremonies for ancestor creatures 'on their own ground': now they had a God that was in the sky, and whose light was the Word. It is hard to say how much such old men knew about or cared for Christian metaphysics; the extent to which their hearts and minds could encompass two religions at a time. Even Strehlow does not test his understanding with an attempt to answer the question. Suffice to say that he was acutely aware of the riddled coexistence of the two worlds of Hermannsburg. For while he was recording the old songs with a kind of sad triumph, he was also working on the final proofs of his translation of the New Testament.

Only a few months earlier (quite independently of the ANU fellowship) he had been at the mission, worrying further details about the New Testament. There had been discussions with Pastor Albrecht about the literal translation of the verb 'to follow' as in 'the disciples followed Jesus.' An earlier version had 'track' as the equivalent. But that had overtones of an intent to kill. Strehlow substituted a term that meant 'walking in front of' Jesus, a term that indicated total trust. He also found a new word for the Holy Spirit. The previous word, *ltana*, actually meant 'spook' or 'ghost.' *Enkai* was better. It referred to the spirit of the living person.[17]

Between Two Worlds
This was a time at Hermannsburg when much seemed to be a desperate matter of life and death. The historian of the mission calls it a period

of breakdown. Pastor Albrecht's wife, Minna, had had a physical collapse, followed by a mental one. She joined the line of long-suffering, dedicated Christian wives for whom the rigours of the place proved too much. This was yet another very dry season. The poor health of the people was endemic. In 1948 there was a measles epidemic; tuberculosis was rife. Poor diet and hygiene were chronic. The indolence of the men—what Pastor Albrecht called their 'inability to be on their own and work for themselves,' their lack of the 'determination that they had once had in their struggle for existence before white people'—was a daily source of frustration, if not demoralisation. It required a strong faith on the part of a man like Albrecht to live with the modern Aboriginal tendency to accept 'free feeding' each day without doing a day's work. God alone helped with his fear for the 'impossible consequences' for the future. It was true that at last the Commonwealth government was prepared to help with mission education, but how would the schooling actually fit with the cultural needs of these children? A simplistic policy of assimilation ignored the physical reality of where the children were; and the fact that for all the years of Christian endeavour, their parents still lived between two worlds. It was Pastor Albrecht's phrase, 'between two worlds.' Even as Strehlow was sitting down with old Namatjira, Albrecht was expressing a deep worry for the future of the elder's son, Albert, who was 'a wanderer between two worlds.' For the young painter was in 'the dazzling lights of publicity' and the recipient of money, his own cash flow which a mission could make no claim on. 'One would say nothing against it,' Albrecht wrote to the Aborigines' Friends' Association in Adelaide at a time when Albert was showing some interest in copper deposits, 'if he knew how to handle it to his best advantage and for the benefit of others. But the opposite is the case, it becomes more and more a curse to him and to others who associate with him.' Strehlow is not on record about Namatjira at this time.* But in the end he confirmed Albrecht's view of the seeds of tragedy. Young Albert was dead by 1959, arguably a victim of the impossible task the mission had set itself: that of equipping strong men and women to endure and create from their position as earthborn creatures from 'within' both cultures.

---

* Strehlow began a biography of Namatjira at some time in the early 1960s. Only two handwritten chapters exist, one about Namatjira's kinship and the other about the *Altjira*.

Meanwhile the patriarchy of the mission held fast to its nucleus of Christian disciples. Moses was still alive, but the first generation of evangelical preachers was now passing away. Titus, the man who had done so much to consolidate the ration station and now Christian outpost at Haasts Bluff, died in November 1949; five months later another Christian stalwart, Abel, departed, presumably towards his place in the Christian sky. Both men had been mainstays of the congregation since Albrecht had stepped into the shoes of Pastor Carl Strehlow in 1926.

The loss of Titus made an impression on Strehlow. 'The first man to stick to his gospel work,' he reflected, the man who had stuck it out at Haasts Bluff in the hardest times before it became a government native reserve. For the future, then, much depended on the training of the next generation of preachers. Albrecht kept up his hopes for them, for the training courses in which they enrolled. Men like Conrad were promising. And Nathaniel. For such men—for the next generation—Strehlow's New Testament could be most important. For Albrecht had noticed that over the years there had been some success with the inner life of Aboriginal Christians. While, in the old days, there was the resistance that Moses had so eloquently described, how a man might be sometimes judged in 'the light of the Word of God.' And that judgment, Albrecht had found at the congregational meetings, was often facilitated when the meaning of Scripture was clear. Then 'the person in question would give in or promise to make restitution without question.' So when it came to the future in general and the lifestyle and values of Aboriginals at the mission, Albrecht said, 'much of our hope for the future centres around this Book.' Strehlow's book, that is: his New Testament.

During this visit to Hermannsburg Strehlow made a surprising error of judgment. He was keen to show the 1932 film of himself and the others at Mount Liebig. It was the film that had lovely shots of the country and its people, many of them still looking in the prime of their lives, figures of health. His cinema was the large children's dining hall, the one that had just benefited from Albrecht's own labours with wood and cement: it now had a concrete floor, along with a kitchen, pantry and bakehouse. On the night of 2 October a happy mob of men, women and children crowded in.

All was running smoothly until some sacred objects appeared in the corner of the screen. Chaos ensured. In horror, the women in the audience rose as one and rushed into the night, their children with them. The men remaining were anguished, angry, and although the film whirred to a stop, its showing had repercussions for months. Men at the mission expected trouble from the Haasts Bluff men. At issue was a ceremony in which Loritja men would want to make trouble. Later still there was to be a visit by angry Pitjantjatjara men. Off limits from the mission, there was a pitched battle, the details of which were kept from the likes of Pastor Albrecht, but which all the children knew about.[18]

Equally, some of the church congregation were angry at the affront of the film to them. They brooded. Nathaniel approached Albrecht. Nathaniel accused Strehlow of staging *tjurunga* shows, and warned the pastor of the heathen aspects. Nathaniel, now vulnerably Christian, was afraid of Aranda culture, just as his non-Christian contemporaries were afraid of each other. In the middle—evidently saying little to himself that was self-questioning—was Luther's Caliban. But a careless Luther, in that he did not pause to consider his display of pagan objects. And an unceremonial Caliban, in that he had been careless in exposing what was of sacred significance.

Family Dues
Bertha went with him on the 1949 trip, which was to be her last to the Centre. The children—Theo, aged seven, Shirley, five, and John, three—went with them. They travelled up to Alice Springs ahead of him and stayed for about three months in the Albrechts' residence at the mission station. The white children played, as Strehlow had, with the Aboriginal children, and they joined the Aboriginal children queuing outside for bread and treacle at five in the afternoon. Shirley loved picking the peas in the Albrechts' vegetable garden, but she shuddered at the sight of dead crows strung up to frighten off the live ones.

Young Theo, however, was left with another dominant memory. Before leaving Adelaide his father said, 'I hope you come back a bushman.'

All the way up on the train, Theo wondered what his father meant by that. At the mission he made a few attempts to learn the language, but found it difficult; and besides, staying at the Albrechts' where everyone spoke English made it hardly necessary, especially as the Aboriginal children were taught English at school. He had been there two months when his father arrived. 'He said, "How's your Aranda?" And I was just so taken aback, and I said, "Did you want me to learn that?"

And he said, "Of course I did. It just shows you've got no interest in them, and you're not the right sort of person, because otherwise you could have learnt Aranda in three months with no formal training."' 'The feeling was,' Theo recalled years later (by which time he was an accomplished linguist in Thai), 'that my father was a superman and everybody else was just normal. I was certainly no superman.'

The children already had a complicated relationship to the Aboriginal domain of their father's world. Back in Adelaide they had appreciated their contact with an Aboriginal housekeeper they knew as Ivy. The Strehlows had employed Ivy Mitchell to help with the convalescence of Bertha's mentally ill step-mother, as well as with their own children. Before they were of school age it was Ivy who looked after them at mealtimes and bedtimes. They ate with Ivy until the day came when their father thought they were getting quite out of hand and their table manners were 'appalling.' Ivy left the Strehlow children with warm memories, akin, it would appear, to those Strehlow had for Marianna. But they did not know Ivy in terms of her Aboriginality, and she evidently was hurt that Strehlow did not acknowledge it either.* After Ivy, the Adelaide home did not often see Aboriginal people. Nor did it have many signs around the place of their father's intimate links with the people of Central Australia. There were paintings by Namatjira, but certainly no indication of the growing collection of sacred objects, or the vast writings, the recordings and films. Strehlow did not show the films at home. His private, possessive attitude towards his work conveyed itself powerfully to each of the children. He could be bright company at the dinner table, he enjoyed a story and a joke, and there was, Theo remembers, 'a lot of conversation, a lot of things discussed. But never ever Aboriginal material. That was absolutely out. I remember asking him once, "How did they ever know how old somebody was? Because they never had calendars." And he looked at me and said, "What do you want to know that for?" Then he explained that when some flower or tree was in bloom, they would know by that. Then on the other hand we heard they couldn't count the way we did.'

---

*   According to Strehlow's son, John, Ivy Mitchell was brought up in Quorn, having been separated from her Aboriginal parents at an early age and as a result of which Strehlow preferred to think of her as not an Aborigine. When she left the Strehlows' domestic service she worked in the laundry unit of the South Australian Railways and with the Salvation Army. John Strehlow recalls: 'She was one of the first people to get a car . . . She lived quite near us in Prospect until she died.'

Strehlow's tendency was to leave his elder son puzzled, disconcerted, incomplete. There was one thing about himself he impressed clearly on the children: the fact that his own father, the strict Pastor Carl Strehlow, had exercised all the patriarchal authority that had made such a dark imprint on the soul of the young Luther.* Ted Strehlow's children knew about this from their father's own hand, as he liked to tell them, either before, during or after: they knew that their punishment was by no means as harsh as he had received. Strehlow's early distance from his children was, it seems, regularly underlined by strappings of his daughter as well as the boys. For minor misdemeanours they met their father's righteous rage, a rage that insisted, even as they lined up for the strap, on abject verbal apologies, so that they were, in her words, 'punished twice over.' As much as for herself she felt for her brothers, who had to take things in their stride. Her father's rages, Shirley recalls, the outbursts her younger brother calls tantrums, were sufficiently acute for the doctor to issue a warning: they were a danger to his health; they put his heart at risk; unless he learnt to control them he was in danger of collapse.†

Strehlow's heavy-handedness was different in one way from his father's: he did not use religion to justify it. He was a strict father pure and simple; not a doctrinal one. And yet week after week while the children were young he insisted on sending them to Sunday school. When they were older they accompanied their mother to church.

---

* The organic connection between the child-in-the-man and the punitive father is drawn by Luther's most psychological biographer: 'The device of beating children down—by superior force, by contrived logic, or by vicious sweetness—makes it unnecessary for the adult to become adult. He need not develop that true inner superiority which is naturally persuasive. Instead, he is authorised to remain significantly inconsistent and arbitrary, or in other words, childish, while beating into the child the desirability of growing up. The child, forced out of fear to pretend that he is better when seen than when unseen, is left to anticipate the day when he will have the brute power to make others more moral than he ever intends to be himself' (Erikson 1958: 66).

† Grief and the tantrum have an 'anthropological' history. Ruth Benedict began her biographical sketch with: 'The story of my life begins when I was twenty-one months old, at the time my father died' and she tells how she idealised his appearance as Christ-like, all the while 'violently repudiating' the cult of grief made by her mother. On her tantrums produced by this conflict, she wrote: 'I was violent to myself or to anyone else within reach . . . I was guilty enough about that, but it was a guilt towards myself, not a social guilt.' When, after her mother persuaded her to swear on the Bible to stop, she did, and depression supplanted the 'devil' of the tantrum (Benedict 1959: 97, 100, 108).

Strehlow, however, seldom went to church himself in those days, and his laxity did not escape the children, Theo especially, who was well aware of the work his father was doing translating the New Testament. His father did not go to church, Theo judged, because his view was that 'he knew more about what was in the Bible than the Pastor.'

In what terms to speak of patriarchy? This picture is based on conversations with his children and, while they agree in general, they differ in emphasis. Despite his tart anecdotes, Theo is inclined to think that his father was no stricter than many others of that period. Shirley, however, has vivid memories of the tears she shed on behalf of her brothers as they lined up in the bedroom to be thrashed. And John Strehlow is adamant about one aspect of his father in particular: his emotional volatility, his frequent tantrums at home.* The picture is of a broodingly self-centred and remote man whose important work left little time for his children. Once his work was disrupted, or if it was not going well, his father could, like a man persecuted by misfortune, fly completely off the handle. He might take hours to cool down, and in that time everyone near him had to tread delicately and even apologise for something they felt they had not done. It was a household that had to constantly appease the father, a home where the father was at liberty to bemoan melodramatically the burdens that fell on him, and as a result his other attributes—his laughter, his gaiety at table, the extent to which he could shine in conversation with some colleagues and friends (though he seemed not to have many friends)—were dampened somewhat. Still, the home was a happy place when Beethoven and Wagner were on the first-class gramophone. It was happier still when their father played and sang at the piano, and their mother joined in. The sight of Ted and Bertha singing together delighted their guests, as it did the children.†

---

* For cultural theory a key question for Benedict, and for Mead, was: 'how a given temperamental approach to living could become so dominant in a culture?' (Benedict 1959: 206). Benedict's journals, like Strehlow's and Malinowski's, are preoccupied with 'love,' as journals have a wont to be. Her observation, 'If we trusted love it would not obsess us' (148) might be a universal epigraph for Western diarists since Rousseau.

† As to the type of music, memories differ. Shirley mentions German songs; songs from the Hermannsburg Mission Hymn Book and, when Strehlow came back from England and Europe in 1951, songs from the Oxford Hymnal. John Strehlow cannot remember any German songs, but lists the Oxford collection of carols and 'all manner of songs' that were popular at the time (personal communication, April 2001).

But at Hermannsburg in the summer of 1949–50 gaiety and music seem not to have been the order of the day. Strehlow was busy with research: more often than not, while the children played along the riverbed, he was off in Alice Springs or further afield. There were outings with both parents, but then Bertha fell and damaged her leg. For weeks she put up with the injury, and her husband thought her very 'game' to do so. But eventually it meant she would be better off at home than struggling on in the Outback. So Bertha and the children left for Adelaide, leaving him there.

He was alone then, at Hermannsburg, with his project, the manuscript that was still unfolding, which he was adding to all the time, the book that was, in its own patriarchal way, becoming his life.

Death of Informants, Life in Films

Strehlow was no sooner back in Adelaide, by February 1950, than he was obliged to go to Canberra. The ANU wanted to confer with its research fellow, who in turn wanted to talk to various people about his project and the films he was about to make. We have no reason to think he had anything but a warm and civil welcome; there was no sign of the wrangle to come and his work was held in wide respect. But we do know that on this visit to Canberra he chose to show his colleagues one of the early films about the expedition to Mount Liebig. And we know that his mood after this visit to Canberra was not good. He told his diary: 'It's time I gave in and admitted myself beaten. I am now well over 41 years of age. My early enthusiasms have all turned into bitter cynicism. One man cannot change the sentiments of a community in his own life time. It's not opposition that has beaten me, my foe has always been indifference—sheer absolute cold indifference . . . My life should have been different and almost certain a much happier one had I gone in for a trade.'

Clearly his showing of films—what it meant and the satisfactions it provided—was contextual. His misery in Canberra in 1950 is not easy to understand. He was still on the fellowship; in fact he had another year to go, during which he would enhance his reputation in Europe. Perhaps it was increasingly clear that an academic future in Canberra was unlikely, and that the incentive he had put before the university— his grand plan for sharing and curating his collection—was not going to yield any more than the short-term support of the fellowship. All this meant, then, that, despite the support for his fieldwork and the polite interest his Canberra visits generated, his future was still uncertain both in Canberra and, if it came to that, at the University of Adelaide.

In early March 1950, he went back to Alice Springs to finish the work for which he had been funded. He was sad and contemplative. He even thought of working not so much on the songs and myths but the Aranda sense of country and its plants. His spirit was further dampened by the closing of a chapter, long anticipated. Gurra, his earliest informant, one of the key Northern Aranda speakers, died soon after his arrival.

A few years older than Rauwiraka, Gurra was another elder who could remember Spencer and Gillen, and like Rauwiraka he had trusted Strehlow with his secret name; he had exhorted Strehlow to look after the chants and the *tjurunga*. In 1933, it had been Gurra who most eloquently urged Strehlow to sanctify Aboriginal nostalgia for what had been lost. It was Gurra who had, in terms identical to Moses, spoken of how the traditional elders had no sense of sin before the white man came. 'We were morally blameless.'[19] Strehlow had last seen Gurra in September the previous year and felt guilty. He had gone to visit him at the Bungalow, the Aboriginal hostel established by the white authorities to help keep the half-castes and others—the wanderers between two worlds—out of the way of white people in town. Gurra had moved out: he had made his own camp two miles along the Todd. Strehlow felt that he was 'an old and broken man.' He wrote: 'Time had been hard on my friend Gurra—I had done little for him since 1933, the year when he showed me the Ilbalintja ceremonies. It was he who had first offered to have ceremonies staged for me when I did not even know that such things were still available.' Gurra died in April 1950, and in his bones Strehlow seems to have known one of the fundamental truths of anthropology: as Clifford Geertz puts it, 'great informants make great anthropologists.'[20]

None of this Strehlow was to tell Canberra when he came to report on this second trip for the fellowship. It was perhaps too personally poignant for him to specify. The same seems to have applied to another sad development that must have sharpened his sense of responsibility to the Centre. Gurra was dead, that was one thing. His other oldest informant, Tom Ljonga, a man more subtly positioned with regard to the traditional ways, was now old as well. In 1933 Ljonga had encouraged his people to part with their *tjurunga*; he thought it could be the black man's way of getting money and increasing his freedom to have the benefits of white men. Now he was even clearer about what he wanted and what his people deserved. A few weeks after Gurra died, Ljonga told Strehlow that when he got back to the south he should send some sheets of iron and cement. Ljonga wanted to build a permanent hut: he wanted to set it down in a place from where no white man could move him. 'We lifted you high today with our ceremonies,' Ljonga told Strehlow: 'You have been nursed in the lap of the dark men. Other white men look up at you as a leader. So do something for us too, to strengthen us when you go back to where all the great ingkata are sitting. We want permanent houses, we want pensions when we are too old to work. You can walk about anywhere you like, you can live anywhere you like; but we have only this country to die in. We don't want to be thrown about always like yalke [bush onion grass] that are being husked.'[21]

Strehlow made the films out at Jay Creek, where he had those tough, formative years as a patrol officer. He did not stay in the old camp but moved into the rock hills about three miles to the north, where he made three clearings, what he called three 'stages' which became the sets for the shooting. On 18 April, at last, the ANU's Bell and Howell camera started to roll. In the next five and a half weeks Strehlow filmed 77 ceremonial acts. 'Approximately 3,600 feet of ceremonial shots were taken in Kodachrome at sound film speed,' he was to report. 'The total footage of Kodachrome film exposed for the National University was 5,800 ft; the balance of 200 ft was sold to a private buyer.'

They were ceremonial films of the first importance—secret men's business which involved keeping women and children, as well as uninitiated men, well clear of the camp. On to each stage would come a totemic clan. They had a stage each. They performed an act a day, with Strehlow moving from one stage to another with his camera. Thus, in honour of the Kangaroo totem, three performances were staged—by the Aranda clan of Krantji, the Loritja totemic clan of Ajaii and the Pitjantjatjara clan of Malupiti. For the Honey Ant totem, Strehlow filmed the Aranda clan of Ljaba and the Loritja totemic clan of Popanja. And for the Native Cat, various acts associated with the Loritja centre of Watarke were staged by the appropriate totemic clan.

All through the shoot, of course, Strehlow fed and sheltered his native friends. For this the university had provided £150 and in the end Strehlow added £11 15s. 5d. from his own funds because he had obtained 'rather more than I had bargained for.' He handed over the tent and the groundsheet to two senior men. It was rain, eventually, that brought things to a close. Five to six inches fell in the first part of June. It swept in torrentially, in a way that must have reminded Strehlow of the dramatic downfalls back in 1937, when the 'roaring, turbulent waters of the re-awakened Jay' tore through the country like 'a primeval giant—an awe-inspiring sight to see Nature's own life blood returning into the dying body of the parched land.' The clouds then, as they must have in 1950, had darkened the 'wilderness of stone hills' and turned the nearby peaks and twin-crested mountain bluff behind Standley's chasm so dark as to be almost black; the mountains had then stood 'rugged, immovable, silent . . . in proud array, their roots fixed firmly in the hidden fastness of the earth, defying time and eternity.'[22]

The films he had made were for all time: they were of matters eternal and to be handled accordingly. When the shooting was done, they were yet to be pieced together, of course. But what he had done was unique and could be properly placed in the amphitheatre of his self-proclaimed achievements, which were now as much of a piece as an open-air theatre is at one with nature. They were the first movie films to depict a complete series of native secret ceremonies in Central Australia. Other men might have been privileged to see the performances (Spencer and Gillen, for example; and indeed Strehlow had seen whole cycles in Alice Springs and Horseshoe Bend in 1933; and then at Altunga in 1935); and some had obtained black-and-white film. But no one had managed to get colour footage of complete secret-sacred ceremonies. As he was able to report to the ANU: 'Consequently my success during the past few months has been most gratifying to me. I would recommend that copies be made of all films after they have been pieced together, and that the originals be stored in a safe place as they are unique. I had to give my personal word of honour to the ceremonial leaders that these films would not be shown publicly; and I would therefore urge that they be reserved for use in Universities only.'[23]

He shot the report off on 27 June 1950. On 13 July he was on the *Orion*, sailing for London. There he hoped to put the ceremonial acts together, give them their proper sequence according to their totemic headings, making them more whole, that much more his own. And there, he hoped, he would be able to show what he then called his 'Chants Ms' to the right people so that they could see what had emerged from all his years of travelling and translation. For no one yet knew—possibly not even himself, not fully—what manner of thing he had made. The work was still becoming; he was yet to fully define himself in translation.

Disciple of the Word

So what *had* he done?

Broadly speaking he had done many things at once, as we do when we write out of a whole life.

He had translated an oral culture into a written one.

He had assembled 'broken' songs as if he were Homer.

He had displayed their forms, and sung their praises, like an Israelite. Then he had made a case for the songs and their culture.

In a word, he had created a dense, sometimes brilliant mix of affirmations and denials as elaborate as a primeval forest.

In the middle of everything he claimed to have found the secret of the songs.

All the while he had been deepening his exchanges with the Aranda men, assimilating the songs he had been given, collecting the myths and the *tjurunga*, accumulating debt, and creating conditions that solicited restitution.

Much he had done in the course of filling out what his father's ethnology had missed: the music. As a Christian who had to eschew all pagan ceremony, the pastor had to sever the words from their rhythm and melody. Strehlow's project was to recover the music his father had shunned, to enliven the words that were meant to be danced and intoned, words that belonged to the cosmic pulse of desire, the words which were part of a fabric for sustaining desire. The Christian father had plucked the song from the passionate body of the pagan culture. His son came, like Orpheus, to play the music back in, or to at least point to where the music belonged.

With this in mind Strehlow organised his magnum opus. At first the music was annotated. The links of sacred words with sacred ceremony were made via the music—and not, as had been done by Spencer and Gillen, merely according to descriptions of ceremony. Having done that, he would more or less leave music alone. He was able to do so because he had created his own emphasis by giving priority to words over the music. They were songs, but: '*In these aboriginal songs, however, music is still the servant of the words.*'

'Music is the servant of the words' is the pivotal proposition of Strehlow's whole work.[24]

How the words worked in the company of the music constituted, in fact, their secret, their cryptic power. After years immersed in the sounds of Aranda, this is what he fished up, as if from the inland sea. He laid the words down the page, like immemorial shells.

Hence the great paradox of *Songs of Central Australia*. It is a book of song that Strehlow's translations have appropriated as poetry. He enshrined the songs as verse—as text, in fact—that had been put together from the oral tradition. The two movements here—from song into poetry, from the oral to the literary mode—went hand in hand. It was this manoeuvre that created the grandeur of his achievement, but also its social and aesthetic complexity as a work of translation.

Here are the songs—no, the poetry, we say—as we move through his huge book: he has brought them to us out of his own journeys in the desert. But then we have to ask: in so doing, what did he bring to them? To what extent are these old songs strangely of his own making? And, having played his part in their recovery—as reconstruction, or re-making—how, exactly, did he affirm their value? On what grounds, for what reasons? *Songs of Central Australia* involved a profound identification with the Aboriginal voice (Strehlow as Caliban), but in that act of valuation what became of his work of Christian translation (Strehlow as Luther)? The short answer is that it was tropically transmuted: by circuitous and defensive reasoning; with affirmations often woven out of his own most personal material, intellectual and emotional, spiritual and sexual. Always, with Strehlow, there is a kind of double movement, a doubled and divided act, where practice makes a mixed marriage with value, and love is never entirely straight.

The Secret of the Song

If Aranda was the black circle, Strehlow claimed to have located the dot at its centre, which was the secret name of the ancestor being, of which the song sang, and whose name lay cunningly concealed in the line of the song.

His word for that concealment was masking. The notion of the mask he hit upon by reference to the *Personae* of ancient Greek theatre, which were worn by actors playing the parts of the Gods. They were masked to disguise the realism of ordinary life, and their particular personalities, all the better to accentuate the impersonal presence of the divine. The mask had another function: its mouthpiece accentuated what was spoken, or sung, creating for the voice a clarity and resonance. Thus the

optic and the acoustic function together projected supernatural
presence—divine expressiveness, and divine speech, all on the principle
of impersonation.[25]

And so, Strehlow thought, Aranda men did in their ceremonies;
they 'were interested in watching not human actors, but living imper-
sonations of supernatural being.'[26] With faces and bodies painted up,
their personal bodies masked by totemic designs, their heads transporting elaborate and sacred headgear that belonged to no one but their
ancestors, they would, once launched into performance, cease to utter
any ordinary speech and be speaking only 'divine' words, those first
spoken by the ancestor being on the ceremonial ground.

The secret-sacred word was masked in two ways: acoustically and
semantically. Acoustically, because it could be disguised by the rhythm
and measure of the song; and semantically because it could be subject
to syllabic disguise—syllables might be added, vowels might be broken,
speech accents eliminated. Sometimes the word itself might be an
archaic word, long ago lost from ordinary speech, if indeed it had ever
lived there; it was a 'cryptic' verse and, as the song unfolded couplet by
couplet, the song might altogether sustain its secrecy as it thrummed
across its mythic country.

Songs exalted under the ancient belief that there was power in
naming, especially if those words were the names of supernatural
beings: a conviction that moved the ancient Hebrew, who could not say
the name of God, and the Egyptians, who gave their deities secret
names, knowledge of which empowered the magicians as well as the
sun god, Ra, and Isis the witch, 'a woman mighty in words.'[27] Words
had power over nature; they could create and they could destroy, and
their utterance, their making, was the thing: as entities unto themselves
they had power.

In Aranda life, terms for composing a verse doubled for naming: to
make a verse was to 'throw out a name,' 'call out a name,' 'call out one's
own name'—and so on, in a series that created a union between the
ancestor who called out, and the song the performer would sing.
The vitality of this concept, its energising power, the fecundity of
grandiloquence, is caught by Strehlow:

According to the aboriginal theory, the ancestor first called out his own
name; and this gave rise to the most sacred and secret couplet or
couplets of his song. Then he 'named' (tneuka) the place where he had

originated, the trees or rocks growing near his home, the animals sporting about nearby, any strangers that came to visit him, and so forth. He gave names to all of these, and thereby gained the power of calling them by their names; this enabled him to control them and to bind them to his will. In each instance he not merely gave them a name, but also described them briefly within the narrow limits of his couplet. In this way a series of couplets, loosely associated by time, space, and story, was brought into being; and this series constituted the song that each ancestor left behind for the benefit of those human beings who were to be reincarnated from himself and from his own supernatural children.[28]

Strehlow, irresistibly, speaks of Adam: by giving names Adam is the Lord of creation.

In the Aranda performance the chants are lords; they have the names of the first creative beings, they are known by those names themselves, and the only man who can sing them is the one with the knowledge—the deep, true, initiated knowledge, the inside knowledge of what the song *is*—he is the one who throws his name out, by singing the song out. And he is no actor who does this. He is the ancestor being himself resuscitated into the present by song. Revived, re-aroused, returned to the living present by song. Not brought back, for he was never departed, but called up out of the ground by feet dancing to song on the sacred ground.

The cryptic nature of the song, which throws the names up, takes the very idea of acting and hurls it from the ceremonial ground. Of course, these singers are men in performance; that is ordinary fact. But the performance itself is not representational. There is no one behind the mask of the totemic designs, just as there is no secret in the song, except to say the secret song is itself. There is 'acting' to the extent that there are better and worse dancers, expert and even more expert singers, and men of higher degree than others: and this is clear amongst performers, as it is in the lulls—informal, humorous, deceptively routine—between performances. Every man is in a way a double agent at all times, but again, no one is acting when they are *in* performance. Nor are they in roles, as ancestor beings. They are the beings, as much as one breath arises out of another breath. They are existing in the time it takes to be the supernatural beings of song, the original authors of song, the songs that are the names of themselves, sacredly, called out—as if, if it can be imagined, the names are nuclei, or seed syllables, as the Tibetans would say, of existence. On the dancing breath the song goes, being and song, song and being on the sacred ground. The essence of things called out, sparking by the fire. Life itself called out, up from the ground. Everything is in song: starlight, night, sun, blood, man, woman, spirit, and more spirit.

And that, in essence, is what Strehlow was writing a book about—had almost finished writing about by 1949. The shell that he held in his hand, which he had translated after years of listening to Aranda sounds, he called the *cryptic poetic diction* of the songs. And the wonder was that he alone among white men could hear what was there to be heard when the shell was held to his ear.

Three questions immediately press in on him as a translator. Given the integral union of song with performance, how was it possible for Strehlow to turn it into literature? As 'literature' what was it? And what was it to him?

The Hard Task of Translation
In his introduction to *Aranda Traditions*, Strehlow took pains to draw attention to the nature of his achievement.

> The difficulties of translation from Aranda to English are considerable. The originals abound in archaic and obsolete words, no longer used in current diction, but traditionally preserved in these instances. The verb stem in Aranda can take about a thousand combinations of suffixes; and many of these change the original force of the verb in such a way that a whole sentence may be necessary in English in order to express the new shade of meaning. Again, in the chant verses, the original word components are always run together and then re-subdivided into metrical feet: this pattern of versification ensures that no uninitiated person can readily understand a verse that he has not had explained to him by his elders.
>
> It follows that an English translation which tries to convey the artistic force of these chants and legends must often use a whole sentence where the Aranda version uses only one verb. It must also use archaic words or turns of expression where the native version employs them. It must frequently paraphrase native words for which there is no exact English equivalent. Since the translator cannot hope to run together archaic English words into a single verse-unit, and re-subdivide it into a regular verse pattern, he has to use inversion and

certain poetical turns in an attempt to capture some of the dramatic effect of the original.

An instance of the application of these principles as regards chants is afforded by the translation of the opening verse of the Ulamba Chant:

(K)erare / tjaritji / kalbitje /
Kankinja / batuare / ulalbitje

These two lines must first be reduced to prose as

Eraritjaritjaka albutjika
Nkinjaba iturala albutjika

'Eraritjaritjaka' is an archaic-poetic term, meaning 'full of longing for something that has been lost,' or 'filled with longing to return home.' 'Albutjika' is an infinitive meaning 'to go home,' 'to turn homeward.' The translation 'His heart is filled with longing to turn home' tries to express the force of this Aranda line; it uses the poetic phrase 'his heart is filled with longing' in order to express the force of the archaic poetic term 'eraritjaritjaka.' Again, 'nkinja' means both 'sun' and 'afternoon'; and the translation 'afternoon sun' combines both these meanings. 'Iturala' means either 'in the heat of the sun' or 'in the brightness of the sun.' 'Nkinjaba iturala' means, then, 'at that time in the afternoon when the sun is glowing in all its heat and brightness.' The translation 'High in the heavens gleams the afternoon sun' attempts to put this into poetic language. The original rhythm of the verse—which is very effective when it is being chanted mournfully—naturally defies all efforts at recapture.[29]

This is rather hard going, and it is meant to be. Strehlow is showing off as much as he is trying to help the reader. Still, it is about the longest illustrated passage he wrote about translation, and is revealing because of that. It demonstrates, first of all, the nature of his respect for the original. More particularly, for the archaic nature of the diction of the original—so archaic, in fact, it is often obsolete. Secondly, Strehlow is making it clear that the best he can offer is a prose paraphrase, one that has been derived from an unpacking of the cryptic verse chant. The result is:

His heart is filled with longing to turn home
High in the Heavens gleams the afternoon sun.

Thirdly, Strehlow makes it clear that 'the original rhythm for the verse' is beyond him, that it 'defies all efforts at recapture.' To put Strehlow in a more general scheme of things regarding translation: we can say that on the last point he was at one with Ezra Pound (who said that the *melopoeia* was untranslatable), and that with regard to respect for the original he did not get bogged down with the pedantry which John Dryden warned against; nor did he risk the conceits of imitation, but rather settled for paraphrase. But that is not to say that the stamp of his own personality, and his own literary compulsion, is not apparent, if not decisive.

The diction that Strehlow has chosen is strikingly his own. Each line has a term that goes beyond the literal meanings Strehlow has given. Thus 'his heart' is not exactly in keeping with what is given as the Aranda phrase 'full of longing for something that has been lost.' 'Heart' is from the lexicon of European Romanticism. It does not naturally spring from a culture which locates emotions in other parts of the body, where the deepest yearnings, as Strehlow can so vividly point out in other contexts, might belong to the stomach. 'Heart' in Strehlow's placement is metaphoric: it may even be completely wrong in terms of the concrete tacit meaning of Aranda 'yearning.'

Then there is the 'Heaven,' from which the second line gets its rhetorical power. It hardly needs saying that 'Heaven' does not belong, that it cannot have been the meaning of the original, least of all the 'archaic' original that predates the Christian arrival under Central Australian skies. That another term did not occur to Strehlow is disturbing. I would also want to quarrel—given the evidence he has presented— with 'gleams.' From his literal translations of the root term which he says is 'heat' and 'brightness' with regard to the sun close to the summit of the day, 'gleams' is surely too ornamental. Idiomatically, the context Strehlow gives seems to call out for a term that is more active, more dynamic, closer to the burning force of the sun near the middle of the afternoon.

It is rather striking that Strehlow shied away from the simple power of something closer to the original.

Looking for home
Yearning to go back
High burning sun
Swollen to go home.

But what is lacking here, of course, is a sense of the archaic. All I have done is the usual modernist thing: find the vernacular for what seems, from the translated paraphrase, to be true to the propositional direction of the original. In so doing, I have, by the way, apparently broken the couplet to which Strehlow says the Aranda are committed. Okay then:

> *Looking for home. Yearning.*
> *High burning sun. Longing to return.*

But this is still insufficiently compacted, to judge from the look of the original. So, and still holding to a couplet:

> *Lost home yearnings*
> *Bright sun home turning,*

or

> *To return, yearning*
> *Sun-blazed homecoming.*

You could play with these: and a satisfying play it would be too, because the Aranda couplet—again it seems so from Strehlow's literal offerings—might be treated as a seed pod to be opened. The result would at least partly depend on what you needed to do with the sun, and how much refrain there should be with the homecoming. It would be a matter of digging into the images and the action, the better to create the feeling. But enough of that for now. The point about Strehlow is that he does not play: it was not in his nature, the serious game of substitution could never be a light matter for him; too much was at stake. He was too preoccupied with what he called the 'archaic' and with the whole problem of making a case for the songs, defending them in the arena of world 'literature,' even though, of course, they were never a literature at all.

Strehlow as Homer

The simple truth is that, for better and worse, in *Songs of Central Australia* Strehlow sought to honour the Aranda song, especially its archaic aspect, by bringing two of his own gifts to it; his Greek scholarship, and his biblical cast of mind. In general the Greek references and analysis allowed him to sing the praises of the Aranda as poetry, while at the same time promoting it somewhat closer to the major achievements of Classical civilisation: as Strehlow extols his Aranda singers, the pre-Homeric poets can be heard reciting on the horizon. As Strehlow wrote down his songs, he was serving the function of the poet or poets who assembled the poems we now attribute to Homer. A translator becomes the 'author' of the songs in the way that 'Homer' became the author of *The Iliad* and *The Odyssey* as they took shape in writing.[30]

How then did Strehlow use the Greek, and the Greeks? The answer is threefold, and in each part it is hard to get away from Strehlow's special pleading, his need to make a case for the Aboriginal poetry and poets, to enshrine them in the Pantheon of European value.

Firstly he wanted to show that link between poetry and music was as it had been in Ancient Greece. He used the Greek examples to illustrate his pivotal claim, that 'in these aboriginal songs . . . music is still the servant of the words.'[31] Thus, in Greece, where the Greek chorus was a synthesis of music, poetry and dance, which was, incidentally, in tune with the Wagnerian operatic ideals of performance elements in harmony, Strehlow wanted to emphasise that 'The words of the singer were the dominant element'[32] He was emphasising, as is so often the case in *Songs*, the words of another scholar, in this case the author of a book on *Greek Lyric Metre*. Strehlow also stressed: 'Down to the middle of the fifth century, the flute player played, and the dancer danced, in time with the natural rhythm of the poetry.' And then in his own words: 'probably Homer's poems, too, were once chanted to the accompaniment of the lyre.'[33]

There was a lot at stake in this emphasis. It was linked to the claim that prose and poetry do *not* always have the same rhythmic basis. The conventional view among English prosodists was to say that in Europe the chant was musically designed to bend to fit every verbal rhythm, when that rhythm was determined by spoken speech patterns. By contrast Strehlow was saying 'the native Australian chants unreservedly refuse to accept speech accent into their strong rhythmical verse patterns.'[34] This was the case because that verse had its own *poetic diction*.

This is Strehlow's second prop in his 'Greek argument' for Aranda. Because of its poetic diction Aranda song was similar to the Greek of Homer, which was 'language never to be spoken.' Strehlow's authority here was the Oxford Classicist C.M. Bowra, upon whose thoughts on the structure of *The Iliad*, and the nature of Romanticism, Strehlow substantially relied. The substantive point here was to consolidate the notion of poetic diction as 'not a spoken language' because it was 'too rich and artificial.'[35] In its richness and artificiality, it could be difficult to the point of obscurity. Archaic words belonged to it. They were words the clear meanings of which had slipped out of sight to history, or words that had come into the diction from foreign sources. Most importantly, they were 'the invention of the poets' as Bowra wrote (and Strehlow repeated). 'The conclusion to be drawn from these cases is that the Homeric language is highly artificial, and its creation seems to be not the work of a single poet but a series of poets who used the old material as well as the different dialects of the Greek world in which they lived.'[36] The Aranda poets were in good company. Their prospects improved with the idea that from this they might go forward, which seems to be the implication of Strehlow's remark that 'the glorious style of *The Iliad* was derived from such an ancient vocabulary, the exclusive poetic diction native to that place.'

But the argument, really, was not grounded: Strehlow was making his case by analogy. That Homer's Ionic Greek—and, if it came to that, old Anglo-Saxon—had refined a poetic diction did not necessarily establish the nature of, or the quality of, the Aranda poetry. To do this Strehlow had to get down to the details of poetic technique, which he did at some length in the middle of his book. Much of what he wants to establish as to the status of the Aboriginal poetry as poetry stands or falls with this part of his argument. At issue, really, is the legitimacy of judging the Aranda poetry as relatively 'primitive' beside European traditions; or to put this in a literary context (as Bowra did in his last book on Homer, when he was comparing the Greek to the Macedonian oralists), or of lesser 'quality.'[37] What Strehlow had to show—given the way he had set the scene— was that the natives' poetic diction was worthy of the evaluative weight he gave to 'poetic.' He does so with very mixed success.

Take the matter of the simile, a fundamental poetic technique, the art of comparing like with like so that perception is freshened, widened.

He fell as an oak falls or a tall pine, which craftsman carve with newly sharpened axes to be a ship's timber.[38]

Strehlow reaches for his Bowra to say that 'with Homer we find the simile fully developed, and this is almost unique in early narrative poetry . . . The simile of Milton or Dante is drawn from Virgil, and Virgil drew his from Homer. So what we take for an essential part of poetry has derived life and strength from a single source.'[39] Bowra was comparing Homer to other early European examples to be found in *Beowulf*, and the Scandinavian *Edda* poems—both of which Strehlow wanted to acknowledge also, especially the Old Saxon from which he cited a long passage. Having shown all that, how does Aranda fare?

Strehlow makes a case for Aranda's compound words. This was Strehlow's third prop. We are vividly treated with examples rather proudly plucked from the major songs, the long runs of couplets arising from ceremonies for kangaroo, native cat, yam, honey ant ancestors and so on. There are the compound nouns—'serpent lake,' 'jagged-mountain edge,' 'the sun's flaming face'; there are the compound adjectives—'sprouting blossoms on their branch tips,' 'with averted motionless heads,' 'having a lofty forehead.' In addition there are what Strehlow calls compound or 'the highly elaborated periphrastic verb forms' that sustain the action of the long songs, just as you would expect from a suffixed language, and as he had pointed out in his earlier work. The examples he gives—'send out intertwined roots,' 'to gleam black with respect to one's head,' 'to put rings of down around the waist'—reinvoke the most vital aspects of his songs in English.[40] They bear the brunt of the songs' pleasing repetitions because they actively vary down the line, or rather, through the time they were taken to sing and dance.

At the same time, though, they do not necessarily constitute the workings of simile. Strehlow has to say as much. 'In the Central Australian songs, as in Anglo-Saxon verse, elaborate similes of the classic type are *entirely lacking*, although the germs for such similes can be recognised without difficulty in the metaphorical and substitute words with which the aboriginal songs abound' (emphasis added). He does not elaborate on this. When is a 'germ' a 'germ,' and when does it rank as reasonably kin to simile? None of the compacted phrases above get near 'he fell as an oak falls.' And Strehlow knows why: 'In our aboriginal songs the two objects between which a relationship is being established are generally identified rather than compared, and this identification precludes the independent poetic elaboration of the thought or action conjured up by the introduction of the substitute term.' Strehlow rightly sings the praises of the compound terms for their 'apt and clever comparison and identifications' and 'their pictorial and descriptive qualities which have been regarded at all times as a hallmark of good verse.' But that does not compensate for what he has in effect said: they tend to point ('identify') to similarities rather than develop thought or action ('compare'). In short, they are rudimentary.[41]

Strehlow the Psalmist

Strehlow's biblical frame took him back to the Hebrew poets, the men and maybe the women who wrote the psalms. By couching the Aranda biblically, the native singers could be heard as part of a long tradition of prayer, and exhortation. Again, they were closer to the tradition of civilised religion, and as poets in control of the profound techniques that made the psalms great.

The focus here was on the couplet, which Strehlow claimed to be the basic unit of Aboriginal poetry, and the way the lines worked together according to the techniques of parallelism. Unlike the ancient Greek, in which the hexameter line was brought to perfection, where the form of the poem was much determined by its measure of feet, Hebrew applied another measure of symmetry: it had a symmetry of units to which Medieval Jewish commentators gave a scientific name— parallelism membrorum. More than 200 years ago the Jewish scholar Robert Lowth named the three types of parallelism: sameness, antithesis, and complement.

> *I am like a pelican in the wilderness*
> *I have become like an owl of the ruins*   (Psalm 102)

is a clear example of the first. For antithesis, there is no better example of antithesis than

> *A time to weep*
> *And a time to laugh*   (Ecclesiastes 3:4)

while the more complex, complementary parallelism might be

> *A man may have many plans in his mind;*
> *But the counsel of the Lord—that will stand.*[42]

The general point is that the poet strove for a symmetric perfection of form and content. Acoustically, we cannot recover the precise nature of the match, except to say that Hebrew remains a concentrated language, and that it seems that the fit of the lines (and/or the phrases that composed the lines) was tight: a pregnant sound/sense unit. It needed little rhetorical elaboration to work psychologically, or poetically. Each couplet could be a most satisfying unit.

When the couplets were arranged on a larger scale the pleasures were more complex. Applying the principle of sameness, the poet could develop a repertoire of similarities which would develop a lively variety of descriptive designations. Then, enriching the semantics— enlivening a list with thoughtful analogy—is enabled by the application of anti-thesis. One says 'thoughtful' advisedly. Antithesis is an intellectual man-oeuvre as much as it is poetic. The epigrammatic nature of the couplet is inseparable from its propostional quality. Add to this the principle of complementarity, and an aspect of Hebrew verse comes to a head, you might say. It is a poetry of teaching and proclamation: the song of it, the soul music out of which it arose in a religious sense, rises to a high level of articulated abstraction. From an awed and yearning heart, Hebrew poetry makes a *philosophic* appeal. And, crucially, this is achieved by the refined use of poetic forms, the mastery of each of the different types of parallelism, 'concentrating the rays of meaning to a white-hot point.'*

On the nature of parallelism for the Aranda, Strehlow begins: 'As a general rule each couplet, like the Hebrew psalm verse, falls into two halves: the second half either reiterates or restates, in slightly different words, a subject already expressed by the first half, or it introduces a new *thought* or *statement*, thereby advancing or completing the subject that has been expressed in the first half' (emphasis added).[43] By way of illustration Strehlow gives us five verses of the 'Ankota Song'—the one initially presented in 1933 when he wrote up his first myth, the story of Ankotaritja (see above). The first verse

---

* We might get the feel of the dynamic from Robert Alter's remarks in *The Art of Biblical Poetry* (1985:19): 'In the abundant instances . . . in which semantic parallelism does occur in a line, the characteristic movement of meaning is one of heightening or intensificaton . . . of focusing, specification, concretisation, even what could be called dramatisation. There is, of course, a certain overlap among these categories, but . . . the rule of thumb . . . is that the general term occurs in the first verset and a more specific instance of the general category in the second verset. "Your granaries will be filled with *abundance*, / with *new wine* your vats will burst" (Prov. 3.10). (The verbs in this line reflect a movement not of specification but of intensification, from being filled to bursting.) "His heart is as solid *as stone* / as solid as the *nether millstone*" (Job 41: 16).'

I am red like the burning fire
I am covered with glowing red down

is enough to remind us that the first line is repeated three times before it unfolds into

I am red like the heart of a fire, and then
A tjurunga is standing on my head.

So far Strehlow is laying out one type of parallelism: sameness. There is no mention of the other two types: antithesis and complement. With regard to the 'sameness' type (which he does not label in this way) he says: 'The reader will have noted that there is a great deal of repetition in Aranda couplets translated so far. In most of them the two component lines of each couplet differ from each other only in point of one word, or at most two. This is the kind of repetitive, antithetical expression that characterises numerous other ancient poems. It can, for instance, be found in many verses of the *Gilgamesh Epic*.'[44]

This is an odd slide. Strehlow alludes to one other type of paral-lelism, yet does not give an Aranda example of it. Instead he rushes on to the Gilgamesh Epic. We read the Gilgamesh (which is convincingly analogous to some Aranda aspects of narrative rather than verse patterns) and then we are given an extract from a ritual song from Semang, which is followed by a secondary source citing another sec-ondary source. Strehlow quotes from John Drinkwater's, *The Outline of Literature*: '*Parallelism of thought and expression*—a sort of magnified allit-eration—is the distinctive mark of all Hebrew poetry, of its proverbial literature, and of much of its narrative. Professor Moulton well described its movement: "Like the swing of a pendulum to and fro, like the tramp of an army marching in step, the versification of the Bible moves with the rhythm of parallel lines."'[45]

With regard to the Aranda poetry, all this takes us around a small circle. But what Strehlow is insisting on—and this is my main point—is the fullness of the comparison with Hebrew poetics and achieve-ment, even though he has not gone much further than roughly illustrating the working of one type of parallelism, the type that is most rudimentary with regard to the parallelism of thought and expression. Yet it is on the basis of this type he writes: 'it is clear that we find in the Central Australian songs not merely a balance of rhythms but also a balance of *thought*' (emphasis added).[46] Later, to make this point about 'the same manner and method of expression (as Aranda), he cites Psalm 105, which turns out to be similar in its development of narrative, perhaps, but is much more developed thematically than anything in Aranda that Strehlow presents.

Aranda poetry is honoured by the comparison with Hebrew. To the Aranda tribe Strehlow brought the tradition of another tribe, seeking to elevate one by virtue of another. But his own song of praise tends to dance around the matter at hand; in seeking so much to praise, he paradoxically underlines one culture's poetic power of religious articulation at the expense of the other. That at least is the impression he creates with his English *prose* versions of the native songs, and in this, of course, we have to place our trust, since we are in the invidious position of most readers of translations: of not having the language of the other. We are in the translator's hands, at the mercy of *his* linguistic lyre. And that is what Strehlow's strategies fostered: the 'key' was with him, and no one else.

The Buried Persona

To point all of this out is not implying a challenge to the accuracy of Strehlow's analysis, or to diminish the greatness of *Songs*. It remains a central text, central in more ways than one: of a region, of an ancient and living culture, and of a continent that has come to mythologise its centre, even as the nature of black and white histories are being contested there. *Songs of Central Australia* stands as a book of teachings, a kind of Torah, for black and white citizens, and this is the way Strehlow obviously intended it. By laying out the songs in the way he did, with all those ladders of couplets and their trellis work of commentary, he was able to take us up and down with his cultural essay, leading us in, if we want to go in, towards the religious centre of Aboriginal Australia.* The book was a love song to 'his' people, and to 'his' own life (which he felt was broken early on, rendering it a sad love song). And it was a song that held within it an essay on culture; it affirmed a kind of poetics of culture, via what he brought to the translations.

---

* I am speaking schematically: Strehlow was always careful not to opine about Aborigines outside Central Australia; and yet, at the same time, the reach of his formulations went beyond his biographical region.

Nor is it necessarily implying that what he brought to Aranda song was extraneous: that is for better qualified people to decide, for linguists of Aranda, if they have the political nerve. But I am indicating the nature of Strehlow's cultural gift-offering to his native culture, the extent to which *Songs* is the embodiment of a cultural exchange, the product, if you like, of translation as a communication. To be critically aware of the book in this way is not to detract from it as a text, but to see it as a manifestation of a certain kind of history.

Translation is always personal, in that the stamp of the translator is what creates the possibility of a translation in English that works. 'My reading on the subject of translation,' Christopher Logue wrote, after his struggles with Homer and his scholars, 'has produced at least one important opinion: "we must try its effect as an English poem." Boswell reports Johnson as saying, "that is the way to judge the merit of a translation."'[47]

Nothing can be more personal than the effect—what is sustained by poetic design—of the English. What is sustained there is the result of the whole encounter between the individual being of the translator and the voice of the original. Ezra Pound is the exemplary case: Pound the erudite, Fascist ego, *and* Pound the self-effacing voyager into the poetics of the other—they go together, they compose the man who achieved so much in translation from Greek, Latin, Old English, Medieval Italian, Japanese and Chinese. As Hugh Kenner remarked, the best of Pound's translations

> exist in three ways, as windows into new worlds, as acts of homage, and as personae of Pound's . . . A persona crystallises a modus of sensibility in its context. It derives from an attempt to enter an unfamiliar world, develop in oneself the thoughts and feelings indigenous to that world, and articulate them into English. A translation, by extension, is a rendering of a modus of thought or feeling in its context after it has already been crystallised . . . The same clairvoyant absorption of another world is presupposed; the English poet must absorb the ambience of the text into his blood before he can render it with authority; and when he has done that, what he writes is a poem of his own following the contours of the poem before him. He does not translate words. The words have led him into the thing he expresses; desolate seafaring, or the cult of plum-blossoms, or the structure of sensibility that attended the Tuscan anatomy of love.[48]

The key word is Kenner's: *persona*. It was Pound's social identity as poet that enabled him to voyage so vividly in translation. It was his sense of public self as poet that energised his ability to grasp the original and make it his own (as well as translating it). It has less to do with interior states, or the flux of personal feelings, displacements or defence mechanisms, than with the poet performing in the public arena of language. That language—the modern English that Pound was seeking to firm up from its own poetic archaisms—was the test of the mettle. Among those archaisms was Georgian ornament and Victorian moralisms, all of it infected by the residue of habits formed in the presence of translations from the Classics. Pound was not against the Classics, far from it. But his diction—the diction fired by his persona—was designed to revitalise modern speech, to give it the lustre of luminous images, whether those images were retrieved from contemporary life or the ancient or distant past. Pound the translator was the persona of the poet confident of his public space.

It must be stressed here that Pound was out to make poetry. He was not working to finish a paraphrase. That was a halfway house. His mode was—to use Dryden's terms—towards imitation, and he defied all its dangers of egoism as the way through the alternative danger of pedantry.

Enough. It is enough by way of indicating the distance between Strehlow and the early modern incursion into the serious poetics of translation. To his credit, he did not formally pretend to be producing poetry in English out of the Aranda, and said it was 'beyond my powers': 'My own translations . . . have normally sought merely to render native verse into intelligible English rhythmic prose.' But of course, the burden of his book was to show that the opposite was the case: that we had before our eyes an accurate rendition of the Aranda poetic diction—as much before our eyes as a language without a dictionary could offer. At one stage in *Songs* Strehlow does offer a translation of it as poetry (in English) and the result is abysmal.

The ant workers yonder dwell, ever dwell:
In ring-tiered homes they dwell, ever dwell.

Abdomens adorned they dwell, ever dwell;
In ring-tiered homes they dwell, ever dwell.[49]

This is from the 'Northern Honey-Ant Song of Ljaba,' and in the printing of the verses Strehlow had the English words stressed according to the Aranda rhythms as distinct from the '*recited* English metre.' This is surely a botch. The point of translation into English is to find rhythms in English that might convey that of the original. All Strehlow has done is pedantically apply the pattern of the original when, if he had been translating in any meaningful sense of the term, he would have been working with the English. His fortunately rare demonstration of his translation as *poetry* not only shows that he was no poet, but that what he had been offering as paraphrases was better in its effects in English.

The strange thing about Strehlow, actually, is that he seems to have been so laborious and tone deaf in his English. Strange because by being so he missed an opportunity to make the Aranda as vital to our own ears as it might have been in performance. This is a puzzle until we remember two things. First, the whole emotional history of Strehlow's education in languages, and his cultural compulsions to rank the Aranda in European terms. Second, his other compulsion, which was to try and make the English faithful to its effects on the Aranda speakers. This is an expression of dual commitment—to the English reader and the native listener—with a bias towards the latter, when the latter were, as he says, etymologically underground, unknown to all, expect perhaps sometimes himself. It is not the force of Strehlow's personality that is the difficulty of *Songs of Central Australia* so much as its depth of involution. The paradox is that in his translations he wanted to sing—to sing out—for the Aranda, and that was the persona he cultivated, but deep down the poet in him was lacking or lay buried. He had no persona where it counted.

Instead, he was there all the time as himself, in his personhood, his individuality—struggling with translation all the while. And it was in that mode he was capable of some extraordinary statements that help position what he had done. Scattered through *Songs* are remarks that make it, almost, an open book with regard to translation, and the most important of them comes after the rich exposition of compound words.

He has been illustrating the task of translating some of the 'hundreds of simple, uncompounded words which belong solely to the vocabulary of verse.'[50] He takes us back to the 'Ankota Song,' which was the first to bear his name in print, back in 1933. He cites the first four verses and draws attention to four different poetic words, 'all of which express variations of the one basic statement "I gleam red," "I am burning red," and "the whole of my body is red." Since none of the terms occurs in 'prose in any Aranda dialect' they have to be glossed from the oral tradition, and this Strehlow does, showing how he tried to dig into the roots of the language. Again it is impossible to judge the actual accuracy of the results without having Aranda oneself, but something of Strehlow's open choice might be gleaned from his solution to one of the terms, Urkurkala nopanama, 'which has been glossed as signifying "gleam red like fire," is derived from the same root as the Western Aranda word urkwarkerama, which means "to be consumed by fire." This poetic term describes the intense colour of the inner flames; and I have rendered the whole line as "I am red like the heart of a fire.""[51]

The passage on 'red' leads to an important confession:

This attempt to differentiate between the root meanings of poetical terms which have been used as synonyms in the songs brings out clearly one of the chief difficulties in translating aboriginal verse into English. The native love for parallelism introduces a host of poetic synonyms into aboriginal verse; and these poetic synonyms are differentiated in meaning by the associations and the imagery introduced by their root syllables. Many of these native roots have no exact equivalents in English, and have to be paraphrased extensively. The associations and the imagery conjured up by the native roots are frequently not identical with those conveyed by their English equivalents even where the basic import is the same. *The two languages do not 'cover' each other very well*; and many of my English paraphrases have purposely been made very full in the hope of suggesting adequately to an English reader the effect that the original lines would make upon a native listener. To use a musical metaphor, the poetic words used in the Central Australian songs are rich in overtones. The root meanings supply, as it were, the fundamental tones; and the associations of the words, coupled with the poetic elaboration of their syllables, produce the varied overtones which necessitate carefully paraphrased translations into English to ensure that the original effects are not missed completely. The glosses provided by native oral tradition are indispensable for a general comprehension of each verse couplet; but the translator needs in addition a sound knowledge of the native dialects and languages themselves, and a thorough acquaintance with other words which are derived from the same roots as some of these rarely-used poetical terms. *In the translation of aboriginal songs a poetic dictionary is an absolute necessity.* This may be defined as a dictionary which lists the poetical words under their roots and gives their appropriate traditional glosses. The compilation of such a poetical dictionary has never yet been attempted either for Aranda or for any of the other aboriginal languages. *Until such a dictionary exists in Aranda, there will remain many scores of Aranda poetical words whose exact significance can only be guessed at* from the general meaning of the verses in which they occur. (emphases added)[52]

It is an important confession. It implies that much of Strehlow's translation might be guesswork and that, at bottom, since the roots of the language did not 'cover' each other particularly well, translation might be inaccurate or even impossible. It is important, too, because it opens us to the idea that for Strehlow, in the absence of sufficient knowledge of Aranda roots, an additional freedom in translation was exercised in the ways I have been suggesting.

His translations might have been quite different if he had taken his own advice and seen the making of the dictionary as a prime and maybe even prior objective, rather than rushing to translate so much. Perhaps it might even have tempered his defensive claim to possession; it might have grounded him in Aranda in ways much closer to its actual nature, more accurately according to its differences. In fact, in the light of the confession, a startling thought becomes possible: that the poetic diction was not itself the defining feature of the Aranda poetry, but rather a product of difficulties in translation. Poetic diction might be an artefact of Strehlow's encounter with the songs, rather than an objective feature of them. Strehlow did not so much define the nature of Aranda poetry so much as its resistant nature found him. What we have been witness to are his very personal struggles with that.

Willing Literature

Strehlow had willed the Aranda literature into being in two simple ways: first of all by deciding that it was, taxonomically, literature. In this his principal mentor was the Cambridge don and scholar of comparative literature. H.M. Chadwick, the author of the three-volume *The Growth of Literature*.[53] Chadwick wrote of 'independent literatures,' or 'native' literatures that were independent of Latin. Ancient Greek, Icelandic and Norse, Celtic and Old English—all were literature to Chadwick. 'Purists may perhaps object to the use of the word [literature] on the ground that etymologically it implies writing. But there is no other term available, apart from cumbrous circumlocutions. Commonly we use the expression "poetry and saga"; but this is not entirely comprehensive. The reader will doubtless understand what we mean, and that is enough.'[54] This was written in 1932 and it was enough for Strehlow for the rest of his life.

Chadwick was trying to steer clear of literary evaluations; his mode was descriptive. He was prepared to set a benchmark with such remarks as: 'There can be little doubt that in the civilised world literature has had a history of several thousand years' (which rather suggests that the written might be worthy of a category of its own); and he spoke of 'backward literature,' both ancient and modern. But he was not going to use the term 'primitive'—that could be left to those who wanted to study 'the most primitive peoples.' He referred to 'literature' that 'must have consisted of records of intellectual activities preserved in speech, not in writing. A man's memory was his library.' Admittedly, in written literature there was what he calls 'the literature of thought' that was written down, eventually. But that was not the literature (oral) of 'celebration' and 'entertainment'—his two other genre categories. These categories pointed further back—in the direction of backwardness, if you like, but more importantly towards another truth: 'It will be seen that we believe (unwritten) literary tradition to have been a more developed and potent force and to have had a longer life than many scholars are willing to allow.'[55]

This set the scene for Chadwick's massive project: to survey genres across time and place—from pre-Homeric song to the Bantu—in the hope of sketching a comparative typology of literatures. In this context Strehlow's work can be located quite simply. He was writing the Australian chapter for the Cambridge scheme of things: he was putting Aranda song on the world map. In a way—the way of the civilised scholar, a master of reading and writing—he was doing the primitive culture the favour, performing it the service, of placing it rightfully, if not newly, in the most desirable company of the time.

But the good intentions—the act of translating an oral to a written culture—were acutely imperialistic at every level: as a practice in the field; and as a mode of representation of the culture—the poetry—that had been gathered. As a disciple of *logos*, the question has to be asked, if only to sketch the parameters of answers: what did Strehlow *do* to the Aranda songs by writing them down?

In the field he was at one with his notebook. By being there with the skill of writing, he had 'a hold' over the others as much as a pastor with the Bible or himself with the patrol officer's log. The power of writing in the colonial field was sharply noticed by Lévi-Strauss when he was with his Brazilian natives in the same years as Strehlow's early life in Central Australia. In Brazil a native chief tried to mimic Lévi-Strauss' handwriting, making wavy signs on the page as if the meaning might 'leap up from the page.' The chief had cottoned on to the fact that writing had something to do with control, and it was that he was trying to display to his fellow tribesmen, illustrating as he did a nice connection between writing and deceit. Lévi-Strauss went on to reflect that even though some civilisations had managed great feats without or before writing, in others the 'primary function of written communication was to facilitate slavery': writing was historically bound to the exercise of 'dominion'.[56]

Strehlow, in the field, had no such experience of an Aranda singer seeking to mimic his record-keeping—whether it be his record of their rations and payments, the *tjurunga* count, or his record of their songs. They were in his company dependently, and most acutely needing to transmit their sacred song in the hope of securing it in some way, but they were not cognisant of how the writing would do that, exactly. How could they know when they lived in a pre-literate culture? From Strehlow's records it is not clear, either, the extent to which he was able to explain to his informants the ramifications of his record-keeping. Nor did he, in any of his writings, contemplate the possibility that his written record of 'their' songs would one day be useful to them. Beyond that, he would also have had to reflect on the difference all his collecting was making. It was not in his nature to address such intellectually self-conscious questions.

As a disciple of *logos* Strehlow was in a crossroad position analogous to Plato in the age of Homer. Havelock's reflections in his *A Preface to Plato* are extremely useful here. Before Homer, the poet was the singer and the seer, the prophetic, divine muse at one with music and dance. After Homer, the poet was weaned from the religious functions belonging to the oral culture because of the advent of writing. Plato wanted to shift the Greek mind from one way of being to the other. Prior to writing, the oral tradition exalted poetry and poets as the best vehicle of 'preserved communication,' and the techniques of poetry increased the powers of memory by cultivating an unquestioning commitment to the tradition by all manner of means: repetitions, music, rhythms, dance and, most importantly, the practice of a *mimesis*, whereby the audience was seduced into full sympathy with performances that involved re-enactments and identification with the figures of whom the poets sang. This was the state of mind that went with this spell-binding poetry, and it has been described as a 'total state of mind' that belonged with the poetry that was a total method, a 'total technology.' The state of mind was 'esoteric'; it was akin to hypnosis, when the audience had to submit to the poet[57]; it altogether fostered automatists in the realm of the irrational, which was inimical to knowledge as critical self-awareness.

Plato wanted to ban poets from his Republic because they were possessed and not quite in their right mind, and could not even understand the meaning of their own words. Ultimately their poems were not open to interpretation; they were a kind of irrational, unpremeditated cry removed from the poet's intention and reflective consciousness. And so it was Plato's project to argue for an alternative, a society where another state of mind was desirable. That was a state where a self-knowing was possible, where the knower was separate from the known, and where the mind was able to contemplate its own objects. Such a cultural order was facilitated by a repositioning of the poet—moving him, one might say, from the realm of oral mystifications to the space of the written and scrutinisable; from the domain of unreason to reason, from poetry to philosophy. And it was the arrival of writing, which Plato contemplated, that brought all of these contrasts to a head. In the past lay the collective memory, unanalysed but transported by poetry. In the future lay the text, where memory was objectified, and endlessly open to interpretation.

All of the above can be couched in numerous ways, with the key terms loaded and pointed in different directions. But the essential notion here is that in Homeric, pre-literate times, the poet and audience were involved in an overall body of experience that was not tantamount to knowledge as critical self-awareness. That overall body of experience was joined uncritically, and engaged with palpably, through all the senses, through the music and the dancing, and its dramatic, erotic appeal came from that: it sustained exercises in techniques of desire. The level of absorption was primary, such was 'the immemorial habit of self-identification with the poem.' But then, once that identification was broken—what? 'Once I end my absorption in the poem, I have ended the poem, too.'[58]

In this sense Strehlow ended the Aranda poems. By writing them down for strangers, for those who had not been part of the dance, he had ended them there. He did not desire to do so, but that was the upshot of his recording. He had translated from a set of symbols which inhabited one state of mind into another. And that state of mind was one that prided itself—thanks to the dominion of writing—on a distinct mode of intellection. What was once active and becoming in the previous state of mind was now a matter of being, of being subject to objective analysis. If the earlier world—Havelock refers to Greece's 'Dark Age'—was warmed by live performances by unknowing subjects at one with their poesis, the new age of reason had been stilled by quiet private contemplation of its cool mental objects, intellectually received.

Again, the formulations could go on. But enough has been said to indicate how it is possible to say that by writing down the Aranda poetry Strehlow had imperialistically applied his faith in *logos* to the detriment of the lived, true nature of the original. He had wrenched the poems into the Platonic daylight of rational analysis where they were not meant to *be*. He had, in a way, *domesticated* them.[59]

Taming His Twin

This aspect of Strehlow's writing, the taming and framing of the Aranda material, also extended to his treatment of some myths. Oh, the savageries were still there in some of the ceremonial detail that accompanies the songs, but the emphasis is no longer upon the primal horde and its deeds. Nowhere was this more apparent than in Strehlow's treatment of the myth that was his own Dreaming: the story of the two boys of Hermannsburg, the twins of *Ntaria*.

His own story took him right back to the Manangananga cave, the name of which meant two children. His father had translated *ratapa*, spirit boys. They were also 'the two boys who always remained children.'[60] Pastor Strehlow judged that the term *ratapa* probably came from ratama—'to emerge, exit or originate from, stem from.'[61] The first translation went:

[Holding] into the small tjurunga like crutches
[The two ratapa] slide back and forth.

'Let us two crawl about,
Together let us crawl about.'

'Let us crawl about on the ridge of the sandhills,
Let us crawl about on the red sandhills.'

'Let us crawl up the short hill,
Let us crawl up the ridge of the sandhill.'

'Let us slide down on the moist [ground]
Onto the soft earth let us slide down.'

'Let us slide down while dragging gum tree fibre,
Let us slide down with gum-tree fibres.

'Let us crawl about in the soft riverbed,
Let us two crawl about.'

'Let us two dive under [in the water],
Making bubbles [on the surface] let us dive under.'

'Let us crawl up on the surface of the rock plates
At the bend [of the creek] let us crawl up.'

'We split [it] for us,
We split the jimbara [sic]-shrub.'

Jartaka wants to climb up,
She wants to climb up onto the ridge of the sandhill.

'In the cave [Jartaka] shivers [for cold],
She shakes herself in the cave [for cold],

'We hitters want to lie down,
Having laid all the [lizard] tails in a heap we want to lie down.'[62]

Pastor Carl glossed the story as:

At *Manangananga* there once lived a *tneera*, by the name of *Jartaka*, and her two *ratapa*, who always remained children. Using their *tjurunga*-woods as crutches and clasping them with both hands, the *ratapa* crawled to and fro on the ground, climbed on top of a sand-hill, and climbed down again onto the plain. Then they lowered themselves into the bed of the Finke river, dragging gum tree bark fibres behind them and dove into a waterhole. Then they climbed up the rocky bank and cut down *jinbara* sticks. They used these to make themselves spears while the mother yearningly kept looking out for them. Having killed many *takintjara*—lizards and put their tails in a heap, they entered the *arknanaua* at *Manangananga* in company of the *ramaia*-men, who had come from the north. There they solidified as *tjurungeraka*.

What on earth was the story about?

The song, as well as the gloss, is cryptic. This was typical. The full meaning of the lines was inseparable from teachings to initiates and the acting out of the song in ceremony. The 'meaning,' if it could be unpacked at all, was embedded in full-blooded performances from which the pastor had exiled himself, Aranda or no Aranda.

What can be said—as ethnographic background to twins stories in the 'primitive' cultures of the world—is that in most such stories the twins are differentiated: one twin is the good one, the other bad; one the harbinger of the evil spirit, the other not; one worth saving, the other not. In real life, as distinct from myth, the first-born of twins is often killed at birth. As the Hungarian psychoanalyst Geza Roheim pointed out on the basis of his fieldwork at Hermannsburg in 1929, 'the first born is called aldoparinja (after the infernal west wind), and is believed to be the child of an evil wind which entered into the already pregnant woman. This child is a demon. The grandmother puts coal or sand into the new-born infant's mouth or beats its head with a stick.'[63]

The strange thing is that Strehlow chose not to explore his father's version. Although he made sound recordings of the song, he did not report the story in his book, nor translate the song, leaving it as a mystery. No: he did more than that. He withdrew from telling the reader about the significance and nature of the myth.

What he does say is that the twins were born of the ereakura bulb woman; he explains that the point of the detail about the lizard hunting is that no living creature must be killed near *pmara kutata*, the home place of ancestors, in this case the Manangananga cave; he quotes the lines from their song that tells of the boys' ceremonial piercing of their nose bone; and he embraces the general proposition of Sir James Frazer that mythical twin children possess magical powers over nature, especially over rain and the weather. But he does not link this theme to the *Ntaria* twins.

And none of this elucidates Strehlow's 'own' story. The one enticing detail is when the twins, 'first looked down upon the *Ntaria* waterhole from the top of the range four miles away, the waterhole is said to have suddenly come to life, showing its excitement by raising large waves on its surface. It was welcoming these twins who were to dive into its depths forever.' Strehlow does not explain why the twins dived into the depths forever. His focus is on the animation of the water, how the waves were rippling, 'tossing about lustily' even though there was no wind.

The idea Strehlow is driving at is the one expressed by 'the Hebrew poet' of the Old Testament who celebrated Israel, 'the house of Jacob' escaping from Egypt, when man's joy was shared by nature. The raging breakers strike as violently as boomerangs, 'angry boomerangs.'

Let the waves turn into raging breakers!

This is Strehlow's preferred translation. By his own account, another version might be:

Let the waves violently strike the boys

which hints at nature's punishment of the boys for some crime. Strehlow writes, 'The Ntaria incident is only a minor episode in the Western Aranda Ratapa myth,' and drops the story.[64]

This is extraordinarily evasive and misleading. The authoritative contemporary version of the story is as follows. The story begins in Palm Valley, in the vicinity of a fertility rock called Itaratara.

A pregnant woman travelled along Palm Creek. She came towards Itaratara from the east. As she approached the site, she left marks in the creek bed—a perfectly semi spherical mound in a rockhole and a row of other rockholes, each of which formed as she felt her labour pains or sat down to rest because of them. Finally reaching Itaratara, she gave birth to twin boys. One was fat. His name was Rengkaraaka. And one was skinny. His name was Ratora.

On a rock place at Itaratara there are marks that look like two sacred objects or bull roarers with strings attached. One mark is much larger than the other, indicating that one of the twins was bigger and healthier than the other. These marks can magically induce strength and weakness in people if they rub against them, and the twins themselves are said to be traditional healers. The two 'strings,' are the twins' umbilical cords. Directly next to the twins, on their eastern side, is a patch of what looks like naturally weathered stone. This is the twins' 'first' camping place, or their 'map' (actually their afterbirth).

The twins proved to be 'cheeky.' They played around all over Palm Valley and were especially fond of hunting with magical sticks. Their mother had a hard time keeping an eye on them, as they would constantly and deliberately run away from her for more adventures. At one point she followed them along Palm Creek towards the east, where she left her marks as a partly white faced, upright rock. The twins travelled on towards Hermannsburg and the mother followed them all the way.

Here at Ntaria, the twins swam at Ntaria Kuku waterhole, and hunted takintjarra (small red-headed lizards which live in the sand dunes and run very fast). They threw the lizard bones into mounds which became the sand dunes. The mother placed the boys in a coolamon which she put on a small hill called Alkumpaturra (low round hills west of Hermannsburg). At one stage the boys stole her coolamon and threw it away.

She climbed Mt Hermannsburg to catch sight of them and tracked them all around the Hermannsburg area. The boys had by now grown into men and had set up a camp at Alkumbadora, just west of Hermannsburg. There used to be two desert oaks at Hermannsburg, which were the boys' marks.

The boys travelled west along the range and hid at Manangananga cave. They dressed for ceremony there and became violently angry when their mother saw them. They speared and killed her there. Her body can now be seen as a large rock on Manangananga Creek.

Eventually the boys went to Ntaria waterhole, along the Finke a little to the north west of the mission. They took a swim in the waterhole but did not remain there. They rose into the sky as rainclouds and travelled to Santa Teresa, where they finished up.*

The truth, then, is that the key event of the twins' story is the execution of their mother. After many years of disrespect for her—the cheek that included stealing her coolamon—they finally killed her because she saw them painted up for their men's initiation. The swim they took was after her death, and the waves had every reason to rise up 'violently.'

There can be no more fundamentally transgressional story. The mother, the earthly life source, is destroyed. At another level it is the

---

* This version is a synthesis of versions in the private and public domain, and is set down here with the permission of its custodian, Denis Ebarintja.

story, par excellence, that most ruthlessly defends the secret-sacred domain of men. Thus the metaphysical life source—ancestor creatures tended by male religious rites—is sustained.

Uncomprehendingly, Pastor Carl wrote the story down and translated the song for it. If he had been able to penetrate its meaning he could not as a Christian have afforded to show any sympathy for it. That his son might not have had a clear view of its meaning when he was a boy may be the case. The story was in the air that he breathed. What matters is that it was the myth—with all its power and opaqueness, its primal ambiguity with regard to the practice of infanticide and the mythic event of matricide—which was the mantle that he chose to adopt. He became happy and proud to make the story his own by virtue of his birth—the emergence of his own *ratapa*—at *Ntaria*. But that adoption had to remain blank because of the incendiary nature of the myth, its necessary repression, since Strehlow was still the Christian son of a missionary.

Strehlow could, perhaps, have publicly explored the story if the twins had been differentiated in some way—one as the good boy, the other as the bad. But in the *Ntaria* story the two boys were united in their demonic ferocity. It is as if Esau and Jacob were not two brothers, but somehow one, in a merger of that Genesis story. An individual intimating tensions in a compound self might say, along with John Berryman, 'My twin, the nameless one, wild in the woods,' and let his sympathies flow precisely because the wild one still implied its civilised opposite. But when there is no such articulation, that cannot happen: a dumbness sets in, internal cultural tensions fall silent, any creative psychological ambivalence is blocked from expression. The primal nature of the *Ntaria* twins closes the door on choice.

There is another aspect that might have closed Strehlow on the topic. The mother's death is justified in the story simply as a defence of male secrets. For Strehlow, the *ingkata* who was to stand accused of violating men's business by handing them over to a woman, the story might have become, in effect, literally unmentionable. He could not make a song and dance about his own myth because it said too much.

Overcoming Desire

We are still answering the question, what had Strehlow done? What was it that he took with him to London in 1950?

He had made a literary text of his struggle with the powerful sexuality of Aranda culture. The nature of this struggle—for him, and for his cultural argument—is most apparent in the passionate chapter on 'Songs of human beauty and love-charms'[65] in which Strehlow starts out with what he calls 'the *problem* of love and sex among the Central Australian native people' (emphasis added). On the nature of that 'problem' he is both declaratory and anxious about sex among the natives and sex in the West.

It was a problem because, even though 'love and desire are highly complex emotional experiences' and there was an 'essential sameness of the passion of love in many of its vital aspects in all human communities,' it was a fact that 'among "civilised" peoples generally, the *spiritual* nature of love is emphasised much more than its physical character; among "primitive" peoples it is the obvious physical basis of love-making that is singled out for notice.'[66] It was then a double problem: the Aranda were less spiritualised about Eros, which created, as we might say today, an issue of perception.

Strehlow begins, too, by recognising others in the field, which is unusual for him.* He mentions Geza Roheim 'of the Freudian school' whose theories could be, if understood, an antidote to any feelings of 'disgust or horror' at certain accounts of 'love-making.' In the same breath Strehlow introduces the then recently published Kinsey Report, 'an eye-opener to millions of American citizens in its details of the actual sexual and marital practices current in the U.S.A.,' and which, if applied locally, would cause a 'rude shock to many Australian citizens.'[67]

It is a nervous beginning. The scene is set for something, but the reader does not know what, until Strehlow introduces the 'Song of the Kwalba [the Spectacled Hare-Wallaby] Chief of Tera,' the marvellously frank verses that are one of the treasures of his book. In English it has, Strehlow thinks, 'a crude and offensive tone' whereas it 'does not sound offensively indecent or obscene to native ears in the original Aranda':

This interesting fact illustrates the difference between Aranda and English as media for expressing such topics. The Aranda terms are merely frank and descriptive; the corresponding English words have been withdrawn from polite conversation for so long and have been so degraded by foul usage that they have become virtually unusable even

---

* A footnote was to be added acknowledging the 'honesty of purpose' of his colleagues, Catherine and Ronald Berndt, whose marvellously full and frank account of the Arnhem Land song cycle, *Djanggawul*, was to be published in 1952.

in print. Even the Latin terms normally adopted in translations offend some readers. Herein Aranda and English reflect the differences in the basic public attitudes towards sex held respectively by the nudist, plain-spoken natives and the repressed and clothed whites, whom religion and civilisation have taught in the past to look upon sex as something unclean and immodest. Having been reared in both cultures, I am capable of experiencing both of these attitudes. I was able to record the Aranda verses without any embarrassment whatever, *but I have felt a con-siderable measure of dislike about translating them into English*; for it is inad-visable for any author to ignore the feelings of his potential audience. I have done so, however, in order to make clear to my readers this basic difference between the two attitudes on sex. The native viewpoint given here may help to explain some points of their behaviour in their original state, which otherwise would seem merely animal-like to us.[68] (emphasis added)

He sweated on this passage, which is the clearest expression of divided feeling in all of his work, the statement that reveals most about his inner struggle. He would draft and redraft the key sentence where *dislike* was originally written as *disgust* and was modified as *trepidation* before finally going into print as *dislike*. With the first response he was writing in key with Roheim, with the primal candour of the Freudian school in mind, with the 'horror' of the savage in mind. The word echoes as it was meant to: right back to the nineteenth-century registrations of the savage as the one with the heart of darkness, as the one outside the bounds of civilised conduct, as primitive in every way, and in particular sexually, since his was a life of brutish licentiousness, group marriage, girl marriage and all the rest of it that appealed to the repressed Christian, European pornographic imagination. *Trepidation*, then, was a way of pulling back from this stock misrepresentation of native mores. But it was changed. Why? Because it said too much the other way? I think so. Trepidation signals approach . . . desire on the pathway into the forest? It is hard to say, and Strehlow never kept notes on textual revisions. In any case, *trepidation* reveals enough. And *dislike* says more as proof, if proof be needed, that Strehlow passed through to a considered resolution of agitated feeling. With *dislike* he had made up his mind not to go there: he had pulled back from his sense of the primitive; he had suppressed that aspect of what he was 'capable of experiencing' in Aranda culture. He would translate Caliban favourably, but he would not become Caliban.[69]

Rather, he would lay out the songs of Caliban, all the while under-going his sense of what it was and had been to be European and Christian under the heading of desire. And with the songs he lays out in this chapter, in the pages that pulse with Aboriginal carnality, and the integrations of sexual consciousness with spiritual belief, Strehlow works at a pitch with the diction he feels he can use, supplementing his failures of nerve with explicit footnotes and exegesis. Overall, he is fixed on the idea that his hands were tied in the English translation, that certain English words had 'been withdrawn from polite conversa-tion' and so he could not use them at all. It is not clear whether he is referring to obscene words or merely plain words. It is certainly clear, however, that he had learnt nothing from the ways in which Joyce, or Lawrence, or Miller had tried to rescue literary means from conven-tional prudery.

Yet, despite all this, the 'Song of the Kwalba' runs out into fourteen pages of text, pulsing all the way. It is a saga of the ancestor sire's frus-trated desire and quest for a mate; of her arrival and arousal to him; of their copulation and settlement with each other—their 'marriage' in Strehlow's parlance. It is soon followed by the secret love charm of the native cat ancestor. This is even more passionate, even more full of arousal, eroticising all action and much of the landscape. It is tempting to quote runs of them here, but possibly that would be too intrusive, even today, on Aboriginal belief.

Strehlow struggles much of the way. He uses the words 'penis' and 'womb,' and the sexual action, its passion and force, is conveyed by reference to 'spearing' (the term that Strehlow says is used by the Southern Aranda poet, rather than the usual term for intercourse, a puzzling fact considering the statements about Aranda plain-spoken-ness elsewhere). In a footnote—a coy placement—Strehlow gives the details about the erotic landscape, the connection between 'serpent lake' and the arousal of 'the deepest recesses of the female body.' Without doubt, the cumulative effect of Strehlow's translation is charged, and frankly informative, but a puritan's linguistic convolutions are also there, and they are telling.

He cannot bring himself to use the simple terms that would be used by the Berndts only a few years later. He is rather wonderful when he uses, apparently literally, a phrase such as 'in the deepest lakes of their bodies,' but in his shy search for synonyms he is immensely keen on 'chalices':

In their chalices of nectar they are churning with passion,—
In the deepest lakes of their bodies they are churning with passion.
In their chalices of nectar let them shiver violently!
Let their very navels shiver violently![70]

This formality, its archaic religiosity, is what counts most for Strehlow. On the stage of world literature, his Christian need was to address the simple fact that: 'To the aboriginal mind, sex stood for life and for joy, never for filth,'[71] and from that try to integrate illusions and realities about 'them' and 'us.' The result was the longest and most convoluted chapter of the book, and an argument that steadily gathered ambivalences until it was hugely bow shaped: looping widely one way and then back the other way, only to loop one more time and then back again, looking for its neat knot in the middle, a resolution that would not come.

Thus: Strehlow concedes that the Tera song is a 'cave-man story' and therefore a model example of the 'primitive'; then he points out that there were in real life (the song was after all a myth) marriage rules, and that, anyway, those rules were massively dislocated by the arrival of the white man. The first Aranda checked unbridled desire in ways that protected the family group, which is more than can said for the sexual freedoms of modern life; and, anyway, regarding myth, who are we—the 'civilised ones'—to overlook the sexual savageries recounted in Greek or Northern European literature? Lengthy textual illustrations are provided. Furthermore, as to our own 'civilised' past, our spiritual valuation of love is as recent as the rise of chivalric love in the Middle Ages, which became the font of the romantic model we value now, examples of which also abound. But that is not to say—a typical *volte face* by Strehlow again—that marriage founded on romantic love is successful. The Christian essayist on love, C.S. Lewis, is pithily evoked: 'Any idealisation of sexual love, in a society where marriage is purely utilitarian, must begin by being an idealisation of adultery.'[72] Yet the Aranda know no such marriage, or have no such tradition of courtly love, and therefore have no 'love' as we know it; and yet Strehlow also wants to speak of the 'essential sameness'[73] of human beings with regard to love and desire, even though 'as regards love, there is a yawning gulf between the conventional attitudes of the natives and ourselves.'[74]

Strehlow goes on for 100 pages in this vein, and near the end of it he remarks, 'A great deal of *outside* European matter has found its way into this discussion of Central Australian love charms' (emphasis added),[75] which it had, yet he was compelled to put it in. He wrote at one point: 'on the whole it seems true to say that Primitive Man sought his escape in superstition, while Modern Man tends to seek refuge in sophistication and cynicism,'[76] and then rails against those 'intellectual giants,' Swift and Shaw, who would disillusion us about romantic love, a cynicism refined by the wit of Noel Coward's

In this hurly burly of insanity
Your dreams cannot last long.[77]

What Strehlow wanted to affirm, really, was the idea of true love finding its match. He considers the Aranda love charms in the context of European tales of unrequited love. He speaks of 'the insoluble difficulties' of individuals 'who had no hope of winning permanently the partner whom they really wanted more than anything else in the world,' and of 'the situation where a man is deeply in love with a woman who does not return his affections, or who, worse, still, loves someone else.'[78] He quotes Heine, 'unrequited love of this kind hurts so deeply because of its essential hopelessness,' and writes at length about the tragedy of Tristan and Isolde. It was the spiritual quality of love, he repeats, which demarcates it from the Aranda 'type of love.'[79] And so on, ad nauseam, really, and one can't help but hear, not only all that he had boned up on in his solitary academic hours on the theme of love, but the sad tinkling of his piano at Horseshoe Bend in 1933: that, and more.

As to marriage, and those who would condemn it to failure: 'Gifted with a cold, clear intellectual vision, these writers have seen and described the decline of the "rosy fingered dawn" of first love into the heat and glare of the dust-laden day of many marriages. But instead of advocating that the dawn should be made as drab as the day, perhaps it would have been better to suggest ways and means of improving the quality of the day,—of turning a stifling summer day into a glorious spring afternoon, in which it is still a joy to be alive.'[80]

The Aranda, carnally speaking, had that joy. What of them, then, in the contemporary setting? What of those who once sang the carnally candid songs, and whose marriage system has been broken by the white invasion? For them, Strehlow seems to say, we can only hope for the best; and he recalls, most revealingly, what Sister M. Skinner told the 1947

Science Conference in Perth when she gave a paper on 'adolescent half-castes.'* The half-caste girls were behaving 'exactly the same way as did the aboriginals,' which was to say 'their sex urge is tremendous,' they did not know 'the meaning of shame,' and yet all the time, 'they were so proud and valiant in their way, so merry and strong and pleased with life. So certain it is their lot to procreate, to make the most of their beautiful structure.' That 'structure' was Skinner's way of referring to the physical. 'They care for their bodies, bathing them and oiling them, dressing their hair, painting their faces, making the best of their clothes.'[81]

For these girls Strehlow wished a Christian marriage, that seems to go without saying. So too does the presence of other pretty Aboriginal girls Sister Skinner must have helped conjure up: starting with the black Juliets of his boyhood, the belles of his homecoming, and the innumerable girls consorting with bushmen during his years as a patrol officer. Strehlow says he does not wish to predict the future, but his argument has almost come full circle. The best present might come from the best of the past. He began by speaking well of passion treated naturalistically, and he ends by speaking of 'uninhibited aboriginal laughter' which, even if it did not belong with 'the tender love lyrics of European verse,' was nonetheless 'guiltless.'[82] *Disgust, trepidation, dislike* have run their course. *Like* is the final note: a vision of female Aboriginal bodies blessed in Christian wedlock.

Strehlow had performed an altogether complicated dance, and the position he has arrived at is a strange one. It is a shy defence of matter-of-fact carnalities, combined with a lament for courtly love. It is both a dance with the vital innocence of celebratory lusts and fecundities, and a Western idealisation of Christian restraints. He casts his own spell upon Aranda *amours*, for all the word resurrecting them as both free in their instincts *and* constrained in their own good ways. It was all as if to say: when it comes to love, 'our' Aranda are noble savages whereas 'we' or, rather, the Western married man, might be the driftwood of the Romantic tradition, but there was hope for him yet. Perhaps.

It was time to set off for London.

He did so on 13 July 1950. He took with him a manuscript swollen with ambivalence. It had much—too much, really—about love in it. And it had that cynical note he had located in the song by Noel Coward, 'Twentieth Century Blues.'

---

* This is Mollie Skinner who co-wrote with D.H. Lawrence *The Boy in the Bush*.

Native Abroad
Tearful Native Son

Setting sail from Fremantle he shed tears, telling himself that he would have no peace until he had come back home. In a spasm of homesickness before reaching London he had a 'vision of home.' With Mount Hermannsburg and Mount Sonder on the horizon, the gums of the Finke nearby, he could hear a voice saying:

> We are the sheltering mountains that stood guard over your cradle. Are we not more beautiful than the green and snow capped mountains in foreign lands? . . . We are beautiful in our own strength: our colours shall never fade . . .
>
> And I saw the landscape fresh in the glory of that beauty that was timeless. The young dawn of eternity was upon the scene. Mt Sonder now . . . gazed below upon the plains still sleeping in his shadow. I could hear his voice. He said, 'Come back to us: in us there is strength and truth.' The dark waters of Japalpa called out. 'In our depths there is coolness and relief when the sun, when life itself bears down upon you too fiercely.' The river gums of the Finke said, 'In our shade you will find rest when you are weary, when a hard world has tried to crush your spirit.' The wind, rich with the scent of gum blossoms and mulga blossoms, fanned my hot and tired brow. And I heard, too, the whisperings, in Aranda—'Don't forget us; for we have always remembered you. We alone have always been loyal to you even when your white countrymen and friends deserted you. You have risen in the world because we lifted you up. Our ancient knowledge has made you great. Only because we admitted you to our secrets have your white friends found an honourable place for you in their midst.'[83]

Writing this down, he did not comment on it as a vision that was a hallucination, the usual mode of a religious epiphany, but set it down as a musing, the result of brooding cogitations, shaped for the page in the way that was now so natural to him. The ventriloquisms were pellucid, an antidote to cynicisms of all kinds: in England he would get the recognition his work deserved; the sharing of secret knowledge would get its proper due; he would be rewarded and the Aranda honoured for their trust in him. That would constitute his greatness. Few Australians have gone to London with higher chauvinistic hopes more secretly tuned.

Strehlow was by then also a nationalist in the public arena. A few
months earlier, in a lecture to South Australian librarians, he had held
forth about Australia, the modern world and Aboriginal culture,
advancing a witty, sentimental, post-war and post-colonial argument:
witty because it managed to insinuate an implied comparison between
the savage German tribes* conquered by Rome and all colonised
subjects, including Aborigines; and sentimental because it was a call to
Australians to shed their 'artificial homesickness' for Britain as the
mother country, and 'give way to the fostering of Australian pride and
love of our home.'[84]

Home was everything in Strehlow's argument. 'Too few people
have ever come to love Australia . . . too few really regard the land of
their birth as their spiritual home.' In the army, Strehlow said, he had
been 'greatly heartened' to find that love among young men who 'had
come from the artisan and labouring sections.' They had not been
'indoctrinated with propaganda about the inevitable superiority of
European and English cultural ideas over everything that has originated in this country.' Or to put the point another way, as Strehlow
did in a cryptically personal footnote: 'The average Australian is
actually a transplanted Englishman, or "Pommy" as you call him . . .
They sit down in their fool's paradise, huddled around the fringe of
their continent like a mob of ants on a log in flood time. They dabble
their feet in the waters of the blue Pacific with an empty continent
at their backs.'[†] Strehlow knew it was not empty at all; it was full of
song, 'splendid myths and songs' that showed 'intense devotion to
country' and which made '"our own" aboriginals . . . the best Australians.' He quoted generously from the rain song of Kaporilja, and

---

* Even more gleefully Strehlow asserted that 'special English character and
  ideals' owed much to the German tribes: 'most of these ideals formed part of
  the cultural heritage in the English eighteen hundred years ago, while they
  were still dwelling in Schleswig.' The argument throughout was about culture
  rather than race: 'The concept of the British race is a dangerous fallacy.' It
  was an argument in favour of cultural change and transmission—the
  culturally 'hybrid.' With regard to Australia, however, Strehlow pulled back
  from talking about the Aboriginal hybrid in any way that pertained to the
  racial blending over generations: rather, his message about learning from the
  Aboriginal was meant to be a lesson for 'white Australians' (Strehlow 1950:
  27, 33).

† Strehlow is quoting the protagonist in the novel *Bad Medicine*, by none other
  than Patrol Officer Vic Hall, who stepped into his shoes at Jay Creek (Hall
  1947: 13). Hall, after being sidelined by Anglo-Australians like Abbott, took to
  fiction by way of redress.

went on to make the extraordinary claim that 'there had been no kinder folk anywhere than the Australian natives': 'We could have learned from them how to feel at home in our new environment . . . our natives have found spiritual peace.' The primal horde was a long way off: 'we have to train ourselves to look upon the land of our birth with the eyes, not of conquerors overcoming an enemy, but of children looking at the face of their mother. Only then shall we truly be able to call Australia our home. Our native traditions can help us to become finer and better Australians.'[85]

Many men in Strehlow's position would have asked themselves why they were outward bound for Empire when their love of home was so great; but he did not, which accentuated the enigma of his arrival.

Misfit

For as Strehlow sailed slowly in second class on the *Orion*, at sea for the first time as an adult, it was not only the 'Chants' that he was carrying to Europe. The other text he had with him was Luther's work, the translations into Aranda that he had been preparing for many of the years he had been working on the songs. Pastor Albrecht had asked him to do this work before the war, and Strehlow had obliged as much as he could as a patrol officer. After the war, he set to, doing exactly what his father had done: work in tandem on the translation of the Scriptures while collecting the songs and myths of the same language. His father had doubled up in translation for the last ten years of his life, and the son had been doing that for the same time now, completing the enormous task in 1949, as he was coming to the end of most of his first draft of the songs, which for some reason he was then calling his 'Chants,' perhaps not yet feeling confident enough in them to promote them to 'songs,' let along speak of them as 'poetry.'

Now, on board, he had a draft of the New Testament translation with him. He was revising John by Ceylon; Romans and Corinthians by Aden. He looked out on 'the world of the Old Testament' and reflected, 'How terrifying these grim lands must have been.' He gazed at the desert on either side of the Red Sea. 'One's own heart gets depressed merely by looking at these bleak ranges of deserts from a ship gliding past them over a blue sea.' He does not seem, at this point in his journey, to be either praying to his God, or gaining much joy from the texts before him.[86]

He was preparing for England. When the revision was done he was reading ancient English poems of the sea, thinking how important they were to him in their Englishness. He passed through the straits of Gibraltar quoting Browning in his diary, celebrating his English heritage, and within days of arriving in London, which he found drab, and whose shopping centres disappointed him, he was still remarking upon his inseparability from the literary heritage. 'To me England is great because of Shakespeare,' he exclaimed, and went on to list other great poets (Wordsworth, Shelley, Chaucer) along with Wren, Shaftes- bury and Wilberforce—a list that placed his political sympathies in the Whig tradition.

Strehlow's arrival in London was a mixture of weary literary expec- tations confirmed but he was not telling his diary what it was that troubled him, and perhaps not clearly telling himself. He rushed to the tourist sites, and bought tickets to the theatre. At the Haymarket he enjoyed *The Heiress*, a middlebrow choice for which he found he had to account. 'Tragedy did not appeal to me on the stage. Life has been bitter enough for me far too frequently; and on the stage I prefer to see those scenes that will make me forget the world in which I move.'[87] Still, that show was the first of many palliatives to come. He endured two winters on tight little budgets—no fruit or alcohol—so that he could make a meal of all manner of performances, a list of dozens that he proudly tallied at the end of his stay.

These were the time-fillers. He was not in the city to be idle. His New Testament could be finalised by more work at the headquarters of the British and Foreign Bible Society, where he consulted the latest edition of Nestle's Greek New Testament. He sat in their library in peace, enjoying the refuge of the place that had for so long been a major Christian publishing centre for mission work throughout the world. He would work on these revisions, on and off, for the next year, and finally have the satisfaction of sending them back to Australia, work done as a labour of love and which he seems not to have mentioned to the academy. That after all would not make him great: the work that would was of course his work from the native language.

As a fellow from the Australian National University, he hoped that all his hard work on the songs, with the ethnographic supplement of his films (which he finally retrieved from Customs), would deliver him a doctorate. For this he would have to impress the 'university folk' who mattered. One was the linguist J.R. Firth at the University of London.

The other, who was not related, was Raymond Firth, an anthropologist at the London School of Economics who had taken the chair once held by Malinowski. Strehlow had already had dealings with Raymond Firth and they had not been promising. The occasion was his 1947 language paper to the Perth Science Conference, where he had forcefully told his fellow anthropologists that they should all be versed in the language of the natives they were studying. The paper rankled; Firth had written to him:

> I agree also of course with your emphasis on the need for anthropologists not only to record material in native languages, but to be able to speak those languages fluently. The reverse is also true. I have just had a letter from G.B. Milnar who is a colleague of J.R. Firth, and is studying Fijian in the Islands. He says that he feels that to study a language it is necessary to follow his subjects to their clearings and to their fishing ground as well as to attend their meetings and domestic ceremonies. In other words the student of languages should be trained to understand the context of language. So, as I think you agree, the linguists should have proper training in anthropology.[88]

Strehlow made contact with Raymond Firth early on and immediately found him an over-diplomatic man, and rather too English (for a New Zealander). And sure enough, it was made clear that Strehlow would need some formal training in both anthropology and linguistics. J.R. Firth, when they met, was to insist on the same thing. At the age of 42—after his career had been interrupted by a war rather than any lack of industry on his part—he was obliged to be a student. Most men with twenty years work behind them would have baulked, and Strehlow did.

He went to the open seminars on anthropology thinking; 'I won't get a PhD in any case—so why study or work? It will never get me anywhere ... I have worked enough.'[89] He was tense about the prospect of Firth looking at his 'Chants Treatise': 'If he tears it to pieces I might as well pack up and go home.'

The land where the voices were was a long way away and Strehlow fell into a melancholic homesickness. 'Even in the deserts of Central Australia we knew that one was in one's own country.' Saying this seemed to help: nostalgia would fundamentally warm him in the months to come, especially when he was most conscious of his 'morbidity,' and of being what he called a 'queer person.'[90] He was homesick soon after first meeting Raymond Firth, and the day after recalling that he was 'known' in his own country he treated himself to an outing at the touring Folies Bergère. 'Some, perhaps even most, of the girls were probably English, but only in a French setting would they have been able to look natural and not brazen.'[91] His diary fulminates about the girls, feminine beauty, decency and the embarrassment of the English men in the audience. But pretty girls were not enough when he was still waiting to face the music with Firth. 'Very depressed. London boring,' he told himself in October, and 'wondering what ever made me think that by hard work I should ever get anywhere in the academic world. It's the same here as elsewhere. A few men of genius get to the top—too often after they are broken and old.'

He was supposed to attend a course in phonetics run by Miss Evans. This he dutifully did, until Miss Evans dressed him down for being late—'spoke to me like an ignorant colonial schoolboy,' a humiliation that was still disturbing his sleep two days later. He thought of his own work back in Australia that 'remains undone.' 'The trouble is,' he reflected, 'I don't fit into any system.'[92]

There were good reasons why Strehlow did not fit into the village of anthropology in London. He was not an anthropologist. He was a literary chap groomed in the Classics, albeit one who had, by virtue of his intimacy with a native language, written very well about mythology and, to a limited extent, the sacred objects that might with a stretch be slotted into rather old-fashioned anthropological discussions about totemism. If he had done his anthropology the academic way he'd have been, by 1951, schooled in the functionalism of Durkheim's *The Elementary Forms of Religious Life* and the descriptive elaborations of Bronislaw Malinowski, whose dramatic literary flair seemed to net so much that was coherent about the mental and sexual life of Melanesians. Out of thinking led by Durkheim, biological notions of race, and the associated constructions of the primitive, had given way to a discourse about culture. Before the war, the LSE had been in thrall to Professor Malinowski, whose best students, men like E.E. Evans-Pritchard, were just coming into their own fieldwork, which would, they hoped, be more theoretically advanced than their teachers'. The era of anthropology facing Strehlow was to be suspicious of mere literary flair, and insistent on extreme coherence of descriptive material and theoretical structures, even if the literary mould was as imperialistic as Kipling (which was the case with Evans-Pritchard among the Nuer in Africa) and universal structures were aridly imposed (as was the case with the elegant prose of Radcliffe-Brown).[93] Sterility, formalism,[94] academic conjecture—these tendencies, even when they were so easily caricatured, were as alien to Strehlow as his father's work had been to Sir James Frazer and Baldwin Spencer. 'They' had labelled Carl Strehlow's ethnography as bogus religiously; the son's feeling was that academic anthropology was bogus scientifically.

That was half the point, really: the intellectual culture at LSE was the product of a tradition that, despite its own efforts to reach 'the theological stratum of the savage mind,' had tended to dismiss mission ethnologists. In the twenties, the important new men of anthropology—Rivers, Haddon, Malinowski—went into the field carrying with them Tyler's *Notes and Queries*, a refinement of Frazer's armchair guide for travellers, *Questions on the Customs, Beliefs, and Languages of Savages*. Although they had come round to thinking that myth texts written in native languages were central to fathoming the ideas and beliefs of the natives, the methodological vantage point of missions, which Malinowski had always despised, was still underestimated. Anthropology as a profession had partly defined itself against the nature of missionary 'contact,' and the aim was to build bridges between the natives and themselves, to define a methodology of fieldwork, to make a science of their personal contacts.*

The time had come, Malinowski declared, for the ethnologist to 'relinquish his comfortable position in the long chair on the verandah of the mission compound, Government station, or planter's bungalow, where, armed with pencil and notebook and at times with a whisky and soda, he has been accustomed to collect statements from informants.' Malinowski called for the anthropologists to go out into the villages and see the natives at work in the garden, on the beach, in the jungle, and so on. He was trumpeting 'open-air anthropology,' the

---

* The term 'fieldwork' was adopted by Haddon and apparently derived from field naturalists, who laboured to collect specimens. Rivers' 'concrete method' yielded what even he called 'bodies of dry fact,' only later to give way to his advocacy of an 'ethnographic empathy' and the application of a sympathy, the sincerity of which the natives would quickly recognise as sincere or not. Finally there was Rivers' realisation that 'language is our only key to the correct and complete understanding of the life and thought of a people.' Upon this Malinowski built, creating the myth of 'field work in the classic anthropological mode.' (Stocking 1983: 87, 91, 90, 77.)

epistemological implications of which entailed direct observation of the native, immersion in their languages, long rather than short-term relationships with their whole life, all in favour of sustained intimacies.[95] Malinowski had been heard to say, 'Rivers is the Rider Haggard of anthropology: I shall be the Conrad.'

The man who reported this remark was Ronald Firth, who wrote a study of Malinowski, making a hero of him well before the cult of Lévi-Strauss.[96] My point is that by 1950 the open-air model of long, solitary and arduous excursions in 'the classic mode,' myth though it was, was to anthropology 'as the blood of the martyrs is to the Roman Catholic Church.'[97]

Any disdain by Strehlow towards the legendary cult of the field would have been entirely reasonable. He had come out of the field. He had been born there. He had gone back to that field and proved the worth of his solitary labours. He did not need lessons about the gaps between his own beliefs and theirs, any more than he needed to be told about the need to look into the differences between structures of belief and actual behaviour. He had come from *that* field too: the complex actualities of native life. He also knew something direct about savage life. And what he knew he knew not as Conrad, but rather, if a literary analogy had to be drawn, as a Caliban, which was more to the point of the ethnographic enterprise. In a word, he did not need to be self-conscious about his practice as an 'anthropologist' any more than he needed a critical concept of culture.[*]

Strehlow's impatience may have distorted Raymond Firth's level of interest. Firth and his colleagues must have known that here was a man whose very life answered to so many 'problems of the field.' But Firth couldn't know the depth of Strehlow's solitary tendencies, and the covert myth that had come to envelop him, what with hearing Aboriginal voices speaking of ancient knowledge, secrets and greatness. 'The myth comes into play,' Malinowski wrote, 'when rite, ceremony,

---

[*]   Strehlow's aversion to a critical or formal concept of culture perhaps helped assign him to that in which he was embedded: a Pauline Christianity which allowed very little cultural detachment about matters of the flesh. By contrast, Lévi-Strauss was able, for better and worse, to deal with his sense of 'the folly of the passions' by putting culture on his formal grid of 'language'; and in this he was partly assisted by his affection for Lucretius, 'the Graecophile Roman' who saw man as torn between the pleasure of sex and the pain of emotional loss, the anxiety of which could be alleviated by 'scientific knowledge, which teaches intelligent detachment, equanimity.' (Sontag 1970: 187–88.)

or a social or moral rule demands justification, warrant of antiquity, reality and sanctity.'[98] If the profession was in its tent trying to define its right place in the field, Strehlow was in his, looking out at them.

Drive Dead Slow

Off and on, a mix of things were satisfied. Professor Harwich in person praised *Aranda Traditions* and assured Strehlow of an appointment at the BBC. On 20 March 1951 he had a booking to lecture at the Royal Anthropological Institute, which was certainly something to look forward to. He had met Dr Phyllis Kaberry, who was particularly interested in the belief of Aranda women.[99] He held forth on their first meeting, and enjoyed doing the same at her flat some weeks later, where he met another Australian who had read his book. In his diary he does not name this other reader except to say she had just had a novel called *Come in Spinner* accepted for publication. Dymphna Cusack does not appear again in his diary, but other Australians do, warming him at a time when his refrain was that he had not made a friend of a single English person.

On the way to dinner with Kaberry he walked around in the crowd at Piccadilly thinking to himself, 'there was not one loving soul there that I knew or that would have cared for me.' At that moment his attention was drawn to a few good-looking girls in smart dresses, one of whom called out 'good night.' A platinum blonde caught up with him and he engaged with her enough to learn that she had a flat nearby. '"So did the other girls," she said . . . I went on, and soon another pretty girl with a smile came past, and said good night. I did not stop, for I should have been late for the party if I had done so.'[100]

A few nights later, as it happens, he saw T.S. Eliot's *The Cocktail Party*, a coruscating study of a sterile marriage. No comment is made on this play by Strehlow, even though he was effusive about many later productions he attended. What he is beginning to hate about the English is their reserve. 'They are so useless unless they want something.' They were 'smug self-satisfied, complacent': 'Today I feel I hate England and London and the stupid English university folk,' he wrote on Sunday, 26 November. The next day there was more heavy fog. But the fog and the sense of oppressive reserve lifted the next day when he had a jolly evening with Professor and Mrs Norman Hare, who were Australians. Their talk prompted another expansive footnote in his diary, this time about 'the state of most marriages in

England' and the idea put forward by Mrs Hare that 'men of 47 should not have wives of 45, they should get fresh young women at that age to exhaust them and keep them interested.'[101] Much fun was had with that line of thought, including Mrs Hare's saying she would not mind being a slave girl since she would 'at least be getting a bit of pleasure.'

In the same entry Strehlow notes his decision to take up private dancing classes. For the next few months he makes no other mention of the street girls, but he enjoyed the dance hall in Brompton Road where the conductor's refrain, 'Hold on tight now,' felt like 'we were going to be taken through a Wild West ride through London.' He also liked the conductor's other call, 'Drive dead slow.'

The other dead slow was the whole process of getting recognition from Raymond Firth. Firth kept him waiting until December, and then, on the basis of an incomplete read, he quibbled about the 'old-fashioned' nature of the translation. Strehlow defended his 'old-fashioned English' on the grounds of the formal nature of the Aranda original. He fumed: it would not be long, due to Firth's lack of enthusiasm, before he felt like burning all of his material.[102]

On 31 December 1950, Strehlow declared his time in London an 'absolute flop. I have no grounds for supposing that I shall be able to stir up any interest among the English University folk over here. Has not Raymond Firth himself assured me that all my work on myths and chants has been scientifically worthless? Has not J.R. Firth told me that he would support a grant for me to go back to Australia, only if I studied more phonetics first? . . . Up until the end of September I still thought that England would provide me with opportunities that Australia had denied to me; today I realise that England will never listen to me—the English only want to teach others, not learn anything themselves.'

In the winter of 1951 Strehlow's most animated diary keeping was about the wild, passionate female he had seen on stage; two pages of eloquence on the dance of Salome who was played by 'a perfectly credible girl—furious, passionate, and yet thoroughly feminine and alluring'; and a half page on Carmen, one of those women 'who want to capture a successful man,' the 'secret ambition of every girl.' At *Il Trovatore*, with Leonora, the match of words with music was a 'terrifying masterpiece of passion.'

He was now more fed up than ever. In March Raymond Firth still had not read all of 'Chants Ms III' which was the section of *Songs of*

Central Australia on the 'Subject Matter and Themes of the Songs.' Nor had linguist J.R. Firth yet read Chants I and II, which were on the music and verse structure.

> But all they want to tell me about is their methods! Of tackling of linguistics and social anthropology of the functional type; they don't want to read anything I have written and to help me with my work . . . I'd go home now and admit my utter defeat in the face of English contempt and indifference. But if defeated here I'd do as badly in Australia, where University folk cringe and bow to English opinion. Sometimes I wonder, in fact very frequently,—why I should go on living at all. I am destined to be a failure. No enthusiasm, no courage, no hard work, no devotion, no persistence will ever bring success for me. England will defeat my Australianism, which I have received from the only human beings who have been loyal to me without fail—my aboriginal friends.[103]

Finally, in April 1951, Raymond Firth came good. 'He gave me back my "Chant MS" indicating mainly that he should have like[d] to have seen more references in it to the class-relationships of people—e.g., in my description of the Ilbalintja ceremonies I should have said how the various actors were related to one another. Otherwise he thought that its "literary" merit was considerable, and that my translations—as far as he could judge—were "adequate" . . . He once more praised my colour films and added that they had been much better than he had expected—it was very seldom that any anthropologist had the technical skill to take a grand film.'[104]

Strehlow does not rage at the lukewarm response to his chants. He is tight-lipped about its apparent consequence: that Firth, who was due to work at the Australian National University in the coming academic year, could not promise him any kind of appointment there. Firth told Strehlow that the ANU had no plans for more work to be done on Australian natives. As to the outcome of his fellowship, that remained to be seen, and on 'what money would be available in the future . . . he promised me nothing,' Strehlow wrote. 'I was glad that I had the Adelaide Uni to fall back upon after my return to Australia.'

On 1 May, when he was contemplating his last complete month in England, he let loose. 'What a hell of misery and disappointment has been my lot in London . . . I hate the old world: its people live on the dead glories of their forefathers; but they themselves are not worth one drop of blood or one coin of our money or one parcel of food to help them in their present struggle for existence or the death-conflict that is coming to them soon.' (The death-conflict, presumably, was the war that would come out of the Cold War that Strehlow had been noting from Churchill's utterances.) He went on in a way that summed up all of his themes, running all of his obsessions into one.

> Before I came to England I was proud of being a Lecturer in English Literature. Now I realise that I had no right to lecture on something as far beyond my reach and capacity. Only an Englishman has a right to English literature and the English language,—not foreigners or colonials. Something has died within me: I don't know why I praised our English heritage in 'An Australian Viewpoint': I have been disowned and cast aside by all over here.
>
> And so I shall return home, shamed and dishonoured. England has behaved like a Folies Bergere girl. They are lovely on the stage and excite and thrill at a distance, and charge for a glimpse of their beauty, but can one imagine one of them being attentive to members of an audience outside the theatre? No, they thrill only to disappear, and so does England. Since the middle of August I have been in this accursed island,—and have not yet made an English friend.
>
> Time is—time was—time has been.
>
> England and Europe are hollow and hypocritical, rotten, meretricious, populated with self-seeking hypocrites, tricksters. And when I get home I shall not be able to tell people what I honestly think, for then my home fold, too, will turn against me. For lying propaganda and lying education have painted a picture of a new Trinity and Holy Mother Europe, Holy Mother Russia and Holy Mother England,—benign, charitable and hospitable.
>
> Perhaps I have no country left to me.
>
> Only my Aranda would still be loyal to me. Somewhere there is; somewhere the gums of Iwupataka are shining green in the narrow gap; somewhere Ratjumba still towers over the oldest ranges in the world. Among the eternal mountains of Central Australia there will one day be peace for me forever.[105]

Home to Germany

But all was not as bad as he felt, even then. There had been another homecoming to make, a definitive one, which compounded Strehlow's covert myth and returned him to his blood mother, all in one. In August 1950 he crossed the English Channel.

By train from Ostend he travelled across the still visibly mutilated landscape, heading south-east through Belgium and into Germany. It was his first time on German soil as an adult. He had last been to his parents' mother country in 1911, when he was a little boy, on the visit that resulted in the deposition of his sister, Martha, and his brothers Frederick, Rudolf, Karl and Hermann. He had not seen these siblings since, though his mother's letters to him told him something of their fortunes. He knew, for instance, that Frederick had died in a Russian POW camp, and Hermann in a hospital somewhere. His mother had, somehow, endured the loss of her sons, and indeed she had soldiered on in her own inimitable domestic way, chronicling the grain of loss and destruction, all of which occurred in conjunction with the daily round of things, just as had been the case in that other wilderness called Central Australia.

He crossed into Germany during the night and woke 'travelling through a large bomb-ruined city' and then over a river. He had come to Frankfurt, the city which had had such a deep connection with his mission at home. To Frankfurt Pastor Strehlow had dispatched his ethnology and, along with other mission pastors, many sacred objects. 'And so,' Strehlow wrote in his diary, 'my first view of Germany was of the city that once housed most of the tjurunga of the Western Aranda district, including those of the ratara ancestors from Manangananga from whom the natives once believed that I had become re-incarnated.'[106]

It is a plain entry, quickly followed by 'I got up, shaved and dressed,' but it is one that re-invoked the vision he had when he left home, and the voices of the Aranda speakers calling to him. He is writing with more detachment, but it is one that registers an uncanny truth: he had come all the way to Germany only to be faced with the ghosts of his twin, the ratapa ancestors. 'His' needs qualifying: in his diary entry it was him in their eyes, in terms of Aranda belief. In his mind's eye he is holding up his doubleness by deflection, contemplating it outside himself. Perhaps he had glimpsed the true horror of the story to which he was moulded, where a mother dies at the hands of her sons: he could not take it in more than that. The train rushed on.

He went to Nuremberg and from there he travelled into the

Bavarian countryside to the village of Gunzenhausen, where his mother lived. But no one met him at the station. He caught a little taxi to her street, and the house. 'I rang the door bell. Gertrude S came to the door, looked at me and called out—"Der Theo ist ja hier!" And an old lady came forward, with an aged, kindly unwrinkled face and tears in her eyes and held her face forward for a kiss.'[107]

Strehlow must have hugged his mother, though he does not say so. But the old lady seems to have flooded with joy, and in the company of her daughter and his sister Martha, they spent as much time as they could together. Strehlow had his Australian life to show her, and she had her war diary to show him, and he wondered at the suffering she had been through, at her powers, like Germany's, of survival despite all the destruction.

On that first night he reunited with his brothers Rudolf and Karl, and their wives. He was there, in their midst, while looking on: 'In the evening they all chatted, mainly about their old days at Hbg, and their somewhat hard youth. I did most of the listening. For nineteen years I had talked scarcely any German, and it was difficult for me to join in an all-German conversation. It was a peculiar experience—one Australian among a large number of Germans, to whom he was said to belong by ties of blood, but who otherwise were strangers to him apart from pictures and letters.'[108]

He had arrived in time for Frieda's seventy-fifth birthday, and was there for the relatives—'the clan'—who got themselves to the party by walking over the border of East Germany, avoiding the Soviet police by keeping well apart from each other. They looked at his colour slides, they walked through the oak forest and went to the cinema together. In the days that followed (and on his next two trips to Germany) Strehlow saw as much of his mother as he could, travelling with her and Martha to the Christian performances at Oberammergau, the passion play that elicited the most graphic passages of his German diary-keeping: he watched fighting back tears, moved by the spectacle of the Bavarian peasants who were 'living their parts,' and whose backdrop was the beauty of the German mountains. 'Beyond the grand beauty of the eternal mountains . . . I could sense the screams of the approaching eagles of war . . . Would Christ speak again at Oberammergau in 1960?'[109]

He was, he had already re-discovered, an Australian. But he was a Christian in Germany with a natural tendency to speak of 'our' (the

German) sufferings during the war. He was disconcerted that in the local beer hall one of Hitler's favourite songs was rendered with gusto, and in the street outside at night drunken youths could be heard with their Sieg Heils. But at Nuremberg, where the War Crimes Tribunal had begun, he could only remark upon the ruins; and at Cologne, some months later, when he came back to Germany a second time, he noted the 'satanic violence' of the Allied bombing that had so razed the city. He fumed that those 'who had authorised such barbarity had not been ashamed to hang Germans as "war criminals." I sighed. What good was it preaching the virtue of democracy. But the Dom [sic] still stood . . . Before it, even Westminster Abby looks small.'[110]

Strehlow's nationalism got the better of him—as it had when he wondered whether the allies of the old world had deserved one drop of blood or coin in their forthcoming struggle for existence. His politics were democratic: he was no supporter of Hitler. But here, in this swirl of patriotic recriminations, we can hear the kind of utterances that may have been the trouble in Central Australia before the war, when some people heard him spouting forth for Germany and the Germans, despite the demonic march of Hitler. It seems to me that by the time Strehlow came to witness post-war realities in Germany he was so embittered by the English that nationalism could carry him away. Personal resentments coloured his public politics, as they did everything else.

It was on his return trip, too, that he was able to go to Frankfurt properly, and see the results of the bombing there. He went particularly to the site of the museum where Baron Leonhardi had received Pastor Strehlow's writing, as well as the dozens of *tjurunga* from Hermannsburg. The museum, then, was in the grand Italian villa, the Palais, which belonged to the baron, and the objects had been stored with a mind to exhibitions, along with other treasures from Oceania, most of them from other mission stations. Now the place was in ruins: its interior was gutted, leaving the outside walls and the classical entablature of the gate. Two twined columns still held the iron grille gate with its eagle wings, and above them the carving of the allegoric female figure, with cherubs cavorting to her right and on her left. On her right, three cherubs, on her left, two, perhaps twins.

The place had housed up to 350 Australian objects, about a fifth of them *tjurunga*. The bombs had destroyed 219, leaving 27 *tjurunga*. Some objects, after the bombing, had been exposed to daylight amongst the rubble of the cellar. Some of these were stolen, but somehow, of those eventually gathered together into safer places in Frankfurt, a *tjurunga* of the *ratapa* twins was intact.*

Strehlow must have gazed at the ruins not knowing, of course, that the *tjurunga* of his totem was safe. His mood in his diary is one of personal loss. The unwritten line seems to be: the *tjurunga* had been taken from their homes, which was tragic enough; now they have been entirely destroyed. It was a negative confirmation that their place, and his place, was not Germany but Australia.

But he also had a positive confirmation about being in Germany as an Australian. Nothing consolidated his sense of self more than the success he had with his films when he was on the Continent. The bitter farewell bade to London in May 1951 heralded his tour of prestigious venues in Brussels, Paris, Cologne, Bonn, Freiburg, Frankfurt, Basel and Zurich. At each of these places he had the pleasure of scientific and artistic audiences—as distinct from the dour and unresponsive university audiences in England. In London on one occasion, for example, he had been incensed when his host declared the dances on film lacked interest except for anthropologists, that they were dull and monotonous compared with African dances: he was incensed because 'my native friends revealed their deepest secrets to me as a sacred trust. I have betrayed them by showing their ritual to dammed sneering English eyes.'[111]

His rituals were his films, which have stood the test of time as ethnographic treasures. The respect they deserved was delivered to them, Strehlow felt, on the Continent. In July 1951 he completed his tour and felt himself to be a major success, properly appreciated at last. He calculated that he had shown them to a total of 3,367 people, and done so speaking German to 1,926, French to 960 and English to 481. His largest audience had been at the University in Bonn, where 510 people

---

* The most valuable of the Oceania collection had been freighted to East Germany for safety, but the Australian objects had stayed in Frankfurt and were placed in various storage spaces until the Volkermuseum opened its post-war premises in the 1950s. The storehouse for the remaining objects is in a modern concrete warehouse 30 minutes drive from the centre of town, along with a file card for each item which shows a scale drawing or photograph of the item, its Aranda name, a reference to its relevant literature and the name of the donor. A *ratapa tjurunga* was donated, not sold, by Pastor Strehlow, at an unspecified date.

were in attendance, followed by his success at the university auditorium in Vienna, where 503 people saw the Aranda men and their sacred ceremonies.[112] His last showing in Europe was back at Gunzenhausen, in his mother's village, where he delivered his talk in German and where 350 people packed into the Lutherhaus. Clearly, the audience was not the university group to which the showing of such films should be confined (as he had told ANU), but he let that pass.*

Frieda Strehlow did not want to see her son go. He did not want to go, necessarily, but his time had come to an end. And he knew he did not belong in Germany. 'I am not at home either in England or Germany.'[113] He was pleased to have reconnected with his sister Martha, who had given him a Leica camera—'a real beauty'—which he would put to marvellous use when he got back home. But he had not, when all was said and done, thoroughly warmed to his German family; he was struck by how they disliked each other, and saddened by the relationship between his mother and her daughter. Frieda said Martha, with whom she was living, did not treat her well. She expressed little sympathy for Martha when she was put in an American detention camp as a suspected Nazi sympathiser. And she also said that Martha had never found a husband because 'it was God's punishment for her religious indifference.'[114]

'No Real Home to Return To'
Strehlow packed up sticks from London in January 1952. After two winters in the town he was now thoroughly sick of the place and was even tired of the operas and plays: 'one would need a companion to enjoy these things . . . when I've been I've come back disillusioned and lonely.' He'd seen *The Tempest* and not even enjoyed that. 'Shakespeare himself had done with love. He was now a Prospero, who was giving up the magic by which he had peopled a stage with airy spirits and

---

* He also let pass the suggestion by the left-wing feminist Jessie Street that he show his films in Eastern Europe. Street was on her way to a communist peace conference in Warsaw in April 1951. Strehlow's first thought was to check with Sir Douglas Copland, at Australia House, about going to 'the Iron Curtain Countries.' He sent a copy of *Aranda Traditions* to Street. Strehlow's political caution was repeated a few years later when he sought the advice of Minister for Territories Paul Hasluck about speaking to the leftist group, the Council for Aboriginal Rights. Such timidity made of him a political enigma: a chauvinistic nationalist shy of the left; a post–colonial, radical friend of the Aborigine who curried favour with imperial conservative forces.

living men and women.' And: 'Caliban disappointed me . . . left on the side of the stage, after Prospero and all his company had departed: even "monstrous" hearts feel not immune to loneliness.'[115]

Did Strehlow have a monstrous heart? He might have wondered. And the 'primitive,' the wilder, dark energies, were before his mind from that last show, the one he happened to enjoy more than any other in London. His own airy spirits were fully engaged by Catherine Dunham and her company of coloured artists at the Cambridge Theatre. On a stage a London critic thought 'reek[ed] of blood and sorcery,' Strehlow was mesmerised by Dunham herself 'as an unwilling girl overcome by love magic . . . until she finally took off her skirts and raised her petticoat as she approached the man who had charmed her . . . Passion, sexual desire, the surge of life, hate,—other primal emotions were portrayed with the abandon of sincerity & the skill of true art.'[116]

These were Strehlow's last words written about art while he was in London. Two days later he packed up his 'last things' in his room, completing his cabin trunk. Then he took a taxi from Russell Square to Victoria Station and the train down to Tilbury.

He must have brooded all the way home. In London Strehlow had felt a failure in almost every way. The highpoint was perhaps J.R. Firth's proposal that sound recordings be made of some of his chants, along with translations of the verses; contact had been made with scholars in Paris and Stockholm. That did not compensate for Raymond Firth's lack of promises about an academic career back in Australia. In London Strehlow had felt the pinch of his economic insecurity, and he could not see that changing.

All this was grim enough. But evidently there was something he could never bring himself to proclaim in London: the depth of his allegiance to the singers of his chants. He had had his 'vision' on the way: that was when the Aranda voices spoke to him. In London, where he had most acutely had the feeling 'primitive' singing went over the heads of the 'civilised' audience, he sprang to its most passionate and crucial defence. It was a defence that defined his sense of his life's work.

No more studies for me! Not with volumes and volumes of untranslated poetry and folklore all around me, and the key to its understanding safely hidden away in my brain. Instead of my listening to so much pointless (from my own personal point of view) talk on subjects that I can't use for my own work, I should have assistants to train for carrying on my work in case something should happen to me before it is finished. But it seems impossible to persuade anyone either here or in Australia that the Australian myths and chants are valuable in themselves, and that they are not merely repositories of all sorts of queer or interesting ideas which the learned scientists, linguists, psychologists, etc. can rip out of their context and then weave them together into a fine shimmering fabric of theory.[117]

So he was sailing home to finish his life's work. That much was clear. He would put the theories of others to the side. He would set to using that 'key' he had 'safely hidden away' in his brain and consolidate his translations. All this was reason enough to make good speed home: home to a reinvigorated sense of destiny. But it was a slow boat home, made all the slower by his economising (he had put himself on rations: no alcohol until Fremantle, until the coast of Australia was in sight), and by the weight he was carrying in himself. Strehlow was not to unburden himself of that, its deadening amalgam of depression and guilt, of remorse and self-recrimination, for a few more days.

When he reached Fremantle he felt, he wrote, 'curiously unmoved today at my first sight of Australian soil; yet when the ship was moving away from it, a sudden surge of love for my homeland came to me.' He was then on the way to Adelaide and to his family—the children, and of course Bertha, whom he had hardly mentioned in the London diaries, and then only when she had sent him a food parcel. Soon he would say why.

On his last night at sea—'my last evening away from home'—he asked himself: 'what has been my main emotion this morning when reaching Fremantle? It did not feel like a homecoming.' And he answers his question with a double confession, one which he would keep to himself by sealing the pages of the diary from the world.

I had no real home to return to. [——] no longer wants me—when I left she was crying and swearing her undying love, and now she is unwilling to see me: I had a letter from her the day before I left London urging me to forget her as my sweetheart so that she could be free from the fear of living a double life. [——] I have hurt—needlessly—by telling her of my affection for [——]. And now I return to a home where I have to be on my guard every day and night, where I have no room that is entirely my own, where I don't even own my soul. I have no home anywhere in Australia: even at J[ay] C[reek] I can only be a visitor, and Hbg cannot be my home as long as it is a Mission Station. And there was not even Paul's promised letter waiting for me at Fremantle. If sent in time, it missed the boat, and I must now worry even lest it should fall into Bertha's hands if readdressed. A wild spirit of protest is rising within me: why am I just like a hunted, homeless animal? Have I deserved a little more from life after all the hard work I have done,—and the kindness I have shown to all the people who now either spurn or condemn me? Have I a right to my personality or am I just a married man who has to live only for his family?[118]

Soon enough, on a 'hot and sticky afternoon,' he was sailing up the 'leaden waters' of St Vincent Gulf and there on the wharf were Bertha and the children waiting for him. 'The children and Bertha were very happy to see me, and Bertha drove me home to Prospect last night.'

It was after this homecoming he sat down to write the rest of *Songs of Central Australia*, his 'Final Summary' as he darkly called it—his long, last chapter, with its indictment of the modern world and his restitution of the primitive in poetry. Its author was a self-confessed adulterer in mid-life, a man recently bereft of not one but two mistresses, a man who felt dead in the waters of his life as a 'family man,' one guiltily confined—captivity's captive—by a Christian prison of marriage.

His Final Summary
Acting the Primitive

The pull of some biographical material has its own force: no matter what, it organises itself around the instincts and the vicissitudes of the subject; the material falls to a base level rather than happily sublimating into da Vinci's ravishing line. In Strehlow's case, it has not been a matter of interpretation, necessarily, least of all of the Freudian kind. Strehlow's diaries, his yearnings and melancholia, his lusts and ambivalent abnegations to authority continue to run their own course that pivots around elemental responses to the primitive. As a result, the intellectual tradition which made a business of speaking about the mechanisms of *eros* and *thanatos* within the self and culture uncannily fits: he comes back from London as a kind of guilt-stricken Caliban, with the sounds in his ears of African dance where 'Passion, sexual desire, the surge of life, hate,— other primal emotions were portrayed with the abandon of *sincerity* & the skill of true art' (emphasis added).[119] The 'sincerity' is revealing. After his two years in Metropolitan Europe Strehlow had come to think of the primitive as *the* authentic mode, the way of release after the misery of dark repressions. It was a primitive thought about the primitive, but one in keeping with the allegorical mode in which he lived, and which, arguably, had come to dominate anthropology without him knowing it.

Equally primitive was his drive to possess his knowledge exclusively, to make of his writing a single pole. This was clear even before he had left London (Elkin had said so in his review of *Aranda Traditions*), and was now going to become clearer as he brought his manuscript to a close. In fact, to read Strehlow is to be given the impression that no one else had really translated sacred song. That is far from true, as we know. His father had been among the first to do so, and he was acknowledged, more or less, in the introduction to *Songs* and occasionally in the body of the son's book.* Pastor Reuther is ignored. Among Strehlow's contemporaries, Harold Davies had translated verses from Aranda, but Strehlow barely mentions him either, any more than he was prepared to give credence to the work of Daisy Bates or Norman Tindale. Nor does he mention (it hardly needs saying) Elkin's ambivalent remarks of 1938, where the songs were not necessarily to be judged poetry at all.[120†]

Among Strehlow's closer personal acquaintances, there was the industrious husband and wife team, Ronald and Catherine Berndt, whose early work was based in Oldea, with desert people far to the south of the Aranda, and who made their name as translators of song when they

---

*   Pastor Carl was much more present in Strehlow's field notes. The father is often the basic reference for a myth or song, against which informants are checked. His words are used as prompts, reviving and testing the memories of the son's informants. The scholar who gains permission to work from these field journals will be in an excellent position to gauge, among other things, Strehlow's refrain about the generational decline of knowledge. They will also be able to track Strehlow's own difficulties with his informants, as with: 'It is typical of native story tellers to put in verses and details that are entirely incomprehensible without some knowledge of the other traditions not yet mentioned by them' (Myth Book 1948: 49a). Patience, and yet more exacting patience, in turn often producing only uncertainty, was the order of Strehlow's days as he sat with the men.

†   Elkin could not, however, bring himself to say they were not generically poetry. 'Those texts,' he wrote (1937: 301), 'which are limited to four or five words do no readily suggest poetry to us, although the singing version with its accent, rhythm and repetition and with its variation in accent and rhythm may do so. Moreover, each word or, in some cases, the total verse gives rise in a singer and audience to ideas, pictures and emotions, which can be best translated in poetic form.' That is to say, the poetry of the Aboriginal song was not lost but regained in translation.

published *The Moon Bone Song Cycle*, a translation from Arnhem Land. The Moon Bone song is a wonderful interlinear translation in blank verse which immediately registered in Australian literary circles, if not with Strehlow. But it was only one song, and the first really major book-length work of distinction was the remarkable *Djanggawul*, which the Berndts published in 1952,[121] the year before Strehlow wrote his last chapter for *Songs*. Hardly a mention is made of this achievement in *Songs* and in 1967, when Strehlow wrote his introduction, all that he could bring himself to say was: 'some Arnhem Land song-cycles, collected by R.M. and C.H. Berndt, have appeared in print.'[122]

There was another important difference between Berndt and Strehlow in 1953. It was a difference not simply of faith but of intent. Berndt hoped that his translations would help 'persuade administrators, missionaries and teachers to adopt a more tolerant attitude towards Aboriginal indigenous life.'[123] No such statement appears in *Songs*—perhaps, of course, because Strehlow took it for granted; perhaps also because he had in his own years as an administrator partly given up on 'policy,' such was his felt defeat as a patrol officer. The fact remains, though: *Songs* was predominantly written as an epitaph and *Djanggawul* was not.

And as an epitaph, *Songs* was a monumental and self-absorbed one, a book that finally sought to compensate for its literariness by arguing a case for the primitive. All this and more can be seen in the movement of the chapter Strehlow sat down to write in 1953. He begins it with a major statement, more explicit in its valuations than anywhere else in his big book. It is as if he has, after his embittering experience of Europe, written himself to a point when he must affirm what is fundamentally important to himself, regardless of the consequences:

The reader who has had the persistence to read through the several hundred song verses translated in this book together with the introductions and notes intended to explain them, will already have been able to form a clear personal judgment about the nature of Australian 'primitive verse' and its function in a 'primitive' Australian society. He will have realised that the term 'primitive' when used in this book does *not* mean verse which is crude, backward, simple, undeveloped, or inconsequential. 'Primitive' has been used rather in the senses of 'original,' 'primary' and 'radical.' In point of language, rhythms and forms, Central Australian poetry is highly developed; and the themes of which it treats are of universal interest to mankind. While its full development as verse is hampered by its bonds to the arts of music and dancing, it shows perhaps the highest development of which such a composite form of art is capable. In Central Australian verse we find literary matter probably not unsimilar to the raw material from which poets like Homer's predecessors hammered out poetry as an independent medium of artistic expression.[124]

It is a shame to say so but the statement is both misleading and inconsistent. Several hundred song verses? Nothing of the sort, if we take 'song verses' to mean what it strongly suggests in this sentence: that the book presents several hundred *songs*. In fact it includes several hundred—900, by Strehlow's count—but they are *couplets*. The 900 represents, Strehlow reports, one-fifth of the collection that he had gathered between 1932 and 1967,[125] but in reporting that he used the two terms, 'song verses' and 'couplets.' Strehlow's statistics are his own and he is entitled to them in the light of years of travelling and hours spent in translation. Without detracting from his labours it is possible to worry about his categories: a 'song-verse' does not make a song, any more than a couplet makes much of a 'verse' in the sense of it being a poem. Strehlow knew this; in fact, he was quite capable of acknowledging the fact in his own records.*

In 1965, camped at the foot of Mount Gillen in Alice Springs, he reflected on the songs and traditions that he had 'saved,' and the 'gaps' he had been 'forced to leave behind': 'I counted the songs that I had recorded on paper (and many or most on wire and tape as well), and I reached a total of seventy songs *apart from the scores of verses* which came from a large number of only partly recorded traditions. I could achieve more than that yet, I believe. But I need assistance, if my meals were cooked for me, and all my camp and town chores done for me, I could give the whole of my time, and energy to my work. Instead I still do all my daily chores myself, as I did thirty years ago, when I first began'(emphasis added).[126]

Despite his inflationary figure in his monumental book—perhaps held to because of those many hard, solitary years, those solo chores—the songs put together from the couplets actually number about 44, providing we assume, for argument's sake, that a song on the page is at least three verses

---

*   Furthermore, on 16 November 1960 Catherine Ellis, his part-time musical research assistant, who had been transcribing the rhythmic measures of some of the Aranda songs most featured in *Songs*, wrote to him from Glasgow about definitions, seeking confirmation that '*verse* is used to refer to the musical setting of one verse of the poetry . . . *Song* is used to describe a complete ceremony.'

(or couplets) long. Of this 44 at least 28 run for a page, and about twelve others run for several pages or more. It has to be said here that Strehlow very largely constructed his book with a close analysis of a baker's dozen songs, and that is all. His basic claim—'hundreds'—was a kind of fantasy. It expresses the lifetime project of which he often spoke: that one day he would have the time (and the public funding) to complete his life's work of translating the body of his collection. That day never came.

In this strange opening paragraph, there is the wobbly attempt to rank the songs on the scale of primitive song. As verse bonded to music and dancing, they 'perhaps' show the 'highest development of which such a composite form of art is capable.' 'Perhaps' reads like an evasion. And where in the book has he made the actual comparisons? In general Strehlow has avoided the high / low dichotomy. If he had made the comparison, as his mentor in comparative literature Chadwick had done quite straightforwardly, the observation might have been different, especially since Chadwick praised Polynesian poetry and poets. In any case, after the remarks about 'highest' what is one to make of the 'raw material' in the next sentence? How raw is raw? And even then there is the tricky qualification, 'probably not unsimilar' (to Homer's predecessors).

The stronger and most interesting claim is Strehlow's final outbreak into some direct speech about the primitive. Again it is semantically problematic. After the above, he cannot reasonably say that his ranking of 'raw material' is not in some ways described as 'simple' or 'undeveloped.' Whether his songs can also be described as 'crude' and 'inconsequential' is another matter: that goes to the heart of how one wants to value the whole culture to which the songs belong. *

---

* It is possible to hold to 'simple' and 'undeveloped' in the non-judgmental way that Boas (1955) spoke of primitive art as early as 1927: as art that employed elementary formal structures, which nonetheless were beautiful, powerful, functional and capable of dynamic change. That was the approach of Strehlow's correspondent, Maurice Bowra, from whom he had taken so much in reference to the Greeks. In 1962 Bowra wrote a lucid book plainly called *Primitive Song* in which he placed some of Strehlow's Australian material in some very mixed company, from the single-syllable chants of the Peyote cult in North America to the complicated narratives of the Eskimos. Bowra was perfectly capable of saying that song might rely on very simple repetitions—as did a Bushman tale—and that it also had 'dignity and coherence' (1962: 75). He was prepared to say that how primitive they really were needed to be sorted out, and that that could be done by acknowledging that 'primitive language deals much less with ideas than with impressions' and the special kind of complexity of social

Strehlow is trying to cut a swathe through his own convolutions. "'Primitive" has been used . . . in the senses of "original," "primary" and "radical."' Well and good, we might say, though it comes as a surprise to see a term like 'radical' for the first time in 700 pages; and to have 'original' affirmed in a neo-biblical sense when that has not been addressed before. There is no explication of 'primary' either. Still, the rhetoric is at least now straightforward, and it is the basis of the case for Aranda poetry that is woven through the next 70 pages, and which becomes, as it unfolds, a moody lament and polemic about poets, poetry and the modern world.

At first pontificating, Strehlow defines art as 'the expression of emotion' by the artist who 'feels things more deeply, more keenly, and [has] the power—the trained power—of expressing his feelings.' Strehlow then speaks well of powers of 'sympathy' or empathy and 'fellow feeling' and goes on about the quality of sympathy that Rembrandt had in such abundance that it animated and warmed his work. His key terms here are not his own but they allow him to make the universal point that links with depth of feeling in native song, which is the quality that raises the song above the otherwise limited poetic techniques: that is to say, 'its use of rhythms, archaic diction, substitute words and the rest—cannot on their own make a true poem.'[127] What makes the poem is the way the songs are 'charged with both sympathy and emotion.'

---

life within 'the narrow limits' of economic organisation' (18). Bowra extolled the language of the songs that were 'admirably suited for emotions and sensations and impressions' and had 'the power to evoke strong responses and to create a vivid awareness of the present scene or the unknown powers at work in it' (26). Thus the imaginative and emotional strength of primitive song, its vital force.

Strehlow told Bowra that he liked his book (Strehlow to Bowra, April 1962). This was well after he had written his 'Final Summary,' of course, but Strehlow might have taken stock of how it was possible to approach the material from an undefensive literary point of view. After all, Bowra's own antiquated approach to language (his cut-and-dried distinctions between language that facilitated ideas as distinct from sensations) was the same as Strehlow's, as was his Hellenic scale of value about what constituted 'civlisation.' When a young poet called Ted Hughes reviewed *Primitive Song* in the *Listener* (3 May 1963) he praised the elementary structures for their vitalist virtues, their skill at expressing strong feeling. Hughes also rightly reproached Bowra for schematically avoiding the ethnology that gave complexity to primitive song, and without which it could not be fully appreciated, and simultaneously reminded readers that 'a grasp of the West's intellectual and spiritual inheritance' was necessary to the 'modern poem.' Hughes' unconvoluted approach to primitive song, which did not involve an indictment of modern poetry, was contemporary with Strehlow's special pleading: more's the pity Strehlow could not benefit from it.

As a general case for art this is impoverished, but Strehlow sought to illustrate his drift with runs of Aranda verse where 'the poet'[128] (suddenly the collective work is the product of individual authorship) indicates an indisputable feeling for the local landscape, or a special mood. Strehlow considers Aranda poems dealing with 'night' and we read a wonderful song about the night parrot; but then he has to admit that while a sense of 'night' is there, it is not as vividly so as the single poems from the Hebrew, Persian and English. With regard to the accessibility of the Aranda poetry Strehlow says: 'to appreciate the details fully one should have lived in Central Australia and become imbued with the spirit of its colourful, harsh, yet magnificent countryside'[129]— which both condemns the poems to an obscurity to which he is opposed, and renders of himself one of the few initiates to the poems. Once again, and even by his own argument, Strehlow has put the cryptic Aranda poetry into the primitivist corner. And it is a tight corner, considering he has already had to reiterate (after Chadwick) that the forms of Aranda poetry *are* very limited: no elegies, hymns of adoration; no heroic verse, no prophetic verses, no gnomic verse, and '*no body of true lyric verse*' (Strehlow's italics).[130] Rhetorically, then, Strehlow must now re-establish their worth as something other than mere literature.

His case for his Aranda poetry is passionate, personal and grandly reactionary. It is quite simply a positive presentation of a culture where 'the links between music, verse, and dancing make it easy to fit poetry into . . . everyday existence.'[131] Strehlow values all the functions of the verse—for initiations, honouring of ancestors, increase ceremonies— and the ways in which the verse unites the audience emotionally. 'They sang of their own prowess at the beginning of time, and the whole community joined in their proud songs.'[132] He asserts that the religious concepts of the verse are 'liberating'—they provided outlets to the imagination in areas that were ethically taboo; this because 'the totemic ancestors rarely made any demands upon their worshippers which curbed their drives or throttled their desires.'[133] He defends the cryptic nature of the verse by saying that, even when unintelligible, 'the music form of the sung verse had an immediate appeal,'[134] and that this was connected, in performance, to the 'word pleasure' that belonged to 'the peculiar kind of word-weaving' that went with the music. Finally, he is saying that the total intelligibility of the ritualistic poetry is less important than its trueness of feeling, and where, in general, the power of the poetry comes from the conviction of the singers that their song connects with 'absolute "truth,"' that the matters of which they sing are true for all time because they emanate from eternity. The absolute truth is one affirmed by his Aranda singer, the 'native' who was neither 'illogical' nor 'pre-logical' in his thinking.[135] Strehlow is speaking here of organic wholes, of artistic fusions, of the marriage that can be made—under the heading of feeling, sympathy, emotion—between sound and sense, words and performances. Clearly he is exalting all that is usually meant by 'primitive,' when the term is used neutrally. At the same time, though, his illustrative allusions indicate another model. Speaking of the power of song, he refers to the songs of Schubert, which 'delight multitudes who know not a word of German.' And with regard to the European model of artistic fusion of words and music, he extols Wagner, where 'fine verse' was made to go with great music, where word and tone made a unified whole.[136]

The case for the Aranda poetry here implies a kind of vision by Strehlow: of a society that does not simply have a poetry at its centre, but a religious poetry that is loyally, passionately performed, a culture where poetry is an expression of its unifications by faith, and by faith alone (as distinct from wars and conquests). That is what Strehlow is affirming in his summary re-presentation of 'his' Aranda poets. One says re-presentation because there is much new material here, and not all of it is consistent with what has gone before. The talk of music being servant to the words has slipped away; the special pleading has been vamped up. Strehlow is pressing a case that weaves about—'word-weaving' himself in cultural terms.

Hitherto, as if echoing the gospel truth of St John, Strehlow was belabouring the primacy of the word in the Aranda poetry. 'Music is the servant of the word.' But now, in this embrace about unities, music can be heard rediscovering its place again. And the return of music to the scene is a reminder of how rhetorical and incomplete Strehlow's position had been in the first place. For who is servant, who master, when the two are inseparable? And in what sense master—genetically, in time, in terms of the development of the poetry: or actually, in the social performances of the 'verse-chants' (to use the phrase Strehlow uses when he is less keen to assert the primacy of the word)? Strehlow's earlier general position is under acute strain for several reasons.

For one thing there is a fundamental truth. The poetry was never performed in the absence of music. The poetry was always song. No poetry existed in Aranda culture that was recited as verse, or which was regarded by anyone as standing free from ritual performance. There were no poems or poets in the modern sense, where the words have a life of their own, in terms of both their divorce from ceremony and their individual authorship.

Strehlow knew this, naturally, and there is nothing in *Songs of Central Australia* to suggest otherwise. He knew that even when the old men were sitting with him and chanting him their song, or fragments of their song—when they were not themselves in ceremony, and no music could be heard as Strehlow's pen moved across the page—he knew that the essence of what he put on the page was inseparable from the singing and the dancing, the elaborate ritual performances to which the poetry belonged, and the larger purposes of which poetry served. He knew this most fundamentally with regard to his Aboriginal culture, just as he did by reference to the ancient Greek, when he chose to emphasise the Greek chorus and the oral tradition of Homeric verse accompanied by the lyre.

He knew, too, that his poetic diction, so-called, was embedded in musical structures—so much so that he devotes pages to melody and rhythm at the beginning of his exposition, making of the body of his book a context for the words that are sung. When it comes down to detail, rhythm is crucial to the words of the song, to its power and presence in performance. Ezra Pound comes to mind: 'the rhythm set in a line of poetry connotes its symphony, which, had we a little more skill, we could score for orchestra.'[137] Pound's point is literal and metaphoric. It is a way of saying that the primal form of the poem lies in its roots in music. 'Rhythm is perhaps the most primal of all things known to us.' The texture of Strehlow's argument, his detailed contextualisation of the poetry, is to imply that strongly. His thrust is to show us, even while rationalistically asserting the opposite, that words were the servants of the music.

Paradoxically, however, the closer Strehlow gets us to the music and his full valuation of the primitive the more his 'gospel thesis' breaks down. This indeed has tended to be the direction of scholarship with Aboriginal music since Strehlow, thanks to the work of Catherine Ellis and her students. The power of the music—the 'essence of the singing and the substance of the song' *together*—is the key to the problem created by Strehlow's ambivalence and ambiguity.[138] And nowhere should this be so obvious as at the stage of his argument in 'Final Summary' where he most exalts the organic unities of the religious culture. For the unities hinged on the music, the language Lévi-Strauss called the most intelligible and untranslatable. Furthermore, the experience of the eternal, the full meaning of the eternal, the essence of the dreaming, was most fully realised not just in the ecstatic performance of that which had been played by the ancestor beings, but implemented by the intricate structure of the music itself: in pitch, tempo, melodic variations that were its meaning, and this was especially so with regard to musical time. Catherine Ellis, who did so much to help Strehlow notate his music, was to develop this thought powerfully with her concept that Aboriginal non-linear time is enacted in the flow of the music.[139]

In other words, while we can say that Strehlow was working hard to value the primal unities of music, and dance and song, he did not fully do so in his 'Final Summary.' He held on to his words at the expense of music, and to this extent he was recoiling from the fully fledged nature of the primitive. He was in fact being rather cautious about his primitive: his was an orderly, if not tame primitive. Gone, in his 'Final Summary,' are all references to the primal horde in Aranda culture, the cruelties of initiation, the dire enforcement of marriage rules, the belief in murderous spirits—all that might be felt to be savageries. Strehlow's evaluations are in the other direction: he is leading his reader towards an appreciation of orderly unities, not of dancers who are lost in any frenzy of excess, or divine ecstasy, or who are drunk on song, but to the model of the dancer who 'even in the exaltation of the dance, remains what he is, and retains his civic name.'[140] What he did not want to do was explore that aspect of ritual dance which was a mixture of 'voluptuousness and terror.'[141]

There is another dimension to what Strehlow was doing. He was not simply returning to what he had come to feel about the primitive: he was restoring, to some extent, what he had taken from Aranda culture in the act of appropriating it as literature. What he had taken away he was putting back, and the movement here was an exchange of sorts. Having, as George Steiner would say, made his aggressive incursion into the original, having encircled and ingested, he was faced, inwardly, with what he had done. Steiner's terms are all too apposite to Strehlow's mood of work.

Saint Jerome uses his famous image of meaning brought home captive by the translator. We 'break' a code: decipherment is dissective, leaving the shell smashed and the vital layers stripped. Every schoolchild, but also the eminent translator, will note the shift in substantive presence which follows on a protracted or difficult exercise in translation: the text in the other language has become almost materially thinner, the light seems to pass unhindered through its loosened fibres. For a spell the density of hostile or seductive 'otherness' is dissipated. Ortega y Gasset speaks of the sadness of the translator after failure. There is also a sadness after success, the Augustinian *tristitia* which follows on the cognate acts of erotic and of intellectual possession.[142]

On this model, there follows a process towards rebalancing, exchange, compensation, restitution. In a sense Strehlow was always engaged in this, one way or the other, as we shall see. He was always caught by contexts that required him to negotiate matters of authority, knowledge, ownership—constantly managing, in private and in public, issues of trust. Now the trust involves good or bad faith with regard to language and meaning, culture and its performances. For, having trusted, violently appropriated and incorporated, there is then the translator's re-balancing, his 'enactment of reciprocity.' This is 'the crux of the metier and morals of translation.'

Naturally, Steiner continues, as if he had been travelling with Strehlow with the constancy of a camel boy, the risk here is of overbalancing. 'The overdetermination of the interpretative act is inherently inflationary: it proclaims that "there is more here than meets the eye," that the accord between content and executive form is closer, more delicate than had been observed hitherto.' Steiner is speaking here of the translator getting stuck in the mode of appropriation, and of incorporation—of egoistically holding on to *their* work as mostly *his*. This might happen if the translator lacks the skills and the character to complete the hermeneutic movement towards exchange.

'Fidelity is ethical, but also, in the full sense, economic. By virtue of tact, and tact intensified is moral vision, the translator-interpreter creates a condition of significant exchange. The arrows of meaning, of cultural, psychological benefaction, move both ways. There is, ideally, exchange without loss. In this respect, translation can be pictured as a negation of entropy; order is preserved at both ends of the cycle, source and receptor.

The general model here is that of Lévi-Strauss' *Anthropologie structurale* which regards social structures as attempts at dynamic equilibrium achieved through an exchange of words, women, and material goods.'[143]

Words, women and material goods. The trinity—with regard to Strehlow's whole career as a translator—is evocative: they make a kind of poetic code to much that has been involved in his life in translation. More generally, though, Steiner's orbit takes Strehlow in, since *Songs* is massive demonstration of both appropriation and of public restitution. Strehlow exalted text as a tribute, a gift, to the Aranda culture, even though his text did not assume they would read it. More pointedly, in his 'Final Summary' he was wanting to return the primitive unities to the culture, which he had hitherto appropriated as literature.

Exchange With Loss

But there was something deeply wrong with Strehlow's argumentative movement. Steiner asserts: 'There is, ideally, exchange without loss.' Strehlow had paid his debts to Aranda poetics at the cost of Western culture. That was the loss. For his affirmations of Aranda poetry and culture are the words to the music of his animosity towards and alienation from modern thought, and his own ungainly modern life. His 'Final Summary' steadily becomes a Wagnerian orchestration of dark things—a lament and a wrathful protest, a dirge and a diatribe—all of which hinged on two pessimistic assumptions. The first was that the Aranda songs were broken, their religious culture over, once and for all. The second was that 'the modern poet' was fatally disconnected from the most important things. On both counts Strehlow's argument was drifting and flawed, a tonal statement, an emotional lament—a symptom of his own vicissitudes rather than developed thought.

His coronial certainty about the broken songs does not stand up to the light of his own evidence The most powerful sounds of death knell are when he cites old men like Rauwiraka, who was a boy when the missionaries arrived in 1877 and who had told him, 'Now everything has been closed up, and memory itself has become ignorant.' Strehlow reiterates the tragedy of the generational loss of memory: 'For the survivors the night of complete ignorance followed.' And yet in the very next sentence he refers to 'the loss of *certain* Western Aranda songs' (emphasis added).[144] In other words, not all was lost: there were remnants.* The songs are *completely* broken; only *certain* songs are broken; the songs are held to with a *tenacity* . . . Strehlow held to each position simultaneously, even though he wanted to say in summary that 'their battle was in vain.'

It is a sweepingly pessimistic generalisation, even though he pauses at one stage to speculate on the possibilities of cultural renewal. Might not Aboriginal art have survived like the white man's once 'the power of the old religion was broken'? His answer is no: 'the bonds of the old religion had been too close.' In addition there was the pernicious nature of what the white culture had brought in the place of the organic unity of the old songs. 'To most of the young people the gulf between the Stone Age and the modern Industrial Age—even though the latter at first reached Central Australia in a rather bucolic and curiously alcoholised form—appeared to be too wide to be bridged . . . The white men did not sing healing songs: they possessed efficient drugs.'[145] And so 'the old songs had lost their appeal for the new generation . . . perished, it should be noted, largely because their subject matter had lost its appeal; no objections had been raised against them on formal or artistic grounds.'[146]

The last point is a strange remark, and rather counter to Strehlow's strong gloom. It implies a ghostly continuity to the songs: as if their forms might be in the air, or in the minds of the next generation of Aboriginal people. This turned out to be the case when traditional owners began to step forward to claim their lands: some of the important songs had endured, both in form and content. Ignoring this prospect, Strehlow speculates. He imagines some songs coalescing as people mingled across traditional territories. If this had been allowed to happen, 'The various Aranda native cat songs, for instance, would almost certainly have been fused into a single song.'[147] He tries with difficulty to imagine the

---

* And indeed, in his introduction to *Songs*, written as late as 1967—the year in which an Australian referendum voted overwhelmingly for a census that included Aborigines, a national response that reflected the contemporary political vitality of Aborigines who had not forgotten the basis of their identity; and on the eve of the campaign for land rights which would be based on the notion of *pmara kutata*, the home country which gave birth to the song—Strehlow also writes that 'in the early nineteen sixties Aboriginal men still living in Central Australia who could sing their traditional songs a century after Stuart's exploratory travels through their tribal lands indicates the *tenacity* with which three fast-dwelling generations had clung to their cultural heritage' (emphasis added, xlv).

shedding of the archaic poetic diction in favour of new techniques of 'word-weaving.' Equally hard to imagine is the idea of men of poetic skill inventing new themes, new songs, once freed from the totemic land-scape. The obstacle here, Strehlow says, is the very density with which the totemic landscape was crosshatched with song. Strehlow reinvoked his famous—but since much 'attacked'—1947 statement in *Aranda Traditions* about the 'utter apathy and the mental stagnation that exist amongst the present generation' who had no room for their own literary efforts because the 'thoroughness of their forefathers has left to them not a single unoccupied scene which they could fill with the creatures of their own imagination.'[148] So plotted was the country with mythological sites that there was no space for new song.*

Strehlow's compulsive pessimism is palpable. The point about the lack of space for new song is illogical, since he was actually speculating on the idea of new song once it *had* been freed from the totemic sites. He was trying to imagine the old forms being revived independently of their subject matter, a prospect which remains relatively unaddressed. As to the hide-bound nature of the poetic diction, in other contexts Strehlow has sung the praises of Aranda as a flexible language—idiomatically, and in terms of its reception of new ideas. But this was in defence of the welcome it could extend to Christianity rather than deep continuities in traditional culture. Last things, last days; final themes, the final summary. How is so much under such a heavy shroud of tragic prognostication?

Part of the answer, we might say now, can be laid at the door of the written. For by *inscribing* the oral Strehlow had solicited a certain relationship between what he had written and their lost past. The dis-tinction here is between inscription and transcription; the former is the recording under the unilateral authority of the author while the latter opens up the possibility of interpretation, dialogue, and open-ended prospect for the speakers concerned. Inscriptions, once they have been

---

*   Strehlow's views on the unfreedom of the Aboriginal imagination is connected with something of a musicological debate about the freedom of singers in the traditional songs (Hale 1984). Whatever Strehlow's final emphasis on this issue, he wrote to Catherine Ellis of how much 'licence' the singer had with that Lower Southern Aranda eagle song, of the 'personal whim of the singer . . . to change the words of the verse slightly.' The same applied to the soloists in the rain verses near Idracowra, so much so that he thought they had more freedom than soloists in 'recitative passages of oratorios' and perhaps as much freedom as soloists in 'the older operas, to vary the ornamentation considerably' (Strehlow to Ellis, 8 February 1963).

written, tend of their own accord to be of the past: they belong even more than before to the people or an age that has been lost, and so they represent, almost automatically, fragments, or ruins, in the way that Walter Benjamin once spoke of 'history' as a process of grasping, not inventive life but 'irresistible decay.'[149] By contrast, if from its inception anthropological record makes dialogue of its essence, no written result can be assigned to being the ruins of history.

Transcriptions imply a future, a time and place for other meanings to carry on. As Strehlow's friend Ronald Berndt was to say at his funeral address, after commenting on the fragility of what had been lost from the 'vast repertoires of aesthetic expression,' but which Strehlow had none the less translated by encapsulating 'an Aboriginal flavour': 'The past is never over and done with—unless the people whose past it was have entirely disappeared.'[150] It was as if the more Strehlow wrote, the more the elegiac mode was his lot: the more he had down, the less he could hear of living voices standing upright nearby.*

Equally, Strehlow's coronial tendencies have as much to do with his view of modern Western culture as with his tragedian's view of the Aranda. This is the other paradox. Strehlow embalmed Aranda culture because it was to him an exemplary case of what modernity was not: it was the preferred alternative to the secular, the materialistic, and the

---

* The only passage in *Songs* where Strehlow speaks against the future being a matter of 'despair' is where he says: 'As long as any language remains a living language, and as long as men and women of intelligence and artistic feeling who have a sense for word-music and word-artistry continue to speak it, its literary future cannot be dismissed as hopeless. The inspired genius who could revive and reshape such a language could still appear on the scene some day' (709). It was his friend and teacher, the poet Charles Jury, who pointed out the ambiguity of Strehlow's sense of 'living language' and the extent to which this idea of new songs went against the grain of his book: 'If I've understood your account of it the poetry and the language used in it is not merely archaic, but unintelligible to the Aranda and the Loritja themselves until they have been elaborately educated in it. And how far can the poetry be said to have been a "living" art, even before the irruption of the Europeans? From what I remembered of the parts of your book I had read before, I had taken it that the texts were purely traditional, and that new songs were not being produced.' Jury, who praised *Songs* overall as a 'work of genius,' was alert to other polarising overstatements. He warned Strehlow against the insinuation that Homer was 'a primitif.' On the matter of modern poetry and its shortcomings, he urged Strehlow not to be 'flattering the Philistines' (like Walter Murdoch, whom Strehlow had cited) or to go too far in his arguments about poetry's popular appeal primarily to the emotions. Referring to Strehlow's strictures against 'cleverness,' Jury exclaimed: 'Ted, Ted, beware! Shall I ever find you deprecating the intellect in poetry?' (Jury to Strehlow, undated).

artistic, when the artistic was made by individuals whom had lost their religious roots. Enter, here, Strehlow's strange tirade about 'modern poets.' These modern poets—whom he never names (apart from one entirely insignificant one) or defines in time (when did they become modern?—after Yeats? Eliot? Pound?) are condemned on several grounds. Their work is too complex. They have lost their connection with a wide audience. Their poetry has no links with ordinary life. Strehlow's terms could not be more contemptuous; they were those with 'idle, personal vapourings'[151]; their work was an 'unnecessary excrescence'[152]; they 'had a superior disregard for the feelings of ordinary men and women.'[153] Insofar as they have an intellectual lineage it is as children of the Romantic movement, which made a cult of the imagination, and therefore gave too much free play to the 'fervently subjective.'

It was, after all, a double-edged sword that created the modern poet. Strehlow is firm—and garbled—about this. Modern poetry is free because it is no longer 'hampered' (to use the term applied to the Aranda song), or 'shackled' by its bonds to the arts of music and dancing. It had had its 'divorce from religion'[154] and that had opened the gate to secular themes and freedom of forms, and to the practice of poetry 'as a personal matter for the artist.' 'In the poems of writers such as Horace and Wordsworth, for instance, the verse is made more interesting for the reader largely by the light it throws on the meditations of two psychologically and artistically interesting personalities. Similarly verse adopts simpler metres which can be over-run and expanded into paragraphs more readily; and speech rhythms supersede the old musical rhythms.'[155] Henceforth there was the rise of prose forms over poetry, and then: 'with the invention of printing poets take less and less trouble to define the ends of their lines *acoustically*: many rely largely on the printer to indicate the line-terminations to the *eye* of the reader. The old clearly-defined rhythmic beats are found to be intolerable by some modern poets.'[156] With Strehlow, poetry has been running downhill into modernity: after religion, its fall. And that, he startlingly claims, was sealed by the invention of printing, the writing down of the poetry. Yes, Strehlow reveals, the conversion of the oral into the written is a destructive operation, a diminishment of poetry. Or it was so with European poetry; and thus must have also been with regard to his own work with the Aranda, though he cannot afford to say so outright.

As a reaction to modernity—or a certain middlebrow experience of it—Strehlow's polemic hardly bears analysis. It was a railing. How else explain its gross oversights? Not only is it blind to the canon of Christian thought and poetry that was a sustained response to secular modernity, the critical tradition from Arnold to Eliot,* but by being so blind he misrepresents some of the best poetry of his time.

At the same time as Strehlow was blind to some of the best English-language poetry of his time, he used Aranda poetics for his own argumentative purposes. The Australian, the native culture, the ancient peoples of song and dance and animistic belief, are here used to construct a nationalism at the expense of other forms of cultural sophistication. It is as if Strehlow wants a chauvinistic art deaf and dumb to other cultures, one so local in its regionalism that its meaning turns on a concept as narrowing as a sacred site. This position creatively affirms a poetry that has an organic relationship with place; well and good. But what is one to say of a model that seems to exalt cryptic poetic diction, poetry for secret initiates, while at the same time lamenting modern poetry's distance from 'everyday life'? These contradictory evaluations escape Strehlow as he conducts us through the slow operatic movement of 'Final Summary.'

By the end of his book Strehlow had by implication sketched the culture he desired. It was a religious culture of organic and ritualised unities. It was a culture with poetry at its centre, a poetry that served the archaic functions of propitiation and prayer. It was a culture where doubt, scepticism or intellectual self-consciousness did not separate the dancer from the dance. It was a culture that turned its back on Hamlet (Strehlow's favourite figure of modernity) and on the trap of modernity's intellect—a culture which eschewed the Enlightenment in favour of medieval certainties, pieties, ceremonies. It was a cultural order ordered by the respect which religious poetry centrally

---

* Even as Strehlow wrote, Eliot had reissued *The Sacred Wood*, with the 1928 preface that should have given Strehlow pause: 'And certainly poetry is not the inculcation of morals, or the direction of politics; and no more is it religion or an equivalent of religion, except by some monstrous abuse of words. And certainly poetry is something over and above, and something quite different from, a collection of psychological data about the minds of poets, or about the history of an epoch' (1960: ix). Strehlow's stamp was to start were he had begun: not with poetry, but belief. For a recent overview of this history of spiritual crisis see Joseph Pearce (1999).

deserved. The notion of *enkaritjaritja* springs up here: the feeling of veneration and anxiety that belonged to and issued from the religious things, and from the poetry that embodied that feeling.[157] Strehlow's implicit alternative to modern culture was religious community united by holy awe.

To put the matter more bluntly, Strehlow had a dream of the collective, and even of a *total literature*. The expression was Sartre's and Strehlow calls it up in the context of Sartre's post-war critique of bourgeois writing that fed on alienation from self and other: Sartre posited the idea of a socialist collectivity that understood its mental constructions so well that its literature was at one with community and belief; it was total literature, and a utopian prospect. What Sartre dismissed as historically and politically remote, Strehlow took up as a lesson to be learned from the way primitive verse satisfied 'old needs and longings.'[158] It was a totalising religious thought, penned with the ashes of Europe in mind.*

'Final Summary' was a summa as conservative as could be. Anti-rational; anti-critical; anti-Enlightenment. All Strehlow's thought and feeling—his personal anguish and his persona of belonging to the Aranda song—conspire in the 'Final Summary' to a vision of a culture that was redemptive, and which had a poetic pulse to it, a rhythm, a vitalising truth and force which modernity could not offer. It is not going too far, I think, to say that in the grand scheme of poetics Strehlow desired to affirm, he was singing the praises of all that was, in body and soul, primitive. His Christianity inhibited him from saying so, but that was the purport of his trajectory—back in time, back to lost time, the time that he habitually lamented, the time of being in the beginning, a time of tribal unities, of the organic, Edenic moments.[159]

In the meantime, however—this was the fact he had to admit in his closing movement—the secular modern world was the case. The world had moved on from its beginnings, and Strehlow had no program, as

---

*   Strehlow's axiomatic placement of the *pmara kutata*, the holy home country, at the centre of the singing, and his eschewing of the rhetoric of political 'rights' in favour of something more fundamental to the soul, is akin to Simone Weil's contemporary argument where she asserted human obligation towards home ground and human roots: 'Obligation is not based on any de facto situation . . . obligation is an unconditional one . . . because it is food for a certain number of human souls' (1952: 7). In other words, Strehlow's position had considerable reach, which he failed to explore.

distinct from a set of strong and complicated personal feelings, to turn back the clock. 'Will poetry ever regain its ancient proud place in our community?' he asked three pages before the end. 'Part of the answer rests in the lap of time and in the present and future labours of our modern poets. But our whole society also needs to make a determined effort toward *elevating* its moments of thoughtful enjoyment to a higher plane' (emphasis added). But it was not 'elevation' he meant, really, since he wanted an art 'in harmony with the daily lives of its members.' And he was able to hope for that, he explained, quoting himself from an earlier article, because, despite the contemporary risk of a third world war, such a dreadful calamity 'would not end civilisation' because the invention of writing had ensured that things of the mind could last. 'The written word has outlasted the decay of the spoken language.' And it was precisely there, he hoped, and exactly because his own work had made possible 'a perusal of the ancient material [of] aboriginal sacred songs,' that the future might be rewarding for 'our future poets.' For it was 'the imagery' found in the ancient material that did 'harmonise with the outward shape and the inward spirit of our continent.' Thus the final hope of the 'Final Summary,' its last enigmatically hopeful line: 'It is my belief that when the strong web of future Australian verse comes to be woven, probably some of its strands will be found to be poetic threads spun on the Stone Age hair-spindles of Central Australia.'[160]

Contradictory till the last, Strehlow defended what he had judged to be a dead or dying culture as a *creative* source; and he extolled the continuous aspects of an oral culture, where everything depended on the 'absolute truths' of belief and performance, because he and only he had *written* it down. The ambiguous, prophetic megalomania of these formulations is disturbing, as is, by the way, Strehlow's apparent assumption that the 'strong web of Australian poetry' was still to come. If he thought this in 1953, in the heyday of Australia's culture cringe (and if Strehlow chose to forget his allies the Jindyworobaks), the remark can be absorbed. If it is read in the context of 1967, when he wrote the introduction to his big book, then it becomes an aberration. As it stands, in a book published in 1971, when looms of Australian poetry were thriving, much of it profoundly cognisant of Aboriginal art and feeling,[*]

---

[*] Les Murray, Australia's pre-eminent poet of country (in the sense continuous with the sympathies of the Jindyworobaks), in 1977 wrote the essay 'The Human-Hair Thread,' in which he indicated that he had been writing poems aspiring to 'the rhythm and feeling of Aboriginal poetry' as early as 1968 (Murray, 1984).

then it is a symptom of perverse closure, the mental fortress he had made for himself against the modern world as his 'Final Summary' becomes an archly academic elaboration of reaction, a Spengler-ish monument.

It was not so surprising, either. Not when you consider the other work, the complementary translations, he had been doing during all the time he was wrestling with the songs: his night work for Luther.

1   Elkin to G.F. James at Melbourne University Press, 7 June 1944, MUP Archives.
2   James to Edgar Preece, 2 July 1943, MUP Archives.
3   Strehlow to Preece, 14 July 1943, MUP Archives.
4   James to Preece, 2 July 1943, MUP Archives.
5   Strehlow to James, 9 June 1944, MUP Archives.
6   A.P. Elkin, review of *Aranda Traditions*, *Oceania* 18–19 (1947): 275.
7   Strehlow to Australian National University, November 1948, ANU Archives.
8   Strehlow to Hohnen, 15 February 1950. All such correspondence held in ANU Archives.
9   Strehlow to Hohnen, 19 August 1949.
10 'The various decisions made so far have been made ad hoc, and the sums of money spent have been spent for particular purposes, mainly on Mr Strehlow's initiative, but with no general policy that I can discern.' Stanner to Registrar, 28 November 1956.
11 Strehlow to Hohnen, 14 February 1950.
12 Ibid.
13 T.G.H. Strehlow, *Songs of Central Australia* [*SCA*] (Sydney: Angus & Robertson, 1971), 391.
14 Ibid., 599.
15 Ibid., 621.
16 Ibid., 346–47. In this citation some of Strehlow's Aranda terms have been omitted and his bracketed refinements of translation inserted.
17 Barbara Henson, *A Straight-Out Man: F.W. Albrecht and the Central Australian Aborigines* (Melbourne: Melbourne University Pres, 1992), 185.
18 Personal conversation (February 1997) with Peter Latz, who grew up on the mission in the 1950s. Latz is also on the record for the Oral History Unit of the Northern Territory Archives.
19 *SCA*, 344.
20 Clifford Geertz, *After The Fact: Two Countries, Four Decades, One Anthropologist* (Cambridge, Mass.: Harvard University Press, 1995), 61.
21 *SCA*, 281.
22 'Report on Field Work Carried Out in Central Australia, March to June 1950,' ANU Archives.
23 Ibid.
24 *SCA*, 32.
25 Ibid., 126.
26 Ibid.
27 Ibid., 124.
28 Ibid., 126.

29 T.G.H. Strehlow, *Aranda Traditions* (Melbourne: Melbourne University Press, 1947), xx–xxi
30 G.S. Kirk, *Homer and the Epic* (Cambridge: Cambridge University Press, 1965).
31 *SCA*, 32.
32 Ibid., 13.
33 Ibid.
34 Ibid., 11.
35 Ibid., 209–10.
36 Ibid., 212.
37 Maurice Bowra, *Homer* (London: Duckworth, 1971), 25.
38 Cited in Bowra, *Homer*, 17.
39 Ibid., 186.
40 *SCA*, 185–92.
41 Ibid., 185–86.
42 *Princeton Encyclopedia of Poetics*, ed. Alex Preminger (Princeton, N.J.: Princeton University Press, 1974). 'Hebrew Poetry'; and J.Verson McGee, *Proverbs* (London: Nelson, 1991), x.
43 *SCA*, 110.
44 Ibid., 114.
45 Ibid., 116.
46 Ibid., 114.
47 *War Music* (Harmondsworth: Penguin, 1981), 8.
48 Ezra Pound, *The Translations of Ezra Pound* (London: Faber, 1953), 10–11.
49 *SCA*, 685.
50 Ibid., 194–95.
51 Ibid., 195–97.
52 Ibid.
53 H. Munro Chadwick and N. Kershaw Chadwick, *The Growth of Literature* (Cambridge: Cambridge University Press, 1932), 1:15.
54 Ibid., 1:x, x, xi.
55 Ibid., 1:xiii.
56 Claude Lévi-Strauss, *Tristes Tropiques* (New York: Atheneum, 1974), 299–30.
57 Eric Havelock, *A Preface to Plato* (Cambridge, Mass.: Harvard University Press, 1982), 134–47.
58 My schematic suggestion about the possible purport of Strehlow's application of *logos* is non-committal about Aboriginal states of knowing, but I am assuming that writing as a system of communication, a form of language, is more conducive to abstract thought than exclusively oral modes. This case has been argued by Jack Goody, who explicates 'the Great Divide' assumed to exist between primitive and advanced societies in terms of the division between the oral and the literate: this because it is writing that 'puts distance between man and his verbal acts,' that 'permits a scrutiny of current knowledge' and 'constructive rumination' that is 'not tied to action' (Jack Goody, *The Domestication of the Savage Mind* [Cambridge: Cambridge University Press, 1977], 146 ff.). That is not to say, of course, that writing is the exclusive language of consciousness, or that self-awareness is logically or ontologically dependent on any one form of communication (Mary Douglas, *Purity and Danger: An Analysis of Concepts of Pollution and Taboo* [London: Routledge, 1966], 80); or that Western knowledge systems based on literacy need to be the exemplary paradigm of rationality (Goody, *Domestication of the Savage Mind*, 146 ff.; David Turnbull, *Masons, Tricksters and Cartographers* [Amsterdam: Harwood Academic Publishers, 2000], 10–15); or that meta-knowledge and Aboriginal culture is a contradiction in terms (Peter Sutton, 'Materialism, Sacred Myth and Pluralism: Competing Theories of the Origin

of Australian Languages,' in *Scholar and Sceptic: Australian Aboriginal Studies in Honour of L.R. Hiatt*, ed. F. Merlan, J. Morton and A. Ramsey [Canberra: Aboriginal Studies Press, 1997] and Ian Keen, 'Metaphor and the Meta-Language "Groups" in Northeast Arnhem Land,' *American Ethnologist*, 22 [1995]); or that agency within the thought structures of Aboriginal culture was not possible (John Morton, 'Singing Subjects and Sacred Objects,' *Oceania* 58, no. 2 [1987]: esp. 107–13).

59 Havelock, *Preface to Plato*, 198, 217.

60 Carl Strehlow, '*Die Aranda…*' vol 1. pt 3, 473.

61 Ibid., vol. 1, pt 2, 245.

62 Ibid., vol. 1, pt 3, Song 52.

63 Geza Roheim, *Children of the Desert: The Western Tribes of Central Australia* (New York: Basic Books, 1974), 65–66.

64 *SCA*, 584.

65 Ibid., 462–542.

66 Ibid., 465.

67 Ibid., 463.

68 Ibid., 475.

69 For the concision of the phrasings around 'disgust/trepidation' I am partly in debt to the paper by Shane Hearsey, 'From Disgust to Trepidation: The Debitage of *Songs*,' 1998, unpublished.

70 *SCA*, 514.

71 Ibid., 541.

72 Ibid., 529.

73 Ibid., 465.

74 Ibid., 339.

75 Ibid., 539.

76 Ibid., 525.

77 Ibid.

78 Ibid., 521–22.

79 Ibid., 527.

80 Ibid., 534.

81 Ibid., 540.

82 Ibid., 540–41.

83 T.G.H. Strehlow, diary, 1950 [SD], 4–5. The London diary is less explicit about dates of entry and hence the use of page numbers in this chapter.

84 T.G.H. Strehlow, *An Australian Viewpoint* (Melbourne: Hawthorn Press, 1950), 14.

85 Ibid.

86 SD, 1950, 15–16.

87 Ibid., 37.

88 Firth to Strehlow, 16 November 1948.

89 SD, 4 October 1950.

90 SD, 1951, 12.

91 SD, 3 October 1951.

92 SD, 16 October 1951.

93 For a commentary on the connection between Evans-Pritchard's style and thought, see Clifford Geertz, *Works and Lives: The Anthropologist as Author* (Stanford, Ca.: Stanford University Press, 1988), 49–73; for a comment on Radcliffe-Brown's style and thought, see E.E. Evans-Pritchard, *A History of Anthropological Thought* (London: Faber, 1981), 200–02.

94 'To him [Radcliffe-Brown] culture was a vacuous, nebulous concept, denoting not any concrete reality, but an abstraction . . . a vague abstraction.' David Lipset, *Gregory Bateson: The Legacy of a Scientist* (Boston: Beacon Press, 1982),

124, citing Radcliffe-Brown's *Structure and Function in Primitive Society* (New York: Free Press, 1965), 190–93. A formalism that could almost entirely suffocate writing designed to convey the actuality of epistemological encounter. As anyone with the misfortune to have to read the first twenty years of *Oceania* might discover, the occasions when the writing could convey this level of reality are rare. A fine example is Olive Pink's account of travels with Gurra, 'Spirit Ancestors in a Northern Aranda Horde Country', IV, no. 2 (1933); another is Strehlow's 'Notes on Native Evidence and its Value', VI, no. 3 (1936), but the most stylish and the one that proved that theoretical brilliance was compatible with open-textured prose was Gregory Bateson's first paragraph in one of his essays from Bali, 'Social Structure of the Iatmul People of the Sepik River, Part III', II, no. 4 (1932).

95   Bronislaw Malinowski, *Magic, Science and Religion and Other Essays* (New York: Doubleday, 1948), 147.

96   Susan Sontag, 'The Anthropologist as Hero,' in *Claude Lévi-Strauss: The Anthropologist as Hero*, ed. E. Nelson Hayes and Tanya Hayes (Cambridge, Mass.: MIT Press, 1970).

97   George Stocking, *Observers Observed: Essays on Ethnographic Field Work*, History of Anthropology, vol. 1 (Madison: University of Wisconsin Press, 1983), 84, citing Seligman as quoted by Firth in 1963.

98   Malinowski, *Magic, Science and Religion*, 107.

99   Phyllis Kaberry, *Aboriginal Woman: Sacred and Profane* (London: Routledge & Kegan Paul, 1939).

100   SD, 8 November 1950.

101   SD, 5 December 1950.

102   SD, 11 and 17 December 1950.

103   SD, 12 March 1951.

104   SD, 17 April 1951.

105   SD, 1 May 1951.

106   SD, 28 July 1951.

107   SD, 29–30 July 1951.

108   SD, 30 August 1951.

109   SD, 7 September 1950.

110   SD, 25 July 1951.

111   SD, 30 November 1951.

112   SD, III, 75.

113   SD, 12 March 1951.

114   SD, 22 September 1951

115   SD, 16–18 October 1951.

116   SD, 19 January 1952.

117   SD, 1950, 93.

118   SD, 25 March 1952.

119   SD, 19 January 1952.

120   According to Philip Scherer, Reuther's translations of the songs have been lost, but fragments can be found in Reuther's papers in the Lutheran Archives, Adelaide. For E. Harold Davies, see his 'Aboriginal Songs of Central and Southern Australia,' *Oceania* II, no. 1 (September 1931); for Daisy Bates, see A.P. Elkin, *The Australian Aborigines* (Sydney: Angus & Robertson, 1979), 300–01.

121   R.M. Berndt, *Djanggawul* (London: Routledge, 1952).

122   *SCA*, xv.

123   R.M. Berndt, *Djanggawul* (London: Routledge, 1952), xxii

124   *SCA*, 657.

125   Ibid., xiv, xxxix.

126   SD, xxxiv, 1965.

127   *SCA*, 660.

128   Ibid., 671.

129   Ibid., 670.

130   Ibid., 659.

131   Ibid., 679.

132   Ibid., 681.

133   Ibid., 680.

134   Ibid., 683.

135   Ibid., 694.

136   Ibid., 683.

137   Pound, *Translations*, 24.

138   See Oceania Monograph 46, *The Essence of Singing and the Substance of Song: Recent Responses to the Aboriginal Performing Arts and Other Essays in Honour of Catherine Ellis*, ed. Linda Barwick, Allen Marett and Guy Tunstill (Sydney: University of Sydney, 1995). Ellis' work was in print in time enough for Strehlow to deepen his own case for timeless unities, if he'd had a mind to. In due course he would attack Ellis viciously.

139   Ellis writes of non-linear time as 'moving from past to present to future; it is one in which the long past is ever-present and ties both future and past to the moment when a correct reproduction of a Dreaming performance takes place.' She illustrates this concept musically according to what Westerners call 'Cosmic Time'—'pulses' within 'the incommensurable framework of eternity' (viz. the interlocking patterns of time structures in Aboriginal music, and in particular the manipulation of 'perfect time' 'to produce a reflection of the timelessness inherent in the beliefs of the performers.' Catherine Ellis, 'Time Consciousness of Aboriginal Performers,' in *Problems and Solutions: Occasional Essays in Musicology Presented to Alice M. Moyle*, ed. Jamie C. Kassler and Jill Stubington (Sydney: Hale and Iremonger, 1984), 153, 160, 149.

140   The phrasing is Nietzsche's in *The Birth of Tragedy* and is cited by Ruth Benedict celebrating the good news that her Pueblo Indians have an Apollonian 'slant' in their culture rather than its Nietzschian antithesis, the Dionysian, which applied, she rather primly claimed, to 'very nearly the whole of aboriginal America.' Benedict, 'Psychological Types in Cultures of the South West,' in *Writings of Ruth Benedict: An Anthropologist at Work*, ed. Margaret Mead (New York: Atherton Press, 1959), 249.

141   The phrase was R.G. Collingwood's (*The Principles of Art* [Oxford: Oxford University Press, 1938], 55), and is cited by Strehlow in his essay on Rex Battarbee. Cited, and then passed over. T.G.H. Strehlow, Foreword to Rex Battarbee, *Modern Australian Aboriginal Art* (Sydney: Angus & Robertson, 1951), 4.

142   George Steiner, *After Babel* (Oxford: Oxford University Press, 1975), 298.

143   Ibid., 302.

144   *SCA*, 677.

145   Ibid., 702.

146   Ibid., 703.

147   Ibid., 704.

148   Strehlow, *Aranda Traditions*, 6; *SCA*, 704.

149   James Clifford, *Writing Culture: The Poetics and Politics of Ethnography* (Berkeley and Los Angeles: University of California Press, 1986), 108–81. Clifford is citing Walter Benjamin, *The Origin of German Tragic Drama* (London: NLB, 1977), 178.

150   R.M. Berndt, 'A Time for Remembering,' October 1978, unpublished.

151 *SCA*, 678.
152 Ibid., 702.
153 Ibid., 711.
154 Ibid., 699.
155 Ibid., 700.
156 Ibid., 701.
157 T.G.H. Strehlow, *Aranda Phonetics and Grammar*, Oceania Monograph 7 (Sydney: University of Sydney, 1944), 215.
158 *SCA*, 717.
159 See James Clifford on Raymond Williams' sourcing of this end point in *Writing Culture*, 113.
160 *SCA*, 729.

3   Night Work for Luther

It's my Testament and my translation and it shall continue to be mine.

Martin Luther

The word in language is half someone else's.

Mikhail Bakhtin

The Cross of Translation

A T THE BEGINNING of Lutheranism, at its very heart, was the act of translation. Its genesis story entails the vocational task of carrying the Word from one language to another, with all the faith that that entails. Faith, first of all, that the city of Babel could be re-addressed, that the Lord's injunction that no man would understand the language of his neighbour was capable of revision. Faith also in the capacity of language to transmit the Word across time and space: from one culture to another, even though they might be worlds apart. Faith, finally, that in all the translation of mere words, Christ's message would easily shine through: or if not, be made to.

Luther set to work on his momentous translation of the New Testament in 1521. At the time he was in hiding at the Wartburg Monastery, his books having just been burnt after his condemnation at the Diet of Worms. The translation was a monkish work conducted while he was in defiant captivity, a labour of militant necessity and of verbal defiance. At Wartburg he had to drop the monk's cowl to disguise his identity. Instead he dressed like a Knight, and Cranach, who would do the woodcuts for the first edition of Luther's New Testament, made a portrait of the religious warrior in knight's armour. At Wartburg the first word-work was a response to a Papal bull about good behaviour. Luther declared it written in language worthy of a kitchen boy: he resented the work it took him to translate from the drunken Latin, and the trouble it took to put into intelligible German.[1] After that he turned to more constructive strategies. He wrote a series of sermons on the Gospels and Epistles in the vernacular, a project that would eventually fill a volume. All this was a reminder that translation work was not new to him: he had after all worked the Psalms into German five years earlier, even before his posting of the Ninety-Five Theses. But it was at Wartburg that he started on the whole New Testament.

He took the Latin and the ancient Greek and turned the Gospel into the German of the day. He worked with the flair of a literary man who had—like a Boccaccio or a Rabelais—a farmyard sense of the physical, and a popular storyteller's sense of actuality. He was the master of simplification: he used popular proverbs, and called up illustrations that drew upon the life of the people.[2] A Scripture once confined to scholars and princes could now be read by commoners; it met his intention 'to produce clear language comprehensible to everyone, with an undistorted sense and meaning.'[3] And this meant that text could now be spoken from the pulpit in a language that made its appeal as directly as a warm fire at night, or a cold draught of water on harvest day. It was one thing, in exclusively papal days, to hear the ritualistic Latin and worry about its textual meaning according to the medieval schoolmen, another to have the Word fly directly to one, and know, as one listened to one's Lutheran preacher, that Christ's word now fitted one's own tongue.

'We do not have to inquire of the literal Latin,' Luther wrote with typical vehemence, 'how we are to speak German, as these asses do.'[4] (The asses were the papists who could not translate or speak German and who objected to his doctrinal emphasis.) They challenged the key word 'alone' which sat in his German line from Paul in Romans 3:28: 'We hold that a man is justified without the words of the law, by faith alone.' Luther had inserted the word 'alone' even though it did not originally appear in either the Latin or the Greek texts. His first line of defence was political defiance. 'Luther will have it so, and says that he is a doctor above all the doctors of the whole papacy.'[5] His second was to say, 'I know very well that the word solum is not in the Greek or Latin text; the papists did not have to teach me that. It is a fact that these four letters s o l a are not there. And these blockheads stare at them like cows at a new gate. At the same time they do not see that it conveys the sense of the text; it belongs there if the translation is to be clear and vigorous. I wanted to speak German, not Latin or Greek, since I was German I had undertaken to speak in the translation.' And he went on to illustrate how 'it was in the nature of our German language that in speaking of two things, one of which is affirmed and the other denied, we use the word solum (allein) along with the word nicht (not) or kein (no). For example, we say. "The farmer brings allein grain and kein money."' The example was deliberately rustic, of the people. The literal Latin did not matter 'as we must inquire about this of the mother home, the children in the street, the common man in the marketplace. We must be guided by their language, the way they speak, and do our translating accordingly. That way they will understand it and recognise that we are speaking German to them.'

Another example concerned Christ's remark: 'Ex abundantia cordis os loquitur.'[6] Luther:

> If I am to follow these asses they will lay the original before me literally and translate thus: 'Out of the abundance of the heart the mouth speaks.' Tell me, is that speaking German? What German could understand something like that? No German can say that; unless, perhaps, he was trying to say that someone was altogether too magnanimous or too courageous, though even that would not yet be correct. For 'abundance of the heart' is not German, any more than 'abundance of the house,' 'abundance of the stove,' or 'abundance of the bench' is German. But the mother in the home and the common man says this, 'What fills the heart overflows the mouth.' That is speaking good German, the kind that I have tried for—and unfortunately not always reached or hit upon. For the literal German is a great hindrance to speaking good German.[7]

Thus from the beginning Luther made two moves in the tropics of translation: he declared that the literal version of the original was not his chief quarry; the pursuit of the vernacular in his own host language was. There was also much more to it than that.

The German that Luther employed was the court tongue of the electoral Saxony, enriched from a number of dialects with which he had gained some familiarity in his travels. He went to great pains to find words. He would make a literal translation of the original, take each word separately and make a fertile list of synonyms. He would select according to sense, but also balance and rhythm. Then all of this would be set aside in favour of a free rendering to catch the spirit of the text. At the same time, however—and this was the qualification that saved Luther from license in translation—he was keen to point out, he had

> not just gone ahead anyway and disregarded altogether the exact working of the original. For example, in John 2 (27), Christ says, 'Him has God the father sealed (versiegelt).' It would have been better German to say, 'He it is to whom God the father means (meinet).' But I preferred to do violence to the German language rather than to depart from the word. Ah, translating is not every man's skill as the mad saints imagine. It requires a right, devout, honest, sincere, God-fearing, Christian, trained, informed and experienced heart. Therefore I hold that no false Christian or factious spirit can be a decent translator.[8]

The first edition of Luther's New Testament was published in 1522. It was a big, expensive book that sold for the price of a horse, as Luther said. Its 3,000 copies sold out in a month and successive editions in Luther's lifetime continued to succeed, abetted as they were by his marginal notes and a preface that insisted on justification by faith, the doctrinal emphasis that informed the whole Germanic enterprise. The first preface said that 'Just as the Old Testament is a book in which are written God's laws and commandments . . . so the New Testament is a book in which are written the Gospel and the promises of God, together with the history of those who believe and those who do not believe them.'[9] Luther went on to drive home the central teaching of the Gospel: 'that it demands no works to make us holy and redeem us. Indeed it condemns such works and demands only faith in Christ, because He has overcome sin, death and hell for us.' To prove the point Luther introduced his translation by favouring some Gospels over others, particularly those that were about 'preaching' rather than 'works,' most notably St Paul's epistles and St John. Of the latter, which famously begins, 'In the beginning was the Word,' the translator said it was 'the one, fine, true and chief gospel.'[10] Luther's translation, then, had an essential missionary thrust: to confirm Paul's teaching, and not to make Christ into a Moses, or the Gospel into a book of law or doctrine. It was meant to be a book of grace to show how the law was to be fulfilled.[11]

For Luther, what translation involved was what was native to it: interpretation. And in Luther's case interpretation of Scripture was close to a mystical experience in its appeal to a direct inner relationship with God. One historian speaks of this as a 'warm, living communion with God in the act of interpreting the sacred text.'[12] Such a relationship came forth in Luther's lectures on the Gospels. When he translated, that intimate communion of interpretation was reinvoked, and then issued as text. It became a work of the spirit, first and foremost, and only then one of scholarship. It was this sense of divine presence in the work—in the Word—that placed Luther apart from Erasmus' work on Laurentius Vallas' *Notes on New Testament Translation and Collation*, the scholarship of which he often relied upon. Luther came to object to the way Erasmus revealed contradictions between the church fathers. 'It is not serious,' Luther said, 'it is ambiguous and sophistical.'[13] Erasmus 'promotes linguistics but retards the gospel.' There was too much of the human landscape in it. For Luther the New Testament translation came from and pointed to the divine mystery.

In the course of his labours at Wartburg Luther was sick and insomniac. He suffered from constipation and lacerations of conscience. 'My conscience troubles me because at Worms I yielded to the importunity of my friends and did not play the part of Elijah.' And the solitude plagued him—'because I am so indolent in prayer.' The New Testament was done in an extraordinary eleven weeks. Luther's speed of work was facilitated by the absence of texts he had to hand. He worked mainly from Erasmus and his two-volume edition of the Vulgate. Later, when he had left Wartburg, and came to work on the Old Testament, he would insist on the primacy of scholarship in the ancient languages if the Gospel were to be truly understood: indeed he went so far as to say that without the study of Latin, Greek and Hebrew, there could be no real knowledge of the Word, and no higher education worthy of the name.[14]

The complete Bible was published in 1533, along with copious illustrations of the Old Testament. The woodcuts were as local as the vernacular. Jacob wrestled with his angel in a German forest. And the text itself, for all the scholarship with regard to its ancient idiom, was rendered in an even more contemporary way than the New Testament.

As one commentary says: 'Judea was transplanted to Saxony, and the road from Jericho to Jerusalem ran through the Thuringian forest.' Luther himself was pleased he had tried 'to make Moses so German that no one would suspect he was a Jew.'[15] He sometimes improved on the 'artificial Hebrew.' He did so 'wherever the words could have given or tolerated an improved meaning' rather than the 'inferior' one of the rabbis. Luther's racism was palpable: his sense of 'tribe' as pejorative was complete.

The ancient tribal tongue had its place, however. When the teaching of the text called for it, Luther was prepared to let the Hebrew be. His statement of doctrinal dogmatism and linguistic zeal was:

> But we have also sometimes translated word for word, though we could have done it otherwise and more clearly, and for this reason: the words have something important in them. Psalm 68:18 for example: 'Thou are gone up on high, and hast led captivity captive.' An idiomatic translation would be, 'hast freed the prisoners.' But that is too weak, and does not yield the rich subtle sense of the Hebrew. 'Thou hast led captivity captive'—that is, not only has Christ released the prisoners, but he has in the process taken away the prison, taken it captive, so that it can never take us prisoner, and our redemption is eternal. St Paul speaks in this way when he says, 'by the law I died to the law.' Again, 'Christ has condemned sin by sin.' Again, 'Death is put to death by Christ.' These are the captivities that Christ has taken captive and annihilated, so that death has no further hold on us, and sin cannot accuse us, the law can no longer chastise our conscience; and such rich, exalted, converting teaching does St Paul provide everywhere. To honour such teaching, and for the comfort of our souls, we must retain such words, must put up with them, and so give the Hebrew some room where it does better than the German can.[16]

Thus there is the ancient text, the integrity of which all translators would claim to respect. There is the host tongue, into which the old words are being rendered. The dynamic issue is the extent to which one or the other is thought or felt to be deserving of priority. With Luther, whose doctrinal passion compelled him to oppose Christ to all that had been merely to do with the law, with the tribalism of the Jews, the choice of direction was laid out. It would be a move away from the original old tribe, and a battle for the vernacular in German for two reasons: to spite the Pope; to reassert and enshrine what was unique about the Gospel. One might say here that Luther's translation of the Bible into German was his most enduring political achievement. His monumental work of translation transported the ancient teachings into the modern world of German nationhood. In complete command of his own tongue, he conquered the old language in a way that made the German Bible a kind of mission station in its own land. The cultural legitimacy of his linguistic direction did not enter his mind. 'Translation,' he declared, 'is a special grace and gift of God,' and it went without saying that he, as the translator, had been blessed with that gift, and that he especially had 'learned from experience what an art and what a task translating is.'[17]

That was why, really, he had to 'talk so much about translating.' He had learned the hard way. He had done the work without ulterior motives, not taking or seeking a single penny for it. 'Neither have I sought my own honour by it: God, my Lord, knows this. Rather I have done it as a service to the dear Christians and to the Honour of the One who sitteth above.' All this was the inspiration for the work of translation which might look deceptively easy once it had been done. 'One now runs his eyes over three or four pages and does not stumble once—without realising what boulders and clods had once lain there where he now goes along over a smoothly planed board. We had to sweat and toil there before we got those boulders and clods out of the way, so that one could go along so nicely. The ploughing goes well when the field is cleared. But rooting out the wood and stumps, and getting the field ready—this is a job nobody wants. There is no such thing as earning the world's thanks.'[18]

And so forth. Luther militantly put himself at the centre of things, driven by evangelical zeal, doctrinal certainty. His aims were pedagogical and political, his translations a vehicle for all of these at once. To these ends he applied his ferocious, penitent, arrogant and pious personality, making himself more captive to these traits as he laboured in translation. The actual work of translation involved all manner of judgments, the rules for which could only be expressed post hoc, after the experience of involvement in many tongues. One historian speaks of the Vulgate having once been, when Luther was a monk, his flesh and blood; and the implication of the analogy with regard to his later work on the New Testament is to say its translation was a matter of transforming that flesh and blood, reconstituting his own body, Love's body, with the divine message of the Gospel.

To this extent, Luther's German gospel as an athletic rendition of his own freedom, his gigantic labour of love, led to a paradox. 'Only those who at least accepted an outline of Luther's concept of religion could accept his reading of scripture. His reading of the Bible was not to be proved by the bare text; it was rather to be validated by the experience of the "true Christians" whom he addressed, an experience very much like his.'[19] The Gospel to which he had led the reader was in a unique way his own. Translation enabled him to conduct his truths in his way. 'It is my Testament and my translation and it shall continue to be mine.'[20] The way was now open to a new era of 'fundamental' disagreement about the meaning of a Scripture.

Or to use another metaphor, which is perhaps the most useful one to bring to the Strehlow patriarchy, and one often used in the discourse on translation: we should see the translator as a musician rendering a work. He is the pianist interpreting the Scripture of Beethoven. There is no such thing as a literal version of any great work: there are, rather, performances of the moment, renditions in time, activities that reach and sustain the right note for the passionate master of texts, as well as his moment in history.

So it was with Luther. The vernacular was more than vernacular. The language of his Bible soon established itself as Germany's literary language, High German in a land of dialects.[21] It was one that sustained the music of Bach, and which moved Goethe through each moon of his literary life. There would be other German translations of the Bible (as there had been before Luther) and his own translation had provoked a Catholic German version by Jerome Emser that plagiarised his own even while praising it for sounding better and therefore being dangerously seductive to 'common folk' because 'amid the sweet words they swallow the hook before they know it.'[22]

In due course, Luther's work would be modernised in the late nineteenth century, in the period when Lutheran missions were importing the Word into the New World, where Luther's tongue would meet tribal tongues other than Hebrew, but still it was sufficiently dominant into the early decades of last century for it to be re-approached with extreme diplomacy when the time came for it to be fundamentally challenged, as it was, finally, in 1925, by the Jewish theologians Martin Buber and Franz Rosenzweig. We attend to their approach in order to map the terrain of choices before young Strehlow when he started his labours in Central Australia.

Buber and Rosenzweig fully acknowledged Luther's command of the old texts. They were excruciatingly conscious of his great condescension towards Hebrew. They highlighted the way Luther's faith in Faith collared so much of his renderings. They did not condemn Luther for his religious motivations, for that would have been to subvert the integrity of their own. They were similarly vocational. Their personal purposes were nothing less than to bring the force of the original Hebrew text into the light of the modern day, to renew what Buber called 'the dialogue between heaven and earth.' Having said as much, their method was the antidote to Luther's Germanisation of the Word. Instead of the vernacular, they would hold to the Hebrew roots of words. In addition they would retain all the poetic techniques—the allusion, repetitions, the 'breath' of the line breaks—of the original. In so doing they were asserting the essential unity of the Old Testament, its sound shape, if you like, as a document that sprang from an oral tradition. Most of all they were intent on rendering the spokenness of the ancient text. Into this they poured their own scholarly and brilliant poetic voices so that the voice of their original tribal language spoke out.

That was the project, at any rate. What it led to is perhaps beyond the scope of our interests, except to note that Buber and Rosenzweig published their Old Testament in 1936, at a time when their German leader was devilishly intent on squashing any challenge to Aryan tribalism. Young Strehlow started his work in 1938 in a very different setting, and yet one which aroused some of the basic dilemmas that arise from the Lutheran legacy of translation. Fundamental questions for biblical translation, and perhaps all translation in the land of Babel, are these: is meaning to be gained from the Word, or something beyond it? What lies in the word, in its written and its spoken forms? Is the difference crucial? Is it possible to express the same meaning in two different tongues? Luther was happy with the difference between languages because he had faith in the meaning of the gospel shining through the Word. That was half the point of Paul's teaching: to hear the message above all, to receive the good news. And so the tribal tongue could be largely written out, and then in the fullness of time preached away. The unity that would come of people speaking different languages would be forged elsewhere, in their redeemable futures.

By contrast, Buber and Rosenzweig had another dream. It was of a sacred text that took its true speakers back, travelling towards the other side of Babel. 'There is only one language,' declared Rosenzweig. And he developed a metaphor that may be useful when we try to account for Strehlow's work with the Bible, on the one hand, and his other considerable labour with an ancient Aboriginal language on the other. Rosenzweig:

> The unity of all languages lies more deeply hidden as regards the element of the word than as regards the totality of a sentence. The sentence presents itself even to the superficial glance as a form, and so as both formable and transformable. Grammar, then, both in syntax and in morphology—which after all refers the individual words to their environing sentence—habitually sets up simple analogies between languages. But the aerial view of a language's verbal landscape seems at first glance too severed and radically diverse from that of every other language: and even the maps of these landscapes, the dictionaries with their enumerations of various senses, only construct for each word in the one language an environing circle of a certain diameter that intersects several circles surrounding words of the other language. There come into being a certain number of common areas—which all, however, apparently lie apart, unrelated and unconnected. The picture alters only through a more geological approach. In the roots of words the severed areas lie together; and still deeper, at the roots of meaning, the roots of physicality, there is, apart from questions regarding some possible original relatedness of languages, that unity of all human speech which the surfaces of words only let us dimly intuit. The translator must dare to descend to these lower layers.[23]

The range of Strehlow's aerial view, his intellectual interest and religious tenor, and his descent into lower layers, its psychological complexity, is precisely what interests us here. For with the Aranda he had already taken a step similar to Buber and Rosenzweig: he had called for the construction of a dictionary that would enable a 'geological approach.' After his elaborate promotion of Aranda songs to literature that is what he had ended up proposing: a return to the roots of the tribal tongue. The issue before him now with Scripture was acute. In what direction would he travel—towards or away from which host tongue? It is irresistible, here, to note that the Hebrew root for travelling does not mean traveller but 'resident alien.' Put the question another way: where would Strehlow make his home? In the bedrock of the Word, which even Luther imposed his evangelical will upon; or in some other place, even more his own?

Book for Blackfellows

It was the German text, not the scholar's Greek and Latin Scriptures that the Lutheran missionaries carried into the New World—at first to Africa, and then to North America, New Guinea and Australia. The German spirit that soldiered forth was pietistic, intent on rooting out evil ways, and replacing them with a devout comprehension of revelation. Here we might see Lutheranism as part of a broader thrust. Even in China, for instance, at a time when Pastor Carl Strehlow was labouring in the wilderness of Hermannsburg, compatriots such as the learned Ernst Faber were intent upon correcting the excesses of Confucianism with the weapon of translation. This involved a judicious selection of German texts that would properly represent the believers who had come from Europe, and a penetration of the Chinese culture with distinctively European terms. The key notions of Holy Ghost, Prophet, Revelation and Saviour were inserted into Chinese thought, along with Progress, Perfection and Evolution. The life of Confucius himself was revised. Christian German belief in China advanced the view that Confucius had experienced revelation through the Holy Ghost, but that his revelation, like those of other pagans after Babel, was incomplete or imperfect. To this extent Confucius was as primitive as other heathens, his mind less developed, and his legacy all the more needful of missionary correction.[24]

Thus German was destined to engage with the other languages of the world, the so-called primitive tongues of the forest, the plains, the desert. It was a short step, in the tenacious missionary endeavour of bringing the Good News to heathens, to write some of their message down in the language of the other, especially if the heathens had no writing of their own. Native peoples from the Americas to the Congo heard strangers bless them in their own language, according to the thoughts of a man called Jesus Christ. What kind of language they heard in their tongue is difficult to specify: one would have to be, quite literally, a speaker of the other's tongue to know and to idiomatically suggest an answer, the possibilities of which are remote because so many traditional languages have died at their roots or changed through time, and those that continue seem disconnected from academic discourse. What can be said, however, is that on the whole the Lutherans held to a faith in the vernacular akin to Luther's. In this they tended to differ from the more doctrinally oriented missionaries of other denominations. As we have seen, they believed that the best way to teach the gospel was to render its message as close to the native tongue as possible, while at the same time, naturally, holding to the meaning of the Scripture. But how to do both at the same time?

In Australia, the first step was always a word list: Sun, Moon, Father, Mother, Water, Fire, Camp, Spear, Dance, Snake . . . and so on. You could sit with the native and draw in the dust till kingdom come. There was no end to naming. It is what unites all cultures. And on a one-to-one basis there could be a tight fit between a primitive tongue and German. A list invites the prospect of a literal translation, one grounded in a common human truth, a notion that disposes of Babel. Or, as Pastor Schurmann in Adelaide reported in 1838, 'I asked some of them words for the sun and different parts of their bodies, and they were very willing to answer.'[25] It was this kind of thing that prompted Elkin to argue—rather unfairly—that the mission method of translation was 'atomistic.'[26]

In South Australia, Pastors Schurmann and Teichelmann wanted conversation with the natives, and made the ethnographic observation that 'If the natives blended with the Europeans, the language of the natives would be lost.'[27] They realised that colonisation was already damaging traditional Aboriginal society, and that good mission work would need two-way comprehensions. Schurmann was especially gentle and insightful in the language domain. Once he had a grip on Kaurna, the language of the Adelaide area, he was able to say: 'I gained an important insight into the religious imaginings of the natives. But I enjoyed a no-less-great pleasure in teaching some of them the main principles of the Christian religions. I told them that . . . Jesus had been circumcised like the black men, had thought well, spoken and done well, then was hanged by his country people, but on the third day he went to heaven.'[28]

It was an approach via native language that clearly relied on an easy dialogue, trusting exchanges rather than doctrinaire instruction from a text. The text arrived soon enough, however: Schurmann and Teichelmann's outline of grammar and phraseology was needed for their efforts at schooling the Aboriginal children. This they did with mixed success, even though many did become literate as well as Christians.[29] There was some sound hope in mission work until George Grey replaced the evangelist Gawler as governor; Grey insisted that Aboriginal education should be exclusively in English. The state wanted to replace the missions. It also wanted, perhaps, to sidestep the German influence altogether. Up until then it was the case that: 'The Germans were the only ministers among the Aborigines. They alone of the ministry mastered their languages and were intimate with the feelings, customs and modes of the Aboriginal people.'[30]

The 'feelings, customs and modes' remained of central concern to Schurmann when he went on to work in the Port Lincoln area where, as a protector and a missionary, he was witness to the blatant shooting of many Aboriginal friends whose language he spoke and whose hearts he knew.[31] So intimate was Schurmann with the customs that he made a strong case against the authorities and vengeful white settlers that 'it is a mistake to try these people by the white man's law': 'They have laws and customs of their own for the punishment of a crime and they do not hesitate to carry them out, therefore more would be achieved if they were tried and punished according to their own laws.'[32] It was a remarkably enlightened view for the time, and inseparable from the Lutheran care and intimate touch for the native tongue. Schurmann's life points up a simple fact about mission history: that while the evangelical project had as its aim the substitution of one culture for another, and to that extent Christianity was the enemy of Aboriginal religion, a handmaiden of colonisation, much would depend on the quality of person who happened to be the missionary at a particular place at a particular time. This historical truth is a general one. As Edwin Smith, the missionary and anthropologist and past president of the Royal Anthropological Institute, has remarked, 'there are missionaries and missionaries.'[33]

At Killalpaninna in 1890, when Pastor Carl Strehlow arrived at the mission, he despaired, as we have seen, at the tenacity of pagan ways. This feeling among missionaries fed the conviction that the Gospel should take priority, and that the work of translating it should be the vanguard of evangelical efforts.* The fresh start at Killalpaninna was

---

* The first book of the Bible translated into an Aboriginal language was done by the Reverend Lancelot Edward Threlkeld of the London Missionary Society in 1830, when he worked from the Awabakal language near Lake Macquarie in New South Wales. This was precisely because of his conviction that it was best to 'Christianise' before 'civilising' the natives, a view which would have the support of the 1837 House of Commons Select Committee, though not that of Threlkeld's superior, the Reverend Samuel Marsden, who thought that 'men must be polished and refined in their manners before they can be properly enlightened in religious truths.' Threlkeld's Gospel of Luke was quickly followed by the Reverend William Watson's translation of Genesis and selections from the Gospel of Matthew into Wiradjuri in 1834, a work that evidently pleased some of his congregation who exclaimed, 'Book for blackfellows! Book for blackfellows' and thought it proved he had 'been a blackfellow once.' Watson was at the Wellington Mission in the Blue Mountains, along with the German Lutheran, the Reverend Johann Handt (Harris 1990: 52, 82, 79, 66, 76).

made with Reuther's diary entry for 10 April 1893: 'We began to translate the Gospels. God grant that we have the health of body and soul that this may redound to His glory and become a blessing to many.'[34]

It was evening work done with the help of four or five Aboriginal elders, men called in from the sandhills after the missionaries had done their duty. The men came to sit in Reuther's astonishingly book-lined study, in the cave of Lutheran books that had been transported for that purpose into the desert. Reuther seems to have had a dogged talent with the language, Strehlow the more natural one.[35]

After nearly three years the New Testament was done. It was the first full translation of the New Testament into an Aboriginal language. The 600 pages were a celebrated achievement among mission circles in Australia as well as Germany, and stood as two heavily bound titles called 'Testament Marra,' the Diyari subtitles of which meant, 'Words Praying to Jesus and Translated into the Diyari Language.'[36] The 'Words Praying' is important. The Testament was not merely a textual exercise, but rather an advent for the spoken word, a tabling of new speech acts for the heathen.

Such a work of translation, the Lutherans learnt at Killalpaninna, was most easily done once they had lived with the natives for a few years; in the words of the Pastor Reidel who succeeded Reuther, after 'the spirit of the language and the people have become one's own.' Reidel addressed these remarks to Strehlow by way of drawing his attention to inaccuracies.

The crucial struggle was for the 'word concept' that did justice to both languages and the Divine Word. It might be clear, for example, that 'Neyi,' with its Diyari connotations for older brother, might serve for 'Christ.' But a 'big brother' who might die on the cross for our sins was not quite right. Less straightforward was the notion of 'soul.' Reidel settled on the Diyari word 'tepi,' a word which the Diyari might use for the shadow of a shadow of a stick lying on still water, its shadow's shadow thrown on the bottom of a pool. The Lutherans seized on this suggestion of something between the material and the immaterial world. That seemed valid enough—or rather a neat move from what was Aboriginal and concrete to a concept that was abstract in a European way. 'Grace' was less easy. Reidel asked his old men what they would use when they felt sorry for someone they were about to execute. 'After a long silence, one man replied. "We never let the man go. We would hurry up and kill him, but our livers become soft and we let him go.'"[37] In the Aboriginal scheme, the liver was the seat of the emotions. But how could 'liver' enter a realm as sacred as the Christian concept of grace? Reuther thought it too indelicate. When central concepts remained elusive in the host language, the Christians were left with their deeds rather than words as the means of instruction. But there was still no getting away from Luther's own legacy: his determination to wrench, if necessary, the meaning out of the tribal tongue and convert its sense and sound in the service of the Lord.

When Pastor Carl went up to Hermannsburg he had Reuther's great example behind him. For Reuther had not only done the New Testament: his legacy after eighteen years included grammars and dictionaries and ethnographic material. Reuther approached the myths as allegories of good and evil, and of those who recounted them as having the law of good and evil 'written in their hearts,' just as Luther had emphasised in his sermons about the tribes in Romans. The social morality of Aboriginal law, Reuther thought, was kin to the biblical Ten Commandments, even if the people themselves might have 'sunken to such low depths.' All heathens would require faith, and once they had that, of course, the words would be there to work for the Word.

Carl Strehlow was to swim in matters of translation as well. He gave his first sermon in Aranda in 1897, and by 1904 put out a 264-page Aranda service book. He was quick to appreciate the linguistic toil of his predecessor Pastor Kempe. Over his eleven hard years, Kempe had compiled word lists and key phrases and an instructional book for children and adults. Kempe was the first to face the strange new language, and all that it meant:

> The difficulty of acquiring the language lies not only in the structure of the language, nor in the scarcity of concrete terms, but in the lack of abstract terms and moral ideas, of which they have no conception. We would not claim that we have mastered the language. If we wish to converse with the Natives in their language, we immediately notice our inability to arrange our ideas in the proper form of verb, noun, and adverb. The difficulty is great for us missionaries, since we must rely on our own scanty experience, having no help, nor anyone to advise, assist, or correct, even if the enunciation of our Natives themselves leaves much to be desired.[38]

'May God grant us the right wisdom in all things,' said Kempe, as if to summon all the virtues that Luther had identified as necessary for the translator, 'and help us over the difficulties in learning the language, so that we may be able to proclaim to these Natives the Gospel of God for their salvation.' In the meantime, he concluded, nothing would be gained by rash haste.[39] There would have to be lessons in reading and writing for the children, memory work and singing; sermons and the Bible stories from Genesis and the New Testament. Kempe produced the first Aranda book of Christian instruction and worship. It contained Old and New Testament stories, psalms, prayers, and 53 hymns, and was an admirable effort, even if it did flounder when Christian concepts could not be put into Aranda. On such occasions Kempe reached for his Latin.

Pastor Strehlow set about improving on Kempe. Among other things, he removed Kempe's Latinisms so that such terms as 'Holy,' 'Servant,' 'Kingdom' and 'Lord' were adapted exclusively from the Aranda. He was in general both correcting and loosening Kempe's work. His own shortcomings, however, included an ignorance of the past tense in Aranda, which could create some confusion when the creed ('I believe . . .') was recited, as well as in other places. He also made mistakes of idiom: he might use, for instance, the wrong Aranda word for 'birth'—the term that applied to animals but not creations of deep spiritual significance. All this said, however, his achievement was considerable, a substantial improvement on Kempe. Despite all his other work, including his ethnographic studies, he toiled on it from 1913 until his last days at the mission, all in the spirit of what Luther so eloquently said was required of a translator: 'a right, devout, honest, sincere, God-fearing, Christian, trained, informed and experienced heart.' Strehlow's Gospel according to St Luke was published by the British and Foreign Bible Society in 1925. Four other Gospels followed. On top of all this he published many hymns in Aranda.[40]

Improving Aranda

Will you revise your father's work for us? Will you help us revive the Gospel for the present era? Albrecht first asked Strehlow to revisit the New Testament in 1938. For a time Strehlow worked quietly on his father's text, picking up the inaccuracies, revising some of what his father had written, but he did not commit himself to ever finishing the job.[41] He had his duties as patrol officer; then he was packed off into the army.

And yet he had already entered the fray with regard to Aranda and Christian translation. Ferociously he had done so in his MA thesis, inflamed by Daisy Bates who had once asserted the 'impossibility of translating the Lord's Prayer into an Australian language'. Bates is worth quoting in full because she so well illustrates the radical sceptical hostility that could exist towards mission endeavour in translation. 'My veneration,' she wrote in *My Natives and I*, 'for my own religion is too great for me to reduce it to Pidgin English, and I have found it impossible to translate it into any one of the 115 Aboriginal languages with which I am acquainted':

There are no words, no possible association of idea, in which to convey our own beautiful prayers full of imagery, and the passion of supplication. Many many times have I tried to render the Lord's Prayer in many tongues and failed utterly in all.

'Our Father,' that is simple—'mama ngalia.'

'Which art in Heaven'—'Sky sit down'—'Kalbi nyinnin.'

'Hallowed be Thy Name'—'Big Nam'—'inni boolga.' So far so good. 'Thy kingdom come.'

Any country that they did not know and belong to was the country of enemies and black magic. That would not do. 'Thy will be done, on earth as it is in Heaven.' Again I was baffled. 'Give us this day our daily bread.' That of course was easy . . . But, 'Forgive us our trespasses as we forgive them'—there is no forgiving, the trespasser is punished there and then, with all the revenge and hatred of which the avenger is capable, and the offence wiped out of memory, and very often the offender with it. 'Lead us not into temptation' was equally impossible, and so was 'Deliverance from evil,' with evil lurking in every shadow, and every possible misfortune, and death itself, just magic.[42]

To which Strehlow retorted:

It may be noted here that the Lord's Prayer was translated quite successfully about 60 years ago. All the abstract nouns of this prayer, such as: 'will,' 'temptation,' etc., are derived by means of common noun-forming suffixes from the verb 'to will,' 'to tempt,' and so on. Of course such a translation had to be carefully explained to the first generation of native pupils. This was no drawback in the eyes of the natives, however, since their own dark and obscure archaic chant verses also have had to be explained over and over again in the past before the young generation could grasp their meaning fully. In any case, even if the abstract nouns in question had not been used in the translation, the difficult sentences could have been paraphrased by turning the abstract nouns into verbs. For instance, 'Thy will be done, on earth as it is in Heaven' could have been rendered into 'May everyone on earth and in Heaven do as Thou desirist.'[43]

What was at issue, Strehlow went on, was the capacity of the native language to admit change and be like other languages of the world—Old Saxon, for instance, which had long ago been invaded by new words and meanings. He had to admit that Aranda did have some limitations with regard to the 'imagination and abstract reasoning' which did not permit 'Hamlet like thoughts,' but this was a concession that did not affect the work of Christian mission. This was where 'the genius of the native language' for analogy came in, and its flexibility 'in adapting itself to the expression of new ideas.' His thesis was published in *Oceania* between 1942 and 1944.

After the war Albrecht put the question again: would Strehlow help prepare the New Testament for publication? Albrecht was looking for new momentum to Christian teaching. The new reserves of Haasts Bluff and Areyonga had opened and, with the demobilisation of Aborigines from the army, mission work was even more imperative. A personal revelation years earlier had sharpened his faith in some individuals. His biographer relates the incident: 'A woman called Frieda died at the mission in July. She was overweight and had a weak heart. In her last hours of life, she saw visions. Her mother, long dead, came to her. A great light was all around her, and Carl Strehlow was there, with a huge book in his hands. As Albrecht sat with her, he felt humbled.'[44]

Albrecht's experience might have touched Strehlow: cued by the vision of a 'Frieda' as well as the task left to him by his father, he had at least two reasons for committing himself to the 'huge book.' But he had been hesitating for a good while. Pastor Philip Scherer, who was to help Strehlow with his translation, later reflected on the 'long time Mr Strehlow remained rather diffident about the matter':

Even the modest revision that he might undertake would mean several years of hard work. But eventually his love and feeling for the Aranda people, of whose relative spiritual helplessness he felt increasingly conscious, inspired him to do something about it. He had lived among them for many years, and had brought with him a rich spiritual heritage from their world of religious thought and culture. What greater contribution could he now give in return than to offer them the Word of God in their own language,—the one thing alone that could give them back a firm anchorage in a confused 'new' world? Besides was not the Aranda language, after all, his special academic field?[45]

In November 1947, Strehlow started work wholeheartedly. In 1948, when he was visiting Hermannsburg to check words and renderings, Albrecht was alarmed to see that the son was doing more than correct his father's mistakes. He was retranslating. 'The older, more literal translation of the verb "follow," as in "the disciples followed Jesus", had used an Aranda word meaning "tracking" which carried the connotation of following someone to kill him. The new translation had the disciples walking in front of Jesus, to indicate a total trust. Strehlow had also established beyond any doubt that the word "Itana" previously used for the Holy Spirit referred only to the departed spirit—more colloquially, a "spook" or "ghost"—and should never have been used. "Enka", referring to the spirit of the living person, was far the better word.'[46] In time, Albrecht came to think that Strehlow's work was 'truly remarkable,' a superior version, much better than he could ever have done himself.

Strehlow had three main texts at work beside his father's. He had the modern German translation by Menge, an English translation by Moffatt, and the Greek text of Nestle. There was no Luther at Strehlow's elbow. His was a twentieth-century work, after a fashion. 'My main object,' Strehlow said when it was all done, 'was to transform the language of the existing version so that it should have the genuine ring of a true and original Aranda document.'[47]

To some extent much of the translation was straightforward. This was partly because of the early work of Pastors Kempe and Strehlow, both of whom received uncharacteristic acknowledgment by Strehlow when the job was finally done, but also because, as he had pointed out in his scornful remarks about Daisy Bates, many key words of the Christian faith had been established in the Aranda language. *Altjira*: God; *Tnakintja*: faith; and *Kamerintja*: resurrection. Strehlow was pleased and relieved that these terms were currency in the Hermannsburg area. They included a wide range of terms and expressions, each of which he carefully checked. In only a few instances were better native words found.[48] And when Christian concepts were not established, Strehlow reported: 'the language that generations of pagan worshippers had once coined for their ancient beliefs was found to furnish an adequate basis for the expression of the greatest and deepest truths of the Christian religion.' Furthermore: 'Often the old words were used with an enriched and deepened significance. At other times the terms used in the New Testament were new abstract nouns, formed by the addition of the correct suffixes to existing Aranda verb-stems. In all cases, the new contexts in which these words are to be found in the New Testament, and their explanations by the mission-aries and native helpers, have ensured that these new meanings are readily grasped and appreciated.'[49]

This is a gloss of several considerations at once, as well as one that tilts the whole enterprise towards praise of the translator. It does not say much about the work that went into the laborious testing process with Aboriginal elders. Strehlow tells us about the 'very fine and sincere Christian preacher, Old Blind Moses,' who had also helped his father; and how much the final text was the result of a panel of men working with Moses who 'suggested, formulated and modelled.' The translation team included Conrad, Rauwiraka, Utnadata, Jakobus, Nathaniel— venerable and authoritative men who checked and rechecked difficult sentences, and each of whom (except Conrad) had been 'well trained in the ancient lore of the tribe.'

Strehlow was adding to the language, using Scripture as a vehicle for cultural change. When linguistic penetration is a tool of cultural trans-formation the host language becomes a Trojan horse for the translator with a cultural mission. There was no hesitation on Strehlow's part to make the necessary incursions upon the native language. As Luther was imperialistically emboldened by the German vernacular, the tongue that would revitalise the Word from the Vulgate, Strehlow did not hesitate to add more Greek conceptions to the Aranda. In effect, he 'Hellenised' the Aranda. To add to the difficulty were Strehlow's diacritics with the Aranda: they were so technical, and idiosyncratic, that he had made the sounds of the words unreadable for anyone who did not know them. The upshot was, as the present leading authority has put it: 'The Gospels once in simple Aranda appeared in a different dress. There were words the congregation did not know, and words from other dialects. The result was a text that was, as mission workers after him were to discover, unnecessarily formal and often difficult.' [50] Strehlow had in a sense turned his back on Luther and his father: they had wanted to ground the Gospel in the vernacular of the host tongue; he had served to move in the other direction, ultimately away from the roots of the language.*

He saw this as enriching the tribal language, adding to its ancient verbal landscape, you might say. In so doing he was merely speeding up an inevitable historical process: languages had always cross-fertilised each other. The result was good for the host language precisely because it 'had the full and highly appreciative approval of the old men,' those best 'educated' in the native tongue. This was the second great benefit: to appreciate his New Testament, the younger men would have to be worthy of what they now had before them. As he wrote to Pastor Scherer: 'the younger men and women of Hermannsburg, whose command of Aranda is no better than the command of English possessed by white Australians who have never received any worthwhile

---

* Something of the flavour of Strehlow's version can be gained by comparing his version of Romans with the one that came into use later on. The English of Strehlow's Aranda tends to be as follows:

'1. Paulus, a slave of Christ Jesus, I being called as an apostle, I also being chosen for the gospel of God, 2. which he had first promised through his prophets in the holy writings, 3. that is the message about his son, he was born from David's seed according to the flesh, 4. But who was appointed God's Son by power from the Holy Spirit after resurrection from the dead ones,—that is Jesus Christ, our Lord, 5. from him we received grace and the work belonging to an apostle, so that all amongst the heathen we would work the obedience belonging to faith for the sake of his name; 6. to them you also belong, you also are called unto Jesus Christ: 7. (now I) to all of you in Rome, to all of God's loved one, to all the holy ones called (send word): May grace be with our, also peace from God our father, and from the Lord Jesus Christ.'

By contrast, the more relaxed version would read:

'I Paul, Jesus Christ's worker, send this letter to you. It was God who chose me to be his apostle. He also commanded me to teach the people the Good News. About the Good News, God has been telling Abraham's family for a long time, through his messengers. The messengers also wrote down this Good News. It can be found in God's old writings. This Good News tells us about God's Son. He belonged to the family of David. He is also God's powerful son. This the Holy Spirit showed us by raising him from among the dead ones. This Jesus is also the Christ, our Lord. Through him God showed us apostles his grace. Also through him, he chose us, and then also sent us as messengers to the heathen, wherever they are living. He sent us to teach them that they should obey Christ correctly, by believing him. You are also part of his group, the group Jesus chose to be his own. I sent this letter to you Romans. God loves you. He also chose you to be his holy people. God our father, and the Lord Jesus Christ, shows you grace and peace.'

(Both translations are by Pastor Paul Albrecht, son of F.W., who has spent many years translating for the mission, much of it a simplification of Strehlow's work.)

education in literature or English writing, will have to do a bit of work in re-learning the beautiful language of their fathers.' To which he added, as if suddenly self-conscious about his imperial position: 'There is nothing startling about this statement. Luther's translation of the Bible helped create Modern High German;—the Authorised Version has had a strong influence on Modern English.'[51]

Strehlow was also trying to consolidate a religious tone in the Aranda of his Scripture. He wanted the music of his Aranda to have the appropriate spiritual elevation. He spoke of this very clearly later on, as if it had been as much in his mind as the quest for the right idiom and the right Greek term. He did not want his text to become 'ultra-pedestrian,' which was the criticism T.S. Eliot had brought to bear on the New English Bible translation. Strehlow wrote to Scherer: 'I wholeheartedly agree with [Eliot's] claim that "the music of the phrase, of the paragraph, or the period is an essential constituent of good English prose," and "that the life of a reading of Gospel and Epistle in the liturgy is in this music of the spoken word." That is true also of Aranda prose; and it has been my aim to achieve similar musical idiomatic effects.'[52]

There was another dimension to Strehlow's cultivation of 'high' Aranda. It was not something he advertised himself, probably because of its acute sensitivity, and perhaps because of his own sense of transgression. But it was a feature of his work that was celebrated by Pastor Scherer when the New Testament was published. His translation brought secret-sacred words into the public domain for the first time. He even incorporated the most sacred Aranda words for circumcision into his New Testament, as the Christian text in Romans so often demanded. It is difficult to say what his expert panel felt about this, but there is no escaping the radical nature of the move: the Christian text was used to break ancient taboos with regard to tribal language and law. The proselytising significance of this step was not lost on those still at work in the fields of the Lord; Pastor Scherer praised Strehlow's 'classical' Aranda:

The New Testament in Aranda will serve as educator and text-book for future generations of Aranda people. It has resurrected that fine part of their language which, under the age long spell of secretive ceremonial taboos, lay suppressed and hidden from the common eye and ear. But with time and constant usage this revived language will become the 'people's' very own for the first time,—not remain the exclusive property of the privileged few initiates as it was originally, and perish together with them. What therefore the secret rites of a heathen religion had subdued, the Christian religion has restored to its fullest richness.[53]

And there was even more to Strehlow's translation work than that. As he was completing his work on the New Testament, he turned to the psalms, a job that began in October 1948 with the revision of the seven already translated by his father, and which he soon extended to 44. Strehlow wanted the list to include 'the best known and most loved sacred poems by Christian readers everywhere' and he delighted in his 'critical audience of Aranda elders who were capable of speaking their language in all its power and beauty.' Not only that: he found that some formal stylistic features of the psalms (the couplets and their parallelisms) 'aroused the deep admiration of the elders.'[54]

The harder work, it seems, was recovering the authentic Aranda. 'One of the greatest challenges in translation was afforded by Psalm 119—not because of its length, but because of the large number of synonyms needed to express distinctions in words like "laws," "ordinances," "statutes" and "precepts." Many of these were rare Aranda words even when they were given to me by my well-educated informants. In fact modern Aranda speakers everywhere tend to use the English word "law" in preference to any of their own terms—an unintentional tribute to the power of the Old Norse word which was added to the English vocabulary as a result of the fierce Viking raids on English coasts more than a thousand years ago.'

Strehlow's point about linguistic change and history is valid, but more interesting is the one he does not develop: that in Aranda culture before the arrival of the missionaries, there was more than one word for 'law' and therefore, more than likely, a deeper refinement of concepts of authority in the culture. These terms had gone under to the monoterm, 'law,' just as the ancestor creatures were supposed to have gone under to monotheism. What is striking in this context of Strehlow reflecting on original meanings in Aranda is his relative lack of interest in the idea of the Aranda dictionary. He had a passion for this when translating the Aranda poetry into English: when the movement was from the original language to the host tongue of his own culture. But here, translating Scripture, he is not so compelled to go back to the roots of words, but rather prefers to shape his preferences by other criteria.

Other psalms presented other challenges. It was not that a word had died away in the Aranda: it was rather that a psalm would continue to have 'added depth of meaning for a Christian reader,' by which Strehlow meant a reader other than Aranda. There was 'the magnificent couplet from Psalm 119: "Thy word is a lamp to my feet and a light to my path."' It is an odd example of relative untranslatability for Strehlow to choose, considering the emphasis he had placed on Aranda powers of analogy in his early writings. What seems to come through these reflections on his translations of the psalms is some greater awareness of the uniqueness of the Christian formulations, his intimacy with them, and their inevitable distance from Aranda phrasings, if not understandings.

With the psalms, Strehlow also confessed to a limitation of his own. 'The translator regrets that he does not know Hebrew.' The remark is placed in a way reminiscent of Luther. Strehlow then acknowledges his debt to 'the English Authorised Version and the German Luther-Bible from his childhood,' as well as 'the scholarly German version of that great linguist, the late Dr H. Menge (who died in January 1939).' That said, he expressed the hope that despite all difficulties of translation, 'the Aranda singers of these psalms will experience, across the gulf of ages, and the divisions and cultures, a sense of communion with the long dead great company of saints whose prayers and cries, and whose songs of praise too, found expression in the ancient Hebrew psalms.'

The Black Missionary

What emerges so strikingly through all Strehlow's opining about translation is his devotional work for the mission. He would place the Christian message where it needed to be, in the hearts of the natives whose songs had been broken. Sometimes he doubted the extent to which that could be done, as with some psalms, but all the while that was the motive: to make the deep historical corrective, to place himself at the centre of the traditional mission enterprise. His night work for Luther has its apotheosis in the following remarks to Scherer in 1954, after Scherer had written his laudatory article for the *Lutheran Herald*. Strehlow wrote:

My main endeavour was, however, to transmute the whole existing translation into genuine Aranda idiom. The translation of a *white missionary* inevitably has a slightly 'foreign' ring to the natives. We, for instance, would not think of asking a Russian, a French, or an Italian scholar to translate the Bible from the original tongues into English: such a translation would always be lacking in these idiomatic touches which only a native speaker of a language can achieve.

I soon found that an alteration in the order of these words here, a subtle twist in the sentence there, the use of an entirely different Aranda phrase somewhere else, would change a formal, literal, and heavily Europeanised 'Aranda' translation into something which had the true ring of the Aranda tongue. Aranda has been one of my own mother tongues; and I endeavoured to make my translation sound like an original Aranda version. (emphasis added) [55]

Strehlow's luminously important implication is clear. His was the superior text because Aranda was his 'mother tongue.' He was not like 'a white missionary.' He was something else, though he pulls back from finally saying it: namely that he was a 'black missionary,' one who spoke the heathen tongue with the authority of a tribal man. He had named himself at last as the gospel teacher, the supreme translator of the Word, both the authority on the liturgical music of words, and the master of idioms. As 'black missionary,' he was his father transmuted.

Hitherto, as we have seen, his sense of authority was straightforward. As the one who had translated the songs and myths, and won the trust of tribal men sufficiently to be called *ingkata*, he had become something of a language master. That did not make him, however, an initiated man, as he had never been through ceremony, but he had become a kind of living archive 'to save their memory from complete extinction.'[56] Now he was more, much more. His Aranda authority was now enveloped with the habit of Christian authority. As the 'Black Missionary' he was Caliban with Gospel.

He finished his translation in September 1949, after nearly two years work.

The New Testament took three years to set in type, but was not published until 1956. The delay was inseparable from the diacritics that Strehlow had invented to render Aranda sounds. Enormous care went into their creation and, thereafter, their reproduction: they would always be a nightmare for typists and printers. The book that finally arrived was a firmly bound, earth-coloured volume of 539 pages, the *Testamenta Ljatinja: Ankatja Arandauna Knatiwumala*. Strehlow would have preferred the inscribed lettering to be in the Aboriginal colours of black, red, yellow and white, but that was not to be. The Council of the British and Foreign Bible Society in Australia printed 2,000 copies, to retail at £2 6s. 0d. and £1 1s. 0d. less for the native people. The publishers handed a newly printed edition to the Finke River Mission at a ceremony at the Adelaide Town Hall on 3 December 1956. The head of the Lutheran synod appealed to members of the church for donations so an honorarium could be given to the translator. A modest sum was raised.

There was a momentous finishing touch to the publication. Pastor Scherer had asked Strehlow to make a design for the title cover of the presentation volume. The Black Missionary did it in the manner of a ground painting and it shows, rather beautifully, a series of concentric circles with a three-pronged pattern emanating from its centre. Strehlow called it the Symbol of Trinity, and explained to Scherer:

> Circles denote eternity (i.e. circle is a curved line that has no beginning and or end). In centre of this system of circles can be see three figures,— the normal Aranda symbol for a person. The three central ones, linked and joined to each other by circles, denote the three Persons of the Trinity, eternally linked and joined to each other in an indivisibly Unity. But each Person of the Trinity has also manifested itself separately at various moments. Hence these are repeated on the outer edge of the Symbol. But even here they are still enclosed by the final circle: God remains One at all times.[57]

There was another figure below the Trinity. There was a symbol that resembled the Aboriginal symbol for a camp, and on either side Strehlow's symbol for the person. 'These,' he told Scherer, 'are two human persons facing each other. They could here symbolise a man and a woman, listening to the Word of God, which comes to them from the Symbol above.'

It is hard to imagine a finer Christian apotheosis for Strehlow, and the Lutherans embraced it with both hands. The symbol was reproduced in the *Lutheran Herald* and Pastor Scherer developed the Christian gloss: the man and the woman were 'representative of all men, women and children of the locality.' In this particular instance they are understood to be listening to the divine Word which is spoken to them by the Triune God above.'[58]

Well and good. The book was for the believers. But so, absolutely, was it for Strehlow, in its incorporation of the Aboriginal motif. The Presentation Volume was finished with black for charcoal, the white of pipe-clay and the red of ochre. And that design of the man and the woman happened to be the design for *Ntaria*, and the pair of twins. Scherer told readers of the *Lutheran Herald* that this was 'quite incidental.' But that has to be nonsense.

What Strehlow had done was take the ground painting of Manangananga, the totem for Twins Dreaming, and transform it for his Christian purposes. In the totem the larger circle has Aboriginal designs, most likely containing the camp in the middle: at the lower edge of the larger circle are the two symbols for persons, perhaps the twins. They seem to be attached to the main circle as appendages. For the Trinity, Strehlow has freed these symbols and relocated them to sit at the camp he has created below. He has, so to speak, separated the twins from the larger circle and set them down below, at their own camp. The whole design of the Trinity was the grand complement to traditional Manangananga symbol on the frontispiece of *Songs of Central Australia*, a supreme complement really, since by this account the Trinity was intended to swallow the other with the ease of a snake an egg. Unbeknown to most, since the Trinity was never published anywhere else, Strehlow had given the Christian symbol his imprimatur of superior authority.[59]

Battle of Words

Before Strehlow's New Testament went to press, dissent arose in the garden of the mission. It seems to have begun in the stock camp. Manasse Armstrong, a drover, fencer, maintenance man, among many other things, a man generally regarded as 'the most capable worker at Hermannsburg,'[60] was unhappy with Strehlow's language work. He and others were worried about some of the words in the hymns. There were words such as: *Eritjalama*: to happen, to arrive; *Eterintja knatiwulama*: to change, to turn into; and *watnupura*: single file.

It is hard to say, now, why these words in particular were offensive. What was clear was that Strehlow had put words in a new order. And he had introduced foreign words into the hymns, words from other tribes. Furthermore, he had left the simple language of the older versions (by Pastor Carl Strehlow and others) and had made things 'difficult and dark.'

The latter expression was Strehlow's own, when he fumed about the incident in his diary. These men were causing enough trouble amongst the congregation for Pastors Albrecht and Reuther to draw Strehlow's attention to it. They also told him that the voices raised against him at Hermannsburg were to the effect that he had been away from the place so long that he had lost his Aranda, and had little feeling for it. As a result, on the weekend of 15 August 1953 'the spokesmen of the dissatisfied' were brought into Alice Springs for a meeting.

They met for two days. The debate was public and intense, and, from Strehlow's ferocious account, Armstrong seems to have had to justify himself in an inquisitional atmosphere. Strehlow challenged him to name any foreign words. 'He failed to produce a single instance.' Strehlow asked for instances of 'dark renderings' and 'When these were produced, I read the sections out slowly, explained one or two words which were new to them; and they agreed that they were perfectly clear.' Then the so-called 'meaningless words' were stoutly defended by Blind Moses. 'The opposition was quickly reduced to Manasse alone.' Armstrong alone, however, was still insisting that he spoke for a large number of dissenters who wanted the Aranda language of the old versions.

'At this stage I began the attack,' Strehlow records, striking a note that harks to Luther:

I explained that these 'dark' and 'wrong' words and passages had in fact been produced by me in close collaboration with Moses, Utnadata, Rauwiraka, Nathaniel, Ronald and Jakobus—all of them gifted and respected old men of the Hermannsburg area, who were undoubted authorities on the Western Aranda dialect. It was, in fact, not my version that was being attacked, but the undoubted speech of their own fathers. Moses corroborated all these statements with great vehemence. Wasn't it true rather that the real reason for the difficulty some had had in understanding the new version was that 1) the 'younger' men of Hbg.— i.e., all people under fifty years of age—had never received any training in the myths and traditions of their forefathers and had therefore never outgrown the simple speech of childhood; 2) they had refused to acknowledge their ignorance and therefore rejected the new translation in which the full vocabulary and constructions of the Western Aranda tongue had found expression?[61]

To the last point, most of the others assented, Strehlow says. But Armstrong held out, maintaining that places other than Hermannsburg would

'NEVER' accept the new version (the capitalisation was Strehlow's). Already, he said, they had made their protest by refusing to sing the hymns.

And so the meeting ended. The Hermannsburg people said they would go back and set things right; Armstrong and the others would be reported as the troublemakers of Hermannsburg. And Strehlow told himself: 'the true Ntaria people had always been certain that I was right, and had learned the new terms assiduously.' What Strehlow does not mention was that Armstrong was a custodian of Jay Creek.

Strehlow was also deceiving himself. 'The battle of words is on again,' Scherer wrote to him in April 1959, 'and I don't know where it is going to end. It is said that some men in the tannery made some unguarded remarks which were overheard, and that this ignited the whole argument.' The New Testament had been in circulation for two years.

It was Armstrong once more, supported by Lukas and Reuben amongst others. Scherer told Strehlow that the staunch evangelists were for him, and named nine other supporters. This was not surprising: Scherer was referring to only one of the two groups at the mission; the Christian converts would not object to any usage of their old language, as opposed to those closer to their traditional life and who had a sacred interest in their own tongue. Among the former was of course Moses, who nonetheless saw how hard it was to go all the way with the white teachings, and the policy of assimilation. 'We tried to become like white men, but found we couldn't. Our law was too strong.' By contrast, men like Reuben and Lukas wanted to uphold the traditional ways, even as they had to adapt them to changing conditions. Somewhere in the middle of these groups was Manasse Armstrong, who believed that Strehlow was destroying the traditional culture.[62]

The dispute was once again about words in the hymns—especially the term *eritjalama*. But it also extended to the language of the New Testament. By the time Pastor Scherer called a meeting passions were high. Already he had tried to explain to Armstrong, imploring him to worry about linguistic matters in private; and he had told a meeting of 34 evangelists, elders and senior men that his conscience was clear with regard to the language he used to administer the Sacrament. Scherer wrote to Strehlow for linguistic advice and to reassure him that mission hearts were in the right place.

Conrad left the first meeting with tears in his eyes, when they argued about the Lord's Prayer. He told me he would remain loyal to this

Testament until his dying day, as Moses asked him to do. I have left no doubt whatever where I stand, too, and my acceptance of this translation as a correct representation of the Word of God is an act of faith. I will not stand judge over the men who have given us that Book and I have asked the meeting whether anyone today considers himself competent to act as a judge over those men who are not here to speak for themselves. If they were debating about false doctrines, they would be justified. But what missionary, evangelist, elder or layman has ever come forward with a charge of false doctrine? I said we are here to work together and build up the Church of God, not to tear it apart; to fight the devil, and not each other. Men are fighting about words, and overlooking the Spirit Who gives life. I have also said that against their objections that the Aranda N[ew] T[estament] has included words from other dialects: why shouldn't it? Shall the N.T. remain the exclusive property of the W[estern] A[randa] people, or shall it become the Book of all the Aranda people? Luther translated the Bible when numerous German dialects existed, but his Bible welded the people and the language together; like-wise the English language is a conglomeration of languages, it has borrowed from everywhere, but today is probably the most universal language in the world.[63]

Strehlow took the high ground of scorn, a place to which he naturally ascended when under pressure. He said that Armstrong was one of those people who 'refuse to be convinced by argument' even when all the evidence was against them. He told Scherer the details of the 1953 meeting in Alice Springs and sent a page of his diary as corroboration. Of Armstrong he said: 'He is attempting to fight both against the meaning of the original Greek text and against the language of the "educated" Western Aranda. This language Manasse, who comes from the Alice Springs area, and who is a half-caste was never fully trained in the A.S. dialect, never learnt decently.'[64]

All Strehlow's absolute terms of evaluation are here. His claim to superior knowledge both of the Classics and Western Aranda, which is to say the mother tongue of the place where he was born. The man of the Twins Dreaming is doubly rooted by this claim: his mother tongue is of the place that he knows best. And so to the doubly dismissive point: that Armstrong comes merely from Alice Springs, is not of the right place, and is not of full-blooded birth. The Black Missionary, himself of two cultures, casts the stone that says much about himself. But of course he cannot spell out the inner logic of his 'black' authority to a pastor so eloquently defending the white faith. To conclude, Strehlow wrenches himself into piety. 'As you know I have no vested interests in my N.T. translations, I rest on the work of the older missionaries, on the language of the educated Western Aranda men, and on the Greek New Testament, I have merely tried to reproduce truthfully and exactly what the sacred text has said. If my work is rejected at Hermannsburg, I can only let God himself be the judge about the merits of the dispute.'[65]

Some years later Scherer wanted Strehlow to resume work on the hymnal. Strehlow, inflamed, recalled the 'rejection' he had suffered at Hermannsburg. 'After some ten years abuse,' he told Scherer, massively exaggerating, 'I have little enthusiasm left for any further translations.'[66] And in August: 'to give up evenings and weekends to this sort of work for months and years,—then to be accused by people who have not lifted up one finger to render any assistance themselves, of "confusing the people" and of "darkening the word of God" is something that kills all the endeavour. For the last ten years I have often deeply regretted ever having allowed myself to be drawn into any translation work at all.'[67]

There is cursing here. Strehlow speaks as if he is buried in a hole, as if he has been driven back into a cell.

Strehlow is admonishing those who should know better: namely those who speak the black tongue that his culture has, ultimately, learnt from theirs. And there is much more to it than that. All those myths and songs, the translations of which into English Strehlow had collected and improved upon for the magnum opus that he had prepared in all the years of thankless overtime on the New Testament, were the felt measure of his homage to their tongue, and the vehicle by which he mapped the landscape of their language. In so mapping he had, had he not, been bringing all to an appreciation of a country animated by spirits: he was in effect employing the other language to re-enchant the world, bringing as much wonder to it as a Prospero. All the more reason then for the Black Missionary to curse like a Caliban.* Embittered,

---

* After showing his guests all the quality of his isle, 'The fresh springs, brine-pits, barren place and fertile,' Caliban found himself rejected in love and accused of being a 'lying slave':

> You taught me language, and my profit on't
> Is, I know how to curse: the red-plague rid you,
> for learning me your language.

Strehlow will now cease from translation from Christian texts. Much has happened to him by now, as we shall see. His cursing partly comes for good reason.

But let us look back for a moment. What we have been considering before now looks rather different. He had translated the songs and fashioned them as literature, and then, in a kind of re-balancing, had sought to return them to the primitive domain. We take that to be partly an act of restitution, an exchange, a corrective to all the acts of appropriation that had occurred in the first place. It was also, however, a primitivist argument in its own right, an expression of Strehlow's romantic reaction to secular modernity. Now, with this display of imperialism in translation, a wilfulness to rival Luther's, what do we have? We would have to say two things. Firstly, that his primitivism is not what it might have seemed. He had drawn back from any savage version of the primitive and his notion of the tribe became a tame one in the course of advocacy. The reason for that is now clear. The collective unities Strehlow was harking back to were not tribal on the model of indigenous people, or even the pagans of the Classical world. They were ones that belonged to the medieval world of Christianity, the kind of order that Huizinga had described, and to which every mission station, in its heart of hearts, deferred. That is to say, all the time *Songs of Central Australia* was being written by Caliban, the Black Missionary was riding along at the same time, shadowing the creation as if the old tribal songs might one day be called to prayer.

And this brings one to the second crucial thing about the totality of Strehlow's translations. They could not, finally, complete their hermeneutic movement of exchange, of the gift-giving and equalising that so exalts the humanising hope of translation. They could not do this because, on the strict, Lutheran model, translation was an exercise in embattled authority rather than relationship, of delivering the Word when the Word was conceived as an inspired act of zealotry. That is not the Lutheran mode today. But in its tradition of translation with which Strehlow identified—possibly even more so than his father—it was so. As a result he could not pull back from his appropriations of the Aranda to engage in any negotiation. He could only go forward dogmatically and, when thwarted, sullenly express a false modesty: 'I can only let God himself be the judge . . .'

This was in 1963. A different man from the one who had finished the New Testament in 1956 was speaking. Much had happened, most notably his attempt to rescue an Aboriginal man from judgment. To this strange, disastrous episode in Strehlow's life—when he cast himself before others for judgment—we now turn.

1 James Mackinnon, *Luther and the Reformation* (New York: Russell & Russell, 1962), 3:63.
2 Ibid., 3:64.
3 Luther in his Preface to the book of Job: cited in Martin Buber and Franz Rosenzweig, *Scripture and Translation* (Bloomington: University of Indiana Press, 1994), 48.
4 'On Translating: An Open Letter' (1530), *Luther's Works* [*LW*], vol. 35 (Philadelphia: Fortress Press, 1970), 189.
5 Ibid., 3:187.
6 Matthew 12: 34; Luke 6: 45.
7 *LW*, 35:189–90.
8 Ibid., 35:194.
9 Ibid., 35:349.
10 Ibid., 35:362.
11 Richard Marius, *Martin Luther: The Christian Between God and Death* (Cambridge, Mass.: Harvard University Press, 1999), 360.
12 Ibid., 104.
13 Ibid., 353.
14 Mackinnon, 3:219.
15 Roland H. Bainton, *Here I Stand: A Life of Martin Luther* (Hodder & Stoughton, London, 1951), 329, 327.
16 Cited in Buber and Rosenzweig, *Scripture and Translation*, 49.
17 Ibid., 193.
18 Ibid., 188.
19 Marius, *Martin Luther*, 363.
20 *LW*, 35:183.
21 Marius, *Martin Luther*, 361.
22 *LW*, 35:184–84.
23 Buber and Rosenzweig, *Scripture and Translation*, 67.
24 Leslie R. Marchant, *Ernst Faber's Scholarly Mission to Convert the Confucian Literati in the Late Ch'ing Period* (Nedlands: University of Western Australia, Centre for East Asian Studies, 1984), 14–16.
25 John Harris, *One Blood: 200 Years of Aboriginal Encounter with Christianity: A Story of Hope* (Sutherland, N.S.W.: Albatross Books, 1990), 317.
26 'The Nature of Australian Languages,' *Oceania* VIII, no. 3 (1937).
27 Harris, *One Blood*, 316.
28 Ibid., 319.
29 Ibid., 321.
30 Ibid., 321, quoting Advocate General William Smillie at the 1842 meeting held by colonists in support of missionaries.
31 Ibid, 328, gives details of a shockingly violent incident.
32 Ibid., 326.
33 Kenelm Burridge, 'Aborigines and Christianity: An Overview,' in *Aboriginal Australians and Christian Missions*, ed. Tony Swain, Tony and Deborah Bird Rose (Bedford Park, S.A.: Australian Association for the Study of Religions, 1988), 25.
34 Christine Stevens, *White Man's Dreaming: Killalpaninna Mission, 1866–1915* (Melbourne: Oxford University Press, 1994), 209.
35 Ibid., 210.

36 Ibid., 212.
37 Ibid., 212.
38 M. Lohe, 'The Modern Chapter,' in *Hermannsburg: A Vision and a Mission*, ed. Everard Leske (Adelaide: Lutheran Publishing House, 1977), 15.
39 Ibid.
40 Ibid., 34.
41 Barbara Henson, *The Straight-Out Man: F.W. Albrecht and Central Australian Aborigines* (Melbourne: Melbourne University Press, 1992), 168–69.
42 T.G.H. Strehlow *Aranda Phonetics and Grammar*, Oceania Monograph 7 (Sydney: University of Sydney, 1944), 62–63.
43 Ibid., 64.
44 Henson, *The Straight-Out Man*, 168.
45 P.A. Scherer in *Lutheran Herald*, 24 November 1956, 346.
46 Henson, *Straight-Out Man*, 186.
47 T.G.H. Strehlow, 'Thoughts of a Translator,' *Lutheran Herald*, 12 January 1957.
48 P.A. Scherer, personal conversation, September 1994.
49 Strehlow, 'Thoughts of a Translator.'
50 Paul Albrecht, personal conversations, 1994, 2002.
51 Strehlow to Scherer, 17 November 1954.
52 Strehlow to Scherer, 5 August 1963.
53 Scherer, *Lutheran Herald*, 8 December 1956, 361.
54 Strehlow's typed two-page report on his translation of the psalms is undated. All commentary on psalms draws on this document.
55 Strehlow to Scherer, 17 November 1954.
56 Strehlow to Scherer, 16 January 1960.
57 Strehlow to Scherer, 13 December 1956.
58 P.A. Scherer in *Lutheran Herald*, 13 February 1957, 57.
59 See James Clifford, *The Predicament of Culture* (Cambridge, Mass.: Harvard University Press, 1988), 21–54, for a vivid illustration of how the anthropological text signals the presence or absence of reflexivity, and possible dialogue with its subjects, as against monological authority like Strehlow's Trinity/Totem. Clifford compares the frontispiece of Father Lafitau's 1724 *Moeurs des sauvages amériqains*, where the ethnography is portrayed as a young woman among allegorical figures presided over by the Hebrew script for Yahweh, with the one for Malinowski's 1922 *Argonauts of the Western Pacific*, where native figures engaged in an act of symbolic exchange may be seen looking at the camera. No Australian text in Malinowski's period was ever so enticing, certainly nothing by Spencer and Gillen. Pastor Carl Strehlow, however, used a photograph of his four main informants as the frontispiece of his work when it was published in Germany: figures credited as they were framed by confident authority.
60 P. Latz, personal conversation, February 1997.
61 Strehlow to Scherer, 13 April 1959, and citing his diary for 18 August 1953.
62 P. Latz, personal conversation, February 1997.
63 Scherer to Strehlow, 3 April 1959.
64 Strehlow to Scherer, 13 April 1959.
65 Ibid.
66 Strehlow to Scherer, 28 February 1963.
67 Strehlow to Scherer, 3 August 1963.

4 Saving Caliban

IN 1958 a 27-year-old Aborigine, a strongly built, good-looking single man—a drinker, sideshow hand, tent boxer and stockman—fell foul of the law in the little seaside town of Ceduna on the far west coast of South Australia. His name was Rupert Max Stuart and he was charged with the savage murder and rape of a nine-year-old girl. He was the grandson of Tom Ljonga, and as a small boy had been one of Patrol Officer Strehlow's charges at Jay Creek. Strehlow had seen Stuart now and then over the years that he was growing up on various cattle stations, but they had not met for some time before Stuart's arrest; nor did Strehlow get in touch during the trial in Adelaide in April 1959 when Stuart was found guilty and sentenced to death.

Strehlow had been away then, working in Sydney, and had in fact chosen rather to steer clear of the case that was so connected to his roots. But he was drawn in once the case went to the High Court on appeal.

On the evening of Saturday 16 May Strehlow was back in Adelaide, working on *Songs*, trying to thread yet another series of couplets, when there was a knock on the door of his rooms at the university. Strehlow let the man in. The visitor was Father Thomas Dixon, who had a few years before worked at the Santa Teresa Mission north-east of Alice Springs. Dixon got to know some of the Aranda people there, and he had learnt his Aranda language from Strehlow's thesis in phonetics and grammar. He much admired Strehlow's work and explained the nature of his mission: he was on a desperate rescue mission for the condemned man. He was going to draw Strehlow into the tropics of translation with regard to the nature of Aboriginal English.

The Work of a Darky

Stuart had arrived in Ceduna with the Funland Carnival on 19 December 1958, a Friday, having hitched a ride from Perth. He worked on a casual basis that night, helping set up the fair. By the Sunday morning he had been given his marching orders and gone off to get a job at the Wheat Board at Thevenard, two miles along the beach from Ceduna, where he was picked up by the police the next evening. Between the Friday and the Sunday, he reportedly told them, he was on a bender. On the Saturday morning: 'I awoke and started work at the show. I had a drink of tea first but nothing to eat.' About ten that morning he drifted off the job and went down to the jetty with a work mate. They talked and drank with 'one half caste bloke . . . that lives around the beach.' Then:

'We walked down the beach near the Jetty and into a little cave. The three of us sat down and drank a flagon of wine.' The workmate went back to the show. 'It was then about half past eleven I think. I got a flagon off a white fellow I met near the Ceduna pub. He was drunk . . . I went down to the same place. I stopped there by myself and drank the flagon. No, I only drank half of it. I put the other half flagon in a sugar bag. I came into town carrying the bag. I left the bag with the flagon in it down behind the Picture Show wall. I jumped in a taxi.'[1]

He went to the Thevenard pub, sat around outside 'about an hour' and accepted a drink from a man with a bottle of wine. The man gave him the bottle for nothing, and he started walking back. 'It was one o'clock I think.' He finished the bottle, walked back to the pub, and then back to the beach.

Then I saw this little girl. I was pretty full then. She was standing in a pool of water playing. I said to the little girl, 'There is some little birds over there.' I pointed up towards the cave. She said 'I will go and have a look.' She walked in the cave. No I am wrong, I crawled in the cave first and she crawled after me. She said, 'Where's the birds?' I said 'They are gone now.' I punched her on the side of the head. She went unconscious. I took her bathers off. Then I raped her. She was hard to root. I done her. Then I hit her with a stone. Before I raped her I took my clothes off. I was wearing a shirt and pants. I also took my boots off. I think I hit her six times with a stone. I left her. I think she was dead. I went and had a wash in the sea. I had no clothes on. I went back to near the cave where I had taken my clothes off and put them on.

The signed confession goes on to say he started walking along the beach back towards Ceduna, then around the back streets to the caravan park to get the flagon in the sugar bag. 'I drank that. I then went back to the Show' for two hours. 'About sun-down me and another fellow went down to the Jetty. We were looking for other fellows drinking . . . I had more wine that night with them.'

The police found his tent at the wheat stacks on the Monday night and took him to the station. They had been directed to Stuart by his work mate, Allan Moir. The confession concludes: 'I killed her because I did not want her to tell what I had done. I cannot read English. I have heard this statement read to me and it is true and correct in every detail.'

The dead girl was Mary Olive Hattam, aged nine, whose savagely battered body had been found in the cave just after midnight on the Saturday. 'The body looked as though it had been savaged by a wild beast,' Sir Roderic Chamberlain wrote when he looked back on the case in which he had been passionately involved as prosecutor and royal commissioner (and after which the state saw fit to elevate him to the bench).[2] The police had no suspect in mind until the Ceduna station got a phone call from Detective Sergeant Phin in Whyalla. The Funland Carnival had arrived in town and during a routine check Phin had questioned Stuart's drinking mate and been told that, among other things, Stuart had spoken of having had 'a maiden' on the beach, and of having had to wash blood from his chest after having 'done a man in.'

Whatever the truth of that, Phin had warmed to it. He told the *Whyalla Times* in 1960, after his retirement: 'When I was told over the phone . . . that a little child's body had been fouly [*sic*] murdered, and that the head had been battered in and was in a cave on the beach, although approximately 300 miles away and engaged on another murder, I did not for a moment consider that outrage as the work of a white man. I immediately thought it was the work of a darky.'

As to the language of this 'half-caste': 'yes, Stuart is one of them . . . under the influence of wine . . . he is an untamed animal,' Phin said. 'I know their language or shall I say gibberish; they have a different monkey gibberish for every tribe.'[3]

The Confession

Phin knew he could freely express his primitive opinions to the news-papers. His phrases signal the part that language was to play in the whole case: the language of racist stereotyping, and the status of the language spoken by the defendant—although Stuart never exercised the same freedom of expression. At the trial a typed confession signed by him was the main evidence for the prosecution, who claimed—and the police under O'Sullivan's blunt cross-questioning maintained—that the confession had been recorded accurately (though it had been typed up two days after the interview without reference to any notes), and that the statement was 'exactly as he said it.'[4] There was an unsworn counter-statement, written up for Stuart by his lawyers, that recounted details of an alleged bashing by police as they 'interviewed' him. This statement was never shown to the court. It did not reappear until the Royal Commission, where the nature of the English, and Stuart's evident skills in the white man's language, became a matter of supreme concern in another startling way: for not only was it to be seen as a statement as much shaped by the writing as the confession had been, it suggested a command of English that Stuart's defence had always denied. At the trial, Stuart had elected not to go into the witness box: to do so while making accusations against the police would have in turn opened him up to cross-examination, where his previous convic-tions—two of which involved physical encounters with females (a nine-year-old girl and a nurse)—could be used against him. O'Sullivan sought leave to have Stuart's unsworn statement read out, on the grounds that Stuart was illiterate and could not read it himself. This request was blocked by the prosecuting counsel, Roderic Chamberlain, and upheld by Judge Reed, on the grounds that illiteracy was insuffi-cient justification for a departure from the normal procedure of a defendant reading his own statement. (When it came to the trackers who had identified Stuart's tracks on the beach near the cave (tracks the police had neglected to photograph or take casts of), Judge Reed had however seen fit to allow Sonny Jim 'a swearing-in ritual used for aborigines. Did he go to church? Did he believe in God? Did he know that if he swore to tell the truth he might be punished if he told lies? He did. "When you die you're dead and gone," he added.'[5])

Rather than hear the statement, the bench put Stuart in the dock to be prompted with regard to the contents. From there he managed to say: 'I cannot read and write. Never been to school. I did not see the little girl. I did not kill her. Police hit me. Choke me. Make me said these words. They say I kill her.' He added, 'That is what I want to say,' and waved the typed statement: 'Someone to read this out for me.'

The judge asked if he wanted to say anything about the police evidence 'as to what happened at the police station.' 'No,' Stuart said, and O'Sullivan requested that no more questions be put to him and that the statement be read. When Stuart would not say anything further from the dock, the judge refused. All that the court heard were his references to its contents in his summing-up. Right to the end of the trial and into the appeal hearings, Stuart had not, arguably, told his own story, because his illiteracy was allowed to be a crucial factor to his disadvantage. The very idea of the court accommodating this fact was scoffed at by Chief Justice Abbott at the Supreme Court appeal: 'Because you have a man you regard as illiterate and incapable of understanding and expressing himself, you want a special system of justice build up for him which is not in existence.'[6]

As it happened, the issue of language was not so easily dismissed. Might the typed statement have been a more effective defence if Stuart's lawyer had been able to communicate with him in Aranda? At the trial O'Sullivan did not raise the matter of Stuart's adequacy in English: it was only to become significant at the appeal stage, first to the Supreme Court and then the High Court. So the trial jury heard the circum-stantial evidence against the accused in the face of his silence and the shelving of his written statement. The defence's attempt to challenge the credibility of the police was fully allowed by Reed, but there was a clue to the Bench's sympathies in the summing-up: 'I do not know that we are here to criticise or enquire into the methods by which the police obtain information or conduct enquiries, except so far as it is alleged that they have made unfair use of their powers or have committed acts of violence or made threats.' At the Supreme Court appeal, the defence claim that Stuart 'would say "Yes" to anything because he thought he was going to be killed' was dismissed as 'utter rubbish' by Chief Justice Napier. As for Justice Abbott, 'he could never understand how a few blows from a policeman could force a confession of a serious nature out of anybody.'[7] This was in 1959: the exposure of police culture that would come with the Commission of Inquiry into Aboriginal Deaths in Custody was 30 years away. Stuart was convicted on the grounds of the police evidence embodied in his confession. The police word was upheld against his; he had been effectively silenced.

On 24 April 1959, Stuart was convicted of murder and sentenced to be hanged on 22 May. On the day before, he would be moved from his ordinary cell at the Adelaide prison to spend the night in the room beside the gallows. There, after making what peace he could with his maker, he would go into the Hanging Tower, where the white hood and the noose were waiting. His spiritual adviser in those last weeks, Father Thomas Dixon, had not initially believed in Stuart's innocence. Rather, he had concentrated on preparing the man for a death premised upon his guilt. When Dixon realised that Stuart was not a baptised Catholic, he set to:

> It had been two years since I had heard a word of Aranda spoken. I had no option but to take down off the shelves my battered copy of T.G.H. Strehlow's 'Aranda Phonetics and Grammar' and the two volumes of words that I had bought for $50. I stretched my religious scruples and purchased a Lutheran Aranda New Testament . . .
>
> The Ten Commandments were my first approach. We talked in simple English with the odd Aranda phrase if I knew it, and a deal of 'pidgin English,' that broken sort of English that every Territorian uses to communicate with the aboriginals. To make sure he understood I made him translate back as I slowly read from the Aranda New Testament. He was unable to read Aranda and had trouble in recognising some of the technical Aranda words that cropped up in the written language. Special attention was paid to the fifth 'Thou shalt not kill' and the sixth 'Thou shalt not commit adultery.'[8]

Dixon worked though many stories and parables from the New Testament. The wise and foolish virgins, the last judgment and the goats being separated from sheep, the 'prodigal son who wasted his time and his money.' He 'concentrated' on Aranda words for 'kill' and 'murder' and 'intercourse'; there was no word for 'rape' in his Aranda dictionary.

> At length I plucked up the courage to ask him straightout whether he had raped and killed the little girl but to all my enquiries came the consistent but calm 'itja' or 'arangua,' the Aranda No! No! My conclusion was that he was lying.
>
> I continued with the Gospel stories of the passion and death of Jesus Christ, the penitent thief, the tale of Judas, the betrayal of Peter in an effort to get Stuart to express some inkling of sorrow, perhaps even to

mention the crime even if he did not admit it in some small way but I produced not the slightest trace of anything remotely related to the crime. Eventually I suggested to him, 'Perhaps you were so drunk that you can't remember doing it?' and with a shrug of his shoulders he grunted the aboriginal 'Mai-it,' which is another way of saying, 'I don't know anything about it.'[9]

In fact Dixon did not really doubt Stuart's guilt until the day he visited the chambers of the defending solicitors, O'Sullivan and Devaney, to find out the date Stuart was to be hanged. They drew his attention to the confession, which the police had all along claimed was in Stuart's 'exact words.' Dixon read it a second time: 'This time the pattern stood out. There were words and combinations of words clearly beyond Stuart's English usage. When I finished reading it I denied the police assertion that this confession of guilt was dictated in the words of Stuart himself. This fitted my suspicions that Stuart knew little of the actual murder.'[10]

Dixon then told the lawyers about Strehlow. He wanted a man with Strehlow's language skills to see the confession and the transcript of the evidence. It was too late for a retrial, but not too late to have the death sentence commuted to life imprisonment. There was to be an appeal to the High Court.

Strehlow the Senior Man

Dixon was approaching Strehlow at a key period in the linguist's life. Strehlow, who had been Reader in Linguistics since 1954, had only recently translated himself into a senior Aranda man. Eighteen months earlier he had finished an autobiographical sketch, 'Land of Altjira,' a deceptively plain account of his first two years back in the Centre, in which he tracks his field diaries for that time. Its movement is similar to the account given in earlier chapters here, and its mix is rather similar too: encounters with the hard country and its hard settlers, the dramatising of some Aboriginal material; the poignant moments at the last cave, the relentless moments collecting songs, and the illumination of the landscape by reference to some of the most powerful myth stories—the Eater of Dead Men, the Avenging Ancestress, the Bird of Death. They were selected not according to their ethnographic significance but rather according to their appeal to the literary imagination, which is not to say that the book has any style worth speaking of.

The diaries are richer texts. As with the journals of Giles, their relentless graininess is the thing: the writing calibrates the poetics of hard travelling without much effort, without any poetry having to be thrown in. They are also more truthful in several ways. In the diary, for instance, the *tjurunga* collection went hand in glove with the gathering of the songs. In 'Land of Altjira' this aspect of the reality is muted, and when it is raised it is so that Strehlow can reiterate his stress on their private ownership. His wording seems pointedly designed to deflect from *any* idea of collective ownership.* The diaries, too, are closer to the continuous grain of Strehlow's feelings with regard to his discomforts with the rougher bushmen. The entries are grim, relentless. In 'Land of Altjira' he is trying to work the story up, spin the yarn in a way that might amuse, play in the realm of Bush Gothic. The result is usually wooden. In general, 'Land of Altjira' is all rather contrived, and nowhere more so than in the passages on the landscape, where the purple prose is as purple, really, as the picturesque distant mountains to be seen in any painting by the toiling Namatjira school. And it is so because the whole orchestration is designed to do something that was only latent in the diary: claim the country that lay before the writer's gaze.

In the diary—it is clear enough—Strehlow is deeply engaged in the recording of the myths, writing them down more often than not in the field, at the ancestor place itself, in the spiritual precinct of the sacred site. The power of this conjunction is implicit in the diary, if it is there at all. In 'Land of Altjira' it is loudly stated: 'Already I was finding it impossible to escape the psychological impact of the myths,' he writes in 1957, 23 years after the event. He has just camped at the honey ant site of Ljamba site, where the story recounts, rather beautifully, how the honey ants emerged through the skin of the ancestor being, 'like sweat drops from a man in the heat of a summer day,' who later brushed them off in swarms until they blackened the mulga trees 'now ablaze in the yellow fire of their wattle blossom.' All this had happened, Strehlow had written, in the Aranda 'Golden Age, when time began.' After this, in full flight he goes on: 'My previous nights

---

* For example, in the manuscript Strehlow at first wrote: 'all these rites, songs and traditions were regarded by the natives as being owned, not by the tribe, but by private individuals and *small local clans*' (emphasis added), only to cross that out and write, 'all sacred myth, songs and ceremonies, in brief, all *tjurunga* were in fact the private and personal property of the individuals who have been born into that totem' ('Land of Altjira,' 115). The reference to collective dimensions of ownership has fallen away.

which had been spent close to the precincts of Ljaba had been filled with complete feelings of peace and serenity, but my night work north of [X: the important kangaroo site] seemed to be tainted by a mysterious sensation of the presence of evil.' The site was the place of the Avenger story.

Later, he climbs the rocky hills from where he has a commanding view of these mythic places and all the peaks in the distance. 'Rabuntja, Ulamba, Eritjakwata, Ulaterka'—he listed them so in his diary, and remarked: 'I saw them all today with eyes drunk with delight and wonder.' In 'Land of Altjira' he says more. 'But I was not merely filled with youthful wonder: I was feeling proud of these jagged bluffs and wild mountains, because they were situated in my own Western Aranda territory. *I felt that they belonged to me, as I had come to belong to them*' (emphasis added).[11] In other words, he had by 1957 amply rehearsed his *main* claim: that his affinity with Central Australia was tantamount to a possession, and that by colouring it all in he was defining all of himself. It was a belonging, furthermore, bound to the aesthetics of nostalgia: the quality of the image was less important than the biographical link behind it.

Finally there was the central anecdote to 'Land of Altjira': how he had been invited by the old men to be their *ingkata*. The event was not in his diary (which does not mean it did not happen), but writing it up in 1957 constituted his moral claim to *Ntaria*, and much else. Furthermore, in 'Land of Altjira' we can see him working on the true feelings that would cohere with the claim to be ingkata. On his first return at Hermannsburg in April 1932, remember, he did not have much to say in his diary. But in 1957 he was writing himself deep into affiliation.

'And now I was back in the land that I had secretly loved and openly dreaded,' he began. 'The question was: Would I be able to become a good bushman, and fight my way through and hold my own . . .' And so on. We have seen his struggle. He wrote the above only to cross it out and write: 'Life might be hard in Central Australia . . . *I felt sure I would come to love my home even more than I had grown to dread it*' (emphasis added). The last declaration is less emphatic, more complex, than the first, and might be more honest as a result. Both are, at any rate, declarations of intent: that through the initiations of hard travelling as he collected the songs he could earn the right to his love of home.

That is what 'Land of Altjira' is really about: a ceremonial display of his ordeals of initiation, a recounting of his proof to have become deserving of the title *ingkata*. The text is meant to help put a seal on all he had written in *Songs of Central Australia*, which had now found a publisher and which would prove, when it came out, how much he had earned from the field.

This was the position he had reached in himself when Father Dixon found him at work in his office on that Saturday afternoon. There was a deep belief, deeper than fantasy, a confirmed state within, that Father Dixon could not be expected to detect. Dixon thought he would be simply requesting a linguist and anthropologist to help the case of a half-caste Aranda man incriminated by white justice. The connection between Max Stuart and Strehlow's own life was close and obvious, but how could Dixon or anybody else seeking to help Stuart realise that Strehlow had secretly confirmed himself as a traditional man of the unadulterated Aranda tongue?

A proudly purist, backward-looking Aranda man in a white man's skin, a rather covert Black Missionary, opened the door to Dixon. Ideally, this was not the best figure in the world to help a half-caste so wilfully, it seemed, adrift from the law of his fathers.

Strehlow to the Defence

Strehlow gave Dixon a warm welcome. He knew of the case, at a distance. He knew, but he had not let himself be drawn into it. As he later explained:

> This was partly due to the fact that I seriously believed that the S.A. Aborigines' Dept. would do all that was in its power to help Stuart. But my other reason was that I owed so much to Stuart's grandfather, who had been my trusted companion on thousands of miles of journeyings on camel back in the 1930s. I had been afraid that Stuart, if I went to see him, would confess that he *had* committed this horrible double crime. I should then have felt myself unable to help him to escape his fate—for I could not have given false evidence on oath in his favour (and a subsequent plea for mercy could not have helped him) . . . I had finally gone to the death cell with a very heavy heart, and had been glad to find out that he seemed to be innocent after all. When I saw the confessions later on, I rejoiced even more: for that document was clearly not in his own language.[12]

Dixon was there precisely to put the confession before Strehlow and, on the basis of that, to ask him to meet Stuart. On 18 May, four days before Stuart was due to be hanged, Strehlow, Dixon and O'Sullivan visited him in the condemned cell at Yatala prison. The three white men sat with the black man at a wooden table and Strehlow asked him to describe the events at Ceduna and Thevenard.

> He talked in Aranda—the only language in which he possesses full fluency of expression and a reasonable range of vocabulary . . . My object at this stage was to find out for myself whether Stuart was capable of giving a clear-cut, incisive, coherent and chronologically-exact account of his doings during the period in question, with all details of the related events placed in logical sequence according to our 'white-man's' ideas. I had never seen this happening during all my years of court experience in taking statements and extracting evidence from aboriginal or uneducated half-caste witnesses in the Northern Territory. Stuart proved to be no exception.

At the lawyer's office later Strehlow read with 'growing amazement' a confession that defied belief.

> In my ten years of wide and varied experience of evidence given by aboriginals, part-aboriginals, police officers and white residents, I had never seen a document even faintly resembling the one I was looking at . . . This succinct and purposeful typescript, in point of its contents and the arrangement of its subject matter, began to reveal itself as a document which could have been composed only by some person who was well versed in legal procedure and in the practice of giving court evidence . . .
>
> I first read the Police Confession immediately after I had had a long talk with Stuart himself in Aranda, and after I had listened to the remarks which he made in English to Mr O'Sullivan in plain Australian, my immediate reaction upon reading the Police Confession was 'Rupert Stuart just does not talk like that.'[13]

The 'scientific analysis' he made of the confession document, extracts of which featured prominently in *Nation*, became the basis of his very public position in the national press and the subject of his ferocious cross-examination by Chamberlain during the Royal Commission. A great deal turned not only on his expertise with regard to the authenticity of the language attributed to Stuart, but also on the extent to which the police might have brutally coerced their suspect. In private, Strehlow's feelings about police culture were unequivocal. He told his diary:

We criticise the Communist Courts for convicting people on 'confessions,' even though many of the latter are actually made by the accused in the full hearing of a court. And then the police produce a typewritten confession in one of our own courts and have this read out by someone else since the accused cannot read or write himself, and then have him convicted on the strength of this confession, in spite of the denial of the accused that he made it in that form. On the other hand, a similar typewritten defence statement was not permitted to be read out by the presiding judge. At the very least, the confession made to the police should have been critically and impartially examined by an outside authority in order to ascertain whether there was any likelihood of its having been 'dictated' (!) by the accused. But S.A. is at least consistent. The whole blood-stained history of the Northern Territory and Central Australia from 1860–1911 was made under South Australian Governments; and the infamous Willshire was sent up by a South Australian Government in 1881 'with special powers.' Hence we should not be surprised if South Australian justice remains true to its long-standing traditions.[14]

Stuart's execution was deferred to 19 June to allow him to apply to the High Court for leave to appeal. The hearing took place in Melbourne. Strehlow's affidavit, more temperately expressed than the blunt remarks above, was taken seriously, Chief Justice Sir Owen Dixon professing himself worried about whether 'this aboriginal was capable of really understanding the proceedings and expressing himself,' and troubled by the language of the confession. 'Do not think I am suggesting that he may not have said this; I find some difficulty about what is said as to how he said it.' In the event, after a month of deliberations during which a further reprieve was needed, the High Court refused leave to appeal while admitting in its written statement that 'the case has caused us a good deal of anxiety.'[15]

This remark, based as it was on Strehlow's linguistic critique of the police confession, was just what the would-be saviours of Stuart needed. The campaign against the death sentence escalated. Between

July and September his execution was stayed another five times, a shuf-fling of the death card that concentrated political passions wonderfully. Finally, towards the end of the Royal Commission, the Playford Government commuted the sentence to life imprisonment.

By the time Strehlow stepped in to take upon himself the role of effectively speaking for Stuart, picking up the echo of Stuart's unread statement at the trial and inserting his own voice into the problematic material of the written confession—acts of sympathetic identification made possible by his translations of Stuart's Aranda, the use of which seems to have been inseparable for Strehlow from the deepest bonds of senti-ment—the political storm had already broken. At the prow of the campaign to save Stuart's life were those who opposed capital punishment on principle, notably the Howard League of Penal Reform. They were most passionately abetted by those who saw the case as one that exempli-fied the difficulties of detribalised natives in the era of assimilation—notably the Aboriginal Advancement League. As the campaign gathered it included the gamut of liberal and left-liberal opinion: university teachers, clergymen, lawyers, journalists, as well as those with direct affiliations on all sides of politics. Liberal opinion in Adelaide was adventitiously led by Rohan Rivett, the forthright editor-in-chief at Rupert Murdoch's News Ltd. In the South Australian parliament on the opposition benches, another rising star and a smart lawyer, Don Dunstan, was eloquently in protest. Interstate, the case was under the microscope of *Nation* magazine, which had assigned a scrupulous young historian, Ken Inglis, to report for them. All along, of course, the tabloid press had been having a field day with a case where the twin subtexts of sex and race prejudice could be so easily and sensationally plumbed. But as events developed through two appeal hearings in Australia, and then to the Privy Council in London, the stakes became much higher than the titillating fate of a black man con-victed of the rape and slaughter of a white girl. Politically, the whole justice system in South Australia was under challenge. Premier Thomas Playford, a man hitherto comfortable in the saddle of Adelaide's comfort-able conservatism, was on one side of the barricades. On the other was an alliance that widened to include H.V. Evatt, the leader of the Federal Opposition, who called for a commutation of the death sentence and a testing of the case before the Privy Council.

To its critics the Playford Government represented a pastoral and mining establishment that had shaped a legal system not renowned for progressive tendencies. 'Theirs was a "hanging State" dominated by bloodthirsty country-folk'—to borrow the sally of prosecutor Chamberlain, who saw himself as defending 'the honour and integrity of the South Australian Government, its Police Force, and indeed the very institutions on which the administration of justice depends.'[16] As the parade of execution dates went past—seven reprieves in four months— the outraged humanist and reformist opposition grew. At one high point Playford, who had abused legal process in the House by a passionate defence of the police, sued the *News* and the editor, Rivett, for the archaic offence of 'seditious libel'—a good measure of Tory panic at the use of certain words if ever there was one. All this was to resist, right to the end, those who sought to save the life of a murderer who was a black man, and whose fate deserved no special consideration because he was a black man. It was in such an atmosphere of feverish social division, with the state apparatus drawn up to its most defensive and desperate height, that Strehlow's 'speaking for Stuart' took shape and most publicly entered the battleground.

His first step into the open was the writing of his affidavit for the appeal to the High Court—a statement that he 'laboured' over in late June. His first public appearance in the matter was at the home of Dr Charles Duguid on 1 July. Duguid, the secretary of the Aboriginal Advancement League, had a mission background in common with Strehlow. He had helped found the Presbyterian mission at Ernabella in arid country a long day's journey south of Hermannsburg. Like Strehlow, he had long been a friend of the Aborigines and a critic of strict assimilation policies, which he insisted would detribalise people too quickly without making adequate provision for the generation that had no choice but to acquire the skills to live well in a white culture. Duguid's house was packed with campaigners and Strehlow aired at length his opinion of the confession.

Two days later Strehlow had a chance to deliver it to the government in person. In the company of Dixon and Norval Morris, professor of law at the University of Adelaide, he met with the Attorney-General. The meeting itself seems to have confirmed his worst feelings about the workings of the Adelaide establishment. The government wanted the meeting kept secret. The deputation was most disconcerted, and told the Attorney-General so. Strehlow added that he was already on the public record by virtue of his affidavit.

Then I gave an outline of my own document and handed it in. Morris then asked the A.G. to remember the grave uneasiness that men like Father Dixon and myself felt about the whole business. The A.G. brought out some objections of his own: Stuart's convictions in Perth, Queensland, and Alice Springs which showed that he knew enough English to understand what was going on. I replied that the A[lice] S[prings] transcripts proved my point that Stuart rambled on hopelessly and used certain idioms that I had pointed out as N.T. English. Father Dixon added that he had ascertained that Stuart had had the help of Native Welfare Officers (and educated halfcastes) when making his defence statements in those courts. The A.G. mentioned that he had to get the terrible effects of the photos of the murdered child out of his mind. Some one replied that they should spur him on to look for the real murderer. The A.G. suddenly asked Father Dixon how long had Stuart been a Catholic. Only for the last 7 weeks? Could he be certain that Stuart had a Christians [sic] conscience. Father Dixon then mentioned that Stuart knew all sorts of Bible stories from the Aranda Bible, and said he had been surprised at the many things Stuart knew . . . The A.G. finally demanded—Why had Stuart never produced any of the witnesses to his claims that he had been drinking with various people on Saturday afternoon? Father Dixon had no real answer to that. As we left, I shot in one more remark—that if Stuart died, he would be making anthropological history. For he would be the first aboriginal who had been found guilty of raping a small girl, and subsequently committing a sex murder.[17]

The document Strehlow left with the Attorney-General was the fullest expression of opinion he was to make about Stuart's confession. After the customary review of his own experience and qualifications, it said that all Northern Territory Aborigines and part-Aborigines showed, when giving evidence, an 'irritating vagueness about all dates and clock times.' The court evidence did not indicate whether Stuart had a watch, or whether he could interpret one accurately. 'Yet in his alleged confession, the illiterate Stuart, who has never had any formal education of any sort, is depicted as a person with a perfect obsession for ascertaining clock times at short intervals and for thinking about days in times of the calendar.'

Again Strehlow attacked the validity of the confession, and then went into detail about the language. Inglis gives a sharp summary of

Strehlow's cumbersome case.

As a boy ... Stuart had learned pidgin English, 'and later on he made some headway in the slightly-improved form of it which bears a closer resemblance to what may be termed "Northern Territory English," i.e., the language spoken by most educated part-aboriginals.' Northern Territory English, he explained, was in many ways like ordinary conversational Australian English; 'but it is marked out, firstly, by an extraordinary lack of range in its vocabulary, and secondly, by certain characteristic idioms of its own. Among the latter is the use of "he" or "she" after a noun ... Thus, in Northern Territory English, it is common to hear expressions like "that woman *she* told me" (for "that woman told me"), "that man *he* wants to know" (for "this man wants to know"), and so on. Another Northern Territory English idiom is the use of "them" in place of "those," as in "*them* two blokes came up today" (instead of "*those* two men arrived today") or "I *seen them* two boys standin' on verandah of hotel" (for "I *saw those* two boys standing on *the* verandah of *the* hotel").' Small divergences from normal Australian English, Strehlow suggested, could be seen even in the few words spoken by Stuart during his trial, 'even after he had carefully discussed with his solicitor the statement he was going to make in the Court in his own defence. After these few sentences he apparently broke down, unable to remember what to say next.' Yet the English of the confession owed nothing to Aranda, 'and—with the exception of a few unimportant words and minor phrases—nothing even to pidgin English, or to Northern Territory English either.'

Among particular words and phrases in the confession Strehlow singled out as implausible the word 'awoke' ('how many white Australians, educated or otherwise, say "*I awoke*" instead of the common and normal, "*I woke up*"?'), 'such better-class elements of the English language as "unconscious" and "raped,"' and the following sentences:

'The Show *was situated* at the Ceduna Oval.'

'The *three of us* sat down and drank a flagon of wine.'

'I put *the half flagon* in a sugar bag.'

'I left the bag with the flagon in it down *behind the Picture Show wall*.'

These passages, said Strehlow, were 'in complete opposition to all the stylistic and grammatical features of Northern Territory English.' Strehlow cited the evidence of Constable Jones that the body of the confession represented 'the words exactly as the defendant spoke them,' and wrote: 'In spite of Constable Jones' protestations, the voice that can be heard speaking in the Police Confession is not the voice of Rupert Stuart.' Strehlow remarked that the act of raping small girls was, in his experience, exclusively a white man's crime.[18]

Strehlow's approach here is systematically, if not laboriously, scientific; the upshot is to advance his special claim to knowledge by placing a rather possessive construction on both the capacities and character of the Aboriginal man. By virtue of the Aboriginal language he shares with Stuart, Strehlow is telling the world what he is privileged to know of the man. And what he knows is—there seems to be no doubt about it—the essence of the man. Indeed we might be forgiven for thinking that it is Strehlow's conviction that he knows Stuart better than the man knows himself. At any rate, there is no hesitation about speaking for him. These were indeed paternalistic times; and Strehlow was, even before he was outspoken about such other tragic figures as Albert Namatjira, never hesitant about speaking on an Aborigine's behalf when it came to the practical aspects of assimilation policy. All the more reason, then, as we shall see, to lament the way things turned out when Strehlow had to speak for Stuart in public, when what Strehlow had to say was set, for the first time, against what Stuart was finally able to say for himself. It was the moment that would undo them both.

'The Air Is Now so Poisoned . . .'

In July events dramatically intensified, arousing Strehlow's feelings, and deepening his involvement in Stuart's fate. With leave to appeal to the High Court having failed, the Executive Council met to reconsider commutation. But the death sentence was upheld. 'It was a staggering blow,' Strehlow wrote in his diary. The hanging would proceed unless the defence took the case to the Privy Council in London. A public appeal was set up to fund the move, and Stuart was duly granted a further fortnight's reprieve.

July 6: 'Father Dixon rang. He had been deeply shaken, but he was at least relieved at not having to accompany Stuart to the scaffold tomorrow.' July 7: 'I did not sleep well last night. This morning I sent a telegram to Hasluck.'[19] He also posted the minister a copy of his linguistic analysis of the police confession. 'I felt very shaken, ill and unhappy.' July 8: 'I had a very good sleep last night—I felt I had done everything in my power in the Stuart case, and now all I could do was wait.' Strehlow had planned to make another visit to Central Australia, but 'I would have had to face all of Rupert Stuart's relatives in Alice Springs, and I could not face them if he got executed after all.'[20]

On 25 July, the Privy Council threw out Stuart's appeal. Chamberlain did not have to speak, because the English Lords found no question of law at issue. One of the judges, Lord Tucker, asked O'Sullivan: 'If he [Stuart] was able to convey to you what his defence was, why could he not convey it to the court?' O'Sullivan's reply—in which he had to concede that he had three months leading to the trial in which to prepare Stuart's defence, a defence that had not troubled with witnesses who might substantiate an alibi—did not impress the Judicial Committee. His return to the alleged police brutality also got short shrift. Viscount Simonds told him: 'You are not entitled upon any of the material before us to suggest that the evidence of the police was in any way corrupt or in any way wrong. It was accepted by the jury and the courts through which this case has proceeded have seen no reason to doubt it.'[21]

Stuart would have been hanged by the end of July but for a major development. Father Dixon, having taken his cue from the Attorney-General on the point of defence witnesses, had gone looking for some: he had tracked the Funland troupe as far as Queensland and from there, with a reporter from the *News* in tow (the paper had helped fund the search), announced that proprietors Mr and Mrs Gieseman would testify that Stuart was with them, working on the darts stall, at the time he was supposed to have committed the murder. The story made international news. Stuart's defenders were jubilant. At last there were grounds for re-opening the case. The Playford Government, under acute political pressure, granted Stuart yet another reprieve and announced, finally, the establishment of a Royal Commission.

On 31 July, when the news came through, Strehlow told his diary:

Tonight I was able to listen to the 3rd act of Wagner's 'Die Meistersinger' in the latest brilliant HMV recording (by Rudolf Kempe) on the Hi-Fi machine in my home. The first two acts I had listened to yesterday afternoon and evening (in between the various interruptions). I had purchased this magnificent set on my birthday early in June, and played it though completely only twice before that first dreadful day when news came that the High Court of Australia had rejected Stuart's petition for leave to appeal against his conviction for murder. Since then I had never again felt in any real mood to listen to any great and glorious music.

But now that it seems as though the corner has been turned at long last, I can enjoy 'Die Meistersinger' again. And my thoughts returned tonight to that last glorious night in Bayreuth in 1951, when—after hearing the wonderful performance of 'Die Meistersinger' for the first time after the destruction of the Third Reich—I walked though the old park in the rich silence of the hour after midnight.

It was on a kind of Wagnerian surge that Strehlow seems to have drifted towards his own appearance at the Royal Commission. He was the knight in shining armour now, and the white hope of the Stuart camp. His name was all over the papers, as well it might be, since his scientific opinion had sustained every legal move to date: and now, with the production of witnesses for the defence, it would come into its own in the full and democratic arena of a commission. At this point, Stuart's cause had every reason to think that such a commission would be a whole new start to their defence: tantamount to a retrial, in fact. Strehlow noted proudly: 'my own linguistic analysis is being referred to primarily in a number of papers now.' For the first time he was interviewed on television. He thought he had done rather well: 'Two of the questions were so unexpected as to cause me to falter slightly; but I managed to win through and—I hope—make all my points.' On 15 August, he was the lead story in the magazine *Nation*, the smartest publication tracking the Stuart case. The paper ran a detailed summary of his affidavit and commented: 'At the Royal Commission it is not only Stuart who is in the dock. Sir Thomas Playford's system is up for scrutiny—the system which allowed the Stuart case to get to the point where the accused has the onus of demonstrating his innocence.'[22]

Playford was indeed in the dock. At the announcement of the Royal Commission there was uproar about the government's choice of judges. One, Justice Reed, had presided at the trial; another, Sir Mellis Napier ('Sir Malice' in Strehlow's diary), had heard the appeal. Hitherto, the opposition to the government might have been described as the liberal-minded friends of Aborigines, the philanthropic left of Australian politics, ranged against something of a legal establishment in South Australia. But the composition of the commission also aroused conservative temperaments: Sir John Latham, president of the Australian Association for Cultural Freedom and former

Chief Justice of the Commonwealth, called for a halt to the inquiry and a report as to whether the new evidence justified a retrial. The case was now a political battleground of some dimensions. Strehlow told his diary:

> The air is now so poisoned with distrust, anger, and resentment, that only a complete re-constitution of the tribunal itself could hope to reveal the truth about the Stuart case. Naturally neither the Govt, nor the judges, nor the Crown Law Office, nor the Police would wish to have any of the original evidence against Stuart questioned or set aside. To do so would suggest that the original trial had resulted in a miscarriage of justice. It would also mean that the State and its judicial agencies had then pushed this miscarriage of justice successfully through all the Appeal Courts of Australia and the Commonwealth—i.e. the Full Court of S.A., the High Court of Australia, and the Privy Council in London. Few of the people in power would be prepared even to face up honestly to such a possibility. The next step accordingly will probably be for the Commissioners to smear O'Sullivan and to attempt to push the blame for the whole sorry affair squarely upon his head. I see little hope that any of the witnesses for Stuart will get much of a go while the present Commissioners are conducting this inquiry. It is the police witnesses who will win all the smiles.[23]

The Commission opened on 10 August. Representing Stuart was a top Sydney QC, Mr J.W. Shand. For the first few days the Giesemans were in the box: their evidence did not stand up well under Chamberlain's cross-examination. Stuart, it was announced, would appear later on: he wanted to give evidence through an interpreter. The name of Strehlow was mentioned. Shand expressed a wish to interview the young circus hand, Allan Moir, who had evidently led the police in the direction of Stuart in the first place. While the commission was considering this request, its chairman, Sir Mellis Napier, spoke about the press: 'In the very nature of things we do sometimes read the newspapers,' he remarked, 'and it would be easier for us if we were allowed to go about our business without being told what witnesses are going to say before they are called . . . It has not been helpful to us that we should be told where truth and justice lie without being allowed to discover that for ourselves.'[24]

A few days later he ended an edgy exchange with Shand:

'There has been a campaign of misrepresentation and of abuse that has aroused such a state of uncertainty and distrust in the community that we are on the point of distrusting the verdict of the jury before any evidence has been produced to justify any distrust . . . [At the commission] it is not the police who are the prosecutors but it is the accused who is called upon to disturb the verdict that has been arrived at.'

Shand submitted that Stuart had to satisfy a court only that in the light of new evidence the case might not have been proved against him beyond reasonable doubt. Stuart was not an accused person, the Chairman observed, but a convicted person . . . 'It is no longer upon the Crown to adduce the evidence that justifies the verdict . . . it is you [the defence] who are accusing the police, and accusing them of a very, very serious crime.'[25]

It was now, when Shand had the police in the box, that the hearing broke open. Sergeant Phin was giving evidence about how he had inter-viewed Moir. Shand identified three changes of ground by Phin, and asked which one was the 'real explanation,' at which Napier interrupted: 'He is not obliged to explain anything.' In the exchange that followed, Napier said he was not interrupting the cross-examination when he was, and that 'as far as I am concerned I have heard enough of this':

NAPIER, CJ: If you feel it is helping you to convince us well and good.
MR SHAND: I feel it is impossible to convince Your Honour on this because Your Honour says you don't want to hear any more of it.
REED, J: That is a rather startling remark to make.
MR SHAND: It may be but I make it and maintain it.[26]

Within minutes Shand had sat down, refusing to cross-examine further because it was 'useless.' Next morning he resigned from the case.

Strehlow in the Dock

Stuart now had no defence at the Royal Commission. Within a few weeks Shand would be dead of cancer back in Sydney. Stuart's life—and possible death—was rather lost sight of in the political uproar. The *News* had a poster on the streets before noon.

SHAND QUITS
'YOU WON'T GIVE STUART
FAIR GO'

The headlines incensed Playford, who set about prosecuting the editor. The whole affair had become, as the prosecuting attorney Roderic Chamberlain was to claim some years later, a matter of law and order, of illegitimate railings against the authority of the state. There was, according to one of Playford's backbenchers, 'utter confusion in the minds of the public.'

Meanwhile, O'Sullivan placed Stuart's written statement before the Royal Commission. It ran for two pages, and began:

> I am an aboriginal.
> I cannot read and write.
> I was at Ceduna the day the girl was killed.
> I did not kill her.
> I did not ever see her.
> I went to a taxi to Thevenard to get a drink.
> I did not want a girl.
> I did not tell anyone I did.
> I had some wine there.
> I was not drunk.

Stuart continued systematically to correct the police report about the girl and the cave, the taking clothes off and washing them in the water. At the police station, he said:

> Then Sergeant Walker grabbed me round the throat with two hands.
> He kept pushing his thumbs into my throat . . .
> I was frightened.
> My head and my throat were hurting.
> I could hardly breathe.
> They were all saying things to me.
> I can't remember it all.
> I kept saying, 'I didn't do it.'
> One said. 'We have found the dead girl. You must have done it.'
> I said 'Perhaps it was a white man.' [27]

Stuart said he signed the confession after the policeman threatened to skin him with a razor. Stuart's statement made sense, up to a point. But why did he not mention working at the darts stall? And what of a detail he had previously told O'Sullivan on the day O'Sullivan had come with Strehlow to see him: namely, that in Thevenard he had met up with a girl at the hotel and had intercourse with her?

Stuart's statement was on the commission's table when Strehlow made his first appearance on 4 September. He was the first new witness to be called after Shand had pulled out. The night before his appearance he had hardly slept, and when he went into the witness box at 10.30 the next morning he was filled with defensive anxiety. Strehlow's diary entry accurately portrays the political odds against him, and the disadvantage he was at now that Stuart had no counsel:

> Three silent figures sat on the judges' bench, Of these three Judge Reed had directed the original trial jury to accept the confession *and* the police record—written up from memory two days later without the aid of any notes!—of their conversations with Stuart as being fully authentic. Napier had warned O'Sullivan, at the Full Court hearing not to suggest any charges of perjury or forgery against the police: 'That's utter rubbish,' he had claimed. I knew that these men would be hostile to my analysis, and that they had just been assured by the Premier—who had also publicly backed the police in Parliament—that the Govt was taking full responsibility for the present conduct of the Royal Commission.
>
> These then were the impartial judges.
>
> Ranged against me was sitting a considerable complement of hostile lawyers—those men from the Crown Law Dept, also the two counsel 'assisting the Commission.' And all these men were men of great legal knowledge and ability. There was not a single lawyer present to help me or to ask me any questions that could have given me the chance of establishing the justice of my own contentions. Brazel had, in fact, earlier told me that I was there to give evidence and that I would be cross-examined 'like any other witness.' [28]

J.F. Brazel, QC, was the senior 'counsel assisting the Commission', part of whose job was to help the witnesses.

At 10.30, then, Strehlow found himself in the clutches of the South Australian Crown Prosecutor, Roderic Chamberlain—'a bald-headed man, with slitted eyes.' He opened with questions about Aborigines and time. By and large, Strehlow said, Aborigines thought in terms of the sun and meals rather than clocks; but an intelligent Aborigine who worked among white men in a job where things happened at fixed times would be quite likely to learn to give those times. He had not seen Stuart take an interest in clock times.

'You have not taken the trouble to find out, have you?'
'No I have not, no.'

This took a few tight minutes to establish: it was the first of several points where Chamberlain tried to highlight Strehlow's lack of real inquiry into the facts of the case, including the details of Stuart's previous convictions and the late arrival of his alibi. Chamberlain's knife went in properly when he led: 'Your comments on this matter have received pretty wide coverage, haven't they?' he asked Strehlow.

'Possibly they have.'
'Don't you know?'
'I have seen them in some parts.'
'Have you seen what appeared on the fourth of August: "Rupert Max Stuart's confession to police fell down on three major points." Have you seen that headline?'
'That was published in the *News*, was it?'
'Yes. Have you read that?'
'Yes,' he said, and Chamberlain commented: 'It reads: "Rupert Max Stuart's confession to police fell down on three major points, Mr T.G.H. Strehlow, Reader in Australian Linguistics at Adelaide University, claimed today. These were the time factor, the confession contained only actions and remarks that would help to convict Stuart, and it was not in the style of Northern Territory English by Stuart." Those were the three major points?'
'That is correct.'
'That is a correct record of a statement that you made for publication in the *News*, is it?'
'Yes,' he agreed.
'You realise the implications in what you were saying to the press, do you, as far as the police are concerned? Do you see any implication in relation to the police in that statement?'

'That was a published document which had been stated to be in the exact language of an aboriginal.'

'Perhaps you will answer my question,' Chamberlain asked him. 'If that qualifies the answer give the qualification, but for the time being I want to know: did you think there was any implication against the police in that statement?'

'Only that the police claimed that the statement of confession was word for word in its own terms.'

'That is what you thought they had claimed?'

'I was under that impression, yes,' he said.

'What you were doing in effect there—correct me if I am wrong about this—was saying the confession was a fake?'

'I have this morning said that in terms of linguistic analysis it cannot be accepted as being . . .' Strehlow began, but Sir Geoffrey Reed interrupted him to say, 'The question is whether that statement of yours meant that the confession was a fake,' and Sir Mellis Napier asked, 'Did you want people to think that?'

'It was a published document and I could not accept it as being genuine,' he said.

Chamberlain, 'Let us see if we can use a little plain Australian. I am not a student of linguistics. Let us put it in plain language. Did you want it understood when you made that statement that the confession was a fake?'

'I think it was a case of mistaken identity,' he said.

'The police had the wrong man; is that what you mean?'

'I was not expressing any information upon the facts.'

'Weren't you?'

'No.'

'And you do not want to now; is that the position?'

'As far as the facts are concerned they would be open, if correct, I think to independent verification.'

'Let us understand one another,' Chamberlain said. 'Didn't you mean, when you made that statement to the *News*, to give it out to the world that the police evidence against Stuart was faked?'

'It meant that there was some doubt,' Strehlow said, and Sir Mellis asked, 'Is it possible to give a direct answer to the question? If you could, it would be quicker.'

'Yes or no?' Chamberlain asked him.

'It did not ring true to me.'[29]

It was not just Chamberlain's slitted eyes that Strehlow was conscious of. He thought he had 'thin lips distorted into a perpetual evil grin', and that he was 'obviously a favourite with the judges.'

'You were able to form your opinion quickly, were you?'

'In his case, I can, yes.'

'In his case you did? You did form your opinion quickly?'

'I am a trained linguist and in cases like that I can.'

'Did you form your opinion quickly?'

'I formed it on reasonable grounds.'

'Just one more try,' Chamberlain said. 'Did you form your opinion about Stuart's English quickly?'

'It was quite easy to do so in this case.'

'Could you answer the question?' Sir Mellis asked, and he said, 'Yes, I formed it quickly.'

'Are you having any difficulty with my English or can't you understand me?' said Chamberlain. 'I can understand you quite well,' Strehlow replied.

'How quickly did you form your opinion about Stuart? How long did it take you?'

'About an hour.'

'During which time Mr O'Sullivan was asking him questions in English and Stuart was answering in English, is that it?'

'No, for a period of an hour doing most of the talking. He was asked questions and answering them in English.'

'What is the first question asked in English, and the answer Stuart gave?'

'I could not honestly answer that question,' Strehlow said.[30]

Chamberlain had before him the full text of Strehlow's analysis as given in confidence to the Attorney-General. Soon he would come to that, and make good use of it, taking Strehlow by surprise, since Strehlow was expecting him to work from the affidavit which had been the basis of the *Nation* article. Rather than dissect Strehlow's case directly, Chamberlain went about establishing that Stuart's own statement was a departure from what he had actually said: that it was as much a *written* version of his position as the original police confession. (The strict police defence that it was in Stuart's 'exact words' had rather slipped out of sight on the way to the Royal Commission and

Book I. p. 146. verse 4.

He hears the familiar twittering of the birds as he approaches his mountain.

22. Jĭntjĭtjĕ́ / rūbắŋkārŏ̆u / bằŋkārŏ̆u   (*Intjĭtjirba aŋkắrapaŋkắrama;

Mĭntjĭtjĕ́ / rūbắŋkārŏ̆u / bằŋkārŏ̆u   Ulắmba *ipĭṭipĭṭaia (or pŏ̆ṭapŏ̆ṭa.)[559]

Mūlắmbŏ̆u / jĭbāṭĕ́ / jĭbāṭĕ́

Jŭlắmbŏ̆u / jĭbāṭĕ́ / jĭbāṭĕ́

"The birds are speaking with many voices
    At Ulắmba, chasm-cleft Ulắmba."

Ibid., verse 5.

He reaches his old cave and flings himself down in his deserted hollow.

23. /: Mắpmāṛĕ́ / jĕ̆tjĕrṇĕ́ / tjĕ̆wālĕ́ / tjŭrbārŏ̆u / bŭrbārŏ̆u :/

(Pmắṛa *tjĕ̆ṇaiắtja
Iwŭlatja urbắṛupurbắṛama?)

"My own home, my dear home,—
    Whose [feet] are disfiguring it?"

Ibid., verse 6.

which has been disfigured by the feet of inquisitive birds.

24. /: Mĕ̆ntjŭlkŏ̆u / tĕ̆mbātjĕ́ / tjŭrbārŏ̆u / bŭrbārŏ̆u :/

(Intjĭlkuṭa *imbĭtjitja
Urbắṛupurbắṛama.)

"The mulga parrots are disfiguring it:
    Their [feet] are disfiguring the deserted hollow."[560]

The particularly easy rhythmic measure employed in the Arĭntja Song of Ulắmba (see page 47 above) lends itself to reproduction in an English version. (Verse 11 is the only couplet composed in a different measure.) In the following rhythmic translation of the Ulắmba Song I have attempted also to indicate the effect of Aranda reduplications to the English reader by using double phrases for reduplicated compound words. Thus, in verse 2, inkắritjarĭtja has been rendered as "ardent-keen, eager-keen", and tjắbuṭabŭ̆ṭa as "bold and hard, combat-hard". Similarly, aŋkắrap'-aŋkắrama has been translated as "voices call, voices fall" (verse 7), and urbắṛupurbắṛama as "scar thy ground, mar thy ground" (verse 8). By means of such translations it has in addition been possible to preserve at least some of the

"rhymes" of the Aranda verse original (e.g. ŋắŋkārŏ̆u / bằŋkārŏ̆u//ltjắŋkārŏ̆u / bằŋkārŏ̆u in verse 7, or ṇŭrbārĕ́ / bŭrbārĕ́ (twice) in verse 8. In this rhythmic English translation the prose word Ulắmba has had its stress shifted to its final syllable (Ulambắ): this is the exact form in which it appears in the sung Aranda version.

---

559. On the changing of *Intjĭtjirba to *Intjĭtjerirba in verse 20a and to Intjĭtjeruba in verse 22, see *Aranda Phonetics*, §§82, 83. The word has been translated here as "birds", in obedience to native oral tradition. Perhaps the original meaning of the first line was, "Birds bearing the avengers' stripes are speaking with many voices".

560. *Imbĭtjitja clearly combines the meanings of imbātja (footprints) and imbĭtja (a deserted hollow) = a place where someone has slept.

---

44. A page from *Songs of Central Australia*. 'It commands monological authority . . . it might be read as a kind of Scripture.'

3.

Again they sing
merrily about
themselves
(69(a) + (b)),

69(a) |: mánuŭnăkĕrắ | tắtjĭlpắtwĕi :|
c.f.
v.5 |:   " | tắtbănrjĕrăkŭnjĕt̆ :|

(b) |: mắnuŭ ănăkĕrắ | tătiărĕt̆ :|
c.f.
v.6 |:   " | tắtbănrjĕrăkŭnjĕt̆ :|

as they go over flats
bearing worawora
flowers

(c) |: mắkăwirăwĕt̆ | rắlpăŭpăjălbăŭ :|
c.f.
v.4 |: mắnuŭăkĕrcit̆ | tjălpăŭpăjălbăŭ :|

Kắla Pŭralitnắm' ekŭrarj etŭka ĕtna itŭtŭtjak' erĕnama -

they cross a pebbly
rise,

(d) |: mắtĭlĕtjắ | tjăkĭrjkĕrăŭ :|
c.f.
v.12 |:   " | tjŭnătanbăŭ :|

+ then pass through
tnjima thickets
(69e + f).

(e) |: wắrămbŭrkărĕt̆ :|
c.f.
v.13 |: wắtnjŭmămĭnkărĕt̆ :|

(f) |: wătnjămăŭrkwĕt̆ | tătjĭtbătjĭtbărĕnă :|
c.f.
v.14 |: wắnuŭăkĕrăt̆t̆ | tjătjĭtbătjĭtbărĕnă :|

Pŭr' etŭka (viz. close to Pŭralitnắma) ĕtna ndắratantĕma
arĕrjopanăma: jăn' ekŭrarja jĭrama. °)

they see another
ndĕrjata lizard: it
"is the last that they
see on their journey.

(g) Ltắrjlă wắrăalĕt̆ ndĭtjŏmĕt̆
Ltắrjlă wắrăalĕt̆ ndĭtjŏmăŭ
Ltătĭrkăŭltătĭrkĕt̆ ndĭtjŏmăŭ
Ltătĭrkăŭltătĭrkĕt̆ ndĭtjŏmĕt̆

Kắla pŭr' erĕrja tjărantắma tralkŭerăma, pmắra
Pŭralitnắm' ekŭrantama -°°)

at Pŭralitnắma
the two aged leaders
at the order of the
horde are plagued
by flies, + perform
their phallic dances
verhorpet̆ (verses
69h - 73).

(h) |: Pŭrălĭrjtjeĭrnăŭ :|
|: mắrja mắrjălălĭrjtjeĭrnăŭ :|
70. |: Rămărjălbŏwtrŏŭwĕt̆ :|
|: Răjŭjpĭt̆ărăkălbŏwtrŏŭwĕt̆ :|

71. |: mắmărjăŭrĭrntŭpeĭntăŭ :|
|: măjŭjpĭt̆ărăkă wĭntŭpeĭntăŭ

72.(a) |: Ltbărălbărălĭt̆ | ntjŏŭmălĭntjŏŭmă :|
c.f.
v. 24 (a) |: Nkărkălĭntjŏŭmă :|

45. A page from Strehlow's 'Myth Books'. A working up of his 'foul papers' to masterfully
written translation.

47. Strehlow in the late 1940s: about the time he set off for London.

46. Strehlow and first-born child, Theo, 1941.

48. Strehlow, Bertha and their children: Theo, Shirley and baby John, c. 1946.

49. The Frankfurt Folk Museum, bombed in 1945, with many Aranda *tjurunga* left destroyed in the rubble.

50. Pastors Scherer and Raberaba with Strehlow and his Aranda New Testament, 1956.

February 23, 1957   LUTHERAN

Mission News

Finke River Mission

ARANDA-IZED CHRISTIAN SYMBOLS

P. A. Scherer

The above designs, which appeared on the title cover
of the Presentation Volume handed to Mr. T. G. H. Strehlow
by the Finke River Mission Board in the Adelaide Town
Hall on December 3rd, are here explained and interpreted
by request. Desired to express Christian ideas in nativized
form, they were designed by Mr. Strehlow himself at the
invitation of the writer.

51. The Christian Trinity as a ground painting designed by Strehlow the 'Black Missionary.'

52. Strehlow on the track in the early 1960s: publicly funded but less inclined to share his collection with the national estate.

53. Strehlow and his new family: Kathleen (centre), her daughter, Yaralie Stuart, and her son Julian Stuart holding young Carl Strehlow.

54. Max Stuart, mid-trial and Royal Commission, 1959.

55. Professor Ronald Berndt, the friend who could not save Strehlow from himself. Berndt is opening the exhibition of the Strehlow Research Foundation on 3 October 1978, the day Strehlow died.

56. Strehlow, c. 1978, close to his last days, reading the Book of *Revelation*.

Chamberlain did not seek to maintain that the police confession was entirely verbatim.)

Chamberlain suggested to Strehlow that if he looked right through Stuart's statement he would find three characteristics:

'One. That it is a complete chronological description of events. Two. That it is expressed with correct past tenses. Three. That it does not contain any great trace, at all events, of Aranda or northern dialect. Do you agree with all that?'

'I agree with that,' Strehlow said.

'You don't doubt the genuineness of that document do you?'

'I think I have explained that in the High Court affidavit.'

'Never mind about the High Court affidavit, you are explaining it here,' Chamberlain said, and Strehlow began to answer with, 'I have been told— Mr O'Sullivan showed it . . . ' but Chamberlain interrupted to say: 'You are explaining it to the Commission and answering me at the moment. Do you doubt the authenticity or genuineness of that document?'

'The only reason why I don't doubt it is I was told by Mr O'Sullivan that he had in fact taken Stuart's replies and put them into, shall I say, slightly more correct English,' Strehlow said, and Chamberlain asked, 'So Mr O'Sullivan has turned Stuart's replies into correct and decent English, is that it?'

'Yes, I should say so.'

'Looking a little further along the second page: "It was easy to see my tracks there, any feller could see them." You think that is a translation of something Stuart said or do you think it purports to be a record of Stuart's exact words?'

'That is an idiom you find Northern Territory people using.'

'Isn't that Stuart's own language rather than O'Sullivan's?'

'I should say it is based on Stuart's language.'

'Doesn't it look to you that it purports to be Stuart's own?'

'The whole document?'

'No, that sentence.'

'Yes.'

'Notice the fourth to bottom line on the first page: "I went to have a shit." You read that sentence. It is describing the purpose for which he went down the yard. Do you think that is Mr O'Sullivan's polite translation into English of what Stuart said or do you think it is purporting to be giving Stuart's own words?'

'That would be Stuart's own words,' Strehlow said.

'So that the document is what you might describe, and did describe the police document, as a little bit of hotch potch, partly polite translation, partly Stuart's own words?'

'Yes, that is correct . . .'

'And you do not blame Mr O'Sullivan for producing a document like that, you don't think there is anything wrong with it?'

'He explained to me that was his setting out of information which he got from Stuart, and I agreed with that; I should be prepared to accept it as that.'

'You understood he was doing it essentially as putting before the Court Stuart's story?'

'Yes,' Strehlow said.

'You didn't suspect he was not faithfully recording exactly what Stuart told him?'

'I didn't suspect that.'

'And it is, as a matter of fact, not a connected account?'

'That is correct.'[31]

Thus, in one move, Chamberlain had subverted the dogmatic logic of Strehlow's linguistic presuppositions about the shaping of a written statement from direct speech. He had challenged the tendency of Strehlow to use black-and-white logic about what Stuart could and could not do with his 'Northern Territory English.' The same black-and-white logic came under deadly attack on the question of what was a black man's crime and what was not. If Strehlow had stereotyped Stuart's language, he had done so even more with regard to types of criminal behaviour. The exchange that follows has all parties, including the judge, struggling with what it was to have 'white man's habits' in 1959, and what it was to be 'wild.'

'[Y]ou have expressed the opinion that this is not a black man's crime, in effect?'

'That is correct,' Strehlow said. 'I have expressed that opinion.'

'Do you know of any case of a white man raping and murdering a ten-year-old child?'

'In my own experience, I would not be sure about it; I think rape is by no means uncommon.'

'Rape and murder of small girls?' Chamberlain asked, and Strehlow said, 'I can't give you a definite instance at the moment.'

'It is not a common white man's crime, is it? . . .'

'You hear about rape and murder connected with white man's society.'

'Can you seriously tell us how many cases there are that you have heard of a white man raping and murdering a small girl?'

'Off hand I can't tell you,' Strehlow said.

'One way of testing that theory would be to make some examination of Stuart's own history, wouldn't it.'

'Yes.'

'Did you make such an examination?'

'I have, yes,' he said.

'You questioned him about his own convictions?'

'I have not questioned him, I have seen the various convictions he is supposed to have had.'[32]

Later, when pressed, Strehlow was not that familiar with the details of the case; and the details he trusted were based on Father Dixon's account, which was to prove wrong on the matter of Stuart's having needed linguistic help at his trial in Alice Springs. 'It is the combination of rape and murder that is the basis of my opinion,' Strehlow said.

'You don't suggest black men would not indecently assault a little girl, but only the rape and murder?'

'Rape and murder,' Strehlow answered, and to clarify this point Sir Geoffrey Reed asked, 'Both together?'

'Yes.'

'Either one might stand up, but not together?' Chamberlain asked.

'Not raping and murdering small girls, but adding them together, yes,' Strehlow said. Mr Justice Ross asked him, 'In some cases they would indecently assault small girls?'

'In our terminology they might, but in most cases small girls, or people we might class as small girls, might have reached the age of puberty and I think rape always means unwillingness on the part of the girl, and it would not necessarily mean unwillingness.'

[Chamberlain continued] 'This theory of yours, does it apply to wild aboriginals only, or to the half-caste who has acquired a white man's habits and possibly vices?'

'My theory applies to aboriginals, also to half-castes and part-aboriginals who have grown up in an aboriginal environment.'

'What about people who have lived a good deal of their lives amongst white men, but haven't got used to the white man's alcohol?'

'If you are thinking about part-aboriginals in South Australia, Victoria or Queensland who have no tribal background I would not be surprised if they did pick up the white man's habits too.'[33]

When Chamberlain went to the substance of Strehlow's analysis of the confession, he focused on technical detail about past tenses and the use of personal pronouns. It was the kind of filigree that distracted from Strehlow's more telling points: that words such as 'unconscious' and 'awoke' were not possibly in Stuart's repertoire. At this point in the cross-examination the absence of a defence counsel in the court was telling: Strehlow was right in thinking that he had no room to lay out his own position properly. Certainly, it was not Chamberlain's job to do that. The bench might have chosen to draw out Strehlow's thinking, but it did not. By the end of Strehlow's testimony, Chamberlain had him where he wanted him: Strehlow had to back right off the charge of police brutality that lay behind his linguistic evidence.

'I do not suppose you are really criticising the South Australian police?'
'No.'
'Not even the police officers engaged in this case?'
'I don't know them, and there is no reason why I should criticise them.'
'You do not think that they have done anything improper?'
'I do not think I have said that they have done anything improper.'
'And you have not meant that to be understood from anything you have said?'
'I think I have said that the particular confession has certain unsatisfactory features which might lead one to doubt.'
'That is all you would say about it?'
'Yes.'
'It would not be a case for a dogmatic opinion?'
'No.'
'You haven't one and you have never expressed one?'
'I do not think I have.'
'The most you would say is that there is that possibility that ought to be fairly looked at? That is all you have meant to say, is it?'
'I think so.'[34]

Strehlow stood down. He had been in the box for nearly three hours. At the time he felt he had done pretty well in the face of Chamberlain's 'perpetual evil grin.' He knew that 'Chamberlain was flat out to make me say in so many words that the Confession was a police forgery and that they had framed an innocent man; and I was determined not to give him that satisfaction.' Bertha had been 'squirming with anxiety,' she told him afterwards, but he had 'looked so cool and completely at ease, even though . . . Of course, I wasn't. My mind was completely taut, and I watched every question like a poisoned dart, and tried to look forward several questions ahead . . . Providence itself must have been on my side—how I avoided some of those traps, I still don't know! There must be a God of Justice about even in S.A.'

Bertha also told him that, in the face of his composure, 'Chamberlain must have been particularly irritated with me.' That is unlikely. Chamberlain had got most of what he wanted: a dilution of the case against the police, and the exposure of an expert who had over-stereotyped both the language and the criminal disposition of the accused man. Chamberlain's feelings about the expert witness, if they are of any account, can be summed up as scorn: he made no bones about this in his summing-up, which was most sympathetically embraced by the commissioners in their findings, and in the book he wrote about the case on his retirement. *The Stuart Affair* was published in 1972, when Strehlow was an ailing 64 and deeply embattled on several fronts. In 1959, after his first appearance at the Royal Commission, he does not seem to have had the objectivity about himself to have reflected critically on the substance of his own transcript. Instead, he became melancholic.

By early September he was telling himself: 'I am sick of these events that have taken place since May—sometimes I wonder whether things will ever be quite the same again in my feelings towards S.A. in general and Adelaide in particular. I wish I could see an end to my present troubles and get away for a holiday to another State, where I could once more breathe the air of a free Australia,—a land beyond reach of Playford and the members of the Adelaide club.'[35]

A week later he wrote:

Today [12 September] I am beginning to wonder whether it was not a mistake on my part, after all, when I listened to Father Dixon on 16th May in this very room, and decided that I would go down and see Rupert Stuart. Since that time the whole State of South Australia, the whole of Australia, and men and women in many parts of the world have been aroused and made uneasy about Rupert. And yet, we are all powerless even to stay his execution or to commute his sentence. Sir Mellis Napier and Sir Thomas Playford between them can snub the pleas for justice and fair play of hundreds of thousands of honest men and women; and because of South Australian State rights no power on earth apparently can halt them. The people of S.A. could, if they rose in protest. But is it possible to find anywhere in an English-speaking country a more docile and slave-minded people than the church-going South Australians? And are not the Lutheran country people among the most docile and slave-minded elements of this population? If Rupert Stuart is to live, only God can help him now.

Stuart Speaks Up

The person with most reason to be anguished was Rupert Max Stuart. The sentence of death had come and gone four times by then. On one occasion he had been so shaken by the stay of execution he had to go to bed for a day. The emotional support given to the young Aborigine seems to have been negligible. When the case began his parents had come down to Adelaide from Alice Springs for a few days, and then gone back again. A certain camaraderie had been struck up with the wardens. Father Dixon continued to visit, as did O'Sullivan and his partner Helen Devaney in the course of their preparing Stuart for the Royal Commission. Strehlow seems to have visited Stuart perhaps half a dozen times between May and the time of the commission. He had seen Stuart's parents for an hour when they came to Adelaide, but that was all. His diary is matter-of-fact about his visits to Stuart: the entries tell how long he sat with Stuart, and the job they had to do by way of interview and transcription. What is striking is the tonelessness of Strehlow's records: he cares about the Stuart case, but it does not indulge the nature of his feelings for Stuart. That is how his diary entry comes across in English. It is possible, of course, that what transpired between them in Aranda was full of feeling, that there was a warmth of cultural sympathy between them, but 'Stuart the man' does not emerge in Strehlow's diary entries. Certainly Strehlow cared for Stuart as an individual in so far as he was the grandson of Tom Ljonga. But as for Stuart as a certain type of Aboriginal—a half-caste, apparently detrib-alised man whose habits were on the low side of white civilisation, an Aboriginal who drank and behaved in a way all too reminiscent of the

Outback characters who so repelled young Strehlow when he was a patrol officer—that aroused other feelings. To commemorate traditional Aranda culture in *Songs of Central Australia* was not to reconcile himself to individuals who represented a degeneration from the ways of their fathers. He had personal reasons for loudly adopting the 'Stuart case,' but not necessarily a man like Stuart, or the man Stuart appeared to be.

Strehlow was challenged on this point at a touchy stage in the case. A senior journalist on the *Advertiser*, Stewart Cockburn, came to his house one night. Cockburn, a defender of the Adelaide establishment, was doing a deeper investigative story on Stuart and, having been extensively briefed by the Attorney-General, felt he had all the inside information about Stuart's character and previous convictions that was driving Premier Playford's defence of the police. Cockburn said that, according to various people who had talked to Stuart, he was capable of speaking English fluently—and that he had perhaps cunningly deceived Strehlow about his knowledge of English. He told Strehlow that he 'perhaps—like the rest—was more interested in defending my own reputation' than in the facts relating to Stuart. It seems not to have occurred to Cockburn to turn the same argument on the likes of Playford and the judiciary.

Strehlow spent the next two hours defending himself.

> I replied that surely Eliza Doolittle and her father in 'Pygmalion' were also fluent speakers of English; yet no one would have expected them to speak the *same kind* of English as Professor Higgins, when the latter first burst into their lives. Then I went on about the style and language of the Confession. This was heavy going; for it took some fifteen minutes or so to get into Cockburn's head the difference between strong and weak English verbs and their preterites. However, after a two-hour brisk argument, Cockburn was prepared to admit, upon leaving, that I had put up a most convincing case for my contentions about the falsity of the confessions. He was not so sure whether he should believe the police had been so 'frivolous' as to frame an innocent man on a mere hunch; but Duguid backed me up in the contention that the police did often use force even against white suspects in order to extract evidence from them.[36]

Strehlow had made the comparison with Eliza Doolittle's 'own kind of English' to Chamberlain in the witness box; he was putting himself in the shoes of Professor Henry Higgins, the emotionally withdrawn teacher of the Cockney—the unassimilated—Eliza.

And still, through all this no one had really heard Stuart fully speak for himself, no one except Strehlow, who had done most of the talking in Aranda (as if Henry Higgins could test Eliza for Ascot by speaking to her in cockney!). What Stuart said still counted.

Stuart appeared before the Royal Commission on 13 October. The public gallery was crowded. The black man sat between uniformed warders, for the first time wearing, as Inglis points out, 'the uniform of urban man: shoes and socks, shirt and tie, and a suit coat to match his trousers.' Hardly a savage, but still a man who might well surprise his teachers in the manner of his speech. But just before that, Strehlow was called again. Once more he was to speak for the black man, and this time he would be questioned by the defence counsel, J.E. Starke, who had at last been appointed following the exit of Shand.

During the time Strehlow was back in the box, Stuart was taken back to his cell. His voice, however,

stayed in court, on tape, while the Commissioners pored over phonetic accounts of what they were hearing and Strehlow gave them a lesson on the Aranda language. At Starke's invitation, Strehlow said that on August 19 he and Shand had visited the gaol with a technician and a tape recorder. Strehlow had spoken an Aranda version of the confession, which Stuart translated sentence by sentence into English.

'Do you consider,' Starke asked Strehlow, 'that the reproduction in English of the Aranda translation of the confession should be as good as the original—assuming it to be genuine—or better, or worse?'

Strehlow said that he would expect the reproduction in English to be better than the original, and that in fact it was worse.

'You made a literal translation?' asked Starke.

'Yes, using the correct tenses, and that is why I say that if anything the rendering he gave ought to be better than the original.'

A recording of the exercise was played, after the Commissioners had been supplied with a document setting out, in parallel columns, the original confession, Strehlow's Aranda version of it, and the phonetic account of Stuart's translation back into English. Without doubt Stuart's English, as heard on tape, was worse than that of the confession. Where the confession had 'He offered me a drink,' the listeners in court heard Stuart say: 'He gibb me a drink.' . . .

Where the confession had: 'Just after coming out of Thevenard town I stood and I finished that bottle,' Stuart, said: 'I went out from Sebenard pub. I's standin'. I drank that bottle.'

Further on, the words 'unconscious' and 'rape' were shown to be beyond Stuart's verbal range. Starke questioned Strehlow on other matters, including time. The witness said that he had seen Shand show Stuart a watch. 'He looked at the watch and after a short delay he said: "Quarter past six." That was wrong. Mr Shand said: "You have another look." This time he said: "Oh no, I am wrong, it is a quarter to six." He realised that the certain interval was a quarter hour. The second time he was right.'[37]

Strehlow was in the box all morning. When his science was done, Stuart was let back in order to take the oath and at last to speak. This he did in a soft voice that sometimes dropped too low. When it did Starke asked him to speak up. He spoke for five hours over the next three days.

In the witness box Stuart's English turned out to be much better than the statement written up by his own lawyer, and considerably less 'Northern Territory' than Strehlow had insisted. When it came to his awareness on the fatal day, he was also more cognisant than anyone had previously credited. Inglis gives the most pungent summary:

At twenty-five minutes to three Starke pointed to the clock on the wall opposite Stuart and said: 'What time?' After a slight pause, Stuart said: 'Twenty-five to three.' On the Saturday morning, he said, he got up at nine o'clock. He now described the morning visit to the beach with Moir, the meeting with a half-caste ('He offered 'im drink'), the drinking out of a flagon. He put the flagon in a sugar bag, he said, walked 'up the town,' and 'left 'im down the lavatory behind picture wall.' He went up the street, talked to 'few dark fellas,' and went into a shop, where 'fella in the shop' rang up a taxi. At one o'clock he and Moir 'jumped in' a taxi and 'went down to fun-fair.' 'Allan went out, got off the taxi. I got off the taxi.'

Stuart went on to say how he had gone back to the pub at Thevenard and met a girl he had talked to in the black section of the pictures on the Friday night.

She went with him to the back of the hotel and 'had naughty,' which took about five minutes.

'You have had naughties before in your life?'

'Oh, yes.'

'What would you say about this girl: had she done a naughty before or not?'

'I think she done it before.' He supposed she was about twenty. He gave her 'four quid.' [38]

And later:

Before the trial, asked Starke, had Stuart told O'Sullivan about the girl at Thevenard?

'No ... I was frightened to say ... He might think I was the fella that killed that girl.'

'Who did you first tell about that?' 'Mr Strehlow.'

'After the trial?' 'Yes.'

'You had known him since you were a little boy?' 'Yes.'

Did he see a little girl that Saturday afternoon? No.

Did he have naughties with or rape or kill a little girl? No.[39]

There were confusing moments in the course of Stuart's evidence, not least when he said 'no' and then 'yes' to Chamberlain's question whether he had actually said in his confession, as his unsworn statement had it: 'Perhaps it was a white man.' It was a double-take that led the Crown Solicitor to remark, 'I give up.' Another ambiguous moment was when Chamberlain pressed him as to whether he had said to Detective-Sergeant Turner that a white bloke pulled out a gun and made him carry the little girl into the cave. 'Yes, that was a lie,' said Stuart, confusingly. But there was more English understanding than not running through his evidence. When Chamberlain asked him to give an account of his alleged assault on the nurse in Alice Springs, his reply tested the limits of his defence:

This other fella was drinking and me and him had a bit of an argument and he went up the street and I followed him and I seen him again up the town, and we got more grog and went down to the Todd River and finished the two bottles and went up the street of the town and I told him to watch them policemen and I went in the pub, the Mountain Arms, and got a flagon of wine and then we went up behind Anzac Hill and had a drink up there and he went up Middle Park, up to the reserve and I came down to town and I got some more grog in town there, and went down to Todd River, the same place we were drinking that morning, and when I finished that bottle I was on my own then and I went to this lavatory to get this bottle and when I got inside I heard a mob of women coming and I could not get out, so one of them came in and I grabbed her and throw her to one side and I run away.[40]

It was a statement the coherence of which gave Chamberlain a chance to put Strehlow on the ropes. Having heard all Stuart had said, he was called back for linguistic comment. Inglis:

Starke asked him to compare his account of the assault at Alice Springs with the narrative in his confession. He had noticed, Strehlow said, that in giving the account to Starke, Stuart left out entirely the relevant fact that he had put a bottle in the lavatory. Chamberlain remarked, and the Chairman agreed, that this was a matter for judgment and not for expert evidence. Mr Justice Reed said he would be interested to know whether Strehlow would describe Stuart's account of events at Alice Springs as a 'rambling statement.' Strehlow said: 'A very fluent rambling statement.'

'Why "rambling"?'

'Perhaps I should say irrelevant.'

Would Strehlow say that Stuart was talking in pidgin English, asked Sir Mellis Napier. 'No, it is what I would describe as Northern Territory English.'

'Was it anything but perfectly good English?'

'I think if you took it down phonetically you would still find some of these things.'

'If any of us were taken down phonetically,' observed the Chairman, 'we would be surprised at the result . . . Do you mean to tell me you regard that man as inadequate in the way of English?'

'I would say he has not got full fluency of expression,' replied Strehlow . . .

To Chamberlain, Strehlow said that he heard few subordinate clauses in Stuart's evidence. Nor, he agreed, did he hear many displaced personal pronouns.

'You think his English has improved a lot in the last nine months?' asked Chamberlain.

'It would be a reflection on the warders if it had not improved.'[41]

Strehlow stood down.

As he told his diary, 'But to the surprise of all of us, Stuart stuck to his story and got through the afternoon without any serious damage. *It was almost incredible!*' (emphasis added).

This was an overstatement. It was 'incredible' only if the contingencies of Stuart's speech were set against a pure model, which is what Strehlow's evidence had postulated. It was only 'almost' incredible if the defence had never thought to look into Stuart's social history—as, in fact, it had not. There is no further comment in the diary, no consideration of the full implications of his own remark. It would have meant facing the full implications of the fact that his defence of Stuart had been undone.

Strehlow was followed by a Crown witness, Milton Liddle, a wood merchant and taxi-driver from Alice Springs. Liddle had always spoken to Stuart in English, but had not seen him for about a year. Had his English improved in that time? Chamberlain asked. 'I do not think so.' The opinion of a taxi-driver was now thought by Adelaide's legal establishment to be worth more than that of the Reader in Linguistics at the University of Adelaide.

Still Guilty

Having sat for just on four months, the Royal Commission upheld the verdict. It conceded that the police had been wrong to claim that their account of the oral interrogation was 'word perfect' and the typed confession was 'exactly the petitioner's words.' What it did not concede was that such police 'help' ought to cast doubt on the confession, and hence the conviction. The commissioners had 'no doubt that the witness [Jones] was speaking incautiously, and with less than the care that is expected of a police witness in a case of this kind,' and 'no doubt that the petitioner had more help with the wording of the written confession than Jones was prepared to admit.'[42] Chamberlain had implied as much in his rhetorical dissection of O'Sullivan's version of Stuart's English in the unsworn statement with Strehlow in the box. For them to come out so bluntly with it, however, was to validate Strehlow's initial concern. When someone claims a statement is word perfect, it is reasonable to expect a responsible linguist to begin by taking the claim literally. That said, however, everything hangs on the terms of the linguist's analysis and the conclusions he draws from the social context of an utterance. It was on these grounds that the commissioners set out to rebut Strehlow's argument, mounting an attack executed by sweeping and scornful generalisations and rammed home with a barbed linguistic critique published as an appendix.

Clear in the tone of the report is their resentment of the torrid politics of the case, the 'heat,' the 'element of exaggeration and extravagance, even of misrepresentation' generated largely by Strehlow. His evidence had been crucial and 'definitely misleading.' In their judgment: 'it was, and is, a perversion of the truth to describe Stuart as "unable to speak English" or as being "denied any opportunity of giving his version of the facts to the jury" or to suggest that the trial was a mis-trial, or was not a fair trial on the defence that was submitted to the jury.'[43] When, after all the unsuccessful appeals, the government had agreed to hold a Royal Commission, it 'had conceded something which the practice of the courts would not allow in the normal course of things.' It had yielded to 'the suggestion that the petitioner is an illiterate aboriginal native—incapable of following the course of the evidence, incapable of more than the few halting and almost inarticulate words in which he addressed the jury, and quite incapable of understanding the questions put to him by the police, or of dictating or assenting to the written confession which was given in evidence.'

The letter of the law having been upheld over and above any exercise of the imagination with regard to cultural difference, the way was now open for the commission to dismantle Strehlow's argument, hinging as it did on Stuart's difference. 'Knowing what we now know, namely, that the petitioner was quite capable of giving evidence without the assistance of an interpreter, and that he was not without previous experience of criminal proceedings, we find it difficult to resist the conclusion that the attitude adopted by the defence was designed to play upon the sympathy of the jury, and that the trial judge was discouraged from asking questions, lest the true measure of the petitioner's understanding and command of English should be disclosed to the jury.'[44]

The report cites passages in the transcript where they had caught Strehlow out and constrained him to admit that, for instance, Stuart's 'Northern Territory English' was better than it might appear if taken down phonetically; and that he had been wrong to assume Stuart's ignorance of a word like 'accident,' which he had used under cross-examination in Cloncurry. The evidence of Stuart's court appearances in Alice Springs—where again Strehlow was shown to have taken certain claims on trust—had provided 'ample material to enable us to appreciate the petitioner's capacity to speak English':

> He was obviously bi-lingual in the sense that he was not only speaking, but was actually thinking, in the English language and idiom. His vocabulary may be limited, although it is certainly not as limited as Mr Strehlow would have given us to believe, but for the last two years or more, it has been clearly sufficient for all ordinary purposes . . .
>
> To this we should add that . . . although uneducated, he is—by any standard—intelligent and quick-witted.[45]

The commissioners omitted to mention that the witnesses had disagreed about Stuart's English; and they implied, as Inglis remarks, that he spoke better or worse English by choice, which was 'to attribute to him a sophistication for which there is no other evidence.'[46] Far from deferring to Strehlow's expertise, they tackled his forensic focus on language head-on.

At Shand's suggestion, taken up by Starke, Strehlow had translated the original confession into Aranda and visited Stuart in prison in order to read him his translation on tape and have Stuart turn it sentence by sentence back into English. Any discrepancy between the English in the confession and his oral translation would show whether he could have dictated the confession—the assumption being that a man fluent in Aranda would have no trouble translating from it into his usual English.

Stuart's translation fell a long way short, in fact; but the tape, and the experiment, failed to impress the commissioners. They had a 'simple explanation' for it: 'however fluent he may be in either language—he is not in the habit of turning either into the other, and when he is called upon to do so, he finds it difficult to transpose the Aranda form and idiom into the English convention.' Between Aranda and English, they supposed, Stuart fell back on pidgin as 'a sort of half-way house.' And, to give the linguist the benefit of the doubt: 'It *may be* that this is how Mr Strehlow came to form the impression that pidgin was the best that the petitioner could do in the way of English.' They even wondered if they could take 'Mr Strehlow's word for it that the petitioner is not only as fluent in Aranda as he is in English, but, also, that he was doing his best, and, further, for Mr Strehlow's ability to reproduce—in Aranda—the exact sense and significance of the English words and idioms. That is, we think, a difficult assumption.'[47]

Strehlow had laid himself open to these barbs by arguing from an assumption of his own: that knowing two languages necessarily implies being easily able to translate from one into the other. His own lifelong experience of language learning had been a formal process largely of translation, with the second language being mastered by constant reference back to the first. Having picked up German and Aranda at the mission, he had gone on to refine his knowledge and study English and then Classics, at school and at university. He made an oddly revealing remark in the box, that the strong and irregular English verbs 'must be learnt off by heart by every white child.' Who else in the room—Stuart excepted—would not have picked up these everyday English verbs by trial and error almost as soon as they learned to talk?

For their part, the commissioners saw no need to imagine the black man moving his mind from a pure model of his native tongue across to another pure model, that of standard English. Stuart's life in language had been nowhere near as ghettoed as that implied. The alacrity with which Strehlow applied himself to the tape recording exercise, and the exhaustive translation, was no doubt facilitated by his long intimacy with the noble native tongue in its pre-colonial form. The in-between tongue—pidgin or Northern Territory English—was bastard country, in Strehlow's book, the book he mapped by language. It was a linguistically primitive wilderness between languages: half-caste country. So confined, a man like Stuart was at a disadvantage culturally, and indeed historically. The commissioners spoke as practical men at home in a complexly adaptive world. Language was a tool, and Northern Territory English a tool an 'intelligent and quick-witted' man in Stuart's position could use. Like any survivor between two cultures, Stuart was as bilingual as he needed to be.

For Strehlow, on the contrary, language was always more than a tool, or a science. In him they had a man possessed by language, whose intense engagement with language, his claim to authority as a defence witness, could be a blind spot when it came to specifics: it shone so brightly that he lost sight of the speaker, Stuart the man, with his own unique experience of words and meanings.

Not so the commissioners. They had already come close to accusing the defence of trying to blind them with Strehlow's science. To their minds, Stuart's 'somewhat unconventional expressions,' they declared, 'have an evidentiary value which approximates to that of a fingerprint.'

Summing up, they judged that the circumstantial evidence supported by the police confession was 'clear and coherent' and that none of the evidence against the police had stood up to cross-examination. If Stuart had been bashed, he had never named an assailant, and anyway the alleged violence must have taken place after he confessed. As to the belated alibi, there the evidence that Stuart could, after all, tell the time was crucial; and the testimony as to times of other witnesses apart from the owners of Funland, on whom Father Dixon had desperately relied, had come through as on balance the less unreliable.

The Royal Commission closed a case that could not be reopened, having worked through its own political sympathies, not as grossly as those campaigning to save Stuart might have polemically anticipated, but with sufficient vigour and precision and logic to substantially discredit the star witness for the defence.

Anguish and Driftwood

All this, so far, has been to see Stuart in a strictly legal light. But at all stages of the drama—especially the battle of stereotypes as to what kind of man, black or white, might have done such a crime—there was a wider frame to put him in: what governments at the time called their assimilation policy. The chief architect of the policy was Paul Hasluck, the Federal minister to whom Strehlow had appealed on Stuart's behalf. Hasluck was to make the classic statement on the subject in 1963. His model was not that the modern generation of Aborigines must learn to live in two worlds, but that they must steadily eclipse their traditional world for the new: that they must be 'assimilated.' The goal was an 'abstract homogeneity,' in Tim Rowse's phrase, for the benefit of all.[48]

By these lights Stuart's fate exemplified the failure of the policy. So did that of Albert Namatjira, who had died in the Alice Springs hospital on 25 August, four days after Shand pulled out of the Royal Commission. Strehlow saw the two cases as linked. It had been Pastor Albrecht, the white man most compassionately familiar with Namatjira, who coined the expression '*between* two worlds' for the social space that had exacerbated the artist's inner conflict and alcoholism. With Stuart, whose gifts had not made him famous, the dislocations took place in private. Namatjira's tragic flouting of the assimilation project was there for all to see. The news of his death upset Strehlow, whose diary entry shows a concern for appearances as much as for the man: 'I am glad that at least he did not die earlier this year when he was in confinement. Perhaps it would have been easier had his heart given out a couple of years ago, when he was at the height of his fame. It would have saved him and his friends and relatives many bitter hours. But his achievements will outlast the darker memories of these last years. His character in bygone years, and his sound artistic achievements gave a new dignity to our Aboriginal fellow citizens everywhere.'[49]

The note Strehlow struck here was profoundly true. The integrity of the assimilation policy hinged absolutely on the issue of dignity. If it was to be successful as a humanistic policy—one designed for the well-being of individuals rather than as a race policy—it would not be a question of the best time for hearts to give out. It would be a matter of personally foreseeing the emotional consequences of social policy. To give Strehlow his due—after his formal, rather self-defeating performance in the Stuart case—few people were more cognisant of this than he was.

Only two years earlier he had held forth in a vigorous little pamphlet, *Dark and White Australians*, based on a talk he had given to the South Australian Peace Committee in the Friends' Hall in North Adelaide. There, well ahead of his time, he had proposed a 'new deal' that substantially humanised official policy. While he was at pains to deny a challenge to government thinking, since he agreed that dark and white Australians, had, in the long run, a 'common destiny,' his radical argument was about the extent and timing and methods of the transition. He was against 'ultra-rapid detribalisation.' White Australians still persisted 'too much in thinking that our dark folk *must* lose their human and racial individuality completely before we can receive them into our midst.'[50] He wanted the policy to pivot not on an abstract idea but an understanding that 'our dark Australian fellow citizens are *human beings*'; they should determine the pace of change and be consulted on social policy in different parts of the nation. The alternative would only dislocate the individual's sense of belonging and destroy communities, as in Africa, Latin America and the Pacific, leaving individuals as 'scattered bits of driftwood.' As always, he was strenuously opposed to the policy of forcibly removing indigenous children from their families.

The most radical aspect was his plan for protecting the tribal people. He recommended what was essentially a land rights policy where the older generation could follow traditional ways in their own country, with their sacred sites protected on the ground of religious freedom.

Such reservations, Strehlow hastened to add, would not be ghettoes but communities receiving government aid for food, health, shelter and education. (The trigger for the original talk had been the national debate raging over the appalling health of Aborigines in the Warburton Range of Western Australia.) The other prong of his strategy concerned the generation who wanted to enter white society: to put tradition behind them and take on the modern world.

Their reasons would run along these lines:

> We are finished with all that. You old people always used to go on walk-abouts in order to visit sacred sites. You always tired yourselves out with ceremonies. You were always worrying about your sacred objects in caves and storehouses. But you got little out of it, and you only had kangaroos and emus and grass seeds to eat for your trouble. That's why we want to be like the white people. The white man gets his native 'boys' to do his work for him, while he sits in the camp and does the cooking. He never worries about religion; yet he always has plenty of meat, plenty of bread, plenty of tea and sugar and tobacco, and all other good things. He has plenty of clothes and blankets, and a house to live in. He can get a native woman whenever he likes, and he can go to the hotel and get drunk whenever he likes. That's what we want to do, too.[51]

In his pamphleteering construction, Strehlow made no references to his personal experiences. But this statement echoes one that made a powerful impression on him in 1933, when he was travelling with none other than Max Stuart's grandfather, Tom Ljonga. Ljonga was eager to help him locate and collect *tjurunga* and said: 'Sell the *tjurunga*, I say, sell them, get rid of them.' In his unpublished autobiography, Strehlow recorded that Ljonga told him, 'surely it was better to get rid of these objects by selling them to the whites, and thus being free from all religious restrictions as whites were. The latter had plenty of food to eat and plenty of tea and sugar to drink. They had liquor, and considered no one except themselves, they feared neither God nor the devil. Why should not dark men reach the same level of emancipation?'[52] Ljonga was speaking for himself and his own sense of the future, and incidentally justifying his own position as a go-between for the old men who wanted to trade or give Strehlow their *tjurunga*. For his own reasons—as self-justificatory as they were socially descriptive—Strehlow was, even in

1933, reflecting on the more general point of the younger generation's right to choose and, by implication, the responsibility of democratic white Australians to facilitate that choice.

For those who wanted to leave, the pamphlet argued, there should be community centres set up in towns and cities 'where they would find people interested in their welfare.' The social structure need not suffer while 'their more inquisitive and adventurous members were learning those European skills and crafts which would increase their earning capacity in the new and changed world without.' They could go back to the reserves if they chose, and work in 'special native schools' offering the practical training in the crafts and trades that would bring about a 'rapid economic uplift of the natives themselves.' The schools would foster the 'traditional native crafts and skills that once distinguished native culture.' And, most relevantly to the Stuart case:

> Above all, let us permit native children to keep their own languages,— those beautiful and expressive tongues, rich in true Australian imagery, charged with poetry and with love for all that is great, ancient, and eternal in the continent. There is no need to fear that continued know- ledge of their own languages will interfere with the learning of English as the common medium of expression for all Australians. *In most areas of Australia the natives have been bilingual, probably from time immemorial.* Today white Australians are among the few remaining civilised people who still think that knowledge of one language is the normal limit of linguistic achievement. (emphasis added)[53]

This was an inspiring view of Australia, one which looked both ways in terms of poetic idealism: an idealism based on the German Enlighten- ment assumption that the language we speak contains the best of us, in whatever culture, and that if two cultures are to live together they must by implication know, if not respect, each other's languages. This is democratic realism on Strehlow's part. Bilingualism becomes integral to the citizenship of the Aborigines, and is just as essential for their post- colonial friends.

There is another implication buried in his formulation, however. It is almost as if he is assuming that those who know *no* language well are destined to drift between cultures: driftwood is the result of the ship- wreck of noble tongues. In his work on translation his compulsion was to raise languages up, to improve them on the model of the higher language. The bilingualism that he rates so highly—in the direction of common citizenship—is premised on an exaltation of the more historic mother tongues, whether German or Greek, English or Aranda. Precisely because of his scorn for pidgin, the creole of the Northern Territory, his sympathies were torn between a scholar's regard for a high language and a demotic negotiation of bilingual life.

And it went beyond an academic purism. In *Aranda Traditions* back in 1947 he had denounced the whole ethos of Northern Territory pidgin English, which, he wrote, 'is not English perverted and mangled by the natives; it is English perverted and mangled by ignorant whites, who have in turn taught this ridiculous gibberish to the natives and who then affect to be amused by the childish babbling of these "savages."' He clinched his case with a burlesque version of the story of *Macbeth* in pidgin, and the comment: 'The whole account is an inadequate, untruthful, and malicious caricature of a great story.' As with *Macbeth*, so with the myths as filtered through the pidgin of the elders: 'even after such ridiculous pidgin English versions have been smoothed out into good simple English, the native Australian Legends have still remained poor and childish tales of little interest to any save the anthropologists.'[54]

Here was the sticking-point for the man who had made it his mission to give the world a definitive body of Aboriginal myth in an English that would finally show it in its true light. He had a social policy biographically prompted by the passionate utterance of Stuart's grandfather in 1933. But face to face with the tragic particularities two generations on—those of Rupert Max Stuart's drifting life which had washed up in the white man's court—his broader social imagination was silenced. And the public intellectual, the radical pamphleteer, had to go quiet in the box: his brief was to speak strictly as a linguist—one who, as a linguist, harboured a particular animus towards the Creole of those *between* cultures. Stuart's defence came to grief in Strehlow's hands because the linguist's view of language left such 'driftwood' marooned in no man's land.

The Consolation, the Wounds

Strehlow could not bear to go near the commission the day it delivered its findings. The whole experience by then seems to have confirmed him in a defeatist view of his place in the larger picture. He told his diary: 'Brazel's only reported references to my evidence were intended to ridicule its value. I have never had much luck getting any point of view on natives or anything connected with them accepted in S.A. In this regard the Finke River Mission Board members are in agreement with Sir Mellis Napier, Brazel and Chamberlain. None of these gentlemen ever want to hear what I may wish to say. My supporters have always been inter-state men or men with Overseas degrees.'[55]

Before long he was back to his normal work. It was a great relief. He had now edited most of *Songs of Central Australia*, although publication was still years off. He was gearing up for more trips to Central Australia, which meant, if he was to keep in touch with his patrons at the Institute for Aboriginal Studies, visits to Sydney and Canberra. In both cities the Stuart case had aroused great interest, and some admiration and support. At the Institute McCarthy offered his sincere congratulations and warmest admiration for the tremendous emotional ordeal he had been through in the interests of truth and justice. In Sydney, Elkin congratulated him and John Kerr told him the whole case was more exciting to read than a novel. Such remarks from eminent contemporaries heartened him, but not enough to heal the wounds of the Royal Commission.

Starke had told him one day that 'over here,' in Adelaide, he had found only one person 'convinced 100% of Stuart's innocence' and that was Father Dixon. Once the findings were public, Strehlow re-opened the case in his own mind.

> For my own part I have been reasonably certain that Stuart could not have been the murderer of Mary Hattam. This belief rests on his own protestations of innocence, on my knowledge of his family and cultural background, on the absence of any indisputable factual and scientific evidence against him, and on the untruthful nature of many of the police assertions against him (also on their fear of any possibility of a retrial—a fear which has been obvious ever since June). But I have always said that *if* indisputable factual proof (in the shape of say footprints, fingerprints, or something similar) could be advanced against Stuart, I would naturally be prepared to revise my opinion of him.[56]

Later Strehlow turned more pointedly to what it had all meant to him, as distinct from Rupert Max Stuart:

All [the interstate papers] report the Royal Commission's findings without comment, except the Melbourne 'Herald,' whose leader states that the Stuart Case is now ended, and that the findings of the judges are to be accepted and that there has never been any doubt about their integrity.

And thus the Stuart case ends.

All that effort came to nothing. In monolithic S.A. Playford and Napier between them have all power, and the findings of a Royal Commission cannot be legally challenged.

Perhaps it is a consolation that Stuart's life has been saved. (emphasis added)[57]

Stuart, we can only assume, thought it a consolation, whatever slump the case had created in Strehlow, in whose mind, besides, the case was never closed. He felt that Stuart's guilt had never been established beyond reasonable doubt—which was after all the point that Shand had made to Napier at the most outrageous moment in a case that had many prejudicial outbursts.

By 1972, Stuart had become literate and had been writing regularly to Dixon as well as Strehlow. 'I was so delighted to receive your letter five weeks ago,' Strehlow wrote to Stuart three days before Christmas, 1972, 'and to see you writing so well and so interestingly. It is just forty years ago this Christmas that your grandfather and I came back from our third long camel trip in 1932 to Hermannsburg. I stayed at Hermannsburg for the next two months; but your grandfather went to Alice Springs and Undoolya for his holidays, after taking the camels down to the Palm Valley Paddock. When he left me, his face lit up, and he said—'I am so happy that my daughter has a son. There are almost no dark men of my age who have any children or grandchildren. But I have a [grand]son, and I can hand some of my secrets over to him one day when he grows up."'

This is solicitude towards a man who might be becoming something other than driftwood. At the same time it is a report about Tom that flies in the face of what Strehlow had been reporting at other stages of his and Tom's life: no longer is Tom advocating the selling of the tjurunga so as to be emancipated like the white man: this is Tom wanting to maintain the continuity of his culture. And indeed it has since emerged that Stuart was in tune with the wish. As this book goes to press there is evidence that throughout this whole period Stuart had been more of an Aranda man than even Strehlow realised, or wished to acknowledge. As a young man he had been initiated; his grandfather, and other senior men, *had* taught him 'secrets.' He knew his important songs, most notably the eagle hawk song from Undoolya, and the caterpillar song from the Alice Springs area. It was the knowledge of songs that helped 'buoy him up' during his years in prison. Once out of prison he made it his business to consolidate and extend such knowledge so that by 1990 he had done so sufficiently to become a respected leader in Alice Springs. For three years he was the Chairman of the Central Land Council. In fact he was the figurehead of the Central Land Council as the Alice Springs Native Title Claim was in the Federal Court, a claim inextricably linked to much of Strehlow's ethnography.[58]

If Strehlow had lived to see all this, who knows what he would have said? What aspect of Stuart would he have sought to affirm? The newly literate, self-improving Stuart; a story of uplift out of a dislocated Aboriginal past? Or the Stuart who sat with his songs during the trial, the Royal Commission and all his prison years? The Stuart who significantly knew his culture even as he toured the county as a circus hand? As we shall see, Strehlow gave short shrift to the Aboriginal men of Stuart's generation: their traditional knowledge never really qualified in his eyes, it was never up to their fathers', and their modern politics made matters worse. Maybe 'a case' like Stuart might have tempered Strehlow's colonial taxonomies about driftwood tending to remain driftwood. But I doubt it. The irony of Stuart's story for Strehlow is that the flow of life in Aboriginal culture washes past and around his position, leaving him as stranded as a man on an island in the flooded Finke River.

---

1   The full text of the confession can be found in all three books on the Stuart case: K.S. Inglis, *The Stuart Case* (Melbourne: Melbourne University Press, 1961), Sir Roderic Chamberlain, *The Stuart Affair* (Adelaide: Rigby, 1973), and T.S. Dixon, *The Wizard of Alice* (Morwell, Vic.: Alella Books, 1987).
2   Chamberlain, *Stuart Affair*, 2.
3   Dixon, *Wizard of Alice*, 76–77.
4   Inglis, *Stuart Case*, 26.
5   Ibid., 23.
6   Ibid., 37.
7   Ibid., 39.
8   Dixon, *Wizard of Alice*, 13.
9   Ibid., 14.
10   Ibid., 16.

11 T.G.H. Strehlow, 'Land of Altjira' [LOA], unpublished MS, 1957, 149.
12 T.G.H. Strehlow, diary [SD], 7 June 1959.
13 *Nation*, 15 August 1959.
14 SD, 21 June 1959.
15 Inglis, *Stuart Case*, 47.
16 Chamberlain, *Stuart Affair*, 4.
17 SD, 1 July 1959. Also: 'I added that in the N.T. it had not been uncommon for
    "over-zealous" policemen to regard themselves as the embodiment of British
    Justice, and to forge—no, "manipulate"—the evidence in order to bring about
    more easily what *they believed* to be justice. My first assignment had been with a
    Commonwealth Board of Enquiry, which investigated just such charges of
    excessive zeal and the manipulation of witnesses and evidence.'
18 Inglis, *Stuart Case*, 55–56.
19 Paul Hasluck, as Federal Minister for Territories, had been an enthusiastic
    patron of Strehlow's fieldwork funded and equipped by the Northern Territory
    Welfare Branch: he was also increasingly the clearest and most passionate
    exponent of the Federal government's assimilation policy. See also note 48.
20 SD, 8 July 1959.
21 Chamberlain, *Stuart Affair*, 54–55.
22 *Nation*, 15 August 1959: cover page.
23 SD, 29 August 1959.
24 Inglis, *Stuart Case*, 105.
25 Ibid., 124–25.
26 Ibid., 132.
27 Royal Commission Report [RCR] 1959, Appendix V, 38–40.
28 SD, 7 September 1959.
29 Chamberlain, *Stuart Affair*, 131–32.
30 Ibid., 134–35. Essentially here and elsewhere I am citing Chamberlain as a
    verbatim record of the Commission transcripts I have consulted.
31 Ibid., 142–43.
32 Ibid., 150.
33 Ibid., 151–52.
34 Ibid., 160–61.
35 SD, 8 September 1959.
36 SD, 23 August 1959.
37 Inglis, *Stuart Case*, 214.
38 Ibid., 216.
39 Ibid., 219.
40 Ibid., 225.
41 Ibid., 228–29.
42 RCR, 25.
43 RCR, 11.
44 RCR, 12.
45 RCR, 14.
46 Inglis, *Stuart Case*, 298.
47 RCR, 14.
48 Tim Rowse, *White Flour, White Power* (Melbourne: Cambridge University Press,
    1989), 110. I am using 'assimilation' generally here, since as a postwar policy it
    is difficult to date precisely. The seeds of it as a concept of Aboriginal futures,
    including perhaps citizenship, may be detected as early as Baldwin Spencer's
    notion of 'uplift,' but it was Hasluck's notion that the Aborigines would forget
    their past that most fully expressed the idea as a national policy. Hasluck had
    been essaying on this for some years before the Stuart case.
49 SD, 27 August 1959.

50 T.G.H. Strehlow, *Dark and White Australians* (Melbourne: Riall Bros, 1958), 23.
51 Ibid., 10.
52 LOA, 57–58.
53 Strehlow, *Dark and White Australians*, 27.
54 T.G.H. Strehlow, *Aranda Traditions* (Melbourne: Melbourne University Press, 1947), xviii–xix.
55 SD, 13 November 1959.
56 SD, 22 October 1959.
57 SD, 5 December 1959.
58 'Buoy him up' is from John Morton recalling one of many personal conversations with Max Stuart. The new work on Stuart's post-prison life is forthcoming in the new edition of *The Stuart Case* by Ken Inglis, who has been interviewing Stuart at length, along with his colleagues at the Central Land Council.

PART V: POSSESSION

The healthy man is not so much the one who has
eliminated his contradictions as the one who makes use of them
and drags them into his vital labours.

Maurice Merleau-Ponty

1   Finders Keepers

Black Sun

IT IS CLEAR that Strehlow was a depressive, melancholic man. This is speaking descriptively, not clinically, but our experience of him so far is invitation enough to the clinical. He was living under the black sun.

The allusion is to the poem by that quintessentially needful poet, Gérard de Nerval:

> *Je suis le ténébreux,—le veuf-l'Inconsolé,*
> *Le prince d'Aquitaine à la tour abolie:*
> *Ma seule étoile est morte—et mon luth constellé*
> *Porte le soleil noir de la Mélancolie.*

The poem was called 'El Desdichado' ('The Disinherited'). The gloss on it by Richard Holmes, the doyen of Romantic biographers, is: 'I am the man of shadows—the man in the shadows—the man of darkness—the man lost in the dark—the shadowy man you cannot see. I am the Widower; I am the Unconsoled, the disconsolate, the grief-stricken man. I am the Prince of Aquitaine . . . I am the Prince with the abolished, shattered, stricken, or blasted Tower; or the Prince standing by that Tower. My only Star is dead, burnt out, extinguished . . . And my star-studded lute, or my lute marked with the constellations, or the zodiac signs; my lute carries, or is emblazoned with, the Black Sun of Melancholy or Melancholia.'[1] The poet himself remarked: 'It is a well-known fact that one never sees the sun in a dream, although one is often aware of some far brighter light.'

And so on. Strehlow lives in the forest of Romanticism, and out of that arise clinical designations of various kinds, ones that capture his state of mourning, his yearning for what he cannot name, 'the thing that does not lend itself to signification, the centre of attraction and repulsion, seat of the sexuality from which the object of desire will never become separated.' These are the terms of merely one analyst with some classic theory on her side.[2] He was filled with an impossible mourning for the maternal object.

Leaving aside deceptively hard theory, the most forgiving and accommodating model, the one closest to the domestic grain of Strehlow's private ruminations, is offered by Winnicott in his famous account of transitional objects (a concept that was, incidentally, prefigured by Roheim in his work on Aranda mysteries, *The Eternal Ones of the Dream*).[3] The transitional object is the thing to which the subject transfers libidinal energy in order to resolve the losses and gains of maturation.

On this model object attachments—things of various kinds (from the beloved pillow to the self-created work of art) constitute the person's story. They hold and withhold the self; seek to be held or not; open and close; move backwards and or forwards in their desires; are immobilised or not, grow or not, in their dialectical motions between wishes in the realm of the pleasure principle and actualities in the realm of the reality principle.

Winnicott, who published his definitive paper in 1951 (as Strehlow was sailing away from London), lays out what has to be worked through under the black sun:

The nature of the object
    The infant's capacity to recognise the object as Not-Me.
    The place of the object—outside, inside, at the border.
    The infant's capacity to create, think up, devise, originate, produce an object.
    The initiation of an affectionate type of object relationship.[4]

By 1958 Strehlow had at least 427 *tjurunga*, and he was holding onto them for dear life. For the sake of the old men who had given them to him in sacred trust, because they were giving him their lives; and for the sake of his own life, which had become more entwined with theirs over the years. Strehlow frequently told himself, in times when he was most miserable, when he felt most bereft of the loving respect of colleagues, that they were his because they had been theirs.

Strehlow's grip on the *tjurunga* is a reminder, too, that for one who felt close to their whole significance, they might themselves be conceived as transitional objects and were in fact sensed as such by his own father. In the most general sense the sacred board or stone was the thing that mediated the material and the spiritual world for its owner, the earthly individual self, with the ultimate sources of renewal: one's relationship with one's *tjurunga* was in essence the relationship one had with one's whole life. More particularly, Aboriginal induction into the use of transitional objects began with the significant play with the *papa*, innocently labelled the digging stick, which doubles in child-rearing for the *tjurunga*.

Carl Strehlow's terms for this might have been composed for Winnicott's clinic:

> When the child is born it cries continuously for its *tjurunga*. To quieten it, the grandfather . . . goes to get the *tjurunga* from the secret cave. The women say that the grandfather has gone to find the *tjurunga*, or rather the *papa* (since they are not permitted to use the word *tjurunga*) that the child lost when it went into its mother. The grandfather wraps the *tjurunga* in fur string so that the woman cannot see it and lays it in . . . the wooden tray in which the mother carries the child around for the first year of its life. The child is laid in the tray so that its head comes directly over the *papa tjurunga*, from which it seems that special strength is imparted to the child's body, so that it grows quickly and in health. When the child is grown the *papa* is placed back in the secret cave.[5]

When Strehlow had begun to collect the objects they were received very much as live things—their power resided in their recent functions in the live performances of the ceremonies where they were, in effect, the living presences of the ancestor beings. The *tjurunga* he collected then were valued by the senior men as subjects, and Strehlow's respect for their passions was an acknowledgement of that. In those early years he took a note of the object he had collected, but in reality he had recorded the presence of a subject with which he had been entrusted. Then the years passed.

He kept collecting. In 1948 he added another 32 to his list. Between 1958 and 1962 another 119. 'A number of my dark friends came up today and gave me the news that N [name from diary unpublishable] had died. Among them were N; and a number of others, I was told that N had died recently, and also old N. These things depressed me. I should like to see old N but alcohol ruined him.' And then, further on, he came to a place where an original owner had given him the full story connected with one of the sacred stones. But the new owner had left it lying under a tree and cattle had walked over it and broken the other half. Strehlow wrote: 'this certainly is the sundown of the traditions of the areas north of the S.A. / N.T. borders . . . to be exact, the sun has set: only the last red after glow remains in the sky.' This was in 1965. There has been death and decline all through Strehlow's story of himself as a collector. But there is a new note here because, as a biological fact, the senior men from whom Strehlow had collected thirty years earlier were now dying, so the odds now were that, when he found himself at another storage place, at yet another last cave, the objects were much closer to being objects because their owners were themselves dead.

Some of the *tjurunga* he collected in this period must have been ceremonially dead, which could have only added to his sense of morbidity. When he went back to Horseshoe Bend that year he reflected

I am the only man who knows the grim stories of despair, hate in this country where death first came to them according to Sth Aranda traditions. I have merely hinted at them in these pages, lest I should pass on before I have had the opportunity of writing them down in detail. Now that all the main actors and witnesses have died, there is no longer any need to keep secret their names, and the dramas in which they figured. Perhaps when the time comes for me to write up these stories, I will have found *that peace and serenity in my own heart which I need for such a task* (emphasis added).[6]

He is now collecting, in effect, dead objects, *tjurunga* whose secret names can be revealed, subjects that have become objects with the passage of time. It is arguable, of course, whether the living subjects who once owned the *tjurunga* could ever have conceded that the spirits of what they had given from the land of *Altjira* might not also live for eternity; certainly the *tjurunga* were capable of having a new life, if their owners felt confident in their culture once more. Strehlow would have to deal with that in later years. But for now, once they had been removed from the rejuvenations of ceremony and the *pmara kutata* and placed elsewhere, Strehlow the collector was ruminating on his psychological state and moral worth—his lack of the requisite 'peace and serenity'—that would allow him to write them up for what they were worth as dead things. And this he is deferring, perhaps because they are dead. He has a wish to treat them as if they are alive. But he is bound for disappointment precisely because he has always been so immature in his reality testing, the commonplace practice of separating his own illusions from the world, of knowing the difference between pleasure and reality principles. The dead and uncommemorated objects are in keeping with his own story, which has for so long been an interminable series of illusions followed by disillusionment. The objects have gone cold on him, as he has on himself.

In this mode he increasingly holds onto the objects he has collected because they are to him a massive compensation, a regressive mode of ordering that he is compelled to keep to himself. Baudrillard describes the compulsions of the collector well: 'Surrounded by the objects he possesses, the collector is pre-eminently the sultan of a secret seraglio.'[7] Back in 1948, Strehlow had, probably for the first time, let on to other authorities that he had a collection of 'sacred native objects.' This was when he listed them as a very large collection that included 'manuscripts, photos, negatives, and various documents relating to the early history of the missions and native reserves in Central Australia'—all with a mind to sharing them. But it was not to be because it could not be. In general the collector invests in objects because he finds it impossible to invest in human relationships, and after that act of compensation, it is impossible to let them go. Objects, the collection, are the loyal friends: as if one has collected things to gaze on which cannot gaze back. Furthermore the value of each object derives from its absolute singularity, the fact that 'it is I who possesses it, which in turn allows me to represent myself in it as an absolutely singular being.'

At this level Strehlow's negotiations to exchange his objects were bound to fail. To release the objects would be to let go of who he was; it would be to destroy the time he had made for himself. 'In fact, the profound power exerted by collected objects derives not from their singularity nor their distinct historicity. It is not because of these that we see the time of the collection as diverging from real time, but rather because the setting up of a collection itself displaces real time.'[8] Having the objects makes their time the collector's, since they have no future. These are suggestions. They are meant to be circular, and as closed as some cave. 'The object is that through which we mourn ourselves.'[9] There are no straight lines into an account of what was to become of Strehlow under his black sun, if only because Strehlow himself gives us no clue to his relationship with his objects.* I am trying to invoke the resonance of Strehlow's entanglements with objects, and how those objects themselves, as part of a system of reciprocity in Central Australia, bound him into a set of obligations from which he could not escape, even as the historical situation changed. And for 'objects,' we can of course read: images and words, maps and ideas, all that pertained, really, to the yearning thing that he called himself.

Securing Images

What Strehlow initially wanted from the Australian National University was straightforward enough.[10] He suggested that the films would benefit greatly from a soundtrack: money might be found to synchronise the wire recordings to some of the colour films. He also mooted the idea of copying the films—so they might be sold to interested institutions and experts while the originals, which were irreplaceable, could be protected for posterity. In addition—in a manner that suggested to the ANU, 'while you're on the job'—he thought some further assistance might be granted, so that he could return once again and, though his fellowship had finished, record more of the ceremonies before they were lost for all time.

In May 1952 Strehlow returned to Canberra to discuss the matter. The university paid his way and put him up at Brassey House. There was to be another film evening, and Professor Nadel had asked him to

---

* Unlike, for instance, his good friend Ronald Berndt, who began his reflections on collecting by remarking that 'certain aspects of material culture leave me cold,' and 'my reasons for collecting objects in the field were not immediately apparent to myself.' Berndt came to value some items as 'validatory documents, ethnographic statements,' and then, with those from sacred rituals, as objects still capable of transformation into subjects, which was in turn connected with 'my own personal transformation' as he involved himself in 'a living Aboriginal situation,' which was the curatorial practice of providing a 'permanent home for them, and ensuring their transformation as "living" entities placed within their own cultural social contexts.' The objects came alive for Berndt and rejuvenated him in the act of fostering Aboriginal futures. It is perhaps no accident that Berndt wrote his paper in 1978 after bearing painful witness to Strehlow's self-entombment with a collection self-assigned to the dead time of the past. (Berndt 1978: 143 144, 151.)

attend one or two seminars. Nadel, who specialised in Pacific studies and had met Strehlow at the University of London, had recently taken the foundation chair in anthropology. The seminars and film night went without obvious mishap, though Strehlow was conscious of Nadel's lack of comment after the film. He came to feel that Nadel's interests were not especially sympathetic to his own Australian ones. Even more to the point, he was unhappy with the idea that emerged from the discussions about his films—that the originals might be stored in the film library of his department, while Strehlow would keep copies that he would make available to the ANU whenever required. No, Strehlow was not happy with this idea at all; and when the train delivered him home to Adelaide he wrote on 12 May to the Registrar, R.A. Hohnen, to tell him so:

I am rather uneasy at the thought of these irreplaceable and unique colour films should be stored in a Film Library, where they would be, in my opinion, too readily accessible. Senior members of the Anthropology Department anticipate frequent long periods of absence from Canberra on duty; and I think it would be a tragedy if the only records of *complete cycles* of Central Australian totemic ceremonies which are in existence today should be damaged by being run through a projector. No missionary or anthropologist or other white man has been permitted to view such complete cycles in this area since 1896,—the year when Spencer and Gillen described the Engwura Initiation Festival held at Alice Springs. Such cycles are nowadays almost impossible to obtain; and I had to risk my whole reputation with natives before I was allowed to film these ceremonies in toto—the condition being that I would make myself personally responsible for the audiences to whom they were shown. In any case few Aranda men now remain who still know the patterns and rites employed in these ceremonies; in ten years time they will virtually have died out, since no native man who is today under 50 years of age is likely to have received full training in these rites as performed in the Aranda-speaking area. The younger generation is already completely disinterested and ignorant.

I should therefore like to request the Australian National University that these films not be placed in any library, but should be kept in a strong-room. If the Australian National University has as yet no strong-room, I am certain that the Adelaide University would be prepared to store them in their fire-proof strong room for the time being.

In a private covering note to Hohnen, Strehlow spoke of his 'sacred trust' with regard to the films, whereas 'other anthropologists have merely a "scientific" interest in them.'

Altogether this is a crucial statement. He has the acute concern of a responsible curator, which surely makes sense. He has a well-informed historical view of the uniqueness of the record to be protected. He makes a clear statement about his sense of social responsibility with regard to his cultural acquisition—one which he will repeat over the next months and years to the ANU, as the university decides to stake its claim on the original copies. He stakes his 'whole reputation' on making himself personally responsible for the audiences to whom they were shown.

But what did this mean? Was this understanding to apply for all time? He had not applied any such rules to his screenings in England and the Continent; and indeed, when papers such as the *Listener* wrote them up there was no suggestion of exclusivity. Years later, when Strehlow tragically ruined his own reputation as the scrupulous *ingkata*, he would say that the showing of sacred things in his possession only awaited the death of all the old men who had trusted him; but there is no mention of that understanding here. Did being personally responsible mean that Strehlow would be there in person whenever the films were screened? Could there be no system of delegation? His private note to Hohnen suggests a strong definition of personal responsibility, one finally sealed by the 'sacred trust.' And this was a sacred trust that excluded Aboriginal people of 'the younger generation.' The whole passage is well on the way to a claim of exclusive possession.

Hohnen seems to have baulked at its intensity. 'From your letters of 11th and 12th May I can see that *your sense of parenthood* with regard to your series of Australian films in very strong, and that it is going to be a wrench to hand them over to a foster parent—even though we did provide the test tube.' The university did have a substantial strongroom, Hohnen told Strehlow. With regard to the interest in the films expressed by the Commonwealth's Department of Information (which hoped to make copies), Hohnen went on: 'It is good of you to make available your *private* films for their purposes, and I would have thought that a nice *quid pro quo* (unless you expect to be paid for them) would be to do some work on the soundtrack for the University films' (emphasis added).

It was a silly reply. Strehlow, prickly as ever, took exception to the remark about parenthood—as well he might, considering his links with the old men in Central Australia. He seized on the reference to private films and reminded Hohnen that Mountford had been able to personally profit from the Department of Information's sale of his films. Indignantly he repeated the issue of trust: 'Perhaps there are some anthropologists who don't honour the undertakings they have given to "simple" natives or "primitive" folk; but I cannot see why it should be immaterial to me to risk my whole reputation with my old native friends by taking no further interest at all in the fate of these films.'

And he added: 'Nothing I have said here, of course detracts from the Australian National University's title to the material I gathered in 1949–50. Wherever the films have been shown, the ANU Fellowship has been mentioned; and in all the manuscripts in which I am working now, full credit is being given to the generosity of the Australian National University, whose financial aid made this research possible.'[11]

A rather complicated set of exchanges follows. Hohnen is trying to calm Strehlow down with regard to the Department of Information. Strehlow is happy for them to put a soundtrack to the Native Cat Ceremony, with a copy of the film to be made for the University of Adelaide. He would leave the distribution rights to the university 'so that the undertakings I have given to the natives should be safeguarded.' He then makes a suggestion that someone should have thought of before: that Aborigines be paid. In May he wrote: 'If there were profits from the film then I would like to urge that some commission should be paid to the present old native leaders of those totems who allowed me to take these films; for without their cooperation no films of complete cycles could have been obtained, as other photographers in this area have found to their cost.' Later, perhaps with Tom Ljonga's work in mind, Strehlow suggested that about half the profit should go to the natives.[12]

There the matter lapsed, pretty much, for another two years. Strehlow continued to deal with the ANU: he was still lobbying for funds to help with another trip to the Centre, in which he had the support of A.P. Rowe, his own vice-chancellor in Adelaide. Rowe had written to the ANU's vice-chancellor, Sir Douglas Copeland, saying that: 'Strehlow is a possession of Australia rather than South Australia and I would have thought Canberra should be interested in him . . . it seems all wrong that a man who is most energetic, most likeable and cooperative and who is the acknowledged expert in his field should be paid the emoluments associated with a milk round. Alas, we have not the funds to do better. Have you a brainwave on this?'[13]

Sir Douglas had no brainwave. He passed the matter on to Professor Nadel. Did the ANU have a research fellowship for Strehlow? Nadel demurred. He could not in all conscience recommend an appointment to any senior post: 'Strehlow's scientific qualifications are linguistic rather than anthropological, and I am aware of the high quality of his work in that field.' As to the forthcoming research fellowship in anthropological linguistics, it was a junior post, and Strehlow would have to take his chance. 'Nor should I care to say how great this chance might be.' It was hard-headed attitudes such as these that helped over the years to thicken the chip on Strehlow's shoulder. He did not apply for the 'junior' research fellowship, even though the manuscript of *Songs* was nearly finished, and many a senior fellow, not to mention Nadel himself, might have been well pleased to be the author of it. Instead, Strehlow was pressing on with more trips to the Centre. It was when he asked the Department of Territories if they could provide him with a tape recorder that Nadel came into the picture again, writing to Hohnen in May 1953: 'The Department of Territories rang me up to ask if we could lend Mr Strehlow a tape recorder since they had none to lend but were anxious to support Mr Strehlow "in any way possible." I declined politely explaining that my Department had no recorder to spare.'

With similarly chilling politeness Nadel went on: 'But it is time I think to remind Mr Strehlow again, and finally, to let us have what belongs to us—the originals of his films, his wire recordings, and copies of the sound film recently produced by the Department of Information. I fear that if we do not get these things out of him now we might never be able to do so. He is obviously "a collector" first and foremost, and what he once collects he tries to keep for good.'[14]

The suspicion that Strehlow was at heart a collector, as distinct from the collaborative researcher suggested by his grand plans three years earlier, seems to have driven the ANU's approach to this conflict of 'national interest.' On 12 May 1953, Strehlow tried to stall the matter of physical possession by suggesting that he hold the 1950 ceremonial films until he took some more shots of the sacred—extra pictures not foreseen in 1950. Hohnen had to be firm. 'We do think it time,' he wrote back the next day, 'particularly as you are proposing to go off again, that you lodged with us the originals of your films, your wire recordings and any other copies of films that belong to us. If you wish, I will send someone to Adelaide to take these over as, doubtless, you are busy planning your next campaign.'

Nadel was the man the ANU planned to send to Adelaide. Strehlow was to lodge, please, all the material clearly in the care of Adelaide's librarian. 'When you return from your present trip we would be very glad to make it available for any further editing or work you wish to carry out on it.'[15] Three days later Strehlow seems to have bowed to reality. 'I can either ask the University to dispatch to you the items mentioned in it, or else hand them over to your agent, just as you desire.' And that might have been that, except that Strehlow came back from the Centre to find that the material had not been removed after all. W.H. Stanner, standing in for Professor Nadel, had come to Adelaide, inspected the material, and at first decided not to remove it. He told the library that he did not want to assume responsibility for transporting valuable research material that could be lost or damaged in transit. This was a momentary respite. But in November, when Stanner started to make practical arrangements to ship the films to Canberra, Strehlow rose up.

To A.P. Rowe he wrote an agitated three-page letter that reviewed all the communication—spoken and written—on 'the question of property ownership'. He said he had agreed to hand things over in haste. While the condition of the 1949 fellowship (that equipment be returned, and exposed film remain the property of the university) was 'a reasonable one,' it was a technicality. 'I had no doubts that the exposed films, though technically the property of the ANU, would be left in my care and keeping on behalf of the ANU.' He appealed to Rowe to make an 'authoritative ruling' on the future of the films, especially considering 'the original promises made to me when the 1949 Fellowship was awarded. I cannot believe that its promises have become meaningless.' Finally, Strehlow said that 'the giving up of this research material would deprive me of invaluable documentary evidence of my own research work at Adelaide.'[16]

This is perhaps the moment to comment on the type of letter Strehlow sent on 23 November 1954. It is the kind of self-defeating communication which was to be typical in the years to come. Its tone is indignant and aggrieved. The essential assumption, which the letter seeks to demonstrate by tabling all manner of correspondence and reports of correspondence, is that an injustice has been done him by a person or persons who have in some way been dishonourable, or uncomprehendingly unappreciative, or both. The buttonholing expectation of the letter—perhaps 'demand' is the word—is that the reader should attend to every detail of its contents, and more. Strehlow writes with the intent of gaining emotional support for his interpretation of each nuance of meaning that has, he insists, been conveyed to him by others. His assumption is that the subtleties of his conduct have all along been transparently virtuous. It was not in his nature to concede error. Indeed he pivots on a premise which is eternally present: that his work is unique and invaluable and that he should be treated accordingly. His documentation of mishap and ill-treatment is meant to establish his case 'scientifically.' Emotionally his letters are a *cri de coeur* for the absolute support and applause of authorities: one can detect the hurt child's demand for recognition, along with the propensity of the hurt child to lash out if it does not get its way. Over the years we see this happening in Strehlow's standard letter of complaint: the more his attacking mode cornered authorities into defensive positions, the more he struck out, the more vitriolic and slanderous he became. In the end, the tragedy for him would be the inability to see that acting out a persecution complex is self-fulfilling.

With Strehlow's letter of the 23 November, Rowe did his best. He sent it on to L.G. Melville, the then Vice-Chancellor at the ANU. 'Put rather brutally, the impression here is that your University is interpreting ownership as possession within reach even though such possession is of little value. I feel sure that I can look to you for help in this delicate matter. If a difference of opinion remains it is one which concerns the whole principle of results and uses of research and if, unhappily, we fail to reach agreement we might put the whole matter to the Australian Royal Society,' then in the process of being formed.

Melville replied that there could be no concessions to Strehlow. Not only had the ANU supported his work from the beginning, and continued to express their interest in his valuable work quite tangibly, all they were doing in the present dispute was asking Strehlow: 'to observe the conditions under which the University provided him with funds to conduct his researches.' Melville drew attention to Strehlow's admission that their terms were reasonable and that he had agreed to them.

Quite simply . . . we do not have in our possession even a copy, let alone the original, of anything he has done other than the recently received copies of the short film sponsored by the Department of Information . . . We have no wish to place difficulties in Strehlow's way in obtaining material needed for his researches. We would be willing to pay the cost of copying the wire recordings so that he may have copies in his possession and we would be willing to consider any reasonable proposal he may make for the copying of original material which is our property. [17]

In other words Canberra still wanted its material to be sent to them from Adelaide. A fresh demand was penned two days before Christmas 1953, but that prompted Strehlow to escalate his resistance in the new year: to Rowe he fired off a five-page letter with nine pages of appendices. The latter included an inventory of correspondence, the first entry of which is dated 3 February 1953. There is no mention of the letters of 14 and 15 February 1950, when Strehlow was sounding so collaborative with regard to his work. Rather, his tone is penny-pinching and carping. He is at pains to point out that the ANU have granted £3,040 of assistance, not the £3,600 they claimed. He points out that many of the expenses of the trip were paid by himself. He gives some details and adds: 'The total expenses were, as a matter of fact, rather higher than the figures given here. I personally added to the "Payments of Natives" grant (of £161.15.5) a considerable amount of money from my private income at various times.' He repeats his claims about the uniqueness of the films and the dangers to the original copies, and he goes on to exclaim: 'Why must my films form part of the work of the school of Pacific Studies' and be 'available for consultation by scholars who may from time to time be working here'? 'My own final practical suggestion would be as follows. Two copies should be made of all recordings and all films. One copy could then stay with me at the Adelaide University; the other could be sent to the Australian National University. The originals should be stored at some place where they would be absolutely safe . . . The Commonwealth Film Bureau's vaults would ensure absolute safety.'[18]

It was that 'final' that got backs up, added to the fact that his request that the ANU cover costs of copying made no sense if the university still had no clear picture of all the film in Strehlow's hands. Could he please give these details. Meanwhile they still wanted the 1950 material lodged with them. They did not want the matter to run on any longer.

Strehlow at last gave in. 'I am sorry if my phrasing was such that it could be misunderstood as a demand,' he wrote on 27 January 1954.

Over the next two months we find him precisely listing the films in his possession and reasonably discussing what might be copied. He also conceded that the four copies of the originals should go to the ANU, and he promised to provide explanatory notes for the films. The only satisfaction must have been the reassurances that enabled him to write: 'Your agreement in principle to conceding me the right to first use of the material collected by me under the auspices of the Australian National University in 1949/50 is noted with pleasure, and also your promise to ascertain my view before allowing any other research worker to make use of my material.' In all, this was a resolution that somewhat deflated all the early talk about sacred trust. The ANU took in the material with the secular insouciant aplomb of a contemporary scientific academy.

Payment to natives? That seems to have been lost sight of soon after Strehlow first mentioned it in 1952, with regard to the Department of Information. It was never mentioned with regard to the rights of access the ANU planned to exercise. In theory, the ANU now had much to add to a useful body of teaching materials. But it was all still in raw form nearly three years later: there were unedited films, and wire and tape recordings unedited and unannotated. When Deputy Registrar W.H. Stanner took stock of 'the long and tangled' Strehlow affair, he found that the policy had been 'thoughtless' and 'ad hoc,' with no general funding policy. Stanner was concerned that if copies of the films were made, they would be useless unless Strehlow agreed to give full translations and annotations. He wanted this to be the condition if the university was paying for permanent microgroove sound recordings.

Various things *were* done with the films between 1956 and 1960. Soundtracks were added to two films (Kangaroo Ceremonies linking Ajaii and Malupiti and Honey Ant Ceremonies in Ljaba) by the Commonwealth Film Bureau (CFB) in Burwood. Then, as agreed with Strehlow, the CFB sent copies to Strehlow. He received them in 1957, checked the soundtracks and sent them back. But the general status and whereabouts of things was still sufficiently unclear by 1960 for Canberra to write to Strehlow again. There was, for example, the Honey Ant Film; did Strehlow have a copy of that?

No, replied Strehlow, on 5 May 1960. The CFB had promised to send him one on 'extended loan' but it had not arrived. Strehlow said he still did not have a copy of Kangaroo and the Honey Ant films with soundtrack and would very much appreciate them 'on loan.'

The rest of what Strehlow had to say should perhaps make us pause, after this long episode in the epic tale of Strehlow and Aboriginal possession. It is a detail that can only vindicate Strehlow in his anxiety about the safety of his ethnographic treasure trove of images and sounds. We have seen how he could go overboard with concern—or possessively fret like an over-anxious parent (to use Hohnen's benevolent if sardonic term). But many a parent's worst worries come true, as we know: strange and terrible things can happen to one's children.

Strehlow wrote to Stanner:

> Some time during the Stuart trial last year a package of my own original landscape and ceremonial films that I had taken on some of my more recent trips to Central Australia (in 1953 and 1955) was returned to me by the Department of Interior Film Division in Burwood without any accompanying letter. I find that among the films that have been returned from Burwood last year there is also the original films of the Kangaroo Increase Ceremonies of Krantji and Imbatjik; Iwuka, which I had sent to the ANU in 1954. How this film comes to be among the private material returned to me from Burwood, seems rather a mystery. You could perhaps tell me what to do with it; since it is the original film of these increase ceremonies, it should not, of course, be screened at all, but kept in safe storage for future sound-tracking.[19]

This must have felt like square one to Strehlow. After all that, his objects had come back to him. How could it not have confirmed in him—in his guts, if we locate his feelings in Aranda terms—that he should never have parted with them in the first place?

'We Collect and Collect'

In 1964 in a grant application to the Australian Institute for Aboriginal Studies in Canberra, Strehlow wrote that:

> in my thirty years of research in Central Australia *I have never asked any totemic clan leaders to reveal their acts and traditions to me, or to sing their songs for my benefit.* Such requests would have been regarded in my case as a serious breach of the ceremonial rules, for which I, having grown up in an aboriginal community, could not have pleaded ignorance as an excuse. I have accordingly always waited for the older men to approach me of their own volition. I knew, for instance, of the existence of the

Uletjapota Eastern Aranda euro traditions and sacred acts in 1933; for they are linked by myth with the Northern Aranda euro traditions and acts of Kaput' Urbula, which I recorded in that year. But the invitation to witness the Eastern Aranda series came to me only thirty-one years later. (emphasis added)

He is quibbling. What does 'ask' mean in this context? Strehlow always travelled in hope and expectation. He did not have to ask because his linguistic liaisons had put him in exactly the right place as a collector, as he knew all through the years. In real time he had lived with the relationships and patiently solicited the objects whether the objects were songs, or myths or sounds or images. To posit, as the above statement tends to do, an imaginary time when things simply came to him is to place himself in the realm favoured by the classic collector, who can somehow stay time by using the collection to reverse the 'relentless passage from birth to death.' In their dislocations and sometimes their mourning, the Aranda had given him their secrets. In his living he now had them, out of their time, and in his own time he had always shied away from recounting the total circumstances of his collecting when that included objects. Baudrillard again comes to mind: *the setting up of the collection itself displaces real time*.

Throughout this period he was increasingly dependent on public bodies to fund his trips and further his collecting. The Northern Territory sometimes helped. The University of Adelaide, apart from paying his salary, was especially helpful with recording and film equipment and sometimes travel costs. But his main patronage still came from Canberra, the place that continued to have its eye on the national significance of his work.

His connection with the ANU had dwindled by 1959. In its place emerged another body, the Australian Institute of Aboriginal Studies (AIAS), upon which Strehlow became increasingly dependent in the years when he most craved recognition for all the travel and work he had done in Central Australia, all that he had asserted by way of his tenacious, scholarly independence. His affair with the Institute was as lively as any a man might have on the Orient Express: a perfect expression of desperate dealings on a fast track that we can see—with hindsight—sped him into a tunnel. By the time Strehlow re-emerged from this affair— when he resigned from the Institute in the most melodramatic and jilted way in 1973—his virile years were strangely over.

The Institute was set up in 1961, with the support of Paul Hasluck and the then Minister for Aboriginal Affairs, W.C. Wentworth. Wentworth had been inspired, at least in part, by papers he had read by anthropologists Berndt and Strehlow, and he hoped that research would help 'contemporary aboriginal life during the transition from the tribal state to assimilation in the Australian community,' a notion that Senator John Gorton supported when the Bill for the Institute went through Parliament.[20] For the first two years W.E.H. Stanner was the Institute's deputy chairman and executive officer, and the Interim Council did not include Strehlow, or, for that matter, Berndt. Instead it had a range of academics relatively distant from anthropology,* and it was only after various protests that Berndt, along with W.R. Geddes, Professor of Anthropology at the University of Western Australia, joined the Interim Council. But Strehlow was left out, because, he thought, even though he had been a nominee of the Governor-General, he had been vetoed by the government in 1968.[21] He was merely a member of the Institute's sub-committee on language.

Strehlow's academic reputation at this time could be seen to be in the doldrums. *Aranda Traditions* was fourteen years behind him. *Songs* was another ten in the future. At the research conference which inaugurated the Institute he played a minor part: he was there to comment on the paper by E.A. Worms on Aboriginal religion, and when he did he deflected from the most general issues and spoke of local details with the Aranda. He called for more local studies of an intense nature by people with 'a good knowledge of the local Aboriginal languages.' In the session on languages, S.A. Wurm gave the keynote paper and Strehlow spoke up in discussion, emphasising that the linguist should also understand social structure, and stressing that there was as yet no dictionary of any Aboriginal language. He mentioned, too, that he had a manuscript 'containing his analysis of song metres, poetical language, and the use of song in ritual, which . . . had been awaiting publication for eight years.'[22]

So he was present at this conference, but decidedly out of account when it came to general matters of language or religion. He seems not

---

* It included R.M. Crawford and J.T. Burke, professors of history and fine arts (respectively) at Melbourne; F.J. Fenner, professor of microbiology at ANU, and A.D. Trindall, Classicist and master of the ANU's University House, and G.H. Lawton, professor of geography at the University of Adelaide. A mere geographer from his own campus galled Strehlow, a feeling that metamorphosed to rage when Lawton supported an honorary degree to Charles Mountford for his works on Aborigines.

to have taken part at all in the discussion of artistic life conducted by Catherine Berndt, including the ethnomusicology survey by Trevor Jones. In general his work received passing reference by others. In other words, at the historic moment of Australian anthropology fully profes- sionalising itself, Strehlow's career was in abeyance. After his brilliant start 25 years earlier, he was slipping into shadow, waiting.

He was not unaware of this. He was acutely conscious, and had been since the thirties, that his research work had been interrupted by taking the job of patrol officer, just as the World War had postponed his academic career. *Aranda Traditions* saved his literary reputation, but did little for him in London. Following his miserable return, and the com- pletion of his 'Chants' manuscript, the long wait for the publication of *Songs of Central Australia* began. These years were corrosive. His whole life, arguably, would have been different if recognition for that work had come to him earlier, if his life could have been seen by others to have come to its just fruition, with all the songs laid out in celebration of Aranda culture, as well as himself. But his dominant note by 1960 is that of a man singularly thwarted. We should bear this in mind with all his dealings with those upon whom he felt dependent.

Strehlow first asked for help from the Institute in 1962, and in March of that year Elkin had made Strehlow aware of their expectations and of the profession's need to have access to his invaluable findings. 'The question that the Council will certainly ask,' Elkin advised him, 'is when will your work be written up in a form which either could be published or, if anything happened to you, could be prepared for pub- lication by someone else? As you know, the great problem is that we collect and collect, but do not get the material really organised and written up for the enlightenment and use of other workers.'[23]

Strehlow tried to be reassuring. He had 'no intention of letting any of the information gathered on my field trips remain unused or in an unusable condition.'[24] He was referring to his genealogical material and sound recordings. He told Elkin the *Songs* had been ready for the printer since 1956, and would have been published by now but for lack of finance at his publishers. But a start on printing the book would be made soon, Strehlow added reassuringly. Meanwhile, if he could have the help of a typist, one who could put the information on to local maps, all that could be 'ready for publication about two years after serious work had been resumed on it.' It was material that must 'gain in importance with each new generation.' 'I fully realise, of course,' he concluded, 'the importance of writing up and publishing the results of our researches. I hope therefore that the Institute will use whatever influence it possesses to procure funds for engaging assistants in order to speed up the labours of research workers and for publishing their completed findings in permanent form for the use of scholars everywhere.'

In March Strehlow got some of the assistance he wanted from the Institute. He had made it clear that the genealogies and the carding of genealogical material was the necessary preparatory work for a full-scale research project: 'Pre-white organisation of the Aranda and adjoining tribes in Central Australia.' This must have helped his application. Still, there was some worry on Elkin's part that they did not know how much of the £400 was to be spent on petrol and how much on maintaining and rewarding informants. It was Elkin's opinion that the cost of petrol for about 7,000 miles might be £150, and that 'for the balance of the £400 the researcher could maintain and reward many more informants than he could use in the short period available to him.' But a full-time typist was 'unhesitatingly rejected' by Elkin: he said no other anthropologist seemed to need someone to type out genealogies, yet others—he named the Berndts—had material just as encyclopaedic.[25]

Still, in May 1962 Strehlow was informed by the Institute that he had the vehicle and travel money he had requested. In his initial notice no mention was made of publication—it seems to have been taken for granted. But another undertaking was gently requested: he might help the Institute collect artefacts for its museum, since 'time was running out for the making of a representative collection.'[26] The Institute was expressing its alertness to what Strehlow (and others) had been saying for the previous 30 years: that the pace of social change in the Centre was causing, if not the death of the traditional culture, then a decline which would seriously deplete what could be gathered. Strehlow seems to have made no response at the time, and F.D. McCarthy, the principal of the Institute, repeated the request two years later as Strehlow was about to set off to the Centre: 'On this trip and at any other time, I wonder whether it would be possible for you to obtain, or arrange to secure, specimens of *waninga*, *nurtunja* and other decorated ceremonial material, for the National Ethnographic Collection, which completely lacks this kind of material for display.'[27]

'I'll do what I can about the suggested ceremonial material,' Strehlow replied. But there is no record of his having done anything, and the Institute was perhaps conscious that a mere £400 for petrol and travel, even with Elkin's extra calculation for payment to informants, could not really buy goods for their museum.

Besides, what Strehlow had undertaken to do—and what they had officially supported in 1963 and 1964—were three activities other than collecting objects (which he continued to do for himself). They were 'the compilation of the genealogies; an Aranda dictionary; maps of the dreaming sites, as well as, of course, other publications that might be born of the material.' By 1964 Strehlow had finally managed to persuade the Institute to provide him with a research assistant after all. Her job would be to collate the genealogies and word lists. A Miss Crowley was to devote herself to this until 1969, when her grant was not renewed. In addition, Strehlow managed to get a second assistant in the person of Pastor Philip Scherer, formerly of the Hermannsburg Mission, who had been helping him with the New Testament. Scherer would help with the dictionary.

The Institute had, in other words, substantially committed itself to Strehlow by 1964—not without a good deal of consternation on the part of its senior members. After Elkin it was Berndt who expressed most concern that they receive regular reports on the work of Strehlow's assistants, and that the 'projects be designed so that they produce results in stages.'[28] 'My own personal view is that he should sit down and write up his material before engaging in more research. However, I fully appreciate the urgency of this research and the fact that "these are the last years, in the Centre": in the words of Strehlow's 1962 application: they are the last years in many other areas too. It seems to me, then, *that he should be given the opportunity to carry out this project*: it could well be argued that the collection of ethnographic material is just as vital as its early publication. I would hold this view myself.'[29]

There had been other worries, at least initially. There was a concern about Strehlow's 'whole system' or perhaps lack of it. Stanner, while supporting Strehlow, had expressed some doubt as to whether Crowley would do the job in the right way. Members did not understand why she needed to take time out to learn Aranda. Stanner and Wentworth wondered whether a young person based in Canberra, given a period of training, could do the collating. The overall feeling was that they should send someone to Adelaide to assess Strehlow's needs. Elkin supported the dictionary idea strongly, just as he had supported

Strehlow's earlier linguistic work. Berndt supported the genealogy and the dictionary, but thought it 'should be one project or the other, but not both, as Strehlow would have to devote a lot of time to each to supervise both Miss Crowley and Pastor Scherer.'

The upshot was that by 1964, when Strehlow received his third grant from the Institute, the expectations upon him had been made plain. He had to supervise his helpers and report regularly on their work. He had to publish. And—if another Institute discussion is any guide—he had been informed that others might be interested in his sound recordings. He should provide them with copies of the tapes. Berndt also thought that the tapes should be annotated in some way. In due course Strehlow agreed to give copies of tapes for the Institute archive—'a set in a sealed container'[30]—as McCarthy put it five years later. 'But nothing has come of this proposal yet,' McCarthy lamented. It never did.

Strehlow was nonetheless taking pains to report in the right way. He had made two successful trips to the Centre in 1964 and told his patrons something about it. In March that year he had spent valuable time with several Eastern Aranda men at Ujitja, 30 miles south-east of Alice Springs. 'The Rain Cycle of Ujitja that I witnessed will constitute the only full-scale rain cycle ever to be recorded in Central Australia,' he proudly declared. (And competitively, one might add, since he goes on to remark that Spencer and Gillen's book *The Arunta* had made 'no mention of any rain *tjurunga*' and omitted to name the rain centre.) He then moved on to Uraiura Swamp on Mr Tom Gorey's property, about 50 miles from Ujitja, 80 from Alice Springs, and saw a number of further interesting Eastern Aranda acts—rat kangaroo, bat, native cat and kangaroo ceremonies. In the movement between camps, Strehlow added, he had been much helped by 'a part-aboriginal station owner, Mr Willy Smith' who 'also supplied beef on several occasions in this difficult country where six years of drought seemed to have killed (or driven away) almost all native game animals.'

Difficult country. The theme is familiar, and in his two reports for 1964 Strehlow cannot help himself. The fieldwork is all the more valuable, Strehlow is compelled to show, for being hard won. He tells his patrons that because of the drought all supplies had to come from Alice Springs, and water had to be carried from ten miles away when he was at Ujitja. 'Heat, flies, and dust made out-door work rather unpleasant on many days.' As for the Uraiura Swamp camp: 'Here too water had to be carted for my men, whose number varied from eight to eleven. Dust gales, clouds, and some rain all combined to interfere with the smooth progress of my work, and sometimes work was made impossible for days on end.'[31]

When he returned to the Centre in June he had been faced with a privileged choice as a fieldworker: three different groups of Aboriginal men wanted him to witness and record their ceremonies. One wanted him to go 55 miles north-east of Alice to the Uletjapota area for the euro ceremonies; another to see the honey ant and native cat boys' ceremonies at Alcoota, 110 miles to the north-east; a third called him to Finke on the South Australian and Northern Territory border, to 'witness various Andekerinja acts'. 'None of these ceremonial series or songs had ever been recorded; and it was difficult to choose between them.' He decided on the euro acts.

Difficult work, again. In his chosen area the euro sites were scattered through 200 square miles of territory, and some had to be visited more than once. All up, Strehlow had to travel more than 3,600 miles in the Land Rover, and the work was made even harder because he could not hire a caravan in Alice Springs. 'This meant that the front cabin of the landrover was the only place where the cameras and the tape recorder could be stored; and all writing had to be done here too. My three camps in 1964 were by far the most uncomfortable camps I have ever had to endure in my whole field experience.'[32]

Strehlow loved advertising his hardships, especially to patrons he has already construed as reluctant. Just as tactless, perhaps, was the graphic description Strehlow gave of the ceremonial objects involved in the euro songs, the outstanding feature of which was the painting of many shields. 'No less than ninety painted shields were produced during this series—a profusion not even distantly approached in any other Central Australian totemic cycle. The thirteen shields in the camp had to be used over and over again, the painted designs being rubbed off after the completion of each act.'[33] There were 25 acts, all of which he photographed. But there is no mention of a shield or two for the Institute museum, any more than there is of writing these ceremonies up in the foreseeable future.

After Strehlow had approval of his next grant in 1965, for travel to Alcoota and Finke, he took pains to make himself look accountable and productively responsive to the Institute's expectations.[34] He had been away in the field, he wrote in August 1965, and altogether had travelled 5,400 miles in the past fourteen weeks—hence the late report. He immediately mentioned two publications almost to hand (even though they had not sprung from fieldwork funded by the Institute). One was the essay, 'Culture, Social Structure and Environment in Aboriginal Central Australia,' for Elkin's festschrift, *Aboriginal Man in Australia*, copies of which the publishers were yet to supply him with; and the other, 'Central Australian Religion: Personal Monototemism in a Polytotemic Community,' his contribution to the festschrift for A.E. Jensen, had been published by the Frobenius Institute in Germany and copies had just arrived.

He went on to describe his assistants' painstaking work: how, because there were so many identical names, they had had to go back through the genealogies identifying each individual and then Miss Crowley had re-typed them with the names 'labelled with Roman figures' for clarity; how Mr Scherer, 'a first-class map drawer,' was doing the kind of invaluable work that would help systematise family grouping in relation to place. It was this kind of work, Strehlow was at pains to point out, that would result in the kind of studies the Institute wanted. By way of indicating the value of Scherer's work, Strehlow wrote that to cover the area in his essay for the Elkin festschrift, 'some sixteen large-scale maps are necessary . . . Mr Scherer has so far drawn about half of these, and I have put on to these maps over 900 aboriginal place names to date.'

With the maps done, Strehlow said, Scherer would 'be able to go ahead with his dictionary cards with much more efficiency and fuller authority.' Samples of Scherer's maps and dictionary cards would be sent to Canberra, Strehlow said, as well as some of Miss Crowley's work. Meanwhile, the applicant concluded, he hoped the salaries of his assistants would once again be approved.

Strehlow's hopes came true: the salaries were approved. But that was all, and hardly worth the candle. If the atmosphere between him and the Institute was icy by the end of 1965, it was soon to freeze over due to several major incidents. The first concerned Scherer and the maps; the second was the silencing of Strehlow after his notorious review of the work of Charles Mountford; and the third, really, was the scandalous leap he took into a new life, after which the surface of his dealings with the Institute cracked completely.

Maps (Ground Level)

Every tree—any tree; any rock—that one; the hill over there, and the water beneath it, the soak beside it; the cave, the creek, the pile of stones at the edge of the claypan . . . these places can have names. The names usually refer to the ancestor creature that was born there or stopped to eat, sleep, drink, fight, copulate or be killed there. Name the place and you name a creature or an event that animates the country with story. Tell the story, or sing the song of the story, and you express a connection with the country. If you are at the place, you might show the connection by pointing; by walking around in the right way, respectfully, calling out, or throwing a stone ahead of you if you are approaching a strong place, one especially sacred in the story. And if you are not there at the place, you might use symbols to represent its arrangement of names. In a sand painting, for example, the lines and shapes might indicate the camp and the track taken by the ancestor creature. Call that a map of sorts.*

The Aranda people did not have a word for map. It seems that they did not need it. They were in the map, and their conception of their habitat was a matter of continuous enactment of the map's meaning. The meaning was its value for its inhabitants. You are in the country and all representations of it (in dance, song, painting) are one and the same.

Maps, as we know them, are representations. They are not what the country is, because the making of the map has been an activity of symbol formation. Concepts have distanced one from the real thing. There is no essential connection between the map and the ownership of the country shown on it. Our mapmaking lifts us from the physical reality.[35]

By comparison, a map of Aboriginal country is like the skin on the human face, and on the throat and chest; and on the belly, the spiritual centre of feeling. In the final analysis, there can be no doubt who owns the map of Aboriginal country.

What is striking about Strehlow's early remarks about maps is that the question of ownership did not seem to arise. Strehlow felt that he had walked over so much of the ground that he had earned certain rights to it. This feeling, it seems, went deeper than his more 'official' claims to entitlement when he told his stories about the old men who

---

*   The first to fully articulate this notion in Central Australia was not Spencer or Gillen but the astute and opinionated policeman Ernest Cowle, who wrote to Spencer 28 May 1900: 'I believe that every water hole, Spring, Plain, Hill, Big Tree, Big Rock, Gutters, and every peculiar or striking feature of the Country, not even leaving out Sandhills, without any exception whatsoever is connected with some tradition' (Mulvaney 2000: 38, 140).

chose to sing their songs to him, and give him their *tjurunga*, the objects that often bore designs that served as maps. He had more than walked: he had laboured across country, and in the country. In the heat and the dust. In rain and in the biting winter winds. He had done this for years, he had worked for a whole lifetime, and like all puritans believed certain kinds of work made one deserving. That was the point, in report after report, when he set down his mileage for other people. We could make a list of those mileages of Strehlow's, and he would think that it spoke for itself. It would begin in 1932 and would be still going strong when he was counting miles for ANU and for the AIAS, when he made his last field trip to the Centre.* The list would be a code for the map that he had made in the most primitive way: by moving through the country, stopping at the most sacred places and walking there. The maps he wanted to make were enactments of his story about the country.

They were being made, too, because they *were* of Aboriginal country. That's what most interested his patrons, after all. Not what Strehlow had walked—though that was interesting, since he had the social skills and wherewithal to be taken, for example, over those square miles of euro sites—but the fact that here was a detailed map of the grain of Aboriginal belief in Central Australia. Strehlow had given them the profound term for it: 'totemic geography.'† Already that lifted the map out of the country and onto the shelf of scientific endeavour. Now his map was there for all the world to see, providing a bird's eye view of all the sacred places in reality, locating the most secret places with an eye as calculating as an eagle's, where no thought has been given to the possible violations of country.

It is striking that neither Strehlow nor the Institute seems to have paused, initially, to consider the full implications of the existence of such maps, or, secondly, the issue of who would be able to look at them. The anthropological literature was yet to swell with qualms about indigenous rights to privacy about their sacred beliefs.

Strehlow's zestful helper with maps was Pastor Philip Scherer, who was as indifferent to any transgressional aspect of them as he had been

---

*   In 1968 he calculated 80,028 miles travelled by motor vehicle and 7,000 by camel. 'Research Trips' comprised 42,020 of the total: the rest was his travelling as patrol officer.
†   Refined rather than created: 'Totemic Geography' was a chapter heading in Spencer and Gillen's *The Arunta* (1927), along with elevation drawings of sites.

to the appropriation of sacred words in their work on the New Testament. It was meticulous, beaverish work on Scherer's part, who had no training as a mapmaker. He worked from military survey maps as a template, transcribing all the place names from Strehlow's diaries, myth books and genealogies. He had been employed, as far as the Institute in Canberra was concerned, to work on the dictionary, but Strehlow had had him, first of all, working on the Lutheran hymnal, and then redirected him to the maps, especially the map for *Songs of Central Australia*. He was in an invidious position.

By the middle of 1965 Scherer was anxious about the standing of his work, as well as his occupational status with Strehlow and the Institute. In July he wrote to Strehlow in Alice Springs to explain that his 'mental frustration or worry' was affecting his health. He had noticed in the Institute newsletter that a research project had been sponsored for an assistant to compile a dictionary from a 30-year collection of myths and songs. He presumed that referred to him; and yet Strehlow had not mentioned it, and had started him off listing the dictionary words from the Aranda New Testament. 'As I now look back,' the letter went on, 'I can see that my work on the NT [New Testament] can be regarded as a preliminary exercise for methods of writing up etc. . . . My only regret in this connection is that you don't seem to have checked the writing-up which I prepared on fullscap [*sic*] sheets for your perusal, so that there have been no corrections of possible mistakes, and that no gaps of knowledge which I had to leave for you have been filled in. At least I should add that I am not aware of any.'

The other worry Scherer noted was that the Institute would continue to fund only if there were publishable results from the research. But how could that be done when 'I have been working almost exclusively on maps which you directed me to do.' He had no aversion to maps, but would be less worried if 'I had the assurance that this work is within the possible range of duties I owe to you under the Institute.' He suggested that Strehlow might report that this work was 'a legitimate contribution towards the publication of your book . . . As things are at the present however, I can only view my future with the Institute with a certain sense of apprehension and uncertainty.' He was not writing, he added, 'in a spirit of complaint, but merely to have the whole situation clarified.'[36]

Strehlow wrote back promptly what he promised was 'a confidential and friendly letter on the whole business.' He was keen to reassure

Scherer about the value of all of his work and his job security. He had, he began, been granted Institute funding for 'a full-scale Aranda dictionary compiled from my notebooks and all other sources.' But he had not realised until Scherer arrived that the typing out of the hymnal was unfinished. This was no fault of Scherer's, and it was as a 'personal favour' that Scherer had been asked to finish it off. 'For this, of course, I am taking full responsibility' (emphasis added). As to the dictionary work that had been done, and although much more of it had been anticipated, Strehlow said it was a good thing that Scherer was making word lists from the hymnal and the New Testament. 'For it does not matter to the Western portion of the Aranda dictionary whether the words came out of the Hbg translations or out of the Western Aranda myths: they are still correctly used Western Aranda words.'[37]

The other 'necessity,' Strehlow went on, was the map for *Songs*. It only remained for a selection of words to be added to it when he got back from Alice Springs.[*] It had become clear that their whole project—the dictionary and the genealogies—depended on detailed Central Australian sketch maps. Thanks to the ones that Scherer had already drawn and to which Strehlow had laboriously added site names from his notebook, the maps had become a 'vital part of our work' and he would be telling the Institute accordingly. And again, it was not Scherer's fault that the work was slow: 'if anything is worth while doing, it is worth while doing well . . . These are, after all, the only maps of their kind in Australia.' Strehlow went on: 'I am accordingly writing my reports now and I am sending them by air to Canberra. Naturally, I am expressing full satisfaction with the work done to date, and I am making a strong point about your mapping work. Any censure that any Council member might feel like making would be directed against me, not you. I know that some Council members could be difficult; but others are completely fair-minded men who value my work highly. (All mention of the hymnal is, of course, "*out*").'[38]

Scherer was not entirely reassured. Soon he would write to the Institute about the maps. In a matter of months, he would not be working

---

[*]   McNally (1981: 135) notes that: 'Once, while in Central Australia on research for Adelaide University, Strehlow wrote to Scherer suggesting that, in order to make the map absolutely precise, he should make himself available to go to Central Australia and personally visit all the places which Strehlow had listed on three foolscap-sized pages attached to the letter. The pages contained 296 place-names.'

on the maps at all. Inside two years he was out of a job. The Institute was fed up with him, and Strehlow turned all his old compliments to Scherer inside out. Scherer by then was claiming some of the maps as his own, refusing to surrender the copies he had worked on until he had extracted a deal out of the Institute. The two Lutherans who had done so much friendly communing over the Aranda language had fallen out and, much to the consternation of the Institute, were locked in battle over the maps.

In a treacherous confidential report to McCarthy in November 1965, Strehlow explained that Scherer lacked ability with Aranda, and deplored his slow and inefficient work on the card system for the dictionary, especially his reliance on biblical names from the Aranda New Testament, and his inconsistent spelling of these names. Furthermore, Strehlow reported, Scherer had disregarded two of his express instructions about the dictionary cards, as a result of which they had to be sorted and done again—by Strehlow.[39]

In making this report, Strehlow seems not to have seen that it incriminated him as a very poor supervisor—a fact not lost on the Institute. As McCarthy told Berndt:

> The most astonishing and unfortunate aspect of the whole situation is that Strehlow calmly told me that all of the work Scherer did in three years on the Aranda dictionary is useless because the latter has not included the source reference with each word—Strehlow, of course, should have insisted that the entries were complete. We'll get very little, therefore, out of the three years' salary we paid Scherer whose re-appointment each year Strehlow recommended with an increase in salary, and never at any stage complained about Scherer's work—in fact, he reported that it was very good . . . It could be embarrassing if an investigation were made about expenditure on his assistants.[40]

In the end the dictionary that did come out of Strehlow's work—and the date of which seems to suggest that it was done by 1957, before Scherer was on the payroll—was 393 typed pages with about 3,160 entries. In the Aranda to English section, some of the entries are developed—as in the case of the Aranda for 'to instruct, rather thoroughly, to make wise,' followed by five more lines; or conscience, 'the good principle in one's body,' followed by seven lines—but most are not. There are simple entries, for, say, 'throat,' 'kiss,' 'to desire passionately,' 'to keep on building' and so forth, with little indication that Strehlow had been working with much of a system. In the English to Aranda, little effort was put into making linguistic links between the cultures: apart from 'love,' which has four entries, the briefest of meanings are given for 'sacred song,' 'song-verse' and 'story,' the matters at the heart of *Songs of Central Australia*. There is no entry for 'poetry,' for which the Aranda apparently did not have a word, a matter that passes without comment by Strehlow. Whatever merits the dictionary had or might have had, it was a long way from his grand notion of 'a poetic dictionary' absolutely essential for the proper translation of songs. This was the book that would list the poetical words under their roots and give the appropriate traditional glosses, thus revealing, Strehlow hoped, the archaic foundations of the poetic diction. Alas for this grandiose but thrilling project, which would have fertilised all aspects of his contribution to Australian poetics.

And alas, too, for critical transparency on Strehlow's part with regard to words that were at issue. There was, for instance, still the matter of defining *Altjira*, and its connection with Spencer and Gillen's term for the Dreaming. The Strehlows, recall, wanted to sever the Dreaming from any notion of 'dream.' Strehlow had been making much of this since 1932. But in his dictionary, his entry for 'dream' as a verb is *altjirarama*, and as a noun, *ankatja altjirarintja*. 'Dream' would clearly seem to be in the root of the term for *Altjira*. But in his entry for *Altjira* the entry simply says: 'Root meaning appears to be "eternal," "uncreated." It is a rare word, used in the Aranda sacred traditions mainly in set phrases, such as . . . *altjirana nambakala* (born out of eternity), *pmara altjira* (eternal home), etc.' Taking the entries for 'dream' and *Altjira* together, this is not an impressive address of the problem, and rather suggests that Strehlow was putting his dictionary to polemical purposes.

It might have been embarrassing, too, if the Institute had reflected on the fact that, despite Strehlow's condemnation of Scherer's Aranda, the pastor had been a considerable help as a Biblical translator for many years on the New Testament, not to mention the hymnal. The whole revision of perspective on Scherer had more to it than met the official eye.

To see what was happening, McCarthy had to take time out to visit Strehlow's office in Adelaide. There he had a secret meeting with Scherer—a meeting that incensed Strehlow because it was held 'behind a closed door.'[41] According to McCarthy he and Scherer had cleared up the situation, 'but then Strehlow insisted upon a legal document being drawn up to give him unqualified and unconditional rights to the use of the annotated maps.'[42]

Back in Canberra, McCarthy had to get legal advice about the maps. His letter to Berndt is about how one damn thing had led to another. 'No legal agreement can be reached on this matter; apparently the copyright or ownership can only be settled in a court. Now if Strehlow completes the work in two years for publication then one of Scherer's main objections will be removed—you remember he was willing to allow Strehlow five years in which to publish but he believed that we would be lucky if it eventuated in ten years! Strehlow has thus misled the Institute very badly for several years in this matter.'[43]

By this stage Scherer was claiming copyright on the outline maps he had supplied. The legal advice the Institute obtained was that the annotations on the maps—drawn from Strehlow's notebooks—belonged to Strehlow alone. The Institute finally suggested to Strehlow that he make his own outline maps and transfer the annotations to the new maps. They wanted to be supplied with a list of all the maps which he held 'on behalf of the Institute.' Beyond that, they regretted the situation that had arisen but felt that it was basically a matter between himself and Scherer.

What, though, *had* happened? Nothing in the official correspondence makes sense of what had so changed the fortunes of Scherer with regard to the maps. Nothing, that is, until the name of Kathleen Stuart begins to crop up.

Ward McNally, Strehlow's biographer, tells us that Strehlow met Kathleen Stuart—'an attractive woman of about thirty'—when she and her husband Donald moved from Perth to Adelaide towards the end of 1964. On Berndt's recommendation they contacted Strehlow, who had read one of Stuart's books and liked it. The couple came to dinner with Ted and Bertha. Other dinners followed. Strehlow helped Donald Stuart get a job as a groundsman at a bowling club and Kathleen a job teaching at a high school, and he undertook to coach her in English literature.

Strehlow's eldest son Theodor told McNally:

My father often picked up Kathleen Stuart at the caravan the family rented, and took her to his rooms at the University. On some of these occasions I was with him, getting a lift to the city. But I never went home with him; I was never sure of what time I would be returning home. I always assumed he took her back to the caravan park. On all the occasions I was present when he picked up Kathleen Stuart, my father seemed to treat her as a pupil. I didn't think anything of the arrangement until I heard that people around the University were talking.

Meanwhile Scherer was trying to go on with the maps, while seeking reassurance that he would get some credit for them. When, Scherer told McNally, he asked Strehlow directly about sharing the credit: 'Strehlow looked at me strangely for several seconds, then he said: "Well, Philip, I suppose we both own it. I'll have to make some provision for you, won't I?"' But Strehlow never did that, and avoided the topic afterwards. 'Finally, we had a row over it. He told me Kathleen Stuart was coming to work for him, and that she would finish it for him. He took the map from me then.'[44]

What could the Institute do with a situation like this? There is no reason to doubt the facts in McNally's account. The maps had become intractable trouble because they had become enmeshed in the emotional affairs of Strehlow, who seems to have been smitten like one possessed. When a man is in love, all creation—all that he has created—is a vitalising force and a direct measure of the world being *his.*

The 'audacity' of Scherer, Strehlow roared to the Institute. That someone in his position (such an underling), should go behind his back in such a way and make such a claim on his property![45]

But Strehlow in his new happiness had overlooked a simple thing. Scherer was a faithful married man who still looked at the world as a Lutheran pastor. Strehlow had hurt his friend; and the friend, as he worked away on the maps and saw Strehlow and Kathleen Stuart coming and going in the offices at the university, had every Christian reason in the world to judge the man harshly.

By contrast, the simple, wonderful fact for Strehlow was that his present had been ecstatically invaded by the experience of eternity we call love. Everything, for once, was in the glorious moment. He was experiencing what the Greeks called *Kairos,* and about which he had recently written as passionately as he had written about anything. Before we contemplate the potential pathos of a late middle-aged man throwing everything up for an attractive woman twenty years younger than his wife of three decades, let us glance at the metaphysical plain he was on, when he was writing at his best.

Maps (Eternal)

Kairos is fulfilled time, the moment of time which is invaded by eternity. But kairos is not perfect completion of time. To act and wait in the sense of kairos means to wait upon the invasion of the eternal and to act accordingly, not to wait and act as though the eternal were a fixed quantity which could be introduced into time, as a social structure which represents the end and goal of history for instance. The eternal is that which invades; it is not something tangible and objective. There are societies which are turned away from the eternal, which rest content in time and finiteness, and there are other societies which are turned towards the eternal and which express their forms and judgment which they have experienced as proceeding from it. But there are no societies that possess the eternal.[46]

The writer was the Protestant theologian Paul Tillich, whom Strehlow quotes in his 1964 paper later published as *Central Australian Religion*, which was his most important single paper in anthropology.* It was an essay that proved, to his colleagues who needed it, that he could do anthropology in some detail and not merely gloss the myths and songs. But what was neo-Christian theology doing in an exposition of Aranda religion?

The turgid subtitle of the paper, 'Personal Monototemism in a Poly-totemic Community,' flagged the more technical aspects of the topic: the connections he would make between the mythology in general, and the totemic sites, along with notions of ownership of song and ceremony connected with the sites. At one level he was revisiting the problem of individual ownership, first raised in *Aranda Traditions*, where

---

* 'Culture, Social Structure, and Environment in Aboriginal Central Australia,' published in 1965, was both longer and more systematic in its overview of geography, local knowledge, survival and emotional attachments to place, myths and kinship, but it is doggedly impersonal and less resonant overall. It is also, by the way, unusual for the credit it gives to the work of others, specifically Berndt and Elkin. Strehlow's fresh contribution is mainly linguistic, but even here he refrains overall from injecting much of himself into the paper, writing as dryly as the Berndts who were editing him for their *Aboriginal Man in Australia* (1965).

the argument happened to help justify the collection he was accumulating. At another level, he was revisiting the songs and the ceremonies on a very local totemic map—he mainly focused on the Ellery Creek area—with which he wanted to show the workings of what he called 'the eternal landscape.' And then, at still another level, he was tabling the topic of eternity in general, and developing that in a way that was remarkable.

Central Australian Religion is one of Strehlow's papers the reading of which becomes an uncanny experience. The feeling at first is of topics rather randomly brought together, linked by association almost, rather than any consistent thesis. The result is a sensation of dislocation, of encountering material in a serial form that is both familiar and unfamiliar, and where the argument never quite comes home. This is mainly because Strehlow never argues from theory; nor does he use concepts that seek to link belief systems with social structures or, if it comes to that, social structures with any analysis of material life. Rather, he moves from one realm to the other, from one richly descriptive moment in his essay to the other, wandering, so to speak, from one watering hole to the other, as if there is no map, or no map he is prepared to share.

At the same time, however, there is another aspect to the experience of reading his richer papers. Despite the above, his material even more strangely converges. The underlying feeling is that everything is actually connected to everything else. His essay is a thickly woven tapestry where it is impossible to unravel the material of one section without pulling at material somewhere else. In addition, once one part has been engaged at one level, it immediately offers itself as an emblem of another. Obviously, since the topic in this case is *Central Australian Religion*, the subject matter itself—a culture that has woven a seamless web of belief and ritual and social organisation—contributes to this reading experience. But there is more to it than that. Strehlow himself was becoming a writer who compulsively wove his personal experience into the framing of his discussion, and who was constantly responding to its ethnographic content as if some aspect of his own life depended on it. Nothing, with Strehlow, could be entirely impersonal.

Central Australian Religion is about, among other things, sex, the carnality at the heart of the most secret-sacred men's ceremonies. Strehlow goes into some detail about the kangaroo ceremony of Krantji, extensively treated in *Songs of Central Australia,* but here even more pointedly with regard to the sexual symbolism at the climax of the ritual. Strehlow describes what happens, a frank disclosure of which would lead to murder if a stranger happened upon the Aboriginal performance: the trangressional body would then be buried on the ceremonial ground. What Strehlow reveals is just as sensitive as the map he encloses a few pages on, which pinpoints the most sacred sites of the clan that has 'inalienable rights' to the land in that area, including the routes of the main ancestor beings: dancing women, carpet snakes, dingoes, rain, black hawk and honey ant. Thus, in various ways, he was choosing to expose the eternal landscape that was so secret-sacred to his Aboriginal friends (this in 1964, when most of them were still alive, and then again with its reprinting in 1978, when to do so was also a provocative, defiant act against his own profession as well).

His motives in 1964 seem to have been mainly polemical. With the sacred kangaroo he wanted to prove another person wrong: namely the German Freudian, Joseph Winthuis, who thought he had seen, in these men living in a state of nature, sexual symbolism unified around one basic concept of 'a single, august, incomparable, powerful, eternally fertile, Original Being (Urwesen).'[47] Strehlow wanted to rebut the monotheistic, and Eurocentric construction. And this he does. He also wanted to qualify the sexual focus of Winthuis—which he does by a light remark about the fellow going too far, like 'Roheim in his more exuberant moments.'[48] Strehlow wanted to stress the 'many sidedness of aboriginal religious thought.' He mentioned the 'survival motives' the Aranda would have appreciated for themselves. All well and good, except that overall Strehlow does not attempt to refute the general point about sexuality. He agreed that 'in large measure ' the sexual symbolism formed a 'considerable part of Central Australian sacred ritual.'

So the sexuality was there, desire informed the heart of the rituals; the religion with which he was so intimate was fundamentally about that. Still, the other thing that Strehlow wanted to enter as central to belief and ritual was not just 'survival,' but eternity. The whole rationale of the initiation ceremonies was to recreate the conditions that existed at the beginning of time. Precisely because the performers had re-created the sacred ground—with the ground painting, with their decorated shield—and then re-enacted, in good faith that they were the ancestor creatures themselves—all this was possible. 'The final scene, which was regarded as the climax and the most sacred act of the cycle, generally revealed the source of life itself at the *pmara kutata* whence the totemic ancestors had first emerged at the dawn of Time.'[49]

Strehlow goes on:

> It is clear from all of these instances that the great mystery revealed to
> the human totemites in the final acts of the ceremonial cycles was the
> eternal union, in an unbreakable embrace, of the separate male and
> female 'principles' which had always coexisted at each sacred site.
> Whereas human unions were only of a brief and transient nature, the
> supernatural union of the male and female 'principles' was the eternal
> and immutable. That was the reason why life continued to emanate
> from these all-important major sacred sites, and why they were called
> *pmara kutata*—a term which has been translated earlier as 'everlasting
> home.'[50]

There is no need to query Strehlow's anthropology to notice the over-tones of his language, evoking the passions of Christian mysticism. The sentence that takes us to Tillich is: 'During the performance of totemic ritual, transient Time and timeless Eternity became completely fused into a single Reality in the minds of the participants.' And then what follows Tillich's assertion that 'there are no societies that possess the eternal' is Strehlow's monumental claim: 'Before the invasion of this home country, the Central Australian totemite certainly believed that he "possessed the eternal" in his own lifetime.'

The rest of the paper grapples with the relationship between individuals—'self-centred persons'—'separate sparks of the life fire of individual supernatural beings'—and the community that held them together at the *pmara kutata*. Again, Strehlow is 'technical'—he presents his maps of totem sites and skin groups—but the embrace is more general, and designed to do more than merely appeal to the religious reader. After speaking of the 'death penalty,' and the 'high solemnity of the festival' he goes on to say:

> Every full-scale ceremonial festival was, in fact, regarded as an occasion
> when Time and Eternity became one, when the border line dividing
> visible human beings and invisible totemic ancestors became temporar-
> ily obliterated, and when in a sense, even the dead once more joined
> the company of the living: for the sacred stone and wooden tjurunga,
> which had been brought out of their sacred stones houses and which

were being stored temporarily on trees at the edge of the ceremonial ground, represented 'the other bodies' not only of all men and women who were still living in the [skin] section area, but also of those who had died.[51]

Strehlow's own visceral response to these elemental ceremonies remains masked. But there is a struggle going on. His awe comes through, and he was by then on record as saying he had 'overpowering' feelings of being face to face with such 'haunting, intricate rhythms' in the 'untamed' landscape. The wild, the savage—he withdrew from those terms, but he was prepared to say that these acts revealed to the Aranda their belief that 'Nature and Man shared the same Life.'[52] And that sharing was so palpably close, of course—with the blood and the fire, the nakedness and the sexual simulations, the sustaining of desire through the passionate duration of the ceremonial cycles—that a witness could not help but be aware of the dynamic possibility of somehow falling back into nature. Culture was displaying its timeless primitivism.

In time, too, Strehlow claimed that he had been to *all* the ceremonial festivals in the Aranda area between 1933 and 1975,[53] an astonishing claim, really, since other men were also shown many things by Aborigines, and since he was not, after all, a blood initiate—which is to say he had never surrendered to subincision in the hands of the senior Aboriginal men he revered. Still, here is the passion of his tremulous reports as witness, and as a witness who had often subtly solicited the performances, a kind of master of ceremonies. These too—his close witnessing, and empathetic sacred awe—are what press through the technical detail of his essay. As a result the reader is driven to feel that Strehlow wants to do something with his own sympathies, that he must in fact do something with them since he would not and could not join those pagan dances and songs.

What he does is sermonise. This is the most remarkable feature of the paper. Strehlow upholds Aborigines as an exemplary case of good human beings, from whom the 'Common Man' of the 'Modern Age' might learn. By 'Modern Man' Strehlow meant 'Secular Man'—the theme readers would meet at length when *Songs of Central Australia* was eventually published, an event still seven years off. Here he is taking his argument further than he had in his 'Final Summary.' He is proposing Aboriginal religion as a model reminder of 'that vital sense and deep conviction of contact with verities and values passionately believed to be eternal . . . For it was the Aborigines' sense of oneness with Eternity [that] made them more kindly, tolerant, and helpful towards their human fellows everywhere.' If there is a touch of fatuousness and vacuity in Strehlow's choice of phrasing that does not, for the moment, matter. The syncreticism of his special pleading is the important thing: 'in Central Australia the longing for the immortality of the *whole* human personality was as strong as anywhere else.'[54] They are Strehlow's italics, and fully indicative of his Christian gloss on the pagan yearnings. And all this, finally, allows him to give advice to anthropology itself, which had for too long seen its material as a study of 'dead museum specimens, abstract social theories, and neat, cold, and boring dissections of human institutions.'[55]

Strehlow's preaching is indeed the antithesis of what was neat and cold. On the basis of eternity, he wanted anthropology to be motivated not in order to gain 'fleeting academic honours' but to 'derive from their studies a fuller knowledge of spiritual concepts and norms of behaviour that could help their own fellows in their quest to evolve more enlightened ways of living together.'[56] He was referring, at an earthly level, to the Aboriginal attunement to environment: their powers of cooperation and survival in the desert. But he was also alluding above all to their metaphysical passion for eternity. In effect, he was exalting the pagan as a means of reviving what was of essence to the Christian.

The further implication was heretical and unsayable but it was there, like a snake by the fire of his own passion: it was that the blood ceremonies and sacrificial intent of the Central Australian religion were, under the banner of eternity, analogous to and of equal worth to Christianity. They were of equal worth because—before the 'collapse of the unique system'[57] to colonisation—the original totemite possessed the eternal in his own lifetime.

'All men are priests—with a difference,' he wrote of the dancers and singers on the sacred ground of their 'everlasting home.'[58] This again was polemical. Strehlow was rebutting the famous Sir James Frazer's dictum 'all men in Australia are magicians, but not one is a priest,' which was the Oxford mythicist's pompous way of saying that Aboriginal beliefs did not qualify as a higher religion. But it was more than polemic: Strehlow was affirming the daily spirituality of the Aboriginal men, and how they were all priests because of the nature of their spiritual inductions into integrated beliefs. And by saying so in the way that he did he was presenting himself as their supreme witness, a kind of proxy high priest in their own terms, a claim he meant for the moment and for eternity. In fact his dictionary had an entry for high priest (*Kinjinta prista*).

Thus, by 1964 Strehlow had declared himself, for those who could read him in the right way. He knew exactly where he was, metaphysically. It only remained to pull the threads of his writing together, and perhaps, out of that single-minded address, grasp some wholeness in his own life.

---

1 Richard Holmes, *Footsteps: Adventures of a Romantic Biographer* (London: Harper Collins, 1996), 211–12.

2 Julia Kristeva, *Black Sun: Depression and Melancholia* (New York: Columbia University Press, 1989), 9, 11. 'According to the classic psychoanalytic theory (Abraham, Freud, Melanie Klein), depression, like mourning, conceals an aggressiveness toward the lost object, thus revealing the ambivalence of the depressed person with respect to the object of mourning. "I love that object" is what that person seems to say about the lost object, "but even more so I hate it; because I love it, and in order not to lose it, I imbed it in myself; but because I hate it, that other within myself is a bad self, I am bad, I am non-existent, I shall kill myself." The complaint against oneself would therefore be a complaint against another, and putting oneself to death but a tragic disguise for massacring an other.'

3 John Morton, 1989, 'Mama, Papa, and the Space Between: Children, Sacred Objects, and Transitional Phenomena in Aboriginal Central Australia,' in *The Psychoanalytic Study of Society*, ed. L. Bryce Boyer and Simon Grolnich, vol. 14 (London: The Analytic Press, 1989), 191.

4 D.W. Winnicott, 'Transitional Objects and Transitional Phenomena,' in *Collected Papers* (London: Tavistock, 1958), 229.

5 Morton, 'Mama, Papa. and the Space Between,' 194. He is citing Carl Strehlow (1908, vol. II, at 80 and 82, and 1913, 3), and goes on to remark: 'Whether the *papa* was just a stick or proper *tjurunga* object was the main subject of the controversy between Strehlow and Spencer. The latter, denying the authenticity of Strehlow's account, gives in its place a different one more in line with Roheim's 1933 version.' That debate needs no resolution here, since my point is that for T.G.H. Strehlow, the psychic resonance of the *papa* and *tjurunga* must have been established by his father, who sold *tjurunga* while he collected them.

6 T.G.H. Strehlow, diary, 9 May 1965.

7 Jean Baudrillard, Jean, 'The System of Collecting,' in *The Cultures of Collecting*, ed. John Elsner and Roger Cardinal (Melbourne: Melbourne University Press, 1994), 10.

8 Ibid., 12.

9 Ibid., 17.

10 Report on Second Year of Fellowship: 1951 (undated).

11 Strehlow to Hohnen, 30 May 1950.

12 Strehlow to Hohnen, 2 July 1952 and 7 April 1953. In the 1953 letter Strehlow expressed a liking for Hohnen's suggestion that 50 per cent be added to the actual cost of the films to allow 'from this sum a sound contribution to be made to the natives.'

13 Rowe to Copeland, 4 August 1952.
14 Nadel to Rowe, 29 August 1952.
15 Hohnen to Strehlow, 3 May 1953.
16 Strehlow to Rowe, 23 November 1953.
17 Melville to Rowe, 22 December 1953..
18 Strehlow to Rowe, 10 January 1954.
19 Strehlow to Stanner, 5 May 1960.
20 Jacquie Lambert, 'History of the Australian Institute of Aboriginal Studies, 1959 –1990,' synopsis, 1993, unpublished, 2, 4, 6, 16.
21 Tim Rowse, 'The Collector as Outsider — T.G.H. Strehlow as "Public Intellectual,"' Strehlow Research Centre, *Occasional Paper 2* (October 1999): 92.
22 *Australian Aboriginal Studies: A Symposium of Papers Presented at the 1961 Research Conference*, ed. Helen Shiels (Melbourne: Oxford University Press, 1963), 248–51, 166–67.
23 Elkin to Strehlow, March 1962.
24 Strehlow to Elkin, 3 April 1962.
25 AIAS Minutes of Council Meeting for 5 and 8 March 1962.
26 Judy Inglis, principal administrative assistant, Interim Council, to Strehlow 4 May 1962.
27 McCarthy to Strehlow, 26 November 1964.
28 Interim Council meeting: extract of discussion on Strehlow, 13 December 1963.
29 Berndt to Elkin, 12 November 1963.
30 MacCarthy to Strehlow, 20 October 1969.
31 Strehlow, report to AIAS of field trip, May 1964.
32 Strehlow: report to AIAS of field trip, June–September 1964.
33 Ibid.
34 Strehlow to Boydell, AIAS, August 1964.
35 For more on this dilemma as to the designation of maps see Peter Sutton, *Country: Aboriginal Boundaries and Land Ownership in Australia* (Canberra: Aboriginal History, 1995), and 'Icons of Country: Topographic Representations in Classical Aboriginal Traditions,' in *The History of Cartography*, vol. 2.3, *Cartography in the Traditional African, American, Arctic, Australian, and Pacific Societies*, ed. David Woodward and G. Malcolm Lewis (Chicago: Chicago University Press, 1988). In the latter Sutton writes: 'One of the salient differences between Aboriginal icons and the kind of Aboriginal maps drawn to explain political geography to ethnologists, perhaps until very recently when such ethnological maps have been used in land claims contested by rival groups, has been their difference of emotional temperature. The icons carry the baggage of highly charged local inter-group relations, the sentiment of attachment to home country . . . and the profound emotional meanings that mythic events have for the unconscious. Ethnological maps, whether drawn by Aborigines or others, tend to be less multidimensional and their emotional connotations tend to be more political than spiritual.' The argument tends to run the other way in David Turnbull, *Masons, Tricksters and Cartographers* (Amsterdam: Harwood Academic Publishers, 2000), 32–38.
36 Scherer to Strehlow, 30 July 1965, Scherer Papers [SP].
37 Strehlow to Scherer, 4 August 1965, SP.
38 Ibid.
39 Strehlow to McCarthy, 1 November 1965, SP.
40 McCarthy to Berndt, 17 March 1967.
41 Strehlow to Boydell, 15 February 1967.
42 McCarthy to Berndt, 17 February 1967.
43 Ibid.

44 Ward McNally, *Aborigines, Artefacts and Anguish* (Adelaide: Lutheran Publishing House, 1981), 136–37.
45 Strehlow to Boydell, 15 February 1967.
46 T.G.H. Strehlow, *Central Australian Religion* [1964] (Bedford Park, S.A.: Australian Association for the Study of Religion, 1978), 34.
47 Ibid., 31.
48 Ibid., 60.
49 Ibid., 30.
50 Ibid., 33.
51 Ibid., 43–44.
52 T.G.H. Strehlow, 'Witnessing Ceremonies,' ABC radio broadcast, 9 August 1952.
53 The Alice Springs Aboriginal Land Rights, 1975, unpublished, 14ff.
54 Ibid., 48.
55 Ibid., 53.
56 Ibid., 53.
57 Ibid., 49.
58 Ibid., 39.

2 The New Life

His Poem Called Journey to Horseshoe Bend

'SUFFERING IS THE means by which we exist,' Oscar Wilde wrote in that letter of remonstration and affirmation that came to be his essay *De Profundis*: 'it is the only means by which we become conscious of existence, and the remembrance of suffering in the past is necessary to us as the warrant, the evidence of our continued identity . . . as though my life, whatever it had seemed to myself and to others, had all the while been a real Symphony of Sorrow, passing through its rhythmically-linked movements to its certain resolution, with that inimitableness that in Art characterises the treatment of every great theme.'[1]

It was a grand statement, even more grandly gardened from the life: sentence by sentence Wilde lays his heart bare, too bare, some would say (as they would of Strehlow's or Malinowski's diaries), but in their cadence and generosity of spirit, in their pathos and faith, in their firm beauty of utterance, they become as they are read an object lesson in that 'symphony' itself. Wilde was writing from the conviction that the scandal that had put him in prison was truly ruinous, and despite the risk of sounding self-pitying, which he surely was, he continued to weave his sentences, shape his paragraphs, and complete the pages of his regulation prison paper in a way that was, if nothing else, artfully good and largely true.

He was issuing forth, flowing from the music that his incarceration had hidden: that *suffering is one long moment*. That truth, when it applies to any life, is problematic. How on earth to unfold its nature without the voice running down, as well as the tolerance of the listener? The doggedness of suffering is an aesthetic difficulty, as writers and readers of diaries know too well; but Strehlow, it seems, did not know very well at all. Wilde's letter is immensely long—it is tempting to say as long as Strehlow's unpublished 'Land of Altjira'—but that would be too unfair to Strehlow. Better to say that the men shared a profound sense of injustice, betrayal, loss, and the task of transfiguring an intractable sorrow. Wilde was of the conviction that only art, the Symphony of Sorrow, could do so; and he thought that of all the arts, literature with its 'subtlety of nuances, of suggestions, of strange perspectives,' would do so best, for 'Modern life is complex and relative.'[2] Literature could rise to the complex and the relative.

It was a high Romantic position, and it was one that Strehlow was able to fully adopt, at last, in 1966. He had fallen ill with peritonitis and was in a critical condition for a day and a night. The collapse confined him to the Wakefield Street Hospital for some time and then to weeks of convalescence at home. Loved ones rallied. To his pleasant surprise, even colleagues at the Institute sent him their sympathies, and one detects in Strehlow's note of thanks to McCarthy that he was deeply touched, that a part of him was capable of registering people as worthy of trust.

His brush with death had another effect. It spurred him on to write the book that would enshrine a memory of his childhood, the now famous *Journey to Horseshoe Bend*. He composed quickly—long adjectival sentences that were to give his editors some trouble when the manuscript was typed up. He had finished the first handwritten draft by 12 June, six days after his 59th birthday, and the typed version was finished and revised by October. It was to be his first book published since 1947.

It is a complicated text emotionally, as well as a landmark in Australian literature for the way it so extensively connects topography with Aboriginal myth. In its psychological and cultural reach, it is a major act of recovery. This is the book in which Strehlow most successfully and self-consciously takes possession of his past, including his Aboriginal understandings. The latter make one line of the narrative. The other is the story of his father's life and death. Both lines had of course been in him for many years (his father's for all his life). Writing these two lines into the one book would be his task: it was the *conjunction* of his father's Christianity with Aboriginal lore that made his book unique. Strehlow was the celebrant whose project it was to bring the two spheres into alliance, because that marriage, if it could be made, constituted his constellation.

He had begun his story earlier on, very much earlier if his diaries are read as rehearsals, which so often they were. In his personal diaries, of course, this was not necessarily the case: they still stand as confessional ventings, highly pitched bouts with himself, as well as a sense of himself as the other reader there to witness his suffering. The note of defensiveness, of pathos and of indignation, in those private diaries, also make them feel less private than they might, but they are nonetheless of the closet, written with the pen in-turned. And yet the pen, with Strehlow, always has a split nib: while one keeps the reader in tune with his private self, the other leads the reader out into the field of his work, and in fact to the field diary itself. This was especially the case in the mid-thirties, when an interweaving began to take place in his writings, and what was recorded about the work in the field resonated in his closely felt thoughts and feelings, and vice versa. His entries were becoming almost full dress rehearsals for fully coming out as a writer.

As his diary carried him through the years, it was written with the public gaze increasingly in view. It is 'intended to be not a private but an official diary,' he told himself in 1962, and 'shows how much I am prepared to admit, not merely to myself, but to others, tonight.'[3] He is passing his diary across the table. It is an act of confidence, at 'night.' But the sharing becomes even more considered by 1964, when he wrote to his colleagues in Adelaide: 'You have noticed how very detailed my diary is—I know. Years ago I used to write only brief entries. Today I know that I am recording *the sunset of an age* that will never return—every act that I see is being performed for the last time, and the men who are with me have no successors. When they die, they will take all their knowledge to the grave with them—except that part which I have recorded. Hence I am writing down everything in full detail, so as to give the clearest picture of an age and of a culture that no one else but I have been privileged to witness.'[4]

This was in fact not true. His early diary entries were seldom brief, and the later entries are not, in any case, about the Aranda so much as himself: the field notebooks contain myths and songs rather than his diary. But he has made the necessary disclaimer of privacy. By the mid-sixties he had come to feel that everything he wrote was of moment, that his private and his public writings would cohere, one way or the other, in the interests of posterity's knowledge of the dying culture to which he had been bearing witness.

He first came out in 1957, when he drafted his autobiography, 'Land of Altjira,' a text that became, even though unpublished, a benchmark of his worth as *ingkata*.

Now with that done, and himself an elder, he sat up to write in 1966 what was designed, at every level, to personally transfigure, to turn and return, everything around his unhappy solitary self in comprehensive ways: it was the symphony he had been trying to write in various ways—in diaries, in letters, in the autobiographical sketch, perhaps even in his diaries as a boy, if they could be found, for almost as long as he had been writing. And the writing was now everything: the greater truth was to be found in the art, the literature, rather than the life. Or to put this in a less Wildeish way: having endured the doggedness of Strehlow's suffering untransformed, it is now possible to see that some truth claims in *Horseshoe Bend* are truths in music, rather than truths of life.

The story of his father's death has been recounted already. In its sequence and tone it has the ring of truth, both as chronology and psychology. The boy idealised the father, even as he felt oedipally deprived of him. He exalted the authority of his father as a Christian, even as his father was losing his Christian faith. But that charge, that his father *did* have a crisis of faith, is dubious. It is, for one thing, out of character with the pastor's life and strength of mind. A large, sick man cries out in the wilderness as he is crippled with pain. The man is angry, he feels an injustice; he speaks out, in private, to his loving wife. This does not constitute a crisis of faith.[5] It is, however, easy to imagine it making a terrible impression on a young Christian son in the fold. And it is even easier—now that we have travelled so far with Strehlow on his own journey—to see that his own tests of faith are a part of his story. He was the one who cried out at Horseshoe Bend in 1933, heartbroken by Sheila; then again with his young wife at Piltardi Rockhole in 1935. Thereafter his sorrows went underground to an extent: he does not cry out as a Christian, but rather seems to have lapsed in his churchgoing and focused instead on the place of eternity in the cultural scheme of things. If anyone over the years has shown signs of creaking faith, of faith tested, or of enduring the barrenness of modernity, it had been Strehlow rather than his father. His own condition composed a music of doubt for the story of his father.

At the same time he exalted his father as *ingkata*—'a rock plate' like an ancestor creature—if only to usurp that Aboriginal authority, which he successfully did. In the end, therefore, the story of the father's death serves the purpose of resurrecting the son as the authority over the Calvary journey through the Land of Eternity: a double victory for the son, writ large. And so on: we have seen enough of that. Now, from the vantage point of Strehlow's life between 1922 and 1967 (when he finished his final draft of *Journey to Horseshoe Bend*), we have a sense not only of his book's coherence but its emotional truth to the life: the way its music has come in fact to determine the life. The writing that Strehlow drew out of himself as he was recovering from his mortal shock in 1967 was acutely personal mythology. It was both corrective and a supra–claim, a dream story of his own, his symphony of symphonies.

There was, most fundamentally, his appropriation of the Aboriginal mythology for the purposes of his own story. Not that the myths did not exist in their own right: but he would tell them in his way, writing them into his movement through the country, harnessing them to his psychic purposes. The Aboriginal stories in *Journey to Horseshoe Bend* are about revenge killing, sexual misconduct, the invention of death, vengeful mothers, stolen sons, fire and rain. Themes of 'hate, revenge and death,' as Strehlow told his diary, when he was rehearsing his narrative in 1953. A more elemental list is hard to imagine, and Strehlow stages the myths to maximum theatrical effect.

At Irbmangkara or Running Waters, where the Finke swells into one of the most fertile places in the region, Strehlow tells of a site fecund with legend: duck, cormorant, fish, creatures of all kinds had their dreamings there, but the narrative he chooses to expand upon is a bloody one, a revenge killing, an actual massacre about 50 years earlier. A young initiate had committed sacrilege and had to be punished, and Strehlow's saga of what follows goes on for many pages. It is as if he can only begin the story of his father's journey after a lengthy stay with a story about the law, where fathers must contest with sons about succession. The savagery of that contest was much laid out in the myths recounted in his earlier book, *Aranda Traditions*, written when he was under the sway of Freud's *Totem and Taboo*, and here, in a less theoretical way, are some of its grisly ramifications. Then we move on.

When they reach Henbury, Theo is separated from his parents. The buggy goes on alone, and he will go with the van by a different route, escorted by three Aboriginal companions—Jakobus and Njitiaka, and his wife Lornie. He walks barefoot at night, through the relentless Britannia Sandhills, with 'their haunting loneliness . . . and brooding moonlit sandhills' and where the spectre shapes—the iliaka njemba that scared him so much as a boy—are in every shadow. When they emerge from the sandhills they pass several waterholes that are key ceremonial sites, and the stories attached to them are recounted by reference to such details as stolen fledgling eagles and their 'swooping, screaming pouncing parents'; an emu sire that opens his chest to pour his 'very life blood' on to the ground; bird men who cast dark spells over the ground; and the fish ancestress who could turn into a devouring woman and who is stabbed by the great crayfish ancestor.[6]

From Idracowra (after the betrayal scene with his mother, and his father's spiritual ordeal with the Book of Job) they travel on, past the rain totem site of Mborawatua. The buggy is still travelling ahead. Mborawatua is a place that offers the relief of rain, but alas, they are in marshy country. With the fluids pouring forth from her body, one of the rain ancestresses created a boggy swamp into which sank the two male kangaroo ancestors, also possessed with the power of making rain. Then they come to the tracks of sandhill wallabies, and the trails once carved by the feet of dancing women. There is some animation in this telling, but still it does not rain: the rain ancestresses have not fully woken from their sleep.

They reach the Land of Death. 'The whole country looked like a forbidding desert gripped in the bony clutch of death' Strehlow announces, before tabling the legend.[7] They are some miles south of Idracowra, on the sandy and rocky plain that forms the meander of the Finke as it winds down to Horseshoe Bend. Here the Ntjikantja brothers, twins, were angry with their mother, a shell-parrot woman who had become pregnant from the winds blowing upon her. Once her two boys were born they turned into snakes, the greenish black venomous ilbaralea species. The mother left the boys to fend for themselves, and the abandoned ones grew quickly into men. 'When the mother finally returned to the men, she swooped down from the sky like a bird, changed back to the shape of a woman, and offered one of her breasts to her sons. The younger brother, incensed at having been abandoned at birth, closed his mouth around her breast, turned into a snake and bit it off.'

The rest of the story turns on the events generated by the enraged vengeful mother. Strehlow recounts it with relish. This legend is the fullest in the book, the most dramatically rendered. The mother calls up an avenging party: reformed as a woman, she offers herself to them to give them strength against her sons. But the sons offer a challenge to the other men. 'Let each man stab his spear into the ground and attempt to climb up on it into the sky.' The elder brother goes up into the sky effortlessly when his spear turns into a snake. The younger one goes up by taking the spear between his legs. 'Blazing like two bright stars, the brothers now pronounced the curse that brought Death into the world . . . "You miserable death-doomed wretches, all of you must die now! You may never return from the earth while you are living, and you may never return after you have died!"'[8]

The name of the place where this happened was secret, Strehlow writes, then he seems to name it in the next paragraph. He passed by it during the day. His father, he notes, must have gone by at night 'somewhere about midnight.'

Later on, though, further on, there was the cone-shaped mountain called Kngeitnama, which meant, 'the Father is standing.' It too was a rain-making place, and still it has not rained, and—Strehlow need hardly say it—his father is not yet dead.

Finally Theo stumbles into Horseshoe Bend. There are other legends to tell, the narrative of them has become more dense all the way, and the first that needs to be told—as if he has just opened his eyes the next morning—are stories of heat and of fire. The main story is linked to Pot' Arugutja, the clifftop site north of the hotel. The ntjiri women, two female chiefs, have a nephew with a skin paler than usual. This is the first story, remember, that Strehlow felt like writing out in any full way, when he did so for Tindale back in 1933: for initiation the boy goes off to the fire totem ancestors at Rumbuntja, men with coal black bodies. The Rumbuntja men do not give the boy back. They return with the darker boy, keeping the pale one. In rage, the mother poisons them, and when all the men are dead the two women 'bore themselves triumphantly, and the brilliant red and black cockatoo feathers which rose high from their heads symbolised the flowering tufts of ntjira grass that sprouted everywhere they went.' Where the Rumbuntja men had vomited were heaps of black pebbles, stones that might receive the charms for warmth needed during a freezing spell in mid-winter.[9]

As if this is not enough, Strehlow once again mentions the plight of a mythic offspring, and the neglect and abandonment of young boys. He then comes to the stories about fire.

This main place is Mbalka. Strehlow gives us a most vivid paragraph about a fire, a firestorm that razes the country all around. It is one of primal destruction, after which the pink and the red feathers of the parrots and cockatoos were the 'colour of the leaping flames, the black feathers of the dead bodies of the charred birds, the grey feathers the ashes of birds totally consumed by the blaze.'[10]

Mbalka, as a matter of topography, is south of the hotel: the travellers have not gone that far. But for the purposes of his narrative, Strehlow has the fire that sets the scene for his father's purgatorial end. Mbalka is the flourish that enables Strehlow to mention 'the constant threat of heat and fire over the Horseshoe Bend country,' and to emphasise that all the major Aranda totems 'were of a kind that increased the afflictions of mankind.'

Afflictions of the landscape, afflictions as they were sung in the Aranda culture—yes. But at the same time, in Strehlow's symphonic recounting, afflictions inimitably linked with his sense of himself then, and especially now: now that he had lived through such sorrow towards his present composition.

Relocating the Spear to Heaven

Two crucial returns seem to have created within him the conditions for his creative biographical feat of 1967. He had been coming and going from the whole area along the Lower Finke, but what preoccupied him was the Land of Death, where there was to be found, for those who knew where to look, the secret-sacred ceremonial site for the snake story of Uralterinja. In the myth story, which he had first recorded in 1933, as he came and went from the venomous lack of love of Sheila, his false darling at the hotel, the two poisonous snakes, two boys, twins, flee from the avenging party organised by their vengeful mother with whom they have had incestuous relations: these are the boys who ascend to the sky, defeating and cursing their avengers and bringing the curse of death upon the place, the precise location of which remained secret even to most of the local population. In 1933, Strehlow was shown the place by senior men responsible for the site; he had mapped it, and taken the song and the story. At that time he was saturated with his sense of loss of Sheila, and darkened, though he does not say much to his diary, by the memory of his father who passed that way at midnight, on the way to his death at the hotel.

He was back there in 1936. He has his old maps, he has Tom Ljonga, and he has Bertha with him. In the presence of his new wife he writes nothing about Sheila, who must have still haunted the place. He writes a few words about his father, words of rehearsal, they turned out to be, but he worries at length about the fact that he cannot relocate the precise sacred site of Uralterinja. The faithful Tom can only do his best as they walk about on the dry, pebbly ground—the 'accursed ground' (he wrote much later) with the flat-topped mountains in view:

> After passing Uralterinja we went up the water course leading up to the right. Soon we halted and went to the left over some stone hills, finally reaching the *pmara kutata* . . . Only Tom knew the spot, the other two being ignorant of it; and Tom, too, had merely been here once: the old chief of this district told him of how to locate the site just before he died, and Tom had to find the site for himself. The place cannot be seen except from a few yards away. It is on top of a stone hill, from where you can see a stone cluster plainly about a mile to the east. A heap of black iron stones . . . had been arranged here in a semi circle, all standing up . . . in the middle stood two smaller white stones . . . We all went to the spot, armed with sticks, hit a dry bush at the edge and then walked completely around the spot before we halted and had all explained to us.[11]

Different trips brought different facets of things alive, but no trip was as full of information as the first. The old men were dying, or their memories were fading in a way that Strehlow's notebooks were not. And that was the momentous realisation in 1953, when he went back again, when he had to search, yet again, for the precise location of the key place of the myth that brought death into the country. This time, without Ljonga, and without Bertha, from whom he was estranged, and guiltily disconnected, the whole place flooded the middle-aged, professionally disgruntled Strehlow with a sense of misfortune. 'Faced by Destiny, even Faith, Hope and Love must die. Destiny is stronger than the strength of the strongest man; and there are events which can crush all the idealism of youth. The waters of the mighty Finke have dashed themselves in vain against the cliffs of Horseshoe Bend. The painted cliffs of Horseshoe Bend cast mighty shadows—there is no corner of the earth where they cannot reach me.'[12]

But he still walked round and round looking for the place where the Ntjikantja twins ascended into the sky, pulling their spear up with them, and becoming thereafter the two Magellan Clouds to be seen brightly shining near the Milky Way. In his diary Strehlow explains— as if to justify his preoccupation with the invention of death and the unusual return to the heavens (as distinct from the earth)—that he wants to find the place again in order to photograph it. More particularly, he wanted to do so in Kodachrome, with the splendid Leica camera given to him by his sister Martha. And this he does, at last, after his helpers wander around for two days. He cleans up the site, and takes a picture of unforgettable power, which will be, as destiny will have it, a component of his downfall. But at that moment, in 1953, the return to the death site gives him an opportunity to do something rather wonderful by way of return to the place and the Aboriginal men. It is an act of gift-giving—of, if you like, restitution—which pleases him and seems to lighten some of the mighty shadows.

The men with him have found the *tjurunga* of the place. They have taken them out of their storehouse—a place that Strehlow had been to in 1933, along with Watua, but they did not belong to them directly, or rather, knowledgeably. Strehlow could help. 'We took out the *tjurunga* which were showing signs of damage from many rains. With the aid of my diary I gave out the old sacred verses that belonged to them, while my companions greased and redochred them.'

'I took out those wooden *tjurunga* which had been promised by W twenty years earlier: they still had my tabs on them.' Strehlow was to keep these *tjurunga*, as was his right, he felt.* As for the myth, it was, he added, 'once well known . . . not only among the Southern Aranda, but also among the Loritja Matuntara and the Andekerinja. Now its memory lived on only in my notebooks and photography.'[13]

Its memory lived on only in my notebooks and photography. That he had in the fullness of time become the repository of the myth of the Land of Death, and then been able to return this song, or parts of it, to men at the sacred site, was the necessary prelude to the full orchestration of his responsibilities in *Journey to Horseshoe Bend*. 'It is now one hour before sunset,' he went on. 'After that will come, not twilight, but the sudden onset of a true Australian night,—a night of complete oblivion.'

---

*   It is, however, not at all clear that W had promised them; rather to the contrary if Strehlow's diary entry at the time is considered (see 'Heartbreak and Prowess,' above).

By 1967 there was an immense question before Strehlow as a writer. How to contend with his own 'mighty shadows' of Horseshoe Bend? How to resist a 'true Australian night'?

Holy Family

Strehlow's answer lay in the romantic interfusions of *Journey to Horseshoe Bend*. The Aboriginal appropriations are the great groundswell of Strehlow's symphony. They issue in rain and fire, the archaic powers of destruction and rejuvenation, and they reveal amongst hell-fire, the wrong boy, the right boy. Over and above this there are other movements in the text, orchestrations in perfect pitch that pertain to the white settlers of the Centre, and the great theme, as Wilde would have said, of Desire. There are two other embraces enacted by Strehlow's narrative, two ways in which he was compelled to transfigure his history into myth.

There were, first of all, the 'tough bush people' of Central Australia, the men and women, with so many of whom, to judge from his diaries, as well as in his references in 'Land of Altjira,' he often had such a troubled relationship. There is little of that in *Journey to Horseshoe Bend*. The racism, the brutality, the sexual folly and cunning, the ignorant chauvinisms, and the self-interested treachery that had him labelled as a Nazi—all that has been subsumed by another picture altogether. Instead, there are glowing portraits of the pioneer settlers at Henbury, Idracowra and Horseshoe Bend, stories of their risk-taking and hard work, their investments of time and money, their stoicism and their generosity of spirit. The dark side of the frontier has been considerably brightened up, and often fits the Australian frontiersmen's best view of himself. Strehlow uses the mission's old friend Bob Buck, the man who gave him his donkey, to call the tune. 'As you know, Mr Strehlow,' Buck says to the pastor, 'us tough bush people in these parts always had an unwritten law of mateship and that law says that every man must help everyone else in trouble, never mind whether the poor bugger's been his pal or his enemy . . . all them nasty Southerners are alike under the skin—they don't know what mateship is. They're only interested in squeezing the last penny and the last ounce of sweat out of whoever works for them; and then they kick him out into the bloody gutter and spit on him, after he's no more use to them.'

Ironically, Strehlow was composing these words for Bob Buck just as other workers, the Aborigines of the cattle stations, were about to be kicked into the gutter as a result of the 1967 Equal Wages case which made them too expensive to employ. This too was outside the orbit of *Journey to Horseshoe Bend*, which strangely avoids the grinding economic realities Strehlow knew so well as a patrol officer, even though he writes passionately and discursively about the murderous patrols of Constable Willshire, whose job it was to make the land safe for cattle. The actual social life of Aborigines, especially the modern period of their destitution—the thirties when welfare policies were racist and failing, and also in the forties, when the assimilation policy tried to swallow blatant racisms in a rhetoric of welfarism—tend to be eclipsed by mythmaking. Strehlow stresses the good relationships between station owners and their native workers, and how the bad old days gave way to practical reconciliation: "im good fella boss, quite man altogether' the 'dark employees' were able to say of Allan Breaden at Idracowra station—a quotation that perfectly fits Strehlow's general purposes.

And then, on top of all this, the reader gets—for the first time in Strehlow's writing—a warm embrace of the region's erotic history. This too is a reversal, a plunge into vivid revision on Strehlow's part, and even more astonishingly, with regard to the 'dark feminine attractions of Central Australia,' the reviled Willshire is cited as confirmation that: 'Men would not remain many years in a country like this if there were no women, and perhaps the Almighty meant them for use as He has placed them wherever the pioneers go.'[14] Here, once again, the dark side of the picture, which was such a nightmare to him when he was on patrol and in pursuit of lustful bushmen with Aboriginal girls, has gone. In its place is a wry, worldly account of social realities, told in a way that creates in the reader's mind a model of carnal union between the races, where bygones can be bygones and intimacy between white men and black women perhaps have a dignified future. A hint of this acceptance is given by reference to Bob Buck, whose sexual liaisons with Aboriginal women were well known and, Strehlow says, accepted by his father. With regard to Buck's sexual predilections and conduct, a very different kind of story could also be told,* but that is not Strehlow's wish. Then, in the most resonant way, he sites his promiscegenation tale at his own sacred site: Horseshoe Bend. This is what he has to say about the household at the hotel.

---

* See for instance my passages about Buck as the exemplary bastard from the bush, a man who joked about the connection between the genitals of Aboriginal girls and his bush knife (Hill 1994: 54–57).

The scene—the *mise-en-scène*, really—takes place after his father's death. The focus is on Gus Elliot as patriarch—the middle-aged but once young adventurer who had come to the Centre in the early days of the mission. He had been as far west as Mount Liebig as a prospective cattleman and had settled for a time at the first Glen Helen station, just north of Japalpa, before taking up at Horseshoe Bend. Along the way he had a half-caste son called after him: the Aboriginal Gus Elliot was brought up at Hermannsburg and later christened Michael. Now, in the household of the hotel there are two half-caste 'kitchen women,' Lil and Victoria. Lil was Elliot's companion before he married the beautiful, athletic Ruby, who was more than twenty years his junior, closer to the age of the black women.

In Strehlow's account, Ruby is telling the story to Frieda, 'drawing her into the company of the tea party at least as a listener, so that her mind would be taken off her overwhelming sense of loss.' Ruby began by telling Frieda that Victoria and Lil had spoken with deep affection not only of the Reverend Strehlow but also of his wife. Strehlow: 'From these tales it had become evident that if Strehlow had come to be accepted as the aboriginal father figure at Hermannsburg, then his wife had long since come to fill the role of the great mother at his side. A shy flush came over Mrs Strehlow's wan and care-lined face.' Strehlow goes on:

Mrs Strehlow had learned about the struggles that Mrs Elliot herself had faced when she first arrived at Horseshoe Bend as Gus Elliot's girl bride. Lil, the gentle and kindly, soft-eyed woman who had borne Gus three sons and a daughter, had been most indignant at being displaced from her honoured position in the Elliot household by the arrival of the young 'white kwiai,' who had, in addition, insisted that Lil's children— some of whom were much the same age as the new Mrs Elliot—should change their surname from that of their father to that of their mother. The fiery-tempered and straight-speaking Victoria had taken Lil's part with rebellious vigour; and the dark stockmen had sullenly refused for a considerable time to accept the change in the names of their lighter-coloured mates from Bert, Sonny, and Jimmy Elliot to Bert, Sonny, and Jimmy Swan. But in the end Mrs Elliot had become accepted as the new white mistress of Horseshoe Bend; and both Victoria and Lil had been so won over by her kindness to the whole dark population that they had not only dropped their enmity towards her, but had come to treat her as a daughter who had to be helped and protected in the harsh land where she had made her new home. Both Victoria and Lil had had their three-quarter white daughters taken from them and sent south for their education. Victoria had in this way lost her two daughters Dolly and Florrie, and Lil her daughter Millie; and neither mother had ever become completely reconciled to her bereavement. Both women still hoped that the time might come when they should at least be able to set their eyes once more on their grown-up daughters. In the meantime the 'young white kwiai' had become a kind of daughter-substitute. The bond of affection that now existed between Mrs Elliot, Victoria, and Lil had a strength that was as admirable as it was touching: perhaps it was only Central Australia that could have united in such perfect accord three women whom social forces and influences in the more civilised South would have turned into lifelong antagonists.[15]

It is a galvanising passage, not least because the barbaric removal of Victoria and Lil's children—a loss with which they had never 'completely become reconciled'—is both acknowledged and so quickly passed over. Strehlow disliked such policies and simply does not want to deal with them here. He needs 'Victoria and Lil' to serve his own mythic purposes: to expound, to air, to uphold a brave idea of a family, one united by a perfect accord between two races and where the mothers of both races are at one with their men, or rather their white patriarch, in loving care of their children of the desert. As a child of the desert himself, he renders Lil and Victoria as his sisters. Indeed, a most resonant photograph of Strehlow's childhood, an image of metaphoric power, shows Theo rocking the cradle of an Aboriginal baby called Victoria (see back cover photograph). She is very possibly the Victoria of the perfect domestic accord mentioned above. From the image one is irresistibly drawn to saying: back then, in the years Theo was cradled in Aranda, his impulse was to nurse his Aboriginal sisters into an intimate domesticated life on the frontier.

And there is something else in the air of the passage above. There is an embrace of the idea of Lil and Victoria as paramours. The romantic picture he had given of the big-hearted rough bushmen made them the natural lovers of the Lils and the Victorias, 'the dark female beauties of Central Australia.' And since these men had so lovingly taken in his sick father, they are in effect kin to him; uncles and cousins and older brothers. They may love the dark beauties, so why not him, especially since he had won his stripes as a bushman? Eros inhabits Strehlow's picture of perfect accord. And only 'Central Australia' could do this, finally: not the 'more civilized South.' Typically with Strehlow names phase into landscape: love issues to and from the home place, like nectar at the *pmara kutata*. And so in one long run of elisions, in a river of links under the open sky of desire, with no wish eclipsed, Strehlow lets himself envisage a kind of holy family under the happy Australian sun.

We can see something else now. This is as bright as the Central Australian moon. The Ruby Elliot of *Journey to Horseshoe Bend* is mythic in more ways than one. She has been rendered as the classic bush heroine, obviously. She rode all night, she carried the storm lanterns, she led his ailing father into the shelter of the hotel at Horseshoe Bend. That is one thing. A beauty she may have been—and was, to judge from the photographs—and the boy that was Theo may well have been smitten by her in 1922. But he did not say that in his early diaries. Nor did he say so, specifically, when he was back at the Bend in 1933, or when he returned at any other time. There are no reveries of Ruby at all. The truth, as we know almost too well, after intruding upon his wretched inscribing, was his love of Ruby's pretty daughter, Sheila. In *Journey to Horseshoe Bend* Strehlow displaced all of his passion for Sheila into the figure of Ruby. The glorification of Ruby was his secret way of returning to the love of his life.

Sheila is briefly mentioned in the book. She comes into the story a few lines after the dream of 'perfect accord' between women. 'When Sheila was born, no one could be more proud of the baby than they were—they treated her like their own child and they couldn't fuss enough around me.' The speaker is Ruby, telling Frieda how it was that Lil and Victoria had mothered her baby white girl. Strehlow's holy family now has a very special glow. For Ruby's logic places her daughter close to Theo in a special way. They both have two sets of mothers: their white mothers by blood and black mothers by birth place. They might as well be brother and sister, siblings of the desert. This mythic truth was what Strehlow had wanted to cry out for so long: that they were according to place profoundly doubled, as eternally linked as twins.

Strehlow was in most ways the least conscious of writers. The underground streams of *Journey to Horseshoe Bend* are exactly that: underground, and streams—a movement of desire that crisscrosses large amounts of country unseen, and which converges at surprising points. Sometimes the movement is quite deep: witness how long it has taken him to put Sheila's name in print; and then to do so slyly, as if her presence has never been paramount to him. At other points he is engagingly and innocently self-revealing, as when he mentions that when older Gus Elliot married his much younger new bride 'it seemed to have rejuvenated him and given him the freshness and the vigour of a young man.'[16]

These lines, like all of the text, were composed as Strehlow was standing up out of the sick bed to become strong. He had mentioned Sheila, his first love, as he was about to abandon the girl he had instead married. He gazed back at Gus Elliot, Sheila's carnally liberated father, the free lover of the black girls, as he was about to embark upon a new life with a much younger, dark-haired beauty of his own. That is one of the wonderful aspects of *Journey to Horseshoe Bend*. Its slippages from the realm of factual consistency hardly matter as the writing, the narrative art and semi-conscious compulsions, operatically swirl back into the life.

The New Life

Strehlow has stepped out of Freud's shadow. The pessimism, the dualism, the primal reductions of *Totem and Taboo*, of Freud's misanthropy in general, had been transcended at quite a fundamental level, at least conceptually. In the early days Freud's opposition between the individual and society, his 'doctrine,' as Stanner called it, of 'men born at odds with society for biological reasons,' seemed to fit Strehlow's bent for comparing the linguistic plight of Hamlet with the life of those who lived in Aranda. On both models, the isolation of the individual against the social order was fundamental: the primordial self, with its instincts, pitted against the culture, and as a result the natural tendency was a neurosis which objectified the world out there, which rendered it an 'IT,' evoking the chronic lament, 'The world has let me down.'

The alternative, the one exalted in the construction of the Holy Family, was one of self with others; of relation and relationship rather than 'natural opposition.' This was the world of mutuality that Stanner was trying to suggest when he debunked the scientific status of Freud in Australian anthropology, and in so doing he reached, not for more anthropology, but for a religious model that happened to come from Martin Buber, the modern theologian of the Hebrew 'tribe.' Buber's I–Thou relations, which issued in comradeship and love, in intimacies that retained identity, autonomy and responsibility, were inimical to Freud's world of 'ambivalence, domination, illusion, imbalance, instability, frustration, infantilism.' They were inimical for a central reason: they sprang from dialogic communications, a linguistic practice that demonstrated the interdependence of self and other.

And so with the deeper logic of *Journey to Horseshoe Bend*. The deep divisions have been resolved. People can speak with each other. Their tongues overlap. Their languages may not, so to speak, 'cover each other' to use Strehlow's phrase of early years, but they are with each other in speech. Furthermore, language itself is no longer felt to be the obstacle to understanding and trust. Rather, it was the function of language to facilitate the social fundamentals of being human. Away then with the model of language as a primitive tool of any kind, bound to engender incomprehension and distance. The model that came to Strehlow in the months he was composing his symphony, his poem of unities, was exactly that: the dialogic alternative.

The function of a language is not to make possible soliloquies on topics and in terms that no one but the speaker can ever grasp, but to establish contact and communication between the speaker and some other person or being that can understand his utterances and is interested in them. Strehlow cited the linguist A. Sommerfelt: 'A real language . . . makes communication in the human sense possible with an interplay of question and reply, a stage to which no animal, so far as is known, has arrived. Unlike the spider that seems to be quite content to sit by itself on its own web day after day gorging itself on killed flies, man is a social animal, craving for the company of other human beings.'[17] It is a truism, but how different it is from the kinds of things Strehlow had been saying about language twenty years before.[18] He is writing with a different focus, having moved, one might say, his orientation from the private gloom of soliloquies to the light of relationships, including new relationships of full significance.

Let McNally resume the story about Strehlow's inevitable passage:

Towards the end of 1967, Bertha mentioned at breakfast one morning that she would like to visit Theodor and his wife in Thailand, where Theodor was studying the people and their language. Strehlow told her she could go with his blessing if she had a mind to, and she decided she would.

'Apart from wanting to see Theodor, I thought it might give Ted and John a chance to mend their differences arising out of John's decision to abandon his study of the Classics at university in favour of History. When John had told his father of that intention, Ted hit the roof. There was an awful row, and at one stage I was afraid it might come to blows. I had managed to defuse it, and they were now slowly responding to each other again,' Bertha recalled.

When Bertha returned home from Thailand she was disturbed by her husband's coolness toward her. He complained of not feeling well, and of experiencing sleeplessness at nights. He had moved most of his clothes from their double bedroom and set up a wardrobe and single bed in what, until then, had been a small sitting room at the front of their home. Bertha tried to make light of this, treating it as a joke, urging her husband to move back into the bedroom

He refused, saying: 'You wouldn't get any rest . . . It wouldn't be fair to you. I'll stay where I am.'

Later in the first week after her return home from Thailand, Bertha told Strehlow and John how much she had enjoyed her visit to Theodor, and Strehlow replied: 'Why did you bother to come back, then? I certainly don't need you any more.'[19]

By early 1968 Strehlow had moved out. The moment he chose was when Bertha had gone to England to visit Shirley. Bertha returned to find John living alone in the house. Strehlow had moved in with Kathleen. As if in a nightmare, Bertha went to Kathleen's place. As she told McNally: 'Kathleen Stuart was courteous but cold to me when she answered my knock on the front door, and she called Ted. He looked surprised to see me standing there, and asked what I wanted. I told him I had to know where I stood, and he said: "Can't you see where we stand? I've left you for a country girl . . . I never did like city girls anyway."'[20]

There seems little reason to doubt Bertha. By all accounts she was a simple-hearted, dutiful wife, a woman of scruple in all spheres of life. Strehlow's remark—'I never did like city girls anyway'—is all too human, too true in its vicious resonance to be made up. Hadn't he loved a country girl more than 30 years ago? He had indeed: so much so that the idea of his destiny containing two loves had become something of a family joke between him and Bertha. Their love banter was that there had been two loves, and Bertha was *the* one. Now she was not. That was the thrust of Strehlow's knife at Kathleen's door. He had another country girl. The right one. After all these years.

Twenty-five years younger than Bertha, Kathleen Stuart had been raised at Northam in Western Australia and become a schoolteacher after some university study and completing her Teacher's Certificate at

Claremont Teachers College. She had taught in various schools in Western Australia before coming to Adelaide in 1964. Her husband, Donald Stuart, had by then written two Outback novels, *The Driven* and *Yaralie*, the latter the story of an Aboriginal girl after whom they named their daughter.

Kathleen Stuart was a vivacious woman who knew her own beauty—'the sexiest woman I have ever met,' according to one woman who worked with her. This colleague, who taught in the same high school, remembers Kathleen holding her class in thrall with tales of love stories, and her own ears burning as Kathleen, seated on the table, her legs swinging, held forth. So struck was she by Kathleen's presence that she said: 'You know, she was so sexy, I think I was even attracted to her, and I've never had any interest in women.'

We might as well say it: Strehlow was a lucky man. He must have found in Kathleen a new lease of life when he met her, and even more so after his sudden hospitalisation in 1966. There was a certain amount of primitive—savage—courage in Strehlow's departure at a time when scandal still dogged a man who left a wife. Conventional society was likely to shun him. Anything leading to divorce was a scandal, especially, perhaps, in Adelaide, the city of churches in which the 'paradise of dissent' had not yet impinged on public sexual mores.

The other risk was the gauntlet of a puritan conscience; and what conscience was more puritan, at its roots, than one shaped on a Lutheran mission?

His own children saw the guilt at work. When they sought him out, he hardly wanted to talk. He would awkwardly usher them into his room and remain aloof as they tried to engage him, then say, 'Well, is there anything else you don't want Kathleen to hear?' Both of his sons found the atmosphere intolerable after a few such meetings: it was as if Strehlow was so excruciatingly conscious of his new life that he could not breathe a word about the old. When Shirley wrote to him from London announcing her engagement, he did not reply. She asked him to the wedding. He did not go. She was, like her brothers, still painfully conscious of their mother's suffering and his severance of all contact and withdrawal of financial support.

Strehlow was telling himself many of the things some men do when they abandon a wife. These include the realisation that from the beginning he and Bertha had never really loved each other. Bertha had had 'a searing love affair' with a married man with whom she almost eloped but for the scandal. And so she had, like him, married on the rebound from her true love. In 1935, he now claimed, he was 'in a state of anguish, even near-panic, at the thought of marrying her.'

Then there was the matter of their different backgrounds. His 'German—and Lutheran—background was . . . completely irksome to her' (and later the 'events of World War II deepened the divisions'). Socially he did not belong to her 'set.' Nor could she share his 'complete absorption either in Central Australia or in aboriginal culture.' It was 'only a mistaken sense of duty' that made him go through with it. They struggled together in Central Australia, where he 'tried to make a "success" of my "marriage" by engaging in every kindness' towards her.

Strehlow could go even further in his exculpations. Having dismissed Bertha's years of devotion to him in Central Australia, he could focus on their nightmare at Piltardi Rockhole 'that might easily have cost us *our* lives': 'After my Herculean efforts of bringing her to safety (during which I lost some thirty pounds in weight), Bertha invited her father and step-mother to Jay Creek, where we had set up tents to live in; and I had to bear the acid moods of her cantankerous stepmother during what should have been a period of recuperation for *me*' (emphases added).

Most of all, Strehlow would say, 'the attempt to establish a sense of close spiritual companionship never succeeded.' He later claimed he had moved his bed to the sunroom in 1947, and that an 'ever-deepening chill set down on' their relationship. 'In other words, if conjugal relations indicate a true marriage, then any "marriage" between Bertha and me came to an end more than a decade and a half ago.' Loves me indeed! he would scoff. 'There is a world of difference between "love" and mere possessiveness. Three decades of hypocrisy and heartbreak are enough for any man.'

And so, in this way, he had rendered everything inevitable, and himself blameless, and Bertha as the dark lady, the soiled and dis-honourable, the unappreciative one. As for Kathleen she was 'the true spouse that God, in His mercy, gave to me when all hope had passed.'[21]

---

1 Oscar Wilde to Lord Alfred Douglas, January–March 1897, *The Complete Letters of Oscar Wilde*, ed. Merlin Holland and Rupert Hart-Davis (London: Fourth Estate, 2001), 696.
2 Ibid., 723.
3 T.G.H. Strehlow, diary [SD], 19 September 1962.
4 Strehlow to 'members of his Dpt. At Adel. Univ,' 14 July 1964.

5   This indeed is the firm view of John Strehlow, the second son of T.G.H., who
    is extensively researching the life of his grandfather, Pastor Carl (personal
    communication, June 2001). However, Peter Latz, who grew up on
    Hermannsburg Mission in the 1950s and whose father first worked there in
    1934, holds that by the time Carl Strehlow had to leave the mission he had
    been defeated by the tenacity and depth of Aranda spirituality.
6   T.G.H Strehlow, *Journey to Horseshoe Bend* [*JHB*] (Sydney: Angus & Robertson),
    1969, 88–92.
7   Ibid., 133.
8   Ibid., 133–36.
9   Ibid., 144–46.
10 Ibid., 146.
11 SD, 16 August 1936.
12 SD, 27 June – 1 July 1953.
13 T.G.H. Strehlow, 'One Hour Before Sunset,' public talk, University of Adelaide,
    16 June 1954.
14 Ibid., 154.
15 Ibid., 200–01.
16 Ibid., 157.
17 T.G.H. Strehlow, 'Man and Language,' address to the Adelaide University
    Linguistic Society, 19 September 1967.
18 The other thrust of the argument was to reverse what he had been saying
    twenty years earlier about anthropologists needing to be linguists. Now he
    argued the linguist needed 'a sound knowledge of . . . the society whose
    language he is studying.' Strehlow had taken in what J.R. Firth had had to say
    in London, and wanted to show he had moved away from the preoccupations
    of 'eminently practical phoneticians and grammarian like O. Jespersen [who]
    spent far too much time in spinning doubtful theories about the origins of
    speech.' Strehlow stressed what Firth called 'the living language' and the
    function of language to 'establish contact and communication' rather than make
    'soliloquies on topics and terms that no one but the speaker can ever grasp.' In
    other words, out with Hamlet, and in with language as a social tool that
    defined humankind. Along with this is the claim that had become increasingly
    common by the sixties: that Aboriginal languages are not primitive, if primitive
    languages exist at all. The Australian languages are 'normal, fully developed
    languages,' Strehlow wrote, reiterating a position he stated on a radio talk ten
    years earlier when he listed difficulty, complexity and vocabulary among the
    features of the Aboriginal languages, along with its special sophistication with
    social concepts: 'If it is impossible to discuss the atomic bomb scientifically in
    Aranda, it is equally impossible to discuss the complex aboriginal world of
    social organisation or totemism in English without introducing a large number
    of indispensable aboriginal key-words.' ('Are There Any Primitive Languages?'
    ABC talk, recorded 1 November 1957.)
       As with most of Strehlow's general talks, 'Man and Language' was to the
    Adelaide University Linguistics Society, but it is hard to separate the platitudes
    and citations of his after-dinner mode from his own thinking on the subject.
    Suffice it to make three points. (1) The general structure of his argument is the
    same as it was in 1947; it is equally dualistic but merely reversed. (2) The
    function of his argument is similarly designed to assert his position as a unique
    authority with regard to Aranda: where, in the past, his linguistic access was
    stressed, in 1967 his knowledge of the society is emphasised, indicating an
    orientation to the world of anthropology rather than the increasingly technical
    world of linguistics, which Strehlow generally avoided. (3) At the same time it
    sarcastically declines to credit anthropology with any practical value 'to supply

advice to practical men in affecting changes in native cultures.' Here Strehlow mocks discussions at the London School of Economics which failed to show how anthropologists 'could give such advice purely on scientific grounds.'

19 Ward McNally, *Aborigines, Artefacts and Anguish* (Adelaide: Lutheran Publishing House, 1981), 133–42.
20 Ibid., 142.
21 Strehlow to the Rev. W. Johnson, 8 June 1970, Lutheran Archives, Adelaide.

PART VI: POSSESSED

The romantic transforms the real into a dream,
imprisons the real like a fly caught in dark amber.
Kenelm Burridge

1   The Burning Collection

The Big, Modern, Messy Picture

STREHLOW WAS GROWING old as Aboriginal life in Australia was entering its modern political phase. In 1963 the life of an Aborigine in the Northern Territory could be described as follows:

you are declared a ward and are one of 15,000. If your skin is not too dark, and your lifestyle closely resembles that of some whites, you can appeal against being a ward. Superintendents of missions or settlements and police officers are powerful in your life. The Director of Social Welfare can tell you where to live and take charge of your property (both powers subject to approval by a court of summary jurisdiction). He can make your boss pay part of your wages, which are set below that of non-wards, into a trust fund which the director controls. If you are on social service benefits and live in an institution, only a portion of that money goes into your own pocket. If you live on a cattle station, the boss gets your child endowment. It is only two years since you could not marry without the director's permission. He still controls aspects of your relationship with your children. He can punish you and white people for mixing socially. You cannot buy a drink until later this year.[1]

The pre-war policies for 'uplift' had a new name: assimilation. Its chief architect was the scholarly, compassionate, liberal-minded Paul Hasluck, Minister for Territories, who wrote in 1963 that the policy 'means that all Aborigines and part-Aborigines will attain the same manner of living as other Australians and to live as members of a single Australian community enjoying the same rights and privileges, accepting the same responsibilities, observing the same customs and influenced by the same beliefs, as other Australians.'[2]

It was a vision that one day Aborigines would erase their differences in the sea of white nationhood. The coercive overseeing of Aboriginal life would in theory be dismantled as Aborigines entered the welcoming harbour of white society through the right schooling, good health care, housing and so on. That was the theory. In practice the welfare supervision demeaned Aboriginal culture and perpetuated a counter-productive social dependence—yet another form of what had been called, since the turn of the century, the 'native problem.'

In ten years between 1967 and 1976 the assimilation policy was dismantled. The emphasis shifted towards notions of self-determination. That was not to say that the old social problems evaporated: far from it, as opponents of change were quick to point out. But the social map of that decade has revolutionary signposts. After the 1967 referendum Aborigines were for the first time to be counted in the national census; and the Commonwealth formalised greater powers for its Aboriginal policies. The referendum was won after crucial Aboriginal involvement in the mainstream political process and the emergence of a generation of Aboriginal leaders who would stress the right to vote, hitherto dependent on scattered formulations by the States.[3] In 1965, the Commonwealth Arbitration Court awarded equal pay to Aboriginal pastoral workers, thus ending nearly a hundred years of the colonial presupposition that if a drover was black and had his family on the station he could be paid a pittance that was almost in kind. The impact of this new labour law was profound, and not all good from the Aboriginal point of view.[4] Scores of Aboriginal families moved off the cattle stations, which often meant that they had to leave the country of their dreamings. They drifted then, as Aborigines had always done in times of strife, towards the towns, where they were unemployed and still rootless, the 'driftwood' as it was named 30 years earlier. Or they found places at one of the mass settlements the government had been setting up in Central Australia since the war. These were established with much philanthropic hope at Areyonga, Papunya and Yuendumu, but there were soon shortfalls. Since education, health, and welfare provision were inadequate to the task, and the social regimes of the camp were complicated, the future of the next generation was still uncertain. At Yuendumu the white superintendent had to threaten to shoot the much valued camp dogs to shock mothers into looking after their new babies.[5]

Still, there were greater freedoms gradually emerging. Aborigines were more in the cash economy, even if the money came from a welfare cheque. The restrictions on travel were removed. The Toyota had arrived in Central Australia. If you were black and part of a mob with a family member who had a car you could drive from one end of a songline to another, just about. You could go all over the place, pretty much like a white man. And you could drink so much that the odds of killing yourself on the road were very great, just as they were of dying of renal failure or diabetes twenty years younger than a white man. Or, and equally, you could go out and put that freedom to use by visiting you own country, looking after it, having ceremonies there, and making the culture stronger in ways that the previous regime had made it harder to do. By the end of the sixties the new situation was a mixed bag, but a freer bag.

Land—its significance and its repatriation—was the political focus, and the return of the land to its rightful owners was often spoken of as if such an achievement would be an overnight palliative to all that had gone wrong in Aboriginal life and spirit. In 1967 the stockmen at Wave Hill station sat down demanding equal pay, and the upshot of that was an electrifying boost of confidence to Aboriginal activists.[6] So, too, was the outcome of the claim against a mining company at the bauxite plant on the Gove Peninsula, when the Aboriginal case was lost, technically, and yet led to the setting up of a Federal commission to look into the implementation of land rights. This was the Woodward Commission set up by the Whitlam Government in 1972, which had Dr Nugget Coombs as its adviser. The departure of Hasluck as Minister for Territories in 1963 had left the way open for Coombs' vision of Aboriginal autonomy. Rather than foster uplift into white society, Coombs was trying to create conditions for an Aboriginal intelligentsia, as well as the grassroots structure for healthy communities.[7] Coombs did not at first emphasise land but by 1972, with the election the Labor Government, he had changed his mind. Other key advisers on Aboriginal policy—W.H. Stanner and A.P.

Elkin—agreed, though Elkin was no longer in the centre of the policy picture. The dismantling of the assimilation policy, with all its well-meaning paternalisms, had left him somewhat behind.

The Woodward Commission travelled through Central Australia for some months. What it had to work out were a mechanism for enabling Aborigines to put their case for land, and criteria that were ethnographically right. Strehlow was conspicuously excluded from this process in Central Australia, probably because he had made himself so unpopular with Canberra. In any case, he opposed the Northern Territory Land Rights Act of 1976 and the establishment of Land Councils in Darwin and Alice Springs to implement it. He had had strong views on sacred sites, on the centrality of land ownership, the pmara kutata, the home place, and on the whole belief system that went with land, and he would have much to say as the full implications of the land rights debate unfolded; but he was not part of this movement towards political modernity, the post-colonial developments that the body of his work, all his translations of myths and songs, was going to enrich.

There was another happening, an amazing one, that is essential to the cultural climate of Strehlow's last days. A renaissance without the seeds of tragedy was the flowering of a whole new school of painting at Papunya. When the schoolteacher Geoffrey Bardon gave some senior men some paints to do with what they wanted, he had no idea that the images they created would constitute a life force of their own.[8] The images sprang, at first, straight out of the sacred recesses of the men's dreaming, a dangerous exposing of the most important things they knew. Gradually, more care was taken.[9] But the ground had been newly broken, so to speak. The paintings started to tap back down to the traditional material—the body painting and the songs, the dances and the initiations. The beauty and the power of the paintings were undeniable to the painters and to their white audience, and after a beginning as quiet as murmurs to a ground painting, they broke into the international art market. Out of the most intensely local religious convictions the first generation of painters proved to the world that indigenous culture had not been murdered by colonialism, not entirely, anyway. Another generation followed, with the women stepping in to paint their dreamings.[10] Monies never dreamed of by Vestey's drovers flowed back to many painters, and a whole new cycle of good fortune and loss began at a pitch not seen since the rise and

fall of Albert Namatjira, the Aranda man who had mysteriously translated some of his sacred designs for white eyes before capsizing under
the pressure of modernity.

Much of this was happening in the prism of a decade. White hopes
for Aboriginal futures were high: flight paths were mapped, as easily
as looking across a dot painting, from one water place to another,
the main track being the one that would give the people back their
land, and from that provide income that was no longer welfare, and
community that was proud, and a culture that might flower in its
own terms, even drawing what it wanted from the white economy
and society. This was the mood of the time, even though there
were qualms in the back rooms of policy makers, even among
people around reformers like H.C. Coombs, who later was prepared
to admit that he had some romantic assumptions about Aboriginal
community, just as Hasluck owned up to having started out with
'muddled hopes.'[11]

And there was more than a little opposition to the substance of the
revolution, especially with regard to titles for land. The pastoral
ascendancy, already in a trough of its own for microeconomic reasons,
was not prepared for any psychological surrender to the Aboriginal
cause. So it was no surprise, historically speaking, to see the Northern
Territory government opposing most Aboriginal land claims for the
next ten years on behalf of cattlemen and mining companies. That
story need not be written here. Suffice it to say that the new period,
utopian though it was in some ways, had a firm basis of reality.
Nothing like it had ever happened before and those who could not
grasp it, or who totally and tenaciously resisted it or misrepresented
it, were doomed to become the contemporary driftwood of history.
The axis of colonial history was shifted forever as a result of the land
claims. Finally—though the finally is still being worked out—the
changes that flowed from the political/cultural shifts of the decade
were themselves mixed and complex, as messy and as unresolved as
life itself. Strehlow, always ambivalent himself, was in the thick of
much ambiguity.

National Kitsch

This is perhaps the moment to consider the nexus Strehlow made of
Aboriginal culture and the national culture—how one might or might
not nourish the other under the banner of art. When that art was

poetry, he got himself into trouble, as we have seen. By the 1970s something rather similar is happening with painting and sculpture.

Strehlow's philistine incomprehension of and incoherence about modern art is displayed in his remarks about Rex Battarbee and the Namatjira school, and about William Ricketts. In his introduction to Battarbee's book, *Modern Australian Aboriginal Art*, he begins straightforwardly enough by welcoming the new school of painting for Aboriginal people, only to lapse soon afterwards. He welcomes 'the day of liberation' of Aranda art from its limited number of sacred symbols that depended on the storyteller or the verse chants to 'make the intentions of the design clear beyond doubt to the spectators.' 'Balance, rhythm and intrinsic beauty' there was in the old sacred art, but because of its 'intimate association with religious ideas' it was strongly conservative.[12] That was in 1951. Five years later,[13] Strehlow called the traditional art 'completely fossilised' because 'its patterns were rigorously supervised by the old men of each totemic clan.' It was in this situation of 'the complete collapse of the old native order,' where 'the old order was completely doomed,' that there was no hope for any 'new, geometrical forms of abstract art': that might be possible 'in two or three generations time,' but not now. Hence the 'liberation' brought by Battarbee in 1932 when the Aranda people at the mission saw his techniques for 'painting truthful, sympathetic, and loving pictures of the finest scenes of the Central Australian landscape.' Strehlow goes on about the 'emotional appeal' of the Central Australian landscape, especially for those familiar with its 'fine, grand, and beautiful scenes.' It is hard to imagine him arguing such a case for anywhere else in Australia, which invalidates his general position.

For the next twenty pages Strehlow tries to say something about art in general, and modern art and its audience. On art, he can't get past his attachment to it as conveying 'private emotional reactions' which returns him again to Battarbee and the 'mirror' his work holds up to nature in the Centre with 'its wonderland of magic colours, shapes, and Nature's own hand written lines.' The terms are naïve and compulsively autobiographical. Yet again Strehlow praises art that 'looks on this ancient, magnificent landscape with awe and affection,' and as if this is not local enough, he adds, 'Often it is not appreciated by the art critics either, unless they have actually been to Central Australia.'[14]

Strehlow defends the Namatjira school from claims that it is 'pretty,' 'photographic' and 'saleable'—all claims that double bind the ambitious

Aboriginal artist in the era of assimilation. To some extent, Strehlow rebuts this. He then lets loose against modern art so lacking in the 'intimacy' of 'primitive art . . . with all the great social and ceremonial activities of a closely integrated community.' (At this point the 'liberation' of Aranda artists from 'fossilised' art seems to have been forgotten.) Strehlow portrays modern art as having no positive function in the community, of having contempt for its 'debased public,' and of being a mere outlet for artists' 'personalities.' Terms such as 'the ordinary public' and the 'average citizen' are bandied around, and the role of the critic condemned as the 'ministrations of an enthusiastic apologist,' proof that 'the artist has failed in his own chosen medium of expression.'[15] Strehlow's tone and case would have pleased Robert Menzies, who had spoken against modern art during the dark ages of Australia in the fifties. Or, to put this another way: a fervent Lutheran peasant could not have been more resentful than Strehlow of art's modality of freedom.

Strehlow's single note is the definitional link between art and emotion, or emotionality: 'the real force of true art [is] not explained in cold and rational terms.' The communal dream is his *cri de coeur*: 'Once upon a time art in all its forms gave joy to the community, and established between individual members of the audience that great bond of sympathy.' That time is unspecified, which renders the point as limply nostalgic as his language for landscape is kitsch. Strehlow's populism comes in the end to saying: 'An Australian home possesses an indefinable atmosphere of its own' as distinct from 'the mannered cleverness of contemporary Europe and the dying magnificence of older Europe.'[16] He is pointing to where the Battarbee and Namatjira paintings should be hung, if people had the right love of the Centre. They would be placed on the walls of the Australian 'one-family homes' inhabited, presumably, by people sharing his contempt and ignorance of contemporary art of any critical complexity. The promising future for the art of a 'dispossessed native population' is on the walls of suburbia, along with the flying ducks.

Strehlow's tolerance of kitsch is further illustrated in his warm friendship with William Ricketts, whose sculptures he first saw in Melbourne in 1939, when he was especially taken by a group of 'totemic kangaroo ancestors' that prompted him to think: here was 'true art—a world created by the mind of a man who was so closely attuned to aboriginal thought processes and emotional attitudes that his clay formed works seemed to breathe the same spirit.'[17] Ricketts was confirmed in Strehlow's eyes when he made such an emotional connection with Aranda elders at Haasts Bluff in June 1954. Ricketts laid out his work on the soft, white river sand and an old senior man responded by holding Ricketts tight in his arms; then the others unwrapped their *tjurunga* and sang for him, with Namatjira looking on. 'They straight away recognised me in spirit,' Ricketts wrote to Strehlow.

Ricketts' work, an application of Jindyworobak thinking into clay, was an interminable weaving of an idealised Dreamtime that had more to do with Strehlow's notions of the Aranda 'Golden Age' than anything happening on earth. Still, the entwining of noble male elders, earth emblems, and unharmed Aboriginal children was an expression of goodwill in relationship, if nothing else, and in the years of the assimilation policy it upheld affirmations about an original Aboriginal virtue that united Ricketts and Strehlow. Ricketts, too, saw his Aboriginal connections as a mission, his 'life's true purpose for the world,' which was not to do with buying and selling, which he discouraged the Aborigines from doing, but 'to give back from God what emanates from God. I try to tell them that they are to go back to a Holy Mountain.'

By 1962 Ricketts was back in Victoria, at Mount Dandenong, where he was creating his own Holy Mountain for his sanctuary of sculptures, firing them for caves excavated from the hill. From Strehlow he requested, and gladly received, the Aranda words for 'My love of country is a consuming fire,' which would go into the rock fireplace as a 'shrine.' 'All life is one,' he told Strehlow, whose heart was in accord, and went on to tell him about the 'Ancestral Mother' . . . or as he elaborated on another occasion, 'God Love, ancestral love, enshrined in a rhythm that moves and sweeps through all life.'

What appealed to Strehlow was the idea of unity of all life, and the Aboriginal feeling of oneness with nature: 'Nature and men shared the same life; and Nature could not die.' Strehlow did not hesitate to be the guest of honour to open the Ricketts Sanctuary in 1973, even though Ricketts' thinking was by then incorporating Indian mysticism of the All Being One, and conflating Hindu teaching with the 'Alchera' and the 'inherent Divinity of Man.'[18] As to Ricketts' spiritual journey to the East, Strehlow seems to have been tolerantly bemused, showing no sign of interest with the idea of Aboriginal belief having affinities with any other spiritual tradition. A preference for keeping the Aranda clear of other spiritual consorts might also explain Strehlow's silence with regard to Elkin's adventurous comparisons of Aboriginal 'medicine men' with the shamans of Tibetan mysticism.[19]

At any rate, when Strehlow spoke on the happy occasion of the sanctuary opening in 1973, he managed to avoid alien religions as well as aesthetic refinements: he spoke firmly of Ricketts' themes as an illustrator. He cited Norman Lindsay, another pre-modernist and vitalist of the human figure, who thought Ricketts a 'great master' who gave hope for 'a great future for this country as world civilisation.' Strehlow slighted 'the new fangled Australia and admiration for so called "aboriginal culture" which is only another expression of our national habit of admiring everything that is phoney and false as long as its cult brings high remuneration for its white prophets and salesmen.' He went on to praise what he had seen in the British Museum: Egyptian art illustrating the cult of the dead; 'the Assyrian cult of terror; and the Greek cult of the beautiful.' Against this, Ricketts' work was 'the finest expression so far of the aboriginal Australian veneration of life.'

Not only was this the supreme example of Strehlow's poor taste overriding his yearnings for theological convergence; it was, by 1973, an obliteration of Aboriginal themes by other white artists, including major writers and painters; and, bizarrely, a kind of racist erasure of the contemporary Aboriginal art already in existence.

Ingkata Stocktaking
Still a collation of Strehlow's work and writings around 1970 would have shown him to have been a supporter of the painful growth from assimilation policies to self-determination.

In 1970 he wrote in the widely read *Australian Book Review*: 'The recent events at Gove and Wattie Creek show that full-blood aboriginals are still waiting for the day when an Australian Government will put a stop to the injustice of laws which have turned them into the only human race in the world which owns no land.'[20] It is hard to imagine a stronger statement. Strehlow was reviewing Paul Hasluck's *Black Australia* and taking an opportunity to focus his criticism of twenty years of coercive paternalism.

He had of course written about Hasluck's policies before. In his elegantly written and deeply felt pamphlets between 1949 and 1960 he had asserted the rights of an indigenous culture to be different, as distinct from automatically being the object of erasure into the 'civilised culture.' He had ideas about the education of Aborigines that respected their language and beliefs, and the delicate relationship with the generation that would never live long enough to assimilate. He reiterated that none of the policies could work from a basis of racist attitudes of superiority, and that education in citizenship was not going to sway Aborigines' distrust of those who would improve them. That in turn required that those who would make 'bad blacks' into 'good blacks' also had to understand that Aboriginal culture still had many good attributes, and that Aboriginal people were, despite the ruination white culture had often brought, happy.[21]

All of this was critical enough, and bold for the time, but Strehlow was not really speaking as a radical social critic. Much of what he had to say was grounded in the first person, in what he had been through, and what he had done for the Aborigine in the early part of his life, and in political terms it had been calculatingly muted out of his own sense of self-interest.

As Minister for Territories, Hasluck was 'the single most important patron of Strehlow's career'[22] in helping him with Commonwealth funds for fieldwork; and it was to Hasluck's sedate conservative style that Strehlow had deferred when his own support of land rights put him in the leftist camp of the Council for Aboriginal Rights. It was his policy, Strehlow had rather ingratiatingly written to Hasluck in the heyday of assimilation rhetoric, 'to refrain from making any comments which would embarrass those who are carrying out the administration of Native Affairs in the Northern Territory.' What then should he do about speaking to the Council for Aboriginal Rights? Would he be 'advancing the cause of the natives'?[23]

'I have formed the impression,' Hasluck advised him, 'that they are very eager to believe the worst about the treatment of the aborigines and are rather unwilling to accept any account which does not raise a scare or scandal. From time to time they have sought information from me and in all cases I gained the impression from their inquiries that they are readers of left-wing pamphlets, but I have no solid basis for my opinion except the way they use words like "exploitation" and "rights."'[24]

Solid basis or not for slurring the Council for Aboriginal Rights, it was enough for Strehlow. He did not speak. He again played safe with regard to the left, just as he had with Jessie Street in London, and his anomalous politics is worth a moment's reflection. Strehlow was a nationalist and democrat in the Australian tradition; his temper was democratic, his bias Australian, as Joseph Furphy had almost put it. He was antipathetic to the English and their Empire, and a full blooded friend of native Australians. He was a Lutheran who had never felt himself to be a part of Adelaide's Anglo establishment. He was a 'bushman' who had never sympathised with the prerogatives of pastoralists, and he had found himself in opposition to their powerful friends in the city. He was to all intents and purposes a Labor man, yet he was a loner.

But he had held his peace when it counted. Another level of conservatism informed him and, we would now say, isolated him into a particular kind of chauvinistic nationalism. This was a conservatism that arose out of his Christian embrace of Aboriginal religion. He was a nationalist who would root Australian identity in the metaphysical qualities of its native peoples. He was allied to their notion of eternity rather than, let's say, their communitarian tendencies, even though he had idealised those in one of his pamphlets.[25] Put another way, Strehlow's anti-imperialist, democratic nationalism would normally have found its home in the ideology of the labour movement, and Strehlow himself would have found friends there, thus appeasing his need for fraternity. Alas, the syncretism of the covert Black Missionary offered him no public place to be. This complicated everything.

In a strange way, he was more at home making corrective remarks in conservative circles than joining up with the 'friends' of Aborigines in general. He once told a meeting of the South Australian Country Party that: 'Thirty years ago the discovery of valuable metals on an aboriginal reserve in the Northern Territory would have led to its closing and the expulsion of its black residents to enable private white interests to take over all operations and profits. Today the general Australian public would, I believe, be opposed to such an action.' I am with the most progressive forces, he was saying, while still avoiding the political company of such people.

However, in 1970 he was being absolutely outspoken, and the odd thing was that, even though the tide of opinion had caught up with him on race policies, he was forthright but alone: he was speaking bravely without many signs of friends. Even more remarkable was that now, at last, he had some of the formal recognition he had craved.

In 1970, too, Strehlow had become what he had so long wished to be: a professor. At long last, the university gave him a personal chair in linguistics. His champion throughout had been Ronald Berndt, one of his referees for the appointment. The others were the distinguished poet and classicist A.D. Hope at the Australian National University, and the Professor of French at the University of Melbourne, A.R. Chisholm. It was support from the world of literature rather than anthropology, or even linguistics. Berndt, of course, affirmed the status of Strehlow's anthropology, but in due course essentially appraised Strehlow's achievement as a contribution to Australian literature. That he had arrived at last in the world of Australian letters had already been demonstrated by the critical reception of *Journey to Horseshoe Bend*, which won the C. Weickhardt Award for the best general book published in Australia (with Chisholm as one of the judges).

Much had come to fruition, much was now enshrined. And the man who had done the enshrining—of traditional Aranda culture—had been honoured in his turn. It was the time, if there ever was a time, for him to have many allies in the Aboriginal cause and for some contentment to shine through.

Restoring Faith

No life is ever new. The past moves with us, never more so than when one is living with a complex compound of grief, anger, guilt. In the winter of 1970, before and after his 62nd birthday, Strehlow found himself in correspondence with two men of the church. With the first, he was replying to Bertha's Anglican clergyman, the Reverend W. Johnson, of St Augustine's Rectory in Victor Harbor.

Johnson seems to have written a letter of some reproach on behalf of Bertha. It was also one that sought understanding of a Strehlow who had grown up in 'a particular form of isolation from normal society,' and developed a 'Teutonic drive to work.' Johnson was playing psychologist to Strehlow as much as ally to Bertha.

These are interesting phrases to meet at this stage of our journey, or anybody's journey, with Strehlow. It would appear that Bertha had been speaking her heart about what it was that possessed her husband to so callously deny their 30 years together. The prime explanation has to lie in the workings of the marriage, which is not clarified by third-hand information, least of all by one letter by one party. But at another level it is pertinent to reflect on the forces that did shape a man who was, manifestly, self-centred, and who seemed to so naturally think of each situation only in terms of being the unjustly aggrieved one. To say that he grew up acutely alone, and was unaccustomed to dealing with the feelings of his peers, fits the picture of remoteness from his young Aboriginal friends. It is in keeping with the boy who was a silent and rather lonely presence; a Christian boy who had his head down over Greek and Latin; a white boy with no future with the black girls; and a boy who did not run as free as he might with the Aranda boys, whose physicality never much served to make good bonds. If this is an accurate picture, whose feelings, apart from his own, were there to consider? And what does such a singular one do with their time? They work. The puritan offspring work: with Teutonic will they work themselves to the bone.

When the Reverend Johnson set Bertha's continued 'love' and 'understanding' against Strehlow's 'drive to work,' Strehlow wrote the wild, narcissistic defence from which we earlier gleaned something of the workings of his heart.[26]

His reply went further than the rectory at Victor Harbor. Strehlow also sent the Johnson letter unsolicited to the distinguished President General of the Lutheran Church in South Australia, Dr Max Lohe, with whom he had gone to school. 'I am attaching it purely for your information,' Strehlow wrote.[27] But that was not true. His personal life was now tied up with the Lutheran response to *Journey to Horseshoe Bend*, a book made of deep reconciling harmonies but which also laid a brutal charge against the church. The charge was the monumental one that in 1922 the board of the Finke River Mission, and Pastor J.J. Stolz in particular, had been neglectful, indifferent, mercenary and ultimately un-Christian in not coming to his father's rescue when it counted. Strehlow as much as blamed the church for the death of his father.

Strehlow's most concrete claim was that when the mission had consulted the Adelaide car firm of Mr Murray Aunger they found the cost of £500 to be too expensive and so had fallen back on the idea of the sick man travelling south by buggy while another car could be arranged. This was a fatal decision, and Carl and Frieda Strehlow sensed that when the news reached them. The pastor broke down for the first time. 'For the twenty-eight years, I have held to my post, and now my clerical colleagues are dumping me,' Strehlow quotes his father saying. 'Undoubtedly they think that I will be of no further use to them, and that they are not going to waste any money on giving me a chance to live.' The pastor condemned the church's 'hypocritical piety.'[28]

In *Journey to Horseshoe Bend* Strehlow recounted the terms in which his father might have reproached Pastor Stolz.

He [the pastor] would reproach Stolz in a fatherly way for his failure to come to Hermannsburg on an inspection visit despite repeated requests in former years. For how could anyone be an effective chairman of a mission board if he had never set eyes on the station that he was helping to administer? He would remind Stolz of the Finke River Mission Board's ingratitude for not taking any vigorous steps to save his life while there had been time to do so, and he would compare the indifference of Stolz and his clerical colleagues with the humanity, the sympathy, and above all, the practical helpfulness of the churchless bush people. He would quote Christ's own injunctions to Stolz; for Christ himself had taught in his sermons, and shown in his parables and stories, that practical love towards one's neighbours came second only to the love due to God Himself. He would further stress that even St Paul, whose clear statement that man was justified by faith without the deeds of the law had always been regarded as a cardinal element of Lutheran doctrine, had also rated love as being greater than hope and greater than faith in that magnificent thirteenth chapter of his First Letter to the Corinthians. It was the failure of the Lutheran clergy to give due weight to the God-established supremacy of love that had constituted such a grave weakness in the doctrinal soundness of much of their preaching.[29]

After such an unctuous, sweeping attack Lohe had a certain need to reply, which he did on 29 May 1970. He began quietly: 'Dear Ted, Quite a number of years have passed since we last met, and much has happened in this time—events which have deeply distressed me and which must have left their mark upon yourself.'[30] It must have appeared to Strehlow, not unreasonably, that Lohe was implying that deserting a wife was one of those 'events' which could colour his feelings about the past, his father, and the church: so he sent off the defence he had mounted for Johnson.

As it happened, Lohe did not buy into Strehlow's marital affairs. But with regard to the charges laid out in *Journey to Horseshoe Bend* he was forthright. 'It is a very illuminating book, which will appeal to many people, but, unfortunately, there are quite a number of shadows, not the least being a total misrepresentation of the late J.J. Stolz and the Finke River Mission Board. This reveals clearly that the chips you have had on your shoulders for many years have not been removed. Actually, with the passing of the years, the chips have grown somewhat larger.'

'In all fairness to Dr J.J. Stolz,' Lohe went on, 'it must be said that he did everything humanly possible to assist your father. Reports of the endeavour to get cars from the centre are clearly indicated in letters and minutes.' Lohe said there was no mention of the Aunger car in the minutes, and 'I told you personally, there is a minute in the board meeting stating that no expense would be spared in order to get your father down to the south.' Lohe might have added that even a mention of £500 to save Pastor Strehlow was no small gesture; a pecuniary calculation, yes, but a sum equivalent to three years of the basic wage.

More to the point were the facts about Pastor Strehlow's resignation, and the efforts the church had made to accommodate him. Lohe told Strehlow that, although his father did resign in 1919, Stolz asked him to withdraw his resignation for the time being in favour of six months' leave with full pay, during which a Pastor Jericho would fill in for him. After Strehlow had relaxed for six months his retirement would come into force in March or April 1921, when he and his wife would be fully repatriated to Germany. But Pastor Strehlow declined because he didn't want Pastor Jericho there for a mere six months. He wanted a full-time committed replacement, which the church, despite its efforts, was unable to find immediately. Altogether the church had approached six possible replacements, four of whom were Strehlow's suggestions.

Lohe reproached Strehlow for making, in the absence of documentary evidence, such an unfair judgment on a man of such integrity as Stolz, a man who 'certainly would not gamble with a man's life' and who was 'not here to defend or vindicate himself.' 'You certainly had ample opportunity of interviewing him since you were fourteen years of age. Now you have taken the opportunity of inflicting barbs, which he, however, cannot feel, but which his sons and daughters and many members of the church feel most keenly.'

Lohe's final remarks resound with patriarchal authority:

Personally I don't think your father would have uttered such statements. You have spoken. But the final arbiter will be God himself who knows and searches the human heart. Both Stolz and your late father were men of God, who gave themselves untiringly for the service of God and their fellow men. No greater tribute than this can be paid to them: They served in all humility. It was Dr J. Flierl who wrote: 'Ueber die Toten nur gutes!' You have singularly failed to ask yourself just why it was that God permitted your father to die when he did. Yes, your father himself is dead. But he still continues to speak.[31]

Strehlow's agitation at these remarks is not hard to imagine. They went to the heart of a man's ambivalence about a father. They amount to saying that if he sincerely wished to honour his father, he should behave like him. More particularly, they say that, while honouring his father, he was dishonouring his memory. And, even more pointedly, that he was a lesser man than his father. This deeper implication must have penetrated Strehlow. Here was Lohe, as the patriarch of his father's church, and the successor to the man (Stolz) who succeeded his father, reminding the son of his inadequacies, just as his father would have done.

There is anger in Strehlow's response of 23 June—twenty pages of anger, one way or the other. He protests that Lohe would so challenge his 'integrity as an academic and [his] trustworthiness as an historian' and his 'personal good faith,' and makes a sustained, attacking defence on all fronts, starting with much detail about the church's obstacles to his father's timely resignation. He defends his own reliability as a fourteen-year-old who kept a diary of what went on at the mission, including the dates of botched attempts to get urgent messages down south, and the daily anxious waiting for news that someone in authority was coming to the rescue, and rebuts what Lohe called his 'fantasy' about Pastor Carl's thoughts.

He sketches the floor plan of the mission house, which shows him living cheek by jowl with his parents, the silent presence that heard everything, the 'boyish mind . . . saturated by adult parental observations.' What he reported his father as saying was true. They were his father's words. 'Nowhere in my book have I voiced my own sentiments under the cover of remarks slipped into the mouth of my father.' He chose not to mention how verbatim recall of his father taxed his memory: how, for example, his father's despairing utterance, 'God does not help,' went through three drafts.

He goes on to defend the bush people (half a page), speaks of charity and of the church's lack of it towards his widowed mother (one page), and documents his historical research for the book (over three pages). He returns to the central charge of the church's 'inactivity' over the car, the details of which could only be in the missing documents. 'I feel that Stolz (and the others), like the Player Queen in *Hamlet*, "protest too much."' He defends his father against the posthumous charge that his stubbornness kept him at the mission until he fell ill and a disaster was inevitable; and goes on to say how his father had been tricked into the posting in the first place (three pages). And so on. Strehlow's stamina for self-justifying grievance was at full stretch. Through it all, or rather, despite it all, three clear truths emerge which, taken together, do something to clarify the question of 'blame' for Pastor Strehlow's death.

Firstly, Strehlow's position is mainly shaped by the feelings he had as a boy at the time. He seeks to use his diary as evidence, but what it was mainly evidence of was his own distress at the escalating alarm in his household as his parents anguished over the problem of transport. Their loyal workers, Mr Mattner and Mr Heinrich, along with their Aboriginal helpers, came and went from Alice Springs as telegrams were sent to Adelaide in the last two weeks of September. Increasingly, his parents felt abandoned, but that does not establish the truth of the claim that they were. When he wrote his book, and his first reply to Lohe, he did not have the records of those messages between Alice Springs and Adelaide. Nor did his own diary cover events for two of those crucial weeks, because, as he has to admit, the mission had run out of writing paper. In general. Strehlow's habit of not sourcing his material made a strange book of *Journey to Horseshoe Bend*: he was asserting it as documentary history while plastering its surfaces with his mythologising voice.

The crucial detail—if documentation for it could be found—was whether Murray Aunger had been approached and his car judged to be too expensive to save Strehlow's life. Lohe said the church had no records but would look into the matter. Strehlow, in his indignant reply, had no evidence either. He only had his boyhood diary, and his memory of his father breaking down, and the reconstruction of his father's outburst about 'hypocritical piety.' One does not want to say here that Strehlow manufactured his father's utterances; but then, in his diary he was not playing Boswell to his father, either. It is the emotional pitch of the diary, along with the passion of his book, that invites the possibility that his father's 'statements' were as expressive of the son's grief as they were an accurate transcript. The fact that Strehlow's whole position was such a *cri de coeur* made documentation of any obscene cost-saving business even more essential.

The second truth that emerges from the Lohe–Strehlow exchange is that the Mission Board's 'delay,' the loss of those two weeks in September—seems to have been the result of misunderstanding along the telegraph line. For one week the mission assumed that the pastor was too ill to move. For another they were waiting while thinking the car was being organised from Alice Springs. This reality emerges from the extract from the *Mission News* for 9 October 1922 quoted by Strehlow himself. He read the item as a sign of the board's complacency, but it can more reasonably be read as an explanation for the delay. Once the board realised no car was available from Alice Springs they had one lined up within 24 hours, and it was on its way on the first available train.

Thirdly, Strehlow essayed in even more detail about the trials of Pastor Carl's life of service to the mission, reminding Lohe yet again that his father (and his mother) wanted to leave the mission from late 1918, as soon as the Great War ended, when thoughts of returning to Germany and their other children preoccupied them. He badgered Lohe about the sluggishness and immobility of those people down south. But then, in this context, Strehlow made a concession with regard to these unresponsive, incomprehending ones. It was that *'even if quite unwittingly and without any personal feelings of malice (or of inhumanity)* they were contributing to a man's horrible death' (emphasis added).[32]

Unwitting and without 'malice' or 'inhumanity.' This is a major admission to Lohe about other people's intentions. It is said in passing and begrudgingly, but said: and it seems to come out from between the lines that there may after all had been a dislocation of communications between Alice Springs and Adelaide. Overall, Strehlow's argument becomes rather circular, and a strange combination of feelings reasserted, and of charges of ill-intent crucially qualified, if not partly withdrawn. It is emotionally driven by what he had carried in himself since he was a boy: the grief and the anger, the bewilderment and disillusionment, the sense of betrayal that he claims was his parent's state of mind, as distinct from his own.

Lohe replied four months later, when he returned from overseas. He had turned up the 'vital information' that Strehlow said was missing from the records. It was Pastor Philip Scherer who had had the files 'for very many years.'[33] Lohe sent two pages of details about telegrams and meetings during the four weeks of crisis in 1922. Flying in the face of Strehlow's accusation of 'inactivity,' the record suggested a flurry of worried signals from both ends, as well as urgently called meetings in Adelaide. The records bear out the *Mission News'* explanation for the two weeks before getting cars organised, and the sick Pastor on the move.

As to Aunger's car, there was still no documentation. However, there is one detail that looms in favour of Strehlow's charge. The message Adelaide received from Heinrich on 3 October was: 'Rev Strehlow states Mrs Strehlow breaking down under strain. Prompt action imperative. Suggest hire car *at whatever cost*' (emphasis added). Cost, it seems, might well have been in the air as a consideration. It makes sense to assume that it may have put into the air over Murray Aunger's £500 car hire fee.

Strangely, neither Lohe not Strehlow commented on this telegram. Strehlow seems not to have noticed its significance, and Lohe was more interested in rounding things off. Again he defended Stolz as a humane man and said, 'Even on reading your father's letter of August 18 [to Stolz], I find no trace of rancour; in fact it is a very friendly and understanding letter, in which he shares his experience at Hermannsburg with Stolz. One can understand the tone of deep disillusionment brought about by the isolation of Hermannsburg and the loneliness, resulting in the cry, "My God, my God, why hast Thou forsaken me!"' No good purpose could be served by going into all the facts, Lohe told Strehlow. 'Despite the plan, scheme and intentions of men, God can bring about good, and I think this is the comforting thing as far as your father's ministry at Hermannsburg is concerned, and this is one aspect we shall never forget.'

The exchange had not damaged Strehlow's desire to keep on good terms with the leader of his father's church. In 1972 Lohe, now retired, visited the Strehlows at home, after which Strehlow wrote to him saying that their friendship, 'which began fifty years ago, is something that should not be allowed to die.' He said how happy he and Kathleen had been to see him, announcing at the same time that 'we hope for an increase in our family next March.'[34]

Strehlow let the matter of his father's death lie until June 1973. More letters had come to light which he claimed supplied some of the missing 'proofs' for what he had been arguing in his book. But they provided nothing of the sort. One item merely revealed that a key message from Alice Springs had not been clear enough about needing a car from the south. The other was a letter that had been sent to his mother in 1922, in which it was reported that Aunger had been approached about a car.[35] But the letter did not say when, or if a price had been set or rejected. The key evidence was still missing.

Lohe seems to have declined to take up the issue again. He could perhaps afford to do so because what seems to be a public defence of the Finke River Mission Board was to turn up in the 1974 *Yearbook of the Lutheran Church*.[36] The piece, 'Death on the Line,' was written by Philip Scherer, who had his own hard feelings about Strehlow. In his attempted rebuttal of *Journey to Horseshoe Bend* (which remained unnamed), Scherer regurgitated all the efforts the board had made to find a replacement for Pastor Strehlow before he had fallen seriously ill. Scherer indulged the idea that it was the pastor's reluctance to get medical help earlier which led to his death. In mid-September, by which time Strehlow knew that his escalating condition was the result of untreated pleurisy, 'he declined to go.' Scherer opined: 'Strehlow was known to be a self-willed and, maybe at times, even rather stubborn.'[37]

Scherer defended the integrity of Stolz and made much of the mission's quick response to train a car to Oodnadatta as soon as the urgency of the situation had been pressed upon them from Alice Springs. Again, though, no documentation about the Aunger car. Scherer, the man with the grudge, and now the church apologist, was the least likely historian to dig it up, or even, if he had it in his possession, wish to use it. His article was a highly motivated rebuke of Strehlow.*

Outraged at the status the church had given the article by publishing it in the *Yearbook*, Strehlow demanded an unequivocal retraction—that the article be officially 'disowned.' If not, 'the Lutheran Church of Australia is unworthy to bear the name of its heroic founder.' He did not get his retraction.

With the father of the church, however, he had not fallen out. He was careful not to do so. And Lohe, in turn, retained warm relations with the angry, hurt, son of the church. Strehlow had, with the skilful ambivalence of a wild child, managed to do two things at once: act out his darkest rage while retaining his needful relations with the family of the church. He had been a disagreeable boy, but was still in the fold.

Socrates Poisoned, Christ Crucified

In August 1970 Strehlow was complaining to Berndt about many things at once.

---

* My suspicion that Scherer might be capable of treating documents this way was aroused in September 1994 when, in a casual conversation, he laughingly mentioned how he had 'destroyed' some documents from the Lutheran Archive because his wife found them sexually offensive. Scherer was the Archivist between 1978 and 1989.

The Institute's continued support of Lawton* naturally cannot help but weight heavily in my deliberations. That man has not done a thing in the way of anthropological research; and yet he is still on the AIAS Council by political influence though he was rejected by his peers in the very first Institute election, held in 1964. I, on the other hand, was resolutely turned down in 1968, by the same political forces, even though Council itself had voted for my inclusion. These are facts, not figments of the imagination; and I have survived in my various endeavours, both in the public and in the academic spheres, because I have never allowed myself to forget the hard facts of life and the machinations of envious men who seek to cheat workers who have succeeded in their own fields on the fruits of their honest endeavours. You may or may not have read *Journey to Horseshoe Bend*. If you have, I can assure you that at the age of fourteen I was compelled to realise that, from then on, I had to make my own way in a country in which I had no relatives apart from my widowed mother who had been left penniless by my father's sudden death. Life has been a tough battle for me ever since— lit up sometimes by the kindness and generosity of individuals who helped me when I had come to a dead end in my endeavours, and made intensely tough at other times by other individuals whom I had not hurt but who believed that I could be robbed or even crushed with complete impunity. I have few illusions left about life. Perhaps the last major illusion I have shattered has been about academic integrity; but now I know what far too many—perhaps even most—Australian academics are like. Did I call them 'academics'?! That typical Australian concept of f.a.q.—'fair average quality'—seems to have permeated most academic activities in our Universities too; and 'fair average quality' merely indicates complete lack of real quality. No further comments are necessary. I am still grateful for the fact that I met so many real academics on my overseas travels in England and on the Continent in 1950–2.[38]

It is hard to imagine that, even as Strehlow was writing this letter, the

---

*   He had fallen out with the geographer, G.H. Lawton, over the Mountford affair, among other things. Two years earlier the university had awarded Mountford an honorary Master of Arts for his writings on Aborigines, and Strehlow, incensed that he still did not have a chair, wrote a homicidal essay on Mountford's new book, *Wimbaraku*. The Institute in Canberra thought the essay too intemperate to publish, as did Lawton, who, having supported Mountford's degree, was slandered by Strehlow in the cross-fire.

contemptible academics at the University of Adelaide, Lawton included, were approving his personal chair. Strehlow was becoming deaf and blind in his furies. The strikingly impersonal note to Berndt, his most consistent friend and supporter, is telling. Berndt would have been the first to read *Journey to Horseshoe Bend* with great interest. Was his friend an academic of 'f.a.q.'? And hadn't Berndt heard the biographical details over many a glass of wine for the last twenty years? Who did Strehlow think he was addressing? The high impersonal note seems meant for posterity. It is also phrased, in its fearfulness, very much for himself, though he was probably only dimly conscious of this. His fear of being 'robbed and crushed' would fit a medieval tale of brigandry. The 'crushed' takes us back to his childhood dream of being trampled by cattle. Then it probably symbolised the darkest presence of the white bushmen, with their primal beasts and sexual primitivisms—all that pagan terror transmitted to him by his orderly Christian parents. Now, with the grieving child still in him, he would be crushed by the competitive herd of others, those who would not help him when he had come to his 'dead end.' The craving for recognition bleeds into a fear of extinguishment. By 1970 he seems to have felt, albeit with the defiance of a stoical hero if not a martyr, that he was inhabiting a nightmare. If a man was not to come to a dead end, he would have to fight his way out.

In this fight he had his most ferocious ally in Kathleen. She told Berndt in June 1970 that the treatment of her husband amounted to a slow, wilful murder akin to Christ's crucifixion, Joan of Arc being burnt at the stake, or Socrates poisoned.[39] Berndt fell quiet. Meanwhile, however, Strehlow still needed the patronage of his persecutors: how else could he carry on his good work for the sake of what his wife was increasingly calling 'posterity,' for the sake of 'eternity'? Strehlow hoped Berndt might sound out those who had 'real power in their hands': 'If favourable, perhaps some approach could then be made to me by Council. But I want no strings attached to such an offer which would enslave me.'

The Institute was not interested in enslaving him. It did not waver in its respect for his work, or even quibble about the value of still more trips to the Centre. What it wanted, as always, was copies of his films to be deposited in Canberra, and to see more of the work written up: at the very least, his Aranda notes translated into English. When the Institute considered what it called Berndt's 'shadow application' on

Strehlow's behalf, it made all of this plain. In fact within eighteen months it granted Strehlow $2,000 for another trip. But what it could not and would not do was agree to fund Mrs Stuart as his research assistant in place of Miss Crowley.

Miss Crowley's salary had been paid by the Institute until Strehlow was appointed professor, after which the Institute asked the University of Adelaide to do so. The university, sympathetic to Berndt and Strehlow's view, suggested that the Institute pay half of Kathleen Stuart's salary.[40] But this it categorically refused to do. It was bad enough that the departure of Miss Crowley seemed to herald the end of the dictionary project, which implied a sad waste of funds in the past.* It was even harder to agree to wholeheartedly support a woman who had criticised them as Kathleen Stuart had. They gave no official reason for the decision not to fund her as a cartographer.

In December 1971 Kathleen had written to McCarthy, who told Berndt it was 'a most insulting attack.' Berndt found it a 'most distasteful' letter and thought that in future they should communicate only with Strehlow.[41] Fearing for Strehlow that such letters were being written at all, Berndt tried over the next few years to temper the furies of the Strehlow household, but in vain. Altogether the Strehlows' assault had by the winter of 1971 made a final break with the Institute inevitable: it was only a matter of time.

It must be said here that Strehlow found it increasingly impossible to seek more public money without directly or indirectly impugning the reputations of other beneficiaries. Prime targets were the musicologist Catherine Ellis and the remarkable amateur anthropologist Robert Edwards. In the case of Professor W.H. Stanner, Strehlow did not stoop to discrediting his work; instead he opposed Institute funding on the grounds of the good academic (and military!) salaries Stanner had received in his many distinguished years before retirement.[42]

At the same time, Strehlow had in July 1971 written the most carping of letters to the minister responsible for the Institute, W.C. Wentworth. It is an extraordinary fourteen-page biographical letter in which he sought to put Wentworth right on all manner of things, not the least of

---

*   Only a month earlier the Institute had calculated that it had funded Strehlow $37,375 since 1962, but Strehlow was paying no heed to that.

which was the poor quality of Wentworth's advice in the past and the charge that much of his own 'material is not available to other scholars.'

The tone is familiar as well—that of satisfied, if aggrieved, self-sacrifice by one who has laboured long and hard and probably deserves better. The letter recounts his childhood, his life as a patrol officer, when he was 'a sort of one-man Aboriginal Department for Central Australia,' his victory in improving rations, winning reserves and battling for Aborigines against the likes of pastoralist Kitto and 'their powerful friends in Melbourne and Canberra' and so on. It is a tale of Strehlow as hero, as collector and scholar of world importance, one whom even Lévi-Strauss had congratulated for 'shedding entirely new light on Australian ethnography,' and a supreme friend of the Aborigines.

Strehlow could be oblivious to the effect such a tone could have on others, even those who admired his work, and with Wentworth he was absolutely blunt with his self-justifying rhetoric.

> You asked, I am afraid a little jeeringly; 'Why should the aboriginals have singled you out, and shown their most secret sacred ceremonies to you and to no one else?'; and you suggested that at least some of the acts shown on the screen must have been performances specially composed for my benefit. You were not convinced by my arguments to the contrary in 1961. Perhaps you may be now. The real answer, of course, was that for ten years I had thrown in all my energies, all my money, and all my loyalties with the dark folk, and had stood up for their rights fearlessly against those white persons in Central Australia who had tried to exploit them some even to crush them. Out of gratitude they have revealed to me their most treasured possessions.

His narrative to Wentworth made the central and enduring point: that the knowledge he possessed was fortified by a unique moral claim to authority. This came from his well-earned place among the Aranda men. He did not speak specifically to Wentworth of land rights; it was hardly necessary by then. The more important thing was to put himself forward as a man who had come to feel unjustly forgotten, despite years of publications designed to make sense of and help the Aboriginal people. All of which entitled him, he told Wentworth, to bemoan the latter's earlier choice of advisers: for by leaving him out of account Wentworth had made 'final choices also about me and my work': 'Only you are in the position to know why my requests [for more financial assistance] were

turned down, and why I was permanently excluded from your circle
of advisers despite my decades of unrivalled field experience.' He
accused Wentworth of 'never finding time to see him' when in
Adelaide, and having made his 'final choices' about advisers as early as
1961. Strehlow need hardly have added: 'In view of what has been said
in this letter, I regret to state that there appears to be no point in our
meeting again.'[43]

Wentworth replied from a certain administrative height:

Dear Professor Strehlow,

I have your long letter. Whatever was told to you about 'Wentworth won't have a bar of your plans' was completely untrue. I have
in point of fact supported your work which I believe to be valuable
and, from my memory, you have received something over $50,000
from AIAS which is I think about as much as has been paid to
anybody.

This however is not the point. I still believe that your knowledge is
very valuable and I am anxious naturally that everything should be done
to preserve what is irreplaceable. As against this, neither Strehlow or
Wentworth is really important.

Whether or not your resentments of the past are justified, I would
ask you to forget them in the light of matters of greater moment.[44]

By 'matters of greater moment' Wentworth meant the fate of what
might now be called the Strehlow collection. On the face of things, all
parties—Wentworth, the Institute, the University of Adelaide, not to
mention the South Australian Museum—had a similar right to be concerned about its ultimate welfare. Welfare is a separate concept from
ownership, but the two were impossible to separate as far as the
Strehlows were concerned. Their thinking had been vividly expressed in
a letter from Kathleen to the Institute in July 1971. The 42-page letter
criticised the Institute and the University of Adelaide for being in
alliance against her husband. It accuses the University of Adelaide of
conspiring against Strehlow—to block the establishment of a Department of Anthropology, to keep him from being a professor—and attacks
the Institute for its grants policy.

More disturbing still was that Kathleen, speaking as her husband's protégée and heir and the one charged with the continuity
of his work, implied that if the persecution did not stop and her

husband was not allowed to carry on with his work for posterity the whole collection may as well go up in flames.

McCarthy took it as a serious threat.

Against Magpie Collectors

For some time a public debate had been emerging in Australia about the registration of Aboriginal sacred sites. The Institute was involved in developments towards a national policy and program for site registration. AIAS had identified 'a gap in our knowledge of Aboriginal culture . . . the recording of mythology, an important aspect of which is the mapping of all waterholes, hills, rocks and other places, sacred and otherwise, named in them.'[45] The Institute saw its task as helping to fill that gap in the most sensitive ways possible, by collating what information it could and attempting to think through such a delicate policy area. There was a catch-22 in this, for those who cared for Aboriginal culture: namely, how could the sites be protected if their location was a matter of public knowledge? That in turn raised thorny questions about who could rightfully collate such knowledge of the sites, and all that went with that in terms of Aboriginal authority of transmission and the trustworthiness of the recorder. The whole issue pointed to the struggles over authority that now beset contemporary politics in the Aboriginal domain.

Strehlow had stated his position as early as 1965, when he had gone to Darwin to give evidence to the special committee set up by the Legislative Council of the Northern Territory government to look into their Native and Historical Objects and Areas Preservation Ordinance. The Legislative Council noted that in the last 30 years Strehlow had 'removed many stone churingas from the Territory and although his activities have been known to the Welfare Branch he has never seen a copy of the ordinance.'[46] Nevertheless it heard Strehlow out with respect and gratitude. There was no denying the depth and breadth of his experience, and when their committee heard him present his now mythic biography, including the false claim that he had 'grown up *exclusively* with aboriginal children till the age of fourteen' (emphasis added), they were totally accepting.[47] Strehlow referred to 'the literature and the dramatic wealth of the country' and the basic right in Australia to 'religious freedom' which should, but did not, hold good for the secret religious traditions of the Centre. He argued that if Aboriginal religion was to be granted the religious freedom that applied to 'not only Christian churches, but also Jewish synagogues, Moslem mosques, and Masonic temples' then Aboriginal sacred sites needed the same protection against unauthorised entry and despoliation.

He emphasised three interlocking essentials. First, that 'all things connected with the old religion of Central Australia—myths, songs, dramatic acts, and sacred objects—were privately owned.' He elaborated on the sacred nature of the *tjurunga* as a man's personal tie with a site, and its indisputability as the private property of his sons, whose responsibility was to apply the rules of ownership and inheritance under penalty of death. Second, *tjurunga*, which were the key to the site, had *only* been handed over to him 'in the presence of all totemic clan members according to the correct ritual prescribed in such instances.' The claim was false, as we have seen, but from it followed his third point, namely that 'I am not in a position to divulge a great part of this information while any of the men to whom promises of secrecy have been given remain alive. Most of the myths and songs are hence still in the aboriginal languages in which they were originally recorded, and the film records of most of the dramatic performances have been placed in safe storage as individual strips which have not been pieced together.'

The Northern Territory's gratitude for this advice is perhaps odd, considering its practical uselessness with regard to policy formation. If, strictly speaking, only the older totemic clan authorities of secret-sacred sites should be allowed to 'trespass' on them, how could they be protected from people who lacked respect? Certainly it made sense for Strehlow to advise the Northern Territory that Aboriginal clansmen should not be obliged to let the government or the police know the location of their 'most intimate personal property.' But what use was this safeguard unless they had some authority over movement through their territory?

Strehlow was well aware of the ground-level facts. As he told a pastoralist in Central Australia: 'The old tribal discipline here has broken down completely, I am afraid; and all sorts of aboriginal stockmen, miners, and others are both stealing sacred objects from old caves in order to sell them to the tourists, or are showing sacred cave paintings to white anthropologists, government officials and others in return for minor rewards.'[48] My point here is that Strehlow's overall stance is both defeatist with regard to the fate of traditional Aboriginal culture, and self-seeking with regard to his own place in its 'preservation.' In essence everything he says points to a notion of unique access and possession on his part.

His self-glorifying paternalism had come to a head in March 1971, when he read what Noel Wallace, a recipient of Institute funds, had told the Institute in his field report: 'Pitjantjatjara men at Finke had obtained possession of Aranta sacred objects that were not being cared for in accordance with tribal "law"—they were to be brought to Ernabella and Amata so that they could be looked after properly.'

Strehlow called this theft. If what Wallace reported was true, the Pitjantjatjara men had stolen Aranda objects. Strehlow knew the place, he knew the objects: he had made notes on them. He knew that the Pitjantjatjara men could not have made the supposed 'identifications.' The Aranda *tjurunga* could not be 'cared for' by persons who do not know their 'name verses' or 'the sacred acts associated with them.' Removed from their totemic sites, 'they will become, in an anthropological sense, just so much useless stone and wooden rubbish: this is a fate that has already been suffered by large numbers of the ineptly catalogued Aranda tjurunga which now clutter up the Central Australian collections thrown together by enthusiastic "collectors" in the National Museum, Melbourne, around the beginning of this century.' The last point was another jibe at Baldwin Spencer. But his final remarks hurled the spear at all 'southern museums' and proposed site officers:

> By encouraging AIAS researchers who are ignorant of aboriginal languages to flit around the country and to pick up scraps of songs and traditions indiscriminately, like magpies which swoop down for their random pickings here, there, and everywhere, the AIAS Council may succeed in building up a large Tape Archive, and it may even collect considerable quantities of sacred sticks and stones for stocking up museum rooms; but the quality of these verbal and material scraps is unlikely to merit in the end a better rating than that implied by the familiar label 'fair average quality'; and much of it may well have to be reclassified by posterity as being much lower than that.[49]

McCarthy thanked him for his concern and said they would follow up the matter. McCarthy himself thought that men like Strehlow and Elkin and Stanner—men who had long experience in the field and no personal difficulty with sacred items—would be the best starting point for the 'delicate policy' the Institute had to work out. McCarthy's remarks foreshadowed the real hard work of policy-making to come: 'There are a lot of interests to be consulted and to be satisfied, ranging from Aborigines

themselves, legislation of all levels ranging from Federal and State ministers, through Welfare Officers and on to field workers, past and present
and Museum authorities or holders of archives.' This world, increasingly,
was bigger than Strehlow, and he knew it.

The Great Book at Last

In November 1971 *Songs of Central Australia* was published at last, a
sumptuous book of which the publisher and author were justifiably
proud. Angus & Robertson printed 1,000 copies to be sold at $65. At
a glance, collectors of rare books knew it was for them: the size of the
edition and the price confirmed it. Publisher and author would have
loved to get the price down, but the costs of production had been too
high. Costings had at least doubled since the book had been accepted
for publication in 1957; by 1967 they were to be at least $16,000 before
the cost of plates and binding, a looming total that had only been subsidised to the tune of $3,500.[50] Angus & Robertson had been loyal to
the project, mostly at their own expense, and Strehlow had been quite
right, overall, to moan about the lack of subsidies from public bodies.[51]
Over the years the book was in production, various means of keeping
the cost down had been considered, but had come to nothing. Strehlow
had stuck with his expensive diacritics, as well as the even less dispen-
sable musical notations, both of which were a nightmare for the typesetters. There were no photographs even though Strehlow had his own
archive of wonderful images from which to choose. They were omitted
out of deference to the secret nature of their contents.

The first review Strehlow read of his book was in the *Times Literary
Supplement* in July 1972. Its haughty English tone, sustained by the
valorous anonymity the paper granted to reviewers of the time, was one
Strehlow had known too well when he was in London.

The review began by stating that *Songs* was not 'the major contribution to social anthropology' that might have been expected of the first
complete account of a poetic heritage by 'an intelligent and sympathetic
observer who had grown up in Central Australia who had then devoted
much of thirty-five years to studying their myths, songs and secret
dramatic performances.' While there was much information about the
Aranda, it was scattered among the pages of 'a quick correspondence
course in world literature,' so that 'the reader is compelled to pick out
the Aranda material in the fog of the author's Grand Theory about the
origins of poetry, which takes up about one sixth of the book.'

With regard to 'song' the reviewer noted the contradiction involved in Strehlow calling it a 'literary production.' Strehlow's 'literary production' was reproached for referring to Latin, Greek and German words for what was sung or intoned, rather than Aranda concepts. 'The author's somewhat paternalistic concern for public recognition of the intellectual and artistic ability of "our Central Australian makers of verse" is thereby cancelled out by his refusal to let the Aranda material stand on its own, or to allow Aranda informants to provide their own analytical clues.' With the music Strehlow had used 'the European strait-jacket of bar-lines and rigid time-signatures' rather than Aranda musical concepts. 'The musical analysis of the songs is unlikely to satisfy any ethnomusicologist.'

As for the anthropologists, useful information for them was in the long, third part of the book about subject matter and themes. The reviewer paid respect to Strehlow's material on the Aranda singer and song, the naming and the word weaving. But the book was radically unbalanced by its European exegesis that masked the Aranda 'experience in living': 'The reviewer counted 950 different Aranda couplets, which with their English translations take up about a fifth of the book. This is only a fraction more space than that taken by the quotations from European literature. In the chapter devoted to human beauty and love charms, which is easily the longest section of Part Three and contains more Aranda couplets than usual, there are 32 pages of Aranda poetry, 20 pages of background information and analysis, and 28 pages of quotations and discussion of European attitudes to love!'

There was a strange aside, at least to the Australian reader. The reviewer seemed to think that Strehlow was obliged to question the intrinsic worth of the Aranda culture and its poetry. 'Subsistence in the Australian desert was harsh enough, but an ingenious technology and careful control of resources made life possible and even afforded considerable leisure time. Why was this time not used to improve the standard of living, and why did tribal custom demand yet more suffering in the cruelty, blood, and anger of circumcision and other rituals?' Why, the reviewer seemed to be asking, did things remain so 'primitive'? 'Strehlow shows clearly how much intellectual effort went into the creation of the Aranda poetry, but he does not consider whether it was worth the price or whom it benefited.' Then the last damning paragraph: '*Songs of Central Australia* tells us something of the creativity and intellectual achievements of the Aranda's forebears but

little of the quality of their lives, which poetry is surely intended to
reflect and enhance. It is essentially a shallow and sadly unrewarding
account, which reflects not so much the austerity and efficiency of the
Aranda's subsistence economy in a harsh environment as the verbal
extravagances of their religious superstructures.'[52]

So much for a life's work.

It was a shrewd, hostile review, written by someone who seemed to
be personally familiar with Aranda song and who had an axe to grind
about the cruel chauvinisms of the culture. Its tone, to begin with, is
certainly in tune with the *TLS* house style of English condescension,
but then it changes into something else: a more direct discourse on the
Aranda culture that had to change because as an 'experiment in living'
it left something to be desired in terms of the weight it gave to 'religious superstructures,' a Marxist term that revealed in an instant the
reviewer's hostility to religion, and therefore to the entire poetics of
Strehlow's work.

For Strehlow it was 'a shocking emotional blow,' 'a devastating rub-
bishing,' 'a blow full of deadly malice.' Outraged, trembling, he remonstrated in his diary on 19 July 1972, casting around for enemies:

The firm must have sent them a review copy; the reviewer was probably
the same man who rubbished 'Songs' when the Clarendon Press—at Sir
Maurice Bowra's instance—asked him for an opinion. The reviewer
jeered at the musical transcription (not by me anyway: the most jeered
transcription is by an 'ethnomusicologist' anyway), nagged at there
being no pictures (these could not be put in lest Aboriginal readers be
mortally offended), criticised me for showing how this verse was related
to 'the quality of [Aboriginal] life' (a sign he has not even read the main
text thoroughly), & finally takes the Central Australian folk to task for
not spending their ingenuity to ameliorate their living conditions rather
than spreading poetry over their harsh environment. Clearly the writer
is himself a white racist to whom 'the good life' means only food &
drink, refrigerators, a car, & lots of idle leisure time. The critic also took
me to task for not showing up what Aranda prose was like—when in
fact it was a book on verse—which no one else has ever succeeded in
translating into English at all! Probably the critic was incensed at my
demolishing Spencer as the only divinity on the Aranda! Having
ignored all the positive features of the book—it provides the texts used
on all social & ritual occasions—then he complacently dismissed it as

'shallow.' I strongly suspect the writer was Raymond Firth, & his main prompter was probably my own old treacherous enemy—Stanner.

He was stunned for the rest of the day. Relief only came when Kathleen came back from the doctor: she was pregnant, and well, and 'that gave both of us something stimulating to talk about.'*

There was something not mentioned in the review. The map. The luxurious, sepia-tinted production tucked into its sleeve at the back of the book. The map was designed to demonstrate the terrain animated by song, the country from which the songs came: it was there to peruse in all its Aboriginal significance. Although it did not pinpoint secret

---

* In Australia, Elkin made up for any damage he might have done by declaring, unambiguously, that *Songs* was one of the three highly significant books in the history of Australian anthropology, to be appraised beside Lorimer Fison and Alfred Howitt's *Kamilaroi and Kurnai* of 1880 and Spencer and Gillen's *The Native Tribes of Central Australia* of 1899. Elkin said Strehlow was the 'gifted author' of a 'superb, scholarly work' the aspects of which were 'manifold, illuminating Aboriginal life, thought, belief and custom.'

A long scholarly review would be needed to do justice to the book's strengths, Elkin wrote: 'To mention but one: this is the love of "homeland," of one's own country with its "everlasting" totemic centre,—a concept of fundamental importance these days when the demand for aboriginal Land Rights is both moral and political . . . Another point made by the author is that the poetry is of vital importance to the Central Australian. It opens a pathway into a real world, as real as the every day word—a world of "eternal and unalterable truths."'

Elkin had changed his mind about the terms for Aboriginal song. Years before, when he had published his classic study, *The Australian Aborigine*, he did not rank it as poetry, but now, after experiencing what he called Strehlow's magnum opus, 'a unique and outstanding literary work—a contribution to the world's literary treasure trove,' he did. And he did so partly, he went on to add, because of Strehlow's intimacy with his subjects, the fact that he was 'in a cultural sense an Aranda, having been admitted into that culture by the children first and later by the elders and the aged.' Elkin said Strehlow had gained a 'well-grounded respect for the old men and their predecessors. This book is an expression of that respect.'

In this review, Strehlow was not reproached for being outside the mainstream of anthropology. His work was placed in an ethnographic tradition that had a wider history than the rise and fall of functionalism, and wider still than contemporary schools that were converging on problems of social structure as they pertained to land ownership. That was partly Elkin's point when he emphasised 'homeland.' Strehlow's cultural analysis, which was combined with so much personal knowledge, had made a canvas that was dynamically useful, contemporary. Furthermore, he had been able to do so not simply because of his industry and 'remarkable gift for translating,' but because the knowledge was his in a special way on account of the long, intimate history of his linguistic liaisons. All of which was good for Strehlow, but it would have been better if the review had been published earlier than 1975.

sites exactly, as they might be located on a survey map, it was a grand sketch map that named and located the most important places Strehlow had been to since 1932—the places where the old men had unwrapped their *tjurunga* out of what he memorialised as the 'last caves' and so on. The map was a code to his own Worthsworthian *Prelude*: it showed his own spots in time, where his life's work had begun, the 'fructifying virtue' of which was now there for all to see in the book that was his life.[53] In its own way the map was the secret-sacred seal to the whole literary endeavour. Touch the map the Strehlows had made and you touched the whole nervous system of their increasingly strident identification with 'traditional' Aranda culture.

Strehlow—the Strehlows—seem to have lain low as the various reviews came out. An episode with one correspondent illustrates the edge they were on. It was about the map, the thing in the book most emblematic of the Strehlows' sense of territory.

A couple of weeks after publication Strehlow received a respectful letter from Dick Kimber, a schoolteacher at Alice Springs. Kimber, who was to become the pre-eminent amateur historian of Central Australia, had seen the map before he had the book, and it was not too late to correct a mistake. He had been travelling with a Pintubi guide and friend south-west of Mount Liebig, the area where Strehlow had defined the boundary between Aranda and Pintubi and Kukatja people. Kimber wrote to say he thought the map was incorrect—perhaps by about 20 to 30 miles in favour of the Pintubi/Kukatja. He enclosed a sketch map of his travels and mentioned in passing that Bob Edwards would verify his view. Edwards, employed by the South Australian Museum, and a member of the Institute, was already in the Strehlows' sights over sacred sites matters.

Kathleen, as the one who had drawn the maps, replied by dismissing Edwards as an untrained museum latecomer and reminding Kimber of Strehlow's record in the field. She pointed out, quite rightly, that there was not much difference between Kimber's line and Strehlow's, and that in any case the boundaries of the Western Desert groups, who had to survive in extreme seasons, were rather more fluid than those of the Aranda.

The tone got Kimber's dander up. He wrote back with detailed evidence of his own Aboriginal connections, pointing out how he had been shown 'what no other white man had ever observed.' Kimber, who was a wide and diligent reader, then documented his written sources: he felt his own position had 'not been blasted into obscurity.'[54]

The joust had begun. Despite Kimber's protestations that he was merely trying 'to retain the perfection of the work,' his approach and his defence of Edwards confirmed for the Strehlows that there was more to this stranger than met the eye. Kathleen told Kimber so. With Edwards in her sights, she stressed how only Strehlow had the language and the songs to validate his sense of a map and its boundaries. He was an Aranda man himself, and she was his only partner and his heir. The whole thrust of her letter was to insist that only she and her husband had been entrusted with the records that showed how things were before the white man.

Strehlow as an 'Aranda man' goaded Kimber. Now both parties were choosing to speak on behalf of one or another senior Aboriginal 'informant.' Kimber took the high ground, reminding Kathleen that he had written respectfully on this matter to her man, not to her, and parried in a parody of black man's talk:

Old man Strehlow, I told you true. You lie (Aboriginal sense).

You send a woman on men's business.

Why do you do that, Old Man Strehlow? You do not do it because you are afraid, do you?

Why do you insult me, old man Strehlow? [55]

All were insulted now. It did Kimber no good to go on about his reverence for Strehlow's scholarly work: 'God could not do better if he were to attempt a history and recording of Aranda ways.' He went on: 'I agree with you wholeheartedly that "[the] only way the white man can hope to understand the dark man is through the eyes of the dark man himself"' and assured her: 'I do appreciate that your husband obtained much of his information from "pre-white" sources.' But—and he went on to say what was now crucial in the whole political dynamic towards Aboriginal autonomy in central Australia:

I do not know that that precludes an 'ignorant young fellow' from having any knowledge whatsoever of his traditional, 'proper country' or of other facts of the old way of life. I do not say that 'the present generation of aboriginal people . . . can teach its grandparents how to suck eggs.' But I do believe that in some ways they often suck the same eggs! In matters of teaching, sharing of food, cooking of food, etc. the old ways are still followed quite strongly, at least in certain areas or certain conditions (often as we derive much more from our forefathers than I think we generally believe).

To make matters worse, Kimber made the men's versus women's business even more pointed for Strehlow's heir. The issue was who was entitled to be 'salvaging' the old culture?

> Yes, I realised that your husband has been doing this, and I also know that Spencer and Gillen thought of themselves as doing the same. Me, well, I just feel very privileged to be able to see some of those 'last vestiges' which your husband has experienced, and I record what I see, hear of and am told. I do it because so much has gone forever, and so little has been recorded, and to me it seems very important that even scraps should be retained, for one day they may add a little colour. Most of what I have seen has been in trust, so no one but me sees my records—certainly no woman or children of my colour . . .
>
> I agree with your description of your husband as 'one of the greatest of all scholars, and the greatest man in his field'—I would blazon the latter half in capitals, for no one will equal him in his Aranda knowledge. It is for this reason that I said he could see my notes if he wished . . . They were for his eyes, I am afraid, and not yours, and it is on this condition I still would allow him to see them if he so desired.

Kimber was not to know the depth of bonding between the Strehlows, any more than he was privy to their wars with the Institute. If he had known, he would never have imagined there was anything Strehlow would keep from his wife. So implacably was this the case that Kathleen told Kimber, in her last words before their schism, that she had not wanted Strehlow to reply to Kimber at all and had agreed only on one condition—that the letter be written in a way that *she* could sign it. In all the battles now, they spoke as one. Kimber once more replied, offering an apology and praising *Songs*, which he had purchased and read.

In the wake of the publication of *Songs*, Strehlow was formally separating from Bertha. McNally resumes on the painful divorce proceedings: 'When Bertha recovered from this shock sufficiently, she sued for divorce on the grounds of desertion. The divorce was made final by the Honourable Justice Roma Mitchell only in 1972. Bertha did not seek maintenance. She proudly stated that, as a senior teacher at Wilderness School for Girls, her salary was ample for her needs. But Justice Mitchell said that, in view of Bertha's age, the time might not be far away when she would need some financial help, and that, if such a need arose, she should come back to the court and seek a reassessment of her position.' Bertha never did.

In July 1972, six weeks after the divorce, Kathleen changed her name from Stuart to Strehlow by deed poll. The Strehlows were married in the Adelaide Registry Office on 25 September, a date chosen to mark the wedding anniversary of Strehlow's father and mother at Point Pass in 1895.

In 1973 the new Mrs Strehlow gave birth to their son, who was named after his grandfather, Carl. It was clear almost from the beginning that he was rather a hyperactive child. The dismay of the ageing, meritocratic father can only be imagined, as can the depth of weariness at having to start the rounds of childrearing all over again. From all accounts, however, Strehlow was a tender, devoted father to the demanding Carl, who would, with his mother, inherit everything Strehlow had collected during his working life with Bertha. His children from the first marriage—Theodor, Shirley and John—were completely dispossessed by their father.

Divorcing Canberra

'I don't really think Strehlow looks upon Central Australia as his own preserve,' Berndt was trying to tell the Institute in the summer of 1972, 'or no more than many of us look at our own field work areas as "our own"':

Certainly there are areas in which Catherine [Berndt] and I have worked, intensively, and occasions when we have objected strenuously to others going over ground we have covered *without* reference to us, and without consultations: and coming up with 'new' discoveries of which we have already written! I don't think it's any more than this. It *is* necessary for contemporary research workers to respect the work of others who have worked in the same area as themselves. I would also not feel, myself, that anthropologists 'are becoming very impatient at not being able to consult much more of the results of Strehlow's research.' Strehlow has not been slow in publishing. Many others who have received grants from various sources have done far less. Look over his complete bibliography: the one which was submitted when he was upgraded to professorial status. And his recent volume on *Songs of Central Australia*. This is most impressive. So I think your comment here could justifiably make Strehlow angry—it would me! (I expect there *are* people who say it about me too!)[56]

It is hard to imagine a saner and more open-handed letter in the circumstances. Most of what Berndt said was right, especially with regard to Strehlow's publications. He had a good list to show, including papers in the mainstream of technical anthropology. His work was on-going, and of a sensitive nature that could not automatically be shown to anyone. Further financial assistance to Strehlow should surely not have been out of the question, especially since the Institute under the Whitlam Government was 'dramatically' better funded than before.[57] Putting aside the *TLS* review, Strehlow's work was at its peak in terms of its prestige, and he was right to think that he had a great deal of material still to translate, catalogue, preserve, before his time ran out. 'I need decades in which to continue my own University research work and my own writings if I am to bring my labours of almost forty years in the Centre to a conclusion that will satisfy posterity. Hence I cannot agree to any diversions,' Strehlow wrote in 1971.[58] He would not have decades. All the more reason for a man like Berndt, who knew Strehlow and his work so well, to keep batting for him.

The Institute now had considerable funds to develop a national program of recording 'sites of significance' for the Aboriginal people. The policy was announced by the Minister of Environment, Aborigines and the Arts, Peter Howson, at the 1972 Annual General Meeting of AIAS. In May there was a national seminar to shape a heritage policy. Strehlow was antipathetic to all breaches of secrecy with sacred sites. One resolution in particular incensed him. Moved by the director of the Western Australian Museum, and seconded by the Western Australian registrar of Sacred Sites, it said: 'This seminar recognises that aboriginal sites are an important and non-renewable part of the capital equipment of the Australian tourist industry, and asks the Minister to give consideration to appointing a committee to advise on the exploitation of aboriginal monuments, antiquities and sites for tourism and the best means of providing adequate protection for such sites.'[59]

'Exploitation' and 'capital equipment' were the key words for Strehlow. It meant despoliation and ran counter to any idea of protection. His logic had the sympathy of many, including some at the Institute, but there was no stopping the general trend towards registration. The last straw was when the Institute formed its Sites of Significance committee which he was not on.

In April 1973 Strehlow resigned from the Institute. It was a 'protest against the anti-aboriginal policies of the AIAS, past present and future.' This rather than 'betray' the 'trust' of 'My Central Australian Aboriginal friends . . . by appearing to side with those who seek to exploit them.'[60] His language was polemical in the extreme, fired by a kind of Cold War rhetoric rather than any of the considerations that were beginning to be addressed at the Institute:

> the Australian Government—in typical *fait accompli* style—is now launching an all-out national assault on what remains of the religion and human privileges of the aboriginal population of Central Australia. Under the pretext of 'saving' the sacred sites and 'preserving' the cultural heritage of aboriginal Australians, a body of civil servants, and anthropological researchers is to be appointed by the Government, without any invitation by tribal elders, and given Australia-wide coercive legal powers and ample finance to extract centuries old secret information on sacared [*sic*] sites and religious practices from the remaining tribalised aboriginal and to bring together all remaining sacred objects to storage centres 'protected' by Government officials. This scheme, it should be noted, has not been devised by the aboriginals concerned nor approved by them. On the contrary, the true owners (as opposed to Government stooges) now stand to lose their last possessions—the most important elements of their traditional culture heritage—just as their forefathers lost their lands to white pioneers. Experience has shown that every sacred site known to whites, by gazettal or otherwise, has promptly been desecrated by vandals and looted by predators; and the storage of sacred objects has yielded good salaries for white 'curators of anthropology' 'guarding' them.[61]

As if this was not enough, Strehlow then spoke out in public. An article appeared in the *Australian* in December under the heading 'Jobs for the (White) Boys' with a photograph of Coombs. He attacked the Institute for flouting its purpose, namely the 'preservation of the most comprehensive records of traditional Aboriginal culture in all its multitudinous aspects.' Instead the Institute had, among other vices, 'fostered short field trips by persons eager to gain easy fame through obtaining material for short papers and theses.' Under the aegis of the Institute, researchers had 'gorged themselves mainly on the aboriginal classificatory kinship terms, but had not bothered to obtain the full genealogical records (including all the totemic centres) of all their informants stretching back a couple of generations before any white contact.'[62]

The article was only a small part of what he had to say. By the middle of the year he was telling the anthropologist Derek Freeman in Canberra, 'My isolation has become absolute and complete,' and declaiming: 'Like my dark friends and informants, [I] will not hand over what I have for the glory of greedy white imposters [sic] who have leapt upon the Aboriginal band wagon. It is better for aboriginal culture to die than to be prostituted in this shameful way . . . Let them . . . "produce the goods" out of their own treasuries of aboriginal research—if they can!!'[63]

The range of the Strehlow attack on the Institute became public.[64] In language hardly designed to prompt civilised debate, he was raising issues that went to the heart of the matter of the competitive workings of anthropology as a profession—a topic that had barely seen the light of day in Australia at the time. In general, anthropology was a discipline late to apply an epistemological critique to itself. More particularly, anthropologists attached to the Institute had been working under a charter that tied them to 'fundamental' research in a way that hampered a full address to the intellectual and ethical issues of being in the field with living communities, as distinct from inevitably dying cultures. Therefore the question of the rights to privacy, the safety or otherwise of the secret-sacred, and the quality of the relationship between the anthropologist and the Aborigine were of central importance to sort out. That Strehlow's outburst bloodied the waters did not mean these questions did not have to be addressed.

Strehlow's stance obscured the start that had already been made. In 1971 John Mulvaney had convened an Institute conference on the anthropologist and fieldwork. Two scandals about the publication of visual material revealing the secret-sacred had stirred the Institute into thought about guidelines. The Institute was becoming increasingly conscious that it could not shy away from a critical analysis of anthro-pological history, or research into the contemporary complexities of

Aboriginal Identity.[65] Its membership was shockingly dominated by white academics and only one Aborigine belonged to it in 1974. By that year, in fact, AIAS president Peter Ucko was announcing that 'research and Aboriginal indigenous activity are not separate activities,'[66] a statement that could not have been made a few years before.

Given this movement, Strehlow's outburst might be seen as speeding some things up. Certainly, after Strehlow, the spotlight was on the pointed charge of academic careerism at the expense of Aborigines. There was by 1974 what Mulvaney has called a 'deluge of criticism from Aborigines, bureaucrats, politicians and many academics.'[67] Among the Aborigines were two theatrical players calling themselves 'Eaglehawk and Crow,' whose open letter of 29 March 1974 attacked the logic of the Institute's planned international conference:

Why is this conference being held? . . . We believe that this conference will make no positive contribution to Australian society and in particular to the position of Aborigines in relation to the total Australian society.

For the participants, the conference will, at best, provide an opportunity for academics to come together, socialise, exchange esoteric facts and abstract theories about their 'fascinating subject matter,' and perhaps even arrive at some new abstractions about human societies in general. It will give them a new sense of 'relevance' and assumed importance. At worst it will provide some of the participants with the opportunity to climb the academic ladder, to obtain recognition from the government for their ideas on how to deal with the 'Aboriginal problem,' and secure them more funds for more research. The conference is unlikely to help any of the participants come to any terms of human relationship with the people from whom they learn (usually called 'informants') and the groups. It is unlikely to help them understand the facts of Aboriginal life, and death, in Australia today.

For the Institute, and especially its Principal, Peter Ucko, the conference is a major weapon for gaining international prestige and a modern relevant image. This, we know, is to impress the government enough to make it think the Institute, as it is now constituted and under the guise of its current 'relevant' programs, is worth more money and worth listening to for advice on Aboriginal matters. This will have the effect of extending the power academics exercise over the lives of the people they study.[68]

The authors were Terry Widders and Peter Thompson, Aborigines from New South Wales. They were speaking pure Strehlow, but with a little more political refinement. Strehlow wrote to congratulate them on their 'excellent case' and explained that he could not go to the conference because he had already resigned.[69]

Some re-thinking and refinement of thinking was now taking place at the Institute. It culminated in a 1975 summary paper on the 'secret-sacred dimension' by Berndt and the Aboriginal writer Dick Roughsey. Admittedly, the paper was by no means designed to address Strehlow's focus, as it stated that with the care of the secret-sacred 'the real problem does not focus on professional anthropologists'; and it shirked the issue of defining 'real responsibilities' and what it was to be 'committed' to an Aboriginal field of study. What it did, however, was focus some of the hitherto 'hazy' thinking about sensitive local knowledge of different kinds in different places at different times. 'We,' the authors said, hoping to speak for the profession, 'need to get over [to the Aborigines] our own ideas about scientific research, its importance to Aborigines themselves and to the understanding of human behaviour generally.' The hope was that after careful 'logical explanation' Aborigines would understand that it was in their inter- ests not to let their sacred knowledge 'die with themselves' and that they might see 'the importance of their social–cultural life (all aspects of it) continuing in a different form from what it was when it was a living reality.'[70]

The paper raised as many issues as it finally clarified, but its trans- parency was its virtue. The reader can see where professional self- interest really might be at odds with those of Aborigines. The notion of hope for a culture was also fully articulated, as it always was, by Berndt, whose thinking never assumed that the songs had been broken. For Berndt and the Institute, that was now a politically open issue in ways that it was not for Strehlow.

What was now broken for him was any creative, sustaining link with Canberra. The crucial severance from the Institute was synonymous to severance from insiders at the ANU and others who were advising the government. And that in turn seems to have coloured all that he had to say about the historic moment with land rights. The Whitlam Govern- ment was intent on granting Northern Territory Aborigines land rights. To guide its thinking on this matter, it set up a commission chaired by Justice Woodward and advised by Nicolas Peterson, a bright anthropologist (and Englishman) at ANU. Strehlow, the renowned expert on Central Australia, was not consulted and, it seems, made no submissions to the commission. Peterson is of the opinion that Strehlow was not drawn into the advisory process at least partly because 'his general reputation' had suffered from the row with the Institute. What also deterred the commission was Strehlow 'claiming that he was the traditional owner for Hermannsburg.' Strehlow told a Northern Territory government official with regard to Finke River mythology: 'I already own the myths concerning these sites and have seen their ceremonies—both pieces of information having been given to me by their now-dead aboriginal owners on the promise of strict secrecy.'[71] If the Woodward Commission had known about Strehlow 'the Black Missionary' it would have been even less interested in his advice.

Beyond that, however, it was perhaps the acutely local nature of Strehlow's focus that made him less useful than he might have been. 'Because,' as Peterson puts it, 'the Commission was not primarily concerned with patterns of land ownership but rather with the practicalities of how land could be transferred to Aboriginal people it was also felt that it was unlikely that he would have anything to add to the submissions we already had from Hermannsburg.'[72]

The Commonwealth government passed its Northern Territory Land Rights Act in 1976 and Strehlow was in principle in accord with the Act. Land rights had always been part of his thinking. But he stood back suspiciously, sceptically, on the sidelines, casting doubt on two things that gave succour to those opposed to its implementation: the extent to which the legislation proposed by Woodward could accurately read local indigenous knowledge about ownership; and the suitability of the Land Councils and the Land Trusts as vehicles for delivering land rights. He was especially concerned that 'the only persons who will in the end benefit will be the half-caste bureaucrats and white lawyers . . . the true aboriginal owners will lose out as usual.'[73]

Strehlow was, for a moment, poised to be involved in the workings of the Act in 1975, when it was in a draft stage and a clause allowed for land rights to be granted to traditional owners in Alice Springs (a provision subsequently deleted by the Fraser Government when it passed the Act in 1976). Strehlow was passionate about 'the true aboriginal owners' in Alice Springs, by which he meant the Aranda, whose territory and genealogies he had mapped.

He was keen to establish two things at once: the validity of traditional rights in the town, and of his authority to specify the local
descent group. 'Since their fathers and mothers, their grandfathers and
grandmother were the men and women whose labours helped the old
white pioneers to built up the original Alice Springs and the old telegraph station, surely even the most elementary sense of white justice
could compel our present law-givers to see that the descendants of the
original Paltara-Knguarea group of Alice Springs are not completely
passed over in the rush of land claims at present being put up by the
Central Land Council.'[74]

Strehlow's political thrust here was to cast doubt on claims that
might be made by other groups, especially considering 'the inadequate
and inaccurate information' that went into the Woodward report. He
was keen to draw attention to the ambiguous position of what he
called, as if reaching back into his files as a patrol officer, 'part-aboriginals.' This was his loaded, contemporary political argument about the
rights, or otherwise, of most Aborigines now living in the town. He
wrote:

> The strong racial attitudes inculcated into the Alice Springs part-
> aboriginal children at the Bungalow, wherever located, resulted in the
> isolation of the Alice Springs part-aboriginal population from the
> full-blood population of this area: the part aboriginals looked on
> themselves as members of the white population, and tended to despise
> their full-blood black relatives. None of the institution trained part
> aboriginals were hence regarded as belonging to the full-blood popu-
> lation, and their 'land rights,' if any, were at best illusionary in the eyes
> of the full-blood aboriginals. To what extent this situation persists in
> today's Alice Springs I do not feel competent to judge. However, I do
> feel that all descendants of the original Paltara-Knuarea local group of
> Tjoritja should be regarded as having better 'land rights' in Alice
> Springs than any 'foreigners,' i.e., full-blood aboriginals and others
> who have moved into the Alice Springs area only since the beginning
> of white settlement.[75]

It was a strange argument that seemed, on the face of it, to invest too
much in an impossibly distant time before the white man, rather as if
detribalisation had been a cut and dried process and Aborigines had no
right to reconsider the basis of their on-going inheritance. More

immediately, Strehlow's position seemed to permanently dispossess most of the Aboriginal people in Alice Springs. Short of a policy of expatriation to their original lands, what was to become of them? He mooted the idea of special residential areas for Aborigines, areas that paid respect to the original Aranda owners and the relative 'strangers,' the other language groups. And here he added, rather foresightedly: 'These "aboriginal sections" or future "aboriginal suburbs" should not be introduced by backdoor methods through alleged "claims for aboriginal land rights"; otherwise these areas may develop into future slums, a most terrifying prospect.'

It becomes clear, reading through Strehlow's paper today, that he was thinking with an acute distaste for what many Aborigines had become: the 'driftwood' long feared and anticipated, those whose symptoms of 'runny noses, diseased ears and eyes, alcoholism' were exacerbated by Federal government's 'clumsy interference' over so many years. And it emerges, as he casts his mind back over his own comings and goings in Alice Springs since 1932, that the full force of that distaste came to him in the early sixties when he was camped on the Todd River, and 'running through several cycles and their sacred ceremonies' with a number of elders he had pitched camp with just below Amoonguna. 'The noise of drunken brawls often floated down to us from the Settlement, particularly on 'pay nights,' and I was told by many of my black friends that they far preferred to camp outside Amoonguna than on it.'

The tone, as ever with Strehlow, is proprietorial, his mood pessimistic. He would have more to say about the Alice Springs Aborigines when they challenged his collection of sacred objects. For this period, though—the historic one of enacting the Land Rights legislation—his outlook was determined less by the creativity of that historical moment than his doomsday judgment about the quality of thinking in Canberra. As one historian has put it, 'he set out a lineage of "chaotic" advice to the Commonwealth—Spencer, Cook, Chinnery, Hasluck, Coombs and Stanner,' the likes of whom Strehlow told Minister for Aboriginal Affairs Viner, 'looked on the N.T. aboriginal purely as challenging experimental or administrative material, but never could establish any real personal contacts with them as friends or even as human beings, who had legitimate hopes, fears and aspirations of their own. The present N.T land rights bill may please lawyers, but it will change nothing in the human sphere. All inhuman theorists and advisers should be sacked as a first step.'[76]

The Burning Collection, Burning Letters

While he was fighting with the Institute in Canberra, Strehlow was also digging his grave at the University of Adelaide. With the threat of burning the collection still in the air, negotiations began between the Strehlows and the university to set up a Strehlow Research Centre, an institution of some kind that would house the collection on campus, help Strehlow continue to write up his work, and order and protect the archive for posterity.

During these agonised dealings Strehlow spoke of leaving the country, presumably with his collection in tow.[77] He warned it was better that 'all the knowledge I have should perish' than it fall into the hands of 'ignorant and irresponsible academics.'[78] He said that he had already begun to destroy the collection for fear that one day the state might control it; in fact, he calmly told his deputy vice-chancellor, 'a considerable amount of paper had been burnt, some records and notes were burnt as recently as a few weeks ago.' He explained, apparently with a chilling sangfroid, that 'it was his duty to burn certain Aboriginal material rather than have it fall into the wrong hands. He claimed that a tribal aboriginal who disinherited his son would himself burn his tjurunga, because there would be nobody to whom it could then belong.'[79]

The university was aghast, distressed, outraged and fearful. It had spent years trying to secure the collection in ways that accommodated Strehlow. After the first eighteen months of dealings Strehlow had written to them so libellously that the university took legal advice, sealed the letters and placed them in the strongroom, to be opened only by resolution of its full council. The vice-chancellor wanted the letters burnt, but a member of the council said that then 'a future historian might be led to make even more adverse deductions about their contents.'[80] The letters stayed in the strongroom.

The university's negotiator with the Strehlows was convinced they were part of a 'developing tragedy that could and should have been averted.'[81] The council was worried that Strehlow was 'possibly on the verge of a mental breakdown.'[82] Its negotiator wanted the university to show 'compassion during Professor Strehlow's physical and mental sickness,' but that was easier said than done after the incendiary letters. In the end the university did show some compassion, all things considered; it resigned itself to Strehlow's militant privatisation of the collection, taking pains to reassure their troubled professor that 'the university does not wish to lay claim to any materials assembled by you in the course of your employment with the university.'[83]

In the beginning the plan looked almost feasible. Evidently—a point that helped fuel Strehlow's escalation of the stakes—it was the university's idea to set up some kind of Strehlow Centre. In 1974 Professor Noel Flentje approached Strehlow with this in mind: the idea was to pay Strehlow beyond the point of retirement, as well as his research assistant Kathleen, and to house the collection safely—safely in terms of its secret-sacred material, and safe for the use of further scholarship, which Strehlow as director would oversee when the time was right. For Strehlow, this looked promising as he had no other means of support forthcoming. For the university, it secured the safety of the collection, although not, as was to emerge, necessarily its ownership.

Strehlow seems to have been inspired by one aspect of the further work:

> The unique purpose of the Institute would not only be to translate for posterity my collection of myths and songs so that they could be linguistic texts illustrating the languages of Central Australia, but also give full accounts of the religion, the social structure, and the totemic landscape of Central Australia, *in the words of the Aborigines themselves.* This has not been done for any other part of Australia, where these things have not only been limited by a gravely inadequate amount of basic data, but have often been seriously distorted by researchers who not only could not speak the languages of their informants, but—worse still—consciously or unconsciously distorted their observations far too often to fit in with the white anthropological theories current at the time. In this way the work done in this Institute would offset the many mythical addenda to aboriginal beliefs and institutions which are accepted as present by most Australian anthropologists as the canon of 'aboriginal culture.'

It was Strehlow's emphasis, even if it was not clear how his forthcoming work would differ from any he had done before, which had always been intimate with the Aranda. The statement stood, however, as a coda for Strehlow's unique linguistic liaisons, from which it followed that, despite the research purport of the Institute, he 'would not consider donating information I have gathered during forty-two years of research work to an institute which was controlled—as is AIAS in Canberra—by men who have not been taught by Aboriginal elders.'

When he mentioned films, a familiar note was struck, and it was the one that would help undo any agreement the university was to try to negotiate. 'I feel unable at present to donate the originals containing my data outright to the university. Most of my private funds went into their collection during the past forty-two years, and their possession is my only insurance against the uncertainties, against my financial future in retirement. They also constitute the only "property" I could bequeath to my wife and family. However, I feel sure that my heirs would like to see my complete original records preserved in an appropriate Archives Department, which might well be the Strehlow Institute.'[84]

There was a strong case to be made that some of the rightful 'heirs' were alive and well in Central Australia and still speaking vigorous Aranda. Their time would come. In the meantime Strehlow could only speak in terms of his private property—soon the inverted comma fell away. It was his property because he had been given it in sacred trust. And it was his capital as security for his family when he died. That is to say, he was clarifying two shocking things: that the sacred men's materials were being passed into the hands of a woman; and that the collection, as capital, might one day be up for sale, one way or the other.

The university seems to have been relatively unconcerned about the idea of eventually repatriating objects to Aboriginal people. Nor did it record any worries about the transgressional nature of a woman inheriting the collection. It was focused on the private property issue and the risk to the collection as part of the national estate, and it was on this roundabout they would squirm for the next two years as Strehlow became entrenched in possessive paranoia.

Strehlow frequently expressed fears that 'strong forces at highest government level . . . are lying in wait both here and in Canberra to pounce on my records and materials for themselves.' Strehlow had a conspiracy theory at the centre of which were Coombs and his ally, Stanner. He told Deputy Vice-Chancellor Barnes that there was a law going through the Federal parliament that would empower a judge to seize any property relating to Aborigines and make it available to appropriate institutions: he compared this development to the powers the state gained over universities in Nazi Germany.[85] Barnes did not know what Strehlow was talking about, but on reflection believed it might have been a reference to a State committee of inquiry into museums and collections which had not contemplated powers of seizure but had recommended legislation to control the export of cultural property. Reporting this conjecture to Berndt, Barnes underlined 'export.' [86]

There was much apprehension about the lengths to which the Strehlows might go.

Still, at the beginning all was not lost for an Institute. There was even a moment when Flentje had lined up the petroleum company Ampol for a $1,500 foundation grant. In July 1974 Ampol described itself to the university as a 'benefactor' and said its money would be paid directly to the university to be used at their discretion to further Strehlow's work 'on the unique history of the Aranda tribes.' Ampol was calling the new centre the Aranda Archive. Nothing was to come of this, but again, it flagged things to come. The totemic maps and genealogies of the Strehlow collection would greatly interest mining interests such as Western Mining soon after Strehlow's death.

For some time the university tried to ignore Strehlow's claim to private property rights. A draft for the centre—now to be called the Central Australian Archive—was the university's preference drawn up by Ronald Berndt, and then re-drafted by Strehlow. Strehlow's redraft forced the university's hand, and they sent him a letter in August 1974 saying that they could not agree to set up an archive 'without your agreement that your collected material . . . is already or will become, the property of the university. Moreover, the university would insist that academic traditions are observed and that as various items are catalogued, classified, or brought to their final form, they will be available for scholars to work on them.'[87]

The letter was written by Acting Deputy Vice-Chancellor John Melville, who, much to Strehlow's chagrin, had recently been talking to Coombs and Stanner in Canberra. Without implying any conspiracy, it is possible to put down the bluntness of the letter to the influence of these men who did not have the responsibility of handling Strehlow with kid gloves. Berndt, as always, was Strehlow's loyal buffer. On the issue of a prior complete handover of Strehlow's work, Berndt told Melville, 'I am sure you will appreciate that such a stipulation would not be acceptable to any reputable anthropologist. Professor Strehlow's material is of inestimable value and is of the utmost significance: he is making this available to your University, under particular conditions which seem to me to be definitely reasonable.'[88]

Strehlow was digging into deeper, even more personal formulations about ownership. His collection, he told Melville, was not 'material.' It consisted of his father's early work, personal diaries and notebooks of 42 years, and the sacred songs myths and ceremonies given to me in trustful confidence by the last ceremonial chiefs of the centres to which these sacred traditions and ceremonies were tied. I was on such occasions also given the sacred objects in special acts of surrender which made me—in Aboriginal eyes—one of the ceremonial chiefs of these centres, charged with their preservation and protection from white greed. These 'greedy whites' in Aboriginal eyes, included not only station people, but also (and especially) white government officials, anthropologists, and ignorant halfcastes. I have been working on this material for years to ensure its adequate preservation and am not going to hand over my uncompleted researches so that so called 'scholars' can cannibalise those parts of it which they think they can comprehend, and then claim full credit for it.[89]

He was to become more torrid than this and still the university persisted, looking desperately for a more diplomatic way to continue to facilitate his work and secure the archive for the university. But it was not getting any clarity from Strehlow in terms of specific proposals. Berndt's advice was to set up something 'transitional,' which did not provoke ownership disputes, and the committee dealing with 'the proposed Strehlow Research Foundation' saw some sense in that. When they took stock of the impasse in March 1976 they judged that the question of ownership of the material was 'a complex one':

Some of it, such as his father's diaries, unquestionably belongs to him; so probably does much sacred material given to him in trust. Much of the remainder was acquired when Professor Strehlow was a member of the University staff and his expeditions to Central Australia were supported by University research grants; although the University might be able to lay claim to this, the problems of classification of the material appear to be insuperable. The committee therefore recommends that the Council make no claim to any of Professor Strehlow's material, certainly within his lifetime; however, the Vice-Chancellor should take what steps he can to prevent the dispersal of the material particularly at the time of Professor Strehlow's death. In any event none of the material should leave Australia.

This was put rather sensitively, all things considered. It was recognition of the fact that a collection is not just a collection: it may be a whole life.

In Strehlow's case it also involved his father's life, and those of innumerable Aboriginal men who had given him the essence of their spiritual lives. The university was trying to get its mind around an issue that involved not simply property rights, but human rights. The whole affair was now something other than a sordid wrangle over possessions.

Throughout this period Strehlow wrote his usual indignant letters. But now there was a difference. Hitherto he had been making a shrill bid for recognition, but now, with everything bound up with the collection, he was pressing for a notion of coherence, trying to show—by pointing, proclaiming, reproaching—how his life had shape with regard to the 'material' that included everything. The collection was the collection because it was a whole, the entire worth of his life.

In a sense his collection was indeed the embodiment of the poetic unities of his life: all that was designed to be together—by virtue of his birthplace, his Lutheran legacy, his linguistics. The unity was more important than the linear narrative, even though he tended, in his anxious righteousness, to get stuck in the narrative, to grind on and on. The larger truth was the timelessness of what he had, not simply its metaphysical value with regard to Aboriginal eternity, but the *telos* of what was his. When he was writing so urgently to others he was trying to convey what he seemed unable to say: that the unities of his life were the thing, and therefore they could not be parted from him any more than an arm or a leg. The poetic wholeness of things was not easily conveyed in the pragmatic venue others had chosen. In a sense, what he was saying so angrily, desperately, was: hear my music, this has been my song, here I stand; the collection is the song of myself.

In labouring the chronicle of his life, he was like Walt Whitman making up favourable reviews of *Leaves of Grass*. Whitman had written the abundant, expansive poems of America and included at the centre of it his subtle, faceted *Song of Myself.* The journalism was meant to help the poem within the poem along its way, and journalism, plain reportage, had also been the raw material for many poems in their earlier drafts. But they were not in the end the collection of poems called *Leaves of Grass*. Its greatness lay in the elevation given to different levels of coherence—material and metaphysical, personal and general, flesh and spirit, the contingent and the cosmic, the present and the eternal—and as all of them came together in the reader's mind, that was the *poem*.

Strehlow's letters were a desperate attempt to hold up the *poem* that others could not read. If they had read *Journey to Horseshoe Bend* they might have had the right idea; and if they had put this together with *Songs of Central Australia* then they would have it in focus. Rather than tirades, it might have made sense for Strehlow to send copies of his book to the ignorant and shut them up for a time. Instead, in the mortal stakes of the political pressure, he wrote his letters, bemoaning and pointing, circling his own narratives because they were designed to come full circle. The life that was a collection, and the collection that was his life had begun with the work of his father that was now in the lap of the son who had displaced the father as ceremonial chief. To break into this circle was to violate the deepest poetic integrities of a life.

His translations—his Aranda songs—were at issue right at this point. In January 1975 Strehlow candidly explained what was incensing him. The university had just set up a centre for Catherine Ellis to teach her ethnomusicology. To Strehlow, it was favouritism. In a nine-page letter to Vice-Chancellor Barnes he accused Ellis of the most gross plagiarisms of his work, claiming that her own 'bogus aboriginal elders,' some of whom were her students, were working against him. He quoted a poem that was circulating on campus:

What have you done, Professor Strehlow
To promote the tribal fellow.
You took from him his sacred past
Did you give him something to last?
We see no Professor, Doctor or credit,
Only a passing word, in his merit.
Don't knock us, as we promote the culture:
You should have done that, in respect for his future.
It's not too late now, for you to reach
Others of your race, who want to teach;
Make them see, we have great knowledge.
To promote our people, to your College
So we too can have recognition
As Professor, or Doctor, on the same condition.

To which Strehlow retorted that the poet, a woman who made such a claim on sacred materials, would 'in the not-so-distant past have been clubbed to death for her sacrilegious presumption and had her body thrown into a fire.'

His war dance had another bad object, however. It was the way in which Ellis had redirected his work. For, having 'stolen' his translations of the songs, as well as the fundamentals of his pioneering musical analysis, she had shifted the focus from the songs to the music. 'C. Ellis now claims that aboriginal tribal elders teach, not sacred poems, but aboriginal "music" to children and novices.'[90] That is to say—we can see the resonance of Strehlow's point clearly in the context of his great argument for *logos* in *Songs of Central Australia*— Ellis was in effect trivialising Aranda culture. That was far from the case, as anyone familiar with her work knows: she would champion Aboriginal metaphysics of the eternal. That aside, Strehlow responded as if she had stepped in to castrate the sacred words of the men, the poems that were at the centre of *his* poem. Ellis was not so unkind to Strehlow. On the contrary, she was to essay expansively on the unique, pioneering contribution Strehlow had made to understanding how 'the concept of *sound* (or just the melody) of an ancestral song symbolised the *flavour* or *essence* of that particular ancestor.' It was an appreciation that spoke of Strehlow's 'claim that the rhythm of the music takes structural precedence over song text'—an emphasis that flew in the face of Strehlow finally, pivotally needing to say that 'music is still the servant of the words.'[91]

Strehlow was, in a way, whirling a bullroarer around the heads of men who were not equipped to hear it. His was the wrath of Job that men did not grasp his Beyond. The two went together: the Aboriginal authority, and the Christian one. But neither analogy is adequate considering Strehow's life under the black sun. The crucial truth is that under his black sun there was still the 'Thing'—the inconsolable, unappeasable depth that remained the mystery. Strehlow's potent, brooding animus had to be acknowledged. That was his human right, as much as he had property rights, even as he was abusing his property rights. His poem had to be understood, accepted. The university was trying to understand, but of those directly involved in summit talks over the collection, only Ronald Berndt fully sensed the Strehlow *poem*. A few others knew they were dealing with a man who was in some kind of extreme state that called for compassion. This was the feeling of acting Vice-Chancellor Harry Medlin when he calmly went to visit the Strehlows at home, a diplomatic mission to the lion's den.

By this time the explosions had taken place. Strehlow had had a collapse: driving on the road near Port Augusta his heart gave way and his wife thought he might die (and was already blaming the university for it). Back in Adelaide Strehlow was still weak when he stood up, and had dizzy spells, and it was in this condition that he told Barnes about having already burnt some archive material, and later wrote his incendiary letters. Their arrival seems to have moved the university council to ignore the sensitive advice of its subcommittee on complexities of ownership. The council wrote to propose an agreement he would sign ensuring all the 'material will pass into the custody of the Centre to be held permanently for posterity.' Since the university was now deaf and dumb to his *poem*, Strehlow obviously felt free to release his hellfire. The university was at the stage of calling off all negotiations when Medlin sought out the Strehlows.

It was an amicable conversation. Medlin reported to the university that Strehlow was 'rational, reasonable and articulate.' 'I believe that, in general terms, he thinks that he was invited by the University to consider a certain course of action and then, when he did so, was accused by the university of making demands on it.' The diplomatic implication was clear: the university should try again, less demandingly. Berndt was keen on this. He spoke of a transitional stage, to which the Strehlows might agree.[92]

But the Strehlows had shifted their ground. The foundation they were now talking about would not be at the university at all. It would be at their own home, in Prospect. *The collection will stay at home, where it and I belong*—the dream text, the point of the *poem*, was now in the air that the Strehlows breathed, and which the university had to breathe with them. They told the university they would add on a new building and showed them the plan, and spoke of their costings and a bank loan. All the writing was now on the wall for a privatisation of the foundation.

The university tried to be calm. 'We realise that your plans are at an early stage and that many details will need to be worked out. However, some of the matters we would wish to discuss are,' and they raised the nagging issues: funding, the 'disposition' of the foundation, the role of the university, resources for other scholars.[93] They were on the back foot.

Berndt was most alarmed. He thought a foundation at home was 'fraught with difficulties' and reported to the university that 'in June the Strehlows were speaking of selling some of their material to finance the building.'[94]

The university was also trying to get Strehlow to withdraw his incendiary letters, but he would not. They were a bargaining tool. Medlin visited again, and got some assurance that 'the letters are not seen as an instrument for bargaining and will be withdrawn when Professor Strehlow is convinced that "the University" is NOT out to get him.'[95] The Strehlows were still ready to negotiate for university help, but they had turned the tables: from their bastion at home, they would set the conditions of university involvement.

On 24 November 1976 Registrar Shields wrote to Strehlow to say that the council had discontinued negotiations. The university would not make any claims on the collection, and Strehlow could, if he wished, keep working on campus. The latter proviso was the desperate palliative, the way of reassuring a man destined not to share, and desperate enough to dismantle the collection, if not destroy it in part or in toto. Who was to know? Only the man who knew the *poem*.

The university had been very patient, more patient than Berndt could imagine his University of Western Australia being in the same circumstances. And yet in none of the correspondence had a simple fact been sheeted home to Strehlow: that for three decades he had been on the payroll of the university, and had his trips funded by the university, and had therefore been assembling a collection that was entirely public property.

Strehlow had always claimed that he had funded a lot of his work. 'In my view all my previous research trips have had to dip heavily into my private pocket for a large part of research expenses (and Mrs Strehlow has always paid for herself for her field trips).'[96] And he made a point of this especially with regard to the sacred objects. But he produced no accounts to this effect. He had no ledger for publicly showing in any overall way what was not funded by the public purse. There seems to be no document in existence—in Adelaide, in Canberra, in Darwin or Sydney, to name the places from which funds had come to him over the years—in which any funding body had regarded him as being a private collector. Occasional calculations can be found in Strehlow's journals that show the difference between his public and private expenditures, but these are rare.* For a man as meticulous as Strehlow this pattern of omission is significant. Obviously, he did at times spend some of his own

---

* For example, in November 1962 he notes cash payments for native informants of £385: 'This amount consists of £140 advance from the University, £245 from my own banking accounts.'

money, but whatever those sums amounted to they were infinitesimal compared to the cost of his trips, which were always funded by a public purse, while all of the time he was travelling on research funds that were, after the war, supplementary to his salary from the University of Adelaide. The notion that his collection was morally his for financial reasons is nonsense. And if money was going to decide the moral claim, payment to Aboriginal people would have to be the first place to start, but no one was saying that.

The claim that he had on his collection was a personal one, bound up with his linguistic liaisons. On this basis, not a monetary one, he had made his private garden of collecting. When the time came for others to look over his fence and inspect his acquisitions—as the subcommittee of the university council had done in June 1975—it was too late, really, to separate one thing from another. All the exchanges had translated into each other; everything, from the peach soup denied to men at Arltunga to the songs he was able to give back to other men at Horseshoe Bend, acts of appropriation merged with acts of restitution through an epoch of colonial and post-colonial history so that Strehlow's garden was his, and that was that.

The university held firm on one thing: the role of Kathleen Strehlow. Strehlow insisted from beginning to end on a senior academic position for his wife. He wanted her appointed to the staff. In the beginning the university seems to have made noises of agreement, but as negotiations firmed the appropriateness of such an appointment was questioned. Berndt, ever the conciliator, thought she could be appointed to the position of 'artist in residence,' or 'something with a title like Senior Curator, Senior Research Officer, Research Fellow etc.'[97] The university did not take up the idea.

Strehlow was protesting all the time on his wife's behalf. He made a case that entwined her place as 'heir' with his collection, and her prospective work as research director after his death. He spoke of her as a necessary 'first condition' to any agreement.[98] 'My wife is the only person who has ever shared my vision of an eternal Aboriginal Central Australia.' He talked up all her years of work for him, her undeniable industry and dedication. She was 'the only person with full access to all my materials and unpublished writings, and is the only person in the world beside myself who could even set down any authoritative statement on the traditional land rights of Central Australia, and on their social significance.'[99]

This claim was made over the next few months, as the Northern Territory Land Rights Act came into operation and, in case after case, traditional owners of land were drawn into the white legal system to claim their ancestral inheritance. But that was not the point in Prospect, Adelaide, at that moment. 'My wife is the only person who has ever shared my vision of an eternal Aboriginal Central Australia'— this was the key to it all.

She shared his *poem* and he, in his love of her, had given her the whole heart of it. It was the eternal poem, that contained the secrets of the Land of *Altjira*, the Land of Eternity; it had been eternally gifted to him, and with it Strehlow sought to immortalise himself, to stay time. He was placing himself out of time.

The paradox was, too, that by now he had been honoured by the university itself. In 1975 it made him Doctor of Letters. There is a photograph of him and his new family on the day: a weary, overweight Strehlow in academic dress smiles beside a proud Kathleen holding their baby Carl; Kathleen's other children, Julian and Yaralie, are sullen teenagers on his side. There on the ground is the man highly acknowledged at last. We might imagine his ruefulness about the doctorate, which he had not brought back with him from London a quarter of a century earlier.

The honour was bestowed for all that he had been saying about himself for so long: for the collecting and the translating, for the monumental *Songs of Central Australia*. In the terms of one of the university's referees, Professor Kenelm Burridge from the university of British Columbia,* *Songs* gave Strehlow 'a permanent place in English and Australian letters.' 'Generations hence,' Burridge went on, 'when Chomsky, Lévi-Strauss et al. will have been chopped up, cannibalised and forgotten by their intellectual descendants, scholars and researchers will still be acknowledging their debt, and paying tribute, to T.G.H. Strehlow.'

Burridge, who had worked in Australia, knew the culture of the profession and was the author of a first-class book on the intellectual, ethical and psychological ramifications of contact with Aborigines.[100] But there was a paradox about this accolade with its playful allusions

---

*   The other referee was Professor G.G. Rose, a resident of East Berlin who, after seventeen pages of rather mechanistic Marxist lament about Strehlow's 'philosophical idealism,' had 'no hesitation' in supporting the doctorate on the basis of original work in the oral literature, the 'language prose and poetic' of the Australian Aborigines, and their music, art and religion.

to savage behaviour. It came after Burridge's five-page filleting of Strehlow's oeuvre over time. With regard to Strehlow's 1947 paper on language, Burridge remarked that 'intellectual initiative and originality cannot be said to be his strong points'; and of *Aranda Traditions,* that it lacked 'sociological imagination'; and with regard to *Songs,* its weaknesses were those lengthy quotations from other bodies of literature which 'seem to me to smack at false scholarship where it is not simply a form of self-flattery'; and 'most pertinently,' 'the very definite note of exculpation.' The Aranda and Loritja material could stand up for itself. He thought it 'presumptuous and exiguous to maintain what I detect as a note of excuse.'

Burridge concluded with an indictment. The shortcomings of *Songs* were of a piece with earlier work: 'a consistent failure to make the most of unparalleled opportunities, a consistent failure of intellectual acumen and thrust.'[101] He then remarked—sardonically, drolly—that the trend of his overview would not 'make Strehlow a proud and happy man,' which indeed it would not have, if Strehlow had seen the way his doctorate had been circumscribed.

But the judgment rightly placed Strehlow in the space and time. His work would monumentally stand forever, as would the imprint of his personality on that work; that long river of himself that we have been following, his continuous course as long as the Finke and as old as melancholia: the flow of his compulsive, sad habit of exculpation.

---

1   Tim Rowse, 'Assimilation and After,' in *Australians From 1939,* ed. Anne Cuthoys, A. W. Martin and Tim Rowse (Sydney: Fairfax, Syme & Weldon Associates, 1987).
2   Paul Hasluck, 'The Problem of Administration,' in *Aboriginal Man in Australia,* ed. R.M. Berndt and C.H. Berndt (Sydney: Angus & Robertson, 1965), 449.
3   Bain Attwood and Andrew Markus, *The 1967 Referendum, or When the Aborigines Didn't Get the Vote* (Canberra: Aboriginal Studies Press, 1997), passim.
4   C.D. Rowley, *The Remote Aborigines* (Ringwood: Penguin, 1972); Ann McGrath, *Born in the Cattle* (Sydney: Allen & Unwin, 1987); W.E.H. Stanner, 'Industrial Justice in the Never Never' [1938], in *White Man Got no Dreaming* (Canberra, Australian National University Press, 1979), 1–22.
5   Tim Rowse, *White Flour, White Power* (Melbourne: Cambridge University Press, 1988), passsim, especially 147–84.
6   H.C. Coombs, *Trial Balance: Issues of My Working Life* (Melbourne: Sun Books, 1981), 281–82; Kenneth Maddock, *The Australian Aborigines: A Portrait of Their Society* (Melbourne: Penguin, 1982), 12–14.
7   Tim Rowse, *Obliged to be Difficult: Nugget Coombs' Legacy in Indigenous Affairs* (Melbourne: Cambridge University Press, 2000).
8   Geoffrey Bardon, *Papunya Tula: Art of the Western Desert* (Melbourne: McPhee Gribble, 1991); Paul Carter, 'The Enigma of the Homeland Place,' in *Papunya*

Tula: Genesis and Genius, ed. Hetti Perkins and Hannah Fink (Sydney: Art Gallery of New South Wales, 2000).

9 R.G. Kimber, 'Recollections of Papunya Tula, 1971–1980,' in *Papunya Tula: Genesis and Genius*.

10 Marcia Langton, 'Sacred Geography: Western Desert Traditions of Landscape Art,' in *Papunya Tula: Genesis and Genius*.

11 Rowse, *Obliged to Be Difficult*, 131ff.; Geoffrey Partington, *Hasluck Versus Coombs* (Sydney: Quakers Hill Press, 1996), 20–21, 37.

12 Foreword to Battarbee, *Modern Australian Aboriginal Art* (Sydney: Angus & Robertson, 1951).

13 *Rex Battarbee: Artist and Founder of the Aboriginal Art Movement in Central Australia* (Sydney: The Legend Press, 1956).

14 Ibid., 25–30.

15 Ibid., 30–40.

16 Ibid., 40–41.

17 Opening address at Ricketts exhibition, Mount Dandenong, Victoria, 14 October 1973.

18 Ricketts to Strehlow, 24 March 1973.

19 See A.P. Elkin, *Aboriginal Men of High Degree*, 2nd ed. (St Lucia: University of Queensland Press, 1980).

20 T.G.H. Strehlow, review of *Black Australians*, *Australian Book Review* 9, no.10 (1979): 280–81.

21 Ibid.

22 Tim Rowse, 'The Collector as Outisder—T.G.H. Strehlow as "Public Intellectual,"' Strehlow Research Centre, *Occasional Papers* 2. (December 1999): 78–9 and passim.

23 Strehlow to Hasluck, 27 March 1953.

24 Hasluck to Strehlow, 8 April 1953.

25 T.G.H. Strehlow, *The Sustaining Ideals of Australian Aboriginal Societies* (Adelaide: Aboriginal Advancement League of South Australia, 1956).

26 Strehlow to Johnson, 8 June 1970.

27 Strehlow to Lohe, 22 June 1970.

28 T.G.H. Strehlow, *Journey to Horseshoe Bend* (Sydney: Angus & Robertson, 1969), 17.

29 Ibid., 170.

30 Lohe to Strehlow, 29 May 1970.

31 Ibid.

32 Strehlow to Lohe, 22 June 1970.

33 Lohe to Strehlow, 7 October 1970.

34 Strehlow to Lohe, 21 December 1972.

35 The letter from Mrs Nell Basedow, the wife of Dr Herbert Basedow, was dated 17 November 1922 and noted that 'Dr Basedow happened to meet Mr Murray Aunger in the street and he told him your committee had been to see him.' Strehlow to Lohe. 2 June 1970.

36 P.A. Scherer, 'Death on the Line,' *Yearbook of the Lutheran Church*, 1974.

37 Ibid., 39.

38 Strehlow to Berndt, 4 August 1970.

39 Kathleen Strehlow to Berndt, quoted in Kathleen Strehlow to McCarthy, 2 July 1971.

40 Edgeloe to Sheppard, 13 Jan 1972; Flentje to Sheppard, 17 March 1972.

41 McCarthy to Berndt, 11 January 1972; Berndt to Sheppard, 21 January 1972.

42 Strehlow to Berndt, 4 August 1970.

43 Strehlow to Wentworth 7 July 1971.

44 Wentworth to Strehlow, 13 July 1971.

45 Strehlow to Berndt, 4 August 1970.
46 Tim Rowse, 'Strehlow Damns Coombs: Ethnography and Policy Critique,'
    paper presented to the Australian Anthropological Society, October 1998.
47 Strehlow 'Some Comments' [relating to the Native and Historical Objects and
    Areas Preservation Ordinance], Appendix 2 of the Report from the Select
    Committee on Native and Historical Objects and Areas Preservation
    Ordinance, 1955–1960, Darwin, August 1965.
48 Rowse, 'Collector as Outsider,' 91, citing Strehlow's 1969 letter to Doreen
    Braitling, lessee at Mount Doreen.
49 Strehlow to McIntosh, 9 March 1971.
50 Strehlow had raised £500 each from the Commonwealth Scientific
    Publications Fund, AIAS and the Commonwealth Literary Fund, and £250
    from the University of Adelaide. Strehlow to Chair of Publications Committee,
    University of Adelaide, 2 November 1967.
51 Strehlow to Wentworth, 7 July 1971.
52 *Times Literary Supplement*, 19 May 1972, 582.
53 William Wordsworth, *The Prelude* [1799], lines 288–94:
      There are in our existence spots of time
      Which with distinct preeminence retain
      A fructifying virtue, whence, depressed,
      By trivial occupations and the round
      Of ordinary intercourse, our minds—
      Especially the imaginative power—
      Are nourished and invisibly repaired …
54 17 Kimber to Kathleen Stuart, 18 January 1972.
55 18 Kimber to Kathleen Stuart, 28 January 1972.
56 Berndt to McCarthy, 24 January 1972.
57 John Mulvaney, 'Conflict and the Rituals of Diplomacy: Les Hiatt and the
    AIAS,' in *Scholar and Sceptic: Australian Aboriginal Studies in Honour of L.R. Hiatt*,
    ed. Francesca Merlan, John Morton and Alan Ramsey (Canberra: Aboriginal
    Studies Press, 1997), 34.
58 Strehlow to Harris, 23 February 1971, cited in Rowse, 'Collector as Outsider,' 94.
59 Robert Edwards, *The Preservation of Australia's Aboriginal Heritage* (Canberra:
    AIAS, 1975), 119. The mover was Dr W.D.L. Ride.
60 Strehlow to AIAS, 10 April 1973.
61 Ibid.
62 *Australian*, 9 December 1973, 20.
63 Strehlow to Freeman, 3 July 1973, cited in Rowse, 'Collector as Outsider,' 102.
64 Its texture and angry relevance are well conveyed by Tim Rowse, 'Collector as
    Outsider,' 93–94, in his summary of the rest of Strehlow's position as it was
    published in the Strehlow Research Foundation Pamphlets, 1986–87:
      'The good will of Indigenous informants benefited researchers but not the
    informants themselves, Strehlow asserted. "At times the reader will not gain
    any impression that the researchers were conscious of their common
    humanity with their studied 'subjects'" . . . The researchers made themselves
    "at home on the aboriginal settlements and missions" and rarely ventured
    into "the old tribal territory". They remained ignorant of both country and
    language.
      'When researchers funded by the Institute described indigenous languages,
    they used "difficult technical terms for even the most elementary linguistic
    facts." Linguists' preoccupation with grammatical structures told little of the
    "power of the aboriginal mind." Such researchers were "incapable of
    understanding even ordinary conversations conducted by aboriginal speakers
    among themselves".

'These studies should have been financed by Universities, not by the Institute, Strehlow insisted. Their esoteric concerns were all too typical of an academic world which had now forsaken "ordinary educated readers..." Their ephemeral theoretical concerns had displaced the collection of data and had left no room for Indigenous views. "It is *their* explanations and *their* accounts that should be set down for posterity in the greatest detail, and so far as possible in *their* own words".

'The Institute should abandon "raw city-trained graduates" and support "the small numbers of well-established people whose work has already proved that they have won the full confidence of some defined aboriginal group or groups ... those few dedicated persons who are willing to spend at least several years in their chosen areas in order to investigate and record all aspects of language, culture, and social structure which their 'informants' are willing to divulge to them... For it is the *quality* of the 'informants' (and the dedication of the researchers) that will in the end determine the whole worthwhileness of the final results. My own best 'informants' have always been men whom I respected deeply and admired without reservation for their intelligence and integrity. In their own cultural world these men would have merited a rating as high as that of the best University professors I have known... It was they who *taught me* what *they thought* I should know, see and hear. I always thought of myself as their pupil, not as their smart examiner".'

65 Mulvaney cites Elkin's rejection of his two articles 'questioning the validity, or ethics, of research pioneer anthropologists' as an example of the former ('Conflict and the Rituals of Diplomacy,' 32); and Marcia Langton cites the Institute's 1971 rejection of subsidy for work on 'Aboriginal Identity in Contemporary Australian Society' as an example of the second ('A Fireside Chat,' in *Prehistory to Politics: John Mulvaney, the Humanities, and the Public Intellectual*, ed. Tim Bonyhady and Tom Griffiths [Melbourne: Melbourne University Press, 1996], 136).
66 Mulvaney, 'Conflict and the Rituals of Diplomacy,' 34.
67 Ibid., 33.
68 Cited in Langton, 'Fireside Chat,' 137–38.
69 Strehlow to Eaglehawk and Crow, 9 April 1974. AIAS Archive.
70 R.M. Berndt and Dick Roughsey, 'On the Question of the Secret-Sacred Dimension vis-à-vis Traditional Australian Aboriginal Life,' AIAS, unpublished, 1975.
71 Strehlow to W.T. Hare, 30 January 1973. Hare was director of the Northern Territory Reserves Board. Cited in Rowse, 'Collector as Outsider,' 103–4.
72 Nick Peterson, personal communication, June 2001.
73 Strehlow to Bain, 29 July 1976, cited in Rowse, 'Collector as Outsider,' 105.
74 Strehlow, 'The Alice Springs Aboriginal Land Rights,' unpublished, 1975.
75 Ibid.
76 Rowse, 'Collector as Outsider,' 102–05, citing Strehlow to Viner, 16 March 1977.
77 Strehlow to Berndt, 29 November 1974.
78 Strehlow to Badger, 31 January, 1975.
79 E.S. Barnes to Council Committee of Strehlow Foundation, 19 November 1975.
80 Minutes of Council, 10 September 1976.
81 Medlin to Barnes, 8 November 1976.
82 Minutes of Council, 9 April 1976.
83 A.E. Shields, Registrar, to Strehlow, 24 November 1976.
84 Strehlow to Flentje, 19 March 1974.
85 Barnes to Council Committee on Strehlow Foundation, 19 November 1975.

86 Barnes to Berndt, 16 January 1976.
87 Melville to Strehlow, 16 August 1974.
88 Berndt to Melville, 29 August 1974.
89 Strehlow to Melville, 20 September 1974.
90 Strehlow to Barnes, 31 January 1975.
91 T.G.H. Strehlow, *Songs of Central Australia* (Sydney: Angus & Robertson, 1971), 32; Catherine Ellis, 'Understanding the Profound Structural Knowledge of Central Australian Performers from the Perspective of T.G.H. Strehlow,' Strehlow Research Centre, *Occasional Paper 1* (October 1997): 57.
92 Medlin to Barnes, 7 June 1976.
93 Registrar to Strehlow, 1 September 1976.
94 Berndt to Barnes, 2 September 1976.
95 Medlin to members of the Strehlow Committee, 7 October 1976.
96 Strehlow to Melville, 7 August 1974.
97 Berndt to Barnes, 1 September 1976.
98 Strehlow to Badger, 31 January 1975.
99 Strehlow to Barnes, 29 August 1976.
100 E. Burridge, *Encountering Aborigines: A Case Study: Anthropology and the Australian Aboriginal* (New York: Pergamon Press, 1973), 19.
101 E. Burridge, 'Report on the Published Words of Professor T.G.H. Strehlow,' 13 December 1973, University of Adelaide Archives. P. Jones kindly drew my attention to the Burridge and Rose reports.

2   Last Days

Final Reminders

IN 1977 THE Strehlows went to Hermannsburg to celebrate the centenary of the mission. Everyone was there. Albrecht and his children. Philip Scherer and other pastors who had worked at the mission. The Latz family, who had helped manage it for so long. Mr Heinrich and other schoolteachers. Officials of the Lutheran Church, government officials, station owners, and many residents of Alice Springs. They were all there along with the Hermannsburg Aboriginal community which had recently had their land handed back to them by the church.

The land return was both a philanthropic and necessary political move by the Lutherans. The time had come to do so: they had after all been trying for many decades to educate their flock for some kind of autonomy. In 1973 the mission had made the first tentative moves in this direction. Its board started discussions with the people, ones they hoped would lead to negotiations that would allow the church leases for land to carry on its spiritual ministry, and which would see the church and the school accepted by the Aboriginal community as a continuing part of their lives. With this move, the Lutherans rather tremulously felt, as their official historian Leske put it, that 'the fat was in the fire.'

'What followed in 1974 changed the whole course of the history of Hermannsburg . . . Suddenly people began to pack up and move out from Hermannsburg to settle as kinship or clan groups in their own chosen areas, many of them in areas on the Lease which they claimed were theirs according to *tjurunga* rights.' This was starting off again 'at the grass roots of their culture on the wurlie level.' It might also have been described, as the official account concedes, as the 'exodus from the bondage of Hermannsburg' even though many people took the Gospel with them.

But it was more complicated than that in terms of cultural heritage. Along with the reassertion of '*tjurunga* rights' came the open return of ceremonies. In the satellite settlements out from the mission—the out stations as they were called in the political movement that was heralded at the time by the secular left, material provision was given by the mission. Then, in a remarkable reversal of history, mission leaders were rewarded by a gift from the out station leaders: they were invited to initiation ceremonies. The ceremonies that were once so 'frowned on by the mission and carried out in secret, unbeknown to the staff or administration' were now the gift offering.

The result was consternation among those who knew mission history. In 1977, when the official history was published, it was declared: 'much thought and study will have to go into the questions which this departure from all mission practice poses, and into the place and role of such ceremonies in Christian aboriginal communities in the future.'[1]

Still, the anniversary was communal celebration remarkably free of the political tensions of the time. Most who were there had in mind the long, hard history of the place, which had produced achievements that Aboriginal people in other parts of the Territory had reason to envy. Despite the political tensions at large over the Land Rights Act, more than 200 people heard the Hermannsburg choir sing Christian hymns in Aranda as if all transgressions against their culture had been forgotten.

Strehlow was saddened by the occasion. He watched 'two poor performances given by Walbiri and Warrumunga folk dancers, specially imported from places hundreds of miles away' and felt that they 'left behind a humiliating feeling of crudeness which did nothing to shed any lustre on true aboriginal identity.' He wished an effort had been made to impress upon the audience the fact that the arrival of the mission in 1877 had saved 'all Aranda dialects from extinction.' He lamented that tributes had not been paid to Lutheran mission supporters.

He wished for a Holy Communion. And he was alarmed to find that joint church services for black and white Christians had been abandoned some years before.[2] They were disgruntled thoughts that must have ill-prepared him for the event to come.

After the lunch Mrs Helene Burns, Albrecht's daughter, was standing talking to Manasse Armstrong, the former mission worker of whom she and her family were fond. Armstrong was one of the men who had challenged Strehlow on issues of translation more than twenty years earlier. Strehlow had had to set him right, dressing him down with the militancy of Luther.

Armstrong wanted to know about the woman Strehlow was with. Helene Burns told him: the woman was Strehlow's new wife, Kathleen. What happened to the first Mrs Strehlow? Armstrong asked. And Helene Burns answered to the best of her tactful ability. Armstrong had known and liked Bertha, having been one of her regular helpers at Jay Creek, the country to which he belonged.

Later, Armstrong approached Strehlow who offered his hand in greeting. Armstrong refused it. For some moments Armstrong spoke with Strehlow. Then he spat at the white man's feet and walked off.

Pastor Albrecht was nearby. It was a most distressing episode to him. He carried it forever afterwards, but only confided to one close friend the impact it had had on him.[3] He would have seen it through Strehlow's eyes, and registered the depth of rebuke to the *ingkata*. And he knew and respected Armstrong, a man of integrity who was acting on behalf of his own culture. Albrecht knew full well that the issue was not merely historical (the row Strehlow and Armstrong had had over language). The issue was the living presence of the *tjurunga* Strehlow had in his possession, and of the sacred material Strehlow had in his archives, and which he was now treating as property that could be bequeathed to a woman or, to be more precise, a woman the senior Aboriginal men did not know. Albrecht himself might have raised the matter with Strehlow, but he could not, as Helene Burns puts it, 'get to base one' on the matter. These were years when Strehlow had in important ways closed down to Albrecht.

Later in his stay Strehlow went out to Gilbert Springs, as his parents called it when he was a boy. This was the place a few kilometres west of where he had had that nightmare of being trampled by cattle. Strehlow went there with his 'twin,' Gustav Malbunka. They were not exactly the same age, they were about two years apart, but 'twin' was the term for the man with whom he had been to school and who had once saved his life. Theo had fallen into a waterhole and knocked his head on a rock. Malbunka had pulled him out.

They had kept in touch over the years; Strehlow sent gifts and Christmas cards. Malbunka had stayed with the school and become an evangelical preacher. More than his other brothers, he had left his traditional culture: Strehlow certainly thought he did not know very much.

Gary Stoll, the superintendent of the mission, was driving them out to Gilbert Springs when something astonishing happened to Strehlow. They had been talking about the *tjilpa*, sometimes known as the native cat. The *tjilpa*, a now almost extinct marsupial, the western quoll, is the powerful dreaming story in the area. Indeed it could be said that the *tjilpa* as the dreaming ancestor was one that carried some of the deepest sexual symbolism that was possible for the rituals of 'sustaining desire.' Strehlow had taken down *tjilpa* songs in several areas, starting with the important ritual on the Burt Plain in 1933. He had cited a good run of it in *Songs*, making a lot of the subincision song that was sung by the great Sire, Malbunka himself. In *Songs*, and in *Aranda Traditions*, Strehlow had made the most of the *tjilpa* story as one that vividly illustrated the feelings of initiates towards their fathers—the suffering of the initiates as they waited for the ceremony, and how they had to see the best meat they had caught go to their fathers. In the song, Strehlow points out, Malbunka is a deceptively comic figure with a knobbly nose, and the young men defiantly keep some bits of meat for themselves. 'The hungry Aranda iliara who saw the best cuts of meat vanish into the mouths of their clan leaders must have derived great secret satisfaction and emotional relief.'[4] But that was not the way of things as the story went on. The *tjilpa* father had a 'terrible power' and it would have been sacrilege to mock him.

All of this had been of first importance to Strehlow in his documentation of a culture that had lost its respect for fathers and had, in so doing, died off. His own collection of *tjurunga* were proof of that.

The Aranda name for Gilbert Springs signified the *tjilpa* dreaming.

As Strehlow and Stoll were talking they heard Malbunka in the back seat. He was softly singing.

Strehlow tuned in.

Malbunka was singing the native cat song.

Strehlow could not believe his ears, but it was true: Malbunka knew some *tjilpa* verses. He sang some on the way to Gilbert Springs, and he sang more on the way back.

When Strehlow expressed his astonishment to Stoll, he was told, 'They need things to go on with. Their parents continued to teach them some things, otherwise they'd be living really ignorant.'[5]

Strehlow had two lessons on that centenary celebration of the mission: two omens, you might say. He was confronted by the *rage* of an Aranda man who felt his culture had been mistreated. And he was obliged to recognise the *celebratory truth* that a key song was not, after all, broken. Contact with the dynamic momentum of the new age could not have been more forceful.

Dead Men Speak / Privatising Eternity

A few months after hearing Malbunka sing the native cat song Strehlow was telling readers of the *Centralian Advocate*, 'Nothing in my film or tapes has anything to do with any living person—they are the private acts and songs of dead men.' The occasion was Strehlow's reaction to a claim on his collection by an Aranda leader, Wenton Rubuntja, chairman of the Central Land Council. 'The Aranda people are still on,' Rubuntja told the *Advocate*, 'the ceremonies are still on. The old people and the young people are still learning the sacred ways, all the time, just like a university.'[6] Rubuntja wanted the Strehlows to return the material to its true owners.

This was a landmark in the politics of Strehlow's collection. Hitherto there had hardly been an Aboriginal voice to be heard on the matter. Now the voice that spoke had a potent base in the statutory Land Council, the body set up mainly to help implement the Land Rights Act, but which had quickly become the moral as well as the political authority on Aboriginal rights in Central Australia. Rubuntja was not just speaking for himself and his clan, or even for the Aranda of the region. By implication he was voicing the principle of Aboriginal property rights over Aboriginal culture. He was a living voice speaking on his own behalf, as well as that of the 'dead.'

This was Strehlow's third showdown with the now politicised Aborigines in Alice Springs. About a year earlier he had fired his heavy cannon into their midst with a letter to the *Centralian Advocate*. The issue was land rights in the town, or rather, the social arrangements

Aborigines were beginning to make with regard to their town camps, which housed more than a thousand people in squalid conditions. Strehlow had attacked Legal Aid lawyer Geoff Eames and Native Affairs assistant director Bob Huey for what he claimed was their ignorant and self-interested manipulations of tribal elders, so-called. Strehlow seems to have been set off by the name Rubuntja.

One of the false elders was Wenton Rubuntja, whose name Strehlow insisted was Wintin. Strehlow laid out the family history, which included a slight on Wenton's father, Bob, 'a man of great knowledge of other men's traditions' from whom he had collected some 'particularly valuable fragments' of rites and verses. Old Rubuntja had also been helpful to Spencer and Gillen.[7]

Strehlow was sneering. It was a contemptuous attack on two generations of Rubuntjas for not knowing their own traditions. Strehlow then went further in reply to his indignant though more temperate Alice Springs critics, underlining the way some Aranda had sold their religious inheritance: 'Surely the Alice Springs tjurunga have not vanished without a trace? They filled over three empty 150 lb bags according to Mr Bob Rubuntja when he complained to me about not having been paid for them by Native Affairs.'[8]

This was about as low as you could get. Gone was Strehlow's sympathetic story of colonial circumstance, when Aboriginal men had had to tragically surrender their spiritual inheritance. Now he pushed an image of crass venality, of a vulgar shipment of *tjurunga* by the sugar bag. It was an obscene denial of the integrity of the contemporary desire to revive cultural traditions where possible, and a cruel use of his admittedly superior knowledge of detail against the simple human truth: that Aboriginal men were now looking to history to strengthen their culture. Strehlow's weapon was his ruthless ownership of history.

The upshot was predictable. Two months later the news came down from the Centre that Aborigines were preparing legal action against Professor T.G.H. Strehlow for 'the return of hundreds of sacred objects he has in his Adelaide home.' The report went on: 'A spokesman for the tribes yesterday said: "It's a burning issue up here. Prof. Strehlow claims he came by the objects after attending 'surrender ceremonies' at which Aborigines surrendered their sacred objects to him. But the people up here say they only gave them to him for study and to be returned to them or that he 'bought them for bully beef and tea.'"'[9]

Strehlow's foaming indignation at this abuse of history was predictable. This particular polemic, which he had partly provoked and which was latent in the whole ideological structure of the land rights movement at its height, even before the Northern Territory government made a race war of land by opposing almost every claim, did nothing for Strehlow's reputation. His appropriations could easily be construed as a manifestation of colonial history, obliterating everything else. It was not the historical moment for personalised nuances: nor was it the time for a former mission boy to insist that his life was the only good life in Central Australia. The movement of the great post-colonial argument was high, and Strehlow's grasping, vindictive defiance of it did his own narrative no good.

That is why, perhaps, Pastor Albrecht's defence of Strehlow, which the papers seized upon the next day, reads so lamely:

I find it hard to believe that the men who are preparing legal action against the Professor really know what they are talking about. Strehlow had the fullest confidence of the men who brought their tjurunga to him. They did so because they felt he would be their best guardian, a matter which was of great concern to them. This fact excluded any thought of a loan. They would never have entrusted these treasures to a man who they felt did not know the engravings and secrets connected with their objects. To say that the tribe wants them back is sheer nonsense. Tjurunga were always owned by individuals, not by the tribe.

Secondly, the charges directed against Professor Strehlow are completely out of context with the attitude he has displayed in his dealings with the Aborigines. After the Professor returned south and I was still living in Alice Springs, he would annually send me a cheque for about £100 together with a list of names indicating the amount of money each person should receive of all the men and women who had been his playmates or who had worked with him. This was done at a time when he himself needed this money while arranging his transfer to the South. I am quite certain from what I have observed that there was never a thought of rewarding the people with 'bully beef and tea.' They were paid in cash out of his own pocket. To say otherwise is a blunt lie.[10]

In a calmer moment Strehlow might have written this himself. No one could blame Albrecht for his loyalty. Albrecht, however, pushed the argument to a reactionary point with his closing remarks. He said that if the *tjurunga* were returned, the claimants 'would not know their meanings, as this was always confined to their owners who have died long ago. This means these tjurunga would become dead relics which would be quickly forgotten, or left rotting in some cave in the Centre, instead of being preserved for posterity. To interrupt what the professor is doing at the present time in evaluating these objects is criminal folly because it breaks up a development which is entirely unique in this country.' Albrecht spoke as if the remaining relatives of the 'individual owners' had no rights at all.

This was Albrecht's last public statement on behalf of Strehlow and it is a sad one. It undoes so much of his good work at Hermannsburg by insisting that all Aboriginal knowledge of the *tjurunga* had gone, a wildly inaccurate claim. It also seemed to imply what a collector like Strehlow would have loved: that somehow, by preserving them for posterity away from the neglect of their owners, they might have a better life. Albrecht's dogmatic notion of 'criminal folly' played into the hands of those who wanted to rewrite history as if the mission were the natural enemy of Aboriginal people.

After these two incidents the battle lines were entrenched: the righteously fortified Central Land Council in Alice Springs, and Strehlow in his bunker in Prospect. The third round with Rubuntja, in January 1978, started when the news broke that Strehlow was selling one of the sacred films for $300,000. That was not all. Reports said other parts of the collection could be up for sale. 'It should not be scattered,' Rubunjta claimed, 'or allowed to be desecrated. Even if the material was sold with restrictions on who could see it, it was for the Aranda people, not Professor Strehlow, to set the conditions.'[11]

The proposed selling was the natural consequence of the university's failure to secure a deal with the Strehlows. The Strehlow Research Foundation was now the independent body it had threatened to be, albeit strapped for funds. The ever-helpful Berndt was its chairman, and it had a small interim committee of Lutheran helpers.[12] The university was still liaising in a friendly manner, trying to keep negotiations open.

The constitution of the foundation made the Strehlows unchallengeable research directors, and declared one of its aims to be 'the collection, collating and discriminant publication of such records and films of religious and cultural happenings of the aborigines for the purpose of education.' The 'discriminant publication' was left undefined, and clearly allowed for the sale of material. Less ominous was the clearly stated educational aim—the setting up of libraries, a museum and an art gallery.

There was no mention of any Aboriginal relationship with the collection: no mention of how the descendants of the owners of the *tjurunga* or the songs might approach the place, and certainly no notion of any Aboriginal representation on the board. When Kathleen Strehlow publicised the foundation in the *Australasian Nurses' Journal*, some attempt was made to balance this oversight. There was a 'vision' of having an outpost of the Adelaide archive set up in Alice Springs, and also one out at Hermannsburg, centres which might help in bringing 'the country back to life.' The idea seemed to imply that the descendants of Strehlow's Aranda informants might have access to songs and maps, as well as the genealogies that showed their ancestry and their totemic rights to land in the days before white settlement. But this was not spelt out. Rather, the emphasis was on the research vision for other scholars, dioramas of ceremonies for the dreamt-of museum, and the possible sale of 'copies of material . . . to provide funds.'

The foundation was making gestures towards 'enlightenment' sharing, but only up to a point. Its true spirit was better caught by Kathleen Strehlow telling readers of the *Nurses' Journal* that the collection had the key to 'a dead culture, ancient as the Egyptians' and that her husband was, because of his command of 'secret languages' and his interdisciplinary genius, 'the Australian Rosetta stone.' From its genesis, then, the foundation was an impossible two-headed beast: it would look outwards wanting to be open to the world of carefully shared knowledge; it looked inwards cultivating the closure of an Egyptian tomb, the secrets of which might never be revealed, and if so then only at a price.[13]

But where was the money to come from? The foundation considered the American mining company, Utah. It wrote to the Australian Mining Industry Council. In fact, Berndt made the approach himself, stressing the need for the foundation to be set up within a university; though, as he had told Strehlow earlier, he was 'not that sanguine about what funds can be obtained from mining companies or their associates.'[14] Berndt was aware that the political landscape was not necessarily conducive to mining companies befriending the Aboriginal cause. Strehlow should take into account the radical nature of the changes that had been taking place, and the importance of the collection—'its direct and indirect relevance to living aborigines, as a cultural resource and as an aid to developing Aboriginal heritage and identity.' Basically, he told Strehlow, 'we are interested in all aborigines who identify in those terms, or whether they be traditionally-oriented or otherwise.'[15]

Berndt was also trying to temper the Strehlows' grandiosities. He wanted the foundation to delete all references to 'hereditary succession,' to make 'the personal equation a little less emphasised—especially in terms of handing on "to the third generation."' This was a reference to the inheritance going to Kathleen Strehlow and their son Carl, then aged four and a half.[16] And he told the Strehlows their plans for funds would cover an operation as big as a university and he did not see how they could do it. He wanted them to go more slowly, plan for Aboriginal representation, and open again to the university's overtures, since the new vice-chancellor, Donald Stranks, was prepared to put the past behind him.

The Strehlows dallied with 'six elders' who met to approve of the foundation: the men were then packed off to Premier Don Dunstan. No more was heard about an Aboriginal presence on the Board. The Strehlows resumed talks with the university via Stranks, feeling they now held all the cards. Strehlow had handed over much of the responsibility for the correspondence to his wife. He seems not to have been up to very much at all. The longer letters that come from him are coloured by snarling suspicion, or not in touch with the present. He dates a handwritten 1977 letter 1944.

Expediency even had him back in contact with the Institute for Aboriginal Studies. The bait was films. The director of the institute, Les Hiatt, was interested in the colour film taken between 1950 and 1965—50,000 feet of it according to the foundation—with an asking price of $300,000. The fee was for film that still had not been processed or titled, and there would be further charges for both. And since the age of the film might have led to some shrinkage there might be a further cost for final hand-processing. The Institute—and the government—were being made to pay.

There was talk of showing the films to the Minister of Aboriginal Affairs himself, Ian Viner. Ucko and Hiatt went to Adelaide, saw some films, and reported to Canberra on the exorbitant nature of the deal. Fury at the foundation.

The personal anguish in the bunker at Prospect was not known to the land rights troops in Alice Springs. So many of the Strehlows' strategies seemed to be clandestine, secretive. That the potential buyer of the film was the Institute for Aboriginal Studies in Canberra, hardly a political enemy, was less the issue than the fact of the sale, especially since the news report also said that 'other archival material, including 100 hours of Aboriginal sacred music and replicas of artefacts are being offered for sale all over the world.' The news report disclaimed any 'betrayal of tribal secrets' and said that the full availability of the collection would not happen 'for at least 20 years.' These were Kathleen Strehlow's words—hardly reassuring for Aranda men in Central Australia or anyone else.[17]

Strehlow was stating the rights and wrongs of ownership even more baldly. 'In Adelaide last night Professor Strehlow said everything given to him and sold to him had been the property of private owners. "None of the information or artefacts was ever tribal property—that is a new untruth cooked up by certain people who have no knowledge of sacred rites," Professor Strehlow said.'

Nothing could be less negotiable. Nor could it be more reductive of basic ethnography, even the ethnography Strehlow had laid out in 1934, when he was fresh from his early collecting. Admittedly, some *tjurunga* were private property in the sense that they were personal totems. But the key question was whether they were so private, or individualised, that they eternally excluded forms of collective responsibility.

Strehlow's own arguments never entirely got to grips with this question, as the foundation itself was to be, when it consulted the Canadian anthropologist David Turner. Turner was, to his dismay, brought to Australia with the assistance of the Western Mining Corporation on behalf of the Strehlow Research Foundation. Apart from noting the shambles the archive was in, he reported what no one at the foundation then wanted to hear: that knowledge and objects were owned by the group; they belonged to *others* as well as the *self*, and insofar as they could be discussed in terms of Western law, they were not alienable.[18]

Lost Brotherhood

It is tempting to think, at this stage of Strehlow's desperation, that he was entirely entrenched in the negative: nay-saying about land rights, about everything contemporary in Aboriginal culture, and the politicking around Aboriginal identity and self-determination. It is certainly true that he was chronically embittered, and that his sense of personal isolation, which he had done much to foster over the years, was profound. To this extent he was as incarcerated in defiance as Luther in his castle at the Wartburg, and his embattled, self-justifying energies were as inseparable from his Christian faith. For though he declared himself as *ingkata*, the last of the Aranda, he was simultaneously the Black Missionary, and in this undeniably his father's son. He had never forsaken his Christianity, and a Christian hope lay behind his warfare with the secular modernists, those who would save 'Aborigines' with their narrow faith in 'citizenship.'

That he was a Christian, and that he wished a future for Aborigines as Christians, he could not easily speak into the political fray. It would have placed him beyond the pale in a profession that prided itself as a child of the Enlightenment. But what he could say, when he had the right audience, was that the polemic against mission history was a travesty of the truth, and that 'a common brotherhood of all men in Christ is still, in my opinion, the only message of hope of mankind.'

This much he expressed to an audience of Lutheran students in 1977. He was speaking to them with the warmth of the teacher with his flock, wanting to set the record straight about matters of history as well as matters of faith. On the first issue he rejected the polemical view that the missions had damaged Aboriginal culture and its religion, that they should be seen as the villains of colonial history. Strehlow insisted that the Hermannsburg Mission had indeed been a place of refuge for the Aranda: he spoke of the 'food, clothing and blankets for the black people' and how the mission had 'protected the black populations from the rifles of other white settlers and the police.' Thus not only the converts, but even those black folk who regarded themselves as pillars of the old faiths, came to appreciate the helpful humanity of those who had come to spread the gospel in 'heathen lands.'

He hastened to add that this was not a 'blank cheque' for approving all that the missions had done. He spoke of lazy mission workers. He pointed to the false pieties: 'I have always wished that mission workers would stop comparing the actions of ordinary members of the black community with the professed ideals of the best honest Christian of our white community and draw, from such unfair comparison of non-comparables, the inference that white Australians in general were superior to black Australians.' But none of this was to say that the missions were the agents of harm to Aboriginal culture. Rather, 'no serious aboriginal demands have so far been made anywhere that the white mission staffs should be evicted in the interests of restoring "aboriginal identity." And from this Strehlow drew a religious conclusion: 'I would suggest that the Australian churches everywhere, and the Lutheran Church in particular, should examine carefully what the attitude of Christians should be towards the Lord of the Church himself: for it was *His* command that His servant should go out into the world and carry the good news to all peoples everywhere.'[19] *

The conviction was rock solid in Strehlow: he had affirmed it to Lutheran students nearly 24 years earlier when he had quoted St Paul (Luther's favourite), who said, 'I feel myself under a sort of universal obligation, I owe something to all men, from cultured Greek to ignorant savage' (Romans 5:14). He had also quoted Paul saying: 'For though I am no man's slave, yet I have made myself everyone's slave,

---

* He was simplifying his case for the missions, which he had put even more trenchantly elsewhere in the first pamphlet published by the Strehlow Research Foundation, *Christian Missions: Places of Refuge or Concentration Centres?* (1977). Its indignant thrust was not only to reiterate some of the racist history of the frontier, but to claim that the land settled by the mission was land left over from the neighbouring pastoral leases, not land taken from the Aborigine, and that the mission had never as a matter of policy forcibly removed black people from one place to the other. That had been the policy of governments. As a refuge, the mission had made it possible for the Aranda population to increase, and its language survive: this at a time when other groups were dying off from the white man's diseases. Finally, and this in a way was his key point, and the one most informing his talk with Lutheran students, it was the humane refuge it was precisely because of the nature of the mission project, which was to show people how to live as Christians rather than coerce them. 'My father's oft stated aim was to show this so he could dare to say to them: "Follow me, dear brothers."'
Strehlow was emphasising the historical reality of personal choice for the Aranda. It was a difficult case to consolidate, since, as he admitted in a closing sentence, 'it is true that many of the old cultural traditions and religious observances vanished at these mission centres,' a concession that pointed to what he knew so well about the impact of Christ Militant at Hermannsburg at the time of his return in 1932: the sacking of the Manangananga cave, the triumphant exhibition of sacred objects on the mission house verandah, and the old men who approached him in distress, asking that he be their *ingkata*. His case strengthens when he lists the names of some of the key converts at the mission, the initiated men who had come into the fold without duress, and women who had thrived as Christians. The baptismal records, he argued, suggest biographies of assimilation rather than coercion, and lives lived happily in the two cultures at once. Strehlow did not reflect on the rueful edge to the memories of such good Christians as Blind Moses, who condemned the bullying arrogance of early mission preaching.

that I might win more men to Christ.' This is the passage where Paul says that to the Jews he was a Jew that he might win the Jews, and that he had, in short, 'been all things to all sorts of men that by every possible means I might win some to God. I do this for the sake of the Gospel; I want to play my part in it properly.'

And of course this was not Strehlow thinking alone. He was, as we have seen, citing a passage crucial to the thinking of his father and his missionary uncle, Christian Keysser, when they made the case for their proselytising work. It was work depending on relationships formed in the native language that had been translated with full religious sympathy, a 'labouring' as Strehlow put it, where the mission worker must 'try to become an aboriginal in thought and expression.'[20] All this time, since his beginning, really, he had believed in the Lutheran mission project, one that had the translator at its centre.

In effect then, in 1977, even as Strehlow had been pleading the special case for Aranda religion, and for 'the greatness of the aboriginal mind' in all its difference, he was simultaneously affirming a Christian faith in the Aranda who had forsaken their traditional fathers for the Christian God. All of his life he had tended to condemn the young Aranda men who had forsaken the songs and ceremonies of their fathers. We have seen that over and over again. What has been less obvious until these later, desperate years was that he also thought—held to himself simultaneously, fervently—that the mission teaching was according to divine command and that those who believed should hold to it as a test of their faith. 'Who do you say I am?' Christ asked. 'What should be the message of the Christian Church to a fearful world?' Strehlow asked the Lutheran students, and cited the French poet Saint-Exupéry as reply: 'We need a renewal of our personal faith and of the church . . . that is the equivalent of a resurrection of the dead.' This was the 'eternity' he wanted to emphasise now: the one beyond the Land of *Altjira*. The true believer, black or white, black and white, he hoped would hold to the 'common brotherhood of all men in Christ.'[21]

The two arguments, then, went hand in hand: a defence of mission history, and the call for a spiritual renewal. But it was only on exclusive occasions that Strehlow spelt out his sacred link. There was good reason for such discretion. On the modern political stage he was *ingkata*, the ceremonial chief, the last of the Aranda: well and good. If, at the same time, he stepped out as the Christian missionary, he was exposing a schizoid division. He was pagan *and* Christian, black *and* white, each defined in opposition to the other. The black pagan was radically opposite, while the white Christian could, arguably, employ its universalising philosophy to encompass the former. Both, admittedly, were founded on concepts of eternity, and that must have been solace to Strehlow, since the fundament of his own metaphysical interests was the concept of eternity. Into this space he was able, as the Christian translator of Scriptures into Aranda, to think of himself, subtextually, as a 'Black Missionary.' But that had to be a subterranean self if he was not to make some kind of show of himself as a man divided. So the split stayed, energetically shrouded on most occasions, and he continued to hold forth on behalf of his two sides, oscillating and convoluting his arguments as much as himself. He could never really put his mind to unravelling the bonds of his emotional allegiances. His stance invited madness.

If madness is too strong—unresolved wretchedness will do—we might simply say it was in his nature to be doubled. Born under the sign of Gemini at Ntaria, the place of the Twins Dreaming. The son of Germans, cradled in Aranda. The boy with two mother tongues. The one whose sense of initiation into manhood always ran in tandem. The young man whose body was tested in the Outback fields of the pagan, while dreaming of prestige in the academy. The one who was full of yearning to connect with his home place that was both a mission and a dreaming site. The one who extolled the spiritual virtues of Aboriginal poetry, even as he ambivalently distanced himself from its erotic powers. The one who essayed upon the virtues of religious unities in art, even as he railed against the modern art that sought to address a spiritual crisis. The one who had created his own unifying poem of Australia, which contained within it a vision of love between the races, but who judged the social consequences of miscegenation harshly. And so on. The streams of desire in Strehlow were always divided; they always ran both ways at once. He was a country with two great rivers flowing through him. This need not be a critical point: seen from the air, that's how he was, a rather ancient landscape that is as it is. There was nothing wrong with him. He had simply become, more nakedly than most individuals, the exemplary case of carnal and spiritual divisions arising from a place we simplify by calling it Central Australia. He was both ontologically the case—fully himself—and representative of two cultures that had yet to reconcile. As a twin he was too complex to be heard, especially if others were listening for prophets with a single voice. But as a man of the hour when the hour is eternity, he was perhaps closest to the spiritual waters of the country.

In 1977 he told the Lutheran students one clear thing, as if it might be a sign. When he went back to the mission for its centenary celebrations, he'd made a simple observation. The windows of the modern school, 'and many other buildings put up in recent years from Liberal government funds' had been broken by stones thrown by 'troublesome teenagers.'[22] But not the windows of the old church: they had remained intact.

In God's Hands

In March 1978 *Stern* magazine in Germany published a sumptuous sixteen-page spread on secret-sacred Aranda ceremonies. Under the heading, 'Die Zornigen' (the angry ones) were eight sensational colour photographs displaying Aboriginal men in ceremony. The casual German reader—*Stern* had a circulation of 1.8 million—could contemplate naked men in glorious headgear, in body paint and featherdown, men crouched beside their pulsating ground painting, men lying full out in the red sand. Some of the photographs simply caught the creaturely vitality of ceremony, others the communality of ritual: all of them took the viewer into the sacred domain of Aboriginal belief. The largest reproduction showed two elders standing among a congregation of desert stones in a barren land with a grey stone mountain behind them. It is an immensely powerful image, and, one detects instinctively, the stones are in some way a graveyard. Indeed, readers of *Journey to Horseshoe Bend* would know the place in their mind's eye: it is a picture of country near the lower Finke which the Aranda knew as the Land of the Dead. It is the site called Uralterinja, which Strehlow had 'lost and found' on his formative visits to Horseshoe Bend.

Strehlow had provided *Stern* with 211 colour slides and 78 black-and-white photographs. The selection from which the editors had made such a limited choice represented the span of his life. They included a 1908 shot of his mother wearing a full white blouse among a little black forest of Aboriginal girls. They showed a bright-looking young Strehlow out at Mount Liebig in 1933, kneeling on the ground between two Aboriginal 'informants.' There were candid shots of ordinary Aboriginal life and close-ups of tnatantja poles, woringa and *tjurunga*. There is one stunning photograph of a place where *tjurunga* were stored: from the upper reaches of the rock shelf, one man is passing the sacred boards down to an older man who receives the ancestor spirits from their sacred cave.

For this wealth of material—a mess of pottage in the careless hands of *Stern*—Strehlow was paid $6,000 as an 'honorarium.' *Stern* agreed not to publish the shots elsewhere for the next eight months or to pass them on to any other magazine. All the material was to be returned within six months, because, as Strehlow wrote later, 'it had not been sold.' Also, and crucially, he had made it clear to the magazine's man in Hamburg that he would 'not agree to any of my photographic material (or copies of it) being sold to any Australian magazine. I was assured that such an occasion could never arise.'

Alas. 'A real atom bomb burst on us today,' he told his diary on 3 August 1978.

Unknown to him, Australia's *People* magazine had got hold of the *Stern* article and published it that morning as a front-page story under the headline 'Sacred Secrets Revealed.' Among the other stories advertised on the cover was one for Hitler's sex life.

The news came through to Strehlow by 9 a.m. In the evening he registered the shattering events of the day:

> After that came various rings from various persons, Zanetti the editor of People, who is now being threatened by an injunction brought by the AIAS 'and Alice Springs aboriginals,' and under pressure to recall this edition and to pulp next week's issue of People as well, since this contains more of my pictures.—R. Berndt also rang from Perth, urging me to put pressure on People, to have its issues withdrawn and pulped, otherwise there might be serious repercussions for me as well, including the destruction of my proposed October display in the Public Library . . . Kathie told Zanetti on the phone that our work was now finished, and so were we. A look at my contract with Stern Magazine revealed that I had merely loaned those slides and black and white prints to the Stern Magazine, and not sold them. Hence the Stern Magazine had no right to sell my pictures to People without my knowledge. I certainly would never have authorised such a sale . . .
>
> Everything rests in God's hands. My cunningly devised Stern contract has failed to gain for me any monetary help overseas, and now I may never write or print anything else any more during the remainder of my life. If this is God's will then let it be done.[23]

Strehlow is so shaken that he has to check, like a man watching himself sleepwalking, the nature of the contract he had signed. He exonerates himself, and yet in the same breath, with his mention of a contract that was 'cunningly devised,' seems to incriminate himself. Having done that he throws his hands in the air: he is in the lap of God, writing himself into a fatally passive position, hell-bent on drawing the tempest to him.

On the first day, however, he did manage to write to *People*. He sent its editor Zanetti a copy of the German contract and summarised its contents in English. It was a firm enough letter but it accepted the editor's 'telephone protestations that they were unaware of the contractual restrictions.' It did not assert any property rights against *People* magazine, only that 'I do not concede that the AIAS has any rights over my pictures. These are my private property and mine alone. No "aboriginals" anywhere have any claims to them, I hope our Law still has some force in Australia.'[24]

Ronald Berndt was absolutely intent on prompting him to more decisive action. Berndt had been in Canberra, among anthropologists at AIAS, when the news stunned the room. And of all people at the Institute he was most acutely aware of the issues at stake both for Aborigines and the profession of anthropology. He had been struggling with the unenviable task of helping the Institute shape its thoughts on 'rules' for dealing with the secret-sacred, and he had been documenting matters of which Strehlow must have known. In 1969 the first gross mishap with photographic material had been the distress created among the community in the Warburton Range at the publication of *Yiwara* by the American anthropologist, Richard A. Gould. In the shock waves of that incident was Charles Mountford's *Nomads of the Western Desert*, which was due to be published but the Pitjantjatjara Lands Council put a legal stop to it in 1976: the sumptuously produced book was pulped. Berndt himself had removed all sacred photographs from his 1974 edition of *The First Australians*, and the 1976 edition of *The World of the First Australians.* He had, however, left sacred material in his 1974 Danish publication, *Australian Aboriginal Religion*, because it was published outside Australia, and 'the volume contained a special statement entitled "Readers in Australia Please Note."'[25]

Berndt rang Strehlow straight away. Strehlow seems to have told him that he, too, was currently opposed to the publication of secret-sacred material. In his own defence Strehlow would have been within his rights to mention the times when publication of ceremonial images caused no apparent offence. He had for instance published *Arunda Traditions*, shown his films in London, where *the Listener* had illustrated 'secret rites,' along with explicit remarks of his about nakedness and blood. More recently, in 1963 in the Australian magazine *Hemisphere* he had published pictures of men with their *tjurunga*, their sacred headgear and the tnatantja pole.[26] The simple fact was that the ground of acceptability in these matters had been changing and was still hard to define with clarity.

Back in Perth, Berndt was 'compelled' to address his recalcitrant old friend:

Dear Ted

... the fact remains that the publication of ostensible secret-sacred Aranda photos in a popular journal having a wide general circulation, and not intended as a research or an anthropological medium, can cause, and has caused, from what I gather, a great deal of upset to Aborigines. That it will be, if it has not already been, published by a person of your standing and under your name will undoubtedly have serious repercussions on all of us who are vitally interested in Aboriginal affairs. There are many people, not necessarily Aboriginal, who are only too ready to attack the work of specialists, and the publication of such an article in *People* will undoubtedly provide them with ammunition in this respect.

In our phone conversation, you said that you were categorically opposed to secret-sacred material being published in a general and public sense. Would it therefore be best, for yourself, to serve an interim injunction on the management of *People* for the withdrawal of its issue on Aug 3, and the following number? In those circumstances, an interim injunction could be based on a breach of contract—that is, that the material you supplied should not be used in Australia. I think it is absolutely essential that you yourself should do this. It would then be seen quite clearly that you are *not* supporting the general publication of secret-sacred photos. You also said over the phone that you were prepared to receive objections or complaints concerning the publication of this material. I don't really think this absolves you from making a public statement in which you deny that you gave *People* permission to publish your material. After all, this is directly in line with your own expressed views ...

I should also make it clear that I am emphasising this for 2 reasons: one, that I am of the firm opinion that Aboriginal attitudes towards secret-sacred material must be respected; and, two, that in the event of your not taking action against the publication of the *People* article, the position could ramify and have serious repercussions in relations to Aboriginal research generally.[27]

Berndt asked to be released from the chair of the Strehlow Research Foundation. The publication of the photographs, 'while directly linked with your own name, would also be seen as having the support of the Committee. But, as I have made clear, it does not have my support.'

'Please, Ted,' Berndt concluded, '*do* take my advice on this matter! Re-think the issues involved and take appropriate action.'

But Ted—who told himself that Berndt's letter was 'nasty'—took no action in public. He ignored Berndt's plea that he make a public statement. In private he consulted lawyers, leaving the talking to his wife because 'I have been so disgusted with everyone, and with myself too.' The more he wrote to himself in anger and self-justification the more the self-disgust seemed to grow.

I now know that no one will look at my case with my eyes. I am that complete anomaly—a white-skinned Aranda man of the old sort. No fully white man can be trusted—for to a modern white man money and power are the only things that matter. He has no time for 'eternal values'—he can't afford them . . . the modern white-trained aborigines are all white men cast in the same normal treacherous mould.

I had come under the decisive influence of pre-white settlement fully trained black men like Gura, Makarinja, Kolbarinja, Rauwiraka and others—men of brilliant minds, who trusted me fully. I had always hoped to set down on culture [*sic*] their brilliant thoughts and the greatness of true Aranda culture. But I always lacked the money to do more than pre-liminary sketches. After my retirement I struggled with what poor private resources I had left, and got nowhere except into debt. My last hope was to get some money from overseas—hence my dealings with *Der Stern* and with the West German TV crew, with strict injunctions to these men never to let any of my pictures return to Australia. I now realise that I have been a fool to trust them. All of them were white men first and men of honour second. My own committee men . . . hope to use my present misery to force me to hand over my house and all my 'material' and other possessions in the care of the 'Foundation' so that they can gain complete power over me, and unearned kudos for them-selves.I have lived too long. 'The last Aranda man' is an anachronism in the world of *1878* [*sic*], which is fit only for God's scrap heap. I had no right to trust anyone with what I had been entrusted by the only com-pletely loyal friends I have ever known—those black men who were the guardians of a great culture not affected by white values. May God forgive me for my own unwarranted betrayal of it! I have sinned against God and my dead friends in listening to the voices of white tempters. And now everyone can say with outward justification, that Strehlow too was only a white man after all. And no creatures will savage me more severely than the vile creatures of my own skin colour.[28]

This is wild writing in more ways than one. Strehlow hardly knows what he is saying. With the '1878' he clearly intended the year he was in, 1978, and not the year after the mission had started in the desert of Central Australia. The slippage itself is revealing, as it hurls him back to the begin-ning, when he might have been 'the last of the Aranda' at the mission's point of genesis: he might have been the final authority at the very beginning of mission time! As for the other slips, 'I always hoped to set down on culture' (when he must have meant 'on paper') and his 'with strict injunctions' (rather than 'instructions'), these are errors in the domain of the will. Would that he could in his potency set things down for the culture, and issue injunctions, but what he gives off is omnipo-tence thwarted, and mental operations dislocated as he storms with the furies of Lear on the heath. 'I know that no one will look at the case with my eyes,' he cries out. And since they did not, would he gouge out those eyes? He would not, but his distress and the storms in his rhetoric are sufficient to flash the thought before his reader.

Strehlow believed he had learnt at the lawyers' that it might cost anything from $50,000 to $150,000 to take out an injunction. There was the possibility of action in breach of copyright. Yet still he remained, to all intents and purposes, ill-fatedly silent in the public eye. Those who would understand him had to come to him.

On 8 August, the *Bulletin* journalist Ian Moffitt wrote a sympathetic, rather exonerating article in which Strehlow was able to state the terms of the *Stern* agreement and to say that much of the knowledge he had 'is still stored in my brain.' This was the 'last Aranda man's' way of making a less than veiled threat. 'I need financial help desperately or it will all die with me, but I don't feel as committed now to getting it all out as I did before my heart attacks. Who am I to attempt to force my knowledge on a country that doesn't want it?'[29]

These were desperate fighting words, but they came from the bunker. He was still not taking the initiative as Berndt had urged. His passivity made him increasingly vulnerable. What solace there was to be had from the *Bulletin* article was expunged by the 'nastiest piece of journalese' in the *Adelaide Advertiser*, an article which printed a telegram to Strehlow from Neville Perkins, Aboriginal member of the Northern Territory Legislative Assembly, saying that *People's* publication was a 'disgraceful and insensitive and unethical insult to Central Australian Aborigines. It shows a callous disregard for Aranda laws and secret custom. The publication is an outrage. You and your wife should be ashamed of yourselves for such a blatant violation of Aboriginal secrets for personal gain.'

Strehlow was especially incensed by the *Advertiser* piece because the journalist had completely omitted his 'punchline' that 'the Ilbalintja men had themselves asked me to photograph their sites and record their myths and songs in order to keep their great sacred home alive after their deaths, and urged me to show my photos to decent honourable white men down south.'[30]

By the time the Perkins telegram was published, conveying as it did in one message all the popular charges—betrayal, disrespect, venality, the transgression of having a woman as an accomplice—the second issue of *People* had reached the streets. Strehlow rushed out that night and bought 112 copies. It was as if he wanted to clear the Adelaide streets of them, or as many as he could afford. Meanwhile *People* had agreed not to distribute the magazine in Alice Springs, where the eyes of distressed Aborigines were most likely to fall on them. In response to Strehlow's position and the urgings of AIAS, *People* was doing its best to establish goodwill.

Strehlow was not well, and he was getting worse in body and mind. He had told the *Bulletin* that he was on four pills a day to keep his blood pressure up. What he could not say was what he was scribbling so clearly to himself in his diary: that he was a black man, and that he was the only rightful owner—the last of the rightful black men—of all the secret sacred material at issue. Possession—the crisis of it—had finally drawn him into a final, consolidating primal utterance about identity. His stereotyping of the cultures—the black one with its 'eternal' values, the white one crassly materialistic—was too silly to trot out in public, which he must have sensed as he traded Arunda images for pieces of silver. But it was what he passionately felt, even as he was resting his fate in the hands of the Christian God.

In the midst of this public frenzy he had his thinking on possession—and cultural transmission—tested in another way. On the night he bought the 112 copies of *People* he found himself listening to a tape-recording of an Aranda man appealing to him to share some of his knowledge. It had been sent by Garry Stoll, the pastor at Hermannsburg. 'The Aranda man, from the Glen Helen area, was saying—in a series of requests to me, much repeated requests to me—that he needed to be instructed in several songs of the area. He belonged to the place on his father's side, and he wanted access to the traditional lore because some Pitjantjatara and Walpiri men doubted his affiliations to the place.'[31]

Churlishly, Strehlow listened to the tape. He noted that the man did not offer him any tjauerilja (gifts of meat) 'though in the old days *all* young men had to "loosen" the old guardians of the sacred traditions with tjauerilja for years before they got the information which was their "heritage."' The tone is dismissive. Strehlow seems to have wanted money, not meat. His judgment—that the man did not qualify as deserving of his heritage—is harsh, and acutely personalised:

I was fascinated by the battery of his voice. But after the battering I have myself received because of People's printing some of my photos behind my back, I am conscious only of the fact that my own expensive attempts for 46 years to keep 'aboriginal culture' alive, I am an impoverished man on the scrap heap, with my enemies rushing in for the kill. I am tired. I want to hear nothing more about aboriginal songs, ceremonies, laws and other things. Now even my good name is being attacked. X [a member of the Foundation committee] even told Kathie this morning that all my 'material' should be handed over to the Foundation plus our house, and that 'we' should apologise to the Aborigines for 'upsetting them' (!!!). What about justice for me and recognition of the fact that if I had not worked for 46 years to preserve Central Australian aboriginal culture nothing of what I had gathered would be extant today. Perhaps it is best that all that I have, and all my knowledge too, *should die with me and be lost forever to all mankind,* including our so called Australian anthropologists and 'The aboriginals' (emphasis added).[32]

The tempest, in his mind, has become a firestorm. As the last true Aranda man he is prepared to go up in flames. Rather than surrender—or even share—his knowledge, he will see it destroyed as he is being destroyed.

He and his wife were still negotiating with the lawyers. He had been pressing on with his case for breach of copyright, but *People* had been telling him that his 'weak contract' (Strehlow's terms) had been legitimately exploited by *Stern*. Later, *Stern* said they had merely made a 'stupid blunder.' On 23 August *Stern* proposed an out of court settlement, offering the Strehlows $14,000 to drop the case. The Strehlows accepted. On 1 September they settled and the money went into their private account, not into the coffers of the Foundation. 'Now at least we can pay off our mortgage,' he exclaimed. 'For the first time in three years or so my cheque book account is no longer in the red. This may make it easier for us when we decide to move out of this country.'[33]

Oblivion Without End

In due course the American magazine *Geo* also paid for a selection from the *Stern* issue, to which Strehlow had agreed. 'A Mr Robert Hughes could come over in October from America and get the text straight.' There were payments to come from the permissions he had given *Stern* for magazines in Finland, Italy, Norway, Japan and Brazil, South Africa, and Belgium.[34] 'I had become one of the world's well known men.' But what payments and fame abroad would ever compensate for the scandal his reputation had become? To add to the disaster, *Stern* had broken another part of its agreement. On publication it was supposed to have included the foundation's appeal for funds, but it did not. To top everything was the fear that Strehlow's disrepute might stop the Commonwealth looking favourably on the idea of granting $100,000 per year for five years to the Foundation.

The death of funds. The death of his reputation. The death of the work. He was ruined: '*wir sind reuiniert (oder "es ist aus mit uns")*.' Kathleen feared the shock of it all could kill him. But still he did not step into the public domain to defend himself.

What he did do was prepare a talk in September for the Anthropological Society of South Australia.[35] Entitled 'In the Beginning,' it started with the Ilbalintja myth told to him by Gurra in 1933, and went on: 'Despite Gurra's hopes the whole myth has never been published in English, and perhaps never will be. For even the recent publication of a small number of my photos of secret Central Australian aboriginal ceremonies in "People" magazine, Sydney, without my knowledge or permission has aroused strong personal criticism (so far from one person only with a heavily vested interest) and press hints of alarm regarding my alleged betrayal of the trust placed in me by my aboriginal friends over the years. A word of explanation about the whole business would therefore seem to be most opportune.'

The 'word of explanation' already had two shortcomings: he had not provided *Stern* with a small number of photos; nor had only one person, with or without a vested interest, expressed outrage. The press had done much more than hint at his betrayal, as his own record of suffering well documented. From this denial, his guilt and self-disgust, Strehlow moved to his ultimate justification: *they* had come to him.

In 1933 Gurra had come to him. 'Gurra and his fellow elders dreaded that after their deaths the "sacred traditions, the sacred objects, and the sacred ceremonies of Ilbalintja" would "all pass into oblivion."' So they hit upon the following plan—which was to perform the ceremony fully for him and for posterity. He resisted the idea at first, and only succumbed to it when he realised that 'any further resistance would be taken as a sign that I did not value my friends' greatest treasures, but had the normal white man's contempt for such things.' That camp, near Alice Springs, lasted two months. 'The hills around the camp echoed night after night from the singing of the ancient songs.'

He did the same thing at Horseshoe Bend, and at other places in other years. 'I travelled scores of thousands of miles,' Strehlow added, developing the now habitual travelogue of hardships and expenditure of funds. 'With so many sacred centres entrusted to my keeping, I was now labelled "Urumbulak" ingkata—the ceremonial chief of ceremonial festivals in general in Central Australia.'

He wrote these things down with all the skill at his command. 'But one thing always worried me. How could I keep the memory of the great centres alive, which now lived on only in my records and photographs?' At the age of 24, when Gurra came to him, Strehlow believed it might be possible to find 'a few wise and honourable men in Australia' to whom he might pass on all that had been trusted to him by his Aboriginal friends. 'I had been trained to regard our Universities, not as collections of ivory towers inhabited by owl-like absent-minded professors, but as the very citadels of Truth and Knowledge.'

As time went on it became clear that his 'academic' colleagues were not at all interested in keeping alive either Ilbalintja or any other centre.' Meanwhile he had chosen to keep the photographs of such a place out of all of his publications, including *Songs of Central Australia*. Then, when all his Ilbalintja friends were dead, and he was the 'sole heir they themselves had appointed,' the situation was different. It was possible to consider a plan for keeping 'their revered great centres alive.'

The plan, Strehlow said, was formulated in 1972 with 'the assistance of two high-ranking true scientists in the University of Adelaide.' It was that the university would provide enough funds for him to 'translate all my collected myths and songs from the original languages into English, and prepare all my photos of secret ceremonies for publication, but only after my own death.' Strehlow said he did not want to give further details of the plan. Suffice it to say that it was 'torpedoed for lack of money because a prominent South Australian personage had vetoed the necessary funds.'

Strehlow cited his misfortunes at the university with regard to staff and salary, the 'political' opposition to his work, the 'determinedly anti-aboriginal policies' of the Australian Institute of Aboriginal Studies, and 'the campaign of malicious whisperings and veiled threats' that had begun against his foundation, the chief propagator of which was the ABC. 'With so many "aboriginal advisers" and "aboriginal spokesmen" (not one of them an aboriginal ingkata) warning the politicians against me on trumped up excuses, all Australian government money was also stopped from coming to the assistance of my research.'

'But I still felt that I should save Ilbalintja and all the other centres in my care from death and oblivion.'

And so—he was reaching the end—'To gain a little money for this purpose, I finally agreed early this year that the German magazine "Stern" could publish a short account of my life and work, illustrated by some of my pictures, in Germany.'

The *Stern* story, Strehlow added, was a 'smash hit.' It was only the aftermath—*People*'s publication without permission, which gave an opportunity for 'the false fulmination of those who have been deter-mined for many years (while feathering their own nests and pitiful careers) to destroy my work'—that was the disaster. Now, Strehlow concluded, if his work was to die, so would Ilbalintja and all the great Aranda centres that 'now lived on only in my pictures and records. In that case, the human counterparts of Gurra's creatures of the night will have won their battle against knowledge and enlightenment.' Strehlow called for the 'greatness and the glory of the true culture of the Aboriginal population' to be acknowledged. It was time for Australia to decide whether the great Central Australian sacred centres were to live or die. 'It is now five minutes before midnight, and then will come that oblivion that has no end.'

Oblivion that has no end. These were the last written words in the apocalyptic paper for the meeting of the Anthropological Society of South Australia on Monday 25 September 1978.

Revelation

The paranoid sweep of Strehlow's charges, his vengeful wrath, is clear. So is the egomania of saying Aranda centres will 'die' without him. Strehlow speaks as if only *his* spirit as *ingkata* can animate the old dancing grounds. He omnipotently assumes the worthlessness of Aboriginal generations after Gurra. The argument is false not simply because it obliterates the difference between a dying and a changing culture, but also because the descendants of men like Gurra were alive to disprove Strehlow's *diktat* about cultural death. They were alive when Strehlow wrote his last words for a public forum (just as they are today, having successfully pressed their Native Title Claim to Alice Springs significantly on the basis of their own knowledge that was buttressed by Strehlow's work as well as Spencer and Gillen's geography and genealogies).[36]

Strehlow's doom-laden rhetoric seems even to have shaped his telling of Gurra's Ilbalintja myth. 'In the beginning everything was resting in an impenetrable thicket of night, and all men (i.e., the totemic ancestors) were dwelling in this impenetrable thicket of night. They were waiting.'[37] The story goes on to tell of the first rising of the sun, and of one group of men who rejoiced in it, and of the other group who did not, who 'today are wanderers in the night.' Strehlow claimed that the 'paragraph is a quotation' as told to him by Gurra, but of course it is not a quotation: Strehlow's European literary imagination had given shape to it, especially, most likely, the metaphoric power of the phrases, 'impenetrable thicket of the night' and 'wanderers in the night.'

The night and the impenetrable thicket had become his. There are signs that his mind was wandering between categories of night and day. He was not sleeping well. Between six and eight each morning he read his German Bible—not the one his mother had given him at nineteen, which had fallen apart, but the one his wife had given him. As she put it, during these last months when they were contending with 'the death of our work and the slow death he was himself dying,' their life and their biblical reading 'assumed almost *total symbolism*' (emphasis added).[38] He was bowed over the Book of Revelation: 'He that hath an ear, let him hear what the Spirit saith unto the churches; To him that overcometh will I give to eat of the hidden manna, and will give him a white stone, and in the stone a new name written, which no man knoweth saving him that receiveth it' (Revelation 2:17). According to his wife this was probably the last passage he read 'while on earth.'

Revelation is a cauldron of Christian symbols and pagan portents. With its references to archaic cultures and cults, it solicits both a blurring of boundaries and an electrification of them. Stones, secret signs, the eating of hidden manna must have fed into Strehlow's life among sacred objects and ancestor spirits. Such things—and the Blood of the Lamb, and the litany of totemistic creatures (lion, ox, eagle, the Beast)—make a cryptic surge of images meant for initiates. Revelation could be read as ceremony; as a text meant as a kind of performance for the soul, providing one knew its signs.

A Lutheran must know the signs. He must enter the great battle between the forces of darkness and the forces of light. Revelation is a text designed for personal projections, for those socially aggrieved. What D.H. Lawrence once said about the gospel is telling here. There are two kinds of Christianity, the one focused on Jesus and the command, 'Love one another,' and the other focused, not on Paul or Peter or John the Beloved, but on the Apocalypse. There was the Christianity of tenderness, and there was the Christianity of self-glorification, the glorification of the humble. The Christianity of tenderness relied on the particular strength of the disciples: their inner courage to renounce the world. This was the courage that renounced power. Others did not have the strength. John of Patmos was not like John the Beloved. He was a weak figure of frustrated desire—desire for power. His Revelation was a will to power, even if the world was to be destroyed. Meanwhile John of Patmos lived in exile, with his self-glorifying rant.

During these months Strehlow was drinking more than usual. Friends noticed the single track of his conversation, and into how deep a rut of recriminations and suspicion he had fallen. One night when his wife had gone to bed, Strehlow wept in the presence of a Lutheran pastor who was trying to be his friend. What have I done? What did I do to deserve this fate? My life's a failure, my work finished, everyone is against me. In fact, everyone was not by then against him. The committee of the Strehlow Research Foundation had given him their vote of support, and so to some extent had the University of Adelaide. But that was not enough, his mind was running on the track of ultimate abandonment.

God does not help.

His father's dying words at Horseshoe Bend, the ones the son had transcribed, and possibly composed, must have inhabited him then.

The Bridal Headpiece

There was some hope yet. There was to be the exhibition. The Strehlow Foundation was organising a great show, an opening, celebratory, honouring event that would put the collection, and the prospective research centre, on the map.

That would help set things right, or at least set the foundation on the road to some proper recognition and fund-raising success. Plans had been afoot for months. The exhibition was supported by a grant from Libraries Board of South Australia. The guest list was impressive. The hope, initially, was that the Prime Minister would open it, but that idea was out of the question since his office had registered its disapproval of the *Stern* affair.[39]

The man who had stepped up to do the job was Justice Michael Kirby, then deputy president of the Australian Conciliation and Arbitration Commission and chair of the Law Reform Commission of Australia. Kirby had been a sudden bright light in the Strehlow darkness. On the instruction of the Attorney-General he had been most respectfully consulting Strehlow on customary law, and whether it should be formally recognised side by side with the present system. Strehlow's long, studied response said several things at once: that anthropologists had never agreed on a definition of the law; nor had indigenous people; and that in such 'an agonising time of transition' it was impossible to say what it might be in the near future. The nub of the issue for Strehlow was that the old law that had existed was based on religious beliefs, which were now weak or non-existent. 'The old law rested on the old religious beliefs, and the younger generation will no longer accept these.'[40]

On what basis, then, he was saying to the legal reformers, could customary law be re-established when Aborigines were stranded in a land of unbelief, or in a legal no-man's-land, as one of his articles was headed.[41] His picture was symptomatic of his dualistic allegorical view of Aboriginal culture; namely, that it did exist at one time in a pristine state, presumably before white contact, and never since. It was, as one anthropologist has put it, an all or nothing view of Aborigines. One explanation for this might be to say: 'He must have seen tradition as an inflexible force in Aboriginal Society.' The other is to say what is equally true: that he 'cannot have known or was unimpressed by the many communities in which elements of "black fellow law," and "white fellow law" are mixed together or lie side by side.'[42] This indeed is true, as we have become increasingly aware. Strehlow did not want to embrace that species of mix for a good reason: his Christian hopes for Aborigines. The side by side for which he secretly yearned was the one expressed by his symbol of the Trinity.[43] Given that only the pristine Aboriginal culture was the true one, the only one left was the one lying down in the Christian way, which would enable the moral presence of eternity to live on, to become the new song. Hence his remark, in the context of the customary law discussion: 'Perhaps white Australians, too, are finding themselves in a not very dissimilar "transitional stage."'[44] The transition he was alluding to there was one from secular modernism to something else. But he had no real hope of that, not in the apocalyptic state he had reached.

Strehlow left everyone, really, in a Godless land. The reader of Revelation had spoken. The upshot was that the Law Reform Commission thought Strehlow's views represented 'a counsel of despair'[45]—which in effect it was. There was a despair right though Strehlow at this time and he seemed to apply it to everything, especially Aboriginal futures. 'What can be salvaged now, I do not even dare to guess at: the mess is almost too great for intelligent comprehension.'[46] This Strehlow wrote in 1978, in the Catholic right-wing paper, *News Weekly*. Short of joining the Cattlemen's Association, he had now located himself as far to the right of the reformist labour circles as he could.

At the State Library of South Australia twenty display cabinets were mounted, the first six illustrating the early work of the mission, especially that of Pastor Carl Strehlow. The text of the catalogue paid a rare and straightforward homage to his father's ethnographic work. The lay person coming to the Strehlow saga for the first time would see Theodor's work in its proper context—as a labour of love that had grown quite naturally out of the whole Lutheran enterprise. But then, having seen that, there was no escaping the son's defiant claim to a greater greatness.

A notice said: 'None of the Strehlow collection of sacred objects or pictures of sacred ceremonies are being displayed although they are the major results of his forty five years of research in Central Australia. Thus about two-thirds of the most important material is not displayed. The Strehlow Research Foundation hopes however to make these available to all Mankind in the future, given the facilities with which to continue the research so essential to its preservation.'

One could move from school days through the whole life. Photographs, field notes, manuscripts and maps told the story. Cases 16 and 17 had artefacts carefully noted as 'non-sacred.' In case 15, however, there was the controversial map of Aranda country, which very clearly indicated the sacred sites from which many of the sacred objects came. The caption read: 'No prototype existed for the end map produced by Mrs T.G.H. Strehlow for *Songs of Central Australia*. No other map exists like it or can ever be produced again.' (When Pastor Philip Scherer saw this caption he was very angry indeed. He had in his possession the drafts of the early maps, upon which the final product was based. He consulted lawyers about T.G.H. Strehlow's claims to exclusivity, but did not proceed with the matter.)

In a pharaoh's tomb objects were used to narrate a life and to represent the wealth that lay elsewhere. So with the first and the last exhibition of the Strehlow Research Foundation. One exhibit included a comment on the future, of the sad fate to come. The caption for case 19 read: 'Samples of field notebooks. The Aboriginal myths and songs appear in their original tongues: they have not yet been translated and perhaps now they never shall.' It was a caption that suggested, as did the one about the map, the hand of Kathleen Strehlow.

October 3 was the day of the opening. Despite the *Stern* scandal, Justice Michael Kirby and the ever-faithful Ronald Berndt would still do the honours. When the morning came, the labels for the cabinets had still not been prepared. Strehlow had taken young Carl to kindergarten but was not back by 10 a.m. as expected because their old car—Betsy—had broken down. His rest that morning was impossible. And he had to get his hair cut; he had to receive Pastor John Pfitzner, missionary of Hermannsburg, who had called in to say goodbye before returning north. There was the rush to the library after that, to meet Kirby and Berndt, as well as Professor Castles and Doctors van Der

Hock and Medlin. When they got to the library Strehlow was agitated. There were still no final labels on some of the photographs! They had to check the wording of each one, and type others. He and his wife slipped the label under the glass protecting his self-portrait. It was a line from Psalm 19: 'Thy work is a light unto my path and a lamp unto my feet.'

This, Strehlow told his wife, is to be my epitaph.

They left the library to meet the others in his rooms at the university. At the top of the stairs Strehlow begged his wife not to hurry. When he met Kirby, his wife saw him give the jurist 'a radiant smile.' They went into his rooms. The table was a mess. 'My husband worked harder than any of us,' she wrote. 'Finally, with chairs found for all, his Honour insisted that my husband occupy his old club chair at the head of the large table . . . He was back at his customary place.'[47]

Thus seated, it was the moment for the presentation. Justice Kirby had praised Strehlow and the auspicious occasion, words that had prompted the delighted Strehlow to offer him a copy of the exhibition catalogue. It was a thing of beauty.

On the cover was a magnificent photograph of a bridal headpiece. It was made of bandicoot tails—black and white and brown—photographed against a glowing, blood-red background. The tails were fixed with black spinifex gum, human hair string and bound with kangaroo sinews, and they made a spray, a vigorous bristle of a fan. Thirty animals had been killed to make it, Strehlow told Kirby. The animal, *ingkaia* (the rabbit-eared bandicoot; today we call it the bilby), was almost extinct by the early 1900s. He was displaying the tail tips of the animal, the albetja.

'I asked him to describe the cover of the program,' Kirby remembers, 'and he told me that it was a bridal decoration in the Aranda tribe. He then began to speak as if in metaphors about the bandicoot tail that is demonstrated in the decoration. And it was as if he was going off into a realm of poetry, because he began to say that the bandicoot was no more. The bandicoot had been driven out of the Australian Centre by the rabbit, introduced by the white man, and the metaphor was very vivid. It was the bandicoot with the original Aboriginal people, the rabbit was the invading white man. And as he said *ingkaia* he seemed to collapse, and it was as if it was gurgling out of him. *Ingkaia*, he said . . . and at that he simply expired. And there was a desperate endeavour to revive him but he died, and he died in my arms.'

'I leapt up,' his wife was to write, 'and cradled his head in my arms.'
Into his diary the night before, Strehlow had written the last words.
'Oh God, what have I done to deserve such torment now?'

And Kathleen would add: 'No longer would he continue to force the
real glory of Aboriginal poetry into a hostile Australia. From then on
the mind of real Aboriginal Australia had ceased to exist.'[48]

---

1   L.H. Leske, *A Vision and a Mission* (Adelaide: Lutheran Publishing House, 1977),
    115, 116.
2   T.G.H. Strehlow, 'Aboriginal Religion and the Role of the Christian Missions,'
    Lutheran Student 77, no. 5 (1977): 17.
3   Personal conversations with Helene Burns, daughter of F.W. Albrecht, March
    1996, September 2000. For another account of the event, see also Ward
    McNally, *Aborigines, Artefacts, and Anguish* (Adelaide: Lutheran Publishing House,
    1981), 173.
4   T.G.H. Strehlow, *Songs of Central Australia* [SCA] (Sydney: Angus & Robertson,
    1971), 409.
5   Garry Stoll, personal conversation, November 1999.
6   *Centralian Advocate*, 14 January 1978.
7   *SCA*, xxxvii.
8   *Centralian Advocate*, 2 December 1977, 16 December 1976, 6 January 1977.
9   *Adelaide Advertiser*, 13 April 1977.
10 F.W. Albrecht, press statement, April 1977.
11 *Northern Territory News*, 14 January 1978.
12 Members of the Interim Committee in December 1977 were the Lutheran
    Chaplain John Sabel, convener; Dr John van der Hoek, from Adelaide
    University's Department of Pure Mathematics, secretary; Brian Pietsch,
    treasurer; John Jarick, student representative.
13 *Australasian Nurses' Journal*, September 1977.
14 Berndt to Strehlow, 18 April 1978, Berndt Museum, University of Western
    Australia.
15 Berndt to Strehlow, 20 July 1978.
16 Berndt to Strehlow, 18 January 1978; Berndt to Dr N. Habel, 19 January 1978.
17 *Northern Territory News*, 13 January 1978.
18 David Turner, Report on The Strehlow Research Foundation, 1984, 1–2, 4.
19 Strehlow 'Aboriginal Religion and the Role of the Christian Missions,' 19, 21.
20 T.G.H. Strehlow, 'Christianity and the Australian Aborigine,' an address to
    Lutheran Student Fellowship, Adelaide Teachers College, 1960, 3.
21 Strehlow, 'Aboriginal Religion and the Role of the Christian Missions,' 19, 22,
    23.
22 Ibid., 23.
23 T.G.H. Strehlow, diary [SD], 3 August 1978.
24 Strehlow to Zanetti, 3 August 1978.
25 Ronald Berndt and Dick Roughsey, 'On the Question of the Secret-Sacred
    Dimension *vis-à-vis* Traditional Australian Aboriginal Life,' 18 September 1975
    AIAS, unpublished paper received and carried by council, April 1976.
26 *Listener*, 12 April 1951: *Hemisphere*, July 1963.
27 Berndt to Strehlow, 4 August 1978.
28 SD, 4 August 1978.
29 *Bulletin*, 8 August 1978.
30 SD, 16 August 1978.

31 Personal conversation, September 1996.

32 SD, 21 August 1978.

33 SD, 24 August 1978.

34 SD, 26 August 1978.

35 T.G.H. Strehlow, 'In the Beginning,' *Journal of the Anthropological Society of South Australia* 16, no. 8 (October 1978).

36 Spencer and Gillen's work was also crucial to the Native Title Claim.

37 Strehlow, 'In the Beginning.'

38 K. Strehlow, *Strehlow Research Foundation Newsletter*, 6 October 1978.

39 Dale Budd, Principal Private Secretary to the Prime Minister, to Strehlow, 21 September 1978.

40 *Australian Nurses' Journal*, August 1978.

41 *Adelaide Advertiser*, 19 February 1977.

42 Kenneth Maddock, *The Australian Aborigines: A Portrait of Their Society* (Ringwood: Penguin, 1982), 177.

43 As distinct, say, from Stanner's way of putting it: 'there is a problem of development as well as one of preservation [of the traditional law] . . . That is to say, while it would be "impracticable to institute a distinct and separate system of Aboriginal law for all persons of Aboriginal descent living in every part of Australia" there were communities that might want to develop their own "rights, duties, liabilities and immunities" as their culture became more "self-sustaining" and free of the arbitrariness, the use of violence, the impatience, and the boorish neglect of Aboriginal rules of privacy, decent conduct, and respect for persons and authorities so often shown by the processes of our criminal law.' W.E.H. Stanner, 'Some Notes on Aboriginal Law and its Possible Recognition,' undated, c. 1976.

44 For a summary of Strehlow's position, see *Australasian Nurses' Journal*, August 1978.

45 See Justice M.D. Kirby's overview of Strehlow's position and summary of this view of Strehlow's advice in 'T.G.H. Strehlow and Aboriginal Customary Law,' *Adelaide Law Review*, 7, no. 2 (1980), and Tim Rowse, 'The Collector as Outsider—T.G.H. Strehlow as "Public Intellectual,"' Strehlow Research Centre, *Occasional Paper 2* (December 1999), 90, citing the finding of The Australian Law Reform Commission 1986.

46 Rowse, 'Collector as Outsider,' 90, quoting Strehlow in *News Weekly*, 27 September 1978.

47 *Strehlow Foundation Newsletter* 6 (October 1978).

48 Justice Michael Kirby was speaking to the cameras for Hart Cohen's film, *Mr Strehlow's Films*, screened on SBS television, 7 July 2001; Kathleen Strehlow's recollections were published in the *Strehlow Foundation Newsletter*, 6, October 1978.

Permissions

FOR PERMISSION TO cite in various ways my acknowledgements go to: Paul Albrecht for citations from Pastor F.W. Albrecht; James Bardon; Dr John E. Stanton of the Berndt Museum of Anthropology for citations from Professor Ronald Berndt; W.W. Norton and Company Inc. for citations from Erik Erikson (© 1958, 1962 and renewed 1986, 1990 by Erik H. Erikson); Graham Hall for citations from Vic Hall; Barbara Henson; HarperCollins Publishers Ltd for citations from Richard Holmes (© 1996 Richard Holmes); Ross Burnet and Idriess Enterprises Pty Ltd for citations from Ion Idriess; Eileen Ingamells for citations from Rex Ingamells; Dick Kimber for citations from his letters; Shane McNally for citations from Ward McNally; Adrian Herring of Journocam Productions and The Hon Justice Michael Kirby for citation from *Mr Strehlow's Films*; Neil Murray for lines from 'Broken Song' (© Rondor Music Australia Pty Ltd, reproduced by kind permission of Rondor Music Australia Pty Ltd); Dr Tim Rowse; Sonia Colalancia for citations from Philipp Scherer; Patricia A. Stanner for citations from W.E.H. Stanner; Oxford University Press for citations from George Steiner (© 1975, 1992, 1998); John and Theo Strehlow and Shirley Crawley for citations from Bertha Strehlow and Frieda Strehlow; the Strehlow Research Centre for citations from T.G.H. Strehlow; Dr Peter Sutton; Mutie Tillich Farris for citations from Paul Tillich; Adelaide University Archives; the Australian Institute of Aboriginal and Torres Strait Islander Studies; the Australian National University Archives; the National Archives of Australia.

For the use of photographs I wish to thank the following: The Lutheran Archives in Adelaide (Plates 1, 5 and 51); State Library of South Australia (Plate 3); the Institut für Stadtgeschichte Frankfurt (Plate 49); The University of Sydney (Plate 17); Helene Burns (Plates 22, 24 and 25); Trudy Johannsen (Plate 16); John Mulvaney (Plate 4); Ken Inglis (Plate 54). For the others I am once again grateful to the Strehlow Research Centre and Brett Galt-Smith for obtaining and granting permission in line with the moral rights and intellectual property policies of the SRC.

Every effort has been made to identify copyright holders of extracts in this book. The publishers would be pleased to hear from any copyright holders who have not been acknowledged.

Bibliography

Select Works by T.G.H. Strehlow

Books

1944. *Aranda Phonetics and Grammar*. Oceania Monograph 7. University of Sydney. Sydney.

1947. *Aranda Traditions*. Melbourne University Press. Melbourne.

1956. *Rex Battarbee: Artist and Founder of the Aboriginal Art Movement in Central Australia*. Legend Press. Sydney.

1969. *Journey to Horseshoe Bend*. Angus & Robertson. Sydney.

1971. *Songs of Central Australia*. Angus & Robertson. Sydney.

Pamphlets

1950. *An Australian Viewpoint*. Hawthorn Press. Melbourne.

1956 [reprint]. 'Friendship with South-East Asia.' *Forum*, vol. IX, nos 1 and 2.

1956. *The Sustaining Ideals of Australian Aboriginal Societies*. Aboriginal Advancement League of South Australia. Adelaide.

1958. *Dark and White Australians*. Riall Bros. Melbourne.

1961. *Nomads in No-Man's Land*. Aborigines' Advancement League. Adelaide.

1964. *Assimilation Problems: The Aboriginal Viewpoint*. Aborigines' Advancement League. Adelaide.

1965. 'William Ricketts and the Mount Dandenong Sanctuary,' in *A Living Voice of the Living Bush*. Forests Commission of Victoria. Melbourne.

1967. *Comments on the Journals of John McDouall Stuart*. Libraries Board of South Australia. Adelaide.

1978. *Central Australian Religion: Personal Monototemism in a Polytotemic Community*. Australian Association for the Study of Religions. Adelaide.

Translations Into Aranda

1956. *Testamenta Ljatinja, Ankatja Arandauna Knatiwumala*. Council of the British and Foreign Bible Society in Australia. Adelaide.

1958. *Altjiraka Iltakana Pepa*. The Finke River Mission. Tanunda.

1959. *Mosaka Pepa Arugulinja*. Finke River Mission. Hermannsburg.

1960. *Psalma Urbutja*. Finke River Mission. Hermannsburg.

1962. *Election Speech*. Translation of Mr D. D. Smith's radio talk for ABC Radio. Alice Springs. December.

1981. *Ljelint Jamea-Pepa Lutherarinja*. Finke River Mission Board. Adelaide.

Translations from Aranda

1966. 'Ankotarinja,' 'The Rain Ancestors' and 'Ilingka,' in *Aboriginal Myths and Legends* by Ronald Robinson. Sun Books. Melbourne.

1986. 'The Brother Eagles,' 'The Hollow at Ilbalinja Soak,' 'Ringneck Parrots' 'The Great Beam of the Milky Way,' in *The New Oxford Book of Australian Verse*. Les A. Murray, ed. Oxford University Press. Melbourne.

Articles

1933. 'Ankotarinja, an Aranda Myth.' *Oceania*, vol. IV, no. 2.

1936. 'Notes on Native Evidence and its Value.' *Oceania*, vol. VI, no. 3.

1947. 'Anthropology and the Study of Languages,' in *Report of 26th Meeting of ANZAAS*. Perth. August.

1949. 'The Future of Aboriginal Education in Australia.' *New Horizons in Education*, no. 3, Spring.

1952. 'Trends in Australian Native Policy.' *The Anti-Slavery Reporter and Aborigines' Friend*, series VI, vol. 7, no. 3.

1953. 'Australian Aboriginal Myths and Legends.' *ABC Weekly*, 10 January.

1953. 'The Poetry of Central Australian Songs.' *Sunday Advertiser Supplement*, 28 November and 5 December.

1957. 'Thoughts of a Translator.' *Lutheran Herald*, vol. 37, no. 1, 12 January.

1959. Extracts from Analysis of Rupert Stuart 'Confession.' *Nation*, 15 August.

1959. Affidavit in Stuart Case. *Report of the Royal Commission in Regard to Rupert Max Stuart*. Government Printer. Adelaide. Appl. III, pt 1.

1962. 'Aboriginal Australia: Languages and Literature.' *Hemisphere*, vol. 6, no. 8.

1962. 'Aboriginal Language, Religion, and Society in Central Australia.' *Australian Territories*, vol. 2, no. 1.

1963. 'Documentation on Albert Namatjira.' *Australian Territories*, vol. 3, no. 4.

1963. 'Religion in Aboriginal Australia.' *Hemisphere*, vol. 7, no. 7, July.

1964. 'The Art of Circle, Line and Square,' in *Australian Aboriginal Art*. R. M. Berndt, ed. Ure Smith. Sydney.

1964. 'Commentary on the Magic Beliefs Described in M. J. Barrett's "Walbiri Customs and Beliefs Concerning Teeth."' *Mankind*, vol. 6, no. 3.

1965. 'Culture, Social Structure and Environment in Aboriginal Central Australia,' in *Aboriginal Man in Australia*. R.M. Berndt and C.H. Berndt, eds. Angus & Robertson. Sydney.

1965. 'New Aranda – English Hymnal.' *Lutheran Herald*, vol. 45, no. 5, March.

1965. 'Some Comments' [Relating to the Native and Historical Objects and Areas Preservation Ordinance]. Appendix 2 of the *Report from the Select Committee on Native and Historical Objects and Areas Preservation Ordinance, 1955–1960*, Darwin.

1966. 'Central Australian Research Memories.' [Adelaide University Graduates Union] *Gazette*, vol. 4, no. 12, June.

1966. 'The Story of Hermannsburg.' *Centralian Advocate*, 29 September – 27 October [five articles].

1969. 'Mythology of the Centralian Aborigine.' *The Inland Review*, vol. 3, nos 11 and 12, June–August and September–November.

1970. 'Geography and the Totemic Landscape in Central Australia: A Functional Study,' in *Australian Aboriginal Anthropology*. R. M. Berndt, ed. University of Western Australia Press. Nedlands.

1973. 'Jobs for the (White) Boys.' *The Australian*, 9 December.

1975. 'Aboriginal Religion.' *Australasian Nurses' Journal*, vol. 4, no. 1, July.

1977. 'Aboriginal Religion and the Role of the Christian Missions.' *Lutheran Student*, vol. 77, no. 5, November.

1977. 'Christian Missions: Places of Refuge or Concentration Centres?'. [Strehlow Research Foundation] *Pamphlet*, vol. 1, no. 1, December.

1978. 'Aboriginal Culture in "White" Education.' [Strehlow Research Foundation] *Pamphlet*, vol. 1, nos 2 and 3, February and April.

1978. Review of *Black Australians* by Paul Hasluck (MUP, 1970). *Australian Book Review*, vol. 9, no. 10.

1978. 'In the Beginning.' *Journal of the Anthropological Society of South Australia*, vol. 16, no. 8, October.

Forewords

1951. Foreword to *Modern Australian Aboriginal Art* by Rex Battarbee. Angus & Robertson. Sydney.

1956. Foreword to *The Feathered Serpent* by Roland Robinson. Edwards & Shaw. Sydney.

1968. Foreword to *The People in Between: The Pitjantjatjara People of Ernabella* by Winifred M. Hillliard. Funk & Wagnall. New York.

Talks, Addresses, Lectures

1934. *Some Northern Aranda Myths.* Lecture to the English Association. 10 August. [Later incorporated in *Aranda Traditions* (MUP, 1947) as Part 1.]

1935. *Tjurunga – Ownership.* Paper presented at the ANZAAS Meeting, Melbourne. January. [Later incorporated into *Aranda Traditions* (MUP, 1947) as Part 3.]

1951. *Future of Australian Aborigines.* Talk given at the Orthopaedic Institute. London.

1954. *One Hour Before Sunset.* Public talk given in the Mawson Theatre, University of Adelaide. 16 June.

1955. *Anthropological Research in Central Australia: The Last Opportunities.* U.S.I. Luncheon Talk. 7 March.

1956. *Linguistics and Anthropology.* Talk to the Anthropological Society of South Australia. 25 June.

1960. *Christianity and the Australian Aborigine.* Address to the Lutheran Student Fellowship, Adelaide. March. [Later published in [Strehlow Research Foundation] *Pamphlet*, vol. 3, no. 6 and vol. 4, no. 1.]

[c.1962]. *Full Citizenship for Aboriginal Australians.* Address on National Aboriginal Day.

1965. *The [New] Aranda Lutheran Hymnal.* Address at St Stephen's Lutheran Church, Adelaide. 14 February. [Later published in *Lutheran Herald*, vol. 45, no. 5, March.]

1967. *Man and Language.* Address to Adelaide University Linguistic Society. 19 September.

Radio and TV Talks

1949. *The Importance of Language.* Talk for unknown radio station.

1952. *Witnessing Ceremonies.* ABC radio talk. 9 August.

1957. *Are There Any Primitive Languages?* ABC Radio Talk (5CL), News Review Comment. 1 November.

1964. *Bible Translation Techniques.* Interview for *What's in a Word?* Channel 7. 3 December.

Art Exhibitions

1973. William Ricketts' Exhibition. Opening address at Mount Dandenong. 14 October.

Miscellaneous

1965. *The Aboriginal Australians – Their Past, Present and Future*. [Written as an article for *Le Monde*, Paris, in December.]

1975. *The Alice Springs Aboriginal Land Rights*. [A report commissioned by the Northern Territory Country Liberal Party, December.]

Secondary Sources

Ackerman, Robert. 1990. *J.G. Frazer: His Life and Work*. Cambridge University Press. Cambridge.

Alter, Robert. 1985. *The Art of Biblical Poetry*. Basic Books. New York.

Apter, Ronnie. 1987. *Digging for Treasure: Translation After Pound*. Paragon. New York.

Arnold, Matthew. 1954. *Poetry and Prose*. Rupert Hart-Davis. London.

Attwood, Bain. 1992. *The Making of the Aborigines*. Allen & Unwin. Sydney.

Attwood, Bain, and John Arnold. 1992. *Power, Knowledge and Aborigines*. La Trobe University Press in association with the National Centre for Australian Studies, Monash University. Bundoora, Vic.

Attwood, Bain, and Andrew Markus. 1997. *The 1967 Referendum, or When the Aborigines Didn't Get the Vote*. Aboriginal Studies Press. Canberra.

Austin, Tony. 1987. *Never Trust a Government Man: Northern Territory Aboriginal Policy, 1911–1939*. Northern Territory University Press. Darwin.

Austin, Tony. 1992. *Simply the Survival of the Fittest: Aboriginal Administration in South Australia's Northern Territory, 1863–1910*. Historical Society of the Northern Territory. Darwin.

Austin, Tony. 1993. *'I Can Picture the Old Home so Clearly': The Commonwealth and 'Half-Caste' Youth in the Northern Territory, 1911–1939*. Aboriginal Studies Press. Canberra.

Austin-Broos, Diane J. 1987. *Creating Culture: Profiles in the Study of Culture*. Allen & Unwin. Sydney.

Bainton, Roland H. 1951. *Here I Stand: A Life of Martin Luther*. Hodder & Stoughton. London.

Bardon, Geoffrey. 1991. *Papunya Tula: Art of the Western Desert*. McPhee Gribble. Melbourne.

Bardon, James. 1991. *Revolution by Night*. Local Consumption Publications. Sydney.

Barwick, Linda, Allen Marett and Guy Tunstill, eds. 1995. *The Essence of Singing and the Substance of Song: Recent Responses to the Aboriginal Performing Arts and Other Essays in Honour of Catherine Ellis*. University of Sydney. Sydney.

Baudrillard, Jean. 1994. 'The System of Collecting,' in *The Cultures of Collecting*. John Elsner and Roger Cardinal, eds. Melbourne University Press. Melbourne.

Bate, W. Jackson. 1967. *John Keats*. Oxford University Press. London.

Bates, D.M. 1938. *The Passing of the Aborigines: A Lifetime Spent Among the Natives of Australia*. 2nd edn, 1966. Murray. London.

Bateson, Gregory. 1932. 'Social Structure of the Iatmul People of the Sepik River, Part III.' *Oceania*, vol. II, no. 4.

Batty, Joyce D. 1963. *Namatjira: Wanderer Between Two Worlds*. Hodder & Stoughton. Melbourne.

Bell, D. 1983. *Daughters of the Dreaming*. McPhee Gribble. Melbourne.

Benedict, Ruth. 1930. 'Psychological Types in the Cultures of the Southwest,' in *Writings of Ruth Benedict: An Anthropologist at Work*. Margaret Mead, ed., 1959. Atherton Press. New York.

Benjamin, Walter. 1969. *Illuminations*. Schocken. New York.

Berlin, Isaiah. 1976. *Vico and Herder*. Hogarth. London.

Berman, Morris. 1981. *The Reenchantment of the World*. Cornell University Press. Ithaca, N.Y.

Berndt, Catherine H., and Ronald M. Berndt. 1965. *Aboriginal Man in Australia*. Angus & Robertson. Sydney.

Berndt, Catherine H., and Ronald M. Berndt. 1971. *The Barbarians*. C. A. Watts & Co. London.

Berndt, Ronald. 1948. 'A Wonguri – Mandjikai Song Cycle of the Moon-Bone.' *Oceania*, vol. XVII, no. 4; vol. XVIII, no 1.

Berndt, Ronald. 1952. *Djanggawul: An Aboriginal Religious Cult of North Eastern Arnhem Land*. Routledge & Kegan Paul. London.

Berndt, Ronald. 1978. *Transformation of Person, Objects and Country: Some Comments*. Occasional Papers in Anthropology. Anthropology Museum. University of Queensland.

Berndt, Ronald. 1978, October. 'A Time for Remembering.' Unpublished.

Berndt, R.M., and Dick Roughsey. 1975. 'On the Question of the Secret-Sacred Dimension vis-à-vis Traditional Australian Aboriginal Life.' AIAS. Unpublished.

Blackburn, Julia. 1994. *Daisy Bates in the Desert*. Secker & Warburg. London.

Bleakley, J.W. 1929. *The Aboriginals and the Half-Castes of Central Australia and North Australia*. Commonwealth Government Printer. Canberra.

Boas, Franz. 1955. *Primitive Art*. Dover Publications. New York.

Bowman, Bryan. 1989. *The Glen Helen Story*. Coleman's Printing. Alice Springs.

Bowman, Bryan. 1991. *A History of Central Australia, 1930–1980*. The author. Alice Springs.

Bowra, Maurice. 1962. *Primitive Song*. Weidenfeld & Nicolson. London.

Bowra, Maurice. 1971. *Homer*. Duckworth. London.

Boyle, Nicholas. 1991. *Goethe: The Poet and the Age*. Vol. 1: *The Poetry of Desire (1749–1790)*. Clarendon Press. Oxford.

Buber, Martin, and Franz Rozenzweig. 1994. *Scripture and Translation*. Indiana University Press. Bloomington.

Burke, Kenneth. 1969. *A Rhetoric of Motives*. University of California Press. Berkeley and Los Angeles.

Burridge, Kenelm. 1973. *Encountering Aborigines: A Case Study: Anthropology and the Australian Aboriginal*. Pergamon. New York.

Burridge, Kenelm. 1988. 'Aborigines and Christianity: An Overview,' in *Aboriginal Australians and Christian Missions*. Tony Swain and Deborah Bird Rose, eds. Australian Association for the Study of Religions. Bedford Park, S.A.

Carment, David, and Barbara James, eds. 1992. *Northern Territory Dictionary of Biography*. Vol. 2. Northern Territory University Press. Darwin.

Carment, David, Robyn Maynard and Allan Powell, eds. 1990. *Northern Territory Dictionary of Biography*. Vol. 1. Northern Territory University Press. Darwin.

Carter, Paul. 1996. *The Lie of the Land*. Faber. London.

Carter, Paul. 1999. *Depth of Translation: The Book of Raft*. NMA Publications. Burnley, Vic.

Carter, Paul. 2000. 'The Enigma of the Homeland Place,' in *Papunya Tula: Genesis and Genius*. Hetti Perkins and Hannah Fink, eds. Art Gallery of New South Wales. Sydney.

Chadwick, H. Munro, and N. Kershaw Chadwick. 1932. *The Growth of Literature*. Cambridge University Press. Cambridge.

Charlesworth, M., R.C. Kimber and Noel Wallace. 1990. *Ancestor Spirits*. Deakin University Press. Geelong, Vic.

Charlesworth, Max, Howard Morphy, Diane Bell and Kenneth Maddock, eds. 1984. *Religion in Aboriginal Australia: An Anthology*. University of Queensland Press. St Lucia.

Chamberlain, Sir Roderic. 1973. *The Stuart Affair*. Rigby. Adelaide.

Chatwin, Bruce. 1987. *The Songlines*. Cape. London.

Cleator, P.E. 1973. *Lost Languages*. Robert Hale. London.

Clendinnen, Inga. 1988. *Ambivalent Conquests: Maya and Spaniard in Yucatan, 1517–1570*. Cambridge University Press. Cambridge.

Clifford, James. 1982. *Person and Myth: Maurice Leenhardt in the Melanesian World.* University of California Press. Berkeley and Los Angeles.

Clifford, James. 1986. *Writing Culture: The Poetics and Politics of Ethnography.* University of California Press. Berkeley and Los Angeles.

Clifford, James. 1988. *The Predicament of Culture: Twentieth-Century Ethnography, Literature and Art.* Harvard. Cambridge, Mass.

Coleridge, Samuel Taylor. 1983. *Biographia Literaria.* James Engell and W. Jackson Bate, eds. Princeton University Press. Princeton, N.J.

Collingwood, R.G. 1938. *The Principles of Art.* Oxford University Press. Oxford.

Coombs, H.C. 1981. *Trial Balance: Issues of My Working Life.* Sun Books. Melbourne.

Davies, E. Harold. 1931. 'Aboriginal Songs of Central and Southern Australia.' *Oceania,* vol. II, no. 1.

Delisle, Jean, and Judith Woodsworth, eds. 1995. *Translators Through History.* J. Benjamins. Amsterdam, Philadelphia.

Derrida, Jacques. 1998. *Monolingualism of the Other; or, the Prosthesis of Origin.* Stanford University Press. Stanford, Ca.

Derrida, Jacques. 1992. 'Tours de Babel,' in *Theories of Translation.* Rainer Schulte and John Biguenet, eds. University of Chicago Press. Chicago.

Dixon, Bob. 1939. *Searching for Aboriginal Languages: Memoirs of a Field Worker.* University of Queensland Press. St Lucia.

Dixon, R.M.W. 1980. *The Languages of Australia.* Cambridge University Press. Cambridge.

Dixon, R.M.W., and Martin Duwell. 1990. *The Honey-Ant Men's Love Song and Other Aboriginal Song Poems.* University of Queensland Press. St Lucia.

Dixon, R.M.W., and Grace Koch. 1996. *Dyirbal Song Poetry: The Oral Literature of an Australian Rainforest People.* University of Queensland Press. St Lucia.

Dixon, R.M.W., W.S. Ramson and Mandy Thomas. 1990. *Australian Aboriginal Words in English: Their Origin and Meaning.* Oxford University Press. Melbourne.

Dixon, T.S. 1987. *The Wizard of Alice.* Alella Books. Morwell, Vic.

Douglas, Mary. 1966. *Purity and Danger: An Analysis of Concepts of Pollution and Taboo.* Routledge & Kegan Paul. London.

Dowling, Jim. 1988. *Ngurra Walytja, Country of My Spirit.* Northern Australia Research Unit Monograph. Darwin.

Dryden, John. 1961. *The Works of John Dryden.* Vol. 1. University of California Press. Berkeley and Los Angeles.

Duguid, Charles. 1972. *Doctor and the Aborigines.* Rigby. Adelaide.

Donovan, Peter. 1988. *Alice Springs: Its History and the People Who Made It.* Alice Springs Town Council. Alice Springs.

Eco, Umberto. 1995. *The Search for the Perfect Language*. Blackwell. Oxford.

Edwards, Robert, ed. 1975. *The Preservation of Australia's Aboriginal Heritage: Report of the National Seminar on Aboriginal Antiquities in Australia, May 1972*. Australian Institute of Aboriginal Studies. Canberra.

Eliade, Mircea. 1972. *The Myth of the Eternal Return: or Cosmos and History*. Princeton University Press. Princeton, N.J.

Eliot, T.S. 1920. *The Sacred Wood*. Methuen, 1960. London.

Elkin, A.P. 1932. 'The Secret Life of the Australian Aborigines,' *Oceania*, vol. 3, no. 2.

Elkin, A.P. 1935. 'Anthropology in Australia. Past and Present.' Australian and New Zealand Association for the Advancement of Science.

Elkin, A.P. 1937. 'The Nature of Australian Languages'. *Oceania*, vol. VIII, no. 3.

Elkin, A.P. 1947. Review of *Aranda Traditions*. *Oceania*, vol. XVIII–XIX, no. 2.

Elkin, A.P. 1975. Review of *Songs of Central Australia*. *Oceania*, vol. XLV, no. 2.

Elkin, A.P. 1979. *The Australian Aborigine*. Angus & Robertson. Sydney.

Elkin, A.P. 1980. *Aboriginal Men of High Degree*. 2nd edn. University of Queensland Press. St Lucia.

Elliott, Brian, ed. 1979. *The Jindyworobaks*. University of Queensland Press. St Lucia.

Ellis, Catherine. 1984. 'Time Consciousness of Aboriginal Performers,' in *Problems and Solutions: Occasional Essays in Musicology Presented to Alice M. Moyle*. Jamie C. Kassler and Jill Stubington, eds. Hale & Iremonger. Sydney.

Erickson, Ray. 1978. *Ernest Giles: Explorer and Traveller, 1835–1837*. Heinemann. Melbourne.

Erikson, Eric. 1958. *Young Man Luther*. Faber. London.

Evans-Pritchard, E. 1956. *Nuer Religion*. Clarendon Press. Oxford.

Evans-Pritchard, E. 1981. *A History of Anthropological Thought*. Faber. London.

Faine, Jonathan. 1993. *Lawyers in the Alice: Aboriginals and Whitefellas' Law*. Federation Press. Sydney.

Feld, Steven. 1990. *Sound and Sentiment: Birds, Weeping, Poetics, and Song in Kaluli Expression*. University of Pennsylvania Press. Philadelphia.

Fernandez Retamar, Roberto. 1989. *Caliban and Other Essays*. University of Minnesota Press. Minneapolis.

Firth, Raymond. 1932. 'Anthropology in Australia, 1926–1932—and After.' *Oceania*, vol. III.

Freeman, Derek. 1996. *Margaret Mead and the Heretic: The Making and Unmaking of an Anthropological Myth*. Penguin. Ringwood, Vic.

Gason, S. 1877. 'The Manners and Customs of the Dieyeri Tribe of Australian Aborigines,' in *The Native Tribes of South Australia*. J.D. Wood, ed. Wigg & Son. Adelaide.

Gass, William H. 1999. *Reflections on the Problems of Translation*. Alfred A. Knopf. New York.

Geertz, Clifford. 1988. *Works and Lives: The Anthropologist as Author*. Stanford University Press. Stanford, Ca.

Geertz, Clifford. 1993. *Local Knowledge*. Fontana. London.

Geertz, Clifford. 1993. *The Interpretation of Cultures*. Fontana. London.

Geertz, Clifford. 1994. 'Anti Anti-Relativism?' *American Anthropology*, vol. 86, no. 2.

Geertz, Clifford. 1995. *After the Fact: Two Countries, Four Decades, One Anthropologist*. Harvard University Press. Cambridge, Mass.

Gentzler, Edwin. 1993. *Contemporary Translation Theories*. Routledge. London.

Gill, Sam D. 1997. *Story Tracking: Texts, Stories and Histories in Central Australia*. Oxford University Press. Melbourne.

Gill, Walter. 1968. *Petermann Journey*. Seal Books. Adelaide.

Giles, Ernst. 1889. *Australia Twice Traversed: The Romance of Exploration*. Sampson Low, Marston, Searle & Rivington. London.

Gillespie, Dr Stuart. 1992. *Translation and Literature*. Vol. 1. Edinburgh University Press. Edinburgh.

Goethe, Johann Wolfgang Von. 1976. *Faust: A Tragedy*. W. W. Norton. New York.

Goethe, Johann Wolfgang Von. 1977. 'West–East Divan,' in *Translating Literature: A German Tradition: From Luther to Rosenzweig*. Andre Lefevere, ed. Van Gorcum. Assen.

Goody, Jack. 1977. *The Domestication of the Savage Mind*. Cambridge University Press. Cambridge.

Greenblatt, Stephen. 1991. *Marvelous Possessions: The Wonder of the New World*. University of Chicago Press. Chicago.

Greenblatt, Stephen. 1994. *Marvellous Possessions*. Harvard University Press. Cambridge, Mass.

Groom, Harold. 1950. *I Saw a Strange Land*. Angus & Robertson. Sydney.

Haebich, Anna. 2001. *Broken Circles: Fragmenting Indigenous Families, 1800–2000*. Fremantle Arts Centre Press. Fremantle.

Hale, Ken. 1984. 'Remarks on Creativity in Aboriginal Verse,' in *Problems and Solutions: Occasional Essays in Musicology Presented to Alice. M. Moyle*. Jamie C. Kassler and Jill Stubington, eds. Hale & Iremonger. Sydney.

Hall, Vic. 1947. *Bad Medicine*. Melbourne. Robertson & Mullins.

Hamilton, Annette. 1980. 'Dual Social Systems: Technology, Labour and Women's Secret Rites in the Eastern Western Desert of Australia.' *Oceania*, vol. 51.

Hamilton, Annette. 1997, 'L.R. Hiatt: Life, Thought and Misunderstanding,' in *Scholar and Sceptic: Australian Aboriginal Studies in Honour of L.R. Hiatt*.

Francesca Merlan, John Morton and Alan Ramsey, eds. Aboriginal Studies Press. Canberra.

Hancock, W.K. 1954. *Country and Calling.* Faber. London.

Hansen, D.E., and I.V. Hansen. 1996. *With Wings: A Centenary History of Immanuel College, Adelaide, 1895–1995.* Immanuel College. Adelaide.

Harney, W.E. 1943. *Taboo.* Australasian Publishing Company. Sydney.

Harney, W.E. 1946. *North of 23.* Australasian Publishing Company. Sydney.

Harney, W.E. 1961. *Grief, Gaiety and Aborigines.* Robert Hale. London.

Harris, John. 1990. *One Blood: 200 Years of Aboriginal Encounter With Christianity: A Story of Hope.* Albatross Books. Sutherland, N.S.W.

Hasluck, Paul. 1965. 'The Problem of Administration,' in *Aboriginal Man in Australia.* R.M. and C.H. Berndt, eds. Angus & Robertson. Sydney.

Havelock, Eric. 1982. *A Preface to Plato.* Harvard University Press. Cambridge, Mass.

Hayes, E. Nelson, and Tanya Hayes, eds. 1970. *Claude Lévi-Strauss: The Anthropologist as Hero.* MIT Press. Cambridge, Mass.

Headon, David, ed. 1990. *North of the Ten Commandments.* Hodder & Stoughton. Sydney.

Healy, Chris. 1997. *From the Ruins of Colonialism: History as Social Memory.* Cambridge University Press. Melbourne.

Healy, J.J. 1989. *Literature and the Aborigine in Australia.* University of Queensland Press. St Lucia.

Hearsey, Shane. 1988. 'From Disgust to Trepidation: The Debitage of *Songs.*' Unpublished.

Heidegger, Martin. 1971. *Poetry, Language, Thought.* Harper & Row. New York.

Henson, Barbara. 1992. *A Straight-Out Man: F.W. Albrecht and Central Australian Aborigines.* Melbourne University Press. Melbourne.

Herbert, Xavier. 1938. *Capricornia.* Angus & Robertson. Sydney.

Hercus, Luise, and Grace Koch. 1997. 'Old Yet Always New: Song Traditions of Southern Central Australia,' Strehlow Research Centre. *Occasional Paper 1.*

Hiatt, L.R. 1971, 'Secret Pseudo-Procreation Rites Among the Australian Aborigines,' in *Anthropology in Oceania; Essays Presented to Ian Hogbin.* L.T. Hiatt and C. Jayawarden, eds. Chandler. San Francisco.

Hiatt, L.R. 1987. 'Freud and Anthropology,' in *Creating Culture: Profiles in the Study of Culture.* D.J. Austin-Broos, ed. Allen & Unwin. Sydney.

Hiatt, L.R. 1996. *Arguments About Aborigines: Australia and the Evolution of Social Anthropology.* Cambridge University Press. Cambridge.

Hill, Barry. 1987. 'Freud and Anthropology,' in *Creating Culture: Profiles in the Study of Culture.* D.J. Austin-Broos, ed. Allen & Unwin. Sydney.

Hill, Barry. 1992. 'Welcoming Dance: On Reading Songs of Central Australia.' *Overland*. Autumn.

Hill, Barry. 1994. *The Rock: Travelling to Uluru*. Allen & Unwin. Sydney.

Hill, Barry. 1996. 'Through Larapinta Land: Baldwin Spencer's Glass Case,' in *Exploring Central Australia*. S.R. Morton and D.J. Mulvaney, eds. Surrey Beattie & Co. Sydney.

Hill, Ernestine. 1951. *The Territory*. Angus & Robertson. Sydney.

Hill, Ernestine. 1973. *Kabbarli: A Personal Memoir of Daisy Bates*. Angus & Robertson. Sydney.

Hofstadter, Douglas R. 1997. *Le Ton Beau de Marot*. Basic Books. New York.

Holmes, Richard. 1996. *Footsteps: Adventures of a Romantic Biographer*. Harper-Collins. London.

Howitt, A.W. 1886. 'Notes on Songs and Songmakers of Some Australian Tribes.' *Journal of the Anthropological Institute*, vol. 16.

Howitt, A.W. 1904. *Native Tribes of South-East Australia*. Macmillan. London.

Hugo, David. 1997. 'Acquisition of the Strehlow Collection by the Northern Territory Government—a Chronology.' Strehlow Research Centre. *Occasional Paper 1*.

Huizinga, Johan. 1996. *The Autumn of the Middle Ages*. University of Chicago Press. Chicago.

Ingamells, Rex. 1935. *Gumtops*. Preece & Sons. Adelaide.

Inglis, K.S. 1961. *The Stuart Case*. Melbourne University Press. Melbourne.

Jacobson, Eric. 1992. 'On Linguistic Aspects of Translation,' in *Theories of Translation*. Rainer Schulte and John Biguenet, eds. University of Chicago Press. Chicago.

Jespersen, Otto. 1921. *Language: Its Nature, Development and Origin*. Allen & Unwin. London.

Jones, P.G. 1987. 'South Australian Anthropological History: The Board for Anthropological Research and its Early Expeditions.' *Records of the South Australian Museum*, vol. 20.

Jones, P.G. 1995. 'Objects of Mystery and Concealment: A History of Tjurunga Collecting,' in *Politics of the Secret*. Christopher Anderson, ed. Oceania Monograph 45. University of Sydney. Sydney.

Jones, P.G. 1995. 'Norman B. Tindale: An Obituary,' *Records of the South Australian Museum*, vol. 28, no. 2.

Jones, Philip. 1984. 'Red Ochre Expeditions: An Ethnographic and Historical Analysis of Aboriginal Trade in the Lake Eyre Basin,' *Journal of the Anthropological Society of South Australia*, vol. 22, no. 7.

Jones, Philip. 1990. 'Traveller Between Two Worlds,' in *The Heritage of Namatjira*. Jane Hardy, J.V.S. Megaw and H. Ruth Megaw, eds. Heinemann. Melbourne.

Jury, C.R. 1961. *The Sun in Servitude and Other Plays*. Cheshire. Melbourne.

Kaberry, P. 1939. *Aboriginal Woman: Sacred and Profane*. Routledge. London.

Keeley, Edmund. 2000. *On Translation: Reflections and Conversations*. Harwood Academic Publishers. Amsterdam.

Keen, I. 1995. 'Metaphor and the Meta-Language "Groups" in Northeast Arnhemland.' *American Ethnologist*, vol. 22.

Kermode, Frank, ed. 1954. *The Tempest*. Methuen. London.

Kimber, R.G. 1986. *Man From Arltunga: Walter Smith, Australian Bushman*. Hesperian Press. Victoria Park, W.A.

Kimber, R.G. 1991. *The End of the Bad Old Days: European Settlement in Central Australia, 1871–1894*. State Library of the Northern Territory. Darwin.

Kimber, R.G. 1997. *Genocide or Not? The Situation in Central Australia, 1860–1895*. Genocide Perspectives. Centre for Comparative Genocide Studies. Sydney.

Kimber, R.G. 1998. 'Gillen Time: The Creation of an Era,' in *Connection and Disconnection: Encounters Between Settlers and Indigenous People in the Northern Territory*. Tony Austin and Suzanne Parry, eds. Northern Territory University Press. Darwin.

Kimber, R.G. 2000. 'Recollections of Papunya Tula, 1971–1980,' in *Papunya Tula: Genesis and Genius*. Hetti Perkins and Hannah Fink, eds. Art Galley of New South Wales. Sydney.

Kimber, R.G., and M.A. Smith. 1987. 'An Aranda Ceremony,' in *Australians to 1788*. D.J. Mulvaney and J. Peter White, eds. Fairfax, Syme & Weldon. Sydney.

Kirby, M.D. 1980. 'T.G.H. Strehlow and Aboriginal Customary Law,' *Adelaide Law Review*, vol. 7, no 2.

Kirk, G.S. 1965. *Homer and the Epic*. Cambridge University Press. Cambridge.

Kristeva, Julia. 1989. *Black Sun: Depression and Melancholia*. Columbia University Press. New York.

Kung, Hans. 1990. *Freud and the Problem of God*. Yale University Press. New Haven, Conn.

Langton, Marcia. 1996. 'A Fireside Chat,' in *Prehistory to Politics: John Mulvaney, the Humanities, and the Public Intellectual*. Tim Bonyhady and Tom Griffiths eds. Melbourne University Press. Melbourne.

Latz, Dora. 1996. *A Hermannsburg Love Story: Dora's 1935 Journal*. Eric Fiebig and Ruth Fiebig, eds. Abbott's Copy Centre. Fulham, S.A.

Layton, Robert. 1999. *Uluru: An Aboriginal History of Ayers Rock*. Aboriginal Studies Press. Canberra.

Lefevere, Andre. 1975. *Translating Poetry: Seven Strategies and a Blueprint*. Van Gorcum. Assen.

Lefevere, Andre. 1977. *Translating Literature: The German Tradition From Luther to Rosenzweig.* Van Gorcum. Assen.

Leske, Everard, ed. 1977. *Hermannsburg: A Vision and a Mission.* Lutheran Publishing House. Adelaide.

Levin, Harry. 1970. *The Myth of the Golden Age in the Renaissance.* Faber. London.

Lévi-Strauss, Claude. 1974. *Tristes Tropiques.* Atheneum. New York.

Levy-Bruhl, Lucien. 1923. *Primitive Mentality.* Allen & Unwin. London.

Lipset, David. 1982 *Gregory Bateson: The Legacy of a Scientist.* Beacon Press. Boston.

Logue, Christopher. 1981. *War Music.* Penguin. Harmondsworth.

Lohe, M. 1977. 'The Modern Chapter,' in *Hermannsburg: A Vision and a Mission.* Everard Leske, ed. Lutheran Publishing House. Adelaide.

Long, Jeremy. 1992. *The Go-Betweens: Patrol Officers in Aboriginal Affairs Administration in the Northern Territory.* North Australian Research Unit. Canberra.

Luther, Martin. 1970. *Luther's Works.* Vol. 35. Fortress Press. Philadelphia.

Mackinnon, James. 1962. *Luther and the Reformation.* Russell & Russell. New York.

Maddock, Kenneth. 1982. *The Australian Aborigines: A Portrait of Their Society.* Penguin. Ringwood.

Maddock, Kenneth. 1997. 'The Temptation of Paris Resisted: An Intellectual Portrait of a Sydney Anthropologist,' in *Scholar and Sceptic: Australian Aboriginal Studies in Honour of L.R. Hiatt.* Francesca Merlan, John Morton and Alan Ramsey, eds. Aboriginal Studies Press. Canberra.

Madigan, C.T. 1936. *Central Australia.* Oxford University Press. London.

Malinowski, Bronislaw. 1922. *Argonauts of the Western Pacific.* Routledge. London.

Malinowski, Bronislaw. 1948. *Magic, Science and Religion and Other Essays.* Doubleday. New York.

Malinowski, Bronislaw. 1967. *A Diary in the Strict Sense of the Term.* Stanford University Press. Stanford, Ca.

Marchant, Leslie R. 1984. *Ernst Faber's Scholarly Mission to Convert the Confucian Literati in the Late Ch'ing Period.* Centre for East Asian Studies, University of Western Australia. Nedlands.

Marcus, Andrew. 1990 *Governing Savages.* Allen & Unwin. Sydney.

Marcus, Julie, ed. 1993. *First in Their Field.* Melbourne University Press. Melbourne.

Marius, Richard. 1999. *Martin Luther: The Christian Between God and Death.* Harvard University Press. Cambridge, Mass.

Mauss, Marcel. 1925. *The Gift.* Routledge. London.

McNally, Ward. 1981. *Aborigines, Artefacts and Anguish.* Lutheran Publishing House. Adelaide.

McGee, J. Verson. 1991. *Proverbs* Nelson. London.

McGrath, Ann. 1987. *Born in the Cattle: Aborigines in Cattle Country*. Allen & Unwin. Sydney.

McGregor, Russell. 1998. *Imagined Destinies: Aboriginal Australians and the Doomed Race Theory, 1880–1939*. Melbourne University Press. Melbourne.

Meggitt, M.J. 1962. *The Desert People: A Study of the Walbiri Aborigines of Central Australia*. Angus & Robertson. Sydney.

Meissner, W.W. 1992. *Ignatius of Loyola: The Psychology of a Saint*. Yale University Press. New Haven, Conn.

Merlan, Francesca, John Morton and Alan Ramsey, eds. 1997. *Scholar and Sceptic: Australian Aboriginal Studies in Honour of L.R. Hiatt*. Aboriginal Studies Press. Canberra.

Modell, Judith. 1984. *Ruth Benedict: Patterns of a Life*. Chatto & Windus. London.

Monk, Ray. 2001. *Bertrand Russell: The Ghost of Madness*. Cape. London.

Morton, John. 1985. 'Sustaining Desire.' PhD thesis. Australian National University. Canberra.

Morton, John. 1987. 'Singing Subjects and Sacred Objects.' *Oceania*, vol. LVIII, no. 2.

Morton, John. 1989. 'Mama, Papa, and the Space Between: Children, Sacred Objects, and Transitional Phenomena in Aboriginal Central Australia,' in *The Psychoanalytic Study of Society*. Vol. 14. L. Bryce Boyer and Simon Grolnich, eds. The Analytic Press. London.

Morton, John. 1995. '"Secrets of the Aranda": T.G.H. Strehlow and the Course of Revelation,' in *Politics of the Secret*. Christopher Anderson, ed. Oceania Monograph 45. University of Sydney. Sydney.

Morton, John. 1997. 'The Effectiveness of Totemism: "Increase Ritual" and Resource Control in Central Australia.' *Man*, vol. 22.

Mudrooroo. 1997. *The Indigenous Literature of Australia*. Hyland House. Melbourne.

Mueller-Vollmer, Kurt, and Michael Irmscher, eds. 1998. *Translating Literatures, Translating Cultures*. Erich Schmidt Verlag. Berlin.

Mulvaney, John. 1985. *So Much That Is New*. Melbourne University Press. Melbourne.

Mulvaney, John. 1990. 'The View From the Window,' in *Through White Eyes*. Susan Janson and Stuart Macintyre, eds. Allen & Unwin. Sydney.

Mulvaney, John. 1997. *My Dear Spencer: The Letters of F.J. Gillen to Baldwin Spencer*. Hyland House. Melbourne.

Mulvaney, John. 1997. 'Conflict and the Rituals of Diplomacy: Les Hiatt and the AIAS,' in *Scholar and Sceptic: Australian Aboriginal Studies in Honour of L.R. Hiatt*. Francesca Merlan, John Morton and Alan Ramsey, eds. Aboriginal Studies Press. Canberra.

Mulvaney, John. 2000. *From the Frontier: Outback Letters to Baldwin Spencer*. Allen & Unwin. Sydney.

Munn, Nancy D. 1986. *Walbiri Iconography: Graphic Representation and Cultural Symbolism in a Central Australian Society*. University of Chicago Press. Chicago.

Murray, Les A. 1984. 'The Human-Hair-Thread,' in *Persistence in Folly: Selected Prose Writings*. Angus & Robertson. Sydney.

Myers, Fred R. 1986. *Pintupi Country, Pintupi Self: Sentiment, Place, and Politics Among Western Desert Aborigines*. Smithsonian Institution Press. Washington.

Obst, T.G. 1998. *The Hands Move On: A Brief History and Recollections of Immanuel College, North Adelaide, 1922–1942*. Immanuel College. Adelaide.

Ortega Y Gasset, José. 1992. 'The Misery and Splendor of Translation,' in *Theories of Translation*. Rainer Schulte and John Biguenet, eds. University of Chicago Press. Chicago.

Partington, Geoffrey. 1996. *Hasluck Versus Coombs*. Quakers Hill Press. Sydney.

Paz, Octavio. 1992. 'Translation: Literature and Letters,' in *Theories of Translation*. Rainer Schulte and John Biguenet, eds. University of Chicago Press. Chicago.

Pearce, Joseph. 1999. *Literary Converts: Spiritual Inspiration in an Age of Unbelief*. HarperCollins. London.

Perkins, Hetti, and Hannah Fink, eds. 2000. *Papunya Tula: Genesis and Genius*. Art Gallery of New South Wales in association with Papunya Tula artists. Sydney.

Pike, Douglas. 1967. *Paradise of Dissent*, 2nd edn. Melbourne University Press. Melbourne.

Pink, Olive. 1933. 'Spirit Ancestors in a Northern Aranda Horde Country.' *Oceania*, vol. 4, no. 2.

Pink, Olive. 1936. 'Camouflage: Summary of a Lecture Dealing With Culture Contact in Australia.' *Mankind*, vol. II, no. 3.

Pink, Olive. 1936. 'The Landowners in the Northern Division of the Aranda Tribe.' *Oceania*, vol. IV, no. 2.

Plowman, R.B. 1933. *The Man From Oodnadatta*. Angus & Robertson. Sydney.

Porteus, S.D. 1931. *The Psychology of a Primitive People*. Longman. London.

Porteus, S.D. 1933. 'Mentality of Australian Aborigines.' *Oceania*, vol. IV, no. 1.

Pound, Ezra. 1931. *Literary Essays*. Faber. London.

Pound, Ezra. 1953. *The Translations of Ezra Pound*. Faber. London.

Preminger, Alex, ed. 1974. *Princeton Encyclopedia of Poetry and Poetics*. Princeton University Press. Princeton, N.J.

Radcliffe-Brown, A.R. 1965. *Structure and Function in Primitive Society*. Free Press. New York.

Radin, Paul. 1957. *Primitive Religion*. Dover. New York.

Read, Peter, and J. Read. 1991. *Long Time, Olden Time: Aboriginal Accounts of Northern Territory History.* Institute for Aboriginal Development. Alice Springs.

Reid, Ian. 1992. *Narrative Exchanges.* Routledge. London.

Riemenschneider, Dieter, and Geoffrey V. Davis, eds. 1997. *Aratjara: Aboriginal Culture and Literature in Australia.* Rodopi. Amsterdam; Atlanta, Ga.

Reuther, J.G. 1981. *The Diari.* P.A. Scherer, trans. AIAS. Canberra.

Robinson, Douglas. 1991. *The Translator's Turn.* The Johns Hopkins University Press. Baltimore, Md.

Robinson, Roland. 1956. *The Feathered Serpent.* Edwards & Shaw. Sydney.

Roheim, Geza. 1974. *Children of the Desert: The Western Tribes of Central Australia.* Basic Books. New York.

Roheim, Geza. 1988. *Children of the Desert II: Myths and Dreams of the Aborigines of Central Australia.* John Morton and Werner Muensterberger, eds. Oceania Publications. University of Sydney. Sydney.

Rose, Deborah Bird. 1992. *Dingo Makes Us Human: Life and Land in an Aboriginal Culture.* Cambridge University Press. Cambridge.

Rose, Deborah Bird. 1996. *Nourishing Terrains: Aboriginal Views of Landscape and Wilderness.* Australian Heritage Commission. Canberra.

Roth, W.E. 1984. *The Queensland Aborigines.* Hesperian Press. Victoria Park, W.A.

Rowley, C.D. 1972. *The Remote Aborigines.* Penguin. Ringwood.

Rowse, Tim. 1987. 'Assimilation and After,' in *Australians From 1939.* Ann Curthoys, A.W. Martin and Tim Rowse, eds. Fairfax, Syme & Weldon. Sydney.

Rowse, Tim. 1989. *White Flour, White Power.* Cambridge University Press. Melbourne.

Rowse, Tim. 1990. 'Aboriginals as Historical Actors: Evidence and Inference,' in *Through White Eyes.* Susan Janson and Stuart Macintyre, eds. Allen & Unwin. Sydney.

Rowse, Tim. 1992. 'Strehlow's Strap: Functionalism and Historicism in Colonial Ethnography,' in *Power, Knowledge and Aborigines.* Bain Attwood and John Arnold, eds. LaTrobe University Press in association with the National Centre for Australian Studies, Monash University. Bundoora, Vic.

Rowse, Tim. 1998. 'Strehlow Damns Coombs: Ethnography and Policy Critique.' Paper presented to the Australian Anthropological Society.

Rowse, Tim. 1999. 'The Collector as Outsider—T.G.H. Strehlow as "Public Intellectual."' Strehlow Research Centre. *Occasional Paper* 2.

Rowse, Tim. 2000. *Obliged to Be Difficult: Nugget Coombs' Legacy in Indigenous Affairs.* Cambridge University Press. Melbourne.

Sahlins, Marshall. 1965. *How Natives Think: About Captain Cook, for Example.* University of Chicago Press. Chicago.

Scherer, P.A. 1974. 'Death on the Line.' *Yearbook of the Lutheran Church.*

Scherer, P.A. 1994. *Camel Treks in the Outback.* The author. Tanunda.

Scherer, P.A. 1994. *Select Letters from the Outback.* The author. Tanunda.

Scherer, P.A. 1995. *The Hermannsburg Chronicle.* The author. Tanunda.

Schmiechen. H.J. 1971. 'The Hermannsburg Mission Society in Australia, 1866–1895.' MA thesis. University of Adelaide. Adelaide.

Schmutter, Gerhard M. 1989. *Tomahawk and Cross: Lutheran Missionaries Among the Northern Plains Tribes, 1858–1866.* Centre for Western Studies, Augustana College. Sioux Falls, S.D.

Schubert, David. 1985. *Kavel's People: From Prussia to South Australia.* Lutheran Publishing House. Adelaide.

Schulte, Rainer, and John Biguenet, eds. 1992. *Theories of Translation.* University of Chicago Press. Chicago.

Searle, John. 1999. *Mind, Language and Society.* Weidenfeld & Nicolson. London.

Sennett, Richard. 1980. *Authority.* Alfred A. Knopf. New York.

Shakespeare, Nicolas. 1999. *Bruce Chatwin.* Harvill. London.

Shapin, Steven. 1994. *A Social History of Truth: Civility and Science in Seventeenth-Century England.* University of Chicago Press. Chicago.

Shiels, Helen, ed. 1963. *Australian Aboriginal Studies: A Symposium of Papers Presented at the 1961 Research Conference.* Oxford University Press. Melbourne.

Sontag, Susan. 1970. 'The Anthropologist as Hero,' in *Claude Lévi-Strauss: The Anthropologist as Hero.* E. Nelson Hayes and Tanya Hayes, eds. MIT Press. Cambridge, Mass.

Spencer, Baldwin, ed. 1896. *Report on the Work of the Horn Scientific Expedition . . .* Melville, Mullen & Slade. Melbourne.

Spencer, Baldwin, and Frank Gillen. 1899. *Native Tribes of Central Australia.* Macmillan. London.

Spencer, Baldwin, and Frank Gillen. 1902. *Across Australia.* Macmillan. London.

Spencer, Baldwin, and Frank Gillen. 1927. *The Arunta.* Macmillan. London.

Spencer, Baldwin, and Frank Gillen. 1928. *Wanderings in Wild Australia.* Macmillan. London.

Stanner, W.E.H. 1979. 'Not by Eastern Windows Only: Anthropological Advice to Australian Governments in 1938.' *Aboriginal History,* vol. 3, no. 1.

Stanner, W.E.H. 1979. 'The Aborigines' [1938], in *White Man Got No Dreaming.* Australian National University Press. Canberra.

Stanner, W.E.H. 1982. 'On Freud's Totem and Taboo' [1953–55]. *Canberra Anthropologist.* vol. 5, no. 1.

Stanner, W.E.H. 1989. *On Aboriginal Religion*. Oceania Monograph 36. University of Sydney. Sydney.

Stapleton, Austin. 1992. *Willshire of Alice Springs*. Hesperian Press. Victoria Park, W.A.

Steiner, George. 1975. *After Babel*. Oxford University Press. London.

Stevens, Christine. 1994. *White Man's Dreaming: Killalpaninna Mission, 1866–1915*. Oxford University Press. Melbourne.

Stocking, George, ed. 1983. *Observers Observed: Essays on Ethnographic Field Work. History of Anthropology*. Vol. 1. University of Wisconsin Press. Madison.

Stocking, George, ed. 1989. *Romantic Motives: Essays on the Anthropological Sensibility. History of Anthropology*. Vol. 6. University of Wisconsin Press. Madison.

Stocking, George. 1995. *After Tylor: British Social Anthropology, 1888–1951*. University of Wisconsin Press. Madison.

Strehlow, Bertha. 1940. 'Through Central Australia.' *Walkabout*, August.

Strehlow, Bertha. 1945. 'A Camel Trip to the Petermann Ranges Across Central Australia.' Royal Geographical Society of Australia, *South Australian Branch Proceedings*, vol. XLVI.

Strehlow, Bertha. 1949. 'Glimpses of Lubra Life in Central Australia,' in *AFA Annual Report*, 1949.

Strehlow, Carl. 1907–20. *The Aranda and Loritja Tribes of Central Australia*. M.F. von Leonhardi, ed.; Hans D. Oberscheidt, trans.

Stuart, J. McD. 1983. *Fourth Expedition Journal, 1860*. Sullivan's Cover. Adelaide.

Sutton, Peter. 1988. 'Icons of Country: Topographic Representations in Classical Aboriginal Traditions,' in *The History of Cartography*, vol. 2.3, *Cartography in the Traditional African, American, Arctic, Australian, and Pacific Societies*. David Woodward and G. Malcolm Lewis, eds. Chicago University Press. Chicago.

Sutton, Peter. 1995. *Country: Aboriginal Boundaries and Land Ownership in Australia*. Aboriginal History. Canberra.

Sutton, Peter. 1997. 'Materialism, Sacred Myth and Pluralism: Competing Theories of the Origin of Australian Languages,' in *Scholar and Sceptic: Australian Aboriginal Studies in Honour of L.R. Hiatt*. Francesca Merlan, John Morton and Alan Ramsey, eds. Aboriginal Studies Press. Canberra.

Sutton, Peter, and Jones, Philip. 1986. *Art and Land: Aboriginal Sculptures of the Lake Eyre Region*. South Australian Museum/Wakefield Press. Adelaide.

Swain, Tony, and Deborah Bird Rose, eds. 1988. *Aboriginal Australians and Christian Missions*. Australian Association for the Study of Religions. Adelaide.

Thomas, Nicholas. 1991. *Entangled Objects: Exchange, Material Culture, and Colonialism in the Pacific*. Harvard University Press. Cambridge, Mass.

Tindale, N.B. 1937. 'Native Songs of the South East of South Australia.' *Transactions of the Royal Society of South Australia*, vol. 6.

Tindale, N.B. 1974. *Aboriginal Tribes of Australia*. Australian National University Press. Canberra.

Todorov, Tzvetan. 1992. *The Conquest of America*. Harper Perennial. New York.

Torrance, Rev. G.W. 1886. 'Music of the Australian Aborigines.' *Royal Anthropological Institute*, vol. 16.

Turnbull, David. 2000. *Masons, Tricksters and Cartographers*. Harwood Academic Publishers. Amsterdam.

Turner, David H. 1987. *Life Before Genesis, a Conclusion: An Understanding of the Significance of Australian Aboriginal Culture*. 2nd rev. edn. Peter Lang. New York.

Vanderwal, Ron, ed. 1987. *The Aboriginal Photographs of Baldwin Spencer*. Viking O'Neill and the National Museum of Victoria Council. Melbourne.

Veit, Walter. 1991. 'In Search of Carl Strehlow: Lutheran Missionary and Australian Anthropologist,' in *From Berlin to the Burdekin: The German Contribution to the Development of Australian Science, Exploration and the Arts*. David Walker and Jurgen Tamke, eds. New South Wales University Press. Sydney.

Venuti, Lawrence, ed. 1992. *Rethinking Translation*. Routledge. London.

Warner, W. Lloyd. 1969. *A Black Civilization: A Social Study of an Australian Tribe*. Peter Smith. Gloucester, Mass.

Weil, Simone. 1952. *The Need for Roots: Prelude to a Declaration of Duties Towards Mankind*. ARK edition 19. London.

Wilde, Oscar. 2001. *The Complete Letters of Oscar Wilde*. Merlin Holland and Rupert Hart-Davis, eds. Fourth Estate. London.

Williams, Bernard. 1993. *Shame and Necessity*. University of California Press. Berkeley and Los Angeles.

Williams, Raymond. 1973. *The Country and the City*. Chatto & Windus. London.

Willshire, W.H. 1896. *Land of the Dawning*. W.K. Thomas and Co. Adelaide.

Winnicott, D.W. 1958. 'Transitional Objects and Transitional Phenomena,' in *Collected Papers*. Tavistock. London.

Wise, Tigger. 1985. *The Self-Made Anthropologist: A Life of A.P. Elkin*. Allen & Unwin. Sydney.

Wittgenstein, Ludwig. 1953. *Philosophical Investigations*. Blackwell. Oxford.

Wolfe, Patrick. 1991. 'On Being Woken Up: The Dreamtime in Anthropology and in Australian Settler Culture.' *Comparative Studies in Society and History*, vol. 32, no. 2.

Wolfe, Patrick. 1999. *Settler Colonisation and The Transformation of Anthropology*. Continuum. London.

Zengotita, Thomas de. 1989. 'Speakers of Being: Refusion and Cultural Anthropology,' in *Romantic Motives*. George Stocking, ed. University of Wisconsin Press. Madison.

Index